Index
to
Loudoun County, Virginia Land Deed Books 2V-3D 1817-1822

Patricia B. Duncan

WILLOW BEND BOOKS
2006

WILLOW BEND BOOKS

AN IMPRINT OF HERITAGE BOOKS, INC.

Books, CDs, and more—Worldwide

For our listing of thousands of titles see our website
at
www.HeritageBooks.com

Published 2006 by
HERITAGE BOOKS, INC.
Publishing Division
65 East Main Street
Westminster, Maryland 21157-5026

Copyright © 2006 Patricia B. Duncan

International Standard Book Number: 978-0-7884-3555-8

Introduction

The following is an extended index to Loudoun County, Virginia Deed Books 2V-3D. In addition to providing the basic information of book:page number, parties involved, and type of document, I have also included the date of the document, the date received in court, and a brief description of the item, including adjoining neighbors, and witnesses.

Microfilms of these records are currently available from the Library of Virginia Interlibrary Loan Service. Copies of the documents may be obtained from the Office of Clerk of Circuit Court County of Loudoun, Box 550, Leesburg, VA 20178-0550.

Abbreviations:
Admr - Administrator
A/L – Assignment of lease
AlexDC – Alexandria, District of Columbia
B/S – Bargain and sale
BaltMd – Baltimore, Maryland
beq. - bequeathed
BerkVa – Berkeley County, Virginia
BoS - Bill of sale
br/o – brother of
CamP – Cameron Parish in Loudoun
ChstrPa – Chester County, Pennsylvania
CoE - Certificate of examination [of wife]
CoI – certificate of importation [for slaves]
Commr - commissioner
cnvy/b – conveyed by (to person now selling the land)
dau – daughter
DB letter(s):numbers - deed book:page
delv. – examined and delivered to
dev. – devised to
div. – division (of estate of)
d/o - daughter of
DoE – Deed of Emancipation [for slaves]
Exor – Executor
Ffx – Fairfax County, Virginia
Fqr – Fauquier County, Virginia
FrdkMd – Frederick County, Maryland
FrdkVa – Frederick County, Virginia
Gent. – gentleman
h/o - husband of
HdnNJ – Hunterdon County, New Jersey
Hllb - Hillsborough
int. - interest

KingG – King George County, Virginia
L/L – Lease for life
L/R – Lease/release
Ldn – Loudoun County, Virginia
Lsbg - Leesburg
Mdbg – Middleburg
MontMd – Montgomery County, Maryland
[number]a = number of acres
PhilPa – Philadelphia County, Pa
PoA – Power of attorney
PrG – Prince George County, Maryland
PrWm – Prince William County, Virginia
prch/o – purchase(d) of
RichVa – Richmond County, Virginia
RtCt – returned to court and ordered to be recorded
S/L – Surrender of lease
s/o - son of
ShelP – Shelburne Parish in Loudoun
StafVa – Stafford County, Virginia
und. - undivided
w/o - wife of
WashDC – Washington, D. C.
WashMd – Washington County, Maryland
wd/o – widow of
WstmVa – Westmoreland County, Virginia

Loudoun Co Deed Books 2V-3D

Bk:Pg: 2V:001   Date: 19 Nov 1816   RtCt: 31 May 1817
Barton D. HAWLING & wife Hannah of Ffx to Dean JAMES of Ldn.
B/S of rights of all lands and negroes derived from estate of William
JAMES dec'd and his widow. Wit: Charles LEWIS, Aris BUCKNER.
Delv. to JAMES 2 May 1819.

Bk:Pg: 2V:002   Date: 19 Oct 1816   RtCt: Jun 1817
Joseph HAINS & wife Maria to trustee William HOGE. Trust for debt
to James McGEATH owed at death of Mrs. Mary McGEATH (m/o
said James) using 109¼a. Wit: William CARR, Thomas GREGG,
Wm. H. HANDY. Delv. to HOGUE 12 Mar 1821.

Bk:Pg: 2V:004   Date: 13 Sept 1816   RtCt: 12 May 1817
Joseph DAVIS of Ldn to Henry DAY of Ldn. Trust of 87¾a on
Beaverdam adj Eb. GRUBB, Reuben HIXON, Adam
HOUSEHOLDER, Margaret SAUNDERS. Wit: John H. McCABE,
Abiel JENNERS.

Bk:Pg: 2V:005   Date: 1 Jan 1817   RtCt: 12 May 1817
Robert MARTIN of Ldn to James WORNAL of Ldn. B/S of 62a
allotted MARTIN (part of 300a prch/o William SAVAGE dec'd by
William MARTIN dec'd, but never paid for or rec'd deed; MARTIN's
will of 31 Mar 1814 asks it be paid for and divided between children
John, Edward, Robert, Andrew, Elizabeth [has since died] and Mary
MARTIN.) Wit: Andrew MARTIN, John WORNAL, John MARTIN,
Charles LEWIS.

Bk:Pg: 2V:007   Date: 28 Jan 1817   RtCt: 12 May 1817
Stephen McPHERSON & wife Celia of Ldn to Thomas GREGG (s/o
Stephen) & David LOVETT of Ldn. Trust for debt to Turner
OSBURN and Herod OSBURN & wife Eleanor using 173a. Wit:
Notley C. WILLIAMS, Joshua OSBURNE.

Bk:Pg: 2V:009   Date: 18 Sept 1816   RtCt: 12 May 1817
Patrick B. MILHOLLEN of Ldn and Aaron SCHOOLEY of Ldn.
Agreement on rent of land on road from Waterford to Leesburg (with
exception of house occupied by William HIXON), SCHOOLEY to
have house where MILHOLLEN now lives. Mentions field that
Thomas TEMPLER now uses. Wit: Jacob MENDENHALL.

Bk:Pg: 2V:010   Date: 26 Oct 1816   RtCt: 12 May 1817
David SMITH & Eli PIERPOINT (Exors of Thomas LOVE dec'd) of
Ldn to Morris OSBURN of Ldn. B/S of 159a adj Amos BEANS. Wit:
Thos. GREGG, Mahlon PURSEL, Balaam OSBURN. Delv. to
OSBURN 4 Jan 1830.

Bk:Pg: 2V:012   Date: 28 Jul 1815   RtCt: 12 May 1817
William LEWIS & wife Sarah of Ldn to George GULICK of Ldn. B/S
of 101¾a on road from fork of Little River to Snickers Gap adj

Mathew ADAMS, James SWART, William NOLAND. Delv. to GULICK 10 Feb 1834.

Bk:Pg: 2V:013   Date: 28 Mar 1817   RtCt: 12 May 1817
John B. STEPHENS & wife Sarah of Ldn to John F. SAPPINGTON of Ldn. B/S of ½a Lot #2 adj Wtfd. Wit: Robert BRADEN, John H. McCABE. Delv. to SAPPINGTON 5 Aug 1818.

Bk:Pg: 2V:014   Date: 10 Feb 1817   RtCt: 12 May 1817
David JANNEY & wife Elizabeth of Ldn to John F. SAPPINGTON of Ldn. B/S of Lots #1 & #8 (¼a each) on E side of High St in new part of Wtfd. Wit: Robert BRADEN, John H. McCABE. Delv. to SAPPINGTON 5 Aug 1818.

Bk:Pg: 2V:016   Date: 1 Mar 1817   RtCt: 12 May 1817
John CARR of Ldn to Edward MAGINNIS of Ldn. L/L (on MAGINNIS and present wife) of ½a adj lands of late William MAINS. Wit: William CARR, Daniel LOVETT, Samuel CLAPHAM.

Bk:Pg: 2V:016   Date: 10 Feb 1817   RtCt: 12 May 1817
David JANNEY & wife Elizabeth of Ldn to John TAYLOR of Ldn. B/S of Lots #3 & #4 (½a each) on E side of High St. in new part of Wtfd. Wit: Robert BRADEN, John H. McCABE. Delv. to TAYLOR 13 Feb 1828.

Bk:Pg: 2V:018   Date: 28 Jan 1817   RtCt: 12 May 1817
William WIN & wife Martha of Ldn to Thomas GREGG (s/o Stephen) & David OSBURN. Trust for debt to Turner OSBURN and Herod OSBURN & wife Eleanor of Ldn using 116a. Wit: Notley C. WILLIAMS, Joshua OSBURN. Delv. to LOVETT 11 Feb 1822.

Bk:Pg: 2V:020   Date: 5 Feb 1817   RtCt: 12 May 1817
John YOUNG of Ldn to John STOUTSABERGER of Ldn. BoS for negro man Caleb 18-20 years old. Wit: Henry HUFF, John T. HENDERSON.

Bk:Pg: 2V:020   Date: 31 Dec 1816   RtCt: 12 May 1817
John DRISH & wife Eleanor of Ldn to Isaac LAROWE of Ldn. B/S of 46a on Potomac. Wit: John McCORMICK, Samuel MURREY. Delv. to LAROWE 12 Oct 1818.

Bk:Pg: 2V:022   Date: __ Apr 1817   RtCt: 12 May 1817
Thomas HUMPHREY of Ldn to Abner Howell of Ldn. L/L (on Thomas & sons Jacob & Marcus HUMPHREY) of 116a on Blue Ridge. Wit: William BOXELL, Marcus HUMPHREY, Mason MARKS.

Bk:Pg: 2V:023   Date: 1 May 1817   RtCt: 15 May 1817
Joseph HATCHER & wife Hannah of Ldn to Jonah SANDS of Ldn. B/S of 66a adj John IREY, Hamilton RODGERS, Joseph TAVENNER, James HATCHER's heirs. Wit: Jesse JANNEY, Daniel MILLER, William CARR, Presley CORDELL.

Bk:Pg: 2V:025   Date: 2 Apr 1817   RtCt: 15 May 1817
Joshua FRED & wife Elizabeth of Ldn to Enoch FURR of Ldn. B/S of 1a (part of land of Joseph FRED Sr. dec'd). Wit: N. C. WILLIAMS, Benj. GRAYSON.

Bk:Pg: 2V:026   Date: 2 Apr 1817   RtCt: 15 May 1817
Enoch FURR Sr. & wife Sarah of Ldn to Joshua FRED of Ldn. B/S of 41a (part of land prch/o Thomas FRED). Wit: Benj. GRAYSON, N. C. WILLIAMS.

Bk:Pg: 2V:028   Date: 2 Apr 1817   RtCt: 15 May 1817
Mordecai THROCKMORTON & wife Sarah of Ldn to Enoch FURR of Ldn. B/S of 128a adj George LINCH (part of land prch/o Thomas A. BROOKE of Md). Wit: Benjamin GRAYSON, N. C. WILLIAMS. Delv. to FURR 12 Feb 1822.

Bk:Pg: 2V:029   Date: 7 Nov 1816   RtCt: 15 May 1817
Thomas DRAKE (s/o Jonathan) of Ldn to William GRAYSON of Georgetown, D.C.. B/S 200a (part of land cnvy/b Thomas DRAKE Sr. dec'd to son Jacob DRAKE dec'd) on E side of Beaverdam adj. Mahlon & Demphrey CARTER, Richard MATTHEWS, Abner HUMPHREYS. Wit: Peter MOORE, Benj. GRAYSON Jr., Geo. M. GRAYSON, Alex. GRAYSON, Lewis ELLZEY, Joshua OSBURN. Delv. to GRAYSON 6 Aug 1819.

Bk:Pg: 2V:031   Date: 13 Apr 1817   RtCt: 5 Jun 1817
Joseph P. THOMAS & wife Sarah of Ldn to William S. NEALE & Jesse GOVER of Ldn. Trust for debt to John B. STEPHENS using 2 lots in Wtfd. Wit: John H. McCABE, Robert BRADEN.

Bk:Pg: 2V:033   Date: 27 Mar 1817   RtCt: 23 May 1817
Jozabed WHITE & wife Margaret of Ldn to Emanuel NEWCOMER of Ldn. B/S of 61a adj Isaac & Samuel NICHOLS, Enos POTTS, James BEAVERS, James CRAIG, David BEALL. Wit: Abiel JENNERS, John H. McCABE.

Bk:Pg: 2V:034   Date: 22 May 1817   RtCt: 29 May 1817
Walter BROOKES of Ldn to James Bowie BROOKS of Georgetown, D.C. Mortgage using negro man Thomas abt. aged 28y, man Trent aged abt. 25y, boy John aged abt 9y, woman Iday & her children Clarrissa, Bet & Jefferson, girl Lucy, horses, farm items, furniture. Wit: James BROOKES, Walter BROOKES, John GILPIN.

Bk:Pg: 2V:036   Date: 21 May 1817   RtCt: 29 May 1817
Walter BROOKES of Ldn to Eliza D. BROOKES. BoS for negro girl Phebe. Wit: James BROOKES, Walter BROOKS, John GILPIN.

Bk:Pg: 2V:036   Date: 21 Apr 1817   RtCt: 10 Jun 1817
James TORBERT of Ldn to Joseph CRAWFORD of MontMd. Trust of 110a (cnvy/b Jonathan CARTER to TORBERT) nr Aldie where TORBERT now resides. Wit: Burr POWELL, Abner GIBSON.

Bk:Pg: 2V:037   Date: 27 Feb 1817   RtCt: 10 Jun 1817
William COCKING & wife Anne of WashDC to Abiel JENNERS of Ldn. B/S of 4 lots on W side of Short Hill – 128a Osburn's Lot, 114¾a Morris' Lot, 40a wood lot, 70a lot. Wit: Wm. THORNTON, James M. DARNAM?

Bk:Pg: 2V:038   Date: 3 Dec 1817   RtCt: 10 Jun 1817
Jesse HARRIS & wife Margaret of Licking Co OH and Joseph WHITE & wife Elizabeth of TN to George TAVENNER Jr. of Ldn. B/S of 230a (all 3 are heirs of George NIXON dec'd who owned land) on road from Snickers Gap to Little River. Wit: John CUNNINGHAM, Nathaniel CUNNINGHAM.

Bk:Pg: 2V:040   Date: 14 Sep 1812   RtCt: 11 Jun 1817
Burgess BALL. Division - George W. BALL (503a in Ldn) agt. of Frances Peyton wd/o Col. Burgess BALL dec'd late of Ldn and Mildred T. BALL (500a in Henderson Co KY and 621a in Warren Co, 624a in Logan Co), Fayette BALL (604a in Ldn), Charles B. BALL (Big Spring stream & 155a in Ldn), Frances W. BALL & Martha D. BALL (500a in Henderson Co KY and 621a in Warren Co, 624a in Logan Co). Males also owe money to guardian of females. Armistead T. MASON & Wilson C. SELDON to sell 125a mt. land nr Leesburg – money given to Geo. W. BALL as guardian of minor heirs. Land sold in Ohio to pay debts. Hugh DOUGLAS, Armistead T. MASON, William NOLAND and Samuel CLAPHAM apptd. commrs. to sell personal property. Gives small plat. Certificates & plat with descriptions from Hopkins Co KY & Warren Co KY. Jun 11, 1817 – George W. BALL has died, devising his shares to his brothers and sisters. Martha D. has married Jonathan C. GIBSON.

Bk:Pg: 2V:049   Date: 6 Jun 1817   RtCt: 11 Jun 1817
William T. T. MASON: Col for slaves Mary abt 40y bright mulatto 5'4" and Sam abt 28y bright mulatto 5'6"or 7" acquired by marriage.

Bk:Pg: 2V:050   Date: 1 Jan 1817   RtCt: 9 Jun 1817
Joseph VANDEVANTER & wife Elizabeth of Ldn to Richard H. HENDERSON of Ldn. B/S100a on Kittocton Mt. (part of land allotted Elizabeth from father William MAINES dec'd). Wit: Abiel JENNERS, Robert BRADEN.

Bk:Pg: 2V:051   Date: 26 Mar 1817   RtCt: 9 Jun 1817
Robert BRADEN of Ldn (as trustee for George JANNEY) to John BAKER of Franklin Co PA. Release of trust dated 5 Nov 1814 on 382a.

Bk:Pg: 2V:052   Date: ___   RtCt: 10 Jun 1817
William CARR & wife ___ of Ldn to Prissy BEESEX of Ldn. B/S of 1a.

Bk:Pg: 2V:053   Date: 29 Apr 1817   RtCt: 10 Jun 1817
Stephen DANIEL & wife Catherine of Ldn to George TAVENER Jr. of Ldn. B/S of 112a adj John GARRETT, Abel GARRETT. Wit: William BRONAUGH, Thos. GREGG.

Bk:Pg: 2V:054   Date: 29 Apr 1817   RtCt: 10 Jun 1817
Gabriel MEGETH & wife Martha of Ldn to Garret WALKER of Ldn. B/S of 3a on Beaverdam adj Stephen DANIEL, James BROWN. Wit: William BRONAUGH, Thos. GREGG. Delv. to WALKER 4 Mar 1822.

Bk:Pg: 2V:055   Date: 29 Apr 1817   RtCt: 10 Jun 1817
Cornelius VANDEVANTER of Ldn to George TAVENER Jr. of Ldn. B/S of 115a on great road from Snickers Gap to Centreville adj Joseph GARRET, Lovell JACKSON. Wit: William BRONAUGH, Thomas GREGG.

Bk:Pg: 2V:057   Date: 29 Apr 1817   RtCt: 10 Jun 1817
George TAVENER Jr. of Ldn to Joseph VANDEVANTER of Ldn. Trust for debt to Cornelius VANDEVANTER using above 115a. Wit: William BRONAUGH, Thomas GREGG.

Bk:Pg: 2V:058   Date: 29 Apr 1817   RtCt: 10 Jun 1817
Geo. TAVENER Jr. of Ldn to Joseph GARRETT of Ldn. Trust for debt to Stephen DANIEL using 115a. Wit: Wm. BRONAUGH, Thos. GREGG.

Bk:Pg: 2V:059   Date: 13 May 1817   RtCt: 10 Jun 1817
George TAVENER Jr. & wife Martha of Ldn to Samuel Sr. & Isaac NICHOLS of Ldn. B/S of 112a on long branch of Goose Creek adj Levi TATE, Joseph GARRETT. Wit: William BRONAUGH, Thos. GREGG. Delv. to Dr. HOGUE 28 May 1827.

Bk:Pg: 2V:060   Date: 29 Apr 1817   RtCt: 10 Jun 1817
Thomas SWICK & wife Ann of Ldn to Garret WALKER of Ldn. B/S of interest in 40a held by Sarah VANHORNE wd/o John VANHORNE dec'd as dower (SWICK would get 1/3 at Sarah's death). Wit: William BRONAUGH, Thomas GREGG. Delv. to WALKER 27 Mar 1821.

Bk:Pg: 2V:062   Date: 20 Feb 1817   RtCt: 10 Jun 1817
Notley C. WILLIAMS & wife Francis of Ldn to Benjamin GRAYSON of Ldn. Trust for debt to Daniel EACHES of Ldn using 278a adj James GRADY, Harry MARKS. Wit: Lewis ELLZEY, Joshua OSBURN.

Bk:Pg: 2V:063   Date: 20 Mar 1817   RtCt: 10 Jun 1817
Abiel JENNERS & wife Deborah of Ldn to John WORSLEY of Ldn. Trust for debt to William COCKING of WashDC using 382a (deed from John BAKER). Wit: Robert BRADEN, John H. McCABE. Delv. to WORSLEY 10 May 1819.

Bk:Pg: 2V:066 Date: 6 Jan 1817 RtCt: 10 Jun 1817
Abiel JENNERS & wife Deborah of Ldn to Henry RUSSELL of Ldn.
B/S of 116a adj Adam GRUBB. Wit: Robert BRADEN, John H.
McCABE. Delv. to RUSSELL 13 May 1822.

Bk:Pg: 2V:067 Date: 17 Dec 1816 RtCt: 10 Jun 1817
Moses JAMES & wife Mary of Muskingum Co OH to Abel JAMES of
Ldn. B/S of 166a on Elk Lick adj Thomas ASBURY (residue of tract
prch/o Benjamin BULLETT by Peter ROSELL). Wit: Andrew HEATH
Jr., William H. McKIM, Benjamin JAMES, John BLAKER.

Bk:Pg: 2V:069 Date: 5 Mar 1817 RtCt: 10 Mar 1817
John CHAMBERS of Ldn to John BOOTH Jr. of Ldn. B/S of 60a
(devised by Robert BOOTH to John during his life and after to heirs
of Thos. STUMP and William CHAMBER). Wit: John S. MARLOW,
William DERRY, Frederick HANDSBY.

Bk:Pg: 2V:070 Date: 3 Apr 1817 RtCt: 11 Jun 1817
George JANNEY & wife Susanna of Ldn to Abraham BAKER of Ldn.
B/S of 114½a adj road to Thompson's and Janney's mills, Thomas
PHILIP, William WILLIAMS dec'd, William VERTZ, Robert BRADEN,
Patrick McGARVIC. Wit: William BRONAUGH, Francis M.
LUCKETT. Delv. to grantee 20 Dec 1819.

Bk:Pg: 2V:072 Date: 9 Jun 1817 RtCt: 12 Jun 1817
Dade P. NOLAND & wife Caroline of Ldn to Thomas R. MOTT of
Ldn. Trust for Samuel CLAPHAM & Wm. NOLAND of Ldn, Jno.
McPHERSON & Clement T. HILLERY of FredMd as endorsers for
Dade on note at Frederick Town Branch Bank using 235a on
Potomack adj Samuel CLAPHAM, Samuel NOLAND, Lloyd
NOLAND where Dade resides. Wit: John H. McCABE, Samuel
LUCKETT. Delv. per order 27 Sep 1826.

Bk:Pg: 2V:074 Date: 12 Jun 1817 RtCt: 12 Jun 1817
Presley CORDELL & wife Amelia of Ldn to Isaac STEAR Sr of Ldn.
B/S of 100a occupied and leased by Joseph GORE adj Burgess
BALL, Thomas BOYD and 31a on road leading from Leesburg to
Noland Ferry adj Thomas SWAN. Wit: Samuel CLAPHAM, Pat'k
McINTYRE.

Bk:Pg: 2V:075 Date: 1 Oct 1816 RtCt: 12 Jun 1817
Josiah WHITE 3rd of Ldn to Joshua OSBURN & James HEATON of
Ldn. Trust for debt to Lewis ELLZEY using 2 tracts of land cnvy/b
ELLZEY & wife Rosannah this day. Wit: Jas. McILHANEY, Joseph
COCKERILL, Herod THOMAS.

Bk:Pg: 2V:077 Date: 1 Jan 1817 RtCt: 12 Jun 1817
Richard H. HENDERSON & wife Orra Moore to Joseph
VANDEVANTER. B/S of 153a on W side of Kittoctan Mt. in Diggs
Valley. Wit: Aris BUCKNER, Presley CORDELL. Delv. to
VANDEVANTER 7 Sep 1818.

Bk:Pg: 2V:078   Date: 13 Jun 1817   RtCt: 13 Jun 1817
William MONROE of Ldn to Sarah LOWE, Edward LOWE & Elizabeth LOWE (ch/o his wife Kitty formerly Kitty LOWE). BoS for household items. Wit: R. H. GOVER, John SURGHNOR, Joshua TAYLOR.

Bk:Pg: 2V:078   Date: ___   RtCt: 16 Jun 1817
Benjamin W. PERRY of Lsbg to Joshua TAYLOR. Trust using slave woman Hannah & her 5 children: Trueman, Westley, Jeraid, Mary & Emily, boy Peter, household items for benefit of Verlinda PERRY & her children. Wit: S. BLINCOE, Wm. SMARR, Thos. MORALLEE.

Bk:Pg: 2V:079   Date: 18 Jun 1817   RtCt: 18 Jun 1817
John WILDMAN & wife Ellener of Ldn to Charles B. BALL of Ldn. B/S of remainder of Lot #7 on S side of Loudoun St in Lsbg. Wit: Samuel MURREY, Presley CORDELL.

Bk:Pg: 2V:081   Date: 14 May 1817   RtCt: 24 Jun 1817
Jonah HUMPHREY & wife Elizabeth of Ldn to Thomas JAMES of Ldn. B/S of 56a on E side of Blue Ridge adj Marcus HUMPHREY, Philip THOMAS, Jonathan PALMER. Wit: Marcus HUMPHREY, Thomas MARKS, John ROSE, Presley CORDELL. Delv. to JAMES 24 Oct 1818.

Bk:Pg: 2V:082   Date: 24 Jun 1817   RtCt: 24 Jun 1817
Alexander HARRISON & wife Susannah of Ldn to Thomas JAMES of Ldn. B/S of 37a adj Nancy YOUNG, Hannah BROWN, William McNIGHT. Wit: John ROSE, Presley CORDELL. Delv. to JAMES 24 Oct 1818.

Bk:Pg: 2V:083   Date: 3 Jul 1817   RtCt: Jun 1817
Silas REESE of Ldn to John WILSON & wife Anna of Ldn. B/S of 59¾a (presently L/L to WILSON) adj William H. HANDY. Wit: Presley CORDELL, John ROSE.

Bk:Pg: 2V:084   Date: 2 Jul 1817   RtCt: 3 Jul 1817
John LICKEY & wife Elizabeth of Ldn to Sampson BLINCOE of Ldn. B/S of 58a on Catockton Mt. adj John C. LICKEY, road from Mdbg by Coes Mill to Lsbg and land BLINCOE bought of John JONES & wife Elizabeth. Wit: Samuel CLAPHAM, Presley CORDELL. Delv. to BLINCOE 25 Apr 1819.

Bk:Pg: 2V:086   Date: 27 Jun 1817   RtCt: 30 Jun 1817
Mandley T. RUST & wife Sally and Eli Offutt & wife Margaret SANFORD of Lsbg to William D. DRISH of Lsbg. B/S of 2 lots in occupation by Benjamin W. PERRY. Wit: Presley CORDELL, Patrick McINTYRE. Delv. grantee 19 Oct 1819.

Bk:Pg: 2V:088   Date: 24 Jan 1816   RtCt: 27 Jan 1817
Samuel HOUGH 3rd of Ldn to Isaac STEER & Asa MOORE of Ldn. Trust for debt to Lydia HOUGH, Polly HOUGH & Sarah HOUGH of Ldn and Levi JAMES of Cincinatti OH using 180a (conveyed to

HOUGH by Lydia HOUGH). Wit: John H. McCABE, Abiel JENNERS. Delv. to HOUGH Feb 1819.

Bk:Pg: 2V:089   Date: __ 1817   RtCt: 1 Jul 1817
Fayette BALL of Ldn and George RUST Jr of Ldn. Exchange land on W side of rd from Lsbg to Nolands Ferry allotted Fayette & brother Geo. W. BALL dec'd for land on Potomac.

Bk:Pg: 2V:091   Date: __ 1817   RtCt: 2 Jul 1817
Fayete BALL, Charles B. BALL & Mildred T. BALL (Exors of George Washington BALL dec'd) to George RUST. B/S of 503a (allotted G. W. from father Burgess BALL's estate). Delv. to Jno. SINCLAIR by directive of RUST 15 Feb 1839.

Bk:Pg: 2V:092   Date: 1 Jul 1817   RtCt: 2 Jul 1817
James RUST & wife Sarah of Ldn to Tho. R. MOTT of Ldn. Trust for debt to Exors of George W. BALL using 169a adj Lsbg. Wit: Presley CORDELL, Patrick McINTYRE.

Bk:Pg: 2V:094   Date: 1 July 1817   RtCt: 2 Jul 1817
George RUST Jr. & wife Maria C. of Ldn to Thos. R. MOTT of Ldn. Trust for debt to Exors of George W. BALL using 503a.

Bk:Pg: 2V:096   Date: 20 Mar 1817   RtCt: 5 Jul 1817
Daniel LOVETT of Ldn to Jonathan MILBURNE of Ldn. Loan of mare and colt. Wit: J. L. DRAIN, Geo. C. MANN.

Bk:Pg: 2V:096   Date: 9 Jul 1816   RtCt: Jul 1817
Ludwell LEE & wife Eliza to Bazel STONESTREET. CoE for sale of 151 9/10a. Wit: Samuel MURREY, Presley CORDELL.

Bk:Pg: 2V:097   Date: 24 Jan 1817   RtCt: Aug 1817
George TAVENER Jr. & wife Martha of Ldn to Jonathan CARTER of Ldn. B/S of 230a (cnvy/b Jesse HARRIS). Wit: William BRONAUGH, Francis W. LUCKETT. Delv. to CARTER 31 Aug 1820.

Bk:Pg: 2V:098   Date: 28 Feb 1815   RtCt: 14 Jul 1817
Col. Francis PEYTON. Division of 3000a on Lickey creek in KY to Townshend D. PEYTON, William HALE & Leven LUCKETT. Claims have been made agst land and named three will defend. Wit: W. S. DARRELL, H. B. POWELL, Henry D. HALE.

Bk:Pg: 2V:099   Date: 27 Mar 1817   RtCt: 12 May 1817
Mason FRENCH of Ldn to Bernard HOOE of PrWm. B/S of __a adj Francis AUBRAY, Bernard HOOE. Wit: R. B. BUCKNER, John HENISEY, Richard PRESGRAVES, Hugh COCKERILL, Wm. ROSE. Del to Aris BUCKNER 14 Aug 1820.

Bk:Pg: 2V:100   Date: 14 Jul 1817   RtCt: 14 Jul 1817
Charles DRISH & wife Susannah of Ldn to Samuel CLAPHAM of Ldn. B/S of ½a adj Lot #14 on S side of Market St. Wit: John HAMILTON, Josias CLAPHAM, Presley CORDELL.

Bk:Pg: 2V:101   Date: 10 May 1817   RtCt: 4 Jul 1817
Joseph P. THOMAS of Ldn to Thos. R. MOTT of Ldn. Trust to indemnify Wm. COOKE & Israel LACEY's heirs (THOMAS built mill house on Big Spring stream but may not be sufficient) using 2 lots in Waterford (tavern, storehouse & stable). Wit: Abiel JENNERS, John H. McCABE.

Bk:Pg: 2V:104   Date: 5 Jul 1817   RtCt: 14 Jul 1817
James KINCHELOE & wife Elizabeth of Fqr to Reuben TRIPLETT of Ldn. B/S of 2 lots in Middleburg (conveyed to KINCHELOE by Andrew SMARR), adj Lot #40, Jacob MANN, Dr. COCHRANE in occupation of John BRADY, Saml. HENDERSON. Wit: Burr POWELL, Abner GIBSON.

Bk:Pg: 2V:105   Date: 10 Apr 1817   RtCt: 18 Jul 1817
Thomas REID & wife Catherine of Ldn to Henry PLASTER of Ldn. B/S of 11a Lot #2 on S fork of Beaverdam (from div. of Thomas REID dec'd). Wit: Benjamin GRAYSON, Cuthbert POWELL.

Bk:Pg: 2V:107   Date: 5 Apr 1817   RtCt: 9 Jun 1817
John B. STEVENS & wife Sarah of Ldn to Lewis KLEIN of Ldn. B/S of 26½ sq poles adj Wtfd adj John F. SAPPINGTON, John PALMER. Wit: Abiel JENNERS, John H. McCABE. Delv. to KLEIN 29 Apr 1820

Bk:Pg: 2V:108   Date: 24 Jul 1817   RtCt: 24 Jul 1817
Seth SINCLAIR of Ldn to George SINCLAIR of Ldn. B/S of 50a (devised from intestate of father John SINCLAIR dec'd of Ldn, plat and div. in DB H:101) and 7a from widow's dower (plat in chancery suit for div.). Delv. to Chs. GULLATT who bought the same 14 Nov 1843.

Bk:Pg: 2V:109   Date: 9 Aug 1817   RtCt: 9 Aug 1817
George TAVENER Jr. of Ldn to Saml. M. EDWARDS of Ldn. Trust for debt to Peter BENEDUM using 268a.

Bk:Pg: 2V:110   Date: 21 Jul 1817   RtCt: 21 Jul 1817
John DRISH & wife Eleanor of Lsbg to Richard H. HENDERSON of Lsbg. B/S of lot in Lsbg adj Thomas JACOBS, Jno. H. EVANS, Jno. B. RATTKIN, Jno. NIXEN, C. CORDELL, P. BELTZ, Ignatius NORRIS, Chas. DRISH. Wit: Presley CORDELL, Patrick McINTYRE.

Bk:Pg: 2V:111   Date: 25 Oct 1816   RtCt: 24 Jun 1817
Spencer DONALDSON of Ldn to his children John Bailey, Catherine w/o Joseph D. BELL, Wesley, George, Juliana, Winifred and James William DONALDSON. Gift of negroes Lizzy, Charity, Harry, Jim, Mary, Lewis, Jacob, Sarah, Matilda and Alfred, farm and household items. Wit: James McDANIEL, Archibald McDANIEL.

Bk:Pg: 2V:112   Date: 19 Jul 1817   RtCt: 21 Jul 1817
James H. HAMILTON & wife Margaret of Lsbg to Samuel CLAPHAM of Ldn. B/S of lot on S side of Market St. adj John McCORMICK,

William DRISH. Wit: Tho. R. MOTT, Wm. CHILTON, John McCORMICK, Patrick McINTYRE, Stephen C. ROSZEL. Rec'd the orig'l by direction of CLAPHAM 11 Jun 1823.

Bk:Pg: 2V:114   Date: 26 Jul 1817   RtCt: 1 Aug 1817
Richd. H. HENDERSON of Ldn to Thomas WHITE of OH of Scotland Mills in Ldn. In Sup'r Ct. of chancery for Winchester Thomas WHITE agst Samuel SPENCER dec'd, if SPENCER removes from VA, HENDERSON to give WHITE ½ of 100a & ½ of Scotland Mills.

Bk:Pg: 2V:115   Date: 18 Jun 1817   RtCt: 18 Jun 1817
Charles B. BALL of Ldn to Enos WILDMAN of Ldn. Trust for debt to John WILDMAN using remainder of Lot #7 in Lsbg.

Bk:Pg: 2V:116   Date: 28 Jun 1817   RtCt: 8 Aug 1817
Henry GLASGOW & wife Cath'e of Lsbg to Joshua RILEY of Ldn. B/S of lot & house in Lsbg adj Samuel M. EDWARDS, Peter BOSS. Wit: Saml. M. EDWARDS, Presley CORDELL, John ROSE. Delv. to RILEY 1 Jan 1821.

Bk:Pg: 2V:117   Date: 9 Aug 1817   RtCt: 9 Aug 1817
Peter BENEDUM & wife Catherine of Ldn to George TAVENER Jr. of Ldn. B/S of 268a adj Wm. McGEATH, Joseph JANNEY. Wit: Patrick McINTYRE, Presley CORDELL. Delv. to TAVENER 4 May 1818.

Bk:Pg: 2V:119   Date: 5 Mar 1817   RtCt: 1 Aug 1817
John B. STEVENS and John BRADEN (Exors of Thos. D. STEVENS dec'd) of Ldn to Robert BRADEN of Ldn. B/S of 45 perches in Hllb adj Richard COPELAND. Wit: Abiel JENNERS, J. H. McCABE. Delv. to Fleming W. HIXON 10 Apr 1831.

Bk:Pg: 2V:120   Date: 30 May 1817   RtCt: Aug 1817
John Conrad LICKEY & wife Margaret of Ldn to George CARTER of Oatlands. B/S of 9a adj LICKEY, ___ LOVETT, Robert COE. Wit: Thomas GREGG, Presley CORDELL. Delv. to Jesse TIMMS pr order filed DB XX:85 on 26 Oct 1819.

Bk:Pg: 2V:121   Date: 4 Mar 1811   RtCt: 11 Aug 1817
Henry ASBURY of RichVa to William JAMES Jr. of Ldn. B/S of 102a on Elk Licking Run formerly occupied by Joseph FOX dec'd. Wit: Amos FOX, Reuben SETTLE, Deen JAMES, William ANDERS, Wm. ROSE. Delv. to Dean JAMES Admr of grantee 20 May 1820.

Bk:Pg: 2V:122   Date: 1 Nov 1815   RtCt: 11 Nov 1816/11 Aug 1817
Mary MASON & son Stevens Thomas MASON of Ldn and Isaac S. WHITE of Ldn. Exchange of 10a allotted to Stevens Thomson MASON in div. of raspberry plain estate for 10a allotted to John T. MASON Jr. Wit: W. T. MASON, Thomson MASON, Wm. M. McCARTY, Armstead T. MASON.

Bk:Pg: 2V:124 Date: 2 Jul 1817 RtCt: 13 Aug 1817
Joseph WHITE & wife Elizabeth of Hawkins Co TN to friend William WHITE of Ldn. PoA for sale of land in Ldn.

Bk:Pg: 2V:125 Date: 17 Jun 1817 RtCt: 12 Aug 1817
Abel MARKS dec'd. Division of money and slaves to dower to Mary MARKS (slaves Ralph, Alce, Hannah & her child Eliza, Dinah, James, Charlott, Fanney), Bennet MARKS (slaves Darkus, Nelly & her child Delilale abt 12m old), Mason MARKS (slave Stephen), Mary PEW w/o Elisha PEW (slave Sally & her child John abt 5m), Lydia MARKS (slave Charity), Samuel MARKS, Margaret HUMPHREY w/o Marcus HUMPHREY (slave Uriah), Thomas MARKS (slave Jesse), Abel MARKS (slaves Isaiah and Emly), Elizabeth w/o James WARFORD (slave Phebe), Watts MARKES (slaves Washington and Rachel), Samuel MARKES (slaves Dick and Harriet). Divisors: James COCHRAN, James NICKOLS, Richard OSBURN.

Bk:Pg: 2V:126 Date: 16 Oct 1816 RtCt: 13 Aug 1817
George NICHOLS dec'd. Division of land. widow's dower (39a), Elizabeth NICHOLS (11a), Sarah NICKOLS (11a), Thomas NICKOLS (11a), Jonah NICKOLS (11a), T(h)amar TRACEY (11a), Nancy TRACEY (11a), Bethsheba BYRNES (11a), Eli NICKOLS 11), John NICKOLS (12a), David NICKOLS (11a). Divisors: Stacy TAYLOR, Joshua OSBURN, Charles CHAMBLIN. Gives small plat.

Bk:Pg: 2V:127 Date: 13 Aug 1817 RtCt: 13 Aug 1817
Bernard TAYLOR & wife Sarah of Ldn to Abraham SKILLMAN of Ldn. B/S of 269a adj Abel JANNEY, Thomas BROWN, John VERNON, Nathan BROWN. Wit: Jno. A. BINNS.

Bk:Pg: 2V:129 Date: 11 Aug 1817 RtCt: 11 Aug 1818
Calvin THATCHER, Thomas GREGG of Short Hill & Jno. LOVE. Bond on THATCHER as Constable in __ district. Wit: Tho. R. MOTT.

Bk:Pg: 2V:129 Date: 7 Jul 1817 RtCt: 14 Aug 1817
Appointment of Wilson C. SELDON to continue as Sheriff for two years.

Bk:Pg: 2V:130 Date: 14 Aug 1817 RtCt: 14 Aug 1817
Wilson C. SELDON, Wm. D. DRISH, Robert MOFFETT, Robert M. NEWMAN, John GRAY, Wm. CHILTON, James RUSK, John DRISH, Richd H. HENDERSON, Benjn. SHREVE, Saml. CARR. Bond on SELDON as Sheriff to collect and receive officers fees.

Bk:Pg: 2V:130 Date: 14 Aug 1817 RtCt: 14 Aug 1817
Wilson C. SELDON, Jas. RUST, Robert MOFFETT, William D. DRISH, Robert M. NEWMAN, Wm. CHILDON, Jno. GRAY, Jno. DRISH, Richd H. HENDERSON, Benjamin SHREVE, Saml. CARR. Bond on SELDON as Sheriff to collect levies.

Bk:Pg: 2V:131   Date: 14 Aug 1817   RtCt: 14 Aug 1817
Wilson C. SELDON, Jas. RUST, Robert MOFFETT, William D.
DRISH, Robert M. NEWMAN, Wm. CHILDON, Jno. GRAY, Jno.
DRISH, Richd H. HENDERSON, Benjamin SHREVE, Saml. CARR.
Bond on SELDON as Sheriff to collect taxes.

Bk:Pg: 2V:132   Date: 13 Aug 1817   RtCt: 13 Aug 1817
Abraham SKILLMAN & wife Violinda of Ldn to Thomas BROWN of
Ldn. B/S of 53a adj Bernard TAYLOR, __ TOMLINSON, __
GIBSON. Wit: Jno. A. BINNS. Delv. to BROWN 30 Nov 1826.

Bk:Pg: 2V:133   Date: 1 Jul 1817   RtCt: 11 Aug 1817
Benjamin A. STONESTREET of Ldn to Sarah STONESTREET of
Ldn. B/S of 220a & 152a on Sterling Branch and slaves John, Sam,
Davy, Luce, Pen, Tilda, Jim & Kitty child of Luce, farm and
household items that Benj. is entitled to at death of his mother
Elizabeth from estate of his father Bazil dec'd. Wit: Henry JONES,
Charles OFFUTT. Wit: Johnston CLEVELAND, Charles OFFUTT.
Delv. to Benj. A. STONESTREET 16 Dec 1819.

Bk:Pg: 2V:134   Date: 13 Aug 1817   RtCt: 13 Aug 1817
Abraham SKILLMAN & wife Violinda of Ldn to David SMITH and
Daniel JANNEY of Ldn. Trust for debt to Bernard TAYLOR using
269a. Wit: Jno. A. BINNS. Delv. to TAYLOR 29 Mar 1826.

Bk:Pg: 2V:135   Date: 1 Sept 1817   RtCt: 8 Sep 1817
Henry ELLIS & wife Jane of Ldn to Joseph HART of Ldn. B/S of 2a
on NW fork of Goose Creek adj Samuel GREGG. Wit: Robert
BRADEN, William CARR. Delv. to HART 26 Feb 1823.

Bk:Pg: 2V:137   Date: 27 Mar 1817   RtCt: 8 Sep 1817
Thomas LESLIE & wife Nancy of Ldn to Jesse EVANS of Ldn. B/S
of 75½a. Wit: Abiel JENNERS, Joshua OSBURN. Delv. to EVANS 7
Nov 1823.

Bk:Pg: 2V:138   Date: 15 Dec 1816   RtCt: Sept 1817
James MACKLAN & wife Mary of Ldn to Amos JOHNSON (paid by
Samuel & Nicholas GARRETT) of Ldn. B/S of ½a on old turnpike
road occupied by Enock GLASSCOCK. Wit: Francis M. LUCKETT,
Wm. BRONAUGH. Delv. to JOHNSON 9 Aug 1819.

Bk:Pg: 2V:139   Date: 2 Aug 1817   RtCt: 25 Aug 1817
Joseph BARTON & wife Rachel of Ldn to Abner HUMPHREY of
Ldn. B/S of 4a adj Bloomfield and John RALPH, Benj. GRAYSON
Jr. Wit: Benjamin GRAYSON, William BRONAUGH.

Bk:Pg: 2V:141   Date: 13 Aug 1817   RtCt: 13 Aug 1817
Thomas BROWN of Ldn to Abraham SKILLMAN of Ldn. Trust for
debt to Abraham SKILLMAN using 53a. Wit: Jno. A. BINNS. Delv. to
SKILMAN 14 Aug 1820.

Bk:Pg: 2V:142   Date: 2 Sept 1817   RtCt: 3 Sep 1817
Benjamin BRIDGES & wife Kitturah of Ldn to James B. LANE of
Ldn. Trust for support of Newton KEENE (s/o Kitturah) using 192a

on Little River Turnpike allotted Kitturah as an heir of Hardage LANE dec'd. Wit: William B. HARRISON, Charles LEWIS. Delv. to N. KEENE 8 Sep 1834.

Bk:Pg: 2V:143   Date: 6 Feb 1817   RtCt: 20 Aug 1817
Amos GIBSON & wife Hannah of Ldn to William KENWORTHY & Mahlon TAYLOR of Ldn. Trust for debt to Israel JANNEY using 133¾a. Wit: Benj. BRADFIELD, Wm. NICKOLS, Jesse HURST, Samuel MURRAY, Presley CORDELL.

Bk:Pg: 2V:146   Date: 10 May 1817   RtCt: 11 Aug 1817
Mahlon HOUGH & wife Mary of Ldn to David JANNEY of Ldn. B/S of __a (cnvy/b Thomas SWANN & Jane BYRD). Wit: Joshua OSBURN, John H. McCABE.

Bk:Pg: 2V:148   Date: 11 Aug 1817   RtCt: 11 Aug 1817
Henry PLETCHER & wife Dolly of Ldn to John GEORGE of Ldn. B/S of 100½a (prch/o Christian NIGHSWANGER). Wit: Abiel JENNERS, Robt. BRADEN. Delv. 24 Aug 1820.

Bk:Pg: 2V:149   Date: 11 Aug 1817   RtCt: 11 Aug 1817
Henry PLETCHER & wife Dolly of Ldn to John GEORGE of Ldn. B/S of 25a on side of Short Hill adj Michael EVERHART, Susannah SMITH. Wit: Abiel JENNERS, Robert BRADEN. Delv. 24 Aug 1820.

Bk:Pg: 2V:150   Date: 20 Dec 1816   RtCt: 11 Aug 1817
John MATHIAS of Ldn to Nicholas ROPP of Ldn. B/S of 45a on W side of Short Hill adj John DEMERY, Peter DEMERY. Wit: Peter DEMERY, Walter CURISK, Philip DERRY. Delv. to ROPP 14 Sep 1832.

Bk:Pg: 2V:152   Date: 2 Jun 1817   RtCt: 11 Aug 1817
Thomas DAVIS & wife Elizabeth of Ldn to Adam HOUSHOLDER of Ldn. B/S of 1a where DAVIS now lives adj Sanford RAMEY. Wit: Robert BRADEN, John H. McCABE. Delv. to HOUSEHOLDER 8 Feb 1820.

Bk:Pg: 2V:153   Date: 5 Dec 1816   RtCt: 11 Aug 1817
Joseph P. THOMAS & wife Sarah of Ldn to William S. NEALE of Ldn. Trust for debt to Isaac WALKER & Jacob MENDENHALL of Ldn using Lot #3 adj Wtfd and stone house in Wtfd adj Fleman PATTISON dec'd. Wit: Robert BRADEN, John H. McCABE.

Bk:Pg: 2V:155   Date: 31 May 1817   RtCt: 11 Aug 1817
Jonathan REED & wife Elizabeth of Ldn to Samuel BEAVERS of Ldn. B/S of 62a (cnvy/b Swithin NICKETTS [NICHOLS]). Wit: William BRONAUGH, Francis M. LUCKETT.

Bk:Pg: 2V:157   Date: 7 Apr 1817   RtCt: 11 Aug 1817
David JANNEY & wife Elizabeth of Ldn to Isaac STEER of Wtfd. B/S of Lots # 4 & #5 (½a) on Fairfax St. in new addition to Wtfd. Wit: Abiel JENNERS, John H. McCABE.

Bk:Pg: 2V:158   Date: 1 Mar 1817   RtCt: 11 Aug 1817
David JANNEY & wife Elizabeth of Ldn to William B. STEER of Ldn.
B/S of ¼a Lot #6 in new addition to Wtfd on Fairfax St. Wit: Abiel
JENNERS, John H. McCABE. Delv. grantee 27 May 1829.

Bk:Pg: 2V:160   Date: 21 Mar 1817   RtCt: 1 Sep 1817
James MOORE, Asa MOORE & John WILLIAMS (Exors of Mahlon
JANNEY dec'd) of Wtfd to Joseph WOOD of Ldn. B/S of 80a adj
Joseph TALBOTT, mill race, Jonas POTTS, Stephen BALL,
Benjamin STEER, new addition to Wtfd. Wit: Robert BRADEN, Abiel
JENNERS. Delv. to WOOD 13 Sep 1823.

Bk:Pg: 2V:161   Date: 31 May 1817   RtCt: 13 Aug 1817
Sarah WHITE of Jefferson Co TN to friend William WHITE of Ldn.
PoA to sell land in Ldn. Delv. to Wm. WHITE 30 Sep 1819.

Bk:Pg: 2V:162   Date: 8 Aug 1818 [17]   RtCt: 11 Aug 1817
Jozabed WHITE & wife Margaret of Ldn to William HERRON of Ldn.
B/S of 9a on N fork of Goose Creek adj Jas. BEANS, John
HOLMES. Wit: Abiel JENNERS, J. H. McCABE. Delv. to HERRON
on 25 Nov 1818.

Bk:Pg: 2V:164   Date: 4 Aug 1817   RtCt: 11 Aug 1817
John WITTERMAN & wife Catherine of Ldn to George COOPER of
Ldn. B/S of 29a on E side of Short Hill. Wit: John McCABE, Robert
BRADEN. Delv. to Jno. COOPER Admr of Geo. COOPER dec'd 12
May 1847.

Bk:Pg: 2V:165   Date: 4 Aug 1817   RtCt: 11 Aug 1817
John WITTERMAN & wife Catherine of Ldn to George COOPER of
Ldn. B/S of 109a adj Peter VIRTZ, Joseph SMITH, Christian RUSE,
__ BRADEN. Wit: Robert BRADEN, John H. McCABE. Delv. to Jno.
COOPER Admr. of Geo. COOPER dec'd 12 May 1847.

Bk:Pg: 2V:166   Date: 27 Dec 1816   RtCt: 11 Aug 1817
Presley WILLIAMS & wife Jane of Ldn to Peter COMPHER of Ldn.
B/S of 27a Lot #3 in div. of Reuben HIXSON dec'd. Wit: Robt.
BOGUE, Addison TUTTLE, Joseph HAWKINS, John H. McCABE,
Robert BRADEN. Delv. to COMPHER 18 Jun 1828.

Bk:Pg: 2V:168   Date: 6 Jun 1817   RtCt: 11 Aug 1817
Moses WILSON & wife Tamar of Ldn to Edward WILLSON of Ldn.
B/S of 18a on S ridge of Goose Creek below mouth of Wanapin
Branch adj Jehu BURSON. Wit: Burr POWELL, A. GIBSON.

Bk:Pg: 2V:169   Date: 26 Mar 1817   RtCt: 11 Aug 1817
William WARNER of Ldn to George WARNER of Ldn. B/S of 50a in
Digg's Valley adj Samuel EDWARDS, R. H. HENDERSON. Wit:
Robert BRADEN, Abiel JENNERS. Delv. to WARNER 26 Aug 1826.

Bk:Pg: 2V:170   Date: 6 Aug 1817   RtCt: 11 Aug 1817
Hugh WILEY Jr. & wife Jane of Ldn to James BATTSON of Ldn. B/S
of ½a (cnvy/b John WILLSON as guardian of heirs of John
JOHNSTONE dec'd to Wm. WILEY and by him to Hugh WILEY) on

Snicker's Gap Turnpike road adj Andrew BEATY. Wit: Burr POWELL, A. GIBSON.

Bk:Pg: 2V:171 Date: 5 Apr 1817 RtCt: 11 Aug 1817
Joseph STEER & wife Sarah of Wtfd to John SCHOOLEY of Wtfd. B/S of house and lot in old section of Wtfd adj Flemmon PATTERSON and nearly adj Isaac STEER. Wit: Abiel JENNERS, John H. McCABE.

Bk:Pg: 2V:173 Date: 1 Sep 1817 RtCt: 1 Sep 1817
John TRIPLETT & wife Elizabeth of Lsbg to Anne ECKART of Ldn. B/S of part of lot in Lsbg on E side of King St adj William CLINE. Wit: Presley CORDELL, William CARR. Delv. pr order 22 Oct 1821.

Bk:Pg: 2V:174 Date: 7 Apr 1817 RtCt: 11 Aug 1817
John B. STEVENS & wife Sarah of Ldn to John PALMER of Ldn. B/S of 27 sq pole lot adj Wtfd adj Lewis KLEIN, John F. SAPPINGTON. Wit: John H. McCABE, Robert BRADEN. Delv. to PALMER 4 Jun 1821.

Bk:Pg: 2V:176 Date: 5 Feb 1817 RtCt: 20 Aug 1817
Patrick MILHOLLAND & wife Malinda of Ldn to Sampson BLINCOE of Ldn. Trust for debt to Mathew MITCHELL & Reuben SCHOOLEY of Ldn using Lot #16 in Lsbg on Loudoun & Back St. Wit: Thomas MORALLEE, Jno. DREAN, Geo. K. FOX. Agreement on payment for improvements by MITCHELL based on rent paid by Aaron SCHOOLEY who rents MILHOLLAND's 117a plantation. Delv. to MITCHELL 1 Mar 1819.

Bk:Pg: 2V:178 Date: 1 Mar 1817 RtCt: 26 Aug 1817
Thomas DRAKE of Ldn to Richard MATTHEWS of Ldn. B/S of 1a in Bloomfield. Wit: Benjamin GRAYSON, Notely [Notley] C. WILLIAMS.

Bk:Pg: 2V:180 Date: 3 Feb 1817 RtCt: 15 Aug 1817
Benjamin DAWES & wife Ann D. of Ldn to William C. NEWTON of AlexDC. B/S of parts of Lot #3 and #5 on NE side of main st. in Millsville. Wit: Francis W. LUCKETT, A. GIBSON.

Bk:Pg: 2V:181 Date: 24 Jun 1816 RtCt: 21 Aug 1817
Samuel CLAPHAM & wife Elizabeth. Survey of 61a and CoE for deed dated 24 Jul 1816. Gives plat by surveyor Jno. MATHIAS. Wit: Charles LEWIS, John ROSE.

Bk:Pg: 2V:182 Date: 27 Mar 1817 RtCt: 19 Aug 1817
Sampson GUY of Ldn to Jesse McVEIGH of Ldn. B/S of 18¾a on Turnpike road from Mdbg to Alex'a formerly owned by Jno. Peyton HARRISON now dec'd. Wit: Jas. SIMPSON, John KILE, George KILE, John McKENNEY, Burr POWELL, A. GIBSON. Delv. to McVEIGH 11 Sep 1820.

Bk:Pg: 2V:183 Date: 15 Jul 1817 RtCt: 16 Jul 1817
Thomas N. BINNS of BaltMd to John A. BINNS of Lsbg. Trust for debt to William A. BINNS & Charles Fenton MERCER of Ldn. MERCER assigned to Thomas BINNS towards payment of purchase

money of tract in FredMd debts agst Francis HESEFORD [HEREFORD?] in name of James MERCER's Admrs, Joseph W. MULLENS, Jacob ISH & James SIMPSON, Wm. M. PROSSER, Levi MUNSELL of Mason Co, John G. NELSON of Mason Co, James TORBERT, Benjamin RUST, Ninian EDWARD & Jno. LITTLETON, Hugh DOUGLASS' Exors, John BAYLY, Thomas Biscoe LEE.

Bk:Pg: 2V:185   Date: 29 Sep 1817   RtCt: 13 Jan 1818
Alexander YOUNG & wife Elizabeth of Ldn to Thomas YOUNG of Washington city. B/S of 316a adj James COLEMAN, Horsepen Run. Wit: Johnston CLEVELAND, Abiel JENNERS. Delv. to Johnston CLEVELAND pr order 14 Sep 1818.

Bk:Pg: 2V:186   Date: 30 Apr 1817   RtCt: 20 Aug 1817
Richard H. HENDERSON (trustee of Richard H. LOVE & wife Elizabeth Matilda late of Ffx) of Ldn to Wilson C. SELDON of Ldn. B/S of 217a on Broad Run (to secure payment from LOVE to Edward DULIN, which LOVE failed to pay).

Bk:Pg: 2V:187   Date: 8 Sep 1817   RtCt: 8 Sep 1817
Charles Fenton MERCER of Aldie to Benjamin HAGERMAN of Ldn. B/S of 21¾a in Fqr & Ldn adj where HAGERMAN now lives, Isaac LAKE.

Bk:Pg: 2V:188   Date: 8 Sep 1817   RtCt: 8 Sep 1817
Jesse McVEIGH and Hugh RODGERS. Bond on McVEIGH as commr. Wit: Tho. R. MOTT.

Bk:Pg: 2V:189   Date: 8 Sep 1817   RtCt: 8 Sep 1817
Daniel LOVETT and Rich'd H. HENDERSON. Bond on LOVETT as commr. of revenue. Wit: Tho. R. MOTT.

Bk:Pg: 2V:189   Date: 8 Sep 1817   RtCt: 8 Sep 1817
Jesse TIMMS and Geo. CARTER. Bond on TIMMS as commr.

Bk:Pg: 2V:190   Date: 17 Jun 1817   RtCt: 8 Sep 1817
Samuel SINCLAIR. Division. Amos SINCLAIR & George SINCLAIR vs. Edith SINCLAIR & others in chancery. Some of land bought by Amos & Samuel SINCLAIR jointly from John McELLDOR & wife Ann. Amos SINCLAIR (18a), reps of Samuel SINCLAIR dec'd (18a & 16a), Geo. SINCLAIR (16a). Gives plat. Divisors: Saml. LUCKETT, Edward DULIN, Isaac STEER.

Bk:Pg: 2V:192   Date: 4 Jan 1817   RtCt: 13 Oct 1817
Philip STRIDER & wife Catherine of FredMd to John HOPKINS Jr. of FredMd. Mortgage using 250a nr Harper's Ferry including tenement formerly leased by Abraham TULLYFRANK.

Bk:Pg: 2V:194   Date: 12 Apr 1817   RtCt: Oct [1817]
Jesse McVEIGH & wife Elizabeth of Ldn to John HARRIS of Mdbg. B/S of part of Lot #29 in Mdbg adj Lot #28 of Noble BEVEREDGE on Washington St. Wit: Burr POWELL, Benjamin SMITH, Cuth't POWELL Jr., Hiram McVEIGH, Leven POWELL, A. GIBSON.

Bk:Pg: 2V:195   Date: 6 Mar 1817   RtCt: Oct 1817
Richard MATTHEWS & wife Elizabeth of Ldn to John W. B.
GRAYSON of Ldn. Trust for debt to Stephen McPHERSON of Ldn
using 1a lot in Bloomfield adj William R. COMBS, William
GRAYSON. Wit: Benjamin GRAYSON, Notley C. WILLIAMS. Delv.
to GRAYSON's trustee 8 Dec 1818.

Bk:Pg: 2V:197   Date: 23 Sep 1817   RtCt: 23 Sep 1817
John G. BOWEN of Ldn to William GILPIN of D.C. BoS for furniture.

Bk:Pg: 2V:197   Date: 13 Sep 1817   RtCt: 30 Sep 1817
Charles BINNS & wife Hannah of Lsbg to Richard H. HENDERSON
of Lsbg. B/S of ½a lot in Lsbg on Market St. adj W. WRIGHT's reps.
Wit: Samuel MURREY, John ROSE.

Bk:Pg: 2V:199   Date: 26 Sep 1817   RtCt: 26 Sep 1817
John NIXON Jr. & wife Jane of Ldn to Jacob FADLEY of Ldn. B/S of
4a (part of land allotted to Jane, late Jane CIMMINGS as heir of
Thomas CIMMINGS dec'd). Wit: Samuel MURRAY, Presley
CORDELL. Delv. to FADLEY 26 Apr 1819.

Bk:Pg: 2V:200   Date: 24 Jan 1817   RtCt: 23 Sep 1817
Turner OSBURN and Herod OSBURN & wife Eleanor of Ldn to
Stephen McPHERSON of Ldn. B/S of 173a (prch/o George RUST)
adj John ROMINE now BLAKELEY, Wm. FRANCIS, Peter ROMINE
the elder and the younger. Wit: Notley C. WILIAMS, Joshua
OSBURN. Delv. to McPHERSON 15 Jun 1825.

Bk:Pg: 2V:201   Date: 24 Jan 1817   RtCt: 23 Sep 1817
Turner OSBURN and Herod OSBURN & wife Eleanor of Ldn to
William WIN of Ldn. B/S of 116a (prch/o George RUST) adj John
HANBY, Martin OVERFIELD, William Ludwell LEE. Wit: Notely
[Notley] C. WILLIAMS, Joshua OSBURN. Delv. to WINN 27 Sep
1821.

Bk:Pg: 2V:203   Date: 22 Sep 1817   RtCt: 26 Sep 1817
John NIXON Jr. & wife Jane of Ldn to George RHODES of Ldn. B/S
of 29a adj Jacob FADELY. Wit: Samuel MURREY, Presley
CORDELL. Delv. to RHODES 9 Sep 1836.

Bk:Pg: 2V:204   Date: 6 Mar 1817   RtCt: 23 Sep 1817
Stephen GREGG & wife Harriet of Ldn to John W. B. GRAYSON of
Ldn. Trust for debt to Stephen McPHERSON using 1½a adj John
RALPH, Wm. COMBS, Abner HUMPHREY. Wit: Noteley C.
WILLIAMS, Benjamin GRAYSON.

Bk:Pg: 2V:206   Date: 26 Sep 1817   RtCt: 26 Sep 1817
John NIXON & wife Jane of Ldn to Josiah HALL of Ldn. B/S of 38a
adj Josiah HALL, Joel NIXON, John NIXON (s/o George). Wit:
Presley CORDELL, Samuel MURREY. Delv. to HALL 7 Apr 1820.

Bk:Pg: 2V:207   Date: 12 Apr 1817   RtCt: 2 Oct 1817
Isaac S. GARDNER & wife Martha of Ffx to James B. LANE of Ldn.
B/S of 521a (7 undivided 9ths of estate of Hardage LANE dec'd

encumbered with LS of BLINCOE) adj church road, Abraham BARNS & his sisters. Wit: A. G. MONROE, J. L. DREAN, Henry PEARS?, George LEE, Geo. N. RATTS, Fleet SMITH, W. C. WOODROW.

Bk:Pg: 2V:208   Date: 4 Aug 1817   RtCt: 12 Oct 1817
Nathan HUTCHISON & wife Hannah of Ldn to Charles LEWIS of Ldn. B/S of 320a of Horsepen tract, adj Henry JONES, George BERKLEY, William PRESGREVES, __ STONESTREET. Wit: Aris BUCKNER, John BAYLY.

Bk:Pg: 2V:210   Date: 16 Apr 1817   RtCt: 23 Aug 1817
Samuel ADAMS & wife Catherine of Ldn to John R. ADAMS of Ldn. B/S of 200a on upper side of Goose Creek (remainder of tract sold ADAMS by Jonas POTTS with 100a conveyed to Peter BEMENDAFFER in 1813). Wit: Thomas FOUCH, Stephen C. ROZELL. Delv. to John R. ADAMS 10 Mar 1819.

Bk:Pg: 2V:211   Date: 1 Sep 1817   RtCt: 12 Sep 1817
Thomas W. POWELL & wife Clarissa of Ldn to James RUST of Ldn. B/S of 361a adj John RICHARDS, Henry CARTER, Thomas JOHNS, Burr POWELL Jr. (part of land dev. POWELL by Col. Leven POWELL dec'd). Sarah R. POWELL wd/o William H. POWELL dec'd to remain in possession of her 138a dower land until her death. Wit: Jno. W. B. GRAYSON, Jno. S. RUST, Geo. NOBLE, Samuel BRINK, Cuthbert POWELL, Benjamin GRAYSON. Delv. to RUST 14 Apr 1821.

Bk:Pg: 2V:213   Date: 14 Mar 1817   RtCt: 20 Aug 1817
Jane ELGIN & son Robert of Ldn to Walter ELGIN Sr. of Ldn. Trust for debt to Richard ADAMS using 60a (part of late Francis ELGIN's land allotted to Richard ADAMS' wife Rebecca and conveyed this day to Jane & son Robert). Wit: Gustavus ELGIN Jr., Mordecai ELGIN, John ELGIN.

Bk:Pg: 2V:214   Date: 26 Sep 1817   RtCt: 26 Sep 1817
Jacob FADELY & wife Mary/Polly of Ldn to John NIXON Jr. of Ldn. B/S of 3a (part of land FADELY prch/o Robert CIMMINGS heir of Thos. CIMMINGS dec'd). Wit: Presley CORDELL, Samuel MURREY.

Bk:Pg: 2V:215   Date: 22 Sep 1817   RtCt: 26 Sep 1817
Edward CATING & wife Martha of Ross Co OH to John WALKER of Ldn. B/S of 13¾a (part of land as heir of Jesse HUMPHREY dec'd) adj John WALKER & wife Letitia, Thomas HUMPHREY, Rachel HUMPHREY. Wit: William BRONAUGH, Thos. GREGG. Delv. 1 Jan 1821.

Bk:Pg: 2V:217   Date: 25 Jul 1817   RtCt: 30 Sep 1817
James CROOKS & wife Elizabeth of Ldn to William WARFORD of Ldn. B/S of 50a (where CROOKS now lives cnvy/b Abraham WARFORD) adj Abraham WARFORD, William ALLEN. Wit: Jehu

JONES, Joshua LEE, William CROOKS, Johnston CLEVELAND, Chas. LEWIS, Ariss BUCKNER.

Bk:Pg: 2V:218   Date: 11 Sep 1817   RtCt: 16 Sep 1817
Isaac LAROWE of Ldn to Charles P. TUTT & Charles Fenton MERCER of Ldn. B/S of 386a on E side of Kittockton Mt. on headwaters of little Limestone adj. Capt. ROSE, Elisha GREGG, Brumfield LONG, George GREGG, reps of John A. BINNS. Wit: Geo. STEPHENSON, William CHICHESTER, David EVELAND. Delv. to TUTT 4 Sep 1820.

Bk:Pg: 2V:220   Date: 6 Mar 1817   RtCt: 17 Sep 1817
John VIOLETT Jr. & wife Mary of Ldn to Enoch GLASCOCK of Fqr. B/S of 41a on Goose Creek adj __ TRIPLETT. Wit: Benjamin GRAYSON, Notley C. WILLIAMS. Delv. to GLASSCOCK 22 Jan 1819.

Bk:Pg: 2V:221   Date: 13 Aug 1817   RtCt: 13 Aug 1817
Aaron SAUNDERS to Charles ELGIN. Release of mortgage on land cnvy/b ELGIN dated 13 Apr 1813. (Recorded RR:193)

Bk:Pg: 2V:222   Date: 13 Aug 1817   RtCt: 20 Sep 1817
Richard Marshall SCOTT of Ffx to Presley CORDELL of Ldn. B/S 2 adj lots of 306a. Wit: Tho. R. MOTT. Delv. to CORDELL 27 May 1818.

Bk:Pg: 2V:223   Date: 6 Mar 1817   RtCt: 17 Sep 1817
Hiram SEATON & wife Nancy of Ldn to Enoch GLASCOCK of Fqr. B/S of 39a (exclusive of two ½a lots of Lewis LUNSFORD and lots lying W of turnpike road held by William BERRY & heirs of James HARRUP under leases) S of Goose Creek adj John VIOLETT Jr. Wit: Benjamin GRAYSON, Notley C. WILLIAMS. Delv. to GLASSOCK 22 Jan 1819.

Bk:Pg: 2V:225   Date: 8 Sep 1817   RtCt: 8 Sep 1817
Jno. PURSELL & Tho. GREGG (trustees of James CRAIG) of Ldn to Henry ELLIS of Ldn. Release of mortgage.

Bk:Pg: 2V:225   Date: 2 May 1817   RtCt: 8 Sep 1817
Abiel JENNERS & wife Deborah of Ldn to Jacob COST of Ldn. B/S of 4 lots (prch/o William COCKING) –128a Osburn's Lot adj Wm. GRUBB, Rich'd GRUBB. 40a Morrisses Lot. 70a lot on W side of Short Hill adj reps of David POTT's. 11a lot on N side of Short Hill nr Dawsons Spring Lot, ¼a lot adj Thos. DAVIS, Wm. GRUBB. Wit: Robert BRADEN, John H. McCABE. Delv. to COST 29 Apr 1820.

Bk:Pg: 2V:228   Date: 19 Sep 1817   RtCt: 14 Sep 1817
William WHITE & wife Nancy of Ldn to George TAVENER Jr. of Ldn. B/S of 230¼a on road from Snicker's Gap to Little River. Wit: Samuel MURREY, Presley CORDELL.

Bk:Pg: 2V:229   Date: 13 Oct 1817   RtCt: 13 Oct 1817
James D. FRENCH, Garrison B. FRENCH and Lewis FRENCH. Bond on Jas. D. FRENCH as constable. Wit: Tho. R. MOTT.

Bk:Pg: 2V:230   Date: 13 Oct 1817   RtCt: 13 Oct 1817
John McPHERSON, John MARTIN and Daniel HAINE. Bond on
McPHERSON as constable.

Bk:Pg: 2V:230   Date: 8 Aug 1817   RtCt: 13 Aug 1817
Amos SKINNER. Col for slave Lucinda age 8y Oct 1809, dark
complexion, acquired by marriage.

Bk:Pg: 2V:230   Date: 24 Jan 1817   RtCt: 13 Oct 1817
Henry ROBERT & wife Phebe (nee JOHNSON, sister of James
JOHNSON late of Ldn) of Muskingum Co OH to Leven LUCKETT of
Ldn. B/S of 118½a (from brother James' estate, part of same land
cnvy/b Casper JOHNSON to LUCKETT, John WILSON & others) nr
Goose Creek. Wit: Joseph BEARD, Jacob CROOKS. Delv. to
LUCKETT on ___.

Bk:Pg: 2V:232   Date: 20 Feb 1816   RtCt: 13 Oct 1817
Morris OSBURN, John OSBURN, Thomas OSBURN, Richard
OSBURN, Mary OSBURN, Sarah OSBURN, Joab OSBURN &
Balaam OSBURN of Ldn and John NICKOLS & wife Hannah of OH,
and Thomas GORE & wife Permilia of KY to Joel OSBURN of Ldn.
B/S of 150a adj Thomas HUMPHREY, Thomas OSBURN. Wit:
James GEORGE, Eli NICKOLS, Joshua OSBURN, John WHITE.

Bk:Pg: 2V:234   Date: 19 Mar 1816   RtCt: 13 Oct 1817
William MAINS (child & heir of William MAINS dec'd of Ldn) of Ross
Co OH to brother Archibald MAINS of Ldn. PoA for benefits from
father's estate. Wit: Levin BETT.

Bk:Pg: 2V:235   Date: ___   RtCt: 25 Sep [1817]
Martin N. McDANIEL late of D.C. Col for slave man Sam abt 34y
black with wife Harriot abt 23y black & their 3 children Frank abt 3y,
Tom abt 2y & Sam abt 6m and slave girl Amy abt 13y black.

Bk:Pg: 2V:236   Date: 21 Jun 1815   RtCt: 13 Oct 1817
Thomas HATCHER, Hiram SEATON & Thomas TRIPLET (commrs.
for James HARROP dec'd, the other commr is dead) to Benjamin
PATTERSON. Sold lease to PATTERSON and amt. paid to Patrick
CARRAL, Wm. GIBBS, Mary CARRAL, Jas. HARROP and Thomas
GHEEN. Wit: Joseph HATCHER, Joshua HOGE, Thomas
HATCHER, Rebekah HATCHER.

Bk:Pg: 2V:236   Date: 2 Dec 1816   RtCt: 13 Oct 1817
William ELLIOTT & wife Elizabeth (late FOWKE, d/o Robert D.
FOWKE dec'd) of Lewisville, Jefferson Co KY to John NIXON of
Ldn. B/S of 79a (part of Elms' patent). Delv to heirs of Jno. NIXON
dec'd 20 Sep 1845.

Bk:Pg: 2V:238   Date: 22 May 1817   RtCt: 13 Oct 1817
William Dudley DIGGS & wife Eleanorah of PrG to John CONARD of
Ldn. B/S of 108a on Potomac River adj David NEER, and 183a adj
William DERRY. Wit: Danl. RAPINE, Saml. W. SMALLWOOOD,

Thomas GALES, William GALES, Francis MILLIKIN. Delv. to
CUNNARD 11 Jan 1819.

Bk:Pg: 2V:240   Date: 22 May 1817   RtCt: 13 Oct 1817
William Dudley DIGGS & with Eleanorah of PrG to John DEMORA
of Ldn. B/S of 12a adj __ NICEWANGER. Wit: Danl. RAPINE, Saml.
W. SMALLWOOD, Thomas GALES, William GALES, Francis
MILLIKIN. Delv. to DEMORA 24 Nov 1818.

Bk:Pg: 2V:242   Date: 1 Oct 1817   RtCt: 18 Oct 1817
Joseph MOXLEY of Ldn to Edward KILLY/KELLY of Ldn. B/S of
217a adj old Cornelius HOLDREN's and Thomas CARR's spring
branches, John ALEXANDER, George CARTER, Thomas MOSS,
Thomas CARR and 5a adj Jacob LASSWELL. Wit: S. BLINCOE,
Jesse TIMMS.

Bk:Pg: 2V:243   Date: 12 Apr 1817   RtCt: 13 Oct 1817
John SCHOOLEY, William H. HOUGH & Daniel STONE (Exors of
William HOUGH dec'd) of Ldn to William DANIEL of Wtfd. B/S of lot
in Wtfd on road from Wtfd to Quaker Meeting house adj Robert B.
WHITE. Wit: Johnston CLEVELAND, John H. McCABE.

Bk:Pg: 2V:244   Date: 27 Mar 1817   RtCt: 13 Oct 1817
Emanuel NEWCOMER & wife Catherine of Wtfd to Robert BRADEN
& Josabed WHITE of Ldn. B/S of 57a, a lot adj William HOUGH and
a lot adj Asa MOORE. Wit: Abiel JENNERS, John H. McCABE.
Delv. to Dr. MARLOW per order filed 5 Jul 1822.

Bk:Pg: 2V:246   Date: 13 Oct 1817   RtCt: 13 Oct 1817
John PALMER & wife Nancy of Ldn to Benjamin JAMES of Ldn. B/S
of 36a adj Benj. JAMES. Wit: Charles LEWIS, Arris BUCKNER.
Delv. to JAMES 30 Apr 1824.

Bk:Pg: 2V:247   Date: 21 Aug 1817   RtCt: 13 Oct 1817
Burr POWELL of Mdbg to Humphrey Brooke POWELL. Gift of 50a &
house (exclusive of ½a family graveyard) adj Mdbg formerly
possessed by his grandfather Col. Leven POWELL dec'd, adj where
Madison & Marshall St. intersect, Thomas CHINN dec'd, road from
Mdbg to Guy ford of Goose creek and Lots #34 & #35 in Mdbg of 1a.
Delv. to Saml. J. TEBBS per order 6 Dec 1829.

Bk:Pg: 2V:248   Date: 27 Mar 1817   RtCt: 13 Oct 1817
Jesse EVANS & wife Mary of Ldn to Samuel D. LESLIE of Ldn. B/S
of ¾a in Hllb (cnvy/b William HARNED in 1813). Wit: Joshua
OSBURN, Abiel JENNERS. Delv to grantee 18 Jan 1820.

Bk:Pg: 2V:250   Date: 6 May 1817   RtCt: 13 Oct 1817
Jacob COST & wife Mary of Ldn to Abiel JENNERS of Ldn. Trust for
debt to John BAKER of Franklin Co PA using 4 lots on Short Hill.
Wit: Robert BRADEN, John H. McCABE.

Bk:Pg: 2V:252   Date: 16 Aug 1817   RtCt: 13 Oct 1817
Catherine COMPHER of Ldn to John STOUTSABERGER of Ldn.
B/S of 13a from div. of Peter COMPHER's dec'd estate. Wit: John
HAMILTON, Sam LUCKETT.

Bk:Pg: 2V:253   Date: 9 Oct 1817   RtCt: 13 Oct 1817
Alexander YOUNG of Ldn to John DULIN of Ffx. PoA. Wit: Abiel
JENNERS, Fleet SMITH. Delv. to DULIN 13 Mar 1820.

Bk:Pg: 2V:253   Date: 1 Apr 1817   RtCt: 21 Oct 1817
Enos WILDMAN & wife Jane D. to Wilson Cary SELDON. Mortgage
on 49a. Wit: Jos. LEWIS Jr.

Bk:Pg: 2V:255   Date: 16 Oct 1817   RtCt: 25 Oct 1817
Robert RUSSELL (Exor of Samuel RUSSELL dec'd) of Ldn to
Thomas NICKOLS of Ldn. B/S of 229a on NW fork of Goose Creek
adj S. WILSON, F. STRIBLING, Chas. TAYLOR, Saml. NICKOLS.
Wit: Stacy TAYLOR, Ruth TAYLOR, William CUMINGS. Delv. to
NICKOLS 2 Apr 1822.

Bk:Pg: 2V:255   Date: 1 Apr 1817   RtCt: 21 Oct 1817
Wilson Cary SELDON of Ldn to Enos WILDMAN of Ldn. B/S of 49a
(part of Aubrey's patent). Wit: Jos. LEWIS Jr. Delv. to WILDMAN 31
Dec 1818.

Bk:Pg: 2V:256   Date: 16 Oct 1817   RtCt: 21 Oct 1817
John LICKEY & wife Elizabeth of Ldn to Robert ROBERTS of Ldn.
B/S of ½ of lot part under lease where Marcy THOMPKINS m/o
Elizabeth lived until death and devised ½ to her sons Asahel and
Jonah THOMPKINS who sold to Elizabeth d/o Marcy. Wit: Patrick
McINTYRE, Presley CORDELL. Delv. to ROBERTS 14 Sep 1832.

Bk:Pg: 2V:257   Date: 8 Nov 1817   RtCt: 8 Nov 1817
Joshua MOXLEY of Ldn to John H. CASSADAY of Ldn. B/S of 7a
adj William WRIGHT, Nicholas MONEY and 1a. Wit: Isaac
LAROWE, Tho. R. MOTT. Delv. to CASSADY 4 Jun 1821.

Bk:Pg: 2V:258   Date: 15 Oct 1817   RtCt: 27 Oct 1817
Isaiah MARKS yeoman & wife Elizabeth of Ldn to Edward B.
GRADY of Ldn. B/S of 14a (inherited from estate of father Elisha
MARKS dec'd). wit: Benjamin GRAYSON, Noteley C. WILLIAMS.
Delv. pr order filed TT177 on 25 Mar 1824.

Bk:Pg: 2V:259   Date: 17 Sep 1817   RtCt: 28 Oct 1817
Mahlon CARTER & wife Catherine of Ldn to John W. B. GRAYSON
of Ldn. B/S of 84½a (devised by father James CARTER dec'd) on E
side of Beaverdam adj Mahlon CARTER, Benjamin GRAYSON,
Abner HUMPHREY. Wit: John P. DULANY, Thomas ALLISON, Mary
HUMPHREY, Cuthbert POWELL, Benjamin GRAYSON. Delv. to
GRAYSON 3 Jul 1819.

Bk:Pg: 2V:261   Date: 8 May 1817   RtCt: 1 Jan 1818
Edmund LOVETT & wife Christian of Ldn to Wm. LICKY & John
JONES of Ldn. Trust for debt to James SIMPSON using 57½a on

Goose Creek. Wit: Stephen C. ROSZEL, William CARR. Delv. to SIMPSON 2 Oct 1818.

Bk:Pg: 2V:262   Date: 13 Sep 1817   RtCt: 29 Oct 1817
Burr POWELL of Ldn to Jacob MANN of Ldn. LS of 1a Lot #3 in Mdbg at intersection of Independence & Washington Sts. Wit: Francis M. LUCKETT, Abner GIBSON. Delv. to MANN 24 Jun 1819.

Bk:Pg: 2V:263   Date: 22 Oct 1817   RtCt: 27 Oct 1817
Enos POTTS & wife Lydia of Ldn to Edward B. GRADY of Ldn. Trust for debt to John BROWN using 65a adj John WARFORD. Wit: Notley C. WILLIAMS, Joshua OSBURN. Delv. to L. P. W. BALCH pr order of GRADY 28 Dec 1824.

Bk:Pg: 2V:265   Date: 10 Sep 1817   RtCt: 16 Sep 1817
Richard H. HENDERSON & wife Orra Moore of Ldn to Thomas R. MOTT of Ldn. B/S of 15a on Catoctin Mt. Small plat given. Wit: Patrick McINTYRE, Presley CORDELL. Delv. to MOTT 4 Feb 1819.

Bk:Pg: 2V:266   Date: 30 Sep 1817   RtCt: 30 Sep 1817
Richard H. HENDERSON & wife Orra Moore of Ldn to John THOMAS of Ldn. B/S of lot on Market St in Lsbg, adj Charles BENNETT, William WRIGHT. Wit: Samuel MURREY, John ROSE. Delv. to THOMAS 7 Aug 1820.

Bk:Pg: 2V:267   Date: 12 Sep 1817   RtCt: 16 Sep 1817
Richard H. HENDERSON & wife Orra Moore of Ldn to James RUST of Ldn. B/S of house & lot in Lsbg where HENDERSON now lives except the office and ground. Wit: Presley CORDEL, Patrick McINTYRE. Delv. to RUST 14 Apr 1821.

Bk:Pg: 2V:268   Date: 17 Oct 1817   RtCt: 25 Oct 1817
Thomas NICKOLS of Ldn to Timothy TAYLOR & Stacy TAYLOR of Ldn. Trust for debt to Robert RUSSEL (Exor of Samuel RUSSEL dec'd) using land cnvy/b RUSSEL. Wit: William CUMINGS, William RUSSELL. Delv. to Stacy TAYLOR 11 Mar 1822.

Bk:Pg: 2V:269   Date: 24 Jun 1817   RtCt: 10 Nov 1817
Samuel TORBERT dec'd late of Ldn. Partition of 100a (another survey gives as slightly less) to brothers & sisters. Brother John TORBERT has bought all undivided shares except for that of sister Elizabeth FRED w/o Thomas FREDD. Agreement on div. of land. Wit: William BRONAUGH, Ben. GRAYSON. Delv. to John TORBERT who appeared to be the owner of the land 2 Nov 1833.

Bk:Pg: 2V:271   Date: 13 Oct 1817   RtCt: 13 Oct 1817
Augustine LOVE & wife Mary of Ldn to Presley SAUNDERS of Ldn. B/S of 32a on main branch of Goose Creek. Wit: Joseph EIDSON, Thos. BROWN, Amos FERGUSON.

Bk:Pg: 2V:272   Date: 5 Aug 1817   RtCt: 10 Nov 1817
Betsey TEBBS of Dumfries VA and Mary F. SPENCE (formerly TEBBS) w/o Dr. John SPENCE, Margaret B. TRIPLETT (formerly TEBBS) w/o Dr. Thomas TRIPLETT, Ann F. DUVAL (formerly

TEBBS) w/o John P. DUVAL, Thomas F. TEBBS, Foushee TEBBS, Willowghby William TEBBS and Samuel John TEBBS (ch/o said Betsey TEBBS). Partition: Will of William CARR dec'd of PrWm f/o Betsey TEBBS devised remainder of estate to Robert LUTTERAL, Simon LUTTERAL and Thomas CHAPMAN in trust for his children Betsey TEBBS, William CARR and John CARR. Surviving trustee Thomas CHAPMAN purchased various lands in several counties, some of which Betsey now holds. Brother William and John CARR died without issue. Wit: David BOYLE, Geo. SMITH, Henry ATCHISON, N. McINTIER. Gives a long schedule of lands conveyed beginning in 1743 to Wm. CARR or his Exors.

Bk:Pg: 2V:276   Date: 18 Oct 1817   RtCt: 13 Nov 1817
Thomas STONESTREET. Col – slave given to his wife Polly STONESTREET by her mother Mrs. Priscilla NICHOOLS [NICHOLS?] of Md – boy Richard abt 6y who he will free at age 28y.

Bk:Pg: 2V:277   Date: 4 Nov 1817   RtCt: 4 Nov 1817
John HARRIS of Md. Col from May 1814 for slave Betty abt 8y slender black complexion tolerably well grown in height with no scars, brought from Md about 20-30 days earlier, given by father of his wife.

Bk:Pg: 2V:277   Date: 16 Jul 1817   RtCt: 13 Nov 1817
Daniel GANTT & wife Lucy of Washington, D.C. to Enoch FRANCIS of Ldn. B/S of 40a on Goose Creek adj Matthew HARRISON. Wit: Sam N. SMALLWOOD, Joseph CASSIN.

Bk:Pg: 2V:279   Date: 11 Jun 1817   RtCt: 13 Nov 1817
William CAMPBELL & wife Margaret of Belmont Co OH to Michael PLASTER of Ldn. B/S of 8a (from div. of estate of James REID dec'd), wood lot of 3a and ¼a in Mdbg. Wit: John BEVAN, William PHILPOT, William BRONAUGH, Francis W. LUCKETT.

Bk:Pg: 2V:282   Date: 8 Mar 1817·   RtCt: 5 Dec 1817
Jacob FADELY & wife Mary of Ldn to George & James RUST of Ldn. B/S of a lot on W side of King St between Loudoun & Markett Sts. next to William TAYLOR's house. Wit: John McCORMICK, Presley CORDELL.

Bk:Pg: 2V:283   Date: 13 Mar 1817   RtCt: 10 Nov 1817
Robert BRADEN & wife Elizabeth of Ldn to George JANNEY of Ldn. B/S of 107a adj the german church, Laurence MINK, John MARTIN, __ HICKMAN, __ WETTERMAN. Wit: Abiel JENNERS, John H. McCABE.

Bk:Pg: 2V:284   Date: 24 Nov 1817   RtCt: 5 Dec 1817
George JANNEY & wife Susannah of Ldn to James MOORE of Wtfd. B/S of 185a (JANNEY prch/o Nathaniel MANNING) nr Kittoctin creek, adj Sanford RAIMEY, Patrick McGARACK, Thomas PHILLIPS. Wit: William BRONAUGH, Francis M. LUCKETT. Delv. to MOORE 12 Feb 1820.

Bk:Pg: 2V:285   Date: 23 Nov 1805   RtCt: 10 May 1817
Notley C. WILLIAMS & wife Frances of Ldn to Josiah WHITE of Ldn. B/S of 5a adj George BROWN. Wit: Stacy TAYLOR, James TUCKER, John WHITE, Wm. BRONAUGH. Del'v. to James COCKRANE by direction of Jno. WHITE Exor of Josiah WHITE dec'd 3 Nov 1829.

Bk:Pg: 2V:286   Date: 3 May 1817   RtCt: 28 Nov 1817
Jonah SANDS & wife Esther of Ldn to Jesse JANNEY of Ldn. B/S of 105a adj John HANBY, Stephen JANNEY, William LODGE, __ ROMINE. Wit: David REESE, Moranda SORBOURNE, Patrick McINTYRE, Presley CORDELL.

Bk:Pg: 2V:288   Date: 30 Sep 1817   RtCt: 28 Nov 1817
Presley SAUNDERS Jr. & wife Mary of Ldn to Thomas B. BEATTY of Ldn. B/S of lot in Lsbg on S side of Market adj Samuel CLAPHAM, Thomas R. MOSS, John LITTLEJOHN. Wit: Patrick McINTYRE, Presley CORDELL.

Bk:Pg: 2V:289   Date: 5 Sep 1817   RtCt: 13 Nov 1817
James SIMPSON & wife Elizabeth of Ldn to Humphrey B. POWELL. Trust for debt to Isaac LAKE using 250a in Bull Run Mt. on Hunger Run adj Burr POWELL, Owen SULLIVAN. Wit: Burr POWELL, A. GIBSON. Delv. to H. B. POWELL 21 May 1822.

Bk:Pg: 2V:290   Date: 30 May 1817   RtCt: 8 Dec 1817
David SMITH & Bernard TAYLOR (trustees) & John HESKETT of Ldn to Jehu HOLLINGSWORTH of Ldn. Release of mortgage on 136½a. Wit: Yardley TAYLOR, Jonathan TAYLOR, George FOX.

Bk:Pg: 2V:291   Date: 18 Nov 1817   RtCt: 10 Nov 1817
Francis TRIPLETT Sr of Ldn to Henry PEERS & Eleanor PEERS of Ldn. B/S of Lot #30 on N side of Market St in Lsbg and ½ of Lot #34. Wit: John H. CANBY, Sam. M. BOSS, Thomas C. ROACH. Delv. to Henry PEERS 25 Jun 1821.

Bk:Pg: 2V:292   Date: 5 Sep 1817   RtCt: 13 Nov 1817
Isaac LAKE & wife Sally of Ldn to James SIMPSON of Ldn. B/S of 250a adj Major POWELL. Wit: Burr POWELL, A. GIBSON. Delv. to SIMPSON 13 Dec 1819.

Bk:Pg: 2V:294   Date: 1 Aug 1816   RtCt: 24 Nov 1817
Charles Fenton MERCER of Aldie to William NOLAND of Aldie. LS of lot containing Aldie Mill, Granary, store, distillery house and millars house.

Bk:Pg: 2V:296   Date: 4 Dec 1816   RtCt: 9 Dec 1816
John MATHIAS of Ldn to David POTTS of Ldn. B/S of 163a at foot of Blue Ridge including lease to Robert HERRON and 42a. Delv. to POTTS 20 Oct 1821.

Bk:Pg: 2V:298   Date: 31 Jul 1815   RtCt: 13 Nov 1817
John DOWDELL & wife Terressa of Ldn to heirs of Hanson SIMPSON late of Ldn. B/S of 2a nr Mdbg (per agreement with Elijah

WILLIAMS since dec'd). Wit: Jesse McVEIGH, Noble BEVERIDGE, John HARRIS, Hugh SMITH, Burr POWELL, A. GIBSON.

Bk:Pg: 2V:299   Date: 5 Feb 1816   RtCt: 13 Nov 1816
William Dudley DIGGS & wife Eleanorah of PrG to Frederick HANSHY of Ldn. B/S of 173a adj Potterfields corner. Wit: E. MASON, Tho. SWANN, Jos. LEWIS Jr., Tho. RENOLD, Thomas POWELL, Theodore SHEKELLS.

Bk:Pg: 2V:300   Date: 28 Nov 1817   RtCt: 1 Dec 1817
William CALDWELL of Ldn to Charles DRISH & Elizabeth CALDWELL (d/o DRISH & w/o Joseph CALDWELL) of Ldn. B/S of undivided fourth (306a) of land of Moses CALDWELL dec'd (f/o William) subject to dower of widow Sarah CALDWELL, adj Patrick B. MILLHOLLAND, Armstead T. MASON, heirs of William McGEATH dec'd.

Bk:Pg: 2V:301   Date: 9 Dec 1817   RtCt: 9 Dec 1817
Joseph CIMMINGS & wife Mary of Ldn to John NIXON of Ldn. B/S of 25a (allotted in div. of estate of __ CIMMINGS). Wit: John McCORMICK, Presley CORDELL. Delv. to Exors of Jno. NIXON dec'd 20 Sep 1845.

Bk:Pg: 2V:302   Date: 11 May 1817   RtCt: 13 Nov 1817
John R. ADAMS & wife Lucinda to Richard ADAMS. Trust for debt to Samuel ADAMS using 200a. Wit: Thomas FOUCH, Stephen C. ROSZEL. Delv. to ADAMS 20 Mar 1819.

Bk:Pg: 2V:303   Date: 27 Nov 1818   RtCt: 27 Nov 1817
Robert H. GOVER & wife Catherine of Ldn to James D. FRENCH of Ldn. B/S of lot on E side of westernmost st in Lsbg adj Thos. BIRKLEY. Wit: Stephen C. ROSSZEL, Presley CORDELL.

Bk:Pg: 2V:304   Date: 9 Dec 1816   RtCt: 9 Dec 1816
John NIXON & wife Jane of Ldn to Joseph CIMMINGS of Ldn. B/S of 29a and 1½a (allotted Jane formerly Jane CIMMINGS from estate of father __ CIMMINGS). Wit: John McCORMICK, Presley CORDELL.

Bk:Pg: 2V:306   Date: 3 Oct 1817   RtCt: 14 Nov 1817
Robert BRADEN & wife Elizabeth of Ldn to Joseph WOOD of Ldn. B/S of 37a (part of land prch/o John MARTIN). Wit: John M. McCABE, Abiel JENNERS. Delv. to Joshua PEWSEY per order 7 Jun 1823.

Bk:Pg: 2V:307   Date: 25 Oct 1817   RtCt: 8 Dec 1817
Jonathan BURSON of Ldn (abt to remove to Ohio) to friend Isaac BROWN. PoA. Wit: William BRONAUGH, Francis M. LUCKETT.

Bk:Pg: 2V:307   Date: 25 Oct 1817   RtCt: 8 Dec 1817
Jonathan BURSON & wife Rebecca of Ldn to John BROWN of Ldn. B/S of 133a adj Edin CARTER, George BURSON, John WILLIAMS. Wit: William BRONAUGH, Francis M. LUCKETT. Delv. to BROWN 20 Jul 1822.

Bk:Pg: 2V:309   Date: 10 Apr 1817   RtCt: 8 Dec 1817
Thomas REID & wife Catherine of Ldn to Samuel DUNCAN of Ldn.
B/S of ¼a Lot #3 in Union Town. Wit: Benjamin GRAYSON,
Cuthbert POWELL.

Bk:Pg: 2V:310   Date: 18 Oct 1817   RtCt: 8 Dec 1817
Simon RICARD & wife Molley of Ldn to Adam SANDBOWER &
Christian SANDBOWER of Ldn. B/S of 210a (Molley's share from
father John SANDBOWER dec'd). Wit: Abiel JENNERS, John H.
McCABE. Delv. to Adam SANDBOWER 7 Apr 1825.

Bk:Pg: 2V:311   Date: 29 May 1817   RtCt: 8 Dec 1817
Daniel DAVIS & wife Malinda of Ldn to John SHAFFER of Ldn. B/S
of 1a nr Broad Run adj Daniel DAVIS, late Isaac BALL, Schoolhouse
lot. Wit: John H. McCABE, Robert BRADEN. Delv. to SHAFFER 13
Feb 1821.

Bk:Pg: 2V:313   Date: 28 Aug 1817   RtCt: 8 Dec 1817
Francis HEREFORD of Fqr to Burr POWELL. Trust for debt to John
Taliaferro BROOKE and James Mercer GARNET (Admrs of James
MERCER dec'd of Fredericksburg VA) tracts of land. Wit: Chas. G.
ESKRIDGE, John MATHIAS, Tho. R. MOTT, James RUST.

Bk:Pg: 2V:314   Date: 9 Dec 1817   RtCt: 9 Dec 1817
Garrison D. FRENCH, Jas. D. FRENCH, Jno. PALMER & Wm.
CHILTON. Bond on Garrison D. FRENCH as constable. Wit: Tho. R.
MOTT.

Bk:Pg: 2V:315   Date: 9 Dec 1817   RtCt: 9 Dec 1817
Jno. L. GILL, Aron BURSON & John WEADEN. Bond on GILL as
constable. Wit: Tho. R. MOTT.

Bk:Pg: 2V:315   Date: 30 Aug 1817   RtCt: 9 Dec 1817
Isaac HARRIS of Ldn. DoE for slave man Jacob, formerly the
property of John WREN, abt 37y of age.

Bk:Pg: 2V:315   Date: 21 Jul 1817   RtCt: 8 Dec 1817
Thomas L. LAWRENCE & wife Anne Louisa of BaltMd to Richard
LAWRENCE of BaltMd. B/S of 1/10th of 'Clover Hill' land (dev. Anne
Louisa in will of John A. BINNS the elder dec'd, dower of widow
Dewanner). Wit: Peter GALT, Matthew BENNETT. Delv. to A. L.
LAURENCE widow Dec 1828.

Bk:Pg: 2V:317   Date: 24 Jul 1817   RtCt: 8 Dec 1817
Richard LAWRENCE of BaltMd to Thomas L. LAWRENCE & wife
Anne Louisa of BaltMd. Deed of conveyance of interest in above
land. Wit: Peter GALT, Matthew BENNETT. Delv. to A. L.
LAWRENCE widow Dec 1828.

Bk:Pg: 2V:318   Date: 14 Apr 1817   RtCt: 9 Dec 1817
Henry CLAGETT & wife Julia of Ldn to John HAWLING of Ldn. B/S
of 59a (part of Carter's patent) adj John WILDMAN. Wit: Chas. G.
ESKRIDGE, J. L. DREAN, George D. SWEARINGER, Patrick
McINTYRE, Presley CORDELL.

Bk:Pg: 2V:319   Date: 9 Dec 1817   RtCt: 9 Dec 1817
Samuel M. EDWARDS & wife Ann of Ldn to Francis TRIPLETT Sr.
B/S of Lot #44 with brick house on King St in Lsbg adj John DRISH,
Richard H. HENDERSON, William KING. Wit: Patrick McINTYRE,
Presley CORDELL.

Bk:Pg: 2V:320   Date: 18 Nov 1817   RtCt: 11 Dec 1817
Henry PEERS & Eleanor PEERS of Lsbg to Richard H.
HENDERSON and Sampson BLINCOE of Lsbg. Trust for debt to
Francis TRIPLETT using 2 lots in Lsbg. Wit: Thos. C. ROACH, John
HANBY, Sam. M. BOSS.

Bk:Pg: 2V:321   Date: 28 Nov 1817   RtCt: 9 Dec 1817
Charles DRISH & Susannah of Ldn to William CALDWELL of Ldn.
B/S of 2 lots in Lsbg on S side of Market St. adj Sally RYAN, George
HEAD Sr., Presbyterian Meeting House. Wit: John ROSE, Presley
CORDELL.

Bk:Pg: 2V:322   Date: 30 Dec 1817   RtCt: 30 Dec 1817
Mountzion WATTS of Ldn to Isaiah POTTS of Ldn. Trust for debt to
Greenbury M. McDONALD of Ldn using farm and household items.

Bk:Pg: 2V:323   Date: 18 Oct 1817   RtCt: 26 Dec 1817
Simon RICKARD & wife Mary of Ldn to Benniah WHITE of Ldn. B/S
of 28a where RICKARD resides (sold by will of Abel JANNEY Sr.
dec'd) adj Peter MILLER dec'd, Archibald MORRISON. Wit: Thomas
WHITE, John CREEN?, M. JANNEY, John H. McCABE, Abiel
JENNERS. Delv. to WHITE 26 May 1821.

Bk:Pg: 2V:324   Date: 6 Nov 1817   RtCt: __ 1817
Israel REDMOND & brother John REDMAN (Israel has PoA) of
Fairfield Co OH to Ariss BUCKNER of Ldn. B/S of 150a from estate
of Andrew REDMOND dec'd, adj William COKE, Nathaniel PEGG,
Sampson TURLEY. Delv. to BUCKNER 15 Feb 1820.

Bk:Pg: 2V:325   Date: 20 Nov 1817   RtCt: 8 Dec 1817
John McPHERSON & wife Cloe and James McPHERSON & wife
Kesiah of Ldn to Benjamin KENT of Ldn. B/S of lot in Union town adj
Henry EVANS, Jacob SILCOT. Wit: Leven LUCKETT, Abner
GIBSON.

Bk:Pg: 2V:326   Date: 31 Dec 1817   RtCt: 9 Jan 1818
Elijah VIOLETT & wife Phebe of Ldn to Saml. M. EDWARDS &
Richard H. HENDERSON of Ldn. Trust for debt to Sanford RAMEY
Sr. using 4a late the property of John VIOLETT dec'd and 60a
adjoining. Wit: Abiel JENNERS, Presley CORDELL.

Bk:Pg: 2V:328   Date: 28 Aug 1815   RtCt: 8 Dec 1817
William ELLZEY & wife Frances H. of Ldn to Philip EVERHART of
Ldn. B/S of 141a adj Peter MILLER, Mich'l STREAM. Wit: John
GOERGE, James WHELUND, Erasmus G. HAMILTON, Thomas
FOUCH, John BAYLY. Delv. pr order 25 Aug 11827

Bk:Pg: 2V:329   Date: 4 Nov 1817   RtCt: 8 Dec 1817
Burr POWELL (acting Exor of Leven POWELL dec'd) to James
GUNN. B/S of 149a adj reps of Thaddeus McCARTY, Leven
LUCKETT. Wit: Asa ROGERS, George TURNER, A. GIBSON,
Hiram McVEIGH, William BRONAUGH, Leven LUCKETT.

Bk:Pg: 2V:330   Date: 28 Oct 1817   RtCt: 11 Dec 1817
Christopher GREENUP of Frankfort KY to John HULLS of Ldn. B/S
of 118a where HULLS now lives adj William A. BINNS, William
CARR, Walter ELLGIN, road separating where Andrew GRIMES
lives. Delv. to HULLS 7 Mar 1821.

Bk:Pg: 2V:330   Date: 13 Jan 1817   RtCt: 8 Dec 1817
William ELLZEY & wife Frances H. of Ldn to Michael STREAM of
Ldn. B/S of 13a on SE side of Short Hill (part of #18 cnvy/b Ferd.
FAIRFAX) adj Conrad ROLLER, Philip EVERHART, __ JANNEY.
Wit: Thomas FOUCH, Stephen C. ROSZEL.

Bk:Pg: 2V:331   Date: 13 Jan 1817   RtCt: 8 Dec 1817
William ELLZEY & wife Frances H. of Ldn to Philip EVERHART of
Ldn. B/S of 13a on SE side of Short Hill (part of #18 cnvy/b Ferd.
FAIRFAX) adj __ JANNEY. Wit: Thos. FOUCH, Stephen C.
ROSZEL

Bk:Pg: 2V:332   Date: 28 Oct 1817   RtCt: 28 Oct 1817
John HULLS of Ldn to Rich'd H. HENDERSON of Ldn. Trust for
Charles BINNS as security in note to Christopher GREENUP of KY
using land derived from GREENUP. Delv. to BINNS 1 May 1830

Bk:Pg: 2V:333   Date: 7 Dec 1817   RtCt: 20 Dec 1817
Lewis P. W. BALCH to Catharine WAGER. Release of mortgage
dated 31 Jul 1815. Wit: Burr W. HARRISON, Chas. G. ESKRIDGE,
J. L. DREAN.

Bk:Pg: 2V:334   Date: 20 Aug 1817   RtCt: 3 Jan 1818
John W. HEREFORD & wife Juliet H. of Orange Co VA to John
LITTLEJOHN of Ldn. B/S of 30a nr Lsbg where LITTLEJOHN now
lives.

Bk:Pg: 2V:335   Date: 7 May 1817   RtCt: 8 Jan 1818
James SIMPSON & wife Elizabeth of Ldn to Edmund LOVETT of
Ldn. B/S of 57½a on Goose Creek (from tract allotted in div. of
estate of Mary SIMPSON dec'd). Wit: John JONES, William
LICKEY, French SIMPSON, Samuel SIMPSON, Burr POWELL, A.
GIBSON. Delv. to LOVETT 13 Mar 1824.

Bk:Pg: 2V:336   Date: 12 Jan 1818   RtCt: 12 Jan 1818
James GREENLEASE of Ldn. DoE for slave Dolly 33y or 34y old
last Oct.

Bk:Pg: 2V:336   Date: 12 Jan 1818   RtCt: 12 Jan 1818
Joseph H. WRIGHT, Joseph P. THOMAS & Elijah PEACOCK. Bond
on WRIGHT as constable. Wit: Jno. A. BINNS.

Bk:Pg: 2V:337   Date: 9 Jan 1818   RtCt: 12 Jan 1818
John DRISH of Ldn to Charles ELGIN of Ldn. B/S of 400a in Monongahala Co Va on Bannes' Run. Delv. to Wm. DRISH Admr of ELGIN 16 Jun 1824.

Bk:Pg: 2V:338   Date: 12 Jan 1818   RtCt: 12 Jan 1818
William BAYLY & wife Jane of Ldn to William WILKINSON of Ldn. B/S of 10a adj Richard VANPELT.

Bk:Pg: 2V:338   Date: 4 Dec 1817   RtCt: 12 Jan 1818
Thomas YOUNG. Col for negro girl Flora abt 16y of a light complexion.

Bk:Pg: 2V:339   Date: 10 Oct 1815   RtCt: 13 Jan 1818
John HANDY dec'd. Division – Widow Given HANDY, Eli Heaton HANDY (147¼a), James MOUNT & wife Hannah (5a mill race exchanged with W. H. HANDY for Lot #3), Maria HAINS (sold to W. H. HANDY and exchanged as above 147¼a), John Carlisle HANDY (147¼a), William H. HANDY (147¼a in his own right). Divisors: Timothy TAYLOR, Daniel VERNON, Daniel EACHES, Sydnor BAILEY. Plat and details given.

Bk:Pg: 2V:342   Date: 12 Jan 1818   RtCt: 12 Jan 1818
John DRISH & wife Helen/Ellen of Ldn to son-in-law Charles ELGIN of Ldn. Gift of part of Lot #13 on King St in Lsbg. Delv. to Mrs. GORE 20 Oct 1833.

Bk:Pg: 2V:343   Date: 13 Jan 1818   RtCt: 13 Jan 1818
Walter BROOKS of Ldn to Wm. CHILTON of Ldn. Trust for debt to James B. BROOKS of D.C. (bound for WALTER's appearance in MontMd court in suit of Dr. John BOWIE) using 600a. Wit: W. D. DRISH, R. J. FLEMING, Charles THORNTON.

Bk:Pg: 2V:344   Date: 15 Jan 1818   RtCt: 17 Jan 1818
Philip JONES of Ldn to Sampson BLINCOE of Ldn. B/S of 8¾a on N side of road leading from Coes Mill to Lsbg adj Isaac HUGHES. Gives small plat. Wit: Samuel A. TILLET, Richard S. JONES, Rowena HOLMES. Delv. to Martha BLINCOE 5 Sep 1832.

Bk:Pg: 2V:345   Date: 13 Jan 1818   RtCt: 13 Jan 1818
Walter BROOKE & James B. BROOKE to William D. DRISH. BoS for negro boy John and girl Phebe. Wit: Wm. CHILTON, Chas. THORNTON.

Bk:Pg: 2V:346   Date: 17 Jan 1818   RtCt: 24 Jan 1818
William H. DORSEY & wife Judith of Ldn to Daniel EACHES of Ldn. Trust for debt to George JANNEY & Elisha JANNEY of Ldn using 154a. Wit: William BRONAUGH, Francis W. LUCKETT.

Bk:Pg: 2V:347   Date: 26 Jan 1818   RtCt: 26 Jan 1818
Daniel HOWELL of Ldn to George LICKEY of Ldn. Mortgage using household items. Delv. to ___ 24 Apr 1820.

Bk:Pg: 2V:348   Date: 31 [30?] Jan 1818   RtCt: 30 Jan 1818
Benjamin KIDWELL of Ldn to his daughters Nancy KIDWELL &
Tamar KIDWELL of Ldn. BoS of farm and household items. Wit:
Thomas BIRKBY, Robert PERCIVAL.

Bk:Pg: 2V:348   Date: 30 Jan 1818   RtCt: 30 Jan 1818
John ROSE & wife Anna of Ldn to Richd H. HENDERSON of Ldn.
B/S of house & ¾a lot on Cornwall St. in Lsbg lately occupied by
ROSE adj William D. DRISH, Ignatius NORRIS?. Wit: Presley
CORDELL, Samuel MURREY.

Bk:Pg: 2V:349   Date: 30 Jan 1818   RtCt: 30 Jan 1818
Richard H. HENDERSON & wife Orra Moore of Ldn to Isaac
HARRIS of Ldn. Trust for debt to Saml MURRAY using above
mentioned lot. Wit: John ROSE, Presley CORDELL.

Bk:Pg: 2V:350   Date: 19 Jan 1818   RtCt: 30 Jan 1818
Samuel MURRAY & wife Betsey of Ldn to John ROSE of Ldn. B/S
of 1a lot on King St in Lsbg. Wit: Patrick McINTYRE, Presley
CORDELL. Delv. to ROSE 22 May 1820.

Bk:Pg: 2V:351   Date: 7 Jun 1817   RtCt: 9 Feb 1818
John MATHIAS of Ldn to David POTTS of Ldn. B/S of 79a at foot on
E side of Blue Ridge adj heirs of Nathan POTTS. Delv. to POTTS 20
Oct 1821.

Bk:Pg: 2V:352   Date: 29 Jan 1818   RtCt: 2 Feb 1818
John THOMAS & wife Margaret of Ldn to Samuel CLAPHAM of Ldn.
B/S of house & lot (part of Lot #18) on Market St in Lsbg. Wit: John
HARDING, Pat'k McINTYRE, William CARR.

Bk:Pg: 2V:353   Date: 1 Feb 1818   RtCt: 4 Feb 1818
John NEWTON & wife Harriot of Ldn to William WRIGHT of Ldn. B/S
of 2 ½a Lots #5 & #6 in Lsbg. Wit: Samuel MURRAY, W. Bradley
TYLER.

Bk:Pg: 2V:354   Date: 8 Oct 1817   RtCt: 7 Feb 1818
George JANNEY & wife Susannah of Ldn to John T. WILSON &
Sampson BLINCOE of Lsbg. Trust for debt to Charles ALEXANDER
of Ldn using 317a adj Christopher GREENUP. Wit: Thomas
MORALEE, John W. DREAN, John DREAN, William BRONAUGH,
Francis W. LUCKETT. Delv. to John T. WILSON 23 Jul 1819.

Bk:Pg: 2V:356   Date: 1 Sep 1817   RtCt: 12 Jan 1818
Aaron BURSON of Ldn to Lewis GRIGSBY of Ldn. Trust for debt to
Joshua PANCOAST using 100a cnvy/b will of James BURSON
dec'd. Wit: Jno. L. GILL, Elias KENT, Mary BURSON. Delv. to Jas.
HAMILTON 1 Feb 1831.

Bk:Pg: 2V:357   Date: 2 Dec 1817   RtCt: 12 Jan 1818
Archibald McVICKERS & wife Elizabeth of Ldn to Moses GULICK of
Ldn. B/S of 70a. Wit: William NOLAND, Leven LUCKETT. Delv. to
___ 5 Mar 1819.

Bk:Pg: 2V:358   Date: 13 Aug 1817   RtCt: 8 Feb 1818
Westwood T. MASON of Ldn to Alfred BELT of Ldn. Release of mortgage. Wit: J. L. DREAN, Chas. G. ESKRIDGE, Edw'd HAMMAT.

Bk:Pg: 2V:358   Date: 11 Oct 1817   RtCt: 12 Jan 1818
Jeremiah HANKS & wife Catherine and Styles HANKS & wife Nancy of Ldn to Isaiah HANKS of Ldn (all heirs of John HANKS dec'd). B/S of rights to 25a on E side of Short hill cnvy/b Peter SANDERS & wife Nancy to Abigail HAUSER (formerly Hanks) Admr of John HANKS dec'd. Wit: Francis McKIMIE, Elijah PEACOCK, William HERVEVES?.

Bk:Pg: 2V:359   Date: 12 Feb [Jan] 1818   RtCt: 12 Jan 1818
Amos GIBSON of Ldn to Stephen C. ROSZEL & John SINCLAIR of Ldn to William LICKEY & wife Abigail of Ldn. Release of trust on debt to Amos GIBSON.

Bk:Pg: 2V:360   Date: 10 Jan 1818   RtCt: 10 Jan 1818
Ludwell LEE (h/o late Flora LEE). Deed of release for 1400a of Broad Run tract to James L. McKENNA & wife Ann Celelia (ch/o Flora) of AlexVa and 600a allotted to Richard H. LEE which has been sold to McKENNA. Delv. to McKENNA 1 Apr 1819.

Bk:Pg: 2V:360   Date: 8 Jan 1818   RtCt: 12 Jan 1818
Samuel CHINN & wife Emily of Ldn to Philip FRY of Ldn. B/S of 20¾a on Goose Creek adj where FRY lives, Phebe SKINNER. Wit: Burr POWELL, Abner GIBSON. Delv. to FRY 11 Feb 1822.

Bk:Pg: 2V:361   Date: 6 Jan 1818   RtCt: 23 Jan 1818
Benjamin HUTCHISON & wife Elizabeth of Pittsylvania Co to William ROSE of Ldn. B/S of all Ldn lands Benjamin HUTCHISON dec'd (f/o Benjamin) died seized of.

Bk:Pg: 2V:362   Date: 7 Jan 1818   RtCt: 12 Jan 1818
Moses GIBSON & wife Lydia of Ldn to Elizabeth GIBSON of Ldn. B/S of 14½a (part of land where Moses now lives) adj James GIBSON (4a), Jeffrie's branch, heirs of John GIBSON dec'd. Wit: Benjamin GRAYSON, William BRONAUGH.

Bk:Pg: 2V:363   Date: 22 Dec 1817   RtCt: Jan 1818
Lloyd NOLAND to Humphrey B. POWELL. Trust for debt to Burr POWELL (who owed Francis HEREFORD) using 300a. Wit: Leven LUCKETT, A. GIBSON. Delv. to __ 25 Apr 1821.

Bk:Pg: 2V:365   Date: 20 Dec 1817   RtCt: 29 Jan 1818
George BURSON & wife Susannah of Ldn to Daniel EACHES of Ldn. Trust for debt to George JANNEY & Elisha JANNEY of Ldn using 5a, 8a & 49a. Wit: William BRONAUGH, Susanna BURSON. Acknowledged by EACHES recorded DB AAA:258.

Bk:Pg: 2V:367   Date: 10 Nov 1817   RtCt: 11 Nov 1817
James TURNER & wife Mary of Randolph Co VA to John M. HART of Randolph Co VA. B/S of 41½a Lot #6 on N side of Panther Skin

below Clifton Mills (formerly owned by John VIOLET dec'd). Delv. to HART 24 Sep 1820.

Bk:Pg: 2V:368 Date: 15 Jun 1817 RtCt: 10 Feb 1818
John S. MARLOW of Ldn to Abraham WINNING of Ldn. B/S of 40a. Wit: Frederick HUNDSLY [?] , Benjamin MOORE, Laurence MINK.

Bk:Pg: 2V:369 Date: 15 Nov 1817 RtCt: 12 Jan 1818
John CHEW of Ldn to Abner HUMPHREY of Ldn. Trust for debt to Jesse Thomas using 84a. Wit: Notley C. WILLIAMS, Joshua OSBURN.

Bk:Pg: 2V:370 Date: 3 Nov 1817 RtCt: 9 Nov 1818
Thomas SMITH & wife Martha of Belmont Co OH to Ebenezer GRUBB of Ldn. B/S of 235a between Short Hill and Blue ridge (cnvy/b Samuel PEARSON to Thomas & George SMITH by contract made with Henry SMITH who died before conveyance) adj Christian MILLER, David POTTS, George ABEL, Jonathan CUNNARD. Wit: Townsend FRASIER, Isaac SIMMONS. Delv. to GRUBB 20 Jun 1822.

Bk:Pg: 2V:371 Date: 13 Sep 1817 RtCt: 9 Feb 1818
John REDMOND of Fairfield Co OH to brother Israel REDMOND of Fairfield Co OH. PoA for sale of land from father Andrew REDMOND dec'd of Ldn.

Bk:Pg: 2V:372 Date: 29 Sep 1817 RtCt: 9 Feb 1818
James BALL & wife Ruth of Jefferson Co OH to Reuben SCHOOLEY of Ldn. B/S of 7a on Kittoctan Mt adj SCHOOLEY, Patrick MILLHOLLINS. Wit: Henry CREW, W. R. BAYHAN, George FULTON, Spencer MINOR. Delv. to Ephraim SCHOOLEY Admr of R. SCHOOLEY 28 Jan 1824 or 26?

Bk:Pg: 2V:374 Date: 18 Nov 1817 RtCt: 9 Feb 1818
Isaac HIBBS & wife Kizsey of Springfield township, Jefferson Co OH to Michael EVERHART of Ldn. B/S of undivided 1/11th of 60a which was in possession of John BOOTH Sr as heir at law of his grandfather [father?] Robert BOOTHE, who claims it in right of his wife Kizsey HIBBS to whom it was devised by her grandfather Robert BOOTH in will of 21 Sep 1759. Wit: William CHAMBERY, William DAVIDSON, foreign name.

Bk:Pg: 2W:001 Date: 12 Dec 1817 RtCt: 30 Jan 1818
Samuel MURRAY & wife Betsey of Ldn to Joseph HILLIARD of Ldn. B/S of land on Back St in Lsbg adj Charles BINN's blacksmith shop, John McCORMICK. Wit: John ROSE, Patrick McINTYRE.

Bk:Pg: 2W:002 Date: 15 Jan 1818 RtCt: 28 Feb 1818
David CONRAD & wife Jane of Ldn to William PAXON Jr. of Ldn. Trust for debt to John B. STEPHENS using lot in Wtfd adj William H. HOUGH, Joseph P. THOMAS. Wit: Abiel JANNERS [JENNERS], John H. McCABE.

Bk:Pg: 2W:004   Date: 3 Feb 1818   RtCt: 9 Feb 1818
Patrick MILHOLLEN of Ldn and Matthew MITCHELL (brother in law of Reuben SCHOOLEY) of Ldn. Agreement – MILHOLLEN rented all his land on Kittockton Mt. adj Joseph CALDWELL, Reuben SCHOOLEY, estate of Richard GRIFFITH, Joshua PUSEY, John WILLIAMS except 10a wood land. MITCHELL can use 10a for 16y if he doesn't waste the timber. Wit: John WILLIAMS, James HIGDON.

Bk:Pg: 2W:006   Date: 7 Mar 1818   RtCt: 7 Mar 1818
John W. COE, Robert COE & David J. COE of Ldn to Edward M. COE of Ldn. B/S of interest (42¾a) in mill tract of Edward COE dec'd father of all parties exclusive of what fell to them at death of Menan COE dec'd. Delv. to Edw'd M. COE 7 Dec 1818.

Bk:Pg: 2W:007   Date: 13 Aug 1817   RtCt: 9 Feb 1818
Nathan JANNEY of JeffVA to Thomas SWANN Esqr of AlexVA. Trust for debt to Craven Peyton THOMPSON and Israel Peyton THOMPSON merchants trading in AlexVA and Robert BRADEN, John MORGAN and Joseph EACHES merchants using Nathan's undivided 1/7th of 245a in Ldn which Amos JANNEY late died seized adj land now occupied by Susannah HOUSEHOLDER, Philip FRY, Adam GRUBB, David EXLINE.

Bk:Pg: 2W:009   Date: 12 Jul 1817   RtCt: 12 Feb 1818
Jozabed WHITE & wife Margaret of Ldn to Enos POTTS of Ldn. B/S of 16a WHITE prch/o Benjamin BRADFIELD. Wit: Robert BRADEN, John H. McCABE.

Bk:Pg: 2W:010   Date: 23 Aug 1817   RtCt: 17 Feb 1818
George TAVENER Jr. of Ldn to Garrett WALKER of Ldn. B/S of 115a on great road from Snicker's Gap to Centerville, adj Joseph GARRETT, Lovel JACKSON. Wit: William BRONAUGH, Thomas GREGG. Delv. to WALKER 27 Mar 1821.

Bk:Pg: 2W:011   Date: 23 Aug 1817   RtCt: 17 Feb 1818
Garrett WALKER of Ldn to William J. BRONAUGH of Ldn. Trust for debt to George TAVENER Jr. using above land. Wit: William BRONAUGH, Thomas GREGG.

Bk:Pg: 2W:012   Date: 23 Feb 1818   RtCt: 23 Feb 1818
William NOLAND of Ldn and William H. LANE of Ldn. Agreement – bond for NOLAND's prch/o portion of lands of Hardage LANE dec'd on Little River Turnpike.

Bk:Pg: 2W:013   Date: 3 Jan 1818   RtCt: 9 Mar 1818
Thomas PRICE & wife Lettitia of Ldn to Richard HIRST of Ldn. B/S of 60a adj James McILHANEY. Wit: Notley C. WILLIAMS, Joshua OSBURN. Delv. to __ 12 Mar 1821.

Bk:Pg: 2W:015   Date: 24 Sep 1817   RtCt: 9 Feb 1818
Enos POTTS & wife Lydia of Ldn to David SMITH of Ldn. B/S of 12a on NW fork of Goose Creek adj SMITH, Giles CRAVEN. Wit: William BRONAUGH, Thomas GREGG. Delv. to SMITH 2 Jul 1825.

Bk:Pg: 2W:016 Date: 26 Sep 1817 RtCt: 13 Jan 1818
Thomas YOUNG of Washington to John DULIN of Ffx. Trust for debt to Alexander YOUNG of Ldn using land on Horsepen Run. Wit: Johnson CLEVELAND, Abiel JENNERS. Delv. to J. CLEVELAND pr order 14 Sep 1818.

Bk:Pg: 2W:018 Date: 9 Oct 1817 RtCt: 25 Feb 1818
William DANIEL & wife Ann of Wtfd to Robert D. WHITE of Ldn. B/S of lot in Wtfd on road to Quaker Meeting House adj another lot owned by WHITE. Wit: John WILLIAMS, Isaac E. STEER, Israel JANNEY, John HAMILTON, John H. McCABE.

Bk:Pg: 2W:020 Date: 17 Dec 1817 RtCt: 10 Feb 1818
Frederick HANDSHY & wife Catherine of Ldn to Asa MOORE & Thomas PHILIPS of Ldn. B/S of 80a on S side of Short Hill adj John S. MARLOW. Wit: Abiel JENNERS, John H. McCABE. Delv. to PHILIPS 13 Aug 1827.

Bk:Pg: 2W:021 Date: 24 Dec 1817 RtCt: 11 Feb 1818
Thomas LAKENAN & wife Margarett to James WARE of FredVA.. B/S of Lots #75 & #76 in Aldie (½a each). Wit: Robert ARMISTEAD, William NOLAND. Delv. to grantee 4 Dec 1819.

Bk:Pg: 2W:023 Date: 3 Feb 1818 RtCt: 9 Feb 1818
Patrick MILHOLLAND and Aaron SCHOOLEY. Agreement – MILHOLLAND rented his farm to SCHOOLEY for 10y period, now they agree to end lease. SCHOOLEY to deliver utensils to Matthew MITCHELL and date for return of stock. Wit: John WILLIAMS, James HIGDON.

Bk:Pg: 2W:024 Date: 9 Jul 1816 RtCt: 25 Feb 1818
Francis TRIPLETT Sr. of Lsbg to daughter Nancy TRIPLETT of Lsbg. Gift of slave girl Jane. Wit: S'n BLINCOE, John TRIPLETT, Francis TRIPLETT Jr.

Bk:Pg: 2W:025 Date: 9 Jul 1816 RtCt: 25 Feb 1818
Francis TRIPLETT Sr. of Lsbg to daughter Nancy TRIPLETT of Lsbg. Gift of slave girl Violett.

Bk:Pg: 2W:025 Date: 22 May 1817 RtCt: 9 Mar 1818
Abraham WINNING & John WINNING of Ldn to John S. MARLOW of Ldn. B/S of 67¼a adj Elias THRASHER, Jacob WALTMAN in "Tankerville's Lands". Wit: Frederick HANDSHY, Benjamin MOORE, Lawrence MINK.

Bk:Pg: 2W:026 Date: 29 Nov 1817 RtCt: 23 Feb 1818
Sampson HOWELL of Ldn to William HOWELL of Ldn. BoS farm and household items. Wit: L. ELLZEY, S. W. COCKERILL.

Bk:Pg: 2W:027 Date: 22 Feb 1803 RtCt: 9 Feb 1818
Abner WILLIAMS of Ldn to John M. HOLLIN of Ldn. Bond to ensure payment on land. Wit: Patrick MILHOLLEN.

Bk:Pg: 2W:028   Date: 3 Mar 1818   RtCt: 3 Mar 1818
Henry BENEDUM of Lsbg to Thomas FLOWERS. Loan of
household items. & horse. Wit: S. BLINCOE, Peter BENEDUM,
George FEITCHTER.

Bk:Pg: 2W:028   Date: 10 Feb 1818   RtCt: 9 Mar 1818
Daniel NICHOLS (Exor of Thomas NICHOLS dec'd late of
Christiana hundred, New Castle Co, DE) to Exor of Henry
NICHOLS. Discharge of bond - Thomas NICHOLS was bound to
Joseph NICHOLS for payment on ½ of 235a in Ldn adj Col.
FAIRFAX, Joseph HOLLINGSWORTH, John MINOR, Edward
NORTON. Joseph NICHOLS died before deed of conveyance
leaving to his only son & heir Samuel NICHOLS. Samuel NICHOLS
assigned over to Henry NICHOLS on 20 Dec 1784. Henry NICHOLS
died appointing wife Susanna (now Susanna LOVE) and brother
Isaac NICHOLS as Exors. Wit: Thomas SMYTH, J. P. FAIRLAMB?,
Nathan BASSETT.

Bk:Pg: 2W:031   Date: 10 Oct 1815   RtCt: 13 Mar 1818
Thomas N. BINNS to Thomas R. MOTT. Trust for debt to Richard H.
HENDERSON (Admr of Alexander SUTHERLAND dec'd) using
62½a on Goose Creek. Wit: Saml. E. EDWARDS, Robert R.
HOUGH, Saml. CARR.

Bk:Pg: 2W:032   Date: 9 May 1812   RtCt: 12 May 1812
Asa MOORE & wife Ann of Ldn to Cornelius SHAWEN of Ldn. B/S
of 19a adj Conrad VERTZ, Reuben HIXON. Wit: Isaac HOUGH, Levi
JAMES, Geo. W. HENRY, Charles BENNETT. Delv. to David?
SHAWEN 24 Mar 1824.

Bk:Pg: 2W:034   Date: 19 Sep 1810   RtCt: 14 Mar 1811/ ___
Asa MOORE of Ldn to Levi JAMES of Ldn. B/S of lot in Wtfd adj
John WILLIAMS, __ SMALLWOOD. Wit: William GOODWIN, Moses
JANNEY, Thomas C. SCOTT.

Bk:Pg: 2W:035   Date: 13 Aug 1817   RtCt: 9 Mar 1817
William HEADMAN (potter) & wife Mary of Philadelphia to son
Andrew HEADMAN. PoA for matters concerning estate of Daniel
LOSCH dec'd in Lsbg. Wit: W. RAWLS, Thomas WHITE.

Bk:Pg: 2W:038   Date: 28 Feb 1818   RtCt: 9 Mar 1818
George JOHNSON. Col for male slave Julian age 9y of dark
complexion acquired by descent.

Bk:Pg: 2W:038   Date: 9 Mar 1818   RtCt: 9 Mar 1818
Joseph HAWKINGS, James H. HAMILTON, Daniel LOVETT. Bond
on HAWKINS as constable. Wit: Jno. A. BINNS.

Bk:Pg: 2W:039   Date: 8 Feb 1813   RtCt: 9 Mar 1818
Josias CLAPHAM. Division on motion of Josias CLAPHAM (Exor. of
Josias CLAPHAM). Divisors to ascertain quantities of land dev.
Aaron SAUNDERS & son Samuel CLAPHAM in trust (then in
England & his children and then by consent of reps of Samuel

CLAPHAM then in England and dec'd who are of age). 249a to Samuel LUCKETT who married with 2 of the daughters of Samuel dec'd, Benjamin JACKSON who married another daughter & George CLAPHAM a son and another part to remain with trustees of heirs under age for further div. 274a to Samuel LUCKETT, Benjamin JACKSON & Geo. CLAPHAM. Gives plat. Divisors: Charles LEWIS, John BAYLY, John L. BERKLEY.

Bk:Pg: 2W:040 Date: 30 Mar 1818 RtCt: 13 Apr 1818
Edward CARTER of Ldn to friend Thomas CARTER of Mason Co KY. PoA for sale of 1000a in Mason Co cnvy/b attorney John B. ARMISTEAD for William C. NEWSON dated 27 Oct 1817. Wit: Lewis P. W. BALCH, Geo. W. ADAMS, Lee W. DURHAM.

Bk:Pg: 2W:041 Date: 4 Oct 1817 RtCt: Mar 1818
Ebenezer GRUBB & Edward DOWLING of Ldn to John CONRAD & Valentine MILLER of Ldn. Trust for debt to Valentine MILLER using 124a on W side of short hill. Wit: Joshua OSBURNE, John WHITE.

Bk:Pg: 2W:043 Date: 7 Oct 1817 RtCt: Apr 1818
Ruth POULTON, James TRIBBY & wife Tamar, Thomas POULTON & wife Eleanor, Charles POULTON, John POULTON, Reed POULTON & wife Anzey of Ldn to Jonathan HEATON of Ldn. B/S of 13a adj Reed POULTON's shops. Wit: Joshua OSBURN, John WHITE. Delv. to HEATON 28 Dec 1818.

Bk:Pg: 2W:044 Date: 20 May 1817 RtCt: 6 Apr 1818
Edmund J. LEE of AlexDC to David LOVETT of Ldn. Indenture of trust of 14 May 1814 from Ferdinando FAIRFAX (for debt to Thomas SWANN & Walter JONES) to LEE for 80a of Lots #8, #9, #10, #11 & #12 on NE end of Short Hill with tenements lately held by Margarett RIDENBAUGH and Jones SPRING and 85a with tenement of Robert WHITE of Shannondale tract nr Hllb. FAIRFAX failed to pay so LEE selling land. Wit: Daniel LOVETT, Robert RUSSELL, Randolph RHODES. Delv. to LOVETT 5 Sep 1821.

Bk:Pg: 2W:047 Date: 4 Oct 1817 RtCt: Apr 1818
Valentine MILLER & wife Sarah of Ldn to Ebenezer GRUBB & Edward DOWLING of Ldn. B/S of 184a on W side of Short Hill adj Christian MILLER, John POTTS, David POTTS. Wit: Joshua OSBURN, John WHITE. Delv. to GRUBB __ Jun 1822.

Bk:Pg: 2W:049 Date: 11 Oct 1817 RtCt: Apr 1818
Mary MILLER (wd/o Christian MILLER dec'd) of Ldn to Valentine MILLER of Ldn. B/S of dower rights to 184a. Wit: John WHITE, Joshua OSBURN.

Bk:Pg: 2W:050 Date: 7 Oct 1817 RtCt: Apr 1818
Ruth POULTON of Ldn to Reed POULTON of Ldn. B/S of 2a where Reed now lives (cnvy/b James TRIBBY & wife Tamar, Thomas POULTON, Charles POULTON, John POULTON & Reid POULTON

to Ruth). Wit: Joshua OSBURN, John WHITE. Delv. to R. POULTON 6 May 1819.

Bk:Pg: 2W:051   Date: 4 Apr 1816   RtCt: Apr 1818
John HOUGH & wife Pleasant of Ldn to John UNDERWOOD of Ldn. B/S of ¼a in Hllb nr road leading to Purcel's Mill. Wit: Evan EVANS, Asa BROWN, Sam. D. LESLIE, Joshua OSBURN, John WHITE. Delv. to grantee 11 Nov 1820.

Bk:Pg: 2W:053   Date: 7 Oct 1817   RtCt: Apr 1818
James TRIBBY & wife Tamar, Thomas POULTON & wife Elenor, Charles POULTON, John POULTON & Reid POULTON & wife Ansey of Ldn to Ruth POULTON of Ldn. B/S of 14a (part of tract held by deed in trust to Martha POULTON for benefit of the parties hereunto her children. Wit: Joshua OSBURN, John WHITE.

Bk:Pg: 2W:055   Date: 29 Dec 1817   RtCt: Apr 1818
John HOUGH & wife Pleasant, Thomas STEPHENS & wife Nancy and Valentine PURSEL of Ldn to Thomas SINCLAIR & George SINCLAIR of Ldn. B/S of 33a adj Hllb. Wit: Joshua OSBURN, John WHITE. Delv. to Thomas SINCLAIR 25 Dec 1818.

Bk:Pg: 2W:057   Date: 25 Sep 1817   RtCt: Apr 1818
David LOVETT of Ldn to Stacy TAYLOR & Craven OSBURN of Ldn. Trust for debt to Jonathan TRIBBY and George TRIBBY of Ldn using 183a. Wit: Joshua OSBURN, John WHITE. Delv. to Stacy TAYLOR 10 Jun 1824.

Bk:Pg: 2W:059   Date: 30 Aug 1817   RtCt: Apr 1818
Joseph PURSELL & wife Susan of Ldn to Christopher SCRIVER of Ldn. B/S of 9a adj George ABEL. Wit: Joshua OSBURN, John WHITE. Delv. to George ABEL 27 Feb 1843.

Bk:Pg: 2W:061   Date: 11 Mar 1818   RtCt: 11 Mar 1818
William KNOX & wife Mary of Ldn to John NIXON of Ldn. B/S of 31a allotted to Mary, formerly Mary NIXON from div. of George NIXON dec'd. Wit: William B. HARRISON, Thomas GREGG. Delv. to Jno. NIXON 1 Nov 1825.

Bk:Pg: 2W:064   Date: 2 May 1817   RtCt: 9 Mar 1818
John HOUGH & wife Pleasant, George PURSEL, Mary PURSEL, Lydia PURSEL & Valentine PURSEL of Ldn to Elisha JANNEY as agent for his son John JANNEY. B/S of 66a adj Hllb, Samuel CLENDINNING, Benjamin LESLIE, heirs of William RUSSEL. Wit: David LOVETT, Asa BROWN, S. H. JACKSON, Joshua OSBURN, John WHITE. Delv. to John JANNEY 30 Mar 1821.

Bk:Pg: 2W:066   Date: 1 Apr 1818   RtCt: 1 Apr 1818
Abraham WINNING of Ldn to John GEORGE of Ldn. B/S of 40a. Wit: Robert BRADEN, Wm. BRONAUGH. Delv. to __ 24 Aug 1820.

Bk:Pg: 2W:067   Date: 6 Apr 1818   RtCt: 6 Apr 1818
Lewis GRIGSBY & wife Hannah of Ldn to Benjamin BRADFIELD of Ldn. B/S of 83a adj Bernard TAYLOR, James COCKRAN. Wit:

Charles LEWIS, Thomas GREGG. Delv. to BRADFIELD 30 Apr 1822.

Bk:Pg: 2W:070   Date: 23 Jan 1817   RtCt: 6 Apr 1818
John AXLINE & wife Christiana of Ldn to Henry AXLINE of Ldn. B/S of 130a adj David AXLINE, Jacob VIRTS, Phillip EVERHART. Wit: R. BRADEN, Daniel HOUSEHOLDER, John BUMCROTS. John H. McCABE. Delv. to __ AXLINE 4 Jan 1824.

Bk:Pg: 2W:071   Date: 6 Mar 1818   RtCt: Apr 1818
John POTTER & wife Elizabeth of Ldn to George RUST of Ldn. B/S of lot in Lsbg on W side of King St between Loudoun & Markett Sts next to Thomas SAUNDERS. Wit: William NOLAND, Leven LUCKETT. Delv. to __ 3 Oct 1818.

Bk:Pg: 2W:073   Date: 2 Apr 1818   RtCt: 3 Apr 1818
Joseph MILHOLLIN of Ldn to Joseph CALDWELL of Ldn. B/S of ½ of undivided 8a (beq. to MILHOLLIN and brother John MILHOLLIN by mother Esther MILHOLLIN dec'd). Wit: Abiel JENNERS, John HAMILTON. Delv. to CALDWELL 30 Nov 1819.

Bk:Pg: 2W:074   Date: 5 Sep 1817   RtCt: 1 Apr 1818
Ruth TRIBBY, Asahel TRIBBY & wife Catherine, George TRIBBY and Jonathan TRIBBY of Ldn to Stacy TAYLOR and Craven OSBURN of Ldn. Under will of father Joseph TRIBBY dec'd, Asahel, George & Jonathan held 136a adj land of James McILHANEY dec'd, Thomas DAVIS, Daniel COOPER and James NIXON. Ruth as wd/o Joseph TRIBBY has life interest. George & Jonathan have sold but not conveyed their shares to Mortimer McILHANEY son of James dec'd who is <21y. George & Jonathan have taken for sale the land of Mortimer McILHANEY dec'd adj land of James BRADFIELD, David LOVETT & Louisa McILHANEY being his part of Elizabeth McILHANY's estate of abt 92a. David LOVETT purchased the shares of Jonathan & George. Trust to cover failure to pay. Wit: Abiel JENNERS, John WHITE. Delv. to LOVETT 10 Jun 1824.

Bk:Pg: 2W:077   Date: 19 Mar 1818   RtCt: Apr 1818
John B. STEVENS & wife Sarah of Ldn to Edward DORSEY of Ldn. B/S of 1a Lot #5 in Wtfd. Wit: Robert BRADEN, Abiel JENNERS. Delv. to DORSEY 11 Feb 1824.

Bk:Pg: 2W:079   Date: 26 Mar 1818   RtCt: 30 Mar 1818
James WORNALL & wife Charlotte of Ldn to Elijah ANDERSON of Ldn. B/S of 31a prch/o Robert MARTIN (his share from father William MARTIN). Wit: William BRONAUGH, Francis W. LUCKETT. Delv. to ANDERSON 2 Apr 1832.

Bk:Pg: 2W:082   Date: 3 Jan 1818   RtCt: 9 Mar 1818
Joseph HAINS & wife Maria of Ldn to John WYNN of Ldn. B/S of 45¼a cnvy/b William HOGUE & wife, Wm. H. HANDEY & wife Eleanor and Stephen MEGEATH dated Apr 1811 and 64a cnvy/b

Mary MEGEATH and the above listed in Mar 1809. Wit: Notely C. WILLIAMS, Thos. GREGG. Delv. to WYNN 9 Dec 1819.

Bk:Pg: 2W:084   Date: 27 Oct 1817   RtCt: 30 Mar 1818
Abner HOWELL & wife Priscilla of Ldn, Abel HOWELL & wife Naomi and Thomas WEST & wife Margaret of OH to Jesse HOWELL of Ldn. B/S of 116a leased land formerly occupied by William HOWEL dec'd and at present by Abner on top of blue ridge adj Elias JAMES, Thomas SUDDEN. Wit: Joshua OSBURN, John WHITE. Delv. grantee 6 May 1820.

Bk:Pg: 2W:086   Date: 31 Dec 1817   RtCt: 9 Mar 1818
Sanford RAMEY & wife Lydia of Ldn to Elijah VIOLETT of Ldn. B/S of 4a. Wit: Sanford J. RAMEY, James McGAVOCK, Samuel MORAN, Abiel JENNERS, Presley CORDELL.

Bk:Pg: 2W:088   Date: 19 Jan 1818   RtCt: 9 Mar 1818
George GIBSON & wife Abigail of Ldn to John MARTIN of Ldn. Trust for debt to Elijah VIOLETT using 8½a nr where old school house stood adj Col. Leven POWELL. Wit: Burr POWELL, A. GIBSON. Delv. to Ashford VIOLETT Exor of E. VIOLETT dec'd [undated]

Bk:Pg: 2W:090   Date: 10 Aug 1817   RtCt: 30 Mar 1818
Colin AULD of AlexDC to Richard VANPELT of Ldn. B/S of 440a adj Mary BOLANS patent on W side of Travers Branch. Wit: Gerrard WYNKOON [WYNKOOP?], William VANPELT, Wm. RUST. Delv. to VANPELT 14 Aug 1818.

Bk:Pg: 2W:091   Date: 3 Mar 1818   RtCt: 29 Mar 1818
Jonathan GIBSON of Ldn to Evi GIBSON of Ldn. Trust to indemnify Moses GIBSON as his security using land & house in Upperville. Wit: Francis W. LUCKETT, A. GIBSON. Delv. to Evi GIBSON 24 Nov 1821.

Bk:Pg: 2W:093   Date: 26 Feb 1818   RtCt: 10 Mar 1818
William VICKERS & wife Ann of Ldn to Mason FRENCH of Ldn. B/S of 7a (a reserve made by James MONTEITH to give him access from his other land to creek independent of his tenant & lessees). Wit: Abner GIBSON, Francis W. LUCKETT.

Bk:Pg: 2W:094   Date: 7 Mar 1818   RtCt: 30 Mar 1818
James LEITH & wife Sarah of Hampshire Co VA to Henry PLAISTER of Ldn. B/S of 76a adj Daniel EACHES. Wit: Chas. LEWIS, James PLAISTER, Robt. POWELL. Delv. to LUCKETT 26 Apr 1822.

Bk:Pg: 2W:096   Date: 12 Apr 1818   RtCt: 11 Mar 1818
John HARRIS & wife Elizabeth of Mdbg to Noble BEVERIDGE. Trust for debt to Jesse McVEIGH using lot in Mdbg cnvy/b McVEIGH to HARRIS. Wit: Burr POWELL, John BRADY, Benj. SMITH, Hiram McVEIGH, A. GIBSON.

Bk:Pg: 2W:097   Date: 11 Dec 1817   RtCt: 9 Mar 1818
Stephen LEWIS and Catharine LEWIS of Ldn to Peter RUST of Ldn.
B/S of rights to their share of 197a from mother Nancy late w/o
Charles LEWIS from her father James LEWIS. Wit: Burr POWELL,
Abner GIBSON. Delv to grantee 2 Aug 1820.

Bk:Pg: 2W:098   Date: 22 Dec 1784   RtCt: 14 Sep 1818
Wilson Cary SELDON Esqr & wife Mary Mason of North River in
Gloucester Co to Cary SELDON of Buck Row in Elizabeth City. B/S
of 4000a (inherited by Mary from brother) except 2000a granted to
William Byrd PAGE 2nd son of Mary MASON by deed dated 22 Mar
1784. Wit: John WHITING, Francis WHITING, Job COLTON. Wit:
Miles KING, Worlich WESTWOOD. Delv. to Wilson C. SELDON 9
Oct 1818.

Bk:Pg: 2W:100   Date: 17 Feb 1818   RtCt: Apr 1818
Enos POTTS & wife Lydia of Ldn to Henry ELLIS of Ldn. B/S of 15a
on NW fork of Goose Creek adj Isaac & Saml. NICHOLLS, Levi
WILLIAMS. Wit: Thomas GREGG, Joshua OSBURN. Delv. to ELLIS
31 Mar 1819.

Bk:Pg: 2W:102   Date: 19 Mar 1818   RtCt: 19 Mar 1818
George NIXON & wife Elizabeth of Ldn to John NIXON of Ldn. B/S
of 5a Lot #7 subject of right of owner of Lot #4 of carrying water from
Spring. Wit: Samuel MURREY, Patrick McINTYRE. Delv. to Jno.
NIXON 1 Nov 1825.

Bk:Pg: 2W:104   Date: 10 Oct 1817   RtCt: Apr 1818
George JANNEY & wife Susanna of Ldn to Robert FULTON of Ldn.
B/S of 319a adj Christopher GREENUP. Wit: William BRONAUGH,
Francis W. LUCKETT. Delv. to FULTON 16 Mar 1819.

Bk:Pg: 2W:105   Date: 24 Nov 1817   RtCt: 10 Mar 1818
Burr POWELL of Ldn to William DISHMAN of Ldn. B/S of 1a Lot
#848 in Mdbg at intersection of Jay & Washington Sts. Wit: Abner
GIBSON, Francis W. LUCKETT.

Bk:Pg: 2W:107   Date: 24 Nov 1817   RtCt: 25 Mar 1818
John P. HEREFORD & wife Elizabeth of Ldn to Elizabeth BOYD.
B/S of Lot #38 and part of #39 on Washington & Pickering Sts. in
Mdbg. Wit: Burr POWELL, Abner GIBSON. Delv'd. to Eliz. BOYD 5
May 1820.

Bk:Pg: 2W:108   Date: 12 Nov 1817   RtCt: 10 Mar 1818
Samuel SINGLETON of Ldn as trustee for Cynthia TRIPLETT (now
w/o William BERRY) to William BERRY of Ldn. Release of trust.

Bk:Pg: 2W:109   Date: 1 Oct 1817   RtCt: 9 Mar 1818
Amos GIBSON & wife Hannah of Ldn to Asa MOORE & Thomas
PHILIPS of Ldn. B/S of 10a (Lots #5, #6 & #7) in Wtfd adj Jas.
TALBOTT dec'd, David JANNEY. Wit: Robert BRADEN, John H.
McCABE. Delv. to PHILIPS 18 Aug 1836.

Bk:Pg: 2W:111   Date: 16 Mar 1818   RtCt: 19 Mar 1818
William P. BAYLY (a son of Pierce BAYLY the elder) & wife Mary L. of StafVA to George BAYLY of FredVA. B/S of his share of land Pierce BAYLY the elder of Ldn dev. son Pierce who died. Wit: Reuben HUTCHISON, Alexander HUTCHISON, Joseph HUTCHISON, Albert BAYLY. Delv. to Geo. BAILEY 15 May 1819.

Bk:Pg: 2W:112   Date: 19 Sep 1817   RtCt: 10 Mar 1818
William VICKERS & wife Anne of Ldn to George JANNEY of Ldn. B/S of 36a adj __WORNELL, __FRENCH. Wit: Abner GIBSON, Francis W. LUCKETT.

Bk:Pg: 2W:113   Date: 20 Sep 1817   RtCt: 10 Mar 1818
George JANNEY of Ldn to William VICKER of Ldn. LS of 36a as above. Wit: William BRONAUGH, Francis W. LUCKETT. Delv. to VICKERS 14 Jan 1820.

Bk:Pg: 2W:114   Date: 14 Mar 1818   RtCt: 14 Mar 1818
John EDWARDS & wife Catharine of Ldn to Joseph CONNER of Ldn. B/S of 1a on W side of King St in Lsbg now occupied by Capt. John ROSE. Wit: Patrick McINTYRE, Presley CORDELL. Delv. to CONNOR 24 Sep 1822.

Bk:Pg: 2W:116   Date: 15 Sep 1817   RtCt: 9 Mar 1818
Robert COE of Ldn to Richard H. HENDERSON of Ldn. Trust for debt to John W. COE Admr. of Menan COE dec'd of Ldn using land cnvy/b Edward COE dec'd (father of Robert & John). Wit: J. L. DREAN, Chas. W. D. BINNS, G. W. ADAMS.

Bk:Pg: 2W:117   Date: 3 Oct 1817   RtCt: Apr 1818
Charles B. ALEXANDER & wife Eliza of Ldn to George JANNEY of Ldn. B/S of 319a adj Christopher GREENUP. Wit: John ROSE, Abiel JENNERS.

Bk:Pg: 2W:119   Date: ___   RtCt: 16 Mar 1818
Charles SHEPHERD (s/o Charles dec'd & Eleanor SHEPHERD) to James W. LEWIS of Ldn. A/L for ¼ part of L/L (on Charles SHEPHERD, wife Elenor & eldest son James) of Aug 1798 from Willoughby TEBBS & wife Betsey of PrWm for 138a adj Samuel PERRY. Wit: John LITTLEJOHN. Delv. to LEWIS 22 Nov 1819.

Bk:Pg: 2W:119   Date: 16 Sep 1817   RtCt: 27 Mar 1818
Thomas GREGG & wife Hannah of Ldn to trustee Fleet SMITH. Trust for debt to John GREGG using 136a. Wit: Notley C. WILLIAMS, William BRONAUGH.

Bk:Pg: 2W:121   Date: 3 Oct 1818   RtCt: 14 Mar 1818
Charles B. ALEXANDER & wife Eliza of Ldn to George JANNEY of Ldn. B/S of 195a adj Robert CARTER's patent, Jacob LASSWELL's patent, Christopher GREENUP. Wit: John ROSE, Abiel JENNERS.

Bk:Pg: 2W:123   Date: 19 Jan 1818   RtCt: 30 Mar 1818
Colin AULD to Reuben HUTCHISON. Release of trust on 174½a.

Bk:Pg: 2W:123   Date: 8 Dec 1817   RtCt: 4 Apr 1818
Edward OWENS and Benjamin OWENS of Ldn to James RUST.
Trust for George JOHNSON as security on bond using farm and
household items.

Bk:Pg: 2W:124   Date: 23 Jan 1817   RtCt: 6 Apr 1818
John AXLINE & wife Christiana of Ldn to John AXLINE Jr. of Ldn.
B/S of 106a (part of land cnvy/b Ferdinando FAIRFAX in Dec 1801).
Wit: Robert BRADEN, Daniel HOUSEHOLDER, John BUMCROTS,
John H. McCABE. Delv. to Jno. AXLINE 10 Jan 1821.

Bk:Pg: 2W:126   Date: 15 Sep 1817   RtCt: 9 Mar 1818
Edward M. COE, John W. COE, William COE & wife Catharine,
David Jamieson COE & Ann SMITH & Emily SMITH infants by
Edward M. COE their guardian for that purpose appointed of Ldn to
Robert COE of Ldn. B/S of 82a Robert COE prch/o Menan COE
before he died part of estate of their father Edward COE dec'd and
42½a Robert bought of Edward COE dec'd. Wit: J. L. DREAN, G. W.
ADAMS, Charles W. D. BINNS, Patrick McINTYRE, Presley
CORDELL. Delv. to Robert COE 22 Jun 1820.

Bk:Pg: 2W:128   Date: 23 Mar 1818   RtCt: 6 Apr 1818
Samuel CLAPHAM & wife Elizabeth of Ldn to Thomas B. BEATTY
of Ldn. B/S of ½a at corner of Lot #14 on S side of Market St in
Lsbg. Wit: Robert BRADEN, Pat'k McINTYRE.

Bk:Pg: 2W:129   Date: 14 Mar 1818   RtCt: 14 Mar 1818
Henry CLAGETT & wife Julia of Ldn to Thomas B. BEATTY of Ldn.
B/S of Lot #17 on Market St in Lsbg. Wit: Samuel MURREY, Presley
CORDELL.

Bk:Pg: 2W:130   Date: 8 Oct 1818   RtCt: 14 Mar 1818
Geo JANNEY & wife Susanna of Ldn to George CARTER of
Oatlands. B/S of 195a adj Robert CARTER Jr.'s patent, Christopher
GREENUP. Wit: William BRONAUGH, Francis W. LUCKETT. Delv.
to Jesse TIMMS pr order filed DB XX:85 on 26 Oct 1819.

Bk:Pg: 2W:132   Date: 12 May 1812   RtCt: 10 Mar 1818
Landon CARTER Esqr (Exor of George CARTER late of StafVA) to
William WRIGHT of Ldn. B/S of 11a adj Dr. SELDEN, B. SHREVE.
Wit: Thomas SWANN, Benjamin SHREVE, Jno. MATTHIAS.

Bk:Pg: 2W:134   Date: 2 Aug 1817   RtCt: 9 Mar 1818
Jehu HOLLINGSWORTH of Ldn to Enos POTTS of Ldn. Trust for
debt to Adam WINEGARNER using 136a on NW fork of Goose
Creek. Wit: David SMITH, William BROWN, Spencer BROWN. Delv.
to Wm. HOGE Exor of Isaac NICHOLLS dec'd 24 Nov 1829.

Bk:Pg: 2W:135   Date: 27 Dec 1817   RtCt: 13 Mar 1818
Anthony CONRAD & wife Mary of Ldn to Burr William HARRISON of
Ldn. Trust for debt to Thomas B. BEATTY using 100a adj Westwood
T. MASON. Wit: J. C. QUICK, Fleet SMITH, Pat'k McINTYRE,
Joseph BEARD, John ROSE, Presley CORDELL.

Bk:Pg: 2W:138   Date: 25 Feb 1818   RtCt: 12 Mar 1818
Jane McCABE, John H. McCABE & wife Mary, John NEWTON & wife Harriet of Ldn to Catharine DOWLING of Ldn. B/S of ½a lot on N side of Market St in W addition to Lsbg. Wit: Abiel JENNERS, Presley CORDELL. Robert BRADEN.

Bk:Pg: 2W:140   Date: 24 Nov 1817   RtCt:
William C. NEWTON & wife Sarah of Ldn to TRIPLETT & WALKER of Ldn. B/S of part of Lot #5 on NE side of main street in Millsville. Wit: William C. NEWTON, Sarah NEWTON. Delv. to THORNTON & WALKER 28 Jan 1820.

Bk:Pg: 2W:141   Date: 4 Apr 1818   RtCt: 7 Apr 1818
Charles ELGIN & wife Roana of Ldn to Edward DORSEY of Ldn. B/S of 19a (bought of Thos. N. BINNS guardian of Elisa S. BINNS). Wit: John HAMILTON, Saml. LUCKETT. Delv. to DORSEY 13 Nov 1820.

Bk:Pg: 2W:143   Date: 23 Mar 1818   RtCt: 27 Mar 1818
George RUST Jr. & wife Maria C. of Ldn to Armstead T. MASON of Ldn. B/S of 503a adj Potomac, road from Lsbg to Nolands Ferry. Wit: Patrick McINTYRE, Presley CORDELL. Delv. to John B. MASON Exor of A. T. MASON 13 May 1819.

Bk:Pg: 2W:144   Date: 19 Dec 1817   RtCt: 10 Mar 1818
Elisha JANNEY and George JANNEY & wife Susannah of Ldn to George BURSON of Ldn. B/S of 5a on N side of Goose Creek, 8a on S side of Goose Creek and 49a on N side of Goose Creek adj Benjamin BROOKE, Robert FULTON. Wit: William BRONAUGH, Francis W. LUCKETT. Delv. to Aaron BURSON pr order filed DB WW:144 on 20 Jan 1820.

Bk:Pg: 2W:146   Date: 1 Apr 1818   RtCt: 21 Apr 1818
Colin AULD of AlexDC to Samuel M. EDWARDS of Lsbg. B/S of Lot #6 in Lsbg. Delv. to EDWARDS by himself on __.

Bk:Pg: 2W:147   Date: 22 Oct 1817   RtCt: 27 Apr 1818
John BROWN yeoman & wife Sarah of Ldn to Enos POTTS of Ldn. B/S of 10a adj John WARFORD. Wit: Notley C. WILLIAMS, Joshua OSBURNE. Delv. to POTTS 13 Jan 1821.

Bk:Pg: 2W:148   Date: 30 Apr 1818   RtCt: 30 Apr 1818
Cornelius BENNETT of Ldn to Robert BENTLEY of Ldn. A/L (lease of 15y from William TAYLOR to William MOXLEY in Mar 1815) of lot in Lsbg between Aaron DIVINE and Nathaniel TRIPLETT) for remainder of term.

Bk:Pg: 2W:149   Date: __ Apr 1818   RtCt: 20 Apr 1818
Lewis P. W. BALCH of Lsbg as commr. for John Lewis SULLIVAN (s/o Murtho SULLIVAN dec'd, Elizabeth SULLIVAN wd/o Murtho) of Ldn to John Lewis SULLIVAN. B/S of 101a. Delv pr order 28 Apr 1838.

Bk:Pg: 2W:150   Date: 27 Feb 1817   RtCt: 31 Mar 1817
Lewis BERKLEY (trustee of Gen. Thomas NELSON) of PrWm to
John HUTCHISON Jr. of Ldn. Release of trust. Wit: Geo. B.
WHITING, P. B. REED, Carter B. THORNTON, R. H. LITTLE. Delv.
to HUTCHISON 21 Aug 1820.

Bk:Pg: 2W:151   Date: 30 May 1817   RtCt: 21 [?] May 1817
Peter COMPHER & wife Margaret and Levi COLLINS & wife
Margaret of Ldn to Thomas GASSAWAY of Ldn. B/S of 26¾a
(shares of land of Peter COMPHER dec'd) adj Edward MARLOW,
__ STOUTSEBURGER. Wit: John HAMILTON, Samuel LUCKETT.

Bk:Pg: 2W:153   Date: 7 Feb 1818   RtCt: 13 Apr 1818
Philip THOMAS of Ldn to Isaiah PAIN of Ldn. B/S of 2a on SE side
of Blue Ridge where PAIN now lives, adj Thomas JAMES. Wit:
Joshua OSBURNE, John WHITE.

Bk:Pg: 2W:154   Date: 9 Feb 1818   RtCt: 13 Apr 1818
Levi WILLIAMS of Ldn to James RUST of Ldn. Trust for debt to
John PANCOAST using land on NW fork of Goose Creek adj
Samuel & Isaac NICKOLS, William HERRON. Wit: Joshua
OSBURNE, Thos. GREGG. Delv. to John PANCOAST 9 Mar 1819.

Bk:Pg: 2W:155   Date: __ 1818   RtCt: 13 Apr 1818
Levi TATE of Ldn to Samuel & Isaac NICKOLS of Ldn. Stephen
DANIEL of Ldn indebted to David HIRST formerly of Ldn. Stephen
made trust with Levi TATE using 112a which Daniel sold to George
TAVENER who sold to Samuel & Isaac NICKOLS. Wit: James
HOGE, Joel CRAVEN, Phebe NICKOLS. Delv. to Saml. NICKOLLS
9 Nov 1825.

Bk:Pg: 2W:157   Date: 7 Jul 1817   RtCt: 5 May 1818
Betsy TEBBS (wd/o Willoughby TEBBS) of PrWm to James M.
LEWIS of Ldn. B/S 162a leased to Abraham B. T. MASON now
dec'd and at present occupied by reps of Hugh DOUGLASS and
188a leased to Charles SHEPHERD now dec'd now with Benjamin
JACKSON as tenent. Wit: Jno. P. DUVAL, J. MACRAE, Thomas F.
TEBBS. Delv. to LEWIS 22 Nov 1819.

Bk:Pg: 2W:158   Date: 9 Feb 1818   RtCt: 27 Apr 1818
Levi WILLIAMS & wife Sarah of Ldn to Enos POTTS of Ldn. B/S of
80a adj John WARFORD, Jehu HOLLINGSWORTH. Wit: Thomas
GREGG, Joshua OSBURNE. Delv. to POTTS 13 Jan 1821.

Bk:Pg: 2W:159   Date: 25 Mar 1818   RtCt: 10 Apr 1818
Bernard TAYLOR & wife Sarah of Ldn to Walter KERRICK of Ldn.
B/S of 3a adj Benjamin BRADFIELD, Stephen WILSON, heirs of
James McILHANEY. Wit: Samuel MURREY, John McCORMICK.
Delv. to KERRICK 27 Dec 1823.

Bk:Pg: 2W:161   Date: 25 Mar 1818   RtCt: 16 Apr 1818
Bernard TAYLOR & wife Sarah of Ldn to Walter KERRICK of Ldn.
B/S of 3a adj KERRICK. Wit: Samuel MURREY, John McCORMICK.
Delv. to KERRICK 27 Dec 1823.

Bk:Pg: 2W:163   Date: 20 Dec 1817   RtCt: 13 Apr 1818
William NOLAND & John SINCLAIR (Commrs apptd 1 Jun 1817 in
chancery PULLER vs PULLER) to Leven LUCKETT of Ldn. B/S of
1/15th of 100+a late the property of James JOHNSTON dec'd and
being also ½ share of land allotted to Joseph PULLER, James
PULLER, Susannah BOZEL w/o Walter BOZZEL, Samuel PULLER
& Elizabeth PULLER heirs of Hannah PULLER dec'd. Wit: T. D.
PEYTON, Samuel NOLAND, Lloyd NOLAND, John THOMAS, Albert
O. POWELL, J. L. DREAN. Delv. pr order filed 14 Feb 1825.

Bk:Pg: 2W:164   Date: 13 Apr 1818   RtCt: 13 Apr 1818
Joseph GARRET & Seth SMITH to Stephen DANIEL. Release of
trust on land nr widow ROZZELL's in Ldn to secure notes given to
Jacob SMITH late of Ldn but now of Belmont Co OH.

Bk:Pg: 2W:164   Date: 12 Apr 1818   RtCt: 13 Apr 1818
John ROMINE to Benjamin KENT. B/S of 14a on Snickers Gap
Turnpike inherited from father John ROMINE dec'd exclusive of
widow's dower, adj Jessee JANNEY's heirs, Susan ROMINE. Wit
William BRONAUGH, Francis W. LUCKETT.

Bk:Pg: 2W:165   Date: 26 Dec 1817   RtCt: 13 Apr 1818
William NOLAND & John SINCLAIR (Commrs for Elizabeth
JOHNSON, Jane JOHNSON the younger, James JOHNSON &
Rachel RANDAL w/o William RANDALL heirs of John JOHNSON
dec'd) to Leven LUCKETT. B/S of land of James JOHNSON's estate
allotted to his mother Jane JOHNSON dec'd and now allotted to
commrs. Wit: T. D. PEYTON, Samuel NOLAND, Lloyd NOLAND,
John THOMAS, Albert O. POWELL, J. L. DREAN. Delv. to
LUCKETT on ___

Bk:Pg: 2W:166   Date: 5 Sep 1817   RtCt: 13 Apr 1818
James SIMPSON & wife Eliza of Ldn to Humphry B. POWELL. Trust
for debt to Isaac LAKE who owes same to Benjamin HIXSON using
250a in Bull Run Mt. on Hunger run adj Burr POWELL, Owen
SULLIVAN. Wit: Burr POWELL, A. GIBSON.

Bk:Pg: 2W:168   Date: 20 Jan 1818   RtCt: 13 Apr 1818
Sanford RAMEY & wife Lydia of Ldn to Hiram SEATON of Ldn. B/S
of 41½a from div. of John VIOLETT dec'd. Wit: Robert BRADEN,
Abiel JENNERS. Delv. to SEATON 30 Sep 1847.

Bk:Pg: 2W:169   Date: 10 Jan 1818   RtCt: 13 Apr 1818
William NOLAND & wife Catharine of Ldn to Reuben HUTCHISON
of Ldn. B/S of 174a prch/o Colin AULD. Wit: Henry McKENZIE, Levi
BARTON, Thomas NOLAND, Chs. G. ESKRIDGE, Albert O.

POWELL, J. L. DREAN, Charles LEWIS, John BAYLEY. Delv. to HUTCHISON 8 Mar 1821.

Bk:Pg: 2W:171 Date: 27 Apr 1818 RtCt: 1 May 1818
Francis STRIBLING & wife Cecilia of Ldn to Joshua PANCOAST of Ldn & William WILSON of MontMD. Trust for debt to Stephen WILSON using 140a. Wit: Thomas GREGG, John WHITE.

Bk:Pg: 2W:173 Date: 9 Jan 1818 RtCt: 13 Apr 1818
John MATHIAS of Ldn to Philip DERRY of Ldn. B/S of 23½a adj __ DEMORY, __ BURNS. Wit: Peter DERRY, Hiram CARNEY, John J. MATHIAS.

Bk:Pg: 2W:174 Date: 13 Apr 1818 RtCt: 13 Apr 1818
John MATHIAS of Ldn to Casper EVERHART of Ldn. B/S of 19a Lot #28 on W side of short hill adj John CONARD. Delv. to EVERHART 11 Mar 1822.

Bk:Pg: 2W:175 Date: 27 Mar 1818 RtCt: 13 Apr 1818
Benjamin KINN (free blackman) & wife Letetia/Letty of Ldn to Asa MOORE & Thomas PHILIPS of Ldn. B/S of 2a on N side of Kittocton creek adj PHILIPS. Wit: Robert BRADEN, John H. McCABE. Delv. to PHILLIPS 3 May 1824.

Bk:Pg: 2W:177 Date: 13 Apr 1818 RtCt: 3 [13?] Apr 1818
Benjamin KENT & wife Sarah of Ldn to Notley C. WILLIAMS. Trust for debt to John ROMINE using 14a. Wit: William BRONAUGH, Francis W. LUCKET. Delv. to ROMINE 9 Apr 1821.

Bk:Pg: 2W:178 Date: 6 Jan 1818 RtCt: 6 Jan1818
William R. McCARTY of Ldn to Joab & Balaam OSBURN of Ldn. B/S of 127a (part of land of Thadeus McCARTY beq. to son William R.). Wit: Burr POWELL, Abner GIBSON. Delv. to Balaam OSBURN 13 Apr 1821.

Bk:Pg: 2W:179 Date: 6 Nov 1817 RtCt: 13 Apr 1818
James GUNN & wife Milley of Ldn to John BEVERIDGE of Ldn. B/S of 149a adj Leven LUCKETT, William R. McCARTY. Wit: Burr POWELL, Abner GIBSON. Delv. to John BEVERIDGE 14 Mar 1820.

Bk:Pg: 2W:181 Date: 18 Apr 1818 RtCt: 18 Apr 1818
William NICKOLS & Bernard TAYLOR (Exors of Jesse JANNEY dec'd) of Ldn to Hannah JANNEY of Ldn. B/S of 1a George TAVENER. Delv. to Henry H. NICKOLS by order of Thos. NICHOLS.

Bk:Pg: 2W:182 Date: 29 Oct 1817 RtCt: 13 Apr 1818
Joseph LEWIS Jr. of Ldn to Thomas T. GANTT cashier of Central Bank of Georgetown. Trust using all 203a of 'Clifton' where LEWIS now lives. Wit: D. RANDALL, L. WASHINGTON, Daries CLAGETT, J. YERBY, Chas. G. ESKRIDGE, Geo. W. ADAMS, J. L. DREAN.

Bk:Pg: 2W:185 Date: 16 Apr 1818 RtCt: 16 Apr 1818
Thomas HATCHER & wife Rebecca of Ldn to Bernard TAYLOR of Ldn. B/S of 172a (cnvy/b Exors of William HATCHER dec'd). Wit:

Samuel MURREY, John McCORMICK. Delv. to TAYLOR 9 Feb 1836.

Bk:Pg: 2W:186 Date: 1 Apr 1818 RtCt: 13 Apr 1818
John HOPKINS of FredVA to Frederick HANDSCHY of Ldn. B/S of 250a on NW side of Short Hill and Potomac. Delv. to HANDSHEY 26 May 1819.

Bk:Pg: 2W:187 Date: 15 Apr 1818 RtCt: 16 Apr 1818
Samuel HATCHER, David SMITH & Bernard TAYLOR (Exors of William HATCHER dec'd) of Ldn to Thomas HATCHER of Ldn. B/S of 307a adj George FAIRHURST, James COCHRAN. Delv. to C. PARKER pr order 22 Sep 1821.

Bk:Pg: 2W:188 Date: 1 Mar 1818 RtCt: 13 Apr 1818
John GREGG & wife Phebe of Ldn to David YOUNG & Isaac NICKOLS Jr. of Ldn. Trust for debt to Isaac & Samuel NICKOLS of Ldn using land on Goose Creek adj John DIXSON. Wit: Jno. McCORMICK, Jno. ROSE. Delv. to Saml. NICKOLLS' Exors 9 Nov 1825.

Bk:Pg: 2W:190 Date: 2 Apr 1817 RtCt: 2 Apr 1818
Enoch FURR Sr. & wife Sarah of Ldn to John W. B. GRAYSON of Ldn. Trust for debt to Mordeica THROCKMORTON using 128a. Wit: Benjamin GRAYSON, N. C. WILLIAMS.

Bk:Pg: 2W:192 Date: 20 Dec 1817 RtCt: 30 Apr 1818
William H. HANDY of Ldn to James RUST of Ldn. Trust for debt to John PANCOAST Jr. using 5a with mill. Wit: Thomas GREGG, John WYNN. Delv. to PANCOAST 26 Mar 1819.

Bk:Pg: 2W:193 Date: 1 Apr 1818 RtCt: 21 Apr 1818
Samuel M. EDWARDS & wife __ of Ldn to Richard H. HENDERSON of Ldn. Trust for debt to Colin AULD using Lot #6 in Lsbg.

Bk:Pg: 2W:195 Date: 13 Apr 1818 RtCt: 13 Apr 1818
Daniel EACHES of Ldn to Matthew BEANS [also given as Martin] of Ldn. B/S of part of land cnvy/b Jonah THOMPSON to George JANNEY & EACHES as joint tenants. Wit: J. L. DREAN, Geo. W. ADAMS, Jno. A. BINNS.

Bk:Pg: 2W:196 Date: 2 Sep 1817 RtCt: 13 Apr 1818
John DIXON (trustee for Ferdinando FAIRFAX) of JeffVA to Jacob WALTMAN Sr. of Ldn. Deed to trust date Jun 1812 from FAIRFAX to DIXON to secure payment to Elijah CHAMBERLAIN. DIXON held sale at Harper's Ferry and sold to WALTMAN. Delv. to WALTMAN 9 Oct 1819.

Bk:Pg: 2W:196 Date: 15 Nov 1816 RtCt: 13 Apr 1818
Jacob ISH of Ldn to John HUTCHISON of PrWm. B/S of 168a adj Reuben HUTCHISON, Pierce BAYLEY, Robert ARMISTEAD, Sampson HUTCHISON. Wit: Johnston CLEVELAND, William NOLAND, Chas. LEWIS. Delv. to HUTCHISON 12 Aug 1820.

Bk:Pg: 2W:198 Date: 4 Apr 1818 RtCt: 13 Apr 1818
Lewis LEIDER of Ldn to Stephen JANNEY & Joshua GREGG of Ldn. Trust for debt to Elijah WARFORD using 130a adj Nicholas OSBURN, Eli McNIGHT. Wit: Stacy TAYLOR, John WHITE.

Bk:Pg: 2W:200 Date: 15 Nov 1816 RtCt: 11 Mar 1818
Jacob ISH of Ldn to John HUTCHERSON/HUTCHISON of PrWm. Trust for debt to Nathan HUTCHISON of Ldn using 303a. Wit: Johnston CLEVELAND, William NOLAND, Chas. LEWIS. Delv to John HUTCHISON 12 Aug 1820.

Bk:Pg: 2W:202 Date: 12 May 1818 RtCt: 12 May 1818
James HALL, George GRAYSON & James MACHLAN. Bond on HALL as constable.

Bk:Pg: 2W:203 Date: 12 May 1818 RtCt: 12 May 1818
John MULLEN, Robt. R. HOUGH & Saml. SUMMERS. Bond on MULLEN as constable.

Bk:Pg: 2W:203 Date: 8 Sep 1817 RtCt: 11 May 1818
Elizabeth FIELDS of Mason Co KY to John JONES of Ldn. PoA to receive money from Thomas FIELDS, William MILLER and Nathan HEDDLESON or anyone else in Va. Wit: Jas. N. COBRERN, Wm. SMITH.

Bk:Pg: 2W:204 Date: 9 Apr 1818 RtCt: 11 May 1818
Daniel GANTT & wife Lucy of D.C. to Enoch FRANCIS of Ldn. Correction of deed for sale dated 16 Jul 1817 of 40a with water grist mill adj Thomas FOUCH, Mathew HARRISON, Goose Creek, Amos THOMPSON. Wit: Benj. G. ORR, Wm. HEWITT.

Bk:Pg: 2W:206 Date: 25 Mar 1811 RtCt: 14 May 1818
Richard H. HENDERSON of Lsbg to Samuel CLAPHAM of Ldn. BoS for negro Jinny & her three children Matilda, Henry & Caroline. Wit: C. BINNS, Saml. M. EDWARDS.

Bk:Pg: 2W:207 Date: 12 May 1818 RtCt: 12 May 1818
William SHREVE of Ldn to Robert MOFFETT of Ldn. PoA.

Bk:Pg: 2W:208 Date: 11 Mar 1818 RtCt: 11 May 1818
John KILE Jr. & wife Winney M. of Ldn to John MARTIN of Ldn. B/S of 12a allotted Winney from land of father Elisha POWELL dec'd. Wit: William BRONAUGH, Francis W. LUCKETT.

Bk:Pg: 2W:209 Date: 2 Jun 1818 RtCt: 2 Jun 1818
John H. BUTCHER to John PANCOAST Jr. Trust for debt to John PANCOAST Sr. using 31a. Delv. to John PANCOAST Jr. 16 Aug 1819.

Bk:Pg: 2W:210 Date: 16 Sep 1817 RtCt: 11 May 1818
Jeremiah W. BRONAUGH of Georgetown D.C. to Burr POWELL of Ldn. Trust for debt to Hugh & James JOHNSTON using 150a. Wit: Wm. BRONAUGH. Delv. pr order 5 Feb 1827.

Bk:Pg: 2W:211 Date: 20 Oct 1817 RtCt: 5 Jun 1818
Jacob ARNOLD & wife Mary of Ldn to Simon SHOEMAKER Jr. of Ldn. B/S of 8a (¼th part of 33a late property of Jacob EMERY dec'd after widow's dower) adj John JACKSON, George COOPER and 1/5th part of 75a widow's dower. Wit: W. S. NEALE, George VINSEL, John BUMCROTS, Robert BRADEN, Abiel JENNERS. Delv to grantee 31 Mar 1820.

Bk:Pg: 2W:212 Date: 12 Oct 1817 RtCt: 3 Jun 1818
Simon SHOEMAKER Jr. & wife Catharine of Ldn to John BUMCROATS of Ldn. B/S of 34a (part of lands of Jacob EMERY dec'd) adj Jacob ARNOLD, John AXLINE and 5¾a (cnvy/b Christopher BURNHOUSE to SHOEMAKER) on short hill adj Elizabeth POTTERFIELD. Wit: W. S. NEALE, George VINSEL, Jacob ARNOLD, Abiel JENNERS, Robert BRADEN. Delv. to BUMCROTES 14 Apr 1821.

Bk:Pg: 2W:215 Date: 20 Oct 1817 RtCt: 3 Jun 1818
Simon SHOEMAKER Jr. & wife Catharine of Ldn to Elizabeth POTTERFIELD of Ldn. B/S of 5¾a (cnvy/b Ferdinando FAIRFAX to SHOEMAKER) on short hill adj John BUMCROATS and 2a (cnvy/b Christopher BURNHOUSE) on side of short hill adj widow EMERY, John BUMCROATS. Wit: W. S. NEALE, George VINSEL, Jacob ARNOLD, Abiel JENNERS, Robert BRADEN.

Bk:Pg: 2W:216 Date: 20 Oct 1817 RtCt: 3 Jun 1818
Simon SHOEMAKER Jr. & wife Catharine of Ldn to Jacob ARNOLD of Ldn. B/S of 50a (cnvy/b Admrs of Jacob EMERY dec'd) adj John AXLINE, John BUMCROATS and 3½a wood lot adj AXLINE & BUMCROATS and 5¾a (cnvy/b Ferdinando FAIRFAX to EMORY) on short hill and 2a (cnvy/b Christopher BURNHOUSE to EMORY). Wit: W. S. NEALE, George VINSEL, John BUMCROATS, Abiel JENNERS, Robert BRADEN. Delv. to ARNOLD 18 May 1820.

Bk:Pg: 2W:219 Date: 26 Mar 1818 RtCt: 14 May 1818
Nathaniel MANNING & wife Euphamia of Ldn to Matthew BEANS/BAYNES of Ldn. B/S of 2a on main road from Wtfd to Hllb. Wit: Abiel JENNERS, R. BRADEN. Delv. to David REESE Admr of grantee on 11 Oct 1823.

Bk:Pg: 2W:220 Date: 6 May 1818 RtCt: 11 May 1818
Isaac STEER & wife Phebe of Ldn to William PAXSON of Ldn. B/S of 87a adj Pattison WRIGHT. Wit: Robert BRADEN, John H. McCABE. Delv. to PAXON 2 Aug 1821.

Bk:Pg: 2W:222 Date: 16 May 1818 RtCt: 27 May 1818
Peter OVERFIELD & wife Deborah of Harrison Co Va to John H. BUTCHER of Ldn. B/S of 37½a (part of land where Benjamin OVERFIELD & wife Mary lived & died). Delv to BUTCHER 12 Jun 1819.

Bk:Pg: 2W:223 Date: 20 Nov 1817 RtCt: 2 Jun 1818
Samuel OVERFIELD & wife Mary of Harrison Co Va to John H.
BUTCHER of Ldn. B/S of 31a (part of land where Benjamin
OVERFIELD & wife Mary lived & died). Delv. to BUTCHER 12 Jun
1819.

Bk:Pg: 2W:224 Date: 4 Apr 1818 RtCt: 12 May 1818
Elijah WARFORD and Mary WARFORD of Ldn to Lewis LEIDER of
Ldn. B/S of 130a where Elijah now lives (part of land formerly held
by John WARFORD now dec'd) adj James WARFORD (br/o Elijah),
Eli McKNIGHT. Wit: Stacey TAYLOR, John WHITE.

Bk:Pg: 2W:225 Date: ___ 1818 RtCt: 23 May 1818
Cuthbert POWELL of Ldn to Mandley TAYLOR of Frederick. B/S of
2a adj said TAYLOR, Jeffries branch. Delv. pr order filed DB PP:263
Dec 1830.

Bk:Pg: 2W:226 Date: 15 Apr 1818 RtCt: 12 May 1818
Mary CALDWELL of Ldn to Joseph CALDWELL of Ldn. B/S of
375½a (¼ share reserving mother's dower to lands of Moses
CALDWELL dec'd to children Joseph, John, Mary & William) adj
Patrick MILLHOLLAND, John WILLIAMS, Stephen SCOTT, John H.
CASSADY. Wit: Robert BRADEN, Abiel JENNERS. Delv. to
CALDWELL 30 Nov 1819.

Bk:Pg: 2W:227 Date: 20 Oct 1817 RtCt: 5 Jun 1818
John BUMCROATS & wife Christiana and Elizabeth POTTERFIELD
of Ldn to Simon SHOEMAKER Jr. of Ldn. B/S of 16a (undivided
shares or 2/4th of 33a after widow's dower of lands of Jacob EMERY
dec'd) adj John JACKSON, George COOPER. Wit: John H.
McCABE, Robert BRADEN. Delv. to grantee 31 Mar 1820.

Bk:Pg: 2W:229 Date: 2 Dec 1817 RtCt: 11 May 1818
Nathaniel MANNING & wife Euphramia of Ldn to Benjamin
GRAYSON of Ldn. Trust for debt to Daniel EACHES 357a adj
Robert BRADEN, Matthew BEANS, Jeremiah MILLER, N branch of
Kittocton Creek. Wit: Abiel JENNERS, John H. McCABE. Delv. to
John W. GRAYSON as pr order from Benj. GRAYSON on ___.

Bk:Pg: 2W:231 Date: 20 Apr 1818 RtCt: 11 May 1818
Frederick HANDSHY & wife Catharine of Ldn to Michael BOGER of
Ldn. B/S of 93a (conveyed to HANDSHY by William D. DIGGS) adj
John S. MARLOW. Wit: Robert BRADEN, John H. McCABE. Delv.
to BOGER 18 Feb 1820.

Bk:Pg: 2W:233 Date: 1 Oct 1817 RtCt: 11 May 1818
Amos GIBSON & wife Hannah of Ldn to Joseph STEER of Ldn. B/S
of 4a Lot #1 in Wtfd adj Mahlon JANNEY, Joseph TALBOTT. Wit:
Robert BRADEN, John H. McCABE. Delv. to STEER 15 Mar 1821.

Bk:Pg: 2W:234 Date: 1 Jan 1817 RtCt: 14 May 1818
Daniel BROWN & wife Rachel of Ldn to Johnathan SCHOFFIELD of
Alexandria. B/S of 80a with water grist and saw mill on Goose

Creek. Wit: William COOMES, R. H. CLEMENTS, Presley JACOBS, Ephraim GILMAN, William BRONAUGH, Thos. GREGG.

Bk:Pg: 2W:236   Date: 16 Sep 1817   RtCt: 11 May 1818
Hugh JOHNSTON & James JOHNSTON of Ldn to Jeremiah W. BRONAUGH of Georgetown D.C. B/S of 150a (former property of father George JOHNSTON dec'd) adj William SMITH, William BRONAUGH, Thomas OWSLEY. Delv. to Wm. BRONAUGH per order 8 Apr 1822.

Bk:Pg: 2W:237   Date: 1 Oct 1817   RtCt: 11 May 1818
Joseph STEER of Ldn to John WILLIAMS & Thos. PHILIPS of Ldn. Trust for debt to Amos GIBSON of Ldn using 4a adj Mahlon JANNEY, Joseph TALBOTT dec'd. Wit: Robert BRADEN, John H. McCABE.

Bk:Pg: 2W:239   Date: 15 Oct 1817   RtCt: 30 May 1818
Isaiah MARKS & wife Elizabeth of Ldn to Stephen McPHERSON of Ldn. B/S of 197a where Isaiah now lives adj Isaiah B. BEANS, Dr. Edward B. GRADY. Wit: Benjamin GRAYSON, Notley C. WILLIAMS.

Bk:Pg: 2W:241   Date: 15 Apr 1818   RtCt: 11 May 1818
John WHITE of Ldn to Bernard TAYLOR of Ldn. B/S of 75a. Wit: Robert BRADEN, Abiel JENNERS. Delv. to TAYLOR 27 Jan 1835.

Bk:Pg: 2W:243   Date: 1 Oct 1817   RtCt: 29 May 1818
Jozabed WHITE of Ldn to Enos POTTS of Ldn. Trust for debt to Jehu HOLLINGSWORTH using 63a adj Wtfd (cnvy/b Emanuel NEWCOMER to WHITE & R. BRADEN in Apr 1817). Wit: Elijah WARFORD, Spencer BROWN.

Bk:Pg: 2W:244   Date: 1 Jan 1818   RtCt: 19 May 1818
John ROSE & wife Anna of Ldn to Charles ELGIN of Ldn. B/S of 7a adj John ROSE, Charles ELGIN, heirs of Henry OXLEY decd. Wit: Enos WILDMAN, Wm. AUSTIN, Benjamin SMITH, Patrick McINTYRE, Presley CORDELL. Delv. to ELGIN 26 Dec 1823.

Bk:Pg: 2W:246   Date: 18 Oct 1817   RtCt: 30 May 1818
Jonas POTTS & wife Nancy of Ldn to Herod OSBURNE of Ldn. B/S of 147a and 110¾a (2 undivided shares on SE side of blue ridge formerly occupied by father Nathan POTTS dec'd – shares of Jonas, his brother Enos & sister Hannah). Wit: Joshua OSBURNE, John WHITE. Delv. to OSBORNE 20 Oct 1821.

Bk:Pg: 2W:247   Date: 18 Oct 1817   RtCt: 30 May 1818
Susannah POTTS of Ldn to Herod OSBURNE of Ldn. B/S of 147a (POTTS' share to two undivided tracts on SE side of blue ridge formerly occupied by her father Nathan POTTS dec'd, she entitled to 1/9th share) adj William POTTS, Turner & Hector OSBURNE and 110a. Wit: Craven OSBURNE, David W. HERRON, William POTTS, Joshua OSBURNE, John WHITE. Delv. to OSBURNE 20 Oct 1821.

Bk:Pg: 2W:249   Date: 20 Jun 1818   RtCt: 25 Jun 1817
Thomas GREGG of Ldn to Samuel GREGG of Ldn. B/S of 136a
where Thomas lives. Wit: Hamilton ROGERS.

Bk:Pg: 2W:250   Date: 13 Apr 1818   RtCt: 11 May 1817
Enoch FRANCIS & wife Nancy of Ldn to Casper ECHART of Ldn.
B/S of 7a. Wit: John DULIN, Jno. J. MATHIAS, Jno. MATHIAS, John
ROSE, John McCORMICK. Delv. per order filed 22 Oct 1821.

Bk:Pg: 2W:251   Date: 26 May 1818   RtCt: 27 May 1818
Polly DAWSON (wd/o James DAWSON) of Lsbg to John T.
WILSON of Lsbg. B/S of DAWSON's interest in 2-story brick house
& lot on Loudoun St in Lsbg now occupied by WILSON. Wit: S.
BLINCOE, Thos. GREGG, Robt. R. HOUGH.

Bk:Pg: 2W:253   Date: 11 May 1818   RtCt: 11 May 1818
William I. WELDON of Ldn to Enoch FRANCIS of Ldn. Trust using
40a & grist mill on Goose Creek where WELDON now lives adj
Thomas FOUCH, heirs of Matthew HARRISON, Amos THOMPSON.
Delv. to FRANCIS 19 Jan 1822.

Bk:Pg: 2W:254   Date: 7 May 1818   RtCt: 11 May 1818
Enoch FRANCIS & wife Nancy of Ldn to William I. WELDON of Ldn.
B/S of 40a and plantation with water grist mill adj Thomas FOUCH,
Matthew HARRISON, Amos THOMPSON. Wit: Thomas FOUCH,
Fielding BROWN, Richard BROWN, John McCORMICK. Delv. to
WELDON 7 Jan 1819.

Bk:Pg: 2W:257   Date: 6 Sep 1817   RtCt: 29 May 1818
Gent. Richard Henry LEE (ch/o Flora LEE, br/o Eliza M. & Ann C.
LEE) of Augusta Co VA to Gent. James L. McKENNA of AlexDC.
B/S of 600a on S side of Kilgore's mill road, George LEE, Mrs.
Matilda LANE. Delv. to McKENNA 4 Oct 1819.

Bk:Pg: 2W:259   Date: 24 Sep 1817   RtCt: 11 May 1818
Enos POTTS & wife Lydia of Ldn to Giles CRAVEN of Ldn. B/S of
18a adj Samuel & Isaac NICKOLS, David SMITH. Wit: William
BRONAUGH, Thos. GREGG. Delv. to grantee Mar 1820.

Bk:Pg: 2W:261   Date: 22 Apr 1818   RtCt: 11 May 1818
Enos POTTS & wife Lydia of Ldn to Elizabeth BOWLEN of Ldn. B/S
of 10a on NW fork of Goose Creek adj Henry ELLIS, Levi
WILLIAMS. Wit: Thos. GREGG, N. C. WILLIAMS. Delv. to BOLEN
28 Jan 1823.

Bk:Pg: 2W:263   Date: 3 Apr 1815   RtCt: 23 May 1818
James RUSSELL & wife Susannah of Ldn to Aaron SCHOOLEY of
Ldn. B/S of part of 2 lots bought of Thomas HURST adj Mahlon
JANNEY, William HOUGH. Wit: Robert BRADEN, Abiel JENNERS.

Bk:Pg: 2W:265   Date: 22 May 1818   RtCt: 22 May 1818
Peter BENEDUM Sr. & wife Catharine of Ldn to Sampson BLINCOE
& Saml. M. EDWARDS of Ldn. Trust for debt to John WALKER of

FredMd using numerous pieces of land. Wit: John McCORMICK, Thos. GREGG. Delv. to WALKER 5 Apr 1820.

Bk:Pg: 2W:268   Date: 31 Jan 1818   RtCt: 13 Apr 1818
Ferdinando FAIRFAX of Washington D.C. to Jacob WALTMAN of Ldn. B/S of 45a (Lot #3, #4 & #5 on side of short hill adj M. BOGER & Lot #6) and 50a river mill lot on Potomack below NW end of short hill and 124a adj Thomas SHOVER. Wit: William WENNER Sr., Fred'k SCHLATZ, Jno. MATHIAS. Delv. to Jacob WALTMAN Sr. on 4 Oct 1819.

Bk:Pg: 2W:270   Date: __ Jun 1818   RtCt: 12 Jun 1818
Albert O. POWELL of Ldn and his guardian Edward SUMMERS of Fqr to Charles BINNS of Ldn. POWELL bound to BINNS, clerk of co ct, to apprentice and dwell with him until age 19y & 6m (on 1 Jan 1824). Wit: Chs. G. ESKRIDGE.

Bk:Pg: 2W:271   Date: 15 Apr 1818   RtCt: 12 Jun 1818
Menan COE. Division – Case of COE vs COE in Chancery Mar 12 & 18. William COE & wife Catharine (35a), Emily SMITH and Ann SMITH infant ch/o Emily SMITH dec'd w/o Charles SMITH (10a with dwelling house, orchard, etc.), Edward M. COE (23a), Robert COE (23a) John W. COE (20a wood lot), David J. COE (7½a cleared & 4a wooded). Divisors: John SINCLAIR, John SIMPSON, Edmund LOVETT. Gives plat and details.

Bk:Pg: 2W:274   Date: 1 Mar 1802   RtCt: 8 Jun 1818
James MAHONEY/McHONEY to Negro Cyrus. BoS for negro woman Lucy. Wit: Wm. H. POWELL, Elijah ANDERSON.

Bk:Pg: 2W:274   Date: 9 Jun 1818   RtCt: 9 Jun 1818
L. P. W. BALCH, Fleet SMITH & Hugh SMITH. Bond on BALCH as treasurer of the board of school commrs. Wit: Bur W. HARRISON.

Bk:Pg: 2W:275   Date: 8 Jun 1818   RtCt: 8 Jun 1818
Hanson ELLIOTT & Turner OSBURNE. Bond on ELLIOTT as constable.

Bk:Pg: 2W:276   Date: 8 Jun 1818   RtCt: 8 Jun 1818
George W. FRENCH, James D. FRENCH, Garrison FRENCH & Daniel LOVETT. Bond on Geo. W. FRENCH as constable.

Bk:Pg: 2W:276   Date: 21 Oct 1817   RtCt: 11 Jun 1818
Joshua BAKER and William YATES & wife Sarah of AlexDC to Robert BRADEN of Ldn. B/S of Lot #1 & #2 in Wtfd now in possession of BRADEN (cnvy/b Mahlon JANNEY to Joshua BAKER and Sarah CAVANS now YATES). Wit: John SIMPSON, John MORGAN, Joseph EACHES, H. W. BRADEN, N. S. BRADEN, Abraham FAW, Adam LYNN. Delv. to BRADEN 31 May 1822.

Bk:Pg: 2W:278   Date: 3 Jun 1818   RtCt: 8 Jun 1818
Thomas CLAGETT of Ldn present in Piscattaway Co MD to John P. DULANY of Ldn. Trust using negro man Stephen age abt 50y, woman Nancy age abt 46y and her children 2 boys & 2 girls aged

from 6y downward, woman Caroline age abt 20y and woman Catharine age abt 60y also farm animals and items. Wit: Geo. E. LLOYDS, John B. HASKINS, B. DULANEY, Wm. S. HERBERT, Jno. H. DeBUTTS.

Bk:Pg: 2W:281 Date: 1 Oct 1817 RtCt: 8 Jun 1818
James H. DULANY of AlexDC to John H. DeBUTTS of PrG. B/S of annuity rent on 500a. Wit: J. M. McCARTY, W. HERBERT Jr., S. SNOWDEN, G. T. RHODES. Sent by mail pr order on ___.

Bk:Pg: 2W:283 Date: 13 Jul 1818 RtCt: 13 Jul 1818
Wilson C. SELDEN (sheriff of Ldn), Robert MOFFETT, Hugh SMITH, Townsend McVEIGH & Robert M. NEWMAN. Bond on SELDEN to collect levies.

Bk:Pg: 2W:284 Date: 20 Jun 1818 RtCt: 20 Jun 1818
David BEATTY of Ldn to John BEATTY of Ldn. B/S of land (undivided part of abt 185a devised by David BEATTY to his widow for life and after her death to sons John BEATTY, David BEATTY, William BEATTY & Robert BEATTY, contract made by John with mother Elizabeth BEATTY) adj Samuel CLAPHAM. Wit: Wm. CHILTON, Abel ORRISON.

Bk:Pg: 2W:285 Date: 9 Jun 1818 RtCt: 9 Jun 1818
Israel REDMOND of Fairfield Co OH to Benjamin JAMES of Ldn. B/S of 102a adj John DEBELL, Benjamin JAMES. Delv. to JAMES 30 Apr 1824.

Bk:Pg: 2W:286 Date: 11 Jun 1818 RtCt: 4 Jun 1818
Aaron SCHOOLEY & wife Elizabeth of Ldn to Mary FOX of Ldn. B/S of part of 2 lots bought by James RUSSELL of Thomas HURST and by SCHOOLEY of RUSSELL in Wtfd. Wit: Abiel JENNERS, Robert BRADEN.

Bk:Pg: 2W:287 Date: 15 Jan 1818 RtCt: 10 Jun 1818
John B. STEVENS & wife Sarah of Ldn to David CONRAD of Ldn. B/S of lot in Wtfd adj Joseph THOMAS. Wit: Abiel JENNERS, John H. McCABE. Delv. pr order filed DB WW:287 this 2 Mar 1820.

Bk:Pg: 2W:289 Date: 1 May 1818 RtCt: 8 Jun 1818
Conrad SHAFFER Sr. & wife Elizabeth of Ldn to William SHAFFER, Conrad SHAFFER Jr. & John RASOR all of Gurnsey Co VA. B/S of 820a. Wit: John HAMILTON, Samuel LUCKETT. Delv. to Conrad SHAFFER 1 Jan 1826?

Bk:Pg: 2W:291 Date: 27 May 1818 RtCt: 9 Jun 1818
James BATTSON & wife Sarah of Ldn to Elizabeth GARRETT of Fqr. B/S of ½a on snickers gap turnpike road. Wit: Burr POWELL, Abner GIBSON.

Bk:Pg: 2W:293 Date: 8 Jun 1818 RtCt: 8 Jun 1818
Joseph PERRY of Ldn to Polly CONNER (d/o Polly CONNER dec'd) of Ldn. BoS for farm animals & items. Wit: Wm. H. BRISCOE, Isaac HARRIS, Wm. P. HARRIS.

Bk:Pg: 2W:294   Date: 10 Jun 1818   RtCt: 10 Jun 1818
George TAVENDER Jr. of Ldn to John MATHIAS of Ldn. Trust for debt to John NIXON using lot in Wtfd prch/o Peter BENNEDUM.

Bk:Pg: 2W:296   Date: 7 Oct 1818   RtCt: 10 Jun 1818
Elijah VIOLETT & wife Phebe of Ldn to George GIBSON of Ldn. B/S of 8½a on Welchmans branch of Panther Skin adj Col. Leven POWELL, Joseph LEWIS' 'Clifton', Betsey MARTIN. Wit: Burr POWELL, A. GIBSON.

Bk:Pg: 2W:298   Date: 12 Apr 1818   RtCt: 1 May 1817
Joseph CARR of Ldn to Caldwell CARR of Ldn. B/S of 100a. Wit: Cuthbert POWELL, John McPHERSON, Jas. L. GIBBS Sr., John CARR. Delv. to grantee 11 Oct 1819.

Bk:Pg: 2W:299   Date: 30 Jan 1818   RtCt: 16 Mar 1818
Ferdinando FAIRFAX of Washington D.C. to Josiah WHITE of Ldn. B/S of 38a on W side of short hill. Wit: John MATHIAS, Fred'k SCHLATZ, Emanuel WALTMAN, Jno. Jas. MATHIAS.

Bk:Pg: 2W:300   Date: 23 Apr 1818   RtCt: 8 Jun 1818
John MATHIAS of Ldn to Jesse EVANS of Ldn. B/S of 120a now in possession of EVANS. Wit: Peter GIDEON, Josias FERGUSON, William GIDEON. Delv. to Robert COCKERELL pr order filed 16 Mar 1820.

Bk:Pg: 2W:302   Date: 23 Mar 1818   RtCt: 15 Jun 1818
Nathaniel POLIN & wife Ann of Harrison Co OH to Adrian L. SWART & John SWART of Ldn. B/S of 130a residue of tract cnvy/b Joseph REEDER to Nathaniel PEGG dec'd in 1770 & devised by PEGG to POLEN under life estate of widow Catharine PEGG, on S run of Broad Run. Wit: Wm. LYNE, Thos. R. MOTT, Robert M. NEWMAN, Charles CHAPMAN, John PALMER, John BAYLEY, Charles LEWIS. Delv. to SWART 18 Oct 1819.

Bk:Pg: 2W:303   Date: 27 Apr 1818   RtCt: 8 Jun 1818
Stephen WILSON of Ldn to Francis STRIBLING of Ldn. B/S of 140a on Goose Creek adj __ DAVIS, __ HOLLOWAY, __ DANIEL, __ DILLON, __ WHITE. Wit: Thomas GREGG, John WHITE.

Bk:Pg: 2W:305   Date: 8 Jun 1818   RtCt: 9 Jun 1818
Jacob DERRY & wife Catharine of Ldn to William DERRY of Ldn. B/S of 59a on W side of short hill (prch/o said William DERRY). Wit: Stephen C. ROSZEL, John McCORMICK.

Bk:Pg: 2W:306   Date: 1 Oct 1817   RtCt: 10 Jun 1818
Charles G. EDWARDS of Ldn to John PALMER & John WILLIAMS of Ldn. Trust for debt to Amos GIBSON of Ldn using 4a adj Joseph TALBOTT dec'd. Wit: Joseph THOMAS, Thomas GREGG, Wm. PAXSON Jr., Robert BRADEN, John H. McCABE.

Bk:Pg: 2W:308   Date: 25 Nov 1817   RtCt: 8 Jun 1818
Marcus HUMPHREY & wife Margaret and William BOXWELL of Ldn to Thomas JAMES of Ldn. B/S of 40a on SE side of Blue Ridge adj

Philip THOMAS, Jonah HUMPHREY. Wit: Craven OSBURNE, Saml. W. YOUNG, Wm. SHREVE, John WHITE, Joshua OSBURNE.

Bk:Pg: 2W:310   Date: 9 Jun 1818   RtCt: 10 Jun 1818
Joseph CARR of Ldn to Thomas W. SMITH of Ldn. B/S of 39 poles of land (part of land sold to CARR by Stephen McPHERSON Sr. dec'd) in Upperville on SW side of Turnpike road adj John DEMERY. Wit: John McPHERSON, David CARTER, James HALL, Caldwell CARR, Elijah HALL. Delv. to Jno. FLEMING pr order 14 Jun 1820.

Bk:Pg: 2W:311   Date: 9 Jun 1818   RtCt: 10 Jun 1818
Joseph CARR of Ldn to Thomas W. SMITH of Ldn. B/S of 39 poles of land in Upperville adj lot where SMITH now resides. Wit: John McPHERSON, David CARTER, James HALL, Caldwell CARR, Elijah HALL. Delv. pr order to Jno. FLEMING 14 Jun 1820.

Bk:Pg: 2W:312   Date: 15 Sep 1815   RtCt: 10 Jun 1818
James RUSSELL & wife Susan of Ffx to Mary FOX of Ldn. B/S of part of lot RUSSELL prch/o Thos. HURST in Wtfd adj Lewis KLEIN, Wm. HOUGH, Mahlon JANNEY, Aaron SCHOOLEY. Wit: Abiel JENNERS, John HAMILTON, Zachariah WARD, John BRONAUGH. Delv. pr order of W. C. SHAWENS 29 Apr 1844.

Bk:Pg: 2W:314   Date: 27 May 1818   RtCt: 5 Jun 1818
John SPENCE & wife Mary of Dumfries, Thomas TRIPLETT & wife Margaret of Ldn, John P. DUVAL & wife Nancy of Dumfries, Thomas F. TEBBS of Lsbg, and Foushee TEBBS. Partition – Will of William CARR the elder in PrWm dev. children Betsey TEBBS, William CARR & John CARR and after death to surviving children. John CARR departed without issue. Betsey surrendered by deed in 1817 to Dr. John SPENCE & wife Mary F., Dr. Thomas TRIPLETT & wife Margaret C., John P. DUVAL & wife Ann F., Thomas F. TEBBS, Foushee TEBBS, Willoughby William TEBBS & Samuel John TEBBS (last 2 infants of Betsey TEBBS) to her children. Long acct.

Bk:Pg: 2W:324   Date: ___   RtCt: 1 Aug 1818
Peter BENEDUM to James RUST. B/S (executions agst BENEDUM in Sup. & Co. Ct by John GRAY ass'ee, William ROSS ass'ee, Isaac FRISHER, Eli OFFUTT, Richard H. HENDERSON and Mandaville LARMOUR?) of lots in Lsbg including 14a prch/o James SHEPHERD by BENEDUM. Deputy Sheriff W. D. DRISH sold at publick auction to RUST all lease hold interests.

Bk:Pg: 2W:324   Date: 1 Aug 1818   RtCt: 1 Aug 1818
Joseph ADAMS of Ldn to William LEACHMAN of Ldn. Trust for use of Nancy L. ADAMS & Delilah ADAMS (ch/o Joseph) during their natural lives, using negro girl Mary Ann aged abt 9y, farm animals, household items.

Bk:Pg: 2W:325   Date: 14 Jul 1818   RtCt: 24 Jul 1818
William CHILTON & wife Sarah H. of Ldn to George RUST Jr. of Ldn. B/S of 44a on road from Lsbg to Nolands ferry adj Dr.

SELDON. Wit: Robert BRADEN, Cuthbert POWELL. Delv. to RUST on 3 May 1824.

Bk:Pg: 2W:327   Date: 24 Jul 1818   RtCt: 24 Jul 1818
William CHILTON & wife Sarah H. of Ldn to Thomas R. MOTT of Ldn. Trust for debt to George RUST Jr. using 193a. Wit: Cuthbert POWELL, Robert BRADEN.

Bk:Pg: 2W:329   Date: 30 May 1818   RtCt: Jul 1818
William CHAMBERS, William ADAMS & wife Drusey, John CRUTCHLEY & wife Nancy of JeffVA to John BOOTH Jr. of Ldn. B/S of 60a (devised by Robert BOOTH to John BOOTH then to heirs of Thos. STUMP and William CHAMBERS.

Bk:Pg: 2W:331   Date: 23 Jun 1818   RtCt: 24 Jul 1818
Richard COCHRAN of Mdbg to Reuben TRIPLETT of Ldn. B/S of ½a Lot #13 in Mdbg. Wit: Burr POWELL, A. GIBSON.

Bk:Pg: 2W:332   Date: 28 Jul 1818   RtCt: 29 Jul 1818
William JOHNSON & wife Margaret of Lsbg to Sally L. ASQUITH of Shepherds Town, JeffVA. B/S of ½a lot & house on Market St in Lsbg where JOHNSON now lives. Wit: Stephen C. ROSZELL, John McCORMICK.

Bk:Pg: 2W:334   Date: 1 Feb 1817   RtCt: 27 Jul 1818
William DARNE of Ldn to Samuel M. EDWARDS of Ldn. Trust for benefit of Mary SAUNDERS w/o Presley SAUNDERS of Lsbg) using female slave Sucky with child Ann. Wit: Thomas SAUNDERS, John SAUNDERS.

Bk:Pg: 2W:335   Date: 22 May 1817   RtCt: 6 Aug 1818
Edward DORSEY & wife Mary of Ldn to William H. HOUGH of Ldn. B/S of lot in Wtfd (part of lot cnvy/b Mahlon JANNEY dec'd and occupied by DORSEY). Wit: Samuel CLAPHAM, Robert BRADEN.

Bk:Pg: 2W:337   Date: 18 Jul 1818   RtCt: 18 Jul 1818
John CALDWELL of Clark Co KY to Joseph CALDWELL of Ldn. B/S of 375½a (John's undivided ¼ reserving his mother's dower). Wit: J. L. DREAN.

Bk:Pg: 2W:338   Date: 5 Mar 1818   RtCt: 9 Jun 1818
Henry FRY & wife Catharine of Ldn to William BROWN of Ldn. B/S of 185½a (cnvy/b Philip FRY & wife Dolley) adj Whitson BIRDSALL, James LOVE, Henry NICKOLS, Conrad BITZER. Wit: Mahlon WALTERS, Simon FRY, Stacey TAYLOR, Robert BRADEN. Delv. to BROWN 10 Sep 1819.

Bk:Pg: 2W:340   Date: 1 Oct 1817   RtCt: 7 Aug 1818
Amos GIBSON & wife Hannah of Ldn to John E. PARMER of Ldn. B/S of 4a Lot #3 nr Wtfd adj Joseph TALBOTT dec'd. Wit: Robert BRADEN, John H. McCABE.

Bk:Pg: 2W:342   Date: 22 Dec 1817   RtCt: 13 Jul 1818
Francis HEREFORD & wife Ann Catharine of Fqr to Townsend D. PEYTON of Ldn. B/S of 270½a adj HEREFORD, James HIXON,

formerly Gen. Stephen Tompson MASON. Wit: Burr POWELL, Abner GIBSON. Delv. to Benjn SNOOT pr order 2 Apr 1823.

Bk:Pg: 2W:344   Date: 9 May 1818   RtCt: 6 Aug 1818
Lucy TRIPLETT (wd/o Cyrus a free blackman late of Ldn) having been prch/o James MAHONEY by Cyrus and emancipated by Cyrus on 11 Sep 1802 in Ldn. CoE for her children Lemmon aged 15y on 20th of last month at age 21y and Peggy aged 13y on 13 Jul next at age 18y. Appoints Daniel JANNEY and Amos GIBSON of Ldn as guardians if she does not live to their majority with GIBSON to take them in. Wit: N. C. WILLIAMS, Francis W. LUCKETT.

Bk:Pg: 2W:346   Date: 3 Apr 1817   RtCt: 4 Apr 1817
Presley SAUNDERS & wife Mary and John SMITH & wife Ruth of Ldn to Thomas R. MOTT of Ldn. B/S of ½a lot on S side of Market St in Lsbg (DB RR:336). Wit: Patrick McINTYRE, W. ELLZEY.

Bk:Pg: 2W:347   Date: 24 Jul 1818   RtCt: 24 Jul 1818
George RUST Jr. & wife Maria C. of Ldn to William CHILTON of Ldn. B/S of 193a on Kattocton Mt. adj John CARR, James RUST. Wit: John ROSE, Pat'k McINTYRE.

Bk:Pg: 2W:349   Date: 10 Jul 1818   RtCt: 24 Jul 1818
Francis Lightfoot LEE of Sully, Ffx to Edmund Jennings LEE of AlexDC Release of mortgage on 562a. Delv. to son 18 Sep 1819.

Bk:Pg: 2W:350   Date: 20 Mar 1818   RtCt: 7 Aug 1818
David JANNEY & wife Elizabeth of Ldn to John B. STEVENS of Ldn. B/S of small piece of ground on S side of lot he prch/o Nathaniel MANNING in Wtfd on Patrick St. Wit: Robert BRADEN, Abiel JENNERS.

Bk:Pg: 2W:353   Date: 13 Jan 1818   RtCt: 23 Jul 1818
William FULKERSON & wife Amelia of Ldn to Thomas FRANCIS of Ldn. B/S of 19¼a (formerly owned by father Benjamin FULKERSON). Wit: Caldwell CARR.

Bk:Pg: 2W:354   Date: 24 Jul 1818   RtCt: 24 Jul 1818
John NEWTON & wife Harriet of Ldn to William CHILTON of Ldn. B/S of 3a. Wit: Samuel CLAPHAM, John ROSE. Marriage contract of John and Harriet on 21 Jan 1808 (DB II:309), Charles BURNS was appointed trustee, now gives consent for sale of land and relinquishes claim as trustee.

Bk:Pg: 2W:357   Date: 6 May 1816   RtCt: 2 Sep 1816
Ludwell LEE Esqr of Ldn to Edmund Jennings LEE Esq of D.C. Trust for debt to Francis Lightfoot LEE using slaves Rippon by trade a carpenter aged abt 30y, Franky his wife aged abt 25y and their son Tom abt 4y, Stephen by trade a stone mason aged abt 30y, Jem aged abt 20y, Sarah a spinner aged abt 42y, Peggy aged abt 40y and Indy & Jenny her daughters & Armstead a boy aged abt 8y, Kingston aged abt 45y, Bridget aged abt 38 his wife and their son Ned abt 9, Moss a man aged abt 36, Esther aged abt 32, Osmond

son of Cebes aged abt 20, Cebes his brother [??] aged abt 9y, Adam aged abt 42y, Harry aged abt 20, John son of Bessie aged abt 12, Sampson abt 30y, Marcus abt 20y, Milly aged abt 40. Wit: Aaron DAILEY, Jos. T. NEWTON.

Bk:Pg: 2W:359   Date: 30 May 1818   RtCt: 24 Jul 1818
Matthew ADAMS & wife Susannah of Ldn to Humphrey B. POWELL of Ldn. Trust for debt of Matthew ADAMS & Abram BROWN to Saml. HATCHER & Joseph HATCHER using tract of land where ADAMS lives for his part of debt. Wit: Burr POWELL, A. GIBSON. Delv. to POWELL 4 Jun 1820

Bk:Pg: 2W:361   Date: 1 Nov 1816   RtCt: 24 Jul 1818
Cuthbert POWELL & wife Catharine of Ldn to Sydnor BAILEY of Ldn. B/S of 340 poles adj POWELL & BAILEY and SE of 11a lot. Wit: Jno. L. DAGG, Joseph FLEMMING, Benjamin GRAYSON.

Bk:Pg: 2W:364   Date: 3 Jan 1818   RtCt: 13 Aug 1818
Nathan NICKOLS. CoE for slave man Samuel (alias Samuel WILLIAMS) aged abt 27y. Wit: John BRADFIELD, Obediah COOKSEY.

Bk:Pg: 2W:364   Date: 13 Aug 1818   RtCt: 13 Aug 1818
Fleet SMITH, Lewis P. W. BALCH, Hugh SMITH. Bond on SMITH as Notary Publick. Wit: Chs. G. ESKRIDGE.

Bk:Pg: 2W:365   Date: 25 Jun 1817   RtCt: 10 Aug 1818
Catharine WATERS (wd/o of Diah WATERS). Dower for 22a adj N. ROPP. Gives plat. PAGE's Admrs agt WATERS in chy: At public sale Catharine WATERS purchased one parcel and George SMITH another.

Bk:Pg: 2W:367   Date: 6 Jun 1818   RtCt: 7 Aug 1818
John SAUNDERS & wife Leanah of Ldn to Margaret SAUNDERS of Ldn. B/S of 3a (part of tract John and George SAUNDERS prch/o George JANNEY). Wit: Robert BRADEN, Abiel JENNERS.

Bk:Pg: 2W:369   Date: 1 Aug 1818   RtCt: 7 Aug 1818
John B. STEVENS & wife Sarah of Wtfd to Robert BRADEN of Wtfd. B/S of lot STEVENS prch/o Nathaniel MANNING on Patrick & Second Sts. Wit: Abiel JENNERS, John H. McCABE.

Bk:Pg: 2W:370   Date: 6 Jun 1818   RtCt: 7 Aug 1818
John SANDERS & wife Leanah of Ldn to Geo SANDERS of Ldn. B/S of 72a (part of tract George & John SANDERS prch/o George JANNEY). Wit: Abiel JENNERS, Robert BRADEN. Delv. to SANDERS 4 Apr 1822.

Bk:Pg: 2W:372   Date: 27 Feb 1818   RtCt: 14 Aug 1818
David MULL. Division – 109a sold by David MULL dec'd to J. BOOTH (2a), Mary MULL wd/o David (36a), Catharine MULL (10a), John MULL (10a), Jacob VERTS (10a), Polly MULL (10a), Jacob VERTS (30a). Gives plat. Divisors: David AXLINE, Mathias SMITLY, Edward CUNNARD. In chancery: Jacob VERTS vs. John GEORGE

Admr of David MULL, John MULL, Mary MULL & Catharine MUʟ inft. children & heirs of David MULL dec'd & Mary MULL widow & relict of David MULL & John BURNHOUSE & Margaret his wife which said Margaret is also one of the heirs and child of said David MULL. Plat ordered to be recorded.

Bk:Pg: 2W:374 Date: 21 May 1818 RtCt: 25 Jul 1818
Mahlon SCHOOLEY of Ldn to John LIVINGSTON of Ldn. B/S of ½a Lots #52 & #53 in Wtfd. Wit: Abiel JENNERS, Robert BRADEN.

Bk:Pg: 2W:375 Date: 22 Aug 1816 RtCt: 10 Aug 1818
James REED. Division – Court order of 14 May 1816. 115a on main road leading into Union Town. Dower land to Rebecca REID wd/o James (26a including mansion house, barn, part of orchard nr house of Thomas REID, wood land), Thomas REID (11a Lot #2), Joseph WILKINSON & wife Elizabeth (8a Lot #3 & 5a #11), William CAMPBELL & wife Margaret (8a Lot #4 & 3a #12), Jonathan REID (6a Lot #5 & 6a #10), James REID (8a Lot #6 & 4a #14), Moses BROWN & wife Mary (8a Lot #7 & 7a #13), John REID (8a Lot #8 & 1a #9). Given in detail by surveyor Wm. KENWORTHY 22 Aug 1816. Gives plat.

Bk:Pg: 2W:386 Date: 12 Apr 1818 RtCt: 11 Aug 1818
John LITTLEJOHN & wife Monica to Marcy TOMPKINS. Agreement on land boundaries for 1a sold in Aug 1800. Gives small plat.

Bk:Pg: 2W:387 Date: 31 Aug 1818 RtCt: 31 Aug 1818
John DUNN of Ldn to Charles BINNS of Ldn. BoS of negro girl Betty abt 17y and dark complexion now in possession of Isaac HARRIS (1 slave for life). Wit: Chs. G. ESKRIDGE, Josiah L. DREAN.

Bk:Pg: 2W:388 Date: 10 Aug 1818 RtCt: 13 Aug 1818
Alexander BRIDGES of Ldn to Benjamin BRIDGES of Ldn. B/S of 215a (DB SS:226 deed cnvy/b James B. LANE to Ketturah then KEENE from estate of Hardage LANE dec'd, Ketturah lately intermarried with Benjamin BRIDGES and in Mar 1818 conveyed land to Alexander.) Delv. to Benjamin BRIDGES 11 Oct 1840.

Bk:Pg: 2W:389 Date: 29 Jul 1818 RtCt: 10 Aug 1818
Mary DUNSMORE of Ldn to John REESE of Ldn. B/S of 2a (part of dower right of land of Isaac SANDS) adj lot where REESE lives. Wit: William STOCKS, George STOCKS, William HIGDON.

Bk:Pg: 2W:390 Date: 19 Jun 1818 RtCt: 13 Sep 1818
Aaron BURSON & wife Esther of Ldn to Daniel BROWN of Ldn. B/S of 52a adj John BALDWIN, John HANN, Thomas TREHORN. Wit: Thos. H. WEY, James MACKLAN, Patrick KING, Francis W. LUCKETT, William BRONAUGH.

Bk:Pg: 2W:391 Date: 19 Jun 1818 RtCt: 3 Sep 1818
James MACKLAN & wife Mary of Ldn to Aaron BURSON of Ldn. B/S of 124a adj F. M. LUCKETT, Edward CARTER, Burson's

milldam. Wit: Daniel BROWN, Thomas H. WEY, Patrick KING, William BRONAUGH, Notely C. WILLIAMS.

Bk:Pg: 2W:393   Date: 28 Jul 1818   RtCt: 11 Aug 1818
Sarah CALDWELL (wd/o Moses CALDWELL dec'd) and John CALDWELL, Mary CALDWELL & William CALDWELL (ch/o Moses) of Ldn to Joseph CALDWELL of Ldn. B/S of land conveyed to Moses by James HAMILTON and not included in prch/o Murtho SULLIVAN dec'd of said Moses for 200a. Wit: Robert BRADEN, John H. McCABE.

Bk:Pg: 2W:395   Date: 22 Apr 1818   RtCt: 10 Aug 1818
Samuel McPHERSON & wife Mary of Ldn to Isaac STEER of Ldn. Mortgage on 10a and 5a. Wit: Robert BRADEN, Abiel JENNERS.

Bk:Pg: 2W:397   Date: 16 Aug 1817   RtCt: 13 Aug 1818
William CHILTON & wife Sarah of Ldn to John DRISH of Ldn. B/S of 11a prch/o Mrs. Fanny LEE. Wit: Chas. G. ESKRIDGE, Saml. CLAPHAM, Presley CORDELL.

Bk:Pg: 2W:399   Date: 20 Jun 1818   RtCt: 3 Sep 1818
Aaron BURSON & wife Esther of Ldn to Francis W. LUCKETT of Ldn. Trust for debt to James MACKLAN. Wit: Thomas H. WEY, Patrick KING, William BRONAUGH, Notley C. WILLIAMS. Delv. to LUCKETT 6 Jan 1820.

Bk:Pg: 2W:401   Date: 8 Aug 1818   RtCt: 10 Aug 1818
James ALDER & wife Hesther of Ldn to Samuel RHODES of PrWm. B/S of 74a on William's Gap branch adj William BLAKELY. Wit: William NOLAND, Thomas GREGG.

Bk:Pg: 2W:403   Date: 17 Mar 1815   RtCt: 12 Sep 1818
Richard H. HENDERSON of Ldn to Enoch FRANCIS of Ldn. Release of mortgage (DB DD:86) conveyed to John A. BINNS now dec'd.

Bk:Pg: 2W:404   Date: 13 Aug 1818   RtCt: 13 Aug 1818
James MOORE, Asa MOORE & John WILLIAMS (Exors of Mahlon JANNEY dec'd) of Ldn to Stephen BALL of Ldn. B/S of 2a adj Mortho SULLIVAN. Wit: Robert BRADEN, Abiel JENNERS.

Bk:Pg: 2W:405   Date: 10 Aug 1818   RtCt: 10 Aug 1818
Jacob KEMERLY of Ldn to Jacob DIXON of Ldn. B/S of 1a. Wit: Jno. A. BINNS. Delv. to John DIXSON 24 Apr 1820.

Bk:Pg: 2W:407   Date: 10 Aug 1818   RtCt: 10 Aug 1818
Jacob LAFFERTY & wife Nancy/Ann A. of Ldn to Aaron SANDERS of Ldn. B/S of 19a Lot #7 of estate of John A. BINNS dec'd on Katocton Mt. allotted to Nancy then Nancy DURHAM. Wit: William ELZEY, Thomas GREGG. Delv to SANDERS 16 May 1827.

Bk:Pg: 2W:408   Date: 28 Feb 1818   RtCt: 10 Aug 1818
John SCHOOLEY, Daniel STONE & William H. HOUGH (Exors of William HOUGH dec'd) of Ldn to Elizabeth GORE of Ldn. B/S of Lot

#3 in Wtfd. Wit: Abiel JENNERS, Robert BRADEN. Delv. to Natha. MINER pr order filed of Elizth GORE 4 Aug 1847.

Bk:Pg: 2W:410 Date: 15 Feb 1817 RtCt: 9 Feb 1818
Matthew MITCHELL & wife Elizabeth and Reuben SCHOOLEY of Ldn to Patrick MILHOLLAND of Ldn. B/S of Lot #16 in Lsbg. Wit: Thos. MORALLEE, Jno. DREAN, Geo. K. FOX.

Bk:Pg: 2W:411 Date: 20 Aug 1818 RtCt: 10 Sep 1818
John LITTLEJOHN & wife Monica of Ldn to James D. FRENCH of Ldn. B/S of ¼a in new bounds of Lsbg on E side of Air St. Wit: Thos. FOUCH, John McCORMICK.

Bk:Pg: 2W:413 Date: 20 Aug 1818 RtCt: 10 Sep 1818
John LITTLEJOHN & wife Monica of Ldn to James BRADY of Ldn. B/S of ¼a part of Lot #3 in new addition of Lsbg. Wit: Thos. FOUCH, John McCORMICK. Delv. to BRADY 2 Feb 1826.

Bk:Pg: 2W:415 Date: 29 Nov 1816 RtCt: 12 Sep 1818
John LITTLEJOHN & wife Monica of Ldn to John CRIDLER of Ldn. B/S of 1 and 1/6a Lot # 12 in new addition to Lsbg adj Joseph SMITH, James GARNER. Wit: Thomas FOUCH, John McCORMICK.

Bk:Pg: 2W:416 Date: 7 Sep 1818 RtCt: 12 Sep 1818
John LITTLEJOHN & wife Monica of Ldn to John CRIDLER of Ldn. B/S of ½a Lot #25 in Lsbg. Wit: Thomas FOUCH, John McCORMICK. Delv. to CRIDLER 27 Jan 1825.

Bk:Pg: 2W:418 Date: 13 May 1818 RtCt: 24 Jun 1818
Henry JENKINS & wife Margaret of Ldn to Joseph T. NEWTON of Ldn. B/S of 87¾a on N side of Tuscarora adj Ellis JENKINS, Alexandria road. Wit: Chas. THRIFT, Robert ELGIN, Gustavus ELGIN, John McCORMICK, Thos. GREGG.

Bk:Pg: 2W:420 Date: 17 Jan 1818 RtCt: 13 Apr 1818
Ferdinando FAIRFAX of Washington D.C. to Jonathan MATHEWS of Loudoun. B/S of 19a (part of Shannondale). Wit: Jno. MATHIAS, Amos HARVEY, Jesse EVANS, John CAMPBELL.

Bk:Pg: 2X:001 Date: 10 Sep 1818 RtCt: 10 Sep 1818
Samuel PLEASANTS, John FIELDS and Joseph JANNEY (firm of Joseph Janney & Co) to John LITTLEJOHN. Release of mortgage from indenture of 13 Sep 1788 (DB R:125) by atty Thomas SWANN.

Bk:Pg: 2X:001 Date: 14 Sep 1818 RtCt: 4 Sep 1818
Benjamin W. PERRY (PERRY committed to jail, long list of debts) to John H. CASSADAY and Joseph P. THOMAS. Trust using his interest in lease lot devised from his father now in occupation of James FRENCH (prch/o brother Samuel W. PERRY) adj Thompson MASON, and slaves of dec'd father. Wit: Wm. CHILTON, Presley CORDELL.

Bk:Pg: 2X:003   Date: 27 Aug 1818   RtCt: 17 Sep 1818
William NOLAND & wife Catherine of Ldn to Nelson NORRIS of BaltMD. B/S of 150a nr head of valley nr old Snickers Gap road adj Aquilla BRISCOE. Wit: Jane LOVE, Wm. L. POWELL, Burr POWELL, Abner GIBSON.

Bk:Pg: 2X:005   Date: 9 Feb 1818   RtCt: 8 Sept 1818
Enos POTTS & wife Lydia of Ldn to Levi WILLIAMS of Ldn. B/S of 63a on NW fork of Goose Creek adj Isaac & Samuel NICKOLS, James BEANS, David F. BEALE, Henry ELLIS. Wit: Thomas GREGG, Joshua OSBURN.

Bk:Pg: 2X:007   Date: 3 Jul 1818   RtCt: 10 Aug 1818
Burr POWELL & wife Catharine of Ldn to Abner GIBSON of Ldn. B/S of Lots #45, #46, #51 & #52 in Mdbg. Wit: Francis W. LUCKETT, Cuthbert POWELL. Delv. to GIBSON 14 Nov 1822.

Bk:Pg: 2X:009   Date: 18 Apr 1818   RtCt: 3 Sep 1818
Robert M. POWELL & wife Betty of Hampshier Co Va to William VICKERS of Ldn. B/S 82a (part of tract lately occupied by widow Mary LEITH excepting the burying ground with free access for heirs of James LEITH dec'd and William & Betty POWELL) adj James PLAISTER, Wm. LEITH, Elisha POWELL. Delv. to VICKERS 14 Jan 1820.

Bk:Pg: 2X:011   Date: 10 Aug 1818   RtCt: Sep 1818
Samuel RHODES of PrWm to Notley C. WILLIAMS of Ldn. Trust for debt to William FRANCIS of Licking Co OH using tract on Williams Gap branch which RHODES prch/o James ALDER. Wit: John SINCLAIR.

Bk:Pg: 2X:012   Date: 14 Apr 1817   RtCt: 10 Feb 1818
James RICE & with Bethany of Ldn to Isaac E. STEER of Ldn. B/S of 71¼a adj STEER. Wit: Abner WILLIAMS, Thomas PHILLIPS, Thomas GREEN. Delv. to W. S. NEALE pr order 5 Nov 1819

Bk:Pg: 2X:014   Date: 10 Aug 1818   RtCt: 12 Sep 1818
John RAMSEY & wife Clarissa of AlexDC to Edward HAMMETT of Ldn. B/S of part of Lot #7 in Lsbg on Royal St. Wit: Newton KEENE, Christopher NEALE. Delv. to HAMMETT 10 Jul 1819.

Bk:Pg: 2X:016   Date: 1 Apr 1818   RtCt: 10 Aug 1818
Isaac STEER & wife Phebe of Ldn to Samuel McPHERSON of Ldn. B/S of 10a where STEER now lives and 5a wood land on Kittocton Creek adj STEER, William PAXSON. Wit: Robert BRADEN, Abiel JENNERS. Delv. to grantee 27 May1820.

Bk:Pg: 2X:018   Date: 13 Aug 1818   RtCt: 10 Aug 1818
Elizabeth SULLIVAN and sons Samuel SULLIVAN & William SULLIVAN (infants under 21y by Elizabeth their Guardian) of Ldn to Stephen BALL of Ldn. B/S of 20a (Murtho SULLIVAN dec'd in life made agreement with BALL to exchange saw mill lot prch/o Moses COLDWELL for lot conveyed to BALL by Exors of Mahlon JANNEY

dec'd & Isaac E STEER, adj his home plantation which has been lately conveyed to Elizabeth SULLIVAN & sons by heirs of Moses COLDWELL) on branch of Limestone Run in breaks of Catocton Mt. Wit: Isaac LAROWE, Robert BENTLEY, Jonas POTTS.

Bk:Pg: 2X:020   Date: 9 Sep 1818   RtCt: 8 [?] Sept 1818
Thomas SWANN to Jacob FADELEY. Release of mortgage given to Swann by Thomas KIMMINS dec'd.

Bk:Pg: 2X:020   Date: 14 Aug 1818   RtCt: 3 Sep 1818
Anthony SWICK & wife Martha of Ldn to Thomas SWICK of Ldn. B/S of 38a conveyed to Anthony by said Thomas & wife Anne on 20 Mar 1818. Wit: William BRONAUGH, Thomas GREGG.

Bk:Pg: 2X:022   Date: 20 Mar 1818   RtCt: 3 Sep 1818
Thomas SWICK & wife Anne of Ldn to Anthony SWICK of Ldn. B/S of 38a (Anne's share of land of father John VANHORNE dec'd). Wit: William BRONAUGH and Thomas GREGG.

Bk:Pg: 2X:023   Date: 19 Apr 1818   RtCt: 3 Sep 1818
Yeoman William VICKERS & wife Anne of Ldn to Daniel EACHES of Ldn. Trust for debt to Robert M. POWELL & wife Betty using 82a of land lately occupied by widow Mary LEITH and 109a. Wit: William BRONAUGH, Francis W. LUCKETT.

Bk:Pg: 2X:025   Date: 9 Feb 1818   RtCt: 8 Sep 1818
Levi WILLIAMS & wife Sarah of Ldn to John HOLLINGSWORTH of Ldn. B/S of 63a on NW fork of Goose Creek. Wit: Joshua OSBURN, Thos. GREGG. Delv. pr order 6 Apr 1821.

Bk:Pg: 2X:027   Date: 28 May 1818   RtCt: 2 Jul 1818
Joseph T. NEWTON & wife Nelly Smith of Ldn to Samuel CARR & Hamilton ELLGIN of Ldn. Trust for debt to Henry JENKINS late of Ldn using 87a on N side of Tuscarora. Wit: Stephen C. ROSZEL, Thos. GREGG, Pat'k McINTYRE.

Bk:Pg: 2X:029   Date: 24 Aug 1818   RtCt: 24 Aug 1818
Jonah NIXON & wife Nancy of Ldn to Geo TAVENDER Jr. B/S Jonah's interest in 365a his grandfather George NIXON dec'd bought of Augustine LOVE and 36a adj Ezekiel MOUNT, Jonathan CARTER. Wit: Samuel MURREY, John McCORMICK.

Bk:Pg: 2X:031   Date: 4 Aug 1818   RtCt: 14 Sep 1818
John W. EVANS & wife Mary F. of AlexDC to William GILHAM of AlexDC B/S of ¼a on S side of King St in Lsbg adj James DAWSON, John DRISH.

Bk:Pg: 2X:033   Date: 14 Sep 1818   RtCt: 14 Sep 1818
Charles DUNCAN & Jesse TIMMS. Bond on DUNCAN as constable.

Bk:Pg: 2X:034   Date: 14 Sep 1818   RtCt: 14 Sep 1818
Jesse McVEIGH & Archibald MEANS. Bond on McVEIGH as commr. of revenue.

Bk:Pg: 2X:034   Date: 14 Sep 1818   RtCt: 14 Sep 1818
Daniel LOVETT & Richard H. HENDERSON. Bond on LOVETT as
commr. of revenue.

Bk:Pg: 2X:035   Date: 14 Sep 1818   RtCt: 14 Sep 1818
Jesse TIMMS & George CARTER. Bond on TIMMS as commr. of
revenue.

**Bk:Pg: 2X:035   Date: 29 Apr 1813   RtCt: 11 May 1813/14 Sep
1818**
Enoch FRANCIS of Ldn to Cornelius SHAWEN of Ldn. Release of
mortgage on 19a. Wit: John LITTLEJOHN, William CLINE, Saml.
CARR. Delv. to David SHAWEN 25 Mar 1824.

Bk:Pg: 2X:037   Date: 18 Apr 1817   RtCt: 14 Sep 1818
Joseph MILHOLLEN to Patrick B. MILHOLLEN. Receipt for $400 in
part of real & personal estate of Esther MILHOLLEN. Wit: John
LITTLEJOHN. Delv. to Patrick B. MILHOLLAND 13 Sep 1819.

Bk:Pg: 2X:038   Date: 14 Sep 1818   RtCt: 14 Sep 1818
Jacob WALTMAN & wife Rachel of Ldn to Emanuel WALTMAN of
Ldn. B/S of 57a adj Potomac, SW side of little Dutchman, where
RIDDLEMIRE lived. Delv. to grantee 20 Nov 1820.

Bk:Pg: 2X:039   Date: 1 Feb 1818   RtCt: 14 Sep 1818
Jacob WALTMAN & wife Rachel of Ldn to Emanuel WALTMAN of
Ldn. B/S of wood lots #3, #4 & #5 in 'Piedmont tract' on short hill mt
on Potomack and mill lot. Wit: Fred'k SCHLATZ, Jno. MATTHIAS.
Delv. to grantee 20 Nov 1820.

Bk:Pg: 2X:041   Date: 14 Aug 1818   RtCt: 14 Sep 1818
R. HOOE & Charles LITTLE to Christian CLYMORE & Murtie
SULLIVAN. Receipt for payments to mortgage with Henry A.
BENNETT. Mortgage recorded DB W:245.

Bk:Pg: 2X:041   Date: 21 Feb 1818   RtCt: 14 Sep 1818
Colin AULD of AlexDC to Rezin WILCOXEN of Ffx. B/S of 150a
(claimed by heirs of Capt Robert LYLE Sr then conveyed to John
MONROE who conveyed to AULD) nr Gum Spring adj Johnston
CLEVELAND. Wit: John RAMSAY, John HOOFF, Edm. J. LEE, R. J.
TAYLOR, Thomson F. MASON. Delv. to Burr W. HARRISON pr
order 20 Feb 1854.

Bk:Pg: 2X:043   Date: 21 Jun 1816   RtCt: 20 Sep 1818
Elizabeth D. PEYTON of KingG to William ELLZEY of Ldn. B/S of
259a (dev. PEYTON by father Henry Alex'r ASHTON). Wit: George
D. ASHTON, Geo. ROGERS, William FRANK, Henry
ALLENSWORTH. Delv. pr order 27 Jul 1824.

Bk:Pg: 2X:045   Date: 12 May 1818   RtCt: 10 Sep 1818
David JANNEY & wife Elizabeth of Ldn to Samuel GOVER of Ldn.
B/S of ¼a Lot #9 in new addition to Wtfd. Wit: Abiel JENNERS,
Robert BRADEN. Delv. to grantee pr order 4 Sep 1820.

Bk:Pg: 2X:046   Date: 30 May 1818   RtCt: 14 Sep 1818
Matthew ADAMS & wife Susanna and Abraham BROWN & wife
Margaret of Ldn to Humphrey B. POWELL of Ldn. Trust for debt to
Samuel HATCHER & Joseph HATCHER using 2 lots of land. Wit:
Burr POWELL, A. GIBSON. Delv. to trustee 10 May 1820.

Bk:Pg: 2X:049   Date: 19 May 1818   RtCt: 14 Sep 1818
Thomas BATTSON & wife Rachel of Ldn to Edwin C. BROWN of
Ldn. Trust for debt to Nancy, Mahaly, Elizabeth & James BATTSON
(to secure div. of £100 when they become of age paid by Exor Jesse
McVEIGH) using 7a on Goose Creek (allotted to BATTSON of
George BARR Sr. dec'd). Wit: Burr POWELL, Abner GIBSON. Delv.
to Jesse McVEIGH 14 Dec 1824.

Bk:Pg: 2X:052   Date: 18 Apr 1818   RtCt: 14 Sep 1818
Robert M. POWELL & wife Betty of Hampshire Co VA to James
PLAISTER of Ldn. B/S of 50a (part of land lately occupied by Mary
LEITH wd/o Jas. LEITH dec'd) adj Henry PLAISTER. Wit: Frederick
BUZZARD, Jacob JENKINS. Dev. to PLAISTER 25 Feb 1823.

Bk:Pg: 2X:053   Date: 16 Mar 1818   RtCt: 20 Jul 1818
Strother M. HELM of Ldn to Fleet SMITH of Ldn. Trust for debt to
James SHIP of FredVA using 240a where HELM lives adj Joseph
LEWIS Sr., John TURLEY Jr., William SMALLY, heirs of Matthew
HARRISON dec'd. Wit: John TURLEY, James TURLEY Jr., Fleet S.
CLOPTON. Delv. to Geo. BAYLY pr order from Jas. SHIP 9 Jul
1819.

Bk:Pg: 2X:056   Date: 3 Sep 1818   RtCt: 14 Sep 1818
Peter STONEBURNER & wife Susanna of Ldn to John HAMILTON
of Ldn. B/S of 90½a adj HAMILTON, Andrew SPRING, Philip
SOUDER. Wit: Robert BRADEN, John H. McCABE.

Bk:Pg: 2X:058   Date: 28 Jul 1818   RtCt: 14 Sep 1818
Sarah COLDWELL wd/o Moses COLDWELL dec'd, Joseph
COLDWELL & wife Eliza, John COLDWELL & wife, Mary
COLDWELL & William COLDWELL (heirs of Moses dec'd) of Ldn to
Elizabeth SULLIVAN wd/o Mortho SULLIVAN dec'd and Samuel
SULLIVAN & William SULLIVAN (infants of Mortho dec'd) of Ldn.
B/S of 200a sold by Mortho to Stephen BALL before his death but
not conveyed. Wit: Robert BRADEN, John H. McCABE.

Bk:Pg: 2X:061   Date: 9 Sep 1818   RtCt: 15 Sep 1818
John LITTLEJOHN & wife Monica of Ldn to Reuben SCHOOLEY of
Ldn. B/S of 6a in Lsbg adj Martin KITTSMILLER on Loudoun St and
another lot known as Littlejohn's Stable Lot adj Royal & Back Sts.
Wit: Thos. FOUCH, John McCORMICK. Delv. 8 Sep 1821

Bk:Pg: 2X:063   Date: 5 Jul 1818   RtCt: 11 Aug 1818
Charles Fenton MERCER of Aldie to James WATTS of Ldn. L/L of
250a on both sides of Bull Run where Reuben CHICK now resides.
Delv. pr order 11 Nov 1834.

Bk:Pg: 2X:065   Date: 8 Aug 1818   RtCt: 17 Sep 1818
Fanny LEE (Exor of Thomas L. LEE dec'd) of Ldn to John
LITTLEJOHN of Ldn. B/S of 7a and 9a on W side of Goose Creek.
Wit: Ludwell LEE, Wilson C. SELDON. Delv. to LITTLEJOHN 30
Aug 1819.

Bk:Pg: 2X:067   Date: 18 Sep 1818   RtCt: 18 Sep 1818
George RUST Jr. & wife Maria C. and James RUST & wife Sarah of
Ldn to John SHAW of Ldn. B/S of lot on W side of King St in Lsbg
between Loudoun & Market Sts. Wit: John ROSE, Patrick
McINTYRE. Delv. to SHAW 5 Aug 1819.

Bk:Pg: 2X:069   Date: 14 Aug 1818   RtCt: 21 Sep 1818
Ann WRIGHT (wd/o William WRIGHT) of Ldn to Joseph HILLEARD
of Ldn. B/S of 1a lot in new addition of Lsbg on W side of King St.
adj Mr. GREENWALL, David CONNER, John McCABE and opposite
Martin CORDELL.

Bk:Pg: 2X:070   Date: 24 Nov 1817   RtCt: 23 Sep 1818
George JANNEY & wife Susannah and Daniel EACHES of Ldn to
Nathaniel MANNING of Ldn. B/S of 357a adj Robt. BRADEN,
Nathen BEANS, Jeremiah MILLER. Wit: William BRONAUGH,
Francis W. LUCKETT. Delv. to MANNING 12 Feb 1822.

Bk:Pg: 2X:072   Date: 27 May 1818   RtCt: 25 Sep 1818
Betsy TEBBS of PrWm to George RUST Jr. B/S of land where
Joseph SHIELDS now lives sold by Joseph WEST & Jacob
NICKOLLS to William DOUGLAS who mortgaged to William CARR
dec'd f/o Betsy. Wit: David BOYLE, Jesse EWELL.

Bk:Pg: 2X:073   Date: 17 May 1818   RtCt: 25 Sep 1818
Daniel HOUSHOLDER & wife Catharine of Ldn to Jacob WYATT of
Ldn. B/S of 2a adj John SHAFFER, Michael STREAM. Wit: Robert
BRADEN, John H. McCABE.

Bk:Pg: 2X:075   Date: 27 May 1818   RtCt: 25 Sep 1818
John SPENCE & wife Mary F., John P. DUVAL & wife Anne F.,
Thomas T. TEBBS, Fouchee TEBBS of PrWm and Thomas
TRIPLETT & wife Margaret of Ldn to George RUST Jr. of Ldn. B/S
of 287a (formerly of William CARR Sr. of Dumfries), adj William
HATCHER, William RHODES, Nathan SPENCER. Wit: John ROSE,
John McCORMICK.

Bk:Pg: 2X:079   Date: 23 Jun 1818   RtCt: 25 Jul 1818
Sampson BLINCOE and Isaac HUGHES. Agreement on dividing
line of old field on N side of Lsbg between the two.

Bk:Pg: 2X:079   Date: 2 Oct 1818   RtCt: 2 Oct 1818
Rebecca HATCHER (wd/o Thomas HATCHER dec'd) of Ldn to
Joseph HATCHER of Ldn. B/S of 200a dev. Rebecca by her father
Isaac NICKOLLS (and 200a to Mary HOGUE) in both Ldn & Fqr.
Wit: Chas. G. ESKRIDGE, Josiah L. DREAN.

Bk:Pg: 2X:081   Date: 1 Oct 1818   RtCt: 2 Oct 1818
Samuel SUMMERS & wife Sally of Lsbg to Jacob FADELY of Lsbg.
B/S of part of lot #58 in Lsbg adj Mrs. DONOHOE. Wit: Patrick
McINTYRE, Samuel MURREY. Delv. to FADLEY 5 Oct 1819.

Bk:Pg: 2X:082   Date: 13 Mar 1813   RtCt: 1 Oct 1818
Jonah THOMPSON & wife Margaret of AlexDC to George JANNEY
and Daniel EACHES of Ldn. B/S of 767a (formerly of Israel
THOMPSON dec'd) adj Hannah MILLER. Wit: C. BINNS, E.
OFFUTT, Alfred REID.

Bk:Pg: 2X:085   Date: 19 Aug 1818   RtCt: 6 Oct 1818
Richard VANPELT & wife Elizabeth of Ldn to George CARTER of
Ldn. B/S of 150a on road from Lsbg to Gum Spring. Wit: William B.
HARRISON, John BAYLY. Delv. to Jesse TIMMS pr order Geo.
CARTER filed DB XX:85 on 26 Oct 1819.

Bk:Pg: 2X:087   Date: 1 May 1818   RtCt: 8 Oct 1818
Ignatius ELGIN of Ldn to Henry JENKINS of MontMd. B/S of 107a
on Secolon. Wit: S. BLINCOE, Jos. T. NEWTON, Hamilton ELGIN.

Bk:Pg: 2X:087   Date: 10 Apr 1818   RtCt: 9 Oct 1818
David JANNEY & wife Elizabeth of Ldn to John H. McCABE and
Samuel HOUGH 3rd of Ldn. B/S of 80a adj Wtfd dev. Amos GIBSON
by Mahlon JANNEY dec'd then conveyed to David JANNEY. Wit:
Abiel JENNERS, Robert BRADEN. Delv. to McCABE & HOUGH 3
Jul 1819.

Bk:Pg: 2X:091   Date: 12 Mar 1817   RtCt: 14 Mar 1817
John TORBERT of Ldn to Sampson BLINCOE of Ldn. Trust for debt
to John PANCOAST using 100a. Wit: Chas. G. ESKRIDGE, Geo. C.
MAUND, Geo. D. SWEARENGIN. Delv. to PANCOAST by order
BLINCOE 17 Aug 1819.

Bk:Pg: 2X:092   Date: 7 Aug 1818   RtCt: 14 Sep 1818
Jemima VIOLETT of Ldn to William HART and William VICKERS of
Ldn. LS of land below land that runs through her plantation towards
Clifton Mill during her lifetime, nr house where Thomas VIOLETT
now lives. Wit: James VIOLETT, Thos. VIOLETT, William
BRONAUGH, Francis W. LUCKETT.

Bk:Pg: 2X:093   Date: 12 Aug 1816   RtCt: 12 Oct 1818
John HUTCHISON of Ldn and Ariss BUCKNER of Ldn. Agreement
on requirements for leased land. Wit: Isaac HEATH, R. H. LITTLE.

Bk:Pg: 2X:094   Date: 24 May 1818   RtCt: 12 Oct 1818
Walter JONES of Washington D.C. to William HODGSON & wife
Portia of AlexDC Trust to John HUTCHISON of PrWm of 34½a for
benefit of Portia. Gives plat. Wit: Chas. J. CATLETT, Jacob
HOFFMAN, E. HOFFMAN. Delv. to John HUTCHISON 12 Aug
1820.

Bk:Pg: 2X:097   Date: 10 Oct 1818   RtCt: 12 Oct 1818
George RICHARDS. Col (brought in on 20 Sep 1818) for negro man
Sam age abt 26y, negro woman Sinia age abt 22y, mulatto woman
Lethe age abt 20y acquired by marriage with Anne Beale
SAUNDERS (d/o John ROSE of Ldn, who acquired by virtue of deed
constituting him trustee of slaves for benefit of said daughter w/o
Geo. RICHARDS.)

Bk:Pg: 2X:097   Date: 13 Apr 1801   RtCt: 13 Apr 1801/12 Oct 1818
John TODHUNTER of Ldn to brother Jacob TODHUNTER of Ldn.
B/S of 27a (John TODHUNTER died possessed of) on road from
Lsbg to Nolands Ferry. Wit: Saml. CLAPHAM, Saml. LUCKETT,
Wm. WILLIAMS.

Bk:Pg: 2X:099   Date: 31 Mar 1818   RtCt: 12 Oct 1818
James WARFORD & wife Elizabeth and Mary WARFORD of Ldn to
Nicholas OSBURN of Ldn. B/S of 125a where James now lives
(formerly held by John WARFORD now dec'd). Wit: Stacy TAYLOR,
John WHITE, Stephen C. ROSZELL, Patrick McINTYRE. Delv. to
OSBORNE 12 Sep 1821.

Bk:Pg: 2X:101   Date: 11 Aug 1818   RtCt: 12 Oct 1818
Jacob MANN & wife Sally to Bernard MANN. Trust for ½ of
expenses for building a house (to be jointly occupied) on 1a using
½a of lot at Washington & Independence Sts. Wit: Burr POWELL,
Abner GIBSON. Delv. to Townsend McVEIGH pr order of MANN 29
Jun 1819

Bk:Pg: 2X:103   Date: 18 Jun 1818   RtCt: 12 Oct 1818
Samuel EVANS of Ldn to Jesse EVANS of Ldn. B/S of 100a
between short hill and blue ridge. Wit: John CAMPBELL, Robert
LAKNON?, Abraham COCKERAL, Aseph CAMPBELL.

Bk:Pg: 2X:104   Date: 18 Jun 1818   RtCt: 12 Oct 1818
Samuel EVANS and Jesse EVANS. Agreement concerning above
land in the event of death. Wit: Robert COCKRELL, Abraham
COCKERAL, John CAMPBELL, Asaph CAMPBELL.

Bk:Pg: 2X:105   Date: 16 Oct 1818   RtCt: 16 Oct 1818
John TODHUNTER & wife Mary of Ldn to Samuel LUCKETT of Ldn.
B/S of 135 perches. Wit: John ROSE, John McCORMICK.

Bk:Pg: 2X:107   Date: 16 Oct 1818   RtCt: 16 Oct 1818
John MATHIAS of Ldn to Levy PRINCE of Ldn. B/S of 19a on W
side of Short Hill adj __ ROPP, __ DERRY, __ DEMORY.

Bk:Pg: 2X:108   Date: 16 Oct 1818   RtCt: 19 Oct 1818
John WILDMAN of Ldn to John WILDMAN of Ross Co OH. B/S of
1a (part of land formerly owned by Jacob WILDMAN) adj formerly
Joseph WILDMAN.

Bk:Pg: 2X:109   Date: 19 Oct 1818   RtCt: 19 Oct 1818
John WILDMAN & wife Sarah of Ross Co OH to Benjamin SHREVE of Ldn. B/S of 22a on E side of Little Secolin adj SHREVE.

Bk:Pg: 2X:110   Date: 13 Apr 1808   RtCt: 20 Oct 1818
Edmund LOVETT & wife Christian[a?] of Ldn to George CARTER of Ldn. B/S of 19a on Goose Creek adj John SIMPSON. Wit: Fleet SMITH, Jas. SIMPSON, Jno. ROSE, John McCORMICK. Delv. to Jesse TIMMS pr order DB XX:85 on 26 Oct 1819.

Bk:Pg: 2X:112   Date: 20 May 1818   RtCt: 21 Oct 1818
Jonathan SCHOLFIELD & wife Eleanor of AlexVA to William HERBERT Jr. Trust for debt to David ROSS & Jonathan ROSS using 80a. Wit: Thomas JANNEY, Henry NICHOLSON, Jno. PAYNE Jr. Delv to HERBERT 3 Jul 1819.

Bk:Pg: 2X:115   Date: 18 Apr 1818   RtCt: 30 Oct 1818
John RUSE (of Christian) of Ldn to William S. NEALE of Ldn. Trust for debt to Leven Ludwell SANDS of Ldn using 15a and 5a. Wit: Abiel JENNERS, John H. McCABE. Delv. to L. L. SANDS 3 Nov 1831.

Bk:Pg: 2X:117   Date: 13 Apr 1818   RtCt: 30 Oct 1818
Sarah RUSE of Ldn to William PAXSON of Ldn. B/S of 15a (Sarah's allotment of land of father Isaac SANDS dec'd) and 5a on Kittoctan Creek. Wit: Abiel JENNERS, John H. McCABE.

Bk:Pg: 2X:119   Date: 15 Apr 1818   RtCt: 30 Oct 1818
William PAXSON of Ldn to John RUSE (of Christian) of Ldn. B/S of 15a and 5a from above deed. Wit: Abiel JENNERS, John H. McCABE. Delv. to John RUSE 3 Jun 1823.

Bk:Pg: 2X:121   Date: 16 Mar 1818   RtCt: 30 Oct 1818
John HOPKINS Jr. of Winchester, FredVa to John HOPKINS of FredVa. B/S of 250a nr Harpers Ferry (from Philip STRIDER & wife Catharine of Md on 4 Jan 1817).

Bk:Pg: 2X:123   Date: 1 Apr 1818   RtCt: 30 Oct 1818
Frederick HANDSCHY of Ldn to Thomas SWANN of AlexDC Trust for debt to John HOPKINS using 250a on NW end of short hill and Potomac. Delv. pr order on __.

Bk:Pg: 2X:125   Date: 30 Oct 1818   RtCt: 5 Nov 1818
George RUST Jr. & wife Maria of Ldn to Joseph BEARD of Ldn. B/S of lot on W side of King St in Lsbg between Loudoun & Market Sts. Wit: Samuel CLAPHAM, Patrick McINTYRE.

Bk:Pg: 2X:127   Date: 4 Jul 1818   RtCt: 5 Nov 1818
Burr POWELL of Ldn to John HARRIS of Ldn. B/S of Lots #18 & #24 in Mdbg. Wit: William BRONAUGH, A. GIBSON. Delv. to grantee 11 Nov 1820.

Bk:Pg: 2X:128   Date: 3 Jul 1818   RtCt: 5 Nov 1818
Abner GIBSON & wife Peggy to Burr POWELL. B/S of Lot #24 in Mdbg. Wit: Cuthbert POWELL, Francis W. LUCKETT.

Bk:Pg: 2X:130   Date: 19 Mar 1818   RtCt: 9 Nov 1818
John BAYLY & wife Peggy C., Samuel BUCK & wife Mary P.,
William GILLMORE & wife Anna, Reuben HUTCHISON & wife Leah,
William COOK & wife Mariah E., Samuel BAYLY by Mountjoy
BAYLY, Mary BAYLY and Alexander M. BRISCOE & wife Matilda P.
to Geo. BAYLY. B/S of land Pierce BAYLY dec'd prch/o James
MURREY, Joseph BENNET & William MURREY in Sep 1791. Wit:
Alex'r HUTCHISON, Joseph HUTCHISON, William BEVERIDGE,
Chas. LEWIS, Wm. B. HARRISON, Arriss BUCKNER, Robt.
ARMISTEAD. Delv. to grantee 17 Nov 1820.

Bk:Pg: 2X:134   Date: 28 Feb 1818   RtCt: Nov 1818
Blacksmith James PATTERSON of Ldn and yeoman Henry
PLAISTER of Ldn. Exchange of 3 roods nr Millsville. Delv to Francis
LUCKETT 26 Apr 1822.

Bk:Pg: 2X:135   Date: 28 Feb 1818   RtCt: Nov 1818
Yeoman Henry PLAISTER & wife Susanna of Ldn to blacksmith
James PATTERSON of Ldn. Exchange with above using 1 rood in
Millsville. Wit: William BRONAUGH, Francis W. LUCKETT.

Bk:Pg: 2X:136   Date: 19 Aug 1812   RtCt: Nov 1818
William McFARLING & wife Rachel (d/o George LEWIS dec'd) of
Ldn to Samuel MOORE of Ldn. B/S of Rachel's share of father's
land. Wit: Wm. BRONAUGH, Joshua OSBURNE, N. C. WILLIAMS.
CoE of 3 Oct 1818 for Rachel in Culpeper Co.

Bk:Pg: 2X:138   Date: 1 Jul 1818   RtCt: 10 Aug 1818
Wm. BRONAUGH and Silas REESE (trustees for David JAMES) to
Jonathan CARTER. Release of trust DB 22:149.

Bk:Pg: 2X:139   Date: 1 Sep 1818   RtCt: 9 Nov 1818
Abel MARKS dec'd. Division – court order dated 11 Mar 1818.
Dower of widow Mary MARKS (140a), Saml. MARKS (52½a), Watts
MARKS (52¼a), James WARFORD & wife Elizabeth (35a), Lidia
MARKS (40a), Elisha PEW & wife Mary (40a), Mason MARKS (30a),
Thos. MARKS (49a), Abel MARKS (53¼a), Marcus
HUMPHRIE/HUMPHREY & wife Margaret (42a), Bennett MARKS
(30a). Gives plat and details. Divisors: James COCKRAN, James
NICKOLS, Joel OSBURN.

Bk:Pg: 2X:141   Date: 10 Oct 1818   RtCt: 9 Nov 1818
Cartwright TIPPITT. Col on 23 Sep last from Washington D.C. for
slaves: black man Davy abt 45y, yellow man Romelus abt 38y, black
man Richard abt 21y, black woman Kitty abt 22y, yellow boy Robert
abt 6y and yellow girl Heister between 1-2y.

Bk:Pg: 2X:142   Date: 12 Oct 1818   RtCt: 9 Nov 1818
John BOOTH of Jefferson Co Indiana to friend John BOOTH Jr. of
Ldn. PoA for matters from will of Robert BOOTH dec'd. Delv. to
John BOOTH Jr. 25 Sep 1819.

Bk:Pg: 2X:143   Date: 7 Sep 1818   RtCt: 9 Nov 1818
Henry JACKSON & wife Elizabeth (late Elizabeth STUMP) of
Guernsey Co OH to John BOOTH Jr of Ldn. B/S of part of 60a dev.
John BOOTH by Robert BOOTH during his life and after to heirs of
Thomas STUMP and William CHAMBERS. Wit: Barton D. HAWLEY,
Geo. METCALF. Delv. to BOOTH 25 Sep 1819.

Bk:Pg: 2X:145   Date: 14 Sep 1818   RtCt: 9 Nov 1818
Sarah HURLEY of Miami Co OH to John BOOTH Jr. of Ldn. B/S of
land dev. John BOOTH by Robert BOOTH during his life and after to
heirs of Thomas STUMP and William CHAMBERS. Wit: Cornelius
HURLEY, Robert HURLEY. Delv. to BOOTH 25 Sep 1819.

Bk:Pg: 2X:147   Date: ___   RtCt: 9 Nov 1818
Commr. appointing John HAMILTON Sheriff of Loudoun.

Bk:Pg: 2X:148   Date: 9 Nov 1818   RtCt: 9 Nov 1818
John HAMILTON, Benj'a SHREIVE, Robert MOFFETT, Wm. CARR,
William MEAD & Armistead T. MASON. Bond on HAMILTON as
Sheriff.

Bk:Pg: 2X:148   Date: 9 Nov 1818   RtCt: 9 Nov 1818
John HAMILTON, Benjamin SHREVE, Robert MOFFETT, William
CARR, William MEAD & Armistead T. MASON. Bond on HAMILTON
to collect levies.

Bk:Pg: 2X:149   Date: 9 Nov 1818   RtCt: 9 Nov 1818
John HAMILTON, Benj'a SHREVE, Robert MOFFETT, Wm. CARR,
Wm. MEAD & Armistead T. MASON. Bond on [HAMILTON] to
collect taxes.

Bk:Pg: 2X:150   Date: 10 Nov 1818   RtCt: 10 Nov 1818
Simon A. BINNS & John HUFF. Release of interest in estate of
Rebecca WILDMAN dec'd. Wit: Rich'd H. HENDERSON.

Bk:Pg: 2X:150   Date: 1 Jan 1818   RtCt: 11 Nov 1818
Henry SANDERS. Col to negro man Tom (sometimes called
Thomas VENIE). Wit: Thomas SANDERS, John SAUNDERS.

Bk:Pg: 2X:151   Date: 19 Mar 1804   RtCt: 13 Nov 1818
James DAWSON to Peter STUMP. BoS for negro girl Milley. Wit:
Hugh QUINTAN. Delv. to STUMP 23 Oct 1819.

Bk:Pg: 2X:152   Date: 10 Feb 1819   RtCt: 10 Feb 1819
Henry H. HAMILTON & Thomas R. MOTT. Bond on HAMILTON as
Notary Public. Wit: Jno. A. BINNS.

Bk:Pg: 2X:152   Date: 29 Dec 1817   RtCt: 10 Aug 1818
Thomas SINCLAIR & George SINCLAIR of Ldn to David LOVETT of
Ldn. Trust for debt to John HOUGH using 33a adj Hllb (cnvy/b John
HOUGH & wife Pleasant, Thomas STEVENS & wife Nancy and
Valentine PURSEL to SINCLAIR). Wit: Turner OSBURN.

Bk:Pg: 2X:154   Date: 1 Jul 1818   RtCt: 10 Aug 1818
Henley SIMPSON to Jonathan CARTER. Release of trust (DB
RR:62) by Jas. SIMPSON & Wm. BRONAUGH.

Bk:Pg: 2X:154   Date: 13 Nov 1816   RtCt: 9 Nov 1818
George CARNAHAM of Ldn and Margaret HIXSON of Ldn.
Agreement concerning claim to property of Flemmon PATTERSON
dec'd in Wtfd in the event of death. Wit: Jno. SCHOOLEY, Wm. H.
HOUGH, Eleanor HIXSON. Delv. to F. W. P. HIXON the heir on 25
Apr 1831.

Bk:Pg: 2X:155   Date: 20 Oct 1818   RtCt: 9 Nov 1818
George CLAPHAM of Sullivan Co TN to Josias CLAPHAM of Ldn.
PoA for land in Ldn. Wit: James SAUNDERS, R. G. SAUNDERS,
Peter STUCK.

Bk:Pg: 2X:156   Date: 29 Sep 1818   RtCt: 9 Nov 1818
Alexander YOUNG & wife Elizabeth to Thomas YOUNG of
Washington D.C. Release of trust made Sep 1817 with John DULIN
of Ldn. Wit: S. BLINCOE, Josiah L. DREAN, James SCOTT Jr.,
Johnston CLEVELAND.

Bk:Pg: 2X:157   Date: 28 May 1818   RtCt: 9 Nov 1818
Abel JAMES & wife Sarah of Ldn to William NOLAND of Ldn. B/S of
66a adj Jeremiah FOSTER. Wit: Charles LEWIS, Robt.
ARMISTEAD. Delv. to grantee 21 Oct 1820.

Bk:Pg: 2X:159   Date: 28 Mar 1818   RtCt: 9 Nov 1818
Benjamin KENT (plasterer) & wife Sarah of Union to Joseph
LOVETT of Ldn. B/S of 1 rood lot in Union adj Widow GRAVES. Wit:
Thos. GREGG, Wm. BRONAUGH. Delv. to MARMADUKE 15 Mar
1825. [should probably have been for the entry below]

Bk:Pg: 2X:160   Date: 1 Oct 1818   RtCt: 9 Nov 1818
Isaac LAROWE of Mason Co Va late of Ldn to John WHITE &
Craven OSBURN of Ldn. Trust for debt to John A. MARMADUKE of
Ldn using 42a conveyed to LAROWE by John DRISH.

Bk:Pg: 2X:162   Date: 9 Apr 1818   RtCt: 9 Nov 1818
Nathaniel NORTON of Ldn to David YOUNG of Ldn. B/S of 75a adj
John NORTON. Wit: Hugh ROGERS, David F. BEALE, William
YOUNG. Delv to Jno. YOUNG 12 Apr 1827.

Bk:Pg: 2X:164   Date: 3 Sep 1818   RtCt: 9 Nov 1818
Peter STONEBURNER & wife Susannnah of Ldn to Edward
MARLOW of Ldn. B/S of 15a on W side of Catoctin Mt adj Peter
FRY. Wit: Robert BRADEN, John H. McCABE.

Bk:Pg: 2X:166   Date: 27 Oct 1818   RtCt: 9 Nov 1818
Matthew RUST & wife Patty of Ldn to Charles Fenton MERCER of
Ldn. B/S of 43a adj William NOLAND, Amos FERGUSON. Wit:
William NOLAND, Leven LUCKETT. Delv. to MERCER 30 Aug
1820.

Bk:Pg: 2X:168   Date: 30 Sep 1818   RtCt: 9 Nov 1818
John TODHUNTER & wife Mary of Ldn to Charles ELGIN of Ldn.
B/S of 163¼a. Wit: Edward DULIN, W. S. NEALE, Adam KENNER,
Samuel CLAPHAM, John McCORMICK. Delv. to ELGIN 26 Dec
1823.

Bk:Pg: 2X:170   Date: 22 Sep 1818   RtCt: 9 Nov 1818
Thomas YOUNG & wife Margaret of Ldn to Cartwright TIPPETT of
Washington City. B/S of 316a adj James COLEMAN, Richard
COLEMAN. Wit: Chas. LEWIS, Johnston CLEVELAND.

Bk:Pg: 2X:171   Date: 10 Nov 1818   RtCt: 10 Nov 1818
Thomas SWANN of Alexandria to George RUST Jr. of Ldn. Release
of trust for debt to George JANNEY & Nathaniel MANNING.

Bk:Pg: 2X:172   Date: 13 Nov 1818   RtCt: 13 Nov 1818
Benjamin SHREVE to Anthony CONARD. Release of trust for debt
to Abraham B. T. MASON.

Bk:Pg: 2X:173   Date: 12 Nov 1818   RtCt: 14 Nov 1818
John MATHIAS to Anthony CONARD. Release of trust for debt to
John H. CANBY. Delv. to CONARD 6 Jul 1822.

Bk:Pg: 2X:174   Date: 14 Nov 1818   RtCt: 14 Nov 1818
Charles ELGIN & wife Roanna of Ldn to Jacob MARTIN of Ldn. B/S
of house & lot on Market St. in Lsbg now occupied by MARTIN &
Thomas B. BEATTY. Wit: Patrick McINTYRE, Samuel MURREY.

Bk:Pg: 2X:176   Date: 14 Nov 1818   RtCt: 14 Nov 1818
Jacob MARTIN & wife Sophia of Ldn to Charles ELGIN. Trust for
above land. Wit: Samuel MURREY, Patrick McINTYRE. Delv. to
Wm. D. DRISH Admr of Chas. ELGIN 8 Apr 1824.

Bk:Pg: 2X:177   Date: 15 Nov 1818   RtCt: 14 Nov 1818
Joseph CALDWELL & wife Eliza of Ldn to Lewis P. W. BALCH of
Ldn. B/S of 4a on NW side of Katoctan Mt. Wit: Samuel MURREY,
Patrick McINTYRE. Delv. to BALCH 14 Sep 1819.

Bk:Pg: 2X:179   Date: 16 Nov 1818   RtCt: 17 Nov 1818
Thomas PIERCE attorney for Alse PIERCE of Ross Co OH to John
H. BUTCHER of Ldn. B/S of 135a (undivided 1/6th as heir of
Elizabeth BURKINS w/o John BURKINS who was Elizabeth
BUTCHER d/o Samuel BUTCHER dec'd) adj James PHILLIPS,
Benjamin OVERFELT, Jenkin PHILLIPS. Delv. to BUTCHER 16 Jun
1821.

Bk:Pg: 2X:181   Date: 11 Oct 1813   RtCt: 18 Nov 1818
John NIXON & wife Nancy of Ldn to Charles BINNS of Ldn. B/S of
Lot #54 in Lsbg. Wit: E. OFFUTT, Saml. M. EDWARDS, Tho. R.
MOTT, Samuel MURREY, John ROSE. Delv. to BINNS 12 Sep
1836.

Bk:Pg: 2X:183   Date: 2 Nov 1818   RtCt: 19 Nov 1818
John JANNEY & wife Ann of AlexDC to Aaron SAUNDERS of Ldn.
B/S of 49a (cnvy/b Jonus POTTS & wife Phoebe to JANNEY) and
80a. Gives plat. Wit: John ROSE, John McCORMICK.

Bk:Pg: 2X:186   Date: 21 Nov 1818   RtCt: 21 Nov 1818
Ellis WILLIAMS & wife Lener of Ldn to Samuel MULLEN of Ldn. B/S
of lot with log house on W side of King St in Lsbg now occupied by
MULLEN. Delv. to MULLEN 16 Nov 1821.

Bk:Pg: 2X:187   Date: 13 Oct 1817   RtCt: 23 Nov 1818
Augustine LOVE & wife Mary of Ldn to Presley SAUNDERS of Ldn.
B/S of 32a. Wit: Joseph EIDSON, Thos. BROWN, Amos
FERGUSON, William BRONAUGH, Francis W. LUCKETT. Delv. to
SAUNDERS the elder 29 Jul 1819.

Bk:Pg: 2X:189   Date: 5 Nov 1818   RtCt: 25 Nov 1818
Wm. HERRON & wife Malinda of Ldn to John HOLMES of Ldn. B/S
of 9a on N fork of Goose Creek adj James BEANS, John HOLMES.
Wit: John McCORMICK, Patrick McINTYRE. Delv. to HOLMES 9
Oct 1820.

Bk:Pg: 2X:191   Date: 13 Oct 1818   RtCt: 26 Nov 1818
Daniel BROWN & wife Rachel of Ldn to David CARTER of Ldn. B/S
of 92½a on N side of Goose Creek. Wit: John SINCLAIR, George
LOVE, John MITCHELL, William BRONAUGH, Francis W.
LUCKETT. Delv. to grantee 27 Dec 1819.

Bk:Pg: 2X:193   Date: 2 Sep 1818   RtCt: 30 Nov 1818
James W. HAMILTON & wife Margaret of Ldn to Thomas MARKS of
Ldn. B/S of 1a Lot #16 in Hllb. Wit: John McCORMICK, Chas. B.
BALL.

Bk:Pg: 2X:195   Date: 1 Nov 1818   RtCt: 4 Dec 1818
William PIGGOTT (Exor of John PIGGOTT dec'd) of Ldn to William
BROWN of Ldn. B/S of 67a adj William NICKOLLS, William
PIGGOTT, Jesse HIRST. Wit: David SMITH, John PIGGOTT, Isaac
PIGGOTT.

Bk:Pg: 2X:196   Date: 4 Dec 1818   RtCt: 4 Dec 1818
William BROWN & wife Sarah of Ldn to William PIGGOTT of Ldn.
B/S of 67a on NW fork of Goose Creek adj William NICKOLS. Wit:
John McCORMICK, Patrick McINTYRE.

Bk:Pg: 2X:198   Date: 18 Aug 1817   RtCt: 5 Dec 1818
John McKNIGHT of Ldn to Charles CHAMBLIN of Ldn. B/S of 8a on
NW fork of Goose Creek (formerly of William McKNIGHT dec'd) adj
Deborah McKNIGHT. Wit: Thomas HART, Jeremiah GILE, Eli
McKNIGHT Jr., Stacy TAYLOR, John WHITE. Delv. to CHAMBLIN
20 Aug 1827.

Bk:Pg: 2X:199   Date: 6 Jun 1818   RtCt: 8 Dec 1818
George SANDERS & wife Elizabeth of Ldn to John SANDERS of
Ldn. B/S of 104a that George & John SANDERS prch/o George

JANNEY, adj Margaret SANDERS, Archibald MORRISON, Abiel JENNERS, Robert BRADEN.

Bk:Pg: 2X:201   Date: 5 Oct 1818   RtCt: 9 Nov 1818
Anthony WRIGHT dec'd. Widow's dower to Elizabeth WRIGHT of 4½a adj Wm. PAXSON, Pattison WRIGHT. Gives small plat. Divisors: James MOORE, John WILLIAMS, R. BRADEN.

Bk:Pg: 2X:202   Date: 18 Jun 1818   RtCt: 18 Nov 1818
George NIXON the elder dec'd. Division not devised by will: Samuel WHITE & wife Sarah (18a), Jesse HARRIS & wife (18a), Joseph WHITE & wife Betsey (19a), Wm. WHITE & wife Nancy (19a), heirs of Geo. & Patty TAVENDER (19¼a), George TAVENDER Jr. in right of his purchases from John NIXON & Jonah NIXON (7a), Henry BALL & wife Ruth (9a), Isaac BROWN & wife Nancy (9a), Joanna L. NIXON (9a), heirs of George NIXON the dec'd (16a), five children of Hannah BARR (15a), Geo. NIXON son of Jonah (4¼a). Gives plat. Divisors: Wm. BRONAUGH, Jno. MATHIAS. Wm. NIXON, Mahlon GARNER & wife Nancy, Jonathan NIXON, Daniel MINOR & wife Pleasant, Wm. KNOX & wife Mary, Davis NIXON, Joseph HAWKINS & wife Sarah, Joseph WILDMAN & wife Hannah, Geo. NIXON an infant by guardian Saml. HOGUE, Jos. NIXON an infant by guardian Giles CRAVEN, John NIXON an infant by guardian Thomas BROWN, also your orator of the ? of NIXON & your oratrix, being children of Geo. NIXON the second dec'd, Jesse HARRIS & wife Peggy late Peggy NIXON, Sarah WHITE widow of Saml. WHITE late Sarah NIXON, Joseph WHITE & wife Betsy, Jonah NIXON, Geo. NIXON, Isaac BROWN & wife Nancy, Henry BALL & wife Ruth, Joanna NIXON which said Jonah, George, Nancy, Ruth & Joanna are children of Jonah NIXON dec'd, William WHITE & wife Nancy late Nancy NIXON, Geo. TAVENDER & wife Patty late Patty NIXON, Hugh BARR who intermarried with Hannah NIXON since dec'd they children by her, Letty BARR, Nimrod BARR, Mahala BARR, Ketura BARR, Wicus? BARR, infants under the age of 21y by Hugh BARR this next friend. versus John NIXON & Isaac HUGHES who intermarried with Rebecca NIXON since dec'd leaving no child living.

Bk:Pg: 2X:205   Date: 8 Jun 1812   RtCt: 15 Dec 1818
Landon CARTER. Division - By decree in John MINOR & wife Lucy Landon, John LEWIS & wife Mildred A. B. and Eliza Travers CARTER agt. St. Ledger Landon CARTER & Frances Lee CARTER and Anna Maria CARTER inft. by Geo. W. BALL their Guardian, allotments to Exor of Landon CARTER Esqr dec'd (705½a), John LEWIS & wife Mildred (670a), John MINOR & wife Lucy and Eliza Travers CARTER (778¾a), Frances Lee CARTER and Maria CARTER (740½a). In Elizabeth CARTER vs. St. Leger Landon CARTER Exor of Landon CARTER of Clive: dower of widow Elizabeth CARTER (178a and 18a), reps of McCARTY (124a), Exors of Landon CARTER dec'd (384a). Gives plat.

Bk:Pg: 2X:208   Date: 11 Jul 1818   RtCt: 17 Aug 1818
Robert DOWNEY & wife Barbara of Charlestown, JeffVa to Richard
BROOKE of Frederick Town, Md. B/S of 134a adj Catesby
COOKE's patent. Wit: David HUMPHREYS, Rich'd WILLIAMS.

Bk:Pg: 2X:210   Date: 20 Mar 1818   RtCt: 15 Aug 1818
James MACKLAN & wife Mary of Union to George JANNEY of Ldn.
Trust using 124a on Goose Creek. Delv. to F. W. LUCKETT 6 Jan
1820.

Bk:Pg: 2X:212   Date: 24 Jun 1817   RtCt: 19 Aug 1818
Josiah HALL & wife Mary of Ldn to Mary BEATTY of Ldn. B/S of
100a of 209a tract. Wit: Joseph KNOX, John DREAN, J. L. DREAN.
Delv. to BEATTY 28 Jul 1819.

Bk:Pg: 2X:213   Date: 21 May 1818   RtCt: 20 Aug 1818
John LIVINGSTON of Wtfd to Jacob MENDENHALL and John
WILLIAMS of Ldn. Trust for debt to Mahlon SCHOOLEY using Lot
#52 & #53 in new addition to Wtfd. Wit: Abiel JENNERS, Robert
BRADEN. Delv. to SCHOOLEY 21 Jun 1823.

Bk:Pg: 2X:215   Date: 27 Jun 1818   RtCt: 14 Aug 1818
John MARKS of Henderson Co KY by attorney Bennet MARKS of
Ldn to William LODGE. Release of trust on 140a. Wit: Thomas
LODGE, Samuel LODGE.

Bk:Pg: 2X:216   Date: 1 Apr 1818   RtCt: 24 Aug 1818
Isaiah B. BEANS & wife Susan of Ldn to Samuel BEANS of Ldn.
B/S of 58½a (inherited from Susan's father James GRADY dec'd).
Wit: Israel CLAYTON, Samuel SINCLAIR, Benjamin GRAYSON,
Notley C. WILLIAMS.

Bk:Pg: 2X:218   Date: 24 Apr 1818   RtCt: 24 Aug 1818
Samuel BEANS of Ldn to Isaiah B. BEANS of Ldn. B/S of 58½a
(above land). Delv. to Isaiah B. BEANS 12 Aug 1820.

Bk:Pg: 2X:220   Date: 29 Jun 1818   RtCt: 10 Aug 1818
Daniel BROWN & wife Rachel of Ldn to William BRONAUGH of Ldn.
Trust for debt to Stephen McGEATH & John WINN using 52a. Wit:
Francis W. LUCKETT, Notley C. WILLIAMS. Delv. pr order filed.

Bk:Pg: 2X:221   Date: 28 Jul 1818   RtCt: 11 Aug 1818
Charles J. LOVE & wife Frances Peyton of Clermont, Ffx to Charles
Fenton MERCER of Aldie. B/S of 84½a N of Cool Spring road
across the Bull Run Mt. and 63½a to the S chiefly in PrWm. Delv. to
MERCER 30 Aug 1820.

Bk:Pg: 2X:223   Date: 13 Aug 1818   RtCt: 13 Aug 1818
Loveless CORNWELL/CONWELL & wife Elizabeth of Ldn to George
CARTER of Ldn. B/S of 2 lots totaling 5a. Wit: William CARR,
Samuel MURREY. Delv. to Jesse TIMMS pr order filed DB XX:85 on
26 Oct 1819.

Bk:Pg: 2X:225   Date: 15 Dec 1818
George BROWN of Belmont Co OH to John LICKEY of Belmont Co
OH. PoA. Wit: Matthew R. PERRIN.

Bk:Pg: 2X:226   Date: 13 Dec 1818   RtCt: 15 Dec 1818
Commr. William D. DRISH to George TAVENDER Jr. B/S of 178a
where Jesse HARRIS formerly lived adj old Turnpike Road (land
from agreement in 1801 signed by George NIXON the younger
dec'd and Hannah BARR d/o George NIXON the elder dec'd
requiring to convey land to Jesse HARRIS & wife Margaret who sold
to TAVENDER). Wit: S. BLINCOE, Josiah L. DREAN, Jno.
MATHIAS.

Bk:Pg: 2X:228   Date: 20 Oct 1818   RtCt: 15 Dec 1818
John MOUNT & wife Mary Ann of Ldn and Thomas MOUNT & wife
Sarah of Alexandria to Richard WEEDON of Ldn. B/S of ½a lot in
Union cnvy/b Isaac BROWN & wife Sarah.

Bk:Pg: 2X:230   Date: 14 Dec 1818   RtCt: 15 Dec 1818
Charles BINNS of Ldn by his son and attorney Jno. A. BINNS and
Daniel McCarty PAYNE. Agreement on 1500a in Warren Co Oh
between Sciota & Little Miami. Wit: Wm. WHITTEMORE (Fayette Co
KY). Delv. to BINNS 28 Jul 1819.

Bk:Pg: 2X:231   Date: 16 Oct 1818   RtCt: 15 Dec 1818
Alsea PIERCE of Ross Co OH to Thomas PIERCE of Ross Co OH.
PoA. Wit: John GREAVE, John FRANCIS (Ross Co OH).

Bk:Pg: 2X:232   Date: 4 Nov 1818   RtCt: 14 Dec 1818
Sarah WHITE of Jefferson Co TN to George TAVENDER Jr. of Ldn.
B/S of part of 230¼a which George NIXON the elder (f/o Sarah)
died seized of and was conveyed to Jesse HARRIS & wife Margaret.
Wit: George WHITE, Abram SHEKELL, Joseph WHITE Sr. Nov.
1818 in Carter Co TN Ct.

Bk:Pg: 2X:234   Date: 10 Nov 1818   RtCt: 14 Dec 1818
Joseph WHITE & wife Elizabeth of Hawkins Co Tn to George
TAVENDER Jr of Ldn. B/S of rights to land of George NIXON the
elder dec'd (f/o Elizabeth). In Ct. Nov 1818 at Carter Co TN.

Bk:Pg: 2X:236   Date: 20 Nov 1818   RtCt: 14 Dec 1818
John SCHROEDER. Col from Md on 11 Nov acquired by marriage
– negro woman Lucy abt 25y very black complexion abt 5' 4" or 5",
negro boy Yorrick abt 9y of black complexion.

Bk:Pg: 2X:236   Date: 31 Oct 1818   RtCt: 14 Dec 1818
John AXLINE & wife Christiana of Ldn to David AXLINE of Ldn. B/S
of 97a in 'Dutch Settlement' adj Adam HOUSEHOLDER. Wit: Abiel
JENNERS, John H. McCABE. Delv. to David AXLINE 7 Nov 1821.

Bk:Pg: 2X:238   Date: 7 Oct 1816   RtCt: 14 Dec 1818
Stephen BEARD & wife Orpah of Ldn to Strother M. HELM of Ldn.
B/S of 40a (part of land devised by Orpah's father Joseph LACEY
dec'd to his daughters Orpah, Tacey, Naomi, Huldah & Ruth) adj

Geo. LEWIS, Matthew HARRISON and 200a prch/o Sampson TURLEY. Wit: Robert ARMISTEAD, John BAYLY.

Bk:Pg: 2X:239   Date: 27 Jul 1816   RtCt: 14 Dec 1818
Patrick McINTYRE of Ldn to Lewis ELLZEY of Ldn. BoS for negro man Soloman.

Bk:Pg: 2X:240   Date: 14 Dec 1818   RtCt: 14 Dec 1818
Lewis ELLZEY of Ldn to Charles BINNS of Ldn. BoS for negro man Solomon.

Bk:Pg: 2X:240   Date: 14 Nov 1818   RtCt: 14 Dec 1818
Yeoman Moses BROWN & wife Mary of Ldn to yeoman Henry PLAISTER of Ldn. B/S of 2/3 of 7a (except ¼a) in Union allotted to Mary d/o James REED dec'd. Wit: Wm. BRONAUGH, Francis W. LUCKETT.

Bk:Pg: 2X:242   Date: 27 Jul 1818   RtCt: 14 Dec 1818
Robert COE & wife Elizabeth of Ldn to William LICKEY of Ldn. B/S of 9¼a on Goose Creek adj John CONROD, road from N. Fork Meeting House to Coe's Mill. Wit: William CARR, Thos. GREGG. Delv. to LICKEY 11 Oct 1821.

Bk:Pg: 2X:244   Date: 14 Nov 1818   RtCt: 14 Dec 1818
John REED & wife Martha of Belmont Co OH to Henry PLAISTER of Ldn. B/S of Lot #5 in Union (James REED died seized of) adj Isaac BROWN. Wit: William BRONAUGH, Francis W. LUCKETT.

Bk:Pg: 2X:245   Date: 2 Oct 1818   RtCt: 9 Nov 1818
Moses GIBSON & wife Lydia of Ldn to John GIBSON & John W. GRAYSON of Ldn. Trust for debt to Joseph CARR using 226a where Moses now lives. Wit: Jonathan GIBSON, Caldwell CARR, Daniel EACHES, Wm. McDONALD. Delv. to GRAYSON 8 Dec 1819.

Bk:Pg: 2X:247   Date: 8 Dec 1818   RtCt: Dec 1818
William COE & wife Catharine, Edward M. COE & wife Mary, Robert COE & wife Elizabeth, David J. COE and John W. COE of Ldn to Samuel HOGE and Lot JANNEY of Ldn. B/S of 42¾a (formerly of Edward COE dec'd, then to Menan COE now dec'd) adj Beach CARTER. Wit: William CARR, Thos. GREGG.

Bk:Pg: 2X:249   Date: ___   RtCt: 14 Dec 1818
David J. COE of Ldn to John W. COE of Ldn. B/S of 26a on N side of Goose Creek dev. David by father Edward COE dec'd.

Bk:Pg: 2X:250   Date: 21 Nov 1818   RtCt: 18 Dec 1818
John HAWLING of Ldn to Thomas SWANN, Jemima HAWLING & Isaac HAWLING of Ldn. B/S of lots by decree of chancery in Winchester 18 Apr 1818. Wit: R. H. HENDERSON, Thomas A. MOORE. H. H. HAMILTON.

Bk:Pg: 2X:252   Date: 22 May 1818   RtCt: Dec 1818
John HADDOX & wife Barbary/Barbara, William BYRNE & wife Mary/Ann and Jeremiah DEBELL & wife Sarah of Fqr and

Dorchas/Dorcas DEBELL of PrWm to Ariss BUCKNER of Ldn. B/S of 52a of John DEBELL dec'd of PrWm which passed to heirs. Delv. to BUCKNER 13 Feb 1820.

Bk:Pg: 2X:254   Date: 22 Oct 1818   RtCt: 26 Dec 1818
Thomas LESLIE & wife Ann of Ldn to Daniel COOPER of Ldn. B/S of 28a on SE side of short hill. Wit: John WHITE, Abiel JENNERS.

Bk:Pg: 2X:256   Date: 22 Oct 1818   RtCt: 28 Dec 1818
James WHITE & wife Mary of Ldn to Herod OSBURN of Ldn. B/S of interest in 2 undivided lots of 147a & 111a on SE side of Blue Ridge formerly belong and occupied by her father in law Nathan POTTS dec'd. Wit: Abiel JENNERS, John WHITE. Delv. to OSBORNE 20 Oct 1821.

Bk:Pg: 2X:257   Date: 27 Jun 1818   RtCt: 28 Dec 1818
Stephen McPHERSON Jr. & wife Cecelia of Ldn to Charles RUSSELL of Ldn. B/S of 167a (prch/o Turner & Herod OSBURN), dispute over 6a with Saml. BUTCHER. Wit: N. C. WILLIAMS, Jno. L. GILL, William BRADFIELD, Notley C. WILLIAMS, Francis W. LUCKETT. Delv. to RUSSELL 14 Apr 1824.

Bk:Pg: 2X:260   Date: 25 Dec 1818   RtCt: 25 Dec 1818
Robert CAMPBELL & wife Jane of Ldn to William ALT of Ldn. B/S of 118a (prch/o Dr. Henry CLAGGETT). Wit: John ROSE, John McCORMICK. Delv. to ALT 17 Aug 1826.

Bk:Pg: 2X:261   Date: 25 Dec 1818   RtCt: 25 Dec 1818
William ALT to Jacob FADELY and Presley CORDELL. Trust for debt to Robert CAMPBELL using above 118a.

Bk:Pg: 2X:264   Date: 26 Dec 1818   RtCt: 26 Dec 1818
Thomas R. MOTT and wife Mary Chichester of Ldn to Mahlon JANNEY of Ldn. B/S of land prch/o Betsy TEBBS in Feb 1816 (DB TT:344). Wit: Stephen C. ROZZELL, Samuel MURREY.

Bk:Pg: 2X:265   Date: 1 Nov 1818   RtCt: 28 Dec 1818
Conrad LICKEY & wife Margaret of Ldn to William LICKEY of Ldn. B/S of 54a where Conrad now lives on W side of road passing Coe's Mill to Lsbg. Wit: John SINCLAIR, John SILLMAN, George LICKEY, William CARR, Thos. GREGG. Delv. to Wm. LICKEY 11 Oct 1821.

Bk:Pg: 2X:267   Date: 28 Dec 1818   RtCt: 28 Dec 1818
Jacob FADELY & wife Mary/Polly of Ldn to John MONROE of Ldn. B/S of Lot #__ in Lsbg on W side of King St & S side of Cornwall St. (cnvy/b Jos. BENTLEY & wife Catharine in May 1814). Wit: Samuel CLAPHAM, John ROSE. Delv. to MONROE 1 Sep 1819.

Bk:Pg: 2X:268   Date: 20 Jun 1818   RtCt: 31 Dec 1818
William H. HOUGH, John SCHOOLEY & Daniel STONE (Exors of William HOUGH dec'd) of Ldn to Asa MOORE & Thomas PHILLIPS of Ldn. B/S of 53a (prch/o Mahlon ROACH) adj. __ McILHANEY. Delv. to PHILIPS 6 Jun 1826.

Bk:Pg: 2X:269   Date: 31 Dec 1818   RtCt: 31 Dec 1818
Jacob FADELY & wife Polly of Ldn to William COOKE, Maria E.
COOKE, Alexander M. BRISCOE, Matilda P. BRISCOE, Peyton
COOKE, Mary A. COOKE, Robert A LACEY, Westwood A. LACEY,
Armistead J. LACEY & Catharine E. LACEY. B/S of Lot #__ at
corner of King and Royal Sts in Lsbg (prch/o John MYERS & wife
Charlotte in 1810). Wit: William CARR, Patrick McINTYRE.

Bk:Pg: 2X:271   Date: 24 Dec 1818   RtCt: 1 Jan 1819
George TAVENDER & wife Sarah of Ldn to Jonathan CARTER of
Ldn. B/S of land where Jesse HARRIS formerly lived to include 178a
within limits of 230¼a. Wit: John McCORMICK, Patrick McINTYRE.
Delv. to CARTER 31 Aug 1820.

Bk:Pg: 2X:274   Date: 15 Aug 1817   RtCt: 24 Jan 1818
George TAVENDER Jr. to William BRONAUGH of Ldn. Trust for
debt to Hugh & James JOHNSTON using 268a. Wit: Jere. W.
BRONAUGH Jr., Jno. M. MONROE, Mahlon GREGG.

Bk:Pg: 2X:275   Date: 6 Jan 1819   RtCt: 6 Jan 1819
Thomas A. BROOKE of Md to Robert RUSSELL of Va. Release on
194a.

Bk:Pg: 2X:276   Date: 6 Jan 1819   RtCt: 6 Jan 1819
William WILDMAN & wife Mahal(e)y of Ldn to Daniel LOVETT of
Ldn. B/S of 1/9th of undivided 172½a (formerly of Richard CARTER
dec'd f/o Mahaley). Charles BALL, Samuel MURREY. Delv. to
LOVETT 14 Aug 1821.

Bk:Pg: 2X:278   Date: 9 Jan 1819   RtCt: 9 Jan 1819
Luke GOINGS to Joseph BEARD and Presley CORDELL. Trust for
debt to Jacob FADELY using 109a and 49a.

Bk:Pg: 2X:281   Date: 9 Jan 1819   RtCt: 9 Jan 1819
Enos WILDMAN & wife Jane of Ldn to Luke GOINGS of Ldn. B/S of
109a and 49a. Wit: John McCORMICK, Chas. B. BALL. Delv. pr
order 4 Dec 1834.

Bk:Pg: 2X:282   Date: 5 Jan 1819   RtCt: 8 Jan 1819
John R. COOKE & wife Maria P. of Berkley to John CARR of Ldn.
B/S of tract on NW side of Goose Creek bought from Stephen
COOKE & wife Catharine in Jul 1810, adj __ BERRY, Henry
LEFEVER. Wit: John WOLFFE, John S. POTTERFIELD. Delv. to
CARR 28 Sep 1821.

Bk:Pg: 2X:285   Date: 8 Jan 1819   RtCt: 9 Jan 1819
John Brewis STEVENS & wife Sarah of Ldn to James McDANIEL &
Archibald McDANIEL of Ldn. B/S of 71a (cnvy/b T. D. STEVENS)
adj Edward McDANIEL, Richard BROWN, William SMITH. Wit: Abiel
JENNERS, John H. McCABE. Delv. to James McDANIEL 2 Mar
1821.

Bk:Pg: 2X:286   Date: 8 Jan 1819   RtCt: 9 Jan 1819
John Brewis STEVENS & wife Sarah of Ldn to William SMITH of Ldn. B/S of 10a (cnvy/b Thomas Darnal STEVENS) adj William SMITH, Edward MCDANIEL, Robert BRADEN. Wit: Abiel JENNERS, John H. McCABE. Delv. to grantee 18 Mar 1820.

Bk:Pg: 2X:288   Date: 16 Aug 1817   RtCt: 11 Jan 1819
William COMPHER & wife Mary of Ldn to Simon YEACA of Ldn. B/S of 10a (allotted in div. of estate of William's father). Wit: John HAMILTON, Saml. LUCKETT. Delv. to YEACA 22 Oct 1819.

Bk:Pg: 2X:290   Date: 7 Nov 1818   RtCt: 11 Jan 1819
William MOXLEY & wife Jane of Hiland Co OH to Thomas R. MOTT of Lsbg. B/S of lot & house on NW side of Market St. in Lsbg (prch/o Ignatius NORRISS in Feb 1812, DB OO:443) and ½a (prch/o R. H. HENDERSON).

Bk:Pg: 2X:291   Date: 28 Nov 1818   RtCt: 11 Jan 1819
William T. BARRY & wife Catharine (formerly MASON) to Armistead T. MASON. B/S of Catharine's interest - Stephens Thomason MASON the young late of Ldn in will of Sept 1815 dev. brother Armistead T. MASON his interest in 510a 'Rasberry Plain' farm where mother now resides, cnvy/b uncle John T. MASON & his mother to Stephens with condition that should pay to his brother and sisters Catharine & Emily ¼ of worth. CoE taken in Fayette Co KY.

Bk:Pg: 2X:293   Date: 17 Feb 1818   RtCt: 11 Jan 1819
Daniel McCALISTER & wife Catharine of Louisville, KY to William GILMORE of Ldn. B/S of 82a (part of land William WRIGHT dec'd prch/o Exors of Geo. CARTER dec'd). Wit: John LITTLEJOHN, Thomas SANDERS, Presley CORDELL, Saml. M. EDWARDS. Delv. to GILMORE 13 Mar 1821.

Bk:Pg: 2X:295   Date: 11 Jan 1819   RtCt: 12 Jan 1819
Lewis P. W. BALCH (commr. for Ann VANHORN wd/o Garret VANHORNE dec'd & John VANHORNE, Mary VANHORNE & Betsy VANHORNE ch/o Garret) of Ldn to Garrett WALKER of Ldn. B/S of 13 1/3a (from Garret's share of father John VANHORNE dec'd land). Delv. to WALKER 27 Mar 1821.

Bk:Pg: 2X:296   Date: 13 Jan 1819   RtCt: 13 Jan 1819
Alexander CORDELL, Sanford RAMEY, Adam HOUSHOLDER, Mahlon JANNEY & Robert MOFFETT. Bond on CORDELL as constable.

Bk:Pg: 2X:297   Date: 9 Dec 1816.   RtCt: 12 Jan 1819
Benjamin SINCLAIR of Scott Co KY to John SINCLAIR Jr. of Scott Co KY. PoA.

Bk:Pg: 2X:298   Date: 26 Dec 1818   RtCt: 26 Dec 1818
Mahlon JANNEY & wife Rachel of Ldn to James SAUNDERS & Chas. DOUGLAS of Ldn. Trust for debt to Thomas R. MOTT using land (DB TT:344). Delv. to MOTT 20 Apr 1820.

Bk:Pg: 2X:299   Date: 2 Jan 1819   RtCt: 11 Jan 1819
Thomas SINCLAIR & George SINCLAIR of Ldn to Samuel LESLIE
& Joseph LESLIE of Ldn. B/S of 33a adj Samuel PURCEL, B.
LESLIE. Wit: Craven OSBURN, Bernard S. DUFFEY, John HOUGH,
David LOVETT, Edward SAUNDERS. Delv. to Saml. LESLIE 13 Nov
1820.

Bk:Pg: 2X:301   Date: 23 Dec 1818   RtCt: 11 Jan 1819
Catharine E. COOKE of Ldn to William GILMORE of Ldn. B/S of 13a
nr Tuscarora Creek between Gilmore's mill and land of Edmund J.
LEE, adj Samuel CARR. Wit: Britton SANDERS, Robert H.
SANDERS, Kitty E. COOKE, Henry S. COOKE. Delv. to GILMORE
13 Mar 1821.

Bk:Pg: 2X:302   Date: 9 Dec 1818   RtCt: 11 Jan 1819
Samuel HOGE and Lot JANNEY & wife Sophia of Ldn to Lewis P.
W. BALCH of Lsbg. Trust for debt to Edward M. COE & William COE
of Ldn using land and mill. Wit: William CARR, Thos. GREGG. Delv.
to Wm. L. COCKERILLE for Geo. CARTER on order of L. P. W.
BALCH filed DB XX:302 on 11 Dec 1820.

Bk:Pg: 2X:305   Date: 22 Sep 1818   RtCt: 11 Jan 1819
James SIMPSON & wife Elizabeth of Ldn to John SIMPSON of Ldn.
B/S of 37½a (from div. of lands of mother Mary SIMPSON dec'd).
Wit: Burr POWELL, A. GIBSON. Delv. to SIMPSON 16 Mar 1824.

Bk:Pg: 2X:307   Date: 4 Jan 1819   RtCt: 12 Jan 1819
Catharine E. COOKE (wd/o Stephen COOKE dec'd) of Ldn to John
R. COOKE of BerkVA. B/S of land from her dower. Wit: Britton
SANDERS, Robert H. SANDERS, Kitty Esten COOKE.

Bk:Pg: 2X:308   Date: 27 Aug 1818   RtCt: 14 Jan 1819
Nelson NORRIS of BaltMd to Fleet SMITH of Ldn. Trust for debt to
William NOLAND using 150a. Wit: Chas. G. ESKRIDGE, J. L.
DREAN, Alfred HARRISON, Saml. THOMPSON.

Bk:Pg: 2X:309   Date: 7 Jan 1819   RtCt: 18 Jan 1819
Levi WILLIAMS & wife Sarah of Ldn to David Fendall BEALL of Ldn.
B/S of 63a on NW fork of Goose Creek adj James BEANS, David
SMITH. Wit: David SMITH, Lewis GRIGSBY, Nathaniel GRIGSBY,
Notley C. WILLIAMS, Thos. GREGG. Delv. to grantee 16 Jan 1820.

Bk:Pg: 2X:311   Date: 19 Jan 1819   RtCt: 19 Jan 1819
Aaron SANDERS & wife Susanna of Ldn to Sarah CRAVEN of Ldn.
B/S of 80a on both sides of Limestone Run adj Gen. MASON. Wit:
Chas. BENNETT, William CARR. Delv. to CRAVEN 15 Jan 1821.

Bk:Pg: 2X:313   Date: 29 Dec 1818   RtCt: 19 Jan 1819
Isaac WRIGHT & wife Susanna of Ldn to William GILMORE of Ldn.
B/S of 5a. Wit: Presley CORDELL, Thomas SANDERS, Samuel
MURREY, Saml. M. EDWARDS, John McCORMICK. Delv. to
GILMORE 12 Mar 1821.

Bk:Pg: 2X:315   Date: 2 Oct 1818   RtCt: 19 Jan 1819
Isaac WRIGHT & wife Susan of Lsbg to William D. DRISH of Lsbg.
B/S of Lot #40 in Lsbg. Wit: Chas. ELGIN, Presley CORDELL, John
DRISH, Chas. G. ESKRIDGE, Samuel MURREY, John
McCORMICK. Delv. to grantee 19 Oct 1819.

Bk:Pg: 2X:316   Date: 8 Nov 1817   RtCt: 19 Jan 1819
John B. STEVENS & wife Sarah of Ldn to William NETTAL of Ldn.
B/S of 1a adj John F. SAPPINGTON, Edward DORSEY. Wit: Abiel
JENNERS, John H. McCABE. Del'v to Wm. NETTLE 19 Jun 1835.

Bk:Pg: 2X:318   Date: 29 Jul 1818   RtCt: 19 Jan 1819
Emanuel NEWCOMER & wife Catharine of Washington Co Md to
Chas. TURNER of Ldn. B/S of 16a adj James BEANS, James
CRAIG, David F. BEALE. Co E from BerkVa. Delv. to 13 Oct 1819.

Bk:Pg: 2X:319   Date: 10 Dec 1818   RtCt: 20 Jan 1819
Richard CHILTON & wife Eleanor of Campbell Co Va to William
PIGEON of Campbell Co Va. B/S of interest in estate of William
HOUGH dec'd (f/o Eleanor) and house & lot former property of John
WILLIAMS now in occupation of John SCHOOLEY and stable lot,
deed of trust by Daniel STONE.

Bk:Pg: 2X:321   Date: 10 Dec 1818   RtCt: 20 Jan 1819
William PIGEON & wife Mildred of Campbell Co Va to Richard
CHILTON of Campbell Co Va. B/S of all of the above.

Bk:Pg: 2X:323   Date: 4 Jan 1819   RtCt: 20 Jan 1819
Aaron MILLER & wife Rachel of Ldn to John JANNEY of Ldn. B/S of
97¾a from div. of estate of Reuben HIXSON dec'd. Wit: Samuel
HOUGH, John H. McCABE.

Bk:Pg: 2X:325   Date: 11 Mar 1818   RtCt: 21 Jan 1819
George JANNEY & wife Susannah of Ldn to James MACKLAN of
Ldn. B/S of 124¼a. Wit: William BRONAUGH, Francis W.
LUCKETT.

Bk:Pg: 2X:327   Date: 23 Jan 1819   RtCt: 23 Jan 1819
Benjamin WHITE & John NIXON (trustees of Joseph WHITE) to Levi
WHITE. Release of trust.

Bk:Pg: 2X:328   Date: 4 Jul 1818   RtCt: 23 Jan 1819
Charles VEALE of Ldn to daughter Catharine P. VEALE. Gift of
negro Cealia age 11y, Lucey age 10y and Mason age 8y, and farm
animals. Wit: Amos VEALE, Lewis STEELE. Delv. To Catharine P.
VEALE 20 Sep 1820.

Bk:Pg: 2X:328   Date: 23 Jan 1819   RtCt: 23 Jan 1819
Benjamin WHITE & John NIXON (trustee of Joseph WHITE) to
William WHITE. Release of trust. Delv. to Wm. WHITE 11 Sep 1820.

Bk:Pg: 2X:329   Date: 27 Feb 1818   RtCt: 25 Jan 1819
Sarah CALDWELL, Joseph CALDWELL & wife Eliza, William
CALDWELL, Mary CALDWELL and John CALDWELL of Ldn to
Sarah CRAVEN, William CRAVEN, Sophia V. CRAVEN, Samuel

CRAVEN and Sarah CRAVEN of Ldn. B/S of 26a adj A. T. MASON. Wit: Stephen C. ROSZEL, Patrick McINTYRE. Delv. to Sarah CRAVEN 15 Jan 1821.

Bk:Pg: 2X:331   Date: 8 Jun 1818   RtCt: 25 Jan 1819
Arthur WHITEHURST & wife Lucretia (late CRAVEN) of Albemarle Co Va to Sarah CRAVEN of Ldn. B/S of Lucretia's undivided share of land from estate of father Thomas CRAVEN dec'd. Wit: John W. CRAVEN, Wm. WERTENBAKER, Dabney C. GARTH. Delv. to Sarah CRAVEN 15 Jan 1821.

Bk:Pg: 2X:333   Date: 24 Jul 1818   RtCt: 28 Jan 1819
Barnet/Bernard HOUGH (Admr dbn of Patrick CAVANS dec'd) of Ldn to James W. HENSHAW of Ldn. B/S of lease by heirs of James HEREFORD dec'd on 1a between William CARR and Edward RINKER dec'd. From suit of John LITTLEJOHN vs. Bernard HOUGH Admr dbn of Patrick CAVANS dec'd. Wit: Chas. B. BALL, Wm. GILMORE, Charles GULLATT.

Bk:Pg: 2X:335   Date: 1 Jun 1818   RtCt: 28 Jan 1819
Dempsey CARTER of Ldn to John W. GRAYSON of Ldn. Trust for debt to Stephen McPHERSON using land where CARTER lives and will possess after his mother's death. Wit: Thos. GREEN, Mary BATES, Marthann BOYCE.

Bk:Pg: 2X:337   Date: 28 Jan 1819   RtCt: 28 Jan 1819
John CRIDLER & wife __ to Burr William HARRISON. Trust for debt to Thomas B. BEATTY using ½a and 1a. Wit: Presley CORDELL, James D. FRENCH, David SHAWEN.

Bk:Pg: 2X:339   Date: 28 Jan 1819   RtCt: 28 Jan 1819
Thomas B. BEATTY of Ldn to John CRIDLER of Ldn. B/S of 1a in Lsbg on Market St. adj James GARNER, Thomas R. MOTT. Wit: Burr W. HARRISON, Robert R. HOUGH, Isaac WRIGHT.

Bk:Pg: 2X:340   Date: 22 Sep 1818   RtCt: 29 Jan 1819
Aaron BOOTH & wife Sarah of Ldn to David MULL of Ldn. B/S of interest in house & lot devised by Margaret RIDENBAUGH to her daughter Margaret RIDENBAUGH and after death to her 4 other children (Sarah now Sarah BOOTH, Mary, George & Mahaly). Wit: Abiel JENNERS, John H. McCABE.

Bk:Pg: 2X:342   Date: 28 Dec 1818   RtCt: 29 Jan 1819
Wilson C. SELDON of Ldn to Everett SAUNDERS of Ldn. B/S of part of Lot #12 in Lsbg (previously leased) adj heirs of Peter BOSS dec'd.

Bk:Pg: 2X:343   Date: 27 Jan 1819   RtCt: 1 Feb 1819
Thomas CIMMINGS of Ldn to John NIXON of Ldn. B/S of 26a (allotment in div. of father's estate).

Bk:Pg: 2X:344   Date: 13 May 1818   RtCt: 4 Feb 1819
Henry JENKINS & wife Margaret of MontMd to George & James RUST of Ldn. B/S of 321a. Wit: Chas. THRIFT, Gustavus ELGIN, Robert ELGIN, John McCORMICK, Thos. GREGG.

Bk:Pg: 2X:346   Date: 10 Jul 1818   RtCt: 5 Feb 1819
Ailcy KENT of Ldn to daughter Elizabeth KENT. Gift of lot in Union, farm and household items. Wit: Ashford KENT, Thomas KENT.

Bk:Pg: 2X:347   Date: 19 Jan 1819   RtCt: 10 Feb 1819
Henry H. HAMILTON. Appointment by Governor as Notary Public. Delv. to HAMILTON 29 Jun 1821.

Bk:Pg: 2X:347   Date: 28 Nov 1818   RtCt: 8 Feb 1819
John T. MASON to Armistead T. MASON. B/S acquits Armistead of all payments due under will of Stephen T. MASON. Deed acknowledged in Fayette KY Ct.

Bk:Pg: 2X:349   Date: 6 Jan 1819   RtCt: 8 Feb 1819
Isaac S. WHITE & wife Mary M. of Washington Co Md to Armistead T. MASON of Ldn. B/S of 150a (10a exchanged with Mary MASON & Stephen T. MASON Jr. dec'd)

Bk:Pg: 2X:352   Date: 10 Feb 1819   RtCt: 10 Feb 1819
Joseph H. WRIGHT and Francis McKEMIE. Bond on WRIGHT as constable.

Bk:Pg: 2X:352   Date: 12 Sep 1818   RtCt: 11 Feb 1819
Thomas B. BEALE of Georgetown to niece Anne Beale Richards (d/o John ROSE) of Lsbg. Trust for her use of slaves for life at present in Georgetown of Samuel BIASS aged 27y, woman Lethe aged 20y and Sinah WILLIAMS age 21y. Wit: Jno. PETER. Delv. to George RICHARDS pr order 11 Apr 1837.

Bk:Pg: 2X:354   Date: 30 Jan 1819   RtCt: 11 Feb 1819
Members of Leesburg Fire Company: John MINES, Geo. RICHARDS, Wm. CHILTON, John McCORMICK, Saml. M. EDWARDS, L. P. W. BALCH, John MONROE, James COTT, David OGDEN, John HAMMERLY, Isaac HARRIS, Edw'd HAMMAT, George HEAD, Chas. B. BALL, Thomas BIRKBY, John B. RATTIE, Martin CORDELL, Joseph LAMBAG, Thos. McCOWAT, Saml. TUSTIN, John THOMAS, Jas. BROWN, R. H. HENDERSON, Danl. P. CONRAD, Aaron WILDMAN, Jno. HUMPHREYS, Saml. M. BOSS, Jno. J. MATHIAS, P. SAUNDERS, Martin KITZMILLER, Presley FOLEY, Fielding BROWN, Duskin MONROE, Joseph HILLIARD, Giles HAMMATT, Samuel MILLER, Addison MINES, Thomas CLAGGETT, John BURTON, Henry PEERS, Benj'a MAULLSBY, Jno. T. WILSON, Nathan MUSGROVE Jr., Josiah L. DREAN, Joshua RILEY, Joshua DUNICKS, Peter BENEDUM Jr., Henry BENEDUM, William CEDARS, John MOORE, James GARNER, Samuel MURREY, Walter BILLINGSLEY, Aaron SCHOOLEY, Robt. R. HOUGH, Thos. MORRALLEE, Presley

CORDELL, John GRAY, Jacob MARTIN, Thos. R. MOTT, John W. DREAN, Henry T. HARRISON, Isaac WEST, Wm. HOPKINS, Hezekiah PERRY, R. H. GOVER, Thos. WILLIAMS, John MARTIN, Wm. J. HAWLEY, John S. EDWARDS, Jas. MANSFIELD, Thos. B. BEATTY, Merrit TARLTON, Fleet SMITH, Jas. W. HENCHER, John HOUGH, James HAMILTON Jr., H. H. HAMILTON, Saml. C. B. McCLELLAND.

Bk:Pg: 2X:355   Date: 21 Jan 1819   RtCt: 8 Feb 1819
Charles VEALE & wife Catherine to William CULLISON. BoS for slave for life negro boy Moses. Wit: Ger'd L. W. HUNT, John ROLLISSON.

Bk:Pg: 2X:355   Date: 20 Jun 1818   RtCt: 17 Feb 1819
Thomas GREGG to Samuel GREGG. A/L of 50a where Nimrod GRACAN now lives on road leading to North fork meeting house, adj John WRIGHT, Henry FOX, P. McINTYRE. Delv. pr order 5 Mar 1822.

Bk:Pg: 2X:356   Date: 3 Feb 1819   RtCt: 8 Feb 1819
John W. VIOLET of Ldn to James BOLES of Ldn. B/S of 50a on Pantherskin branch (part of estate of John VIOLET dec'd allotted to sister Juliet Ann VIOLET). Delv. to BOLES 27 Jan 1836.

Bk:Pg: 2X:358   Date: 8 Feb 1819   RtCt: 8 Feb 1819
Isaac NICKOLS & James LOVE & wife Susanna (Exors of Henry NICKOLS dec'd who was s/o Thomas NICKOLS of Newcastle Co Del) of Ldn to Nathan GREGG of Ldn. B/S of 125a (of Henry NICKOLS dec'd) adj James LOVE, Rebecca LOVE, Thomas NICKOLS. Delv. to GREGG 24 Aug 1820.

Bk:Pg: 2X:359   Date: 8 Feb 1819   RtCt: 8 Feb 1819
Isaac NICKOLS & James LOVE & wife Susanna (Exors of Henry NICKOLS dec'd) of Ldn to Thomas NICHOLS of Ldn. B/S of 114½a (Henry NICKOLS dec'd purchased of Moses CADWALADER). Delv. to Thos. NICHOLLS 26 Jan 1829.

Bk:Pg: 2X:361   Date: 8 Feb 1819   RtCt: 8 Feb 1819
Isaac NICKOLS & James LOVE & wife Susanna (Exors of Henry NICKOLS dec'd) of Ldn to Rebecca LOVE of Ldn. B/S of 142a (of Henry's estate) adj Wm. SMITH, Nathan GREGG.

Bk:Pg: 2X:362   Date: 8 Feb 1819   RtCt: 8 Feb 1819
Conrad BITZER, John BROWN, Nathan GREGG & Thomas NICKOLS of Ldn. Agreement on land boundaries.

Bk:Pg: 2X:363   Date: 26 Jun 1818   RtCt: 8 Feb 1819
John MATHIAS of Ldn to Thomas KIDWELL of Ldn. B/S of 11a Lot #19 on W side of short hill and 87a part of Lot #21, #22, #22, #24 & #25. Delv. to KIDWELL 16 Jul 1822.

Bk:Pg: 2X:365   Date: 29 Dec 1818   RtCt: 8 Feb 1819
Ann GIBSON of Ldn to Amos GIBSON of Ldn. PoA. Wit: Joseph CARR, Francis W. LUCKETT.

Bk:Pg: 2X:366   Date: 8 Feb 1819   RtCt: 8 Feb 1819
John BROWN & wife Ann of Ldn to David REESE of Ldn. Trust for debt to Thos. NICHOLS using 114½a. Wit: Thomas FOUCH, Stephen C. ROSZEL. Delv. to REESE 25 Jul 1823.

Bk:Pg: 2X:368   Date: 8 Jan 1819   RtCt: 8 Feb 1819
Yeoman Benjamin BROOKE & wife Hannah of Ldn to Isaac NICKOLS Jr. and yeoman Amos GIBSON of Ldn. Trust for debt to Ann GIBSON and William GIBSON using 126a. Wit: Joseph CARR, Francis W. LUCKETT.

Bk:Pg: 2X:370   Date: 8 Feb 1819   RtCt: 8 Feb 1819
Thomas NICHOLS & wife Leatitia of Ldn to John BROWN of Ldn. B/S of 114½a (cnvy/b Moses CADWALLADER to Henry NICKOLS dec'd). Wit: Thomas FOUCH, Stephen C. ROSZEL.

Bk:Pg: 2X:372   Date: 1 Aug 1818   RtCt: 8 Feb 1819
John B. STEVENS of Wtfd to Asa MOORE of Wtfd. Trust for debt to Robert BRADEN, John MORGAN & Joseph EACHES (trading under Braden, Morgan & Co.) using 84a. Wit: John BRADEN, Burr BRADEN, Sanford EDMONDS, George W. HENRY, Thomas PHILLIPS.

Bk:Pg: 2X:374   Date: 30 Nov 1818   RtCt: 9 Feb 1819
James M. ROBERDEAU & wife Mildred L. of Ffx to Richard COCHRAN & Oliver DENHAM of Mdbg. B/S of Lot #22 in Mdbg (owned by late Edmond DENNY). Wit: Jas. L. TRIPLETT, M. L. TRIPLETT, Alex'r WAUGH. Delv pr order filed 10 Nov 1828.

Bk:Pg: 2X:376   Date: 26 Dec 1818   RtCt: 23 Feb 1819
Jacob HOUSER & wife Abigail of Ldn to Cornelius SHAWEN, John KALB, Absalom KALB, Presley WILLIAMS, James WHITE, William COOK, John SANDERS and Aaron MILLER (trustees of Methodist Episcopal Church). B/S of 1a (HOUSER bought from Isaac HOUGH) adj William WOLFORD.

Bk:Pg: 2X:379   Date: 31 Mar 1819   RtCt: 3 Mar 1819
William D. MONROE of Ldn to Arthur GARNER (in right of William's wife Kitty MONROE late Kitty RINKER). Trust of interest in estate of Edward RINKER dec'd. Wit: Josias CLAPHAM, Joseph WILDMAN, Jno. N. BINNS.

Bk:Pg: 2X:380   Date: 2 Mar 1819   RtCt: 4 Mar 1819
Lindsa THOMAS & wife Nancy of Madison Co Va to Edward HAMMATT of Ldn. B/S of ½ of lot cnvy/b M. WEATHERBY and ½ lot (cnvy/b Benjamin SHREVE to Benjamin WOODLEY then conveyed to HAMMATT then to THOMAS) on road from Lsbg to Haymarket adj Benjamin WOOD, Benjamin WOLDLEY, John LITTLEJOHN. Delv. to HAMMETT 7 Aug 1820.

Bk:Pg: 2X:381   Date: 25 Jan 1819   RtCt: 25 Jan 1819
William NOLAND of Ldn to Richard BROOK of FredMd. Release of trust for debt to Samuel B. CLAGETT & Alexander NEILE on 140a. Wit: John J. HARDING, Burr W. HARRISON, Henry T. HARRISON.

Bk:Pg: 2X:383   Date: 4 Sep 1818   RtCt: 4 Mar 1819
James W. HENSHAW & wife Margaret of Ldn to Sampson BLINCOE of Ldn. Trust for debt to Thomas MORALLEE and Jacob THOMAS (as security for HENSHAW as Admr of Edward RINKER dec'd) using interest in RINKER's estate, animals and household items. Wit: John CRAMWELL, Thomas BIRKBY, John DREAN.

Bk:Pg: 2X:385   Date: 8 Jan 1819   RtCt: 8 Mar 1819
Thomson MASON. Col for male slave Philip abt 40y dark colour abt 6' acquired by marriage, Molly abt 40y a bright mulatto abt 5' 5" acquired by marriage, Moses abt 12y a mulatto abt 4'9" or 10" acquired by marriage.

Bk:Pg: 2X:386   Date: 26 Feb 1819   RtCt: 8 Mar 1819
Thomson MASON. Col for slave Harriot a small girl abt 10y a bright mulatto abt 4' 4" acquired by marriage.

Bk:Pg: 2X:386   Date: 18 Nov 1818   RtCt: 8 Mar 1819
Conrad FURST/FEARST & wife Betsey late Betsey WILSON of Athens Co OH to Peter PHILLIPS of Athens Co OH. PoA to receive money from Amos HARVEY of Ldn (revoking PoA to Nicholas PHILLIPS for sale of estate of Ebenezer WILSON dec'd late of Ldn). Wit: Wm. HARPER, Charles HARPER.

Bk:Pg: 2X:387   Date: 16 Nov 1818   RtCt: 8 Mar 1819
David McDONALD & wife Betsey late Betsey WILSON, Hannah WILSON and Polly WILSON of Athens Co OH (heirs of Thomas WILSON dec'd late of Athens Co OH and formerly of Ldn) to Peter PHILLIPS of Athens Co OH. PoA to receive money from Hannah WILSON of Ldn (exor of Ebenezer WILSON late of Ldn). Wit: Henry BARTLETT, Conrad FARST.

Bk:Pg: 2Y:001   Date: 8 Mar 1819   RtCt: 12 Apr 1819
Elizabeth DULANY of AlexDC to James H. DULANY of Ldn. PoA to deal with 250a in Ldn late in possession of Thomas CLAGETT. Wit: P. R. FENDALL Jr, Hugh N. PAGE, Jno. MASON.

Bk:Pg: 2Y:002   Date: 6 Mar 1819   RtCt: 6 Apr 1819
Merrit TARLTON of Lsbg to Macka TARLTON of Lsbg. Trust for debt to Abiel JENNERS of Ldn and James WOOD of Lsbg using household items. Wit: Rich'd H. LEE, Mason PIGGOT, Thomas MORRIS.

Bk:Pg: 2Y:003   Date: 9 Nov 1813   RtCt: 9 Mar 1819
William NOLAND (trustee of Colin AULD & James SANDERSON) to Thomas SWANN. Release. Wit: Colin AULD.

Bk:Pg: 2Y:003   Date: 6 Apr 1819   RtCt: 6 Apr 1819
John SHAW of Lsbg to daughter Catharine SHAW. Gift of house & lot on King St. in Lsbg at present occupied by Saml. B. T. CALDWELL (lately prch/o George & James RUST). Wit: John SHAW Jr. Delv. to Jno. SHAW Sr. 5 Aug 1819.

Bk:Pg: 2Y:004   Date: 6 Apr 1819   RtCt: 6 Apr 1819
John SHAW of Lsbg to son John SHAW Jr. Gift of brick house & lot on SE corner of Loudoun & King Sts in Lsbg adj Dr. John T. WILSON. Wit: Catharine SHAW. Delv. to Jno. SHAW Sr. 5 Aug 1819

Bk:Pg: 2Y:005   Date: 6 Apr 1819   RtCt: 6 Apr 1819
John SHAW of Lsbg to his children Mary SHAW, Sidney SHAW and Elizabeth Ann SHAW. Gift of brick house and wooden dwelling house presently under lease to Joseph HILLIARD in Lsbg. Wit: Catharine SHAW, John SHAW Jr. Delv. to John SHAW Sr. 5 Aug 1819.

Bk:Pg: 2Y:005   Date: ___   RtCt: 12 Jan 1819
Enoch MASON (of StafVa attorney for William Dudley DIGGS) to Hamilton ROGERS. Release of trust. Delv. to Thos. ROGERS 29 Oct 1825.

Bk:Pg: 2Y:006   Date: 22 Mar 1819   RtCt: 29 Mar 1819
Abner HUMPHREY & wife Mary of Ldn to John Gill HUMPHREY of Ldn. B/S of 114a adj Joseph FRED, heirs of Samuel TORBERT dec'd, William GRAY, Stephen GREGG, John RALPH, David THARP, John CHAMBLIN. Wit: Benjamin GRAYSON, John W. GRAYSON. Delv. to HUMPHREY 13 Feb 1822.

Bk:Pg: 2Y:008   Date: 31 Oct 1818   RtCt: 31 Mar 1819
James VIOLETT & wife Sarah of Ldn to Amos DONHAM [DENHAM] of Ldn. B/S of 1/9th undivided share of L/L late property of Elijah VIOLETT dec'd br/o James. Wit: Wm. BRONAUGH, Francis W. LUCKETT.

Bk:Pg: 2Y:010   Date: 15 Mar 1819   RtCt: 9 Apr 1819
Martin BRENT of Ldn to Hiram SEATON of Ldn. B/S of 15a (prch/o Thomas LEWIS). Wit: Charles BENNETT.

Bk:Pg: 2Y:011   Date: 3 Apr 1819   RtCt: 5 Apr 1819
Benjamin GRUBB of Ldn to John GRUBB of Ldn. B/S of interest in 3a bought in partnership former property of Jonah HAGUE dec'd. Wit: Adam HOUSHOLDER, Presley WILLIAMS.

Bk:Pg: 2Y:012   Date: 15 Sep 1818   RtCt: Apr 1819
David JANNEY & wife Elizabeth of Ldn to Lewis COLE of Ldn. B/S of ½a Lots #10 & #11 in Wtfd. Wit: Abiel JENNERS, John H. McCABE. Delv. to COLE 5 Dec 1820.

Bk:Pg: 2Y:014   Date: 12 Mar 1819   RtCt: 12 Mar 1819
Lewis P. W. BALCH (as commr.) of Lsbg to Hannah JANNEY of Ldn. B/S of 1/6th part of 162a (to Elizabeth as heir of Stacey

JANNEY dec'd - interest of Jonah TAVENDER, Lettaria, Jonathan, Stacey, Lot, Mahlon, Hannah, Sarah & Jesse TAVENER ch/o said Jonah his late wife Elizabeth). Delv pr order 23 Dec 1829.

Bk:Pg: 2Y:015   Date: 12 Mar 1819   RtCt: 12 Mar 1819
Hannah JANNEY of Ldn to Jonah TAVENER in own right and as guardian of Maria, Jonathan, Stacey, Lot, Mahlon, Hannah, Jonah & Jesse TAVENER) of Ldn. Trust for debt to Lewis P. W. BALCH of Lsbg using above land. Delv. pr order filed 4 Apr 1837.

Bk:Pg: 2Y:017   Date: 26 Dec 1818   RtCt: 19 Mar 1819
Samuel TAYLOR & wife Ann to Wm. H. HOUGH & Asa MOORE. Trust for debt to Upton REED of BaltMd using 104a adj John TAYLOR. Wit: Abiel JENNERS, John H. McCABE. Delv. to trustee 1 Jan 1820.

Bk:Pg: 2Y:019   Date: 24 Feb 1819   RtCt: 31 Mar 1819
Joseph STEER & wife Sarah of Wtfd to William PAXSON Jr of Wtfd. B/S of lot in Wtfd conveyed to STEER by Anthony P. GOVER adj Richard CHILTON. Wit: Abiel JENNERS, John H. McCABE. Delv. to PAXSON 22 Dec 1821.

Bk:Pg: 2Y:021   Date: 1 Apr 1819   RtCt: 2 Apr 1819
Frederick HENSHA/HANASHY & wife Catharine of Ldn to John Stone MARLOW of Ldn. Trust for debt to Erasmus WEST & Henry FRAZIER using land on Potomac. Wit: Jno. J. MATHIAS, Lee DURHAM, Josiah L. DREAN, Stephen C. ROSZEL. Patrick McINTYRE.

Bk:Pg: 2Y:023   Date: 9 Jan 1819   RtCt: April 1819
Benjamin BROOKE & wife Hannah of Ldn to Jacob SILCOTT of Ldn. B/S of 65a on S fork of Beaverdam (prch/o William HARNED), part of 'Butterlands' tract, adj Isaac COWGILL, Samuel DUNKIN. Wit: Joseph CARR, Francis W. LUCKETT. Delv to SILCOTT 4 Mar 1833.

Bk:Pg: 2Y:025   Date: 23 Jan 1819   RtCt: 8 Mar 1819
Thomas LESLIE, Josiah WHITE Jr., Samuel PURCEL Jr. and Craven OSBURNE (trustees of Town of Hllb) to Thomas MARKS of Ldn. B/S of Lots #17, #18 & #19 in Hillsboro on road leading to Keye's Ferry. Wit: Jesse SILCOTT, Richard ROACH, Isaac CAMP. Delv. to R. H. HENDERSON 27 Apr 1821.

Bk:Pg: 2Y:027   Date: 19 Mar 1818   RtCt: Apr 1819
Robert BRADEN & James MOORE of Ldn to Amos JANNEY of Ldn. B/S of 86 (from trust of Joseph DAVIS dec'd to BRADEN & MOORE) adj Peter SAUNDERS, Beaverdam. Wit: L. DULANEY, J. H. McCABE, Noble S. BRADEN. Delv. to JANNEY 2 Sep 1819.

Bk:Pg: 2Y:029   Date: 1 Apr 1819   RtCt: 2 Apr 1819
Frederick HENSHA/HANDSHY & wife Catharine of Ldn to Erasmus WEST & Henry FRAZIER of FredMd. B/S of part of tract prch/o John HOPKINS adj Potomac, Waltman's mill (reserving 1a for HENSHA).

Wit: Jno. J. MATHIAS, L. W. DURHAM, Josiah L. DREAN, Stephen C. ROSZEL, Patrick McINTYRE. Delv. to Corbin WEST 8 Ma_ 1825.

Bk:Pg: 2Y:032 Date: 16 May 1817 RtCt: 8 Mar 1819
Samuel WILSON of Harpers Ferry, JeffVa to Amos HARVEY of Ldn. B/S of land Samuel entitled to as heir in will of Ebenezer WILSON dec'd late of Ldn entitled after death of widow Hannah. Wit: Jos. D'BELL, George GIDEON, Peter GIDEON.

Bk:Pg: 2Y:033 Date: 21 May 1816 RtCt: 8 Apr 1819
Abiel JENNERS & wife Deborah of Ldn to Henry OREM of Ldn. B/S of 102a held by OREM under lease from George Wm. FAIRFAX dec'd conveyed to JENNERS. Wit: Robert BRADEN, John H. McCABE.

Bk:Pg: 2Y:035 Date: 21 Mar 1819 RtCt: 10 Apr 1819
Sampson BLINCOE & R. H. HENDERSON of Ldn (under decree in suit of William MOXLEY & wife agst Exor of Daniel LOSH) to John GRAY of Ldn. B/S of lot in Lsbg on King St adj William D. DRISH, John J. HARDING, Samuel MILLER, John MINES, Thomas MORALEE.

Bk:Pg: 2Y:036 Date: 9 Apr 1819 RtCt: 9 Apr 1819
William H. LANE of Ldn to William NOLAND of Ldn. B/S of 377a on both sides of little river turnpike adj __ ROSZEL, __ JAMES. Delv. to grantee 20 Oct 1820.

Bk:Pg: 2Y:038 Date: __ 1819 RtCt: 6 Mar 1819
James FARQUHAR of Ldn to James MOORE of Ldn. B/S of Lots #18 & #19 in new addition to Wtfd adj MOORE's other lots. Delv. pr order filed 9 Jul 1830.

Bk:Pg: 2Y:040 Date: 27 Mar 1819 RtCt: 12 Apr 1819
Thomas HUMPHREY of Ldn to William TAYLOR of Ldn. B/S of 1a nr foot of blue ridge adj Marcus HUMPHREY, Thos. HUMPHREY. Wit: John LOVE, David JAMES, Morris OSBURNE. Delv. to TAYLOR 11 Oct 1819.

Bk:Pg: 2Y:041 Date: 31 Aug 1818 RtCt: 8 Mar 1819
John MILLER & wife Catharine of Fqr to Adam MILLER & Jesse MILLER. B/S of Catharine's interest of 1/8th estate devised by Peter MILLER Sr. to wife Catharine MILLER (except that which she has already relinquished to Aaron, John, Daniel, Adam & Jesse MILLER). Delv. to Adam MILLER 14 Aug 1820.

Bk:Pg: 2Y:043 Date: 2 Aug 1818 RtCt: 8 Mar 1819
Aaron MILLER & wife Rachel of Ldn to Adam MILLER & Jesse MILLER of Ldn. B/S of Aaron's 1/8th interest in estate of Peter MILLER Sr to his wife Catharine during her lifetime. Wit: Robert BRADEN, John H. McCABE. Delv. to Adam MILLER 14 Aug 1820.

Bk:Pg: 2Y:046 Date: 27 Mar 1819 RtCt: 27 Mar 1819
Jonah SANDS & wife Hester of Ldn and Hannah JANNEY of Ldn. Partition of 162a held by Stacey JANNEY dec'd late of Ldn with

101a to Jonah and 60a to Hannah. Wit: Patrick McINTYRE, Chas. B. BALL.

Bk:Pg: 2Y:048   Date: 11 Feb 1818   RtCt: 12 Oct 1818
William GHEEN & wife Narrissa to Thomas GREGG. LS of 50a (15 in timber). Wit: Hugh RODGERS, Charlotte GREE, Wm. H. HANDY, Hamilton RODGERS, Samuel GREGG. Delv. to Henry BROWN pr order filed DB YY:48 on 25 Jan 1820.

Bk:Pg: 2Y:050   Date: 24 Nov 1818   RtCt: 11 Mar 1819
Stephen McPHERSON Jr. & wife Cecilia of Ldn to John MARKS of Ldn. B/S of 161a (cnvy/b Isaiah MARKS to McPHERSON) adj Isaiah B. BEANS. Wit: Benjamin GRAYSON, Notley C. WILLIAMS.

Bk:Pg: 2Y:052   Date: 4 May 1818   RtCt: 8 Mar 1819
John SINCLAIR & wife Susannah of Ldn to James SWART of Ldn. B/S of 63a (prch/o Levi BARTON in 1815) on little river. Wit: James SINCLAIR, Esther SINCLAIR, Zanada FOWLES, Abner GIBSON, Francis W. LUCKETT.

Bk:Pg: 2Y:054   Date: 6 Mar 1819   RtCt: 10 Mar 1819
Andrew FINITY/FENTON Jr. of Ldn to Amos DENHAM of Ldn. B/S of his interest in the reversion of his part of 183a lately the property of his grandfather John VIOLETT dec'd subject to L/L by Elijah VIOLETT. Wit: Burr POWELL, A. GIBSON.

Bk:Pg: 2Y:055   Date: 5 Feb 1819   RtCt: 27 Mar 1819
Jonah SANDS & wife Esther of Ldn to William NICHOLS of Ldn. B/S of 66a on NW fork of Goose Creek adj John FREY, Hamilton RODGERS, Joseph TAVENER, James HATCHER dec'd. Wit: William BROWN, Hamilton ROGERS, Bernard TAYLOR, Chas. B. BALL, Pat'k McINTYRE. Delv. to Wm. NICHOLS 7 Aug 1833.

Bk:Pg: 2Y:058   Date: 15 Apr 1817   RtCt: 29 Mar 1819
Thomas SWAN of AlexDC to Jesse RICE of Ldn. B/S of 35a adj reps of Wm. MAINS. Wit: George D. SWEARINGER, Geo. C. MAUND, John W. LITTLEJOHN, Chas. G. ESKRIDGE. Delv. to RICE 20 May 1820.

Bk:Pg: 2Y:059   Date: 11 Mar 1817   RtCt: 30 Mar 1819
George JANNEY & wife Susannah of Ldn to Edward CARTER of Ldn. B/S of 36a. Wit: William BRONAUGH, Francis W. LUCKETT. Delv. to CARTER 2 Sep 1819.

Bk:Pg: 2Y:062   Date: 1 Sep 1818   RtCt: 13 Mar 1819
John DRISH & wife Eleanor of Ldn to William D. DRISH of Ldn. B/S of house & lot on King St in Lsbg adj John GRAY, John J. HARDING, Charles DRISH (cnvy/b Charles BINNS trustee of Rosanna HOUGH m/o Thomas & John HOUGH – DB PP:281 & 481). Delv to DRISH 8 Oct 1833.

Bk:Pg: 2Y:063   Date: 15 Mar 1819   RtCt: 17 Mar 1819
Samuel HOUGH Jr. of Ldn to Peter SANDERS of Ldn. B/S of 180a on Beaverdam creek (dev. Saml by is mother Lydia HOUGH) adj

Robert BRADEN, Michael COOPER, Margaret SANDERS, Joseph POSTON Jr. Wit: Abiel JENNERS, John H. McCABE.

Bk:Pg: 2Y:066   Date: 25 Apr 1818   RtCt: 19 Mar 1819
William H. HANDY & wife Eleanor of Ldn to James MOUNT of Ldn. B/S of 147¼a on Goose Creek. Wit: William BRONAUGH, A. GIBSON. Delv. to HANDY 7 Oct 1823.

Bk:Pg: 2Y:068   Date: 9 Sep 1818   RtCt: 9 Apr 1819
Daniel MILLER & wife Mary of Culpeper Co Va to Margaret SAUNDERS of Ldn. B/S of 16a on Katocton creek. Wit: John H. McCABE, Abiel JENNERS.

Bk:Pg: 2Y:070   Date: 8 Jan 1819   RtCt: Apr 1819
Ann GIBSON, William GIBSON & Solomon GIBSON (heirs of James GIBSON dec'd late of Ldn) to Benjamin BROOKE of Ldn. B/S of 126a (including 4a granted to James by will of mother Alice GIBSON) on Pantherskin branch adj Moses GIBSON original line, John GIBSON's heirs. Wit: Joseph CARR, Francis W. LUCKETT. Delv. to BROOKE 2 Sep 1823.

Bk:Pg: 2Y:072   Date: 25 Apr 1818   RtCt: 19 Mar 1819
James MOUNT & wife Hannah of Ldn to William H. HANDY of Ldn. B/S of 147¼a on Goose Creek (allotted in div. of estate of John HANDY dec'd in right of his wife) adj Points OWSLEY. Wit: William BRONAUGH, A. GIBSON. Delv. to HANDY 11 Oct 1823.

Bk:Pg: 2Y:074   Date: 24 Nov 1818   RtCt: Apr 1819
Stephen McPHERSON & wife Cecilia of Ldn to John MARKS of Ldn. B/S of 26a (cnvy/b Isaiah MARKS & wife Elizabeth). Wit: Benjamin GRAYSON, Notley C. WILLIAMS.

Bk:Pg: 2Y:077   Date: 7 Apr 1819   RtCt: 8 Apr 1819
John NEWTON & wife Harriet of Lsbg to John GRAY of Lsbg. B/S of 1a nr Lsbg adj GRAY on W side of King St. Wit: John ROSE, John McCORMICK.

Bk:Pg: 2Y:079   Date: 14 Jan 1819   RtCt: 31 Mar 1819
Jozabed WHITE of Ldn to William H. HANDY of Ldn. Trust for debt to Benjamin BRADFIELD & Emanuel NEWCOMER of Ldn using 58a.

Bk:Pg: 2Y:081   Date: 28 Jan 1819   RtCt: 12 Apr 1819
Anthony P. GOVER & wife Sarah of AlexDC to Joseph STEER of Ldn. B/S of lot in Wtfd (cnvy/b Levi JAMES) adj Eleanor HOUGH, E. DORSEY. Wit: Amos ALEXANDER, Jno. PELLIMIX.

Bk:Pg: 2Y:085   Date: 9 Dec 1818   RtCt: 8 Mar 1819
Joseph CARR of Ldn to Samuel SINGLETON, Uriah GLASCOCK, James WORNEL & William MORGAN (trustees of Goose Creek Baptist Church at Upperville). B/S of 1a on N side of turnpike road from Ashby's gap to Alexandria. Wit: Peter C. RUST, Reuben TRIPLETT, Caldwell CARR, John JAMES, Sydnor BAILEY, Wm. GILMORE, Benj. BROOKE.

Bk:Pg: 2Y:086 Date: 1 Apr 1819 RtCt: 5 Apr 1819
Barton EWERS & wife Rachel of Ldn to John MARKS of Ldn. B/S of 16a adj Joshua GREGG, Thomas JONES, Benjamin JACKSON, Sam WILLIAMS. Wit: William POWELL, Amy MELLLIN, Malinda JURY, Benjamin GRAYSON, John W. GRAYSON.

Bk:Pg: 2Y:089 Date: 10 Apr 1818 RtCt: 31 Mar 1819
William FULKERSON & Amelia FULKERSON of Ldn to Mandley TAYLOR of FredVa. B/S of 19¼a nr Upperville. Wit: Sydnor BAILEY, Reubin TRIPLETT, Benjamin TRIPLETT, Cuthbert POWELL, Joseph CARR.

Bk:Pg: 2Y:091 Date: 24 Nov 1818 RtCt: 13 Mar 1819
Enoch FRANCIS & wife Nancy of Ldn to Silas REESE of Ldn. B/S of several adj lots totaling 325a (cnvy/b Peter HARBOUR in Apr 1796). Wit: Jno. MATHIAS, John DULIN, Wm. SMARR, Samuel MURREY, Thos. FOUCH. Delv. to REES 26 Oct 1819.

Bk:Pg: 2Y:095 Date: 15 Mar 1819 RtCt: 22 Mar 1819
Peter SANDERS & wife Ann of Ldn to William H. HOUGH & David SHAWEN of Ldn. Trust for debt to Samuel HOUGH Jr., Lydia HOUGH, Mary HOUGH & Sarah HOUGH of Ldn using 180a on Beaverdam adj Joseph POSTON. Wit: Abiel JENNERS, John H. McCABE. Delv. to David SHAWEN on 26 Oct 1821.

Bk:Pg: 2Y:100 Date: 19 Apr 1819 RtCt: 19 Apr 1819
Robert H. GOVER of Lsbg to Joseph WILLIAMS. Trust for debt using household items. Wit: Geo. HEAD, Thos. S. W. BOYD, C. SUTHERLAND.

Bk:Pg: 2Y:101 Date: 27 Jan 1819 RtCt: 12 Apr 1819
William D. DRISH & wife Harriet of Ldn to Richard H. HENDERSON of Ldn. B/S of lot on Cornwall St. in Lsbg adj HENDERSON, Francis TRIPLETT. Wit: John ROSE, Chas. B. BALL.

Bk:Pg: 2Y:102 Date: 14 Apr 1819 RtCt: 6 May 1819
John MARTIN of Lebanon, OH to George RICORD of Ldn. Release of mortgage of 1814 on 130a.

Bk:Pg: 2Y:103 Date: 20 Feb 1819 RtCt: 12 Apr 1819
Annah GALLEHER of Ldn to John JOHNSON of Ldn. B/S of ¼a (cnvy/b father William GALLEHER & wife Mary in 1812) adj Isaac BROWN, William GALLEHER, James REED, Caleb N. GALLEHER. Wit: Seth SMITH, David GALLEHER, C. VANDEVENTER, John H. EVANS. Delv. to JOHNSTON pr order filed DB DDD:15 on 17 May 1822.

Bk:Pg: 2Y:104 Date: 25 Mar 1819 RtCt: 12 Apr 1819
Jonah TAVENER of Ldn to Benjamin WALKER, Stephen DANIEL, Joseph GARRETT, James BROWN, Gabriel McGEATH, James McGEATH, Stephen McPHERSON, Levi TATE, Isaac NICKOLS Jr., Samuel NICHOLS Jr., Stephen McGEATH, George TAVENER Jr., John GREGG, Asa TRAHERN, Johnathan EWERS, Garrett

WALKER, Johnathan REID, Joshu[a] PANCOAST & Isaac NICKOLS Sr. (as trustees of school) of Ldn. B/S of schoolhouse lot reserving use of the lot. Wit: Samuel TRAHERN, Reuben TRIPLETT Jr., Joseph HAMPTON.

Bk:Pg: 2Y:106   Date: 10 Oct 1818   RtCt: 12 Apr 1819
Jonathan CARTER & wife Elizabeth of Ldn to Francis W. LUCKETT of Ldn. Trust for debt to George LOVE of Fqr (trustee for the benefit of Mary LOVE wife and Martha & Jane H. LOVE d/o Augusta LOVE) using 87½a. Wit: Thomas GREGG, Leven LUCKETT. Delv. to LUCKETT 30 Jun 1824.

Bk:Pg: 2Y:108   Date: 8 Apr 1819   RtCt: 27 Apr 1819
John W. GRAYSON to Stephen GREGG of Ldn. Release of trust for debt to Stephen McPHERSON Jr. Wit: Wm. R. COMBS, Jno. L. GILL, L. R. MOUNT.

Bk:Pg: 2Y:110   Date: 3 May 1819   RtCt: 8 May 1819
James W. HANCHER (Admr dbnwwa of Edward RINKER dec'd – decree in MILLER & others vs MONROE & wife dated Dec 1818) of Ldn to John FICHTER of Ldn. B/S of land (Lot #7 in div.) leased by Patrick CAVAN of James HEREFORD dated Aug 1798. Wit: Presley CORDELL, Henry CRANE, John MARTIN.

Bk:Pg: 2Y:111   Date: 10 Oct 1818   RtCt: 12 Apr 1819
David CARTER to Francis W. LUCKETT. Trust for debt to George LOVE (trustee for the benefit of Mary LOVE wife and Martha, Sarah & Jane H. LOVE daus. of Augustine LOVE) using 125a. Wit: John SINCLAIR, Johnathan CARTER, August'e LOVE. Delv. to LUCKETT 30 Jan 1824.

Bk:Pg: 2Y:113   Date: 22 Mar 1819   RtCt: 12 Apr 1819
Mandley TAYLOR of Frederick to Cuthbert POWELL of Ldn. B/S of 4a adj TAYLOR, POWELL, Joseph LEWIS. Benjamin GRAYSON, Joseph CARR. Delv. to POWELL 12 Aug 1823.

Bk:Pg: 2Y:115   Date: 28 Feb 1819   RtCt: 12 Apr 1819
Daniel REESE & wife Linny of Ldn to William SILVER & Joseph EIDSON of Ldn. B/S of 2a adj. heirs of Leven POWELL, Jesse BURSON. Wit: John SINCLAIR, David ALEXANDER, Moses OWSLEY, A. GIBSON, Thos. GREGG. Delv. to EIDSON 24 Aug 1841.

Bk:Pg: 2Y:117   Date: 13 Mar 1819   RtCt: 12 Apr 1819
Jonah NIXON of Ldn and George NIXON of Ldn. Partition of 200a (100a each) dev. them by grandfather George NIXON dec'd. Delv. to Geo. NIXON 16 Feb 1852.

Bk:Pg: 2Y:119   Date: 31 Mar 1819   RtCt: 12 Apr 1819
Moses GULICK & wife Martha and George GULICK & wife Sarah of Ldn to Charles STOVIN of Ldn. B/S of 320a 'Gulick's gum spring tract' on road from gum spring to Lsbg adj Maj. William B. HARRISON. Wit: Burr POWELL, A. GIBSON.

Bk:Pg: 2Y:122   Date: 16 Jan 1819   RtCt: 12 Apr 1819
Stephen McPHERSON & wife Cecilia of Ldn to Samuel SINCLAIR
of Ldn. B/S of 8a (cnvy/b Sarah MARKS) adj mill lot, Isaiah MARKS.
Wit: Benjamin GRAYSON, Notley C. WILLIAMS.

Bk:Pg: 2Y:124   Date: 14 Dec 1818   RtCt: 14 Dec 1819
Peter ISH & wife Harriet of Ldn to Robert BENTLEY of Ldn. B/S of
½a Lot #20 adj Lsbg (now property of James RUST holding deposits
of branch bank of the Valley). Wit: Jno. A. BINNS, Ludwell LEE,
John McCORMICK.

Bk:Pg: 2Y:126   Date: 20 Aug 1818   RtCt: 12 Apr 1819
John LITTLEJOHN & wife Monica of Ldn to Joseph ADAMS of Ldn.
B/S of ¼a in new addition to Lsbg on Loudoun St adj Lot #15. Wit:
Saml. M. EDWARDS, Jesse DAILEY, C. BINNS, Thos. FOUCH,
John McCORMICK.

Bk:Pg: 2Y:128   Date: 12 Apr 1819   RtCt: 12 Apr 1819
Joseph ADAMS & wife Winnah/Winny of Ldn to Gerard L. W. HUNT
of Ldn. B/S of ¼a in new addition to Lsbg adj Lot #15. Wit: Chas. B.
BALL, Presley CORDELL. Delv. to ADAMS 2 Jun 1825.

Bk:Pg: 2Y:130   Date: 30 Mar 1819   RtCt: 12 Apr 1819
Presley WILLIAMS & wife Jane of Ldn to John SHAFFER of Ldn.
B/S of 70a with grist mill on broad run (formerly occupied by John
BALL) adj Peter COMPHER, William HOUGH dec'd, Isaac BALL,
schoolhouse lot, Sanford RAMEY, Reuben HIXON (cnvy/b Isaac
STEER trustees to WILLIAMS Aug 1815 DB TT:172). Wit: John H.
McCABE, Saml. HOUGH Jr. Delv. to SHAFFER 29 Oct 1819.

Bk:Pg: 2Y:132   Date: 1 Apr 1819   RtCt: 12 Apr 1819
Presley WILLIAMS & wife Jane of Ldn to John SHAFFER of Ldn.
B/S of 13a wood lot (as heirs of Reuben HIXSON dec'd) adj John
FAULEY, Margaret SAUNDERS, John WEEST?. Wit: John H.
McCABE, Saml. HOUGH Jr. Delv. to SHAFFER 29 Oct 1819.

Bk:Pg: 2Y:134   Date: 19 Apr 1819   RtCt: 21 Apr 1819
Thomas B. BEATTY of Ldn to William H. LANE of Ldn. B/S of Lot
#17 on Market St in Lsbg. Wit: Thomas C. ROACH. Delv. to LANE
17 Jul 1820.

Bk:Pg: 2Y:136   Date: 15 Mar 1816   RtCt: 7 Apr 1817/1 May 1819
Thomas PARKER, Robert TAYLOR & Richard H. HENDERSON (as
commrs. in decrees in Winchester of Thomas SWANN & Edmund J.
LEE Admrs. of William B. PAGE dec'd agst Ferdinando FAIRFAX
dated Jul 1814) to James & William THOMPSON. B/S of 274a
'Widow HEPBURN's tenement'. Wit: Thos. SWANN, Joshua
POTTS, Joshua OSBURNE, John WHITE. Gives plat and details.
Delv. to Jas. THOMPSON 11 Mar 1820.

Bk:Pg: 2Y:139   Date: 24 Aug 1818   RtCt: 12 Apr 1819
Peter MILLER & wife Mary, Daniel MILLER & wife Mary of Culpeper,
Jno. MILLER & wife Catharine of Fqr and Adam MILLER & Jesse

MILLER of Ldn to Aaron MILLER of Ldn. B/S of 88a (dower's interest of Catharine MILLER wd/o Peter MILLER Sr., who died 14 Apr 1815) adj Peter VERTS, Joseph FRYE, Jeremiah PURDOM. Wit: Robert BRADEN, John H. McCABE. Delv. to grantee 29 Nov 1820.

Bk:Pg: 2Y:143   Date: 15 Apr 1819   RtCt: 15 Apr 1819
Fielding BROWN & wife Hannah of Ldn to John Gill WATT of Ldn. B/S of lot (cnvy/b William M. LITTLEJOHN in Jan 1813, DB 22:1) on Market St. and lot (cnvy/b Samuel M. EDWARDS) and 1a (prch/o overseers of the poor). Wit: Presley CORDELL, Chas. B. BALL. Delv. to WATT 11 Nov 1819.

Bk:Pg: 2Y:145   Date: 19 Aug 1818   RtCt: 14 Apr 1819
Israel JANNEY of Ldn to Daniel JANNEY of Ldn. B/S of 78a adj Israel JANNEY, Solomon GORE. Wit: Solomon GORE. Delv. to Danl. JANNEY 6 Dec 1819.

Bk:Pg: 2Y:148   Date: 20 Oct 1818   RtCt: 6 May 1819
James MOORE & wife Rebekah and James FARQUHAR of Ldn to William JANNEY of JeffVa. B/S of 50a and ¼a. Wit: John WILLIAMS, David JANNEY, John PIERPOINT, John H. McCABE, Saml. HOUGH.

Bk:Pg: 2Y:150   Date: 10 Apr 1819   RtCt: 12 Apr 1819
William NICKOLS & Bernard TAYLOR (Exors of Jesse JANNEY dec'd) of Ldn to Jonathan EWERS of Ldn. B/S of 105a adj Stephen JANNEY, Phinehas THOMAS. Delv. to EWERS 29 Apr 1822.

Bk:Pg: 2Y:152   Date: 25 Feb 1819   RtCt: 27 Apr 1819
William SMITH & wife Sarah of Shenandoah Co Va to Richard H. HENDERSON and John J. HARDING of Ldn. B/S of 2a on N side of Loudoun St. in Lsbg. Notation - Presley CORDELL, Thos. MORALLEE & Wm. D. DRISH are owners of these lots equally with us. Signed Rich'd. H. HENDERSON & John J. HARDING.

Bk:Pg: 2Y:153   Date: 19 Apr 1819   RtCt: 19 Apr 1819
John ROSE (Admr wwa of George KILGORE dec'd) of Ldn to Henry STEVENS of Ldn. B/S of 23a & 9a on broad run. Delv. to STEVENS 11 Apr 1820.

Bk:Pg: 2Y:155   Date: 26 Apr 1819   RtCt: 26 Apr 1819
John ROSE (Admr wwa of George KILGORE dec'd) of Ldn to William SHEID of Ldn. B/S of 224a. Delv. to SHEID 6 Mar 1820.

Bk:Pg: 2Y:156   Date: 16 Apr 1819   RtCt: 31 Apr 1819
John ROSE (Admr wwa of George KILGORE dec'd) of Ldn to George SHEID of Ldn. B/S of 192a. Delv to SHEID 6 Jun 1820.

Bk:Pg: 2Y:158   Date: 16 Apr 1819   RtCt: 19 Apr 1819
Henry STEVENS & wife Eleanor of Ldn to John ROSE of Ldn. B/S of land (cnvy/b Hannah STEVENS - DB Y:371 dated Sep 1798) on side of Kittocton Mt. adj John ROSE, Henry OXLEY. Wit: John McCORMICK, Presley CORDELL. Delv. to ROSE 22 May 1820.

Bk:Pg: 2Y:160   Date: 27 Oct 1818   RtCt: 12 Apr 1819
Moses GIBSON & wife Lydia of Ldn to Sydnor BAILEY & John
GIBSON of Ldn. Trust for debt to Henley BOGGESS using 226a
where GIBSON now lives adj Joseph LEWIS Jr., Pantherskin Run
(subject to sale of 17a to Amos GIBSON and heirs of James
GIBSON dec'd). Wit: Towns'd McVEIGH, Robt. SINGLETON, Minor
FURR, Burr GRAYSON, John W. GRAYSON. Delv. to BALLY [sic] 9
Nov 1819.

Bk:Pg: 2Y:163   Date: 23 Jan 1819   RtCt: 12 Apr 1819
Israel GIBSON (an heir of John GIBSON dec'd late of Ldn) to Isaac
NICKOLS Jr. & Amos GIBSON of Ldn. Trust for debt to Benjamin
BROOKE using his interest from estate of John GIBSON dec'd.
Delv. to BROOKE 20 Dec 1820.

Bk:Pg: 2Y:165   Date: 21 May 1815   RtCt: 12 Apr 1819
Jacob WERTZ & wife Lucy, Peter WERTZ & wife Susan, Michael
EVERHART & wife Christiana and John THOMAS & wife Margaret
of Ldn (heirs of Peter WERTZ dec'd) to John SHAFFER of Ldn. B/S
of 138a (cnvy/b Ferdinando FAIRFAX to Peter WERTZ in 1802) adj
John ROLER, __ BELTZ, __ RHORBACK. Wit: Abiel JENNER, John
H. McCABE. Delv. to SHAFFER 29 Oct 1819.

Bk:Pg: 2Y:167   Date: 15 Apr 1819   RtCt: 15 Apr 1819
John Gill WATT & wife Dewanner of Ldn to Samuel MURREY &
Isaac HARRIS of Ldn. Trust for debt to Fielding BROWN of Ldn
using land prch/o Fielding BROWN & wife Hannah this date.

Bk:Pg: 2Y:170   Date: 17 Apr 1817   RtCt: 3 May 1819
Stephen GREGG & wife Harriet of Ldn to Samuel & Isaac NICHOLS
of Ldn. Trust using house & lot in Bloomfield adj John RALPH, John
G. HUMPHREY. Also signed by Isaac NICHOLS Jr. Delv. to Saml.
NICKOLLS Exors 9 Nov 1825.

Bk:Pg: 2Y:173   Date: 4 May 1819   RtCt: 4 May 1819
Samuel E. TAYLOR (br/o John) of Ldn to Rich'd H. HENDERSON.
Trust for debts to RIGGS & PEABOBY and BRADEN MORGAN &
Co. (3 executions in Superior Ct. agst TAYLOR and John F.
SAPPINGTON) using 103a nr Wtfd (devised from father Jesse
TAYLOR dec'd). Delv. pr Tho. MOORE to trustee 1 Jan 1820.

Bk:Pg: 2Y:175   Date: 27 Sep 1817   RtCt: 12 Apr 1819
Ruth TRIBBY (wd/o Joseph TRIBBY dec'd), Asahel TRIBBY & wife
Catharine, Johnathan TRIBBY & George TRIBBY (heirs of Joseph
TRIBBY dec'd) of Ldn to Mortimer McILHANY of Ldn. B/S of 136a
adj Samuel GREGG, James McILHANY. Wit: Abiel JENNERS, John
WHITE.

Bk:Pg: 2Y:178   Date: 1 May 1819   RtCt: 3 May 1819
Jesse GOVER & wife Miriam of Wtfd to William H. HOUGH & John
WILLIAMS of Ldn. Trust for debt to Isaac WALKER & Jacob
MENDENHALL of Wtfd using 201½a (undivided interest in estate of

Miriam's father Henry TAYLOR dec'd). Wit: Abiel JENNERS, Saml. HOUGH Jr. Delv. pr order 25 Jul 1828.

Bk:Pg: 2Y:181   Date: 20 Mar 1819   RtCt: 12 Apr 1819
Philip COOPER & wife Elizabeth of Ldn to John KALB & William EVERHEART of Ldn. Trust for debt to Absalom KALB using 104a adj George SHOEMAKER, Jeremiah PURDOM, Aaron MILLER. Wit: Saml. HOUGH Jr., John H. McCABE. Delv. to John KALB 8 Apr 1822.

Bk:Pg: 2Y:185   Date: 19 Apr 1819   RtCt: 19 Apr 1819
Henry STEVENS & wife Eleanor of Ldn to John Alex'r BINNS & Saml. M. EDWARDS of Ldn. Trust for debt to John ROSE (Admr of George KILGORE dec'd) using land prch/o ROSE. Delv. to ROSE 12 Apr 1822.

Bk:Pg: 2Y:187   Date: 26 Apr 1819   RtCt: 26 Apr 1819
William SHEID & wife Matilda B. of Ldn to John A. BINNS & Saml. M. EDWARDS. Trust for debt to John ROSE (Admr of George KILGORE dec'd) using land on broad run prch/o ROSE. Wit: Samuel MURREY, Presley CORDELL. Delv. to Jno. A. BINNS 12 Nov 1828.

Bk:Pg: 2Y:190   Date: 28 Aug 1818   RtCt: 14 Apr 1819
Daniel JANNEY & wife Elizabeth of Ldn to William HOGE & Jesse HOGE of Ldn. Trust for debt to Israel JANNEY using 78a adj Israel JANNEY, Solomon GORE. Wit: Solomon GORE, Joel CRAVEN, John BELT, John McCORMICK, Presley CORDELL. Delv. to Exor of JANNEY 18 Aug 1826.

Bk:Pg: 2Y:194   Date: 8 May 1819   RtCt: 8 May 1819
John FEICHTER to Thomas MORALLEE & John THOMAS. Trust for debt to James W. HANCHER (Admr dbn of Edward RINKER dec'd) using land granted to FEICHTER by HANCHER.

Bk:Pg: 2Y:197   Date: __ May 1819   RtCt: 11 May 1819
Lewis P. W. BALCH & Wm. CHILTON. Bond on BALCH as treasurer of the board for commr. for the education of poor children.

Bk:Pg: 2Y:198   Date: 11 May 1819   RtCt: 11 May 1819
Edward HAMMATT, Joseph BEARD, Samuel A. TILLETT & Reuben SCHOOLEY. Bond on HAMMATT as constable.

Bk:Pg: 2Y:198   Date: 11 May 1819   RtCt: 11 May 1819
William ROSE, Chas. LEWIS & Richard COCKERILLE. Bond on ROSE as constable.

Bk:Pg: 2Y:199   Date: 26 Mar 1819   RtCt: 10 May 1819
Joseph THOMAS & wife Ruth, William NICKOLS & wife Mary and Thomas NICKOLS & wife Letitia (heirs at law of Stacey JANNEY dec'd) of Ldn to Jonah SANDS & Hannah JANNEY of Ldn. B/S of 162a (late property of Stacey JANNEY dec'd) adj Jonah SANDS. Wit: Edward DAVIS, Samuel NICKOLS, Isaac NICKOLS, Patrick McINTYRE, Charles B. BALL. Delv. to Jonah SANDS pr order of Hannah JANNEY 25 Apr 1829.

Bk:Pg: 2Y:201   Date: 14 Nov 1818   RtCt: 10 May 1819
John REED & wife Martha of Belmont Co OH, Joseph WILKINSON
& wife Elizabeth, Moses BROWN & wife Mary, Johnathan REED of
Ldn, James REED of Guernsey Co OH, Thomas REED & with
Catharine of ___ to Samuel BEAVERS of Ldn. B/S of 22a and 6a
held in life estate by Rebecca REED wd/o James REED dec'd. Wit:
Wm. BRONAUGH, Francis W. LUCKETT. Delv. to BEAVERS 28
Feb 1825.

Bk:Pg: 2Y:204   Date: 26 Mar 1819   RtCt: 10 May 1819
Nelson NORRIS & wife Eliza of BaltMd to William NOLAND of Ldn.
B/S of 150a nr old Snickers gap road, adj Mathew ADAMS, James
SWART, Aquilla BRISCOE's lot #23 in Aldie. Wit: Henry McKENZIE,
Thomas H. KIRBY, James L. NORRIS.

Bk:Pg: 2Y:207   Date: 23 Sep 1818   RtCt: 10 May 1819
John LEWIS Sr. of Ldn to dau. Rebecca LEWIS. Gift of all his
personal property including negroes, farm animals and household.
Also signed by John LEWIS. Wit: James Henson BRADSHAW,
George ROSE, John ROSE, Kezia HUTCHISON. Delv. to Charles
GULLATT 24 Jan 1822.

Bk:Pg: 2Y:208   Date: 25 Sep 1818   RtCt: 10 May 1819
John LEWIS Sr. of Ldn to dau. Rebecca LEWIS. Gift of 240a where
he now lives adj lot leased of Anthony RUSSEL. Wit: Richard
COLEMAN, Coleman LEWIS, Jos. LEWIS. Delv. to Ch. GULLATT 4
Jan 1822.

Bk:Pg: 2Y:209   Date: 17 May 1819   RtCt: 17 May 1819
John A. WASHINGTON of Ldn to Jno. A. BINNS of Ldn. BoS for
negro man Marlborough commonly called Doctor, a slave for
obtained from estate of my father now dec'd. Delv. to John A.
BINNS 28 Sep 1819.

Bk:Pg: 2Y:209   Date: 7 Jun 1819   RtCt: 7 Jun 1819
Samuel E. TAYLOR to Richard H. HENDERSON. Trust for debt to
Thomas PHILIPS using lot where TAYLOR now lives dev. him by his
father Jesse TAYLOR dec'd. Delv. to trustee 1 Jan 1820.

Bk:Pg: 2Y:210   Date: 18 Dec 1818   RtCt: 10 May 1819
Bernard McCORMICK & wife Isabella of Ldn to William WILKINSON
of Ldn. B/S of 1/3 undivided interest in 10a (Isabella is entitled to
from father Thomas VANANDER late of Ldn) adj WILKINSON,
Andrew CAMPBELL. CoE from FredVa. Delv. to WILKERSON 15
Mar 1822.

Bk:Pg: 2Y:212   Date: ___   RtCt: 22 May 1819
Jacob KIMMERLE/KIMERLY of Ldn and Isaac SHIPLEY of Ldn.
Agreement abt payment - abt 1 Mar 1819 KIMERLE rented for 3y to
SHIPLEY his 60a farm adj S. CLAPHAM, widow HIXON, Wm.
BROWN, Isaac STEER. Wit: S. BLINCOE, Thos. MORALLEE, Thos.
W. MONROE. Delv. to both 23 Nov 1819.

Bk:Pg: 2Y:213   Date: 12 Jun 1819   RtCt: 12 Jun 1819
Sampson BLINCOE (trustee of Philip RAZOR & wife Elizabeth) to
John H. BUTCHER. B/S of RAZOR's land (devised by father to
mother during life and then to children) in trust.

Bk:Pg: 2Y:214   Date: 12 Jun 1819   RtCt: 12 Jun 1819
John H. BUTCHER of Ldn to Joshua B. OVERFIELD of Ldn. B/S of
above land. Delv. to OVERFIELD 1 Mar 1822.

Bk:Pg: 2Y:215   Date: 19 Dec 1817   RtCt: 22 Oct 1818
George BURSON & wife Susannah of Ldn to William H. DORSEY of
Ldn. B/S of 154a adj Joseph BURSON, Jacob HUMPHREY,
Johnathan BURSON, stone quarry. Wit: Wm. BRONAUGH, Francis
W. LUCKETT. Delv. to ___ 25 Apr 1821

Bk:Pg: 2Y:217   Date: 18 May 1819   RtCt: 19 May 1819
Samuel MURRAY of Lsbg to Samuel MILLER of Lsbg. Release of
trust using lot in Lsbg adj Dr. Henry CLAGGETT. Wit: Thomas
SANDERS, Presley SAUNDERS.

Bk:Pg: 2Y:218   Date: 20 May 1819   RtCt: 9 Jun 1819
Isaac HARRIS of Ldn to Isaac CROSBY of Ldn. Release of trust for
debt to Francis TRIPLETT using lot nr Lsbg.

Bk:Pg: 2Y:219   Date: 11 May 1819   RtCt: 11 May 1819
Abner HUMPHREY (trustee for Thomas LEEDOM & wife Hannah
under deed executed by Jesse THOMAS) to John CHEW. Release
of trust on 84a.

Bk:Pg: 2Y:221   Date: 20 May 1819   RtCt: 25 May 1819
Isaac HARRIS & wife Sarah of Ldn to Sarah WRENN (free woman
of color) of Ldn. B/S of ¼a on carolina road nr Lsbg adj James
RUST, Isaac HARRIS. Wit: Samuel MURREY, Saml. M.
EDWARDS.

Bk:Pg: 2Y:222   Date: 12 Mar 1819   RtCt: 18 May 1819
Nancy TURNER of Harrison Co Va to Samuel D. LESLIE of Ldn.
B/S of leased 100a (from George W. FAIRFAX by attorney G.
NICKOLS unto Israel THOMSON guardian of Nancy PHILIPS now
TURNER on 10 Apr 1786). Delv. to LESLIE 13 Nov 1820.

Bk:Pg: 2Y:224   Date: 8 Jan 1819   RtCt: 8 Jan 1819
John CARR of Ldn to Richard H. HENDERSON of Ldn. Trust for
debt to John R. COOKE using land on NW side of Goose Creek
conveyed to CARR by COOKE.

**Bk:Pg: 2Y:226   Date: 10 Oct 1816   RtCt: 23 Sep 1817/24 May
1819**
John JANNEY of AlexVa to Joseph JANNEY of AlexVa. Release of
mortgage on land devised by father Joseph JANNEY dec'd. Delv. to
Joseph JANNEY 4 Apr 1821.

Bk:Pg: 2Y:227　Date: 20 Jan 1819　RtCt: 10 May 1819
David CARTER of Ldn to William H. HANDY & John SINCLAIR of
Ldn. Trust for debt to David ALEXANDER using 65a (cnvy/b
ALEXANDER). Delv. to Jno. SINCLAIR 5 Oct 1822.

Bk:Pg: 2Y:229　Date: 12 Sep 1817　RtCt: 10 May 1819
Robert BRADEN, Ebenezer GRUBB, James RUSSELL & Robt.
RUSSELL (commrs. under ct. decree under suit of Admrs. of William
B. PAGE dec'd agst WALTERS & others) of Ldn to Catharine
WATERS of Ldn. B/S of 22a adj Nich's ROPP, George SMITH. Wit:
Edw'd CUNARD, George SMITH, William DERRY. Delv. to Levi
WALTERS [WATERS] pr order filed 8 May 1824.

Bk:Pg: 2Y:231　Date: 1 Jun 1819　RtCt: 9 Jun 1819
John DREAN & wife Nancy of Ldn to Isaac HARRIS of Ldn. Trust for
debt to Simon SMALE using Lot #56 in Lsbg adj Sampson
BLINCOE, Samuel TUSTIN, heirs of William R. TAYLOR. Wit:
Thomas BIRKLEY, Josiah DREAN, Fielding BROWN, Presley
CORDELL, Saml. M. EDWARDS.

Bk:Pg: 2Y:233　Date: 19 May 1819　RtCt: 19 May 1819
Samuel MILLER & wife Hannah of Ldn to Samuel MURREY of Ldn.
B/S of brick house and lot between Dr. Henry CLAGGETT and
Thomas SANDERS on Loudoun St in Lsbg. Wit: Thomas
SANDERS, P. SAUNDERS, Wm. NOLAND, Saml. M. EDWARDS.

Bk:Pg: 2Y:235　Date: 3 Apr 1818　RtCt: 11 May 1819
Henry NEAR and Amos NEAR & wife Sarah of Ldn to George
SMITH of Ldn. B/S of 50a. Wit: Edward CUNNARD, John CONARD,
David NEER, James NEER. Delv. to SMITH 18 Jan 1822.

Bk:Pg: 2Y:236　Date: 3 Apr 1818　RtCt: 11 May 1819
Henry NEAR and Amos NEAR & wife Sarah of Ldn to James NEAR
of Ldn. B/S of 60a on W side of short hill. Wit: Edw'd CUNARD,
John CONARD, David NEER, George SMITH. Delv. to Jas. NEAR 7
Sep 1825.

Bk:Pg: 2Y:238　Date: 3 May 1819　RtCt: 12 May 1819
Benjamin T. TOWNER of JeffVa to Eve TOWNER of Ldn. Gift of his
interest in Lot #62 in Lsbg at Back & Royal St. Delv. to E TOWNER
8 Apr 1824.

Bk:Pg: 2Y:239　Date: 30 Nov 1818　RtCt: 7 Jun 1819
Robert MOFFETT & wife Ellen of Ldn to Peter COOPER of Ldn. B/S
of ___ part of BINNS patent adj Landon CARTER. Wit: Thos.
FOUCH, Saml. LUCKETT. Delv. to COOPER 12 Mar 1825.

Bk:Pg: 2Y:241　Date: 28 Apr 1819　RtCt: 10 May 1819
Henry ELLIS & wife Jane of Ldn to William ALLEN of Ldn. B/S of
15a on NW fork of Goose Creek adj Isaac & Samuel NICKOLS,
Elizabeth BOLIN, David F. BEALES. Wit: William BRONAUGH,
Thos. GREGG. Delv. to ALLEN 4 Sep 1826.

Bk:Pg: 2Y:243   Date: 1 Sep 1812   RtCt: 12 Apr 1819
Mahlon COMBS & wife Sarah of Ldn to Bernard TAYLOR of Ldn.
B/S of 4a (part of land of Andrew COMBS dec'd). Wit: John WYNN,
Mary BOLON. Delv. to TAYLOR 14 Apr 1826.

Bk:Pg: 2Y:245   Date: 27 Jan 1819   RtCt: 24 May 1819
John NEWTON & wife Harriet of Ldn to Alexander RICHARDSON &
Nelson S. HUTCHISON of Ldn. B/S of 1a nr Lsbg adj John GRAY.
Wit: John ROSE, Samuel MURREY. Delv. to RICHARDSON 21 Feb
1820.

Bk:Pg: 2Y:246   Date: 16 Mar 1819   RtCt: 9 Jun 1819
Joseph GOURLEY (eldest s/o Samuel GOURLEY dec'd), John
GOURLEY, Jabez WILSON & wife Rebecca late Rebecca
GOURLEY and Elizabeth GOURLEY by their attorney in fact (all
ch/o Samuel dec'd and entitled to 1/5th of his real estate) of Ldn to
Gourley REEDER of Ldn. B/S of part of 103a which Joseph
GOURLEY late of Ldn died seized (prch/o David LOVETT) and
share of each who join in this deed is 1/7th part of 1/5th with 1/5th to
said Samuel GOURLEY and at death to his 7 children (3 are
infants). Delv. to REEDER 14 Aug 1820.

Bk:Pg: 2Y:248   Date: 13 Jun 1818   RtCt: 2 Jan 1819
Philip RAZOR & wife Elizabeth of Ldn to Sampson BLINCOE of Ldn.
Trust for debt to John BUTCHER as security using land of George
RAZOR (f/o Philip) dev. his wife during her life and at her death
amongst his children. Wit: M. C. OVERFIELD, Nathaniel TRIPLETT,
Thos. MORALLEE, Wm. C. PALMER.

Bk:Pg: 2Y:250   Date: 6 Dec 1818   RtCt: 7 Jul 1819
Henry HUFF & wife Mary of Ldn to Peter STUCK of Ldn. B/S of
50½a adj Peter FRYE, Peter STUCK, John SHAFFER. Wit: Samuel
MURREY, Presley CORDELL. Delv. to Peter STUCK Jr. 21 Apr
1845.

Bk:Pg: 2Y:253   Date: 13 Mar 1819   RtCt: 18 May 1819
Peter BENEDUM & wife Catharine of Ldn to Samuel BUCK of
Sheandoah Co Va. B/S of ½a Lot #59 in Lsbg adj John A. BINNS.
Wit: Abiel JENNERS, John H. McCABE. Delv. to BUCK 3 Apr 1820.

Bk:Pg: 2Y:255   Date: __ 1818   RtCt: 27 Jan 1819
John NIXON & wife Nancy of Ldn to George TAVENDER Jr. of Ldn.
B/S of rights to land that George NIXON (f/o John) bought of
Augustine LOVE on Goose Creek where Jesse HARRIS formerly
lived. Wit: Samuel MURREY, Presley CORDELL.

Bk:Pg: 2Y:258   Date: 10 Jun 1819   RtCt: 11 Jun 1819
Samuel M. EDWARDS & wife Ann of Ldn to James CAMPBELL of
Ldn. B/S of 130a (prch/o Wm. Dudley DIGGS). Wit: Samuel
MURREY, Presley CORDELL. Delv. to CAMPBELL 14 Aug 1820.

Bk:Pg: 2Y:260 Date: 10 Jun 1819 RtCt: 11 Jun 1819
James CAMPBELL & wife Elizabeth of Ldn to James
GREENLEASE of Ldn. B/S of 72a (prch/o James GREENLEASE in
1815) adj Hamilton RODGERS. Wit: Samuel MURREY, Presley
CORDELL. Delv. to GREENLEASE 1 Feb 1820

Bk:Pg: 2Y:262 Date: 10 Oct 1818 RtCt: 29 May 1819
Jonathan SCHOLFIELD & wife Eleanor of Alexandria to Benjamin
WATERS of Alexandria. Trust for debt to Thomas K. BEALE
(security on bonds to William PATCH) using 80a with grist mill on
Goose Creek. Wit: Elisha TALBOTT, R. H. CLEMENTS, John BALL.

Bk:Pg: 2Y:265 Date: 26 May 1819 RtCt: 26 May 1819
George SHEID & wife Rebecca of Ldn to John A. BINNS of Ldn.
Trust for debt to Anthony CONRAD (as security for SHEID as
guardian of his children Sarah G., James W., John H. & Erasmus
Wilson SHEID, legatees of George KILGORE dec'd) using 192a
(prch/o John ROSE Admr of KILGORE).

Bk:Pg: 2Y:267 Date: 10 May 1819 RtCt: 10 May 1819
Jesse BURSON of Ldn to Sampson BLINCOE of Ldn. Trust for debt
to John PANCOAST of Ldn using 149a adj Edward MUDD. Wit:
John PANCOAST Sr., Josiah L. DREAN, David ALEXANDER, Chs.
G. ESKRIDGE. Delv. to PANCOAST on 14 Aug 1820.

Bk:Pg: 2Y:269 Date: 12 Sep 1817 RtCt: 10 May 1819
Robert BRADEN, Ebenezer GRUBB, James RUSSEL & Robert
RUSSEL (commrs. under decree, mortgage on land by Diah
WATERS) of Ldn to George SMITH of Ldn. B/S of 54¾a and 4¼a.
Wit: Edward CUNNARD, William DERRY, Anth'y WRIGHT. Delv. to
SMITH 18 Jan 1822.

Bk:Pg: 2Y:270 Date: 21 Oct 1818 RtCt: 10 May 1819
Samuel E. TAYLOR of Wtfd to John E. PARMER of Wtfd. Trust for
debt to Charles G. EDWARDS using 104a less 3a sold to Jno.
BINNS. Wit: R. BRADEN, Noble S. BRADEN, John F.
SAPPINGTON, James P. SCHOOLEY. Delv. per order 14 Dec
1826.

Bk:Pg: 2Y:272 Date: 29 Apr 1819 RtCt: 10 May 1819
William ALLEN & wife Elizabeth of Ldn to David SMITH of Ldn. Trust
for debt to Henry ELLIS using 15a on NW fork of Goose Creek
(cnvy/b ELLIS). Wit: William BRONAUGH, Thomas GREGG.

Bk:Pg: 2Y:274 Date: 28 May 1819 RtCt: 28 May 1819
John MATHIAS & John NIXON of Ldn to George TAVENER Jr. of
Ldn. B/S of 249a nr Wtfd (prch/o Peter BENEDUM).

Bk:Pg: 2Y:275 Date: 5 Apr 1819 RtCt: 9 Jun 1819
Mary WILKINSON, Joseph WILKINSON & wife Elizabeth, Hannah
WILKINSON and Anna WILKINSON to Gourley REEDER of Ldn.
B/S of undivided 1/5th part of 103a (prch/o David LOVETT by Joseph
GOURLEY dec'd in Apr 1806, GOURLEY died intestate without heir

so land descended to sister Mary REED, children of John
GOURLEY dec'd of Carolina, children of Margaret FELL (once
GOURLEY) dec'd, children of Samuel GOURLEY dec'd and Mary,
Joseph, Hannah & Anna WILKINSON surviving children of Elizabeth
WILKINSON sister of Joseph dec'd). Delv. to REEDER 14 Aug
1820.

Bk:Pg: 2Y:277   Date: 13 Jan 1819   RtCt: 8 Feb 1819
Charles TURNER & wife Malinda to William HOUGH & Bernard
TAYLOR. Trust for debt to Emanuel NEWCOMER of Washington Co
Md using 61a (less 9a sold to Wm. HERRON and 16a sold to Enos
POTTS) adj Isaac & Saml. NICKOLS, Enos POTTS, James BEANS,
James CRAIG. Wit: Leven LUCKETT, Thos. GREGG. Delv. to
TAYLOR 9 Mar 1829.

Bk:Pg: 2Y:279   Date: 1 Jun 1819   RtCt: 9 Jun 1819
John WILKINSON yeoman of Ldn (attorney in fact for Edward FELL
of Wilkesbarre, Luzerne Co Pa, blacksmith Nathaniel SHEWELL &
wife Cynthia of New Britain Township, Bucks Co Pa and Jane
TITUS (wd/o Seriah TITUS) of Buckingham Township, Bucks Co Pa)
to Gourley REEDER of Ldn. B/S of undivided 1/5th parts of land of
Joseph GOURLEY brother of his sister Margaret FELL (m/o Edward
FELL and others) died seized and FELL's mother being dec'd he
and sisters inherited. Delv. to REEDER 14 Aug 1820.

Bk:Pg: 2Y:281   Date: 15 May 1819   RtCt: 20 May 1819
Jane McCABE, John McCABE & wife Mary, Catharine DOWLING,
John NEWTON & wife Harriet (widow, heirs and reps of Henry
McCABE dec'd late of Ldn) to Samuel G. HAMILTON of Ldn. B/S of
1a on S side of Cornwall St in W addition to Lsbg. Wit: Presley
CORDELL, Saml. M. EDWARDS. Delv. to Erasmus G. HAMILTON
pr order S. G. HAMILTON filed DB YY:281 on 15 Nov 1819.

Bk:Pg: 2Y:283   Date: 15 May 1819   RtCt: 20 May 1819
Jane McCABE, John McCABE & wife Mary, Catharine DOWLING,
John NEWTON & wife Harriet (widow, heirs and reps of Henry
McCABE dec'd late of Ldn) to Samuel G. HAMILTON of Ldn. B/S of
1a on S side of Cornwall St. in W addition to Lsbg adj John
BURTON. Wit: Presley CORDELL, Saml. M. EDWARDS. Delv. to E.
G. HAMILTON pr order S. G. HAMILTON filed DB YY:281 on 14
Nov 1819.

Bk:Pg: 2Y:286   Date: 7 Jun 1819   RtCt: 7 Jun 1819
Peter COOPER & wife Nancy of Ldn to William MEAD of Ldn. Trust
for debt to Robert MOFFETT using 110½a (cnvy/b MOFFETT). Wit:
John McCORMICK, Presley CORDELL. Delv. to MOFFETT 12 Mar
1825.

Bk:Pg: 2Y:289   Date: 16 Jan 1819   RtCt: 12 Jun 1819
John MARKS & wife Lydia of Ldn to John W. GRAYSON of Ldn.
Trust for debt to Stephen McPHERSON using 160a adj George
MARKS, Isaiah B. BEANS, Isaiah MARKS (part of land devised by

will of Elisha MARKS dec'd to son Isaiah MARKS). Wit: Benjamin GRAYSON, Notley C. WILLIAMS.

Bk:Pg: 2Y:292   Date: 16 Jun 1819   RtCt: 17 Jun 1819
Samuel GRAY (insolvent debtor under executions in the name of William DULANEY) to Sheriff John HAMILTON. B/S of all real estate. Wit: S. BLINCOE, Daniel LOVETT, Giles HAMMATT.

Bk:Pg: 2Y:293   Date: 18 Jun 1819   RtCt: 18 Jun 1819
John B. HOOK. Col for slave Nathan abt 32y who lost the first joint of his little finger, Elias abt 29y and Eliza abt 20y old, brought in from FredMd within the last 40 days and owned for more than 5y, received from uncle Jas. T. HOOK.

Bk:Pg: 2Y:293   Date: 15 Jun 1819   RtCt: 15 Jun 1819
Henry FURLONG, Thomas SAUNDERS & Robert R. HOUGH. Bond on FURLONG for his credentials of ordination to perform duties as Methodist minister.

Bk:Pg: 2Y:294   Date: 14 Oct 1818   RtCt: 14 Jun 1819
Sarah EWERS & Nancy EWERS of Ldn to Jonathan EWERS & Richard EWERS of Ldn. PoA concerning lands of John EWERS dec'd (all mentioned are heirs along with William EWERS, David EWERS, Richard EWERS, Robert EWERS, George EWERS & Isabella HARRIS). Wit: Thos. GREGG, Elias JAMES, Moses BROWN.

Bk:Pg: 2Y:295   Date: 4 Sep 1818   RtCt: 14 Jun 1819
Edward FELL and other children of Margaret FELL dec'd to John WILKINSON of Ldn. PoA – Joseph GOURLEY of Ldn died intestate and lands descended to his brothers & sisters the children of John GOURLEY & wife Elizabeth. Margaret GOURLEY dec'd his sister who married Joseph FELL had issue Edward FELL (blacksmith of Wilksbarre, Luzerne Co Pa), Cynthia FELL who m. Nathaniel SHEWELL (yeoman of New britain township, Bucks Co Pa) and Jane FELL (wd/o Buckingham township, Bucks Co Pa) who m. Seriah TITUS late dec'd. Wit: Samuel FELL, Jesse FELL, Edmund SMITH, John ROSS.

Bk:Pg: 2Y:298   Date: 2 Mar 1819   RtCt: 14 Jun 1819
John GOURLEY and other children of Samuel GOURLEY dec'd to Joseph GOURLEY (s/o Samuel dec'd). PoA. Concerns estate of Joseph GOURLEY as above mentioned and issues of brothers Samuel late of Montgomery Co Pa (f/o Joseph, John, Rebecca who m. Jabez WILSON, Elizabeth, Martha, Samuel & Emmor, the last 3 are minors) and John late of N. Carolina and sisters Elizabeth who m. John WILKINSON and Margaret who m. the above mentioned FELL. Wit Frederick SOLLADY, Hirdin McNEILL.

Bk:Pg: 2Y:300   Date: 4 Mar 1818   RtCt: 14 Jun 1819
James L. McKENNA & wife Ann Cecilia of AlexDC to Benjamin C. ASHTON & Richard C. NORTON of AlexDC Trust using Ann interest

in 1400a which Flora LEE m/o Ann and former w/o Ludwell LEE partitions between brother Richard Henry LEE and Ann. Wit: West ASHTON, F. H. KENEDY, Anth'y CREASE. Delv. to A. GILPIN pr order filed DB YY:300 12 May 1820.

Bk:Pg: 2Y:304 Date: 10 Apr 1819 RtCt: 14 Jun 1819
Jacob STONEBURNER dec'd. Division –Barbary DRISH wd/o Jacob (32a), Christian STONEBURNER (7a), Jacob STONEBURNER (7½a), Sally STONEBURNER (7½a), Betzey STONEBURNER (7a), Peggy STONEBURNER (7½a), Susanna FEICHTER w/o Peter FEICHTER (14a), Catharine ELLIOT w/o John ELLIOT (13a), Christena CAMERLY w/o Jacob CAMERLY (9a & 2a), Frederick STONEBURNER (11a & 3a), Barbary McMULLIN (w/o Daniel McMULLIN, 11a & 3a), ch/o Godfrey STONEBURNER dec'd (Jacob, William, John & Francis STONEBURNER) (13a). Gives plat. Divisors: Jno. MATHIAS, Saml. M. EDWARDS, Thomas SANDERS.

Bk:Pg: 2Y:308 Date: 13 Jul 1819 RtCt: 13 Jul 1819
John HAMILTON, Benjamin SHREVE & Robert MOFFETT. Bond on HAMILTON as sheriff to collect poor rate.

Bk:Pg: 2Y:309 Date: __ 1819 RtCt: 13 Jul 1819
Sheriff John HAMILTON, Benjamin SHREVE, Robert MOFFETT & Jno. A. BINNS. Bond on HAMILTON to collect levies.

Bk:Pg: 2Y:309 Date: 2 Jan 1819 RtCt: 15 Jun 1819
Samuel BUTCHER the younger & wife Hannah to Samuel TORBERT. B/S of 14a (from will of father Samuel BUTCHER dec'd when surveyed indicated this additional land, suit agst Samuel by Jenkin PHILIPS & wife Hannah and TORBERT) adj Thomas HEREFORD. Wit: S. BLINCOE, Henry PEERS, Benj. SHREVE. Delv. to John TORBERT 2 Nov 1819.

Bk:Pg: 2Y:312 Date: 17 Jun 1809 RtCt: 13 Jul 1819
William M. LITTLEJOHN (Lt. of Light Dragoons of U.S. army now of New Orleans) to John LITTLEJOHN Esqr of Ldn. PoA.

Bk:Pg: 2Y:313 Date: 7 Jun 1819 RtCt: 7 Jun 1819
Henry BROOKES of Ldn to Susannah BROOKES of Ann Arundel Co Md. B/S of 1/11th of undivided late property of Walter BROOKES dec'd. Wit: A. O. POWELL, Rich'd NORWOOD, Caleb D. BROOKES, Jno. MATHIAS.

Bk:Pg: 2Y:313 Date: 28 Jun 1819 RtCt: 28 Jun 1819
Mary BARNETT (guardian of Joseph BARNETT) of Ldn to Truman GORE of Ldn. Indenture of apprenticeship to learn trade of house-joiner from now until 18 Dec 1825 when Joseph will be 21y old. Wit: Thomas A. MOORE, Josiah L. DREAN.

Bk:Pg: 2Y:314 Date: 20 Aug 1818 RtCt: 9 Jul 1819
John LITTLEJOHN & wife Monica to Gerard L. W. HUNT. Correction for B/S of ¼a in new addition of Lsbg on 20 Aug 1818 to Joseph

ADAMS who sold to G. L. W. HUNT but error was made in length of front of lot. Delv. to G. L. W. ADAMS [HUNT?] 2 Jun 1825.

Bk:Pg: 2Y:315   Date: 7 May 1819   RtCt: 15 Jun 1819
Richard Henry LEE of Ldn to Ludwell LEE of Ldn. B/S of 100a 'Sugarland tract' on Potomac from div. of estate of Philip Ludwell LEE dec'd between heirs Matilda LEE & Flora LEE. Ludwell has possession for life as a tenant.

Bk:Pg: 2Y:316   Date: 14 Jun 1819   RtCt: 14 Jun 1819
Jane McCABE of Ldn to Charles Fenton MERCER & Charles P. TUTT of Ldn. B/S of dower rights to 250½a conveyed to Isaac LAROWE on 15 Nov 1794 by husband Henry McCABE.

Bk:Pg: 2Y:317   Date: 6 Oct 1818   RtCt: 14 Jun 1819
Foushee TEBBS of PrWm to Thomas TRIPLETT of Ldn. B/S of all lands sold to TEBBS by Thomas TRIPLETT & wife Margaret Carr on 5 Oct 1818. Delv. to Wm. RUST pr order 21 Apr 1827.

Bk:Pg: 2Y:318   Date: 14 Oct 1818   RtCt: 14 Jun 1819
Samuel SINCLAIR of Ldn to Francis W. LUCKETT of Ldn. Trust for debt to William BRONAUGH & Abner HUMPHREY. Wit: John W. T. BRONAUGH, Jere. W. BRONAUGH Jr., Jere. W. BRONAUGH.

Bk:Pg: 2Y:319   Date: 21 Mar 1819   RtCt: 14 Jun 1819
Moses GULICK & wife Martha and George GULICK & wife Sarah of Ldn to William LYNE of Ldn. B/S of 12a on 'Gulicks Gum Spring tract. Wit: Burr POWELL, A. GIBSON. Delv. to LYNN 14 Jan 1822.

Bk:Pg: 2Y:321   Date: 27 May 1819   RtCt: 14 Jun 1819
Yeoman John WHITACRE & wife Phebe of Ldn to Seth SMITH of Ldn. Trust for debt to Aaron BURSON of Ldn using land cnvy/b BURSON & wife Esther. Wit: Wm. DUNKIN, David E. BROWN, James MACKLAN, Wm. BRONAUGH, Thos GREGG.

Bk:Pg: 2Y:323   Date: 16 Dec 1818   RtCt: 4 Jun 1819
Fanny LEE (wd/o & Exor of Thomas L. LEE) to Samuel CLAPHAM of Ldn & Edmund J. LEE of AlexDC. B/S of 38a and right of passing from mill on Goose Creek to main road from Lsbg to Alexandria. Gives plats. Wit: Tasker C. QUINLAN, Josias CLAPHAM, Rich'd H. LEE, Jno. LITTLEJOHN, Chs. G. ESKRIDGE. Delv. to CLAPHAM 15 Mar 1821.

Bk:Pg: 2Y:326   Date: 19 Feb 1819   RtCt: 3 Jul 1819
Peter SANDERS & wife Ann of Ldn to Samuel HOUGH Jr of Ldn. B/S of 94a in Piedmont Manor (cnvy/b Henry Jos. FRY). Delv. to HOUGH 26 Oct 1821.

Bk:Pg: 2Y:328   Date: 9 Mar 1818   RtCt: 23 Jun 1819
James MOORE, Asa MOORE & John WILLIAMS (Exors of Mahlon JANNEY dec'd of Wtfd) to Charles G. EDWARDS of Ldn. B/S of lot in Wtfd adj John VANDEVENTER.

Bk:Pg: 2Y:330   Date: 9 Mar 1818   RtCt: 23 Jun 1819
John WILLIAMS & Thomas PHILIPS (Exors of Sarah JANNEY dec'd of Wtfd) to Charles G. EDWARDS of Ldn. B/S of lot in Wtfd adj formerly lot of Sarah CAVAN, Anna BALL.

Bk:Pg: 2Y:332   Date: 21 Jun 1819   RtCt: 3 Jul 1819
John W. GRAYSON of Ldn to Stephen McPHERSON Jr. of Ldn. B/S of 1a lot nr Bloomfield (where Richard MATHEW & wife Elizabeth previously lived but sold by trustees). Wit: Wm. GRAYSON, Notley C. WILLIAMS, Benjamin GRAYSON. Delv. to GRAYSON pr order of McPHERSON 3 Sep 1821.

Bk:Pg: 2Y:333   Date: 19 Feb 1819   RtCt: 3 Jul 1819
Peter SANDERS & wife Ann of Ldn to Samuel HOUGH Jr. of Ldn. B/S of 14¼a on E side of short hill. Wit: Abiel JENNERS, John H. McCABE. Delv. to HOUGH 26 Oct 1821.

Bk:Pg: 2Y:335   Date: 21 Apr 1819   RtCt: 14 Jun 1829
John BOOTH Jr. & wife Catharine of Ldn to John GEORGE of Ldn. B/S of BOOTH's interest in 60a devised by Robert BOOTH to John BOOTH Jr. during his life and after his death to heirs of Thomas STUMP and William CHAMBERS including interest of George CULP & wife Eleanor, John CHAMBERS, William CHAMBERS, William ADAMS & wife Dowzer, John CRUTCHLY & wife Nancy, Henry JACKSON & wife Elizabeth & Sarah HURLEY which BOOTH purchased. Wit: Samuel HOUGH Jr., John H. McCABE. Delv. to __ 24 Aug 1820.

Bk:Pg: 2Y:337   Date: 15 Apr 1819   RtCt: 14 Jun 1819
Bernard MANN & wife Joanna of Ldn to Vincent MOSS of Ldn. B/S of 77a (cnvy/b Nathaniel MOSS & wife Ann in Oct 1798). Wit: Burr POWELL, Abner GIBSON. Delv. to MOSS 16 Apr 1828.

Bk:Pg: 2Y:339   Date: __ 1819   RtCt: 14 Jun 1819
Samuel CLAPHAM & wife Elizabeth of Ldn to Jacob FAWLEY of Ldn. B/S of 17a on Katocton Mt. adj JOHNSON's furnace tract. Wit: E. G. HAMILTON, Lee W. DENHAM, Josiah L. DREAN. Delv. to FAWLEY 19 Dec 1821.

Bk:Pg: 2Y:341   Date: 14 Apr 1819   RtCt: Jun 1819
Burr POWELL & wife Catharine of Ldn to Bernard MANN of Ldn. B/S of Lots #1 & #2 in Mdbg. Wit: A. GIBSON, Towns'd McVEIGH, Asa ROGERS, Francis W. LUCKETT, Wm. NOLAND. Delv. to MANN 23 May 1820.

Bk:Pg: 2Y:343   Date: 27 Mar 1819   RtCt: 15 Jun 1819
Dade P. NOLAND & wife Caroline Francis of Ldn to Elizabeth NOLAND of Ldn. B/S of 32½a (from div. of estate of father Thomas NOLAND dec'd to Dade & brothers Samuel and Lloyd). Wit: Johnston CLEVELAND, Leven LUCKETT. Delv. to B. P. NOLAND on 14 Nov 1859.

Bk:Pg: 2Y:345   Date: 22 Mar 1819   RtCt: 14 Jun 1819
Dempsey CARTER & wife Mary Anne of Ldn to Richard CARTER of Ldn. B/S of 72a adj John W. GRAYSON, Henry CARTER. Wit: Benjamin GRAYSON, John W. GRAYSON. Delv. pr order on 9 Mar 1830.

Bk:Pg: 2Y:347   Date: 10 Jun 1819   RtCt: 14 Jun 1819
James GREENLEASE & wife Catharine of Ldn to Richard H. HENDERSON of Lsbg. Trust for debt to Samuel M. EDWARDS using 72a. Wit: Samuel MURREY, Presley CORDELL.

Bk:Pg: 2Y:350   Date: 10 Jun 1819   RtCt: 11 Jun 1819
James CAMPBELL & wife Elizabeth of Ldn to Richard H. HENDERSON of Lsbg. Trust for debt to Saml. M. EDWARDS using 130a prch/o EDWARDS. Wit: Samuel MURREY, Presley CORDELL. Delv. to EDWARDS 31 Aug 1822.

Bk:Pg: 2Y:353   Date: 22 Jun 1819   RtCt: 9 Aug 1819
Thomas J. MARLOW. Col from Md for black girl Harriet 9y old.

Bk:Pg: 2Y:353   Date: 9 May 1816   RtCt: 19 May 1819
John HARDING of Ldn to Rhodam ROGERS of Hampshire Co Va. BoS for slave boy Gary aged between 8-9y.

Bk:Pg: 2Y:354   Date: 4 Aug 1819   RtCt: 5 Aug 1819
Jane DOWNS of Lsbg to daughter Sarah Eleanor CALDWELL of Lsbg. Gift of all the furniture Jane owns.

Bk:Pg: 2Y:355   Date: 3 Aug 1819   RtCt: 3 Aug 1819
David OGDON and William H. LANE. Agreement on sale of house & lot in Lsbg to Lane for relinquishment of dower rights before 20 Sept and deed of trust. Wit: L. P. W. BALCH.

Bk:Pg: 2Y:355   Date: 8 May 1817   RtCt: 9 Aug 1819
Ann(a) Brown WEST of Logan Co KY to James H. HAMILTON of Ldn. PoA to convey to William ELLZEY of Ldn in trust for benefit of heirs of Mathew HARRISON dec'd 41a or 42a formerly sold to HARRISON by Elizabeth WEST dec'd sister of Ann.

Bk:Pg: 2Y:357   Date: 19 Jul 1819   RtCt: 19 Jul 1819
Bernard HOUGH (Admr of Patrick CAVAN dec'd late of Lsbg) to Nancy THOMAS (wd/o Leonard THOMAS dec'd). LS of 9a leased to CAVAN by James HEREFORD in Aug 1798. Delv. to THOMAS 31 Dec 1821.

Bk:Pg: 2Y:358   Date: 4 Aug 1819   RtCt: 4 Aug 1819
John NEWTON & wife Harriet of Ldn to John H. McCABE. Trust of 42a (devised in right of wife) nr Lsbg sold to George RUST Jr. on 24 Jul 1819 because Harriet in bad health and has since died, in trust for infant children Jane H. NEWTON & Mary Ann NEWTON. Wit: R. H. HENDERSON. Delv. to McCABE on ___.

Bk:Pg: 2Y:360   Date: 23 Nov 1818   RtCt: 10 May 1819
James MOUNT of Ldn to Hugh & James JOHNSON of James Co Va. Trust using 147¼a on Goose Creek. Wit: Francis W. LUCKETT,

George KILE, Joseph LANE. Delv. to Jos. McGEATH pr order filed 6 Sep 1823.

Bk:Pg: 2Y:361   Date: 1 May 1819   RtCt: 3 Aug 1819
Charles HOUGH & wife Mary and Elijah PEACOCK & wife Ann of Ldn to William STEER of Ldn. B/S of 45a (allotted from land of John HOUGH dec'd) adj N. DAVISON, William H. HOUGH, Jacob WINE, Benjamin STEER dec'd. Wit: Wm. H. HOUGH, J. P. THOMAS, Abiel JENNERS, Samuel HOUGH. Delv. to STEER 4 Sep 1820.

Bk:Pg: 2Y:363   Date: 18 Jan 1819   RtCt: 29 Jul 1819
David ALEXANDER & wife Elizabeth of Ldn to David CARTER of Ldn. B/S of 65a on N side of Goose Creek where ALEXANDER now lives adj SCHOLFIELD's mill, John HUMPHREY, Jonathan CARTER, old turnpike road to Snickers Gap. Wit: Leven LUCKETT, Thos. GREGG. Delv. to grantee 27 Dec 1819.

Bk:Pg: 2Y:365   Date: 9 Oct 1818   RtCt: 29 Jul 1819
Augustine LOVE & wife Mary of Ldn to Jonathan CARTER of Ldn. B/S of 87½a on N side of Goose Creek on old turnpike road leading to Snickers Gap nr Johnston's ford. Wit: John SINCLAIR, David CARTER, George LOVE, William BRONAUGH, Francis W. LUCKETT. Delv. to CARTER 31 Aug 1820.

Bk:Pg: 2Y:367   Date: 10 Oct 1818   RtCt: 29 Jul 1819
Augustine LOVE & wife Mary of Ldn to David CARTER of Ldn. B/S of 125a on road that passes nr LOVE's house to Snickers Gap, adj Jonathan CARTER (prch/o David JAMES), Adam BARR. Wit: John SINCLAIR, Jonathan CARTER, George LOVE, William BRONAUGH, Francis W. LUCKETT. Delv. to grantee 27 Dec 1819.

Bk:Pg: 2Y:369   Date: 21 Jul 1819   RtCt: 4 Aug 1819
John LITTLEJOHN late of Ldn to Moses BUTLER (free man of colour) of Ldn. B/S of 10a (convy/b Mrs. Fanny LEE). Delv. to BUTLER 27 Mar 1824.

Bk:Pg: 2Y:370   Date: 10 Jul 1819   RtCt: 10 Jul 1819
Peter BENEDUM Sr. of Ldn to Charles DOUGLASS of Ldn. Trust for debt to John GRAY using 217½a (cnvy/b Thos. N. BINNS & wife). Wit: Chs. G. ESKRIDGE, Robert MOFFETT, E. G. HAMILTON.

Bk:Pg: 2Y:372   Date: 31 Jul 1819   RtCt: 9 Aug 1819
William KEYSER & Sarah KIRK (Exors of Robert W. KIRK dec'd) of Germantown, Philadelphia Co Pa to John LITTLEJOHN late of Ldn. B/S of lot on Back St. in Lsbg which the late James KIRK of Alexandria died seized of. Wit: Jos. REED, Jno. ANTRIM.

Bk:Pg: 2Y:374   Date: 6 Jan 1819   RtCt: 4 Aug 1819
Ann B. WEST of Logan Co Ky to William ELLZAY (trustee under will of Mathew HARRISON dec'd of Ldn). Release on 41½a formerly sold to HARRISON by Elizabeth WEST dec'd sister of Ann B. WEST.

Bk:Pg: 2Y:375   Date: 31 Jul 1819   RtCt: 31 Jul 1819
William CARR & wife Mary of Ldn to Henry CLAGETT of Ldn. B/S of
76a (cnvy/b W. C. SELDON DB EE:539) on Tuscarora adj Carolina
Road.

Bk:Pg: 2Y:377   Date: __ 1819   RtCt: 312 Jul 1819
Ignatius ELGIN of Ldn to John WILDMAN of Ldn. B/S of 82a (prch/o
Exors of George CARTER) adj Samuel DONOHOE and 174a. Delv.
to WILDMAN 3 Mar 1821.

Bk:Pg: 2Y:379   Date: 1 Jul 1817   RtCt: 27 Jul 1819
George RUST Jr. & wife Maria C. of Ldn to James RUST of Ldn. B/S
of 169a adj __ McNELAGE, __ DAILEY, Martin KITZMILLER, __
THOMPKINS, Patrick CAVAN's lease, Mary FOSTER, __
RICHARDSON. Wit: Jno. ROSE, Presley CORDELL. Delv. to RUST
17 Feb 1828.

Bk:Pg: 2Y:381   Date: 22 May 1819   RtCt: 17 Jun 1819
James WILLIAMS dec'd. Division by court order dated 10 May 1819
– widow's dower (38a & 5a and negro man George), Dean JAMES
(101a prch/o Henry ASBERRY being Dean's share and share of
Barton D. HAWLEY & wife Hannah and Enoch HUTCHISON & wife
Abigail which Dean purchased and 60a and negro boy Jerry), Nancy
JAMES (62a and negro Nancy to be free in 8y) William JAMES (53a
and negroes Charlotte & Lorindy), John JAMES (51a and negro
Phillis), Enoch HUTCHISON & wife Abigail (negro Becky & child),
Barton D. HAWLEY & wife Hannah (his share to Dean JAMES
having paid for it). Divisors: Lewis HUTCHISON, Ariss BUCKNER,
Chs. LEWIS, Abel JANNEY.

**Bk:Pg: 2Y:383   Date: 20 Aug 1817   RtCt: 2 Sep 1818/6 Aug
1819**
Thomas PARKER, Robert J. TAYLOR & Richard H. HENDERSON
(commrs. under decree in chancery in Winchester in Thomas
SWANN & Edmund J. LEE Admrs of William B. PAGE dec'd agst
Ferdinando FAIRFAX) to John MATHIAS of Lsbg. B/S of 814a in
Ldn & JeffVa. Wit: Chs. G. ESKRIDGE, S. BLINCOE, L. P. W.
BALCH. Delv. to MATHIAS 6 Apr 1820.

Bk:Pg: 2Y:386   Date: 24 Jul 1819   RtCt: 4 Aug 1819
John NEWTON & wife Harriet of Ldn to George RUST Jr. of Ldn.
B/S of 42a adj J. G. McCABE, Mrs. DOWLING. Wit: Presley
CORDELL, Thomas SANDERS. Delv. to RUST 3 May 1824.

Bk:Pg: 2Y:388   Date: 23 Jul 1819   RtCt: 24 Jul 1819
Isaac HARRIS and Simon SMALE & wife Elizabeth of Ldn to
Sampson BLINCOE of Ldn. B/S of part of Lot #56 in Lsbg (conveyed
to HARRIS in trust for SMALE by John DREAN) adj Samuel
TUSTIN. Wit: John MCCORMICK, Thomas SANDERS. Delv. to
BLINCOE 4 Sep 1826

Bk:Pg: 2Y:390   Date: 1 Jan 1819   RtCt: 7 Jun 1819
James RUST & wife Sarah and George RUST Jr. & wife Maria of
Ldn to Thomas R. MOTT of Ldn. B/S of 321a (prch/o Henry
JENKINS & wife Margaret in May 1818) on Secolon. Wit: John
McCORMICK, Presley CORDELL. Delv. to R. H. HIND the Exor. 24
Sep 1828.

Bk:Pg: 2Y:393   Date: 31 Jul 1819   RtCt: 31 Jul 1819
Henry CLAGETT & wife Julia of Lsbg to Samuel CARR and
Sampson BLINCOE of Lsbg. Trust for debt to William CARR using
76a.

Bk:Pg: 2Y:395   Date: 11 Jan 1819   RtCt: 2 Sep 1819
Sarah PRICE & Samuel CLAPHAM to George BEEMER. BoS for
slave for life woman Betsy & her infant child Hannah. Wit: Jos.
BEARD, Lewis BEARD.

Bk:Pg: 2Y:395   Date: 1 Apr 1818   RtCt: 24 Aug 1819
Andrew FINITY & wife Jemima and Maria FINITY of Ldn to Amos
DENHAM of Ldn. B/S of all interest of Andrew & Jemima and
reversion of 132a lately belonging to John VIOLETT f/o Jemima
subject to L/L by Elijah VIOLETT. Wit: Amos JOHNSON, William
BRENT, Wm. CHADDUCK, Joseph CARR, A. GIBSON.

Bk:Pg: 2Y:397   Date: 20 Mar 1819   RtCt: 21 Aug 1819
Peter PHILIPS of Athens Co OH (attorney in fact for David
McDANIEL & wife Elizabeth late Elizabeth WILSON, Hannah
WILSON & Mary WILSON and as Guardian for John, Porter,
Thomas, Eleanor, Sally & Maria WILSON infants pr order of 15 Dec
1818) to Amos HARVEY of Ldn. B/S of all shares & interest in real
estate in Ldn of ancestor Thomas WILSON dec'd whereupon
Ebenezer WILSON dec'd their grandfather died seized. Delv. to
HARVEY 17 Feb 1827.

Bk:Pg: 2Y:398   Date: 7 Sep 1819   RtCt: 7 Sep 1819
James CURRIE to Richard H. HENDERSON. Trust for debt to
George RHODES & Daniel LOVETT (as CURRIE's security) using
65a nr Lsbg (undivided 1/8th part subject to dower of Elizabeth
CURRIE wd/o Isaac CURRIE dec'd)

Bk:Pg: 2Y:399   Date: 9 Sep 1819   RtCt: 11 Sep 1819
John MONROE & wife Mary of Lsbg to Richard H. HENDERSON of
Lsbg. B/S of ½a adj James RUST, Samuel M. EDWARDS, Thos. R.
MOTT, Robert BENTLEY. Wit: William NOLAND, John
McCORMICK.

Bk:Pg: 2Y:400   Date: 4 Sep 1819   RtCt: 9 Sep 1819
Thos. R. MOTT of Lsbg to Richard H. HENDERSON. B/S on
'Academy lot' in Lsbg (held in trust by MOTT for debt of Thos. N.
BINNS).

Bk:Pg: 2Y:401   Date: 9 Sep 1819   RtCt: 11 Sep 1819
Richard H. HENDERSON & wife Orra Moore to John MONROE. B/S
of house & ' Academy Lot' on Loudoun St in Lsbg adj John A.
BINNS. Wit: William NOLAND, John McCORMICK.

Bk:Pg: 2Y:402   Date: 18 Sep 1818   RtCt: 24 Aug 1819
Edward MARTIN & wife Elizabeth and John MARTIN of Ldn to
Amos DENHAM of Ldn. B/S of all interest in reversion of 133a lately
belonging to John VIOLETT f/o Elizabeth subject to L/L by Elijah
VIOLETT. Wit: Amos JOHNSON, James HARL, Willis BRENT,
Joseph CARR, A. GIBSON.

Bk:Pg: 2Y:404   Date: 10 Jul 1818   RtCt: 13 Aug 1818
Samuel MURREY and Jonas POTTS (under decree of 12 Jun 1795
in chancery between William WILSON & Co agst James BYRNES &
wife Rachel and Geo. Emery GOFF & wife Mary) of Ldn to Andrew
JAMIESON of AlexDC B/S of Lot #61 (purchased by Pat'k CAVAN
as agent for WILSON and conveyed to Wm. HERBERT in trust for
benefit of his children. Trustee assigned right to WILSON who
assigned it to Andrew JAMIESON).

Bk:Pg: 2X:405   Date: 27 Apr 1819   RtCt: 27 Apr 1819
John ROSE (Admr wwa of George KILGORE dec'd) to Geo. K.
FOX. Receipt for payment of part of legacy. Delv to ROSE the Admr.
22 May 1820.

Bk:Pg: 2X:406   Date: 26 Apr 1819   RtCt: 26 Apr 1819
John ROSE (Admr wwa of George KILGORE dec'd) to William
SHEID who m. Martina B. FOX. Receipt for payment for part of
legacy. Delv. to ROSE the Admr 22 May 1820.

Bk:Pg: 2X:406   Date: 27 Apr 1819   RtCt: 27 Apr 1819
John ROSE (Admr wwa of George KILGORE dec'd) to Geo. K. FOX
(apptd. 14 Apr 1819 as guardian to sister Elizabeth F. FOX). Receipt
for payment for part of legacy. Delv. to ROSE the Admr 22 May
1820.

Bk:Pg: 2X:406   Date: 21 Apr 1819   RtCt: 21 Apr 1819
John ROSE (Admr wwa of George KILGORE dec'd) to George
SHEID (apptd 13 Apr 1819 as guardian to his children Sarah G.,
James W., John Henry & Erasmus W. SHEID). Receipt for payment
for part of legacy. Delv. to ROSE the Admr 22 May 1820.

Bk:Pg: 2Z:001   Date: 15 Jun 1819   RtCt: 23 Aug 1819
Joseph WOOD & wife Lydia of Ldn to William STONE of Ldn. B/S of
½a in Wtfd (prch/o Exors of Mahlon JANNEY dec'd). Wit: Samuel
HOUGH Jr., John H. McCABE. Delv. to STONE 12 Jan 1820.

Bk:Pg: 2Z:002   Date: 9 Aug 1819   RtCt: 9 Aug 1819
Peter MILLER and Aaron MILLER (Exors of Peter MILLER dec'd) of
Ldn to Jacob SHOEMAKER of Ldn. B/S of 3a on E side of short hill
adj lands of Peter MILLER dec'd, Philip FRY, Charles CRIM, John &
Benjamin GRUBB. Delv. to grantee Feb 1822.

Bk:Pg: 2Z:004   Date: 22 Mar 1819   RtCt: 1 Sept 1819
Asa CARTER & wife Cynthia of Ham[p]shire Co Va to Dempsey
CARTER of Ldn. B/S of 44a adj William CARTER, Demsey
CARTER, Abner HUMPHREY. Wit: Benjamin GRAYSON, John W.
GRAYSON.

Bk:Pg: 2Z:006   Date: 10 Jun 1819   RtCt: 9 Aug 1819
Joshua PUSEY & wife Mary of Ldn to James NIXON of Ldn. B/S of
36a adj John WORSLEY, Robert SANFORD, James NIXON, James
TEMPLER. Wit: Abiel JENNERS, Saml. HOUGH Jr. Delv. to PUSEY
Exor 10 Mar 1831.

Bk:Pg: 2Z:008   Date: 13 Jul 1819   RtCt: 1 Sep 1819
Demsey CARTER & wife Mary Anne of Ldn to William CARTER of
Ldn. B/S of 44a (cnvy/b brother Asa) adj William CARTER, John W.
GRAYSON. Wit: Benjamin GRAYSON, John W. GRAYSON. Delv.
pr order filed 13 Feb 1827.

Bk:Pg: 2Z:010   Date: 15 Nov 1817   RtCt: 8 Sep 1819
Jesse THOMAS & wife Elizabeth of Ldn to John CHEW of Ldn. B/S
of 84a adj Owen THOMAS. Wit: Notley C. WILLIAMS, Joshua
OSBURN.

Bk:Pg: 2Z:012   Date: 9 Mar 1819   RtCt: 9 Aug 1819
Absalom KALB & wife Susannah of Ldn to Philip COOPER of Ldn.
B/S of 104a adj George SHOEMAKER, Jeremiah PURDOM, Aaron
MILLER. Wit: John H. McCABE, Saml. HOUGH Jr. Delv. to
COOPER 20 Sep 1825.

Bk:Pg: 2Z:014   Date: 13 Aug 1819   RtCt: 30 Aug 1819
John LITTLEJOHN & wife Monica of Ldn to Jesse DAILEY of Ldn.
B/S of 7a (bought of Fanny LEE).

Bk:Pg: 2Z:015   Date: 5 Oct 1818   RtCt: 14 Jun 1819
Thomas TRIPLETT & wife Margaret Carr (d/o Betsy TEBBS of
Dumfries) of Ldn to Foushe TEBBS of PrWm. B/S of Margaret's
interest in estate of grandfather William CARR dec'd. Wit: John
ROSE, Charles B. BALL.

Bk:Pg: 2Z:017   Date: 10 Apr 1819   RtCt: 9 Aug 1819
Joseph WOOD & wife Lydia and John CAVEN of Ldn to Joshua
PEWSEY of Ldn. B/S of 87a on Kattocton Mt. (formerly property of
Joseph CAVEN dec'd) adj John WORSLEY, Robert SANFORD,
James NIXON. Wit: Saml. HOUGH Jr., John H. McCABE. Delv. to
grantee 7 Sep 1820.

Bk:Pg: 2Z:019   Date: 31 Mar 1819   RtCt: 31 Mar 1819
Samuel LUCKETT & wife Rebecca, Benjamin JACKSON & wife
Elizabeth and Josias CLAPHAM of Ldn to William LYNE of Ldn. B/S
of 274a on broadrun (part of tract willed by Josias CLAPHAM dec'd
to Samuel CLAPHAM dec'd). Wit: John ROSE, William CARR. Delv.
to Jas. M. LEWIS pr order filed 27 Jun 1821.

Bk:Pg: 2Z:021   Date: 14 Jun 1819   RtCt: 9 Aug 1819
William NEWTON dec'd. Division by court order dated 11 Mar 1819
of lands on W side of Goose Creek – Lot #1 of 181a to heirs & reps
of William NEWTON dec'd and Lot #2 of 227a to complainant
Joseph T. NEWTON. Gives plat. Divisors. William ELLZEY, Silas
WHERRY, Archibald MAINS, Britton SANDERS.

Bk:Pg: 2Z:024   Date: 5 Aug 1819   RtCt: 9 Aug 1819
James CRAINE (trustee of Jane WEATHERBY formerly Jane
McFARLAND) to Oliver DENHAM. B/S of Lot #21 in Mdbg (Jane
entitled to devise from John McFARLAND during her life who sold to
William SWART & wife Jane who sold to DENHAM). Wit: Burr
POWELL, A. GIBSON.

Bk:Pg: 2Z:027   Date: 25 Aug 1819   RtCt: 26 Aug 1819
Andrew JAMIESON & wife Mary of AlexDC to John A. BINNS of
Ldn. B/S of Lot #61 in Lsbg. Wit: A. O. POWELL, Towns'd
McVEIGH, Lee W. DENHAM, Rich'd H. HENDERSON.

Bk:Pg: 2Z:028   Date: 17 May 1819   RtCt: 10 Sep 1819
Joseph SMITH & wife Mary of AlexDC to Samuel TUSTIN of Ldn.
B/S of lot in Lsbg adj Wm. CARR, SMITH's grass lot, lot occupied by
Charles a free negro, Francis EDWARDS, Saml. M. EDWARDS.
Wit: Samuel MURREY, Saml. M. EDWARDS. Delv. to TUSTIN 4 Oct
1820.

Bk:Pg: 2Z:030   Date: 18 Jan 1819   RtCt: 9 Aug 1819
Ann A. B. HARDING of JeffVa to Peter COMPHER of Ldn. B/S of
18a (allotted to HARDING in div. of John A. BINNS dec'd). Delv. to
COMPHER 12 Dec 1820.

Bk:Pg: 2Z:032   Date: 8 Aug 1814   RtCt: 4 Aug 1819
Fanny LEE (Exor of Thomas Ludwell LEE dec'd) of Ldn to Henry
PEERS of Ldn. B/S of 10a adj __ NEWTON.

Bk:Pg: 2Z:035   Date: 14 Nov 1818   RtCt: 1 Sep 1819
Yeoman Michael PLAISTER & wife Jane of Ldn to Lewis HUNT of
Ldn. B/S of ¼a Lot #4 in Union (James REID died seized of). Wit:
Seth SMITH, Wm. BRONAUGH, N. C. WILLIAMS. Delv. to HUNT 31
Jul 1820.

Bk:Pg: 2Z:036   Date: 5 Apr 1819   RtCt: 24 Aug 1819
Yeoman William VICKERS & wife Ann of Ldn to James RALLS of
Ldn. B/S of 1a (formerly property of James LEITH) adj George
BURSON, Henry BARTLET. Wit: Wm. BRONAUGH, Francis W.
LUCKETT.

Bk:Pg: 2Z:038   Date: 26 May 1819   RtCt: 26 Aug 1819
Aaron BURSON & wife Esther of Ldn to Michael PLAISTER. B/S of
57a (willed to Aaron by father James BURSON dec'd) adj Isaac
BROWN, Joseph BURSON, Michael PLAISTER. With Seth SMITH,
Wm. BRONAUGH, Francis W. LUCKETT. Delv. to grantee 27 Jun
1821.

Bk:Pg: 2Z:040   Date: 26 Apr 1819   RtCt: 27 Aug 1819
William JANNEY of Ldn to John WILLIAMS & Jacob MENDENHALL of Ldn. Trust for debt to James FARQUHAR using 50a on Kattocton creek. Delv. pr order filed 1 Apr 1822.

Bk:Pg: 2Z:043   Date: 26 Aug 1819   RtCt: 11 Sep 1819
Bernard HOUGH (Admr of Patrick CAVANS dec'd) of Lsbg to Samuel M. EDWARDS of Ldn. A/L (James HEREFORD to CAVANS Aug 1798) of lot adj John LITTLEJOHN, Saml. HOUGH including 'federal spring'. Wit: Josiah L. DREAN, A. O. POWELL, E. G. HAMILTON. Delv. to EDWARDS 8 Jun 1822.

Bk:Pg: 2Z:045   Date: 10 Sep 1819   RtCt: 10 Sep 1819
Stephen McPHERSON Jr., Jno. MARKS & Jacob SILCOTT. Bond on McPHERSON as constable.

Bk:Pg: 2Z:046   Date: 9 Sep 1819   RtCt: 13 Sep 1819
Daniel LOVETT & Rich'd H. HENDERSON. Bond on LOVETT as commr. of revenue in 1st district.

Bk:Pg: 2Z:046   Date: 13 Sep 1819   RtCt: 13 Sep 1819
Jesse TIMMS & George CARTER. Bond on TIMMS as commr. of revenue in 2nd district.

Bk:Pg: 2Z:047   Date: 13 Sep 1819   RtCt: 13 Sep 1819
Jesse McVEIGH & Hugh RODGERS. Bond on McVEIGH as commr. of revenue in 3rd district.

Bk:Pg: 2Z:048   Date: 13 Sep 1819   RtCt: 13 Sep 1819
James D. FRENCH, Lewis FRENCH & Garrison B. FRENCH. Bond on James D. FRENCH as constable.

Bk:Pg: 2Z:049   Date: 1 May 1819   RtCt: 13 Sep 1819
John BAYLY (s/o Pierce BAYLY) & wife Peggy of Ldn to Hugh ROGERS of Ldn. B/S of 97½a residue of land formerly held by John KELLEY under L/L after the recovery of SHEARMAN's reps agst WATTSON and 76a formerly held by Thomas SEALOCK under L/L. Wit: Chas. LEWIS, Ariss BUCKNER.

Bk:Pg: 2Z:052   Date: 3 Jan 1818   RtCt: 30 Aug 1819
John WYNN & wife Susannah of Ldn to Joseph HAINS of Ldn. Trust using land sold to WYNN by HAINS. Wit: Notley C. WILLIAMS, Thos. GREGG. Delv. to WINN pr order from Wm. H. HANDY 12 Mar 1821.

Bk:Pg: 2Z:054   Date: 17 May 1819   RtCt: 26 Aug 1819
George BAYLY & wife Mary Ann of Ldn to Stephen BEARD of Ldn. B/S of 334a (will by Pierce BAYLY Sr. to Pierce BAYLY Jr. dec'd). Wit: Ariss BUCKNER, John BAYLY. Delv to Jos. BEARD 18 Dec 1820.

Bk:Pg: 2Z:056   Date: 9 Sep 1819   RtCt: 10 Sep 1819
Tasker Carter QUINLAND of Ldn to Cornelius BENNETT of Ldn. Lease agreement for 5y of 300a on Little river where __ JOHNSON resides.

Bk:Pg: 2Z:058   Date: 19 Jul 1819   RtCt: 27 Aug 1819
Amos JANNEY of Ldn to Abiel JENNERS & Thomas PHILIPS of
Ldn. Trust for debt to James MOORE (Exor of Joseph DAVIS dec'd)
using 200a at foot of short hill. Wit: John WILLIAMS, David JAMES,
James ERVIN. Delv. to Abiel JENNERS 14 Dec 1822.

Bk:Pg: 2Z:060   Date: 26 Feb 1819   RtCt: 13 Sep 1819
Martin SETTLE & wife Ann of Scott Co KY to John HUTCHISON of
Ldn. B/S of 133a. Wit: Jno. BRANHAM, Job STEVENSON. Delv. to
Wm. MERSHON pr order of John HUTCHISON filed 26 Feb 1822.

Bk:Pg: 2Z:065   Date: 1 Sep 1819   RtCt: 11 Sep 1819
John MONROE & wife Mary of Ldn to Robert BENTLEY of Ldn. B/S
of lot on W side of King St in Lsbg adj Thomas MORALLEE, Rev.
John MINES. Wit: E. G. HAMILTON, A. O. POWELL, Josia[h] L.
DREAN, John McCORMICK, Presley CORDELL.

Bk:Pg: 2Z:067   Date: 1 Sep 1819   RtCt: 11 Sep 1819
Robert BENTLEY & wife Catharine Langdon of Ldn to John
MONROE of Ldn. B/S of lot in Lsbg (prch/o Peter ISH) adj Richard
H. HENDERSON's office on S side of Market St, Thomas R. MOTT,
Saml. M. EDWARDS, James RUST. Wit: E. G. HAMILTON, Josiah
L. DREAN, Lee H. DENHAM, John McCORMICK, Presley
CORDELL.

Bk:Pg: 2Z:070   Date: 26 Apr 1819   RtCt: 13 Sep 1819
Benjamin C. ASHTON & Richard C. NORTON of Alexandria D. C.
and James L. McKENNA & wife Ann Cecilia (d/o Flora Lee). Trust to
Robert J. TAYLOR in trust for Charles T. CHAPMAN (as security for
McKENNA. Wit: Anth'y CREASE, West ASHTON, W. C. PAGE, F.
H. KENNEDY, George TAYLOR, Thomas MOSS. Delv. to A. P
GILPIN pr order filed DB YY:300 15 May 1820.

Bk:Pg: 2Z:076   Date: 1 Sep 1819   RtCt: 11 Sep 1819
Robt BENTLEY to William D. DRISH & Presley CORDELL. Trust for
debt to John MONROE using lot on King St in Lsbg adj Thomas
MORALLEE. Wit: E. G. HAMILTON, Josiah L. DREAN, Lee W.
DENHAM. Delv. to CORDELL 30 Apr 1823.

Bk:Pg: 2Z:078   Date: 12 Jun 1819   RtCt: 9 Aug 1819
Nathan BROWN & wife Nancy of Ldn to Isaac NICKOLS Jr. &
James HOGE of Ldn. Trust for debt to Samuel & Isaac NICHOLS
using 135a nr N. fork meeting house where Thomas GREGG now
resides adj heirs of John YOUNG dec'd. Wit: Benjamin GRAYSON,
William CARR. Delv. to James HOGE 28 Jan 1823.

Bk:Pg: 2Z:083   Date: 2 Dec 1818   RtCt: 27 Jul 1819
Richard COCHRAN & Oliver DENHAM of Ldn to James L.
TRIPLETT of Ldn. Trust for debt to James N. ROBERDEAU of
Centreville using Lot #22 in Mdbg. Wit: John SMARR, John UPP,
John W. FRYE. Delv. to Frs. TRIPLETT Jr. pr order filed 8 Aug
1820.

Bk:Pg: 2Z:086 Date: 29 Jun 1818 RtCt: 26 Aug 1819
William NOLAND & wife Catharine of Ldn to Richard H.
HENDERSON. Trust for debt to Farmers Bank of Alexandria using
541a on both sides of Little river turnpike abt 26 miles from
Alexandria. Wit: Leven LUCKETT, Robt. ARMISTEAD.

Bk:Pg: 2Z:091 Date: 11 Oct 1819 RtCt: 11 Oct 1819
Frederick BELTZ of Ldn. DoE for man of colour James WEST. Wit:
Rich'd H. HENDERSON, Thomas A. MOORE.

Bk:Pg: 2Z:091 Date: 1 Oct 1819 RtCt: 11 Oct 1819
Thomson MASON. Col on 3 Sep 1819 of slave Lucy of very dark
complexion abt 17y old and abt 5' acquired by marriage.

Bk:Pg: 2Z:092 Date: 11 Oct 1819 RtCt: 11 Oct 1819
Travis GLASSCOCK, Francis W. LUCKETT, George HEAD Jr. &
Randolph RHODES. Bond on GLASSCOCK as constable.

Bk:Pg: 2Z:093 Date: 11 Oct 1819 RtCt: 11 Oct 1819
Garrison B. FRENCH, James D. FRENCH & William TAYLOR. Bond
on Garrison B. FRENCH as constable.

Bk:Pg: 2Z:094 Date: 9 Oct 1819 RtCt: 9 Oct 1819
Charles DRISH of Ldn to Joseph CALDWELL of Ldn. B/S of
undivided ¼th subject to dower of widow Sarah CALDWELL of
property formerly of Moses CALDWELL dec'd.

Bk:Pg: 2Z:095 Date: 28 Dec 1818 RtCt: 13 Sep 1819
Burr William HARRISON to Anthony CONARD & wife Mary. Release
of trust for debt to Thomas B. BEATTY using land adj where
CONARD lives.

Bk:Pg: 2Z:096 Date: 6 Mar 1819 RtCt: 11 Oct 1819
Washington HOUGH & wife Maria G. of Bridgeport, Fayett Co Pa to
Joseph BOND of Wtfd. B/S of ½ of 5a lot and tanyard in Wtfd (dev.
HOUGH and brother Peyton HOUGH by their grandfather William
HOUGH dec'd) adj Amasa HOUGH, Robt. BRADEN, Wm.
PAXSON, Flemmon PATTISON. Wit: Andrew PORTER, Abiel
JENNER, John H. McCABE. Delv. to Peyton HOUGH pr order filed
19 Mar 1823.

Bk:Pg: 2Z:099 Date: 14 Jun 1819 RtCt: 13 Sep 1819
Jonas POTTS & wife Nancy of Ldn to Benjamin SHREVE & Joshua
OSBURNE of Ldn. Trust for debt to Archibald McVICKER using
151a on SE side of Kattocton Mt. Wit: Leven LUCKETT, Abner
GIBSON. Delv. to Ben. SHREVE 26 Apr 1821.

Bk:Pg: 2Z:102 Date: 3 Mar 1819 RtCt: 13 Sep 1819
Joseph WOOD & wife Lydia of Ldn to William WRIGHT of Ldn. B/S
of 1a Lots #5, #6, #7 & #8 in Wtfd. Wit: Saml. HOUGH Jr., John H.
McCABE.

Bk:Pg: 2Z:104   Date: __ Jun 1819   RtCt: 13 Sep 1819
Archibald McVICKERS & wife Elizabeth of Ldn to Jonas POTTS of
Ldn. B/S of 151a. Wit: Craven OSBURNE, John WHITE. Delv. to
POTTS 4 Mar 1822.

Bk:Pg: 2Z:106   Date: 20 Feb 1819   RtCt: 13 Sep 1819
Moses WILSON & wife Tamar of Ldn to Hugh ROGERS of Ldn. B/S
of 5¾a (prch/o Walter LANGLEY) on Goose Creek adj Capt. Dennis
McCARTY. Wit: Burr POWELL, A. GIBSON.

Bk:Pg: 2Z:109   Date: __ 1819   RtCt: 8 Sep 1819
Francis TRIPLETT Sr. of Ldn to Francis TRIPLETT Jr. of Ldn. B/S of
vacant lot (cnvy/b Samuel M. EDWARDS) between lots of William
KING and Francis TRIPLETT Sr. on King St in Lsbg. Wit: Edw'd
HAMMATT, Benj'n MAULSBY, Andrew MONROE.

Bk:Pg: 2Z:110   Date: 4 Sep 1819   RtCt: 7 Oct 1819
Robert BRADEN & Charles BENNETT Jr. (Exors of James RICE
dec'd) of Ldn to Rebecca RICE of Lsbg. B/S of lot in Lsbg (prch/o
John NIXON & wife Nancy) adj Wm. KING.

Bk:Pg: 2Z:112   Date: 14 Sep 1819   RtCt: 12 Sep 1819
David OGDEN & wife Elizabeth of Ldn to William H. LANE of Ldn.
B/S of lot as corner of Cornwall & Back St. in Lsbg adj William
KLINE. Wit: John ROSE, John McCORMICK. Delv. to Harrison
FITZHUGH pr order 12 Nov 1821.

Bk:Pg: 2Z:114   Date: 3 Aug 1819   RtCt: 6 Oct 1819
Samuel BUTCHER & wife Hannah of Wood Co Va to John H.
BUTCHER of Ldn. B/S of undivided 1/6th of 130a which Samuel
claims as heir of Elizabeth BURKINS w/o John BURKINS and d/o
Samuel BUTCHER dec'd (tract now in possession of John
BURKINS) adj Benjamin OVERFIELD, Jenkin PHILLIPS. Delv. to
John H. BUTCHER 1 Mar 1822.

Bk:Pg: 2Z:116   Date: 7 Aug 1819   RtCt: 13 Sep 1819
Burr POWELL of Ldn to James WEEKS of Ldn. B/S of ½a Lot #31 at
Liberty & Marshall Sts. in Mdbg adj Samuel HENDERSON.

Bk:Pg: 2Z:118   Date: 7 Aug 1819   RtCt: 13 Sep 1819
Major Burr POWELL to Dr. James WEEKS. B/S of ½a Lot #42 at
Hamilton & Marshall Sts. in Mdbg. Wit: Cuth. POWELL Jr., Benjamin
SMITH, Thos. BISCOE.

Bk:Pg: 2Z:120   Date: 1 Jul 1819   RtCt: 11 Oct 1819
Thomas BEATTY & wife Rachel of Harrison Co OH to George
RHODES of Ldn. B/S of 41a (1/9th share of lands of Rachel's father
Thomas CIMMINGS dec'd). Wit: John HURLESS, John DAVIS,
James HARPER. Delv. to RHODES 9 Sep 1836.

Bk:Pg: 2Z:124   Date: 2 Sep 1818   RtCt: 12 Jul 1819
Frederick STONEBURNER & wife Elizabeth of Ldn to Jane MAINS
of Ldn. B/S of 111½a adj Joseph VANDEVENTER, John DODD and
5a (prch/o David LACEY) adj Obed PIERPOINT on road from Lsbg

to Hllb. Wit: Robert BRADEN, Abiel JENNERS. Delv. to Jno? CARR? 26 Apr 1825.

Bk:Pg: 2Z:127   Date: 4 Sep 1819   RtCt: 13 Sep 1819
Burr POWELL & wife Catharine to Abner GIBSON. B/S of 2a nr Mdbg on Wankopin branch. Wit: Francis W. LUCKETT, Leven LUCKETT. Delv. to GIBSON 14 Nov 1822.

Bk:Pg: 2Z:131   Date: 11 Jun 1819   RtCt: 1 Oct 1819
Isaac NICHOLS & James HOGE of Ldn to Nathan BROWN of Ldn. B/S of 135a where Thomas GREGG now resides (formerly held in trust by Isaac & Samuel NICHOLS from Thomas GREGG & wife Hannah) nr north fork meeting house adj heirs of John YOUNG dec'd. Delv. to Nathan NICHOLS 23 Feb 1820.

Bk:Pg: 2Z:133   Date: 3 Jul 1819   RtCt: 14 Sep 1819
Patrick B. MILHOLLAND/MILLHOLLEN of Ldn to Edward HAMMATT of Ldn. Trust for debt to William S. NEALE & James W. HANCHER (as security in 2 suits agt MILHOLLEN by Samuel BIRCHEY & Cupid ROBINSON) using lots on Loudoun St in Lsbg (prch/o Mathew MITCHELL & Reuben SCHOOLEY) and 10a on Kittoctan Mt. leased to Mathew MITCHELL. Delv. to HAMMAT 14 Jan 1820.

Bk:Pg: 2Z:136   Date: 1 Oct 1819   RtCt: 9 Oct 1819
Jacob FADELY & wife Mary of Ldn to Thomas MORALLEE of Ldn. Trust for debt to Simon SMALE using Lot #58 in Lsbg. Wit: Presley CORDELL, Saml. M. EDWARDS.

Bk:Pg: 2Z:139   Date: 6 Oct 1819   RtCt: 7 Oct 1819
Jesse GOVER & wife Meriam of Ldn to John WILLIAMS & William H. HOUGH of Ldn. Trust for debt to Robert BRADEN, John MORGAN & Joseph EACHES (Braden, Morgan & Co) using undivided interest in 201½a of Henry TAYLOR dec'd of Ldn. Wit: John H. McCABE, Saml. HOUGH Jr. Delv. pr order filed 14 Feb 1823.

Bk:Pg: 2Z:143   Date: 1 Oct 1819   RtCt: 9 Oct 1819
Simon SMALE & wife Elizabeth and Thomas MORALLEE of Ldn to Presley CORDELL & Jacob FADLEY of Ldn. Trust for debt to Jacob FADELEY using lot in Lsbg cnvy/b FADLEY to MORALLEE. Wit: Saml. M. EDWARDS, Thomas SANDERS.

Bk:Pg: 2Z:146   Date: 4 Nov 1819   RtCt: 10 Nov 1819
Richard H. HENDERSON (commr. in Joseph HARRIS agst reps of John A. BINNS dec'd) of Ldn to Zachariah DULANY of Ldn. B/S of 2a adj Stephen DANIEL, road from Wtfd to Noland's Ferry.

Bk:Pg: 2Z:147   Date: 26 Sep 1809 [19?]   RtCt: 8 Nov 1819
Thomas LESLIE & wife Ann of Ldn to Edward DOWLING of Ldn. B/S of 4¼a on side of N end of short hill adj Mahlon HOUGH. Wit: Mahlon ROACH, Samuel COOK, Henry DAWES. Delv. to grantee 1 Apr 1820.

Bk:Pg: 2Z:148   Date: 11 Oct 1819   RtCt: 11 Oct 1819
Edward HAZELL & Wm NOLAND. Bond on HAZEL as constable.

Bk:Pg: 2Z:149   Date: 17 Aug 1818   RtCt: 9 Aug 1819
John C. LICKEY & son John LICKEY and Sampson BLINCOE.
Agreement – fence nr road from Mdbg to Coes mill is property diving
line. Wit: A. O. POWELL, Geo. SWEARINGEN, John JONES,
Charles SMITH, Jno. MATHIAS.

Bk:Pg: 2Z:149   Date: 16 Oct 1819   RtCt: 4 Nov 1819
John RALPH of Ldn to Jesse McVEIGH of Ldn. B/S of 4a (cnvy/b
Isaac RICHARDS & Abner HUMPHREY) in Bloomfield adj where
Stephen GREGG now resides, road to Ebenezer meeting house.
Delv. to McVEIGH 11 Sep 1820.

Bk:Pg: 2Z:151   Date: 26 Jun 1819   RtCt: 11 Oct 1819
William NOLAND of Ldn to Amos FERGUSON of Ldn. B/S of 150a
which FERGUSON & Henson SIMPSON conveyed in trust to
NOLAND. Wit: Jonah HOOD, Samuel M. PROSSER, Richard H.
NEALE.

Bk:Pg: 2Z:152   Date: 26 Jun 1819   RtCt: 11 Oct 1819
Amos FERGUSON to William NOLAND. Trust for debt to James
SIMPSON (as rep of infant children of Henson SIMPSON dec'd)
using 150a. Wit: Jonah HOOD, Samuel M. PROSSER, Richard H.
NEALE. Delv. to SIMPSON 16 Sep 1820.

Bk:Pg: 2Z:154   Date: 10 Nov 1819   RtCt: 11 Nov 1819
Thomas HOUGH dec'd. Division – Joseph HOUGH (23a), Clarinda
FRENCH formerly HOUGH (22a & 30a), John W. T. HOUGH (37a),
Anne E. HOUGH (37a). Gives plat. Divisors: Robert BRADEN, John
H. McCABE, Abiel JENNERS. Chancery of 13 Sep 1819 – James D.
FRENCH & wife Clarinda vs. Joseph, Anne Eliz'h & John W. T.
HOUGH (John SCHOOLEY apptd. guardian for these infants).

Bk:Pg: 2Z:158   Date: 20 Oct 1819   RtCt: 21 Oct 1819
Moses WILSON & wife Tamar of Ldn to Miller HOGE of Ldn. B/S of
26¼a (prch/o Walter LANGLEY) adj Capt. Dennis McCARTY. Wit:
Burr POWELL, A. GIBSON. Delv. to Joseph EIDSON pr order filed
DB LL:148 on 10 Apr 1820.

Bk:Pg: 2Z:160   Date: 18 Sep 1819   RtCt: 27 Oct 1819
John ROOFE (Exor of Margaret RIDENBAUGH dec'd) of Ldn to
John BOOTH of Ldn. B/S of 13a (dev. Margaret the younger now
dec'd by mother Margaret RIDENBAUGH dec'd) adj David MULL,
George SHULTS, George COOPER, William WINNER. Delv. to
BOOTH Sr. 8 Mar 1821

Bk:Pg: 2Z:162   Date: 6 May 1819   RtCt: 12 Oct 1819
James BEAVERS of Ldn to William BENTON of Ldn. Trust for debt
to John BEVERIDGE using 50a. Wit: William THRIFT, Chas.
DUNCAN, William BEVERIDGE. Delv. to Wm. SMARR who
purchased land under the deed on ___.

Bk:Pg: 2Z:163   Date: 13 Sep 1819   RtCt: 11 Oct 1819
Ch. RALLS & wife Maria, Margaret Ann RALLS and Geo. N. RALLS
(heirs of G. RALLS dec'd) to Highland CROWE. B/S of 200a and
13a. Wit: Wm. A. LANE, James GREEN Jr.

Bk:Pg: 2Z:166   Date: 17 Feb 1819   RtCt: 16 Oct 1819
Tasker C. QUINLAN of Ldn to Archibald McVICKERS of Hampshire
Co. B/S of 136a. Delv. to McVICKER 22 Jan 1820.

Bk:Pg: 2Z:167   Date: 13 May 1819   RtCt: 11 Oct 1819
Henry CLAGETT & wife Julia of Ldn to John HALLING of Ldn. B/S
of 73a.

Bk:Pg: 2Z:169   Date: 4 Aug 1819   RtCt: 13 Nov 1819
Jacob EVERHART dec'd. Division by court order dated 16 Jun 1819
– widow (60a), Sarah EVERHART (9a), Joseph EVERHART (24a),
Jacob EVERHART (34a), John EVERHART (36a). Gives plat.
Divisors: John S. MARLOW, John GEORGE, Jno. J. MATHIAS.

Bk:Pg: 2Z:173   Date: 18 Sep 1819   RtCt: 12 Oct 1819
John GEORGE & wife Elizabeth of Ldn to Daniel HOUSEHOLDER
of Ldn. B/S of 49a (former prop. of Adam RHORBAUGH dec'd sold
by comm. Richard H. HENDERSON to John GEORGE, DB TT:413)
with life estate to Hannah RHORBAUGH (wd/o Adam). Wit: John
WHITE, Craven OSBURNE. Delv. pr order 22 Dec 1823.

Bk:Pg: 2Z:175   Date: 26 May 1819   RtCt: 11 Oct 1819
Aaron BURSON & wife Esther of Ldn to John WHITACRE of Ldn.
B/S of 55a adj Michael PLAISTER, James BURSON, Joseph
BURSON. Wit: Seth SMITH, Wm. DUNKIN, James MACHLAN, D.
Ellicott BROWN, Wm. BRONAUGH, Francis W. LUCKETT. Delv. to
WHITACRE 24 Jul 1822.

Bk:Pg: 2Z:177   Date: 18 Sep 1819   RtCt: 12 Oct 1819
John GEORGE & wife Elizabeth of Ldn to Daniel HOUSEHOLDER
of Ldn. B/S of 52a (cnvy/b HOUSEHOLDER in Dec 1813, except 2a
sold by GEORGE to Solomon VICKROY) adj Jacob VERTZ, George
& Conrad ROWLER. Wit: Craven OSBURN, John WHITE.

Bk:Pg: 2Z:179   Date: 9 Sep 1819   RtCt: 11 Oct 1819
Lloyd NOLAND & wife Ann W. of Fqr to Burr POWELL of Ldn. B/S of
tract dev. NOLAND by father Thomas NOLAND (tract divided
between Dade P, Samuel N. and Lloyd NOLAND) adj Potomac,
Saml CLAPHAM. Wit: Francis W. LUCKETT, A. GIBSON. Delv. to
Burr W. HARRISON 19 Mar 1840.

Bk:Pg: 2Z:182   Date: 10 Nov 1819   RtCt: 11 Nov 1819
Strother M. HELM now of Ldn to Sheriff John HAMILTON of Ldn.
B/S of 300a in Monogahela Co Va and 200a in Mercer Co Pa. Wit:
S. BLINCOE, R. J. FLEMING, Thomas JONES.

Bk:Pg: 2Z:184   Date: 28 May 1818   RtCt: 2 Nov 1819
Thomas TORBERT and Thomas FRED & Elizabeth FRED late
TORBERT. Partition – Samuel TORBERT (br/o Thomas, Elizabeth &

John TORBERT) has contracted with Eli BUTCHER s/o Samuel for land left by Eli's grandfather Samuel BUTCHER dec'd to Jenkin PHILIPS of which 14a was recovered. Thomas & Elizabeth's share is 1½a and Thomas TORBERT's share as 1½a with John TORBERT to have the remaining. Wit: Benjamin GRAYSON, John W. GRAYSON.

Bk:Pg: 2Z:186   Date: 28 Jul 1819   RtCt: 14 Oct 1819
George JANNEY & wife Susanna of Georgetown D.C. to Richard H. HENDERSON of Ldn. Trust for debt to George RUST Jr. using land prch/o William CARR Sr. dec'd by RUST and conveyed to JANNEY. Wit: Tho. R. MOTT, Henry H. HAMILTON, Martin CORDELL.

Bk:Pg: 2Z:190   Date: 12 Apr 1817   RtCt: Oct 1819
Benjamin BRADFIELD & wife Rachel of Ldn to William KENWORTHY of Ldn. B/S of 60a (cnvy/b Exors of Benjamin MEAD dec'd in Oct 1813, DB 22:434) adj George FAIRHURST, Aquilla MEAD. Wit: Robert BRADEN, Thomas GREGG. Delv. to KENWORTHY 18 Jun 1827.

Bk:Pg: 2Z:193   Date: 31 Jul 1819   RtCt: 9 Nov 1819
John GOURLEY (s/o John GOURLEY dec'd) & wife Rhoda, Michael STANLEY & wife Mary, Jesse STANLEY & wife Lydia (Mary & Lydia d/o John GOURLEY dec'd) of Guilford Co NC to William REEDER of Ldn. B/S of 1/5th of 103a (prch/o David LOVETT by John GOURLEY dec'd). Wit: Hezekiah STARBUCK, Samuel STANLY, James CLEMMONS. Delv. pr order 30 Nov 1821.

Bk:Pg: 2Z:197   Date: 22 Feb 1819   RtCt: 16 Jun 1819
John OVERFIELD & wife Sarah of Henderson Co KY to John BUTCHER of Ldn. B/S of 37½a (John's share of tract where parents Benjamin OVERFIELD & wife Mary lived). Wit: Joshua B. OVERFIELD, Joseph RICHARDSON, Stephen JANNEY. Delv. to BUTCHER 1 Mar 1822.

Bk:Pg: 2Z:201   Date: 12 Oct 1819   RtCt: 13 Oct 1819
Joseph WILDMAN & wife Hannah of Ldn to Benjamin SHREVE Sr. of Ldn. B/S of tract from father Joseph WILDMAN dec'd including interest of Martin WILDMAN a son of Joseph WILDMAN dec'd which Joseph purchased. Wit: Saml. M. EDWARDS, William CARR. Delv. to SHREVE Sr. 20 Jan 1820.

Bk:Pg: 2Z:204   Date: 1 Nov 1819   RtCt: 1 Nov 1819
Anderson JEFFERS & wife Harriet of Ldn to Isaac WRIGHT of Ldn. B/S of undivided ¼th of lot on S side of Market St. in E addition of Lsbg, adj Thomas R. MOTT, Samuel M. EDWARDS. Wit: Thomas SANDERS, Presley CORDELL.

Bk:Pg: 2Z:206   Date: 13 Aug 1819   RtCt: 12 Oct 1819
Ferdinando FAIRFAX of Washington to John CAMPBELL of Ldn. B/S of 28a on side of blue ridge adj Jesse EVANS. Wit: Ebenezer

GRUBB Jr., Jno. J. MATHIAS, Hugh THOMPSON, Asaph CAMPBELL. Delv. to CAMPBELL 4 Feb 1823.

Bk:Pg: 2Z:209   Date: 13 Dec 1819   RtCt: 13 Dec 1819
John ROSE. CoE for slave Joe (alias Joseph CARTRIGHT). Delv. to CARTWRIGHT 29 Sep 1820.

Bk:Pg: 2Z:209   Date: 8 Dec 1819   RtCt: 9 Dec 1819
Joseph SMITH & wife Mary of AlexDC to Samuel MURREY & wife Elizabeth of Ldn. B/S of 2½a on Loudoun St in Lsbg adj lot occupied by Charles STEWART (free man of colour). Wit: E. G. HAMILTON. Delv. to MURREY 4 Mar 1820.

Bk:Pg: 2Z:211   Date: 13 Dec 1819   RtCt: 13 Dec 1819
John L. GILL, Andrew MARTIN, Jas. WORNELL & Stephen R. MOUNT. Bond on GILL as constable.

Bk:Pg: 2Z:212   Date: 19 Nov 1819   RtCt: 15 Dec 1819
John BOOTH of Jefferson Co Indiana to John BOOTH Jr. of Ldn. PoA for land from Robert BOOTH dec'd. Wit: John MEEK. Delv. to John BOOTH Jr. 10 Apr 1820.

Bk:Pg: 2Z:213   Date: 23 Nov 1819   RtCt: 23 Nov 1819
Jacob KEMERLY/KIMMERLE and Isaac SHIPLEY. Agreement to resend arrangement in DB YY:212 made in 1819.

Bk:Pg: 2Z:214   Date: 8 Dec 1819   RtCt: 9 Dec 1819
Richard H. HENDERSON of Ldn to William D. DRISH of Ldn. Release of trust on house & lot in Lsbg for debt of Ignatius NORRIS.

Bk:Pg: 2Z:215   Date: 3 Dec 1819   RtCt: 13 Dec 1819
Thomson MASON. Col for male slave Belcher abt 30y abt 5' 9", brought into Va 20 Nov 1819, acquired by marriage.

Bk:Pg: 2Z:216   Date: 3 Sep 1816   RtCt: 10 Sep 1816
Richard Henry LEE of Ldn to Adam WEAVER of JeffVa. BoS for negro boy Ben. Wit: Thos. DARNE, Thos. T. DRAKE, Lee DURHAM, A. O. POWELL.

Bk:Pg: 2Z:216   Date: 10 Aug 1819   RtCt: 9 Nov 1819
Patrick MILHOLLEN of Ldn to Adam HOUSEHOLDER of Ldn. LS of 14y for frame house & kitchen with corner house where Jane DOWNS now lives and ½ of garden. Wit: Jno. LITTLEJOHN, Saml. M. EDWARDS.

Bk:Pg: 2Z:218   Date: 19 Mar 1818   RtCt: 9 Nov 1819
George NIXON & wife Elizabeth to John NIXON. B/S of part of tract of George NIXON dec'd (DB WW:102). At time NIXON was not legal to make sale of his share but now can.

Bk:Pg: 2Z:220   Date: 1 Jul 1819   RtCt: 8 Nov 1819
Ludwell LUCKETT & wife Lettice of Ldn to Leven LUCKETT of Ldn. B/S of 400a (deeded to Lettice by her father Francis PEYTON dec'd). Wit: Burr POWELL, A. GIBSON.

Bk:Pg: 2Z:220   Date: 28 Jul 1819   RtCt: 8 Nov 1819
Ludwell LUCKETT of Ldn to Leven LUCKETT of Ldn. B/S of 400a.

Bk:Pg: 2Z:221   Date: 20 Nov 1819   RtCt: 20 Nov 1819
John MATHIAS & John NIXON of Ldn to William KING of Ldn.
Release of trust on lot on E side of King St. in Lsbg (DB SS:222).

Bk:Pg: 2Z:223   Date: 29 Nov 1819   RtCt: 29 Nov 1819
Samuel M. EDWARDS of Ldn to George TAVENDER. Release of
trust on debt to Peter BENEDUM.

Bk:Pg: 2Z:224   Date: 27 Dec 1818   RtCt: 14 Jun 1819
John W. VIOLETT and Julian VIOLETT (s/o and d/o Benjamin
VIOLETT of Ldn) of OH to Amos DENHAM of Ldn. B/S of their
interest in reversion of 133a (in L/L to Elijah VIOLETT) of
grandfather John VIOLETT dec'd. Wit: Amos JOHNSON, William
NUTT, Hiram McVEIGH.

Bk:Pg: 2Z:225   Date: 15 Dec 1819   RtCt: 15 Dec 1819
Memorial from the attorneys at law practicing in this court to
maintain dignity of the Bar. Signed: Richard H. HENDERSON, L. P.
W. BALCH, Burr W. HARRISON, Thomas P. KNOX, S. BLINCOE,
John K. MINES, Fleet SMITH, Rich'd Henry LEE, Wm. CHILTON.

Bk:Pg: 2Z:227   Date: 5 Jun 1819   RtCt: 10 Nov 1819
Daniel VERNON & wife Rebecca of Ldn to Benjamin HIXSON of
Ldn. B/S of 4a (conveyed to David GIBSON & Daniel VERNON by
James HIXSON, then in May 1818 from GIBSON to VERNON). Wit:
Burr POWELL, A. GIBSON. Delv. to HIXON 28 Aug 1824.

Bk:Pg: 2Z:229   Date: 21 May 1819   RtCt: 4 Oct 1819
Annah GALLEHER of Ldn to Lewis HUNT of Union. B/S of ¼a (part
of lot in Union conveyed to Annah by her father William GALLAHER
& wife Mary in 1812) adj Isaac BROWN, lot cnvy/b Wm. GALLAHER
to his grandchildren of the name McKENNY, John JOHNSON. Wit:
Seth SMITH, Major HUNT, Joseph MERCER. Delv. to HUNT 21 Jul
1820.

Bk:Pg: 2Z:230   Date: 3 Apr 1819   RtCt: 30 Nov 1819
Samuel DUNCAN & wife Anna of Ldn to George MARKS of Ldn.
B/S of ¼a in Union (Lot #3 in div. of lands of James REED dec'd).

Bk:Pg: 2Z:232   Date: 11 Oct 1819   RtCt: 1 Dec 1819
Jesse McVEIGH & wife Elizabeth of Ldn to John RALPH of Ldn. B/S
of 105a adj Henry PETERSON, John BAYLEY. Wit: Burr POWELL,
A. GIBSON.

Bk:Pg: 2Z:234   Date: 1 Apr 1819   RtCt: 30 Nov 1820
John MARKS & wife Lydia of Ldn to Samuel DUNKIN of Ldn. B/S of
59a (cnvy/b Stephen McPHERSON who bought from Isaiah MARKS
left Isaiah by father Elisha MARKS & brother Thomas MARKS) adj
Edward B. GRADY mill lot, Samuel SINCLAIR. Delv. to Geo. E.
LLOYD pr order 18 Nov 1820.

Bk:Pg: 2Z:236 Date: 8 May 1819 RtCt: 10 Nov 1819
David GIBSON & wife Nancy of Ldn to Daniel VERNON of Ldn. B/S of 4a (jointly purchased in 1804). Wit: John SINCLAIR, Joseph DANIEL, Burr POWELL, A. GIBSON.

Bk:Pg: 2Z:238 Date: 17 Nov 1819 RtCt: 17 Nov 1819
William AULT & wife Susannah of Ldn to Bazil NEWMAN of Ldn. B/S of 20a on road from Edwards ferry road to Clapham's mill. Wit: John McCORMICK, Presley CORDELL. Delv. to John MATHIAS 23 Dec 1820 pr order filed DB LL:238.

Bk:Pg: 2Z:240 Date: 14 Apr 1819 RtCt: 8 Nov 1819
Burr POWELL & wife Catharine of Ldn to Hugh SMITH of Ldn. B/S of Lots #49 & #50 in Mdbg at Jay & Washington Sts. Wit: A. GIBSON, Towns'd McVEIGH, Asa ROGERS, Francis W. LUCKETT, Wm. NOLAND. Delv. to Jos.? SMITH 2 Aug 183?

Bk:Pg: 2Z:243 Date: 17 Oct 1819 RtCt: 23 Nov 1819
Peter BENEDUM & wife Catharine of Ldn to John A. BINNS of Ldn. B/S of lot on S side of Loudoun St in Lsbg adj John A. BINNS (formerly of Dr. McCLEAN now dec'd). Delv. to BINNS 2 Feb 1820.

Bk:Pg: 2Z:244 Date: 17 Nov 1819 RtCt: 5 Dec 1819
Peter BENEDUM of Ldn to John BENEDUM of Ldn. B/S of 105a adj Wm. A. BINNS.

Bk:Pg: 2Z:246 Date: 29 Nov 1819 RtCt: 29 Nov 1819
Ignatius NORRIS & wife Mary of Ldn to William D. DRISH of Ldn. B/S of house & lot on Cornwall St. in Lsbg (prch/o John KIPHEART) adj R. H. HENDERSON, James RUSSELL. Wit: Patrick McINTYRE, Presley CORDELL.

Bk:Pg: 2Z:248 Date: 17 Nov 1819 RtCt: 19 Nov 1819
William LICKEY & wife Abigail of Ldn to John LICKEY of Belmont Co OH. B/S of 40a on Kattocton Mt. and W side of road from Lsbg to Coes Mill. Wit: Edmund LOVETT, Adam BARR, George LICKEY, John McCORMICK, Presley CORDELL. Delv. to LICKEY 8 Sep 1821.

Bk:Pg: 2Z:250 Date: 17 Sep 1819 RtCt: 29 Nov 1819
George TAVENER Jr. & wife Sarah of Ldn to Abiel JENNERS of Ldn. B/S of 250a (cnvy/b Peter BENEDUM in Aug 1817) adj Wm. McGEATH. Wit: John H. McCABE, Saml. HOUGH Jr. Delv. to JENNERS 31 Jan? 1821.

Bk:Pg: 2Z:252 Date: 18 Sep 1819 RtCt: 8 Nov 1819
Barbara ROPP and Nicholas ROPP & wife Elizabeth to John CONARD, James RUSSEL, Peter DEMORY, John DEMORY, George SMITH Jr. and Philip DERRY. B/S of ½a between short hill and blue ridge. Wit: Ebenezer GRUBB, John WHITE.

Bk:Pg: 2Z:255   Date: 7 Sep 1819   RtCt: 8 Nov 1819
Burr POWELL & wife Catharine of Ldn to Hugh SMITH of Ldn. B/S
of 4a nr Mdbg. Wit: Cuthbert POWELL, Francis W. LUCKETT. Delv.
to SMITH ? Aug 1836.

Bk:Pg: 2Z:258   Date: __ Oct 1819   RtCt: __ Oct 1819
Peter BENEDUM to John A. BINNS. B/S of lot in Lsbg lately of John
C. QUICK, adj John A. BINNS (with money in trust for Maria QUICK,
and at her death for benefit any minor children).

Bk:Pg: 2Z:260   Date: 26 Jul 1819   RtCt: 30 Nov 1819
William GRAYSON late of Georgetown now of Ldn to Benjamin
GRAYSON of Ldn. B/S of 200a adj Bloomfield and Demsey
CARTER, John W. GRAYSON, Richard MATHEWS, Abner
HUMPHREY. Wit: James O. GAITHER, Ben GRAYSON Jr., R'd O.
GRAYSON, Mary D. GRAYSON. Delv. pr order to Jas. L.
HAMILTON 31 Dec 1829.

Bk:Pg: 2Z:263   Date: 8 Apr 1819   RtCt: 4 Dec 1819
John HAMILTON & wife Winifred of Ldn to Jacob WALTMAN Jr. (s/o
Samuel dec'd) of Ldn. B/S of 17a on W side of Catocton creek
(prch/o William BROWN). Wit: John WEARING, Thos. N. YOUND
[YOUNG?], Jacob STOUSABERGER, Presley CORDELL, Thomas
SANDERS. Delv. to WALTMAN 21 Mar 1820.

Bk:Pg: 2Z:265   Date: 12 Jun 1819   RtCt: 8 Nov 1819
Samuel HOUGH Jr. of Ldn to Peter HICKMAN of Ldn. B/S of 94a in
Piedmont Manor (cnvy/b Peter SANDERS) adj John MARTIN alias
George RICHARDS, George SHOEMAKER and 14a adj James
HAMILTON dec'd. Wit: John H. McCABE, Abiel JENNERS. Delv. to
John HICKMAN Admr of grantee 14 May 1823.

Bk:Pg: 2Z:269   Date: 26 Apr 1819   RtCt: 24 Nov 1819
Mordecai THROCKMORTON & wife Sarah McCarty of Ldn to
Warner W. THROCKMORTON. Trust for debt to Warner
WASHINGTON of Frederick Co using 400a (part of 660a) adj
Francis & John AWBREY's patent, Robert RUSSEL, John BEAVER,
Enoch FURR and slaves Jack & Fanny with their children James,
Lucy, Arena, Betsy, Jane & Ann and Lucinda & her children Casar,
Mary, William & James and Joseph & Sarah and their dau. Patty,
Anna, Sawney, Harry and Joseph. Wit: Perrin WASHINGTON,
Fairfax WASHINGTON. Wit: Benjamin GRAYSON, John W.
GRAYSON.

Bk:Pg: 2Z:274   Date: 4 Jan 1820   RtCt: 5 Jan 1820
Thomas JACOBS of Lsbg to dau. Matilda McCLELLAND w/o Saml.
McCLELLAND. Gift in trust to Charles BINNS of household items.

Bk:Pg: 2Z:275   Date: 18 Dec 1819   RtCt: 18 Dec 1819
Reuben SCHOOLEY and Mathew MITCHELL & wife Elizabeth to
Patrick B. MILHOLLAND. CoE for Elizabeth in sale of 15 Feb 1817.

Wit: Presley CORDELL, Pat'k McINTYRE. Delv. to MITCHELL & MILHOLLAND DB WW:440.

Bk:Pg: 2Z:277   Date: 27 Dec 1819   RtCt: 27 Dec 1819
Charles SHEPHERD of Ldn to James M. LEWIS of Ldn. B/S of undivided interest (abt 37½a) from will of father Charles SHEPHERD dec'd. Wit: R. H. HENDERSON. Delv to LEWIS 10 Mar 1821.

Bk:Pg: 2Z:278   Date: 20 Oct 1819   RtCt: 13 Dec 1819
George SMITH & wife Eve of Ldn to William DERRY of Ldn. B/S of 11a adj John TENNEY, Anthony WRIGHT. Wit: John WHITE, Craven OSBURNE. Delv. to DERRY 10 Aug 1821

Bk:Pg: 2Z:280   Date: 10 Oct 1817   RtCt: 1 Jan 1818/3 Jan 1819
John VIOLETT now of Ldn to Sanford RAMEY of Ldn. B/S of 41½a (from div. of father's estate). Wit: S. BLINCOE, S. J. RAMEY, Henry HARRISON.

Bk:Pg: 2Z:282   Date: 21 Oct 1819   RtCt: 13 Dec 1819
William DERRY & wife Barbara of Ldn to Anthony WRIGHT of Ldn. B/S of 1a (prch/o George SMITH). Wit: John WHITE, Craven OSBURNE. Delv. to Adam EVANS pr order filed __.

Bk:Pg: 2Z:284   Date: 27 Dec 1819   RtCt: 27 Dec 1819
George RUST Jr of Ldn to John CARR of Ldn. Trust for debt to Joseph CALDWELL of Ldn using 322a prch/o CALDWELL. Delv. to CALDWELL 12 May 1821.

Bk:Pg: 2Z:285   Date: 9 Dec 1819   RtCt: 13 Dec 1819
Sarah RHINE, John RHINE & Mary RHINE of Ldn to John SURGENOR/SURGHNOR of Ldn. B/S of lot adj George HEAD on Loudoun St. in Lsbg (sold to George RINE by Patrick CAVANS DB AA:29). Delv. to SURGHNOR 19 May 1820.

Bk:Pg: 2Z:287   Date: 24 Dec 1819   RtCt: 24 Dec 1819
John BOOTH Jr. attorney in fact of John BOOTH of Jefferson Co Indiana to John WENNER of Ldn. B/S of all claims by John BOOTH of Indiana.

Bk:Pg: 2Z:289   Date: 21 Oct 1819   RtCt: 13 Dec 1819
George SMITH & wife Eve of Ldn to Mathias PRINCE of Ldn. B/S of 5a between short hill & blue ridge adj PRINCE, James NEAR. Wit: Craven OSBURN, John WHITE. Delv. to A. M. SANFORD pr order 15 Jul 1823.

Bk:Pg: 2Z:291   Date: 21 Oct 1818   RtCt: 13 Dec 1819
William DERRY & wife Barbara of Ldn to John DEMORY of Ldn. B/S of 3a between short hill & blue ridge adj lease of Mrs. NEISWANGER, __ PRINCE. Wit: Craven OSBURN, John WHITE. Delv. to DEMORY 10 Aug 1821.

Bk:Pg: 2Z:294   Date: 16 Nov 1819   RtCt: 13 Dec 1819
Joshua OVERFIELD & wife Ann and Joseph RICHARDSON & wife Susannah of Ldn to John H. BUTCHER of Ldn. B/S of 50a where

John H. BUTCHER lived on 28 Feb 1815 and which Martin OVERFIELD the elder died seized. Wit: Notley C. WILLIAMS, John W. GRAYSON. Delv. to BUTCHER 1 Mar 1822.

Bk:Pg: 2Z:296   Date: 13 Nov 1819   RtCt: 13 Dec 1819
Jehu BURSON & wife Ann of Ldn to Harmon BITZER of Ldn. B/S of 72a on both sides of Wancopin branch of Goose Creek where BURSON now lives adj Peter TOWPERMAN, Thomas ATWEL dec'd. Wit: Burr POWELL, A. GIBSON. Delv. to BITZER 12 Jul 1823.

Bk:Pg: 2Z:299   Date: 29 Nov 1819   RtCt: 13 Dec 1819
Jehu BURSON & wife Ann of Ldn to Absalom DENNIS of Ldn. B/S of 44¾a on waters of Goose Creek where BURSON now lives adj John RUSSEL, Moses WILLSON, Edward WILSON. Wit: Burr POWELL, A. GIBSON.

Bk:Pg: 2Z:302   Date: 13 Nov 1819   RtCt: 13 Dec 1819
Edward WILSON & wife Mary Ann of Ldn to William H. HANDY of Ldn. B/S of 2a (prch/o Thomas BISCOE) on N side of Goose Creek. Wit: Burr POWELL, A. GIBSON. Delv. to Townshend McVEIGH pr order of HANDY filed 26 Sep 1822.

Bk:Pg: 2Z:304   Date: 12 Nov 1819   RtCt: 15 Dec 1819
Jacob MANN & wife Sally of Mdbg to Bernard MANN of Mdbg. B/S of ¼a part of Lot #3 in Mdbg. Wit: Burr POWELL, A. GIBSON. Delv. to MANN 23 May 1820.

Bk:Pg: 2Z:306   Date: 21 Oct 1819   RtCt: 13 Dec 1819
Samuel GROVE of Ldn to John DEMORY of Ldn. Trust for debt to William DERRY using land on W side of short hill (prch/o William DERRY & wife Barbara). Delv. to __ 20 Jan 1820.

Bk:Pg: 2Z:309   Date: 11 Dec 1819   RtCt: 16 Dec 1819
Henly BOGGESS of Fqr to Richard H. HENDERSON. Trust for debt to William PATON & Jonathan BUTCHER (surviving partners of Patons & Butcher) and Thomas JANNEY & Douglas BROWN (firm of Thomas JANNEY & Co) of AlexDC using 220a adj George NOBLE, George RUST, Herod THOMAS (formerly owned by brother Samuel BOGGESS dec'd). Wit: John THOMAS, Thomas CLAGETT, Thomas A. MOORE. Delv. to HENDERSON 7 Apr 1823.

Bk:Pg: 2Z:311   Date: 25 Dec 1819   RtCt: 27 Dec 1819
Joseph CALDWELL & wife Eliza of Ldn to George RUST Jr. B/S of 322a where CALDWELL now lives and mother Sarah acknowledges she gave up her dower rights to land. Wit: Presley CORDELL, Thomas SANDERS. Delv. to RUST 23 Apr 1822.

Bk:Pg: 2Z:314   Date: 14 Jan 1819   RtCt: 13 Dec 1819
William DERRY & wife Barbara of Ldn to Mathias PRINCE of Ldn. B/S of 4a (cnvy/b PRINCE in 1816). Wit: Craven OSBURN, John WHITE. Delv. to PRINCE 14 Aug 1827.

Bk:Pg: 2Z:317   Date: 7 Jan 1820   RtCt: 7 Jan 1820
William J. WEADON of Ldn to Samuel CARR & Sampson BLINCOE
of Ldn. Trust for debt to William CARR using 40a plantation with a
water grist mill on Goose Creek adj Thomas FOUCH, Mathew
HARRISON heirs, Rev. Amos THOMPSON dec'd., Daniel GANTT.
Wit: A. O. POWELL, Geo. SWEARINGEN, Chs. G. ESKRIDGE.
Delv. to CARR 25 Apr 1822.

Bk:Pg: 2Z:320   Date: 18 Jan 1819   RtCt: 5 Jan 1820
Nero LOSSON of Wtfd to Noble S. BRADEN of Wtfd. Trust for debt
to Samuel E. HENDERSON using lot in Wtfd (cnvy/b Exors of Wm.
HOUGH dec'd) adj Nathan MINOR.

Bk:Pg: 2Z:323   Date: 15 Nov 1819   RtCt: 13 Dec 1819
Stephen JANNEY & wife Letitia of Ldn to Abner HUMPHREY &
Edward B. GRADY of Ldn. Trust for debt to John H. BUTCHER
using undivided moriety of 110a where Elizabeth OVERFIELD lived
& died which BUTCHER sold to JANNEY. Wit: Benjamin
GRAYSON, N. C. WILLIAMS. Delv. to BUTCHER 1 Mar 1822.

Bk:Pg: 2Z:326   Date: 16 Nov 1819   RtCt: 13 Dec 1819
Thomas DRAKE of Ldn to Abner HUMPHREY & Edward B. GRADY
of Ldn. Trust for debt to John H. BUTCHER using 64a formerly
owned (apart) by Martin OVERFIELD & (apart) by Mary
OVERFIELD. Delv. to BUTCHER 1 Mar 1822.

Bk:Pg: 2Z:329   Date: 16 Nov 1819   RtCt: 13 Dec 1819
Jehu BURSON & wife Ann of Ldn to Abner HUMPHREY & Edward
B. GRADY of Ldn. Trust for debt to John H. BUTCHER using 108a
(former prop. of Mary OVERFIELD). Wit: Notley C. WILLIAMS, John
W. GRAYSON. Delv. to BUTCHER 1 Mar 1822.

Bk:Pg: 2Z:332   Date: 25 Dec 1819   RtCt: 27 Dec 1819
Joseph CALDWELL of Ldn to Stevens Thomson MASON (s/o Gen.
Armstead T. MASON) of Ldn. B/S of 70a & 12a (A. T. MASON
contracted 3 Apr 1819 and 24 Nov 1819 purchases with CALDWELL
but died before conveyance leaving only child said Stevens T.
MASON. Wit: Presley CORDELL, Thomas SANDERS. Delv pr order
6 Sep 1844.

Bk:Pg: 2Z:336   Date: 9 Oct 1819   RtCt: 10 Jan 1820
William NOLAND of Ldn to John BAYLY of Ldn. Trust for debt to
Thomas TRIPLETT of Washington D.C. using 328a prch/o
TRIPLETT & wife Margaret. Delv. to Thomas F. TEBB 16 Aug 1822.

Bk:Pg: 2Z:338   Date: 9 Oct 1819   RtCt: 10 Jan 1820
Thomas TRIPLETT & wife Margaret of Washington D.C. to William
NOLAND of Ldn. B/S of 328a on road from Lucy's old tavern to
Lsbg, Carolina road. Delv to grantee 21 Oct 1820.

Bk:Pg: 2Z:340   Date: 10 Jan 1820   RtCt: 10 Jan 1820
L. P. W. BALCH & Rich'd H. LEE. Bond on BALCH as treasurer of
the board of commrs. for educating poor children.

Bk:Pg: 2Z:341   Date: 16 Jan 1819   RtCt: 11 Jan 1820
Henry CLAGGETT. DoE for mulatto man Phill alias Phil NELSON.
Wit: Saml. M. EDWARDS, R. G. SAUNDERS.

Bk:Pg: 2Z:342   Date: 10 Jan 1820   RtCt: 10 Jan 1820
Joseph H. WRIGHT, Thomas WHITE & John H. CASSADY. Bond
on WRIGHT as constable.

Bk:Pg: 2Z:343   Date: 10 Jan 1820   RtCt: 11 Jan 1820
Thomson MASON. Col on 20 Dec 1829 for black woman Sarah abt
5' 4" and 33y old, yellow woman Letty abt 5' 6" and 22y old, black
woman Sylvy abt 5' 5" and 19y old, black woman Henrieta abt 5' 8"
and 19y, black girl Malvina abt 4' and 9y old, yellow girl Juliet abt 5y
old, black boy Wilfred abt 3y old, girl June abt 6m old and girl Anny
abt 5y old acquired by marriage.

Bk:Pg: 2Z:344   Date: 11 Jan 1820   RtCt: 20 Jan 1820
Francis W. LUCKETT of Ldn to Aaron BURSON of Ldn. Release of
trust on debt to James MACKLAN on 124a.

Bk:Pg: 2Z:345   Date: 17 Oct 1807   RtCt: 14 Jan 1820
Joseph WORTHINGTON & wife Elizabeth (d/o William OSBURN
dec'd) and Craven OSBURN & Landon OSBURN. Agreement –
Elizabeth entitled to child's portion of father's estate at death of his
widow but part of land is held under lease for life – WORTHINGTON
does not wish to sell his share. Wit: William BLINCOE, James
BLINCOE, Thos. BLINCO. Delv. to Craven OSBURN 30 Mar 1821.

Bk:Pg: 2Z:347   Date: 19 Jun 1819   RtCt: 28 Jul 1820
Marcus HUMPHREY & wife Margaret of Ldn to Mary MARKS of Ldn.
Trust for debt to secure Margaret and children using div. from her
father Abel MARKS dec'd of negro Ury abt 22y old. Wit: Thomas
MARKS, Lydia MARKS, Mason MARKS. Delv. pr order 8 Nov 1821.

Bk:Pg: 2Z:348   Date: 26 Nov 1819   RtCt: 10 Jan 1820
Albert BAILEY (s/o Pierce BAYLY the younger) & wife Sarah of Ldn
to George BAILEY of FredVa. B/S of share in land which Pierce
BAYLY the elder prch/o James MURRY, Joseph BENNETT &
William MURREY dated 1791 and Pierce BAYLY the younger
having died intestate. Wit: John BAYLY, Ariss BUCKNER. Delv. to
grantee 17 Nov 1820.

Bk:Pg: 2Z:350   Date: 1 Apr 1819   RtCt: 14 Jan 1820
Ruth POULTON of Ldn to Jonathan HEATON of Ldn. B/S of 12a
where Ruth now resides adj Reed POULTON, Thomas POULTON.
Wit: Calvin HATCHER, Reed POULTON, William HATCHER. Delv.
to HEATON 29 Mar 1824.

Bk:Pg: 2Z:352   Date: 18 Nov 1819   RtCt: 29 Jan 1820
George N. RALL of Culpeper Co Va to Joseph TULLEY of FredVa.
Trust using residue 213a in trust to Hiland CROWE adj CROWE,
Benjamin JAMES.

Bk:Pg: 2Z:354   Date: 15 Jan 1818   RtCt: 14 Jan 1820
William GLASSCOCK & John GLASSCOCK of Fqr to David
LOVETT & Craven OSBURNE of Ldn. B/S of ½a.

Bk:Pg: 2Z:355   Date: 6 Sep 1819   RtCt: 20 Jan 1820
Burr POWELL & wife Catharine of Ldn to Richard COCHRAN of
Ldn. B/S of 16a above Mdbg adj POWELL, Jane WEATHERBY. Wit:
Cuthbert POWELL, Francis W. LUCKETT.

Bk:Pg: 2Z:358   Date: 6 Oct 1819   RtCt: 20 Jan 1820
William NOLAND & wife Catharine of Ldn to Resin WILCOXEN of
Ffx. B/S of Lots #77, #78 & #79 on S side of Mercer St in Aldie. Wit:
Robert ARMSTEAD, Leven LUCKETT.

Bk:Pg: 2Z:360   Date: 26 Jul 1819   RtCt: 12 Jan 1820
Ann TAYLOR and Mary TAYLOR of Ldn to Benjamin SHREVE of
Ldn. Trust for debt to Abraham H. COLLINS using rights to land of
father Henry TAYLOR dec'd. Wit: Elizabeth RICHARDS, Ann
TAYLOR, Isaac GRIFFITH. Delv. to SHREVE 24 Aug 1822.

Bk:Pg: 2Z:362   Date: 15 Oct 1818   RtCt: 14 Feb 1820
Jesse McVEIGH Exor of James BATTSON dec'd to Elizabeth
BATTSON Exor of Jno. BATTSON. Receipt of part of legacy from
JAMES. Wit: Towns'd McVEIGH.

Bk:Pg: 2Z:363   Date: 14 Nov 1818   RtCt: 14 Feb 1820
Jesse McVEIGH Exor to Jas. BATTSON dec'd to Thos. BATTSON.
Receipt of full legacy. Wit: Towns'd McVEIGH.

Bk:Pg: 2Z:363   Date: 21 Nov 1818   RtCt: 14 Feb 1820
Jesse McVEIGH Exor to Jas. BATTSON dec'd to Hannah
BATTSON. Receipt for full legacy. Wit: Elizabeth SWART, Towns'd
McVEIGH.

Bk:Pg: 2Z:364   Date: 17 Oct 1818   RtCt: 14 Feb 1820
Jesse McVEIGH Exor of Jas. BATTSON dec'd to legatees of Jno.
BATTSON dec'd through James CULVERHOUSE Exor. of Jno.
BATTSON dec'd. Wit: Hugh ROGERS

Bk:Pg: 2Z:364   Date: 15 Feb 1820   RtCt: 15 Feb 1820
William D. DRISH. Writ of adquoddammnum (deposition) to
condemn lands of heirs of William C. NEWTON, David RICKETTS &
Joseph T. NEWTON with verdict for $643 which was mislaid on
application of the Leesburg Turnpike Co.

Bk:Pg: 2Z:365   Date: 29 Nov 1819   RtCt: 26 Jan 1820
Jehu BURSON & wife Ann of Ldn to Edward WILSON of Ldn. B/S of
37¾a adj Thomas ATWELL dec'd, Harman BITZER, Edward
WILSON. Wit: Burr POWELL, A. GIBSON.

Bk:Pg: 2Z:367   Date: 4 Nov 1819   RtCt: 14 Jan 1820
John CHEW & wife Margaret of Ldn to Joseph THOMAS of Ldn. B/S
of 37a adj heirs of Owen THOMAS dec'd. Wit: Craven OSBURN,
John WHITE. Delv. to Jonah THOMAS Admr of Ruth THOMAS
dec'd 17 Nov 1851.

Bk:Pg: 2Z:370   Date: 1 Feb 1820   RtCt: 8 Feb 1820
Joseph BOND of Wtfd to Asa MOORE of Wtfd. B/S of 136a (prch/o
Exor of Joseph TALBOTT dec'd) adj Amos JANNEY. Delv. to
Thomas PHILLIPS Exor of Asa MOORE dec'd 12 Aug 1836.

Bk:Pg: 2Z:372   Date: 18 Dec 1819   RtCt: 10 Jan 1820
Sarah STONESTREET of Ldn to Benjamin A. STONESTREET of
Ldn. Release of mortgage on interest in estate of Bazil
STONESTREET. Wit: Johnston CLEVELAND, John J. COLEMAN,
Charles OFFUTT. Delv. to Ben. A. STONESTREET 26 Mar 1821.

Bk:Pg: 2Z:373   Date: 11 Jan 1820   RtCt: 11 Jan 1820
Sampson BLINCOE & Richard H. HENDERSON of Ldn to Fleet
SMITH of Ldn. Release of trust on house & lot in Lsbg. Delv. to
SMITH 23 Feb 1820

Bk:Pg: 2Z:374   Date: 23 Jan 1819   RtCt: 4 Feb 1820
Jozabed WHITE (Exor of Sarah LACEY dec'd) of Ldn to William
WHITE of Ldn. B/S of Lots #38 & #39 in Wtfd. Delv. to WHITE 17
Nov 1823.

Bk:Pg: 2Z:376   Date: 19 Dec 1817   RtCt: 14 Jan 1820
John E. PARMER & wife Mariab of Ldn to Samuel HOUGH 3rd of
Ldn. B/S of 1st lot lying on Second St. in new addition of Wtfd adj
Isaac WALKER. Wit: Abiel JENNERS, J. H. McCABE. Delv. to Saml.
HOUGH Jr. 26 Oct 1821.

Bk:Pg: 2Z:379   Date: 11 Jan 1820   RtCt: 10 [?] Jan 1820
Ann WRIGHT wd/o William WRIGHT dec'd of Ldn to Samuel CARR
of Ldn. B/S of 21a on SW side of turnpike road from Lsbg to Goose
Creek. Wit: Thomas SANDERS, Joseph BEARD, Jno. MOORE.
Delv. to grantee 15 Feb 1821.

Bk:Pg: 2Z:380   Date: 26 Nov 1819   RtCt: 10 Jan 1820
Albert BAYLY & wife Sarah of Ldn and Samuel BAYLY to George
BAYLY of FredVa. B/S of shares in 69a (Pierce BAYLY Sr. dec'd in
his will dev. sons, including Albert & Samuel, adj lands of Ariss
BUCKNER which he leased to Thomas REESE during his life and is
now held by John BLAKER). Wit: John BAYLY, Ariss BUCKNER.
Delv. to grantee 17 Nov 1820.

Bk:Pg: 2Z:383   Date: 21 Dec 1819   RtCt: 26 Jan 1820
Abraham BAKER & wife Catharine of Washington Co. Md to Abiel
JENNERS of Ldn. B/S of 114½a tenanted out to Arther GARNER
(bought of George JANNEY Apr 1817). Wit: John H. McCABE,
Saml. HOUGH Jr.

Bk:Pg: 2Z:385   Date: 5 May 1819   RtCt: 8 Feb 1820
Margaret McILHANY (m/o Elizabeth McILHANY dec'd late of Ldn) to
Elias JAMES, Jonathan JAMES Jr. & Daniel JAMES of Ldn. B/S of
Eliz. share of 87½a 'Gidney CLARKE's land' on NW fork of Goose
Creek. Delv. to Daniel JAMES 27 Oct 1821.

Bk:Pg: 2Z:387   Date: 13 Sep 1819   RtCt: 29 Jan 1820
Hiland CROWE & wife Ann of Ldn to George B. WHITING of Ldn.
Trust for debt to George N. RALLS using 100a where CROWE lives
adj Mary STOKES, James J. RALLS and 13a. Wit: Ariss BUCKNER,
John BAYLY.

Bk:Pg: 2Z:391   Date: 7 Aug 1819   RtCt: 26 Jan 1820
Thomas BISCOE & wife Sarah of Ldn to Edward WILSON of Ldn.
B/S of 15a (prch/o James RACEY) and 25a (prch/o Walter
LANGLEY) and 40a. Wit: Burr POWELL, A. GIBSON.

Bk:Pg: 2Z:393   Date: 29 Jan 1820   RtCt: 4 Feb 1820
Jozabed WHITE & wife Margaret of Ldn to Robert BRADEN of Ldn.
B/S of 47a (prch/o Emanuel NEWCOMER by White & Braden). Wit:
Abiel JENNERS, John H. McCABE. Delv. to BRADEN 31 May 1822.

Bk:Pg: 2Z:396   Date: 23 Aug 1819   RtCt: 11 Jan 1820
William COOKE & Joseph BEARD (trustees of Strother M. HELM) to
John BAYLY. B/S of 145a (defaulted in trust by HELM). Wit: S.
BLINCOE, John MONROE, Tho. SWANN. Delv. to John BAYLY 1
May 1820.

Bk:Pg: 2Z:398   Date: 4 Feb 1820   RtCt: 8 Feb 1820
Asa MOORE of Ldn to Daniel STONE & William H. HOUGH of Ldn.
Trust for debt to James MOORE Exor of Joseph TALBOTT dec'd on
behalf of widow & children using 130a.

Bk:Pg: 2Z:402   Date: 27 Nov 1819   RtCt: ___
Stephen DANIEL & wife Catharine of Fqr to John W. GRAYSON of
Ldn. Trust for benefit of Aaron BURSON & Thompson FURR of Ldn
using house & lot in Alexandria (DANIEL sold BURSON & FURR
land in Fqr prch/o Robert HUNTON late of Fqr of DANIEL). Delv. to
BURSON 5 Apr 1820

Bk:Pg: 2Z:406   Date: 27 Nov 1819   RtCt: 10 Jan 1820
Isaac WRIGHT & wife Susan of Ldn to George FEITCHER of Ldn.
B/S of 4a on NE side of turnpike road from Lsbg to Goose Creek
bridge adj Edmond J. LEE. Wit: Thomas SANDERS, Saml. M.
EDWARDS. Delv to FEICHTER 29 Feb 1820.

Bk:Pg: 2Z:409   Date: 10 Sep 1819   RtCt: 10 Jan 1820
Richard COCHRAN of Mdbg to Lloyd NOLAND. Trust for debt to
Burr POWELL using 16a on S side of turnpike road adj Jane
WEATHERBY. Delv. to H. B. POWELL pr order 26 Sep 1835.

Bk:Pg: 2Z:412   Date: 30 Jan 1820   RtCt: 31 Jan 1820
Charles DRISH & wife Susannah of Ldn to Robert MOFFETT &
Benjamin SHREVE of Ldn. B/S of lot in Lsbg adj William
JOHNSTON on E side of King St, heirs of Henry GLASSGOW
(subject to lease held by James WOOD). Wit: Presley CORDELL,
Saml. M. EDWARDS. Delv. to SHREVE 29 Feb 1820.

Bk:Pg: 2Z:415   Date: 24 Jun 1819   RtCt: 10 Jan 1820
Joseph LEWIS Jr. of Ldn to Aaron R. LEVING, Elisha RIGGS & William THOMSON Jr. of Georgetown D.C. Trust for debt to Central Bank of Georgetown using 203a 'Clifton' where LEWIS resides. Wit: James MELVIN, James A. MAGRUDER, Brooke MACKALL, Jos. B. FOX.

Bk:Pg: 2Z:421   Date: 15 Jan 1820   RtCt: 14 Feb 1820
Elizabeth RICKETTS. Col from Md for negro woman Sucky abt 17y old yellow complexion & well grown, negro boy Bob abt 7y old, both brought to Va on 27 Dec 1819.

Bk:Pg: 2Z:422   Date: Feb 1816   RtCt: 17 Feb 1820
James LEITH dec'd. Division which fell to James LEITH & Patty LEATH by the will of John VIOLETT dec'd their grandfather James LEATH having conveyed his interest to Hiram SEATON. To Patty LEATH (25a), Hiram SEATON (19a and 6a wood land). Divisors: Amos DENHAM, Daniel EACHES & Sydnor BAYLY. Gives plat. [note: see page 444 for commrs. report which should have been recorded before the plat]

Bk:Pg: 2Z:424   Date: 2 Sep 1819   RtCt: 18 Feb 1820
John JOHNSTON dec'd. Division – Rachel RANDEL w/o William RANDLE (33a & 8a), Elizabeth JOHNSTON (35a & 8a), Jane JOHNSTON (41a & 8a), James JOHNSTON (33½a & 8a). Gives plat. Divisors: Jesse McVEIGH, Hugh ROGERS.

Bk:Pg: 2Z:427   Date: 5 Mar 1813   RtCt: 18 Feb 1820
Francis ELGIN dec'd. Division by court order dated 9 Feb 1813 – Gustavus ELGIN (240a), Walter ELGIN (261a), Francis ELGIN (256a). Gives plat. Divisors: Thos. FOUCH, Thomas MOSS, Step. C. ROSZEL.

Bk:Pg: 2Z:429   Date: 13 Dec 1819   RtCt: 14 Feb 1820
James HAMILTON dec'd. Division of slaves by court order of 13 Dec 1819 – Charles & John HAMILTON (negro man Henson & woman Helen), Enos WILDMAN who m. Jane HAMILTON (d/o James) (negro woman Henny), James & Ann HAMILTON (minors) (negro woman Lucy & her children Harriet & Maria). Divisors: R. BRADEN, Abiel JENNERS, Saml. HOUGH Jr.

Bk:Pg: 2Z:430   Date: 9 Oct 1815   RtCt: 18 Feb 1820
Thomas CUMMINGS dec'd. Division by court order dated 15 Aug 1815 – Jane CUMINGS (29a & 1½a), James CUMINGS (18¾a & 9a), Anthony CUMINGS (26a), Nancy CIMINGS (17a), Rachel CIMMINGS (41a), Rebecca CUMINGS (19a & 9a), Joseph CUMMINGS (25a), Thomas CIMMINGS (26a), Robert CIMINGS (25a). Gives plat. Divisors: Jno. MATHIAS, R. BRADEN, Daniel LOVETT.

Bk:Pg: 2Z:435   Date: 19 Sep 1816   RtCt: 18 Feb 1820
Jacob EMERY dec'd. Division by court order of 8 Apr 1816 –
widow's dower to Catharine EMERY – Lot #1 (108a where she
lives), Lot #2 on short hill (11½a), Lot #3 on side of short hill (16a).
Gives plat. Divisors: Geo. HUFF, Jeremiah PURDOM, Cornelius
SHAWEN.

Bk:Pg: 2Z:439   Date: 7 Oct 1819   RtCt: 14 Feb 1820
James MOORE & Asa MOORE (Exors of Joseph TALBOTT dec'd
h/o Rebeccah), Joseph TALBOTT, Elisha TALBOTT, Jesse
TALBOTT, John TALBOTT, Stephen SCOTT & wife Sarah, John
PANCOAST & wife Mary, William COALE & wife Anne and Isaac
WALKER & wife Susannah reversionary heirs of Jos. dec'd to
Joseph BOND of Wtfd. B/S of 136a (prch/o Mahlon JANNEY). CoE
for Mary PANCOAST and Anne COALE of FredMd, Elisha
TALBOTT acknowledged in AlexDC, Joseph TALBOTT
acknowledge in FredMd. John H. TALBOTT, Sarah SCOTT & Susan
WALKER acknowledge in Ldn.

Bk:Pg: 2Z:444   Date: 11 Dec 1815   RtCt: ___
Hiram SEATON vs. Patty LEITH (infant) in chancery. Brother James
LEITH appointed Guardian adlitem of Patty LEITH. Decree that
Sydnor BAYLY, John P. DULANEY, Amos DENHAM, Daniel
EACHES to divide between Hiram SEATON & deft. Patty LEITH
interest in estate of their grandfather John VIOLETT dec'd. See
page 422]

Bk:Pg: 2Z:445   Date: 1 Aug 1819   RtCt: 14 Feb 1820
Elias KENT of Ldn to sons Harrison & William KENT. Gift of beds &
bedding. Wit: Thomas L.HUMPHREY, Jno. M. MONROE.

Bk:Pg: 2Z:445   Date: 10 Jul 1819   RtCt: 21 Feb 1820
James BROWN of Ldn to John BROWN of Ldn. B/S of ¼a leased lot
& house in Wtfd, farm & household items. Wit: John POTTS, Henly
BROWN.

Bk:Pg: 2Z:446   Date: 3 Aug 1816   RtCt: 14 Feb 1820
Philip DERRY & wife Barbara of Ldn to Jasper EVERHART of Ldn.
B/S of 1a. Wit: Ebenezer GRUBB, John WHITE.

Bk:Pg: 2Z:448   Date: 9 Feb 1820   RtCt: 14 Feb 1820
Thomas STUMP, Sarah STUMP & Joseph STUMP (ch/o Thomas
STUMP the younger dec'd) of Ldn to Michael EVERHART of Ldn.
B/S of 60a (devised by Robert BOOTH to Thomas STUMP the elder
& wife d/o BOOTH and William CHAMBERS & wife another dau) adj
late prop. of Thomas D. DIGGS, Michael EVERHART, John
BOOTH, reps of David MULL. Wit: Wm. WERTZ, John SHAFFER,
R. BRADEN, Frederick HANDSHY, Henry STREAM, Joseph
EVERHART. Delv. to trustee Samuel POTTERFIELD 8 Mar 1853

Bk:Pg: 2Z:449 Date: 22 Nov 1819 RtCt: 14 Feb 1820
Eleanor STUMP of Ldn to Michael EVERHART of Ldn. B/S of 60a
(as above). Wit: R. BRADEN, Henry STREAM, Joseph
EVERHEART.

Bk:Pg: 2Z:451 Date: 13 Nov 1819 RtCt: 11 Feb 1820
Jehu BURSON & wife Ann of Ldn to Peter TOWPERMAN of Ldn.
B/S of 22a on wancopen branch of Goose creek where BURSON
now lives on road from Mdbg to Edward WILSON, adj Thomas
BATTSON. Wit: Burr POWELL, A. GIBSON. Delv. to TOWPERMAN
14 Sep 1821.

Bk:Pg: 2Z:453 Date: 19 Mar 1819 RtCt: 15 Feb 1820
Frederick COOPER & wife Molly of Ldn to John DAVIS of Ldn. B/S
of 1a (cnvy/b George HUFF) on N side of Broad run adj Daniel
STONE. Wit: Robert BRADEN, Abiel JENNERS. Delv. to DAVIS 11
Mar 1822.

Bk:Pg: 2Z:455 Date: 16 Nov 1819 RtCt: 2 Mar 1820
Albert BAYLY & wife Sarah to John BAYLY of Ldn. B/S of Albert's
interest in 600a where Pierce BAYLY lived. Wit: John TURLEY,
John SINCLAIR, Sampson HUTCHISON, Thomas GHEEN. Delv. to
John BAYLY 1 May 1820.

Bk:Pg: 2Z:457 Date: 1 Jan 1817 RtCt: 11 Mar 1820
· Charles Burgess BALL & wife Lucy of Ldn to Fayette BALL of Ldn.
B/S of 112a from estate of late Col. B. BALL. Wit: John
McCORMICK, Patrick McINTYRE.

Bk:Pg: 2Z:459 Date: 12 Jul 1819 RtCt: 15 Feb 1820
John HOFFMAN & wife Phebe to Richard H. HENDERSON. Trust
for debts to Enoch FURR, Emery LLOYD, John THOMSON, W. C.
PALMER using interest in late prop. of Nancy CLARKE d/o William
CLAYTON dec'd which interest accrued to Phebe by the death
intestate of Nancy. Wit: John ROSE, Presley CORDELL. Delv. to
HENDERSON by Thos. A. MOORE 24 Aug 1820.

Bk:Pg: 2Z:461 Date: 15 Jan 1820 RtCt: 7 Mar 1820
John BOOTH of Jefferson Co Indiana to George MULL, David
MULL, Elizabeth MULL and their mother Mary MULL of Ldn. B/S of
30a of Lots #5, #6 & #7 (allotted to Jacob VERTS in div. of estate of
David MULL dec'd). Wit: Lee W. DURHAM, George SWEARINGEN,
A. O. POWELL.

Bk:Pg: 2Z:462 Date: 15 Jan 1820 RtCt: 7 Mar 1820
John BOOTH of Jefferson Co Indiana to John MOORE of Ldn. B/S
of 107a. Wit: A. O. POWELL, Lee W. DURHAM. Delv. to MOORE 25
Feb 1825.

Bk:Pg: 2Z:464 Date: 14 Aug 1819 RtCt: 21 Feb 1820
Henry PEERS of Ldn to William CLINE of Ldn. B/S of 10a (prch/o
Fanny LEE). Wit: E. G. HAMILTON, Lee W. DURHAM, Josiah L.
DREAN. Delv. to CLINE 7 Sep 1820.

Bk:Pg: 2Z:465   Date: 21 Oct 1819   RtCt: 14 Feb 1820
Tasker C. QUINLAN of Ldn to James MONROE of Washington D.C.
B/S of 15a.

Bk:Pg: 2Z:467   Date: 14 Dec 1819   RtCt: 16 Mar 1820
William WRIGHT of Ldn and Joseph CALDWELL of Ldn. Agreement
– bound to each other to abide by the decision of Robert BRADEN,
Abiel JENNERS & John H. McCABE respecting legacy left by
Joseph CALDWELL dec'd to Jane WRIGHT being the privilege of
cutting hay annually off land of Moses CALDWELL, legacy which
Joseph wants discharged by payment. Verdict for CALDWELL.

Bk:Pg: 2Z:468   Date: 13 Mar 1820   RtCt: 12 Mar 1820
Samuel HAMMATT & Richard H. HENDERSON. Bond on
HAMMATT as constable.

Bk:Pg: 2Z:468   Date: 13 Mar 1820   RtCt: 12 Mar 1820
Joseph HAWKINS, Jas. H. HAMILTON & Danl. LOVETT. Bond on
HAWKINS as constable.

Bk:Pg: 2Z:469   Date: 3 Feb 1820   RtCt: 3 Mar 1820
Thornton WALKER & wife Fanny of Ldn to Jesse TRAHERN of Ldn.
B/S of ½a adj Samuel DUNKIN, Isaac BROWN, Benjamin KENT,
William H. DORSEY. Wit: Wm. BRONAUGH, Thos. GREGG. Delv.
to Wm. H. DORSEY pr order filed 20 Nov 1820.

Bk:Pg: 2Z:471   Date: 28 Feb 1819   RtCt: 3 Mar 1820
Fleming ROGERS & wife Mary of Shelby Co KY to Margaret
HIXSON of Ldn. B/S of lot adj Patterson WRIGHT and ½a adj Sarah
THOMPSON, Joseph TALBOTT. Wit: Robert BRADEN, Abiel
JENNERS.

Bk:Pg: 2Z:474   Date: 15 Nov 1819   RtCt: 29 Feb 1820
John H. BUTCHER & wife Nancy of Ldn to Stephen JANNEY of
Ldn. B/S of 110a (from deed of Feb 1815 from Elizabeth
OVERFIELD to BUTCHER and Hudson, Joshua, Susannah &
Martin OVERFIELD). Ben. GRAYSON, Notley C. WILLIAMS.

Bk:Pg: 2Z:476   Date: 11 Jan 1820   RtCt: 15 Feb 1820
Archibald McVICKERS & wife Elizabeth of Hampshire Co to
Benjamin MOFFETT of Ldn. B/S of 136a adj Tascoe QUINLAN. Wit:
Francis W. LUCKETT, A. GIBSON.

Bk:Pg: 2Z:478   Date: 8 Jan 1820   RtCt: Feb 1820
Enos POTTS & wife Lydia of Ldn to Levi WILLIAMS of Ldn. B/S of
11½a on NW fork of Goose creek and Henry ELLIS, Elizabeth
BOLEN, David SMITH, Giles CRAVEN (prch/o Stephen WILSON).
Wit: Thos. GREGG, Notley C. WILLIAMS.

Bk:Pg: 2Z:480   Date: 20 Dec 1819   RtCt: 29 Feb 1820
James SIMPSON & wife Elizabeth of Ldn to Humphrey B. POWELL.
Trust for debt to Noble BEVERIDGE using land cnvy/b Isaac LAKE
& wife Sally in 1817. Delv. to Hugh SMITH pr order of H. B.
POWELL filed BBB, 17 Apr 1822.

Bk:Pg: 2Z:482   Date: 25 Feb 1820   RtCt: 29 Feb 1820
John HARRIS & wife Elizabeth of Mdbg to Humphrey B. POWELL of Ldn. Trust for debt to Noble BEVERIDGE using Lot #29 in Mdbg. Wit: Burr POWELL, A. GIBSON. Delv. pr order 24 Nov 1827.

Bk:Pg: 2Z:485   Date: 27 Nov 1819   RtCt: 4 Feb 1820
Lot JANNEY & wife Sophia of Ldn to Samuel HOGE of Ldn. B/S of land conveyed to JANNEY & HOGE in Dec 1818 by William COE & wife Catharine, Edward M. COE & wife Mary, Robert COE & wife Elizabeth and David J. COE. Wit: James H. HAMILTON, Thos. GREGG, Joseph CARRELL. Delv. to HOGE 31 Dec 1824

Bk:Pg: 2Z:487   Date: 14 Feb 1820   RtCt: 10 Mar 1820
William NOLAND & wife Catharine of Ldn to Richard H. HENDERSON. Trust for debt to George SMITH of Dumfries, PrWm using 400a adj Aldie on Little River. Wit: Robert ARMISTEAD, Leven LUCKETT. Delv. to HENDERSON 3 May 1820.

Bk:Pg: 2Z:492   Date: 22 Jan 1820   RtCt: 20 Feb 1820
Benjamin MOFFET & wife Malinda of Ldn to Archibald McVICKER. Release of trust on 135a. Wit: S. BLINCOE, Jonas POTTS, Leven W. SHEPHERD.

Bk:Pg: 2Z:495   Date: 25 May 1810   RtCt: 5 Apr 1820
Benjamin B. THORNTON to Isaac STEERS. BoS for negro woman Lucy & her children Elizabeth & Frank. Wit: John KIPHART, A. O. POWELL, Lee W. DURHAM, Geo. SWEARINGEN.

Bk:Pg: 2Z:497   Date: 6 Apr 1820   RtCt: 6 Apr 1820
Peter BOSS & wife Lydia of Pike Township, Wayne Co OH to Samuel M. BOSS of Lsbg. B/S of undivided interest in lot & 2-story brick house in Lsbg on NE corner of Loudoun & King Sts. and lot adj Robert R. HOUGH, Chas. B. BALL, Joshua RILEY, Saml. M. EDWARDS (land of Peter BOSS late of Lsbg leaving widow Mary and Peter, Saml. M., Daniel C., David & Abraham BOSS and Mary HAWKE (now MARTIN) & Wm. HAWKE {ch/o Margaret HAWKE dec'd d/o Peter dec'd} and Saml. BOSS s/o Jacob BOSS dec'd {s/o Peter dec'd}). Delv. to Saml. M. BOSS 6 Apr 1820.

Bk:Pg: 2Z:499   Date: 8 Feb 1819   RtCt: 23 Feb 1820
Joanna LEWIS (formerly wd/o George BRENT dec'd) to Martin BRENT (s/o George dec'd). Partition – land to widow's dower, Thomas BRENT, Willis BRENT, Martin BRENT. Martin bought undivided shares from Thomas & Willis and Willis bought of Hugh BRENT. Wit: Wm. VICKERS, Hiram SEATON. Gives plat. Divisors: Wm. VICKERS, Hiram SEATON, Seth SMITH.

Bk:Pg: 2Z:504   Date: 29 Jul 1819   RtCt: 8 Nov 1819
John BEVERIDGE of Ldn to son John BEVERIDGE. Gift of negro man James. Wit: Horace LUCKETT, Ludwell LUCKETT, Balaam OSBURN. Delv. to John BEVERAGE Jr. 27 Oct 1822.

Bk:Pg: 2Z:505   Date: 27 Nov 1819   RtCt: 27 Mar 1820
David ALEXANDER & wife Elizabeth of Ldn to Benjamin MOFFETT of Ldn. B/S of 7¼a on N side of Goose creek (residue of 10a conveyed to John HUMPHREY) adj David CARTER. Wit: Wm. NOLAND, Chas. LEWIS.

Bk:Pg: 2Z:507   Date: 28 Mar 1820   RtCt: 29 Mar 1820
Jesse GOVER & wife Miriam of Ldn to Samuel GOVER of Ldn. B/S of part of lot in Wtfd prch/o Israel T. GRIFFITH. Wit: Robert BRADEN, Saml. HOUGH Jr.

Bk:Pg: 2Z:509   Date: 22 Mar 1820   RtCt: 22 Mar 1820
Owen WILLIAMS & wife Rhoda of Pickaway Co OH to Ellis WILLIAMS of Ldn. B/S of undivided 1/5th interest in lands of John WILLIAMS dec'd (f/o Owen & Ellis) left to now dec'd sister Mary WILLIAMS and brother Daniel WILLIAMS who is supposed to be dead (went to sea 20y ago and not heard from in 18y) and dower rights of mother Martha WILLIAMS. Delv. to Ellis WILLIAMS 13 Jul 1836.

Bk:Pg: 2Z:511   Date: 25 Mar 1820   RtCt: 27 Mar 1820
David JANNEY & wife Elizabeth of Ldn to John Randolph WHITE of Ldn. B/S of ¼a in new addition to Wtfd (Sarah BRADEN dec'd prch/o JANNEY and dev. WHITE but never received a deed). Wit: Robert BRADEN, Abiel JENNERS.

Bk:Pg: 2Z:513   Date: 5 Feb 1820   RtCt: 31 Mar 1820
William STONE of Ldn to David SHAWEN of Ldn. B/S of ½a lot in new addition to Wtfd (prch/o Joseph WOOD) adj William H. HOUGH. Delv. to SHAWEN 13 Dec 1822.

Bk:Pg: 2Z:514   Date: 13 Mar 1820   RtCt: 18 Mar 1820
Richard H. HENDERSON of Ldn to Jacob MOCK of Ldn. Release of trust of Samuel E. TAYLOR.

Bk:Pg: 2Z:514   Date: 20 Mar 1820   RtCt: 27 Mar 1820
David JANNEY & wife Elizabeth of Ldn to Joseph LOVETT of Ldn. B/S of ¼a Lot #9 in Wtfd on Fairfax St. adj James MOORE, Lewis COLE. Wit: Robert BRADEN, Abiel JENNERS. Delv. to grantee 12 Mar 1821.

Bk:Pg: 2Z:516   Date: ___   RtCt: 22 Mar 1820
Owen WILLIAMS of Pickaway Co OH to Ellis WILLIAMS of Ldn. Bond concerning transaction on page 509. Delv. to Ellis 13 Jul 1836.

Bk:Pg: 2Z:517   Date: 14 Dec 1813   RtCt: 13 Jun 1814/28 Mar 1820
Thomas A. BROOK of MontMd to Mordecai THROCKMORTIN of Ldn. B/S of 800a adj Robert RUSSEL. Wit: R. J. TAYLOR, Thomson F. MASON, Joseph SMITH, C. AULD.

Bk:Pg: 3A:001   Date: 28 Mar 1820   RtCt: 29 Mar 1820
Asa MOORE & wife Ann of Ldn to Israel T. GRIFFITH of Ldn. B/S of
Lot #3 in Wtfd which GRIFFITH leases adj leased lot of Sarah P.
GRIFFITH, __ BRADEN.

Bk:Pg: 3A:002   Date: 10 Apr 1820   RtCt: 10 Apr 1820
Richard McALISTER, John ROSE & John A. BINNS. Bond on
McALISTER to perform marriages as Methodist minister.

Bk:Pg: 3A:003   Date: 12 Nov 1819   RtCt: 13 Mar 1820
Bernard MANN & wife Joanna of Mdbg to Jacob MANN & wife Sally.
Release of trust on ½a in Mdbg. Wit: Burr POWELL, A. GIBSON.

Bk:Pg: 3A:005   Date: 28 Sep 1819   RtCt: 10 Apr 1820
Richard H. HENDERSON (comm. in case of George HANCOCK
agst Admrs of Robert CARTER) of Ldn to Alfred G. CARTER of Ldn.
B/S of 130a (dev. Robert CARTER dec'd f/o Alfred from his father
John CARTER) adj Andrew HEATH dec'd and 130a occupied by
Isaac HEATH. Delv. to grantee 15 Jan 1821.

Bk:Pg: 3A:007   Date: 18 Mar 1820   RtCt: 18 Mar 1820
Amos JANNEY of Ldn to Henry HICKMAN of Ldn. B/S of 2a. Delv.
to HICKMAN 8 May 1822.

Bk:Pg: 3A:008   Date: 17 Mar 1820   RtCt: 18 Mar 1820
Amos JANNEY of Ldn to John BOGER of Ldn. B/S of 2a opposite
the Lutheran stone church. Delv. to BOGAR 8 May 1822.

Bk:Pg: 3A:009   Date: 28 Mar 1820   RtCt: 29 Mar 1820
Israel T. GRIFFITH of Ldn to Jesse GOVER of Ldn. B/S of Lots #1,
#2 & #3 in Wtfd (devised by Richard GRIFFITH to Israel). Delv. to
GOVER 17 Aug 1820.

Bk:Pg: 3A:011   Date: 21 Mar 1820   RtCt: 27 Mar 1820
John B. STEPHENS & wife Sarah of Ldn to Robert BRADEN of Ldn.
B/S of lot in new addition to Wtfd adj Lewis KLEIN. Wit: John H.
McCABE, Abiel JENNERS. Delv. to BRADEN 31 May 1822.

Bk:Pg: 3A:013   Date: 1 Aug 1818   RtCt: 23 Mar 1820
Thomas FLOWERS of Ldn to John LITTLEJOHN of Ldn. Mortgage
on ¼a at Air & Loudoun Sts. in Lsbg. Wit: Thomas SANDERS, J.
SANDERS.

Bk:Pg: 3A:015   Date: 16 Mar 1820   RtCt: 27 Mar 1820
Alfred H. POWELL of Frederick Co to John CARR of Ldn. Release
of trust for debt to Edward McGUIRE. Wit: John POISAL, Edmund
GRAHAM, Johnston MAGOWEN. Delv. to Jno. CARR 28 Apr 1821.

Bk:Pg: 3A:016   Date: 8 Dec 1818   RtCt: 5 Apr 1820
Maria FENITY of Ldn to Amos JOHNSON of Ldn. B/S of 1/6th part of
56a including 8a of wood lot detached left Jemima FENITY & her
children by John VIOLETT dec'd. Wit: John WILSON, William NUTT,
Hiram McVEIGH. Delv. to JOHNSON 6 Oct 1820.

Bk:Pg: 3A:018   Date: 11 Mar 1820   RtCt: 13 Mar 1820
Margaret HIXON of Ldn to James MOORE of Ldn. Trust for debt to
Jesse RICE of Ldn using ¼a & house in Wtfd (prch/o John E.
PARMER). Delv. to Leven CHILTON 19 Mar 1822.

Bk:Pg: 3A:020   Date: 25 Mar 1820   RtCt: 27 Mar 1820
David JANNEY & wife Elizabeth of Ldn to Isaac WALKER of Ldn.
B/S of lot in new addition to Wtfd on W side of Second St adj Saml
HOUGH Jr., John B. STEVENS. Wit: Robert BRADEN, Abiel
JENNERS. Delv. pr order 19 Jul 1824.

Bk:Pg: 3A:023   Date: __ 1819   RtCt: 18 Mar 1820
Amos JANNEY of Ldn to George JANNEY of D.C. B/S of 34a
(prch/o James MOORE & Robert BRADEN) adj Peter SAUNDERS,
Adam HOUSEHOLDER.

Bk:Pg: 3A:025   Date: 20 Sep 1819   RtCt: 10 Apr 1820
Alfred G. CARTER of Ldn to Richard H. HENDERSON of Ldn. Trust
to Creditors of Robert CARTER dec'd (Fredericksburg Ct. George
HANCOCK &c vs. Admrs. of Robert CARTER dec'd {late of Sudley
s/o John CARTER} &c) using 'Heaths lot', 'Halleys lot', Foleys lot' &
'Hughs lot'. Delv. to Thos. A. MOORE for R. H. HENDERSON 30
May 1820.

Bk:Pg: 3A:027   Date: 15 Mar 1820   RtCt: 10 Apr 1820
Samuel SINCLAIR. Division by court order of 14 Dec 1819. Lot #2
(23½a) & #5 (12a) to widow, Lot #1 (181½a) & #6 (9a) to Craven
SINCLAIR, Lot #3 (30a) to Mary THORNTON, Lot #4 (62¼a) to
Charles THORNTON. Gives plat. Divisors Aaron SANDERS, James
M. LEWIS.

Bk:Pg: 3A:029   Date: 16 Nov 1819   RtCt: 23 Mar 1820
John H. BUTCHER & wife Nancy of Ldn to Thomas DRAKE of Ldn.
B/S of 64a (formerly owned by Martin OVERFIELD & Mary
OVERFIELD). Wit: Notly C. WILLIAMS, John W. GRAYSON. Delv.
pr order filed 1 Nov 1820.

Bk:Pg: 3A:032   Date: 24 Feb 1820   RtCt: 27 Mar 1820
Joseph EIDSON & wife Mahala of Ldn to Catharine LACEY of Ldn.
B/S of 173½a on turnpike road to Wm. H. HANDEY's mill, road from
Mdbg by Capt. McCARTY's house, Hugh WILEY, road to Wilson's
fulling mill. Wit: Burr POWELL, A. GIBSON.

Bk:Pg: 3A:034   Date: 25 Feb 1820   RtCt: 27 Mar 1820
Catharine LACEY of Ldn to Joseph EIDSON of Ldn. B/S of 173½a
as above. Wit: Sarah ROZEL, Phoeba ROZEL, Daniel REESE.
Delv. to EIDSON 21 Mar 1821.

Bk:Pg: 3A:036   Date: 13 Dec 1819   RtCt: 27 Mar 1820
Thomas FRED Sr. & wife Elizabeth of Ldn to Thomas FRED Jr. of
Ldn. B/S of 1½a (part of wood land devised from Samuel TORBERT
dec'd) adj Thomas A. HEREFORD, John BURKINS, Thomas

TORBERT. Wit: Stephen McPHERSON Jr., John TORBERT, Mahaly FRED.

Bk:Pg: 3A:038   Date: 21 Sep 1819   RtCt: 12 Oct 1819
Frances COLEMAN of Ldn to James LEWIS & Charles LEWIS of Ldn. Frances abt to m. Robert M. NEWMAN. Trust for her using 1/6th part of land where family of James COLEMAN dec'd (f/o Frances) lived cnvy/b his father and "Rocky Hill tract" conveyed to James by his father and tract cnvy/b Ludwell LEE and 1/6th part of Cubun tract dev. Hannah COLEMAN (m/o Frances) by her mother and 1/6th part of 1000a in Franklin Co KY on Kentucky River in 1807 and 1/6th part of 100a on Goose Creek in Madison Co KY and undivided interest in slaves Toby, Len, Charles, James, Bill, Charlotte, Caroline, Hannah, Mille, George, Sampson, Richard, Rachael, Silve and the entire interest in slaves Eliza, Newton, Daniel & Penny belonging to Frances as beq. by her grandmother and in farm items and animals. Wit: Johnston CLEVELAND, Ths. DARNE, Nath. S. ODEN. Delv. to Chas. LEWIS 10 May 1830.

Bk:Pg: 3A:040   Date: 20 Mar 1820   RtCt: 28 Mar 1820
Andrew FENITON Jr. to Amos JOHNSON of Ldn. B/S of interest in 56a including 8a wood land detached Lot #3 allotted to Jemima FENITON & her children of lands of John VIOLETT dec'd. Delv. to JOHNSON 6 Oct 1820.

Bk:Pg: 3A:043   Date: 1 Feb 1820   RtCt: 5 Apr 1820
Adam HOUSEHOLDER & wife Sarah of Ldn to John DAVIS of Ldn. B/S of 1a (cnvy/b Thomas DAVIS dec'd & wife Elizabeth) adj Sanford RAMEY. Wit: Samuel HOUGH Jr., John H. McCABE. Delv. to DAVIS 11 Mar 1822.

Bk:Pg: 3A:045   Date: 28 Mar 1820   RtCt: 29 Mar 1820
Jesse GOVER & wife Maryam of Ldn to Noble S. BRADEN. Trust for debt to Israel T.GRIFFITH of Ldn lot in Wtfd prch/o GRIFFITH. Wit: Robert BRADEN, Samuel HOUGH Jr. Delv. pr order 12 Dec 1820.

Bk:Pg: 3A:049   Date: 12 Oct 1819   RtCt: 13 Mar 1820
George ZIMMERMAN & wife Ann of Ffx to Susanna SIMPSON of Ffx. B/S of interest in 49a (from father Henry ZIMMERMAN dec'd). Wit: R. RATCLIFF, O. RATCLIFF, Saml. RATCLIFF.

Bk:Pg: 3A:052   Date: 15 May 1819   RtCt: 13 Mar 1820
Jacob MILLER & wife Elizabeth of Ldn to Adam MILLER & Jesse MILLER of Ldn. B/S of 250a on E side of Short Hill (prop. of Peter MILLER dec'd now in possession of widow Catharine MILLER). Wit: Ebenezer GRUBB, Craven OSBURN. Delv. to Jesse MILLER 5 Dec 1820.

Bk:Pg: 3A:054   Date: 3 Dec 1819   RtCt: 13 Mar 1820
Jacob ZIMMERMAN & wife Jane of Ffx to Susanna SIMPSON of Ffx. B/S of undivided portion of 49a (from father Henry ZIMMERMAN dec'd).

Bk:Pg: 3A:057 Date: 10 Aug 1819 RtCt: 25 Mar 1820
Caleb N. GALLIHER & wife Lucinda of Ldn to Thornton WALKER of Ldn. B/S of ½a adj Samuel DUNKIN, Isaac BROWN, Cornelius VANDEVANTER, Benjamin KENT. Wit: Thos. GREGG, Jno. W. GRAYSON. Delv. to WALKER 16 Nov 1820.

Bk:Pg: 3A:059 Date: 2 Feb 1814 RtCt: 4 Apr 1820
John MATHIAS & wife Nancy of Lsbg to Richard H. HENDERSON (Admr of Alexander SUTHERLAND dec'd) of Lsbg. Trust using Nancy's 1/5th interest in lot & house in Lsbg of father Robert HAMILTON dec'd. Wit: Burr W. HARRISON, Ebenezer MARTIN, James STEPHENSON, Samuel MURREY, John LITTLEJOHN. Delv. to HENDERSON 4 May 1820.

Bk:Pg: 3A:063 Date: 18 Mar 1820 RtCt: 18 Mar 1820
Amos JANNEY of Ldn to Aaron MILLER of Ldn. B/S of 70a adj __ HICKMAN, __MINK, __RICKARD, George COOPER. Delv. to grantee 290 Nov 1820.

Bk:Pg: 3A:065 Date: 1 Aug 1819 RtCt: 23 Mar 1820
John LITTLEJOHN & wife Monica of Ldn to Thomas FLOWERS of Ldn. B/S of ¼a in new addition of Lsbg at corner of Air & Loudoun Sts. Wit: C. BINNS, Jesse DAILEY, Tho. FOUCH, Jno. McCORMICK.

Bk:Pg: 3A:067 Date: 20 Sep 1819 RtCt: 27 Mar 1820
Edward DOWLING of Ldn to Benjamin LESLIE of Ldn. B/S of 24a on E side of Short Hill adj __ McILHANY, __ CLENDENING, __ JANNEY. Wit: Craven OSBURN, Jonas POTTS, Saml. D. LESLIE.

Bk:Pg: 3A:069 Date: 17 Nov 1819 RtCt: 21 Mar 1820
John BENEDUM of Ldn to William CARR of Ldn. Trust for debt to Peter BENEDUM using 105a cnvy/b Peter BENEDUM. Wit: L. P. W. BALCH, Jesse RICE, John J. MATHIAS. Delv. to Saml. M. EDWARDS agent for Peter BENEDUM 18 Feb 1824.

Bk:Pg: 3A:072 Date: 1 Mar 1820 RtCt: 13 Mar 1820
Stephenson HIXON & wife Alice of Ldn to Aaron MILLER of Ldn. B/S of 129a (out of lands of Reuben HIXSON dec'd for dower of Mary HIXON where Mary now resides). Wit: Robert BRADEN, John H. McCABE. Delv. to grantee 29 Nov 1820.

Bk:Pg: 3A:075 Date: 17 Jan 1817 RtCt: 27 Mar 1820
Martha ORENDUFF, Exor of Johnathan PALMER dec'd) of Ldn to James NICHOLLS of Ldn. B/S of 60a on SE side of blue ridge, formerly held & occupied by Johnathan, adj Moriss OSBURN, Thomas JAMES, James NICHOLS. Wit: Craven OSBURN, Joel OSBURN, Joseph THOMAS.

Bk:Pg: 3A:077 Date: 18 Mar 1820 RtCt: 18 Mar 1820
Amos JANNEY of Ldn to John M. SOCKMAN of Ldn. B/S of 2a. Delv to Charles SOCKMAN pr order filed 28 May 1823.

Bk:Pg: 3A:079   Date: 28 Feb 1820   RtCt: 13 Mar 1820
Thomas FRED Jr. of Ldn to Thomas FRED Sr. of Ldn. B/S of 1½a adj Thomas A. HEREFORD (part of 14a sold by Samuel BUTCHER to Samuel TORBERT dec'd).

Bk:Pg: 3A:081   Date: 11 Dec 1819   RtCt: 14 Mar 1820
John LICKEY & wife Elizabeth of Belmont Co OH to Sampson BLINCOE of Ldn. B/S of 23a on road from Mdbg by Coes mill to Lsbg and all land heretofore sold him by BLINCOE. Wit: Henly BOGGESS, Jas. L. HAMILTON, John MATHIAS. Delv. to Martha S. BLINCOE 7 Sep 1832.

Bk:Pg: 3A:087   Date: 28 Feb 1820   RtCt: 13 Mar 1820
Thomas BISCOE & wife Sarah of Ldn to John TOWERMAN of Ldn. B/S of 15a nr Goose Creek where BISCOE now lives adj Edward WILSON, Thomas BATTSON, road from Mdbg to Handey's mill. Wit: Burr POWELL, A. GIBSON.

Bk:Pg: 3A:089   Date: 11 Mar 1820   RtCt: 6 Apr 1820
Thomas Randolph MOTT & wife Mary Chichester of Ldn to James RUST of Ldn. B/S of 20a on Kittocton Mt. (prch/o Richard H. HENDERSON, DB UU:216) and 15a (conveyed to MOTT 10 Sep 1817, DB VV:265). Wit: Presley CORDELL, Saml. M. EDWARDS. Delv. to RUST 27 Nov 1825.

Bk:Pg: 3A:092   Date: 22 Jan 1820   RtCt: 5 Apr 1820
Isaac E. STEER & wife Leah of Ldn to Mahlon SCHOOLEY of Ldn. B/S of 61a (part of tract prch/o James RICE) adj John WORSLEY. Wit: Robert BRADEN, John H. McCABE.

Bk:Pg: 3A:095   Date: 7 Apr 1819   RtCt: 13 Mar 1820
John B. HOOK & wife Jane, Josias CLAPHAM, Hannah CLAPHAM & Maria CLAPHAM of Ldn to James McFARLAN of Ldn. B/S of 249a (part of land willed by Josias CLAPHAM dec'd to Samuel CLAPHAM dec'd). Wit: Wilson C. SELDEN, Charles LEWIS. Delv. to McFARLAN 23 Jan 1828.

Bk:Pg: 3A:099   Date: 15 Apr 1819   RtCt: 13 Mar 1820
James McFARLAN & wife Hannah of Ldn to John B. HOOK, Josias CLAPHAM, Hannah CLAPHAM & Maria CLAPHAM of Ldn. Trust using above 249a. Wit: Charles LEWIS, William B. HARRISON.

Bk:Pg: 3A:102   Date: 26 Oct 1819   RtCt: 13 Mar 1820
Burr POWELL of Ldn to Samuel IDEN of Ldn. B/S of ½a Lot #64 in Mdbg.

Bk:Pg: 3A:105   Date: 22 Oct 1818   RtCt: 13 Mar 1820
David LOVETT of Ldn to James WHITE of Ldn. B/S of 165a adj John WHITE, Samuel WRIGHT, Charles HUMPHREY.

Bk:Pg: 3A:107   Date: 5 Feb 1820   RtCt: 27 Mar 1820
Joseph LEWIS Jr. of Ldn to William GORE. Trust for debt to Josiah LOCKHART of FredVa using 160a, part of Piedmont, now in possession of Johnathan McCARTY and adj 150a in possession of

Andrew THOMPSON (both cnvy/b Jonah THOMPSON). Delv. to John WRIGHT pr LOCKHART 1 Nov 1822.

Bk:Pg: 3A:110   Date: 13 Aug 1819   RtCt: 13 Mar 1820
Ferdinando FAIRFAX of Washington to Hugh THOMSON of Ldn. B/S of 112a in Shannondale tract on side of blue ridge adj Thomas LESLIE, Jesse EVANS. Wit: John CAMPBELL, William CLENDENING, Thomas S. STONE, William GIDEON. Delv. to THOMPSON 6 Mar 1821.

Bk:Pg: 3A:113   Date: 25 Mar 1820   RtCt: 27 Mar 1820
Albert BAYLY of Ldn to Ariss BUCKNER and George B. WHITING of Ldn. Trust to ensure that wife Sarah BAYLY when she arrives at 21y relinquishes all her right of dower of 188a 'Diammond Hill' beq. to Albert by father Pierce BAYLEY which he sold in Nov 1819 to John BAYLEY. Wit: William ROSE, C. DUNCAN, Amos SKINNER, R. H. LITTLE. Delv. to John BAILEY 20 May 1820.

Bk:Pg: 3A:116   Date: 24 Mar 1820   RtCt: 27 Mar 1820
John BAILEY & wife Peggy of Ldn to Albert BAILEY of Ldn. B/S of 188a on old Gum Spring road adj George B. WHITING, Reuben HUTCHISON, Sampson HUTCHISON. Wit: Wm. B. HARRISON, Chs. LEWIS. Delv. to grantee pr order 10 Jul 1820.

Bk:Pg: 3A:119   Date: 10 Nov 1819   RtCt: 14 Mar 1820
John DUNKIN & wife Ruth of Ldn to John CLARK of Ldn. B/S of 89a adj George MARKS, Benjamin JENKINS, Thomas TREHORN. Wit: Notley C. WILLIAMS, Jno. W. GRAYSON.

Bk:Pg: 3A:123   Date: __ Jan 1820   RtCt: 20 Mar 1820
John DREAN & wife Nancy of Lsbg and Sampson BLINCOE of Lsbg. Agreement on dividing line of lots in Lsbg. Wit: Benjamin DAWES, N. C. WILLIAMS, Reuben SCHOOLEY, Thomas SANDERS, Saml. M. EDWARDS. Delv. to BLINCOE 4 Sep 1826

Bk:Pg: 3A:127   Date: 5 Apr 1820   RtCt: 10 Apr 1820
John MATHIAS Sr. of Ldn to John MATHIAS Jr. of Ldn. Trust for sale of 610a on blue ridge mt. & W of sale to David POTTS (part of 3 tracts containing 500a in JeffVa & Ldn cnvy/b commrs. Thomas PARKER dec'd, Robert J. TAYLOR & Richard H. HENDERSON under decree) with John Sr., Thomas SWANN & Edmund J. LEE of AlexDC to divide proceeds of sale and 150 on W side of short hill and S of sale to Thomas KIDWELL. Wit: Saml. M. EDWARDS, Burr W. HARRISON, L. P. W. BALCH. Delv. to Jno. J. MATHIAS 14 Sep 1820.

Bk:Pg: 3A:130   Date: 10 Mar 1820   RtCt: 13 Mar 1820
Samuel SINCLAIR & wife Ruth of Ldn to Edward B. GRADY of Ldn. Trust for debt to John MARKS using 43a formerly prop. of John MARKS & Stephen McPHERSON Jr. where SINCLAIR's merchant mill stands, adj John MARKS, George MARKS, Isaiah MARKS and also 10a prch/o Stephen McPHERSON Jr. Wit: William

BRONAUGH, Francis W. LUCKETT. Delv to John MARKS 27 Jul 1820.

Bk:Pg: 3A:135   Date: 5 May 1819   RtCt: 13 Mar 1820
Elias JAMES & wife Ruth, Johnathan JAMES Jr. & Daniel JAMES of Ldn to James McILHANY & John LOVE of Ldn. Trust for debt to Margaret McIlHANY using 87½a. Wit: L. ELLZEY, Stacy TAYLOR, Edward STONE, Craven OSBURN, John WHITE.

Bk:Pg: 3A:140   Date: 22 Oct 1819   RtCt: 27 Apr 1820
George JANN(E)Y & wife Susanna of D.C. to Amos JANN(E)Y of Ldn. B/S of 107a adj __ MINK, __HICKMAN, __ RICKER. Wit: Daniel BUSSARD, W. S. CHANDLER.

Bk:Pg: 3A:144   Date: 27 Sep 1813   RtCt: 2 May 1820
Catharine STORKS [STOCKS?] and John A. BINNS. Agreement about deed in prch/o 1a including house formerly occupied by Bazzell JOHNSON.

Bk:Pg: 3A:144   Date: 26 Apr 1820   RtCt: 27 Apr 1820
William CHILTON & wife Sarah Harrison to George CARTER. B/S of 33a adj __ CARTER, __ QUINLAN, __ CHILTON. Wit: Presly CORDELL, Thomas SANDERS. Delv. to Wm. L. COCKERIL[L]E pr order filed deed bundle CCC (first bundle) 27 Feb 1822.

Bk:Pg: 3A:147   Date: 20 Apr 1820   RtCt: 21 Apr 1820
George H. SINCLAIR of Ldn to Aaron SANDERS and Charles ELGIN of Ldn. Trust for debt to Mahlon JANNEY using land cnvy/b Thomas R. MOTT. Delv. to Chs. ELGIN 4 Nov 1820

Bk:Pg: 3A:148   Date: 5 Feb 1820   RtCt: 8 May 1820
Joseph LEWIS Jr. of Ldn to Edward McGUIRE and Daniel HARTMAN of Winchester. Trust for debt to Daniel HARTMAN using 300a adj 'Clifton' (prch/o Alfred H. POWELL). Wit: John MACKY, Alfred H. POWELL, W. MAXWELL. Delv. to Major SMITH pr order filed 26 May 1820.

Bk:Pg: 3A:151   Date: 13 Apr 1820   RtCt: 13 Apr 1820
Samuel MURREY & Isaac HARRIS of Ldn to John G. WATT & wife Dewanner of Ldn. Release of trust to Fielding BROWN.

Bk:Pg: 3A:152   Date: 4 Jan 1820   RtCt: 8 May 1820
Hugh BIRKLY of Bullett Co KY agent & attorney in fact for Catharine BIRKLY, Malinda BERKLEY, Robert HOSKINS & wife Matilda late BERKLEY & Marmaduke BERKELEY (heirs of Ann BERKLEY dec'd formerly Ann KEENE an heir of Richard KEENE dec'd) to James ALLEN of Ldn. B/S of 108a adj Richard KEENE. Delv. to ALLEN 24 Jun 1820

Bk:Pg: 3A:156   Date: 14 Oct 1819   RtCt: 5 May 1820
John MARKS & wife Lydia to Samuel SINCLAIR. B/S of 29a conveyed on 26 Dec 1816 to include part not previously conveyed. Wit: John W. GRAYSON, Notley C. WILLIAMS.

Bk:Pg: 3A:159   Date: 16 Feb 1820   RtCt: 10 Apr 1820
Jesse TRAYHORN & wife Harriet of Union to John M. MONROE of
Ldn. B/S of 52 sq poles a little N of Union adj Samuel DUNKIN,
Isaac BROWN. Wit: William BRONAUGH, Thomas GREGG. Delv.
to Henry BROWN pr order of MONROE filed away among deeds 9
Jan 1821.

Bk:Pg: 3A:161   Date: 20 Mar 1820   RtCt: 26 Apr 1820
George TAVENER Jr. of Ldn to Aaron BURSON of Ldn. PoA for
monies as Exor of George NIXON dec'd due from William HARDING
dec'd and Admr Charles BINNS. Wit: Robert CHINN, John
McKINNEY. Delv. to Charles BINNS Exor of Wm. H. HARDING 21
Feb 1828.

Bk:Pg: 3A:163   Date: 26 Apr 1820   RtCt: 9 May 1820
Aaron BURSON. Receipt of monies from Chs. BINNS Admr wwa of
William H. HARDING dec'd – injuction is dissolved in Sup Ct of
Winchester. Wit: R. H. HENDERSON.

Bk:Pg: 3A:163   Date: 19 Apr 1820   RtCt: 21 Apr 1820
David CUNNARD & wife Sarah of Ldn to Mahlon JANNEY. B/S of lot
in Wtfd adj William H. HOUGH, John C. HANDEY. Wit: Robert
BRADEN, Abiel JENNERS.

Bk:Pg: 3A:166   Date: 27 Apr 1820   RtCt: 27 Apr 1820
William CHILTON & wife Sarah H. to Charles B. BALL. B/S of 5-6a
on ferry road to N of Lsbg adj Dr. Wilson C. SELDON. Wit: A.
MINES, Presly CORDELL, Thomas SANDERS.

Bk:Pg: 3A:169   Date: 15 May 1815   RtCt: 9 May 1820
James GRADY dec'd. Division – Lot 1 (66a) to Jane DAGGS heirs
(daus. Susan & Clarissa DAGG), Lot 2 (60a) to Abijah SANDERS &
wife Elizabeth, Lot 3 (66a) to Johnathan WATERS & wife Ann, Lot 4
(56a) to Edward B. GRADY, Lot 5 (13a) & 6 (26a) to Ury GRADY,
Lot 7 (58½a) to Mary GRADY, Lot 8 (58½a) to Susanna GRADY.
Gives plat.

Bk:Pg: 3A:172   Date: 8 May 1820   RtCt: 8 May 1820
Oliver DONHAM/DENHAM & Richard COCKRANE. Bond on
DONHAM as constable in Mdbg district.

Bk:Pg: 3A:173   Date: 14 May 1803   RtCt: ___
John D. ORR & wife Lucinda of JeffVa to Thomas ATWELL of Ldn.
B/S of 198a (indenture to Henry LEE of Westmoreland for 636½a on
Goose Creek only partially proved and not yet legal. LEE sold his
interest in Apr 1807 to Thomas LANG of NY who sold to Thomas
ATWELL) adj Burr POWELL. Wit: Burr POWELL, Noble
BEVERIDGE, John UPP, Daniel VERNON, James ARMSTRONG,
Martin BRENT, Jesse McVEIGH.

Bk:Pg: 3A:176   Date: 8 May 1820   RtCt: 8 May 1820
James M C. HANSON, Thomas SANDERS & Francis HEREFORD.
Bond on HANSON as credentialed Methodist to perform marriages.

Bk:Pg: 3A:177   Date: 20 Apr 1820   RtCt: 21 Apr 1820
Mahlon JANNEY to Aaron SANDERS & Charles ELGIN. Trust for
debt to Thomas R. MOTT using house & lot in Wtfd prch/o David
CONARD. Delv. to ELGIN 4 Dec 1820.

Bk:Pg: 3A:179   Date: 1 Dec 1819   RtCt: 10 Apr 1820
James RUST & wife Sally of Ldn to Robert ROBERTS of Ldn. B/S of
24a adj __ TOMKINS. Wit: Thomas SANDERS, Saml. M.
EDWARDS. Delv. to ROBERTS 14 Sep 1832.

Bk:Pg: 3A:181   Date: 10 Apr 1820   RtCt: 10 Apr 1820
William BRONAUGH of Ldn to George TAVENER Jr. of Ldn.
Release of trust for debt to Hugh & James JOHNSON using 268a.

Bk:Pg: 3A:183   Date: 11 Nov 1819   RtCt: 5 May 1820
Yeoman John CLARK & wife Emily of Ldn to Thornton WALKER of
Ldn. Trust for debt to John DUNKIN using 89a. Wit: Notly C.
WILLIAMS, John W. GRAYSON.

Bk:Pg: 3A:185   Date: 15 Apr 1820   RtCt: 6 May 1820
Bernard TAYLOR & William NICHOLS (Exors of Jesse JANNEY) of
Ldn to Hannah HOWELL (w/o Jesse HOWEL[L]) of Ldn. B/S of 67a
on SE side of blue ridge adj Morise OSBURN, __ KIRKPATRICK,
Joel OSBURN. Wit: Joel OSBURN, John MILDERN, Robt. ROSS.
Delv. to John JANNEY pr order 10 Sep 1825.

Bk:Pg: 3A:187   Date: 12 Feb 1820   RtCt: 10 Apr 1820
Zachariah DULANY & wife Mary E. of Ldn to Joseph CAVENS of
Ldn. B/S of 2a (John A. BINNS sold to Joseph HARRIS but not
conveyed and comm. R. H. HENDERSON conveyed to DULANY)
adj William WRIGHT, Stephen DANIEL, road from Wtfd to Nolands
Ferry. Wit: Abiel JENNERS, John H. McCABE. Delv. to CAVANS 14
Dec 1820.

Bk:Pg: 3A:190   Date: 24 Apr 1820   RtCt: 24 Apr 1820
Jacob KEMERLE/KIMMERLE & wife Christeana of Ldn to David
McGAHA of Ldn. B/S of land on Kettocton Mt. adj J. DIXON (cnvy/b
Samuel CLAPHAM abt 1816). Wit: John McCORMICK, Presley
CORDELL.

Bk:Pg: 3A:192   Date: 24 Apr 1820   RtCt: 24 Apr 1820
Jacob KEMERLE & wife Christina of Ldn to John DIXON. B/S of 1a
(on 10 Aug 1818 KIMERLE conveyed the tract to John DIXON but
deed Jacob DIXON instead of John and wife Christina did not sign)
adj __ CLAPHAM. Wit: John MCCO[R]MICK, Presly CORDELL.
Delv. to DIXSON 25 Mar 1822.

Bk:Pg: 3A:195   Date: 28 Mar 1820   RtCt: 27 Apr 1820
George JANNEY and Susanna JANNEY of Georgetown D.C. to
Joseph GORE of Ldn. B/S of 17a on Great road adj Benjamin
BRADFIELD, Levi WILLIAMS. Wit: H. T. FOXHALL, Danl.
BUSSARD. Delv. to Jos. GORE Exor. of Jos. dec'd 24 Jan 1831.

Bk:Pg: 3A:198   Date: 28 Dec 1819   RtCt: 10 Apr 1820
Joseph STEER & wife Sarah of Wtfd to John WILLIAMS of Ldn. B/S of Lots #4, #5 & #6 in new addition to Wtfd on corner of an ally that adj presbyterian meeting house. Wit: Robert BRADEN, Abiel JENNERS.

Bk:Pg: 3A:201   Date: 1 Jan 1820   RtCt: 17 Apr 1820
Adam ZIMMERMAN & wife Sarah of Ffx to James SIMPSON of Ldn. B/S of 49a (from death of his father __ ZIMMERMAN). Delv. pr order filed ___.

Bk:Pg: 3A:204   Date: 11 Feb 1820   RtCt: 18 Apr 1820
Benjamin HIXSON & wife Tacey of Ldn to Sanford ROGERS of Ldn. B/S of 13½a adj John & Fenton MERCER, __ HEREFORD. Wit: Burr POWELL, A. GIBSON.

Bk:Pg: 3A:208   Date: 14 Mar 1793   RtCt: 8 May 1820
John TAYLOR & wife Anne of RichVa to James McILHANY of Ldn. B/S of 5480a on Catocton (granted to Francis AWBERY on 7 Jul 1731 & transferred to John TAYLOR dec'd 20 Mar 1732 & dev. above John TAYLOR) and 863a on N drains of Goose Creek (granted to Benjamin GRAYSON & transferred to John TAYLOR dec'd & dev. above John TAYLOR). Wit: William BEALLE Jr., William GORDON, William BEALL the younger, John CORBIN.

Bk:Pg: 3A:213   Date: 10 Nov 1819   RtCt: 10 Apr 1820
Sarah WHITE (by attorney William WHITE) of Jefferson Co TN to Thomas BISCOE of Ldn. B/S of Sarah's div. in 18a of George NIXON the elder dec'd. Wit: Jesse McVEIGH, A. GIBSON, B. WEEKS.

Bk:Pg: 3A:216   Date: 25 Mar 1820   RtCt: 10 Apr 1820
Enoch FURR Sr. & wife Sarah of Ldn to Joshua FRED of Ldn. B/S of 8a (cnvy/b Saml. DIXON who conveyed to Joseph FRED dec'd in Jun 1897 [1797?] who gave to son Thomas FRED who conveyed to Enoch FURR Sr.) adj Thomas A. HEREFORD. Wit: Benjamin GRAYSON, Jno. W. GRAYSON. Delv. to FREDD 2 May 1822.

Bk:Pg: 3A:219   Date: 20 Mar 1820   RtCt: 10 Apr 1820
Thomas BISCOE & wife Sarah of Ldn to Jesse McVEIGH of Ldn. Trust for debt to William WHITE using 2 lots (cnvy/b WHITE and Thomas CARRUTHERS & wife Patty). Wit: Burr POWELL, Abner GIBSON. Delv. to Levi WHITE Admr of William WHITE dec'd 25 May 1830.

Bk:Pg: 3A:223   Date: 6 May 1820   RtCt: 6 May 1820
William NICHOLS & Bernard TAYLOR (Exors of Jesse JANNEY dec'd) of Ldn to James NICHOLS of Ldn. B/S of 1a adj. James NICHOLS, Morris OSBURN, Hannah HOWELL.

Bk:Pg: 3A:225   Date: 8 Jan 1820   RtCt: 10 Apr 1820
Levi WILLIAMS & wife Sarah of Ldn to Elizabeth DAY of Ldn. B/S of
1a (prch/o Enos POTTS). Wit: Thomas GREGG, Notly C.
WILLIAMS.

Bk:Pg: 3A:228   Date: __ 1820   RtCt: 10 Apr 1820
Zachariah DULANY & wife Mary of Ldn to David JANNEY of Ldn.
Trust for debt to Joseph CAVINS using land prch/o CAVINS. Wit:
Abiel JENNERS, Saml HOUGH Jr.

Bk:Pg: 3A:231   Date: __ Oct 1819   RtCt: 11 Apr 1820
James W. HANCHER (Admr dbn of Edward RINKER dec'd) of Ldn
to Robert CAMPBELL of Ldn. B/S of residue of lease on Lot #10
leased of James HEREFORD by Patrick CAVEN who conveyed to
John BROWN who conveyed to RINKER (to clear back rents from
death of Mrs. Sarah RINKER dec'd). Wit: S. BLINCOE, Jno. J.
MATHIAS, Thomas MORRALLEE. Delv. to CAMPBELL 5 Jul 1824.

Bk:Pg: 3A:233   Date: 16 Oct 1819   RtCt: 1 May 1820
Robert CAMPBELL of Ldn to Edward HAMMATT & Thomas
MORRALLEE of Ldn. Trust for debt to James W. HANCHER (Admr
of Edward RINKER dec'd) using above lease purchase. Wit: S.
BLINCO, John J. MATHIAS.

Bk:Pg: 3A:236   Date: 10 Nov 1819   RtCt: 10 Apr 1820
William WHITE and Thomas CARRUTHERS & wife Patty of Ldn to
Thomas BISCOE of Ldn. B/S of 19a on Goose Creek (Lot #5
allotted to WHITE and late wife Nancy from estate of George NIXON
dec'd). Wit: A. GIBSON, Burr WEEKS, Jesse McVEIGH, John
McCORMICK, Presly CORDELL. Delv. to N.? COCKERILL 6 Jun
1825.

Bk:Pg: 3A:240   Date: 28 Mar 1820   RtCt: 27 Apr 1820
George JANNEY and Susana JANNEY of Georgetown D.C. to
Daniel COCKERILL of Ldn. B/S of 15a adj Benjamin BRADFIELD.
Wit: Hen'y FOXHALL, Danl. BUSSARD.

Bk:Pg: 3A:244   Date: 28 Mar 1820   RtCt: 27 Apr 1820
George JANNEY and Susanna JANNEY of Georgetown D.C. to
Benjamin BRADFIELD of Ldn. B/S of 29½a on Great road adj
BRADFIELD, Daniel COCKERILL. Wit: Hen'y FOXALL, Daniel
BUSSARD.

Bk:Pg: 3A:249   Date: 14 May 1819   RtCt: 22 Apr 1820
John HAWLING to Henry CLAGGETT. Trust for debt to Mary
HAWLING & Elizabeth HAWLING using177a adj Isaac HAWLING.
Wit: William HAWLING, Thomas RENOE, Sarah RENOE.

Bk:Pg: 3A:253   Date: 13 May 1819   RtCt: 25 Apr 1820
John HAWLING to Presly CORDELL. Trust for debt to Henry
CLAGETT using 73a cnvy/b CLAGETT adj William MEAD, William
HAWLING, John HALLING. Wit: Wm. HAWLING, Thomas RENOE,

Elizabeth HAWLING, Thomas SANDERS, Saml. MILLER, Jno. SANDERS.

Bk:Pg: 3A:258 Date: 20 Dec 1817 RtCt: 5 May 1820
George BURSON & wife Susanna of Ldn to Daniel EACHES. Trust for debt to George JANNY using 5a on N side of Goose Creek and 8a on S side of Goose Creek and 49a on N side of Goose Creek adj Benjamin BROOKE, Robert FULTON. Wit: Francis W. LUCKETT, Wm. BRONAUGH. Delv. to Rich'd H. HENDERSON for EACHES 22 Dec 1822.

Bk:Pg: 3A:264 Date: 28 Mar 1820 RtCt: 27 Apr 1820
George JANNEY and Susanna JANNEY of Georgetown D.C. to Levi WILLIAMS of Ldn. B/S of 7a adj Joseph GORE, Benjamin BRADFIELD, David SMITH. Wit: Hen'y FOXALL, Daniel BUSSARD.

Bk:Pg: 3A:268 Date: 2 May 1820 RtCt: 12 Jun 1820
Dr. William L. POWELL. Qualified to his commission as Lt. in 56th Reg, 6th Brigade, 2nd Div. of Va Militia.

Bk:Pg: 3A:268 Date: 17 Jan 1820 RtCt: 12 Jun 1820
Nelson GREEN. Qualified to his commission as Capt. in 56th Reg, 6th Brigade, 2nd Div. of Va Militia.

Bk:Pg: 3A:269 Date: 25 Apr 1820 RtCt: 8 May 1820
Joseph GOODLY of Ldn to Susanna GOODLY (wd/o of his son Joseph). Gift of farm animals, household items, rights on promissory note of Amos HARVEY. Wit: Craven OSBURN, Thomas HOUGH, Delilah HOWELL.

Bk:Pg: 3A:271 Date: 8 May 1820 RtCt: 8 May 1820
Sampson BLINCOE of Ldn to Martha HOLMES of Ldn. B/S of ½a now in HOLMES' possession adj farm of BLINCOE adj __ ROZZEL (through agreement with John JONES & Martha). Delv. to F. W. LUCKETT pr order 25 Sep 1838.

Bk:Pg: 3A:272 Date: 5 Mar 1820 RtCt: 20 May 1820
Benjamin KENT of Ldn to children Thomas KENT, Benjamin KENT, Elizabeth KENT, Samuel KENT & John KENT. Gift of house on 15a nr Snignears [Snickers] Gap, farm animals, household items. Also signed by Sarah KENT.

Bk:Pg: 3A:273 Date: 21 Dec 1819 RtCt: 6 Jun 1820
Elizabeth T. CRIDLER and John M. FREY & wife Emily of Mdbg to Amos JOHNSON of Mdbg. B/S of 2/6th parts of Lot #20 & #59 and tan house lot in Mdbg formerly prop. of Frederick CRIDER dec'd. Wit: O. DUNHAM, Wm. H. CRIDER, Abner OSBURN. Delv. to JOHNSON 28 May 1823.

Bk:Pg: 3A:275 Date: 3 Jun 1820 RtCt: 3 Jun 1820
Benjamin SMITH of Ldn to Daniel P. CONRAD of Ldn. Trust for debt to Enos WILDMAN of Ldn using 2 chests of tools (list given – carpentry items). Delv to WILDMAN 30 Oct 1826.

Bk:Pg: 3A:277   Date: 1 Mar 1820   RtCt: 5 Jun 1820
Joseph B. MERSHON of Ldn to Joshua HUTCHISON, Thomas
MERSHON & Eli HUTCHISON (2 from Ffx & 1 from Ldn). Trust for
debt to Samuel O'BANNION using 100a prch/o O'BANNION. Wit:
Elijah HUTCHISON, Thomas BRISCOE, George WHALEY.

Bk:Pg: 3A:279   Date: 2 May 1820   RtCt: 20 May 1820
Presley WILLIAMS & wife Jane of Ldn to Benjamin SHRIEVE of
Ldn. Trust for debt to John SHAFFER of Ldn (as security on bonds
to trustees of Susanna BALL pr Sup. Ct. judgment) using interest in
land allotted as dower to Mary HIXON wd/o Reuben HIXON dec'd
and crop of wheat on farm belonging to Susanna CHILTON and
horses. Wit: Robert MOFFETT, Geo. WHITMORE, Jno. BEATY.
Delv. to SHREVE 21 Dec 1820.

Bk:Pg: 3A:281   Date: __ Mar 1820   RtCt: 16 May 1820
Mary Ann BINNS of Ldn to Aaron SANDERS of Ldn. B/S of 33½a
adj widow STARK, __ COOPER, __ GREGG. Wit: Charles BINNS,
Wm. A. BINNS, John A. BINNS. Delv. to Aaron SAUNDERS 16 May
1827.

Bk:Pg: 3A:283   Date: 7 Oct 1816   RtCt: 23 May 1820
Nathaniel POLEN of Harrison Co Oh and Catharine PEGG of Ldn to
Strother HELM of Ldn. B/S of part of 20a where PEGG lives adj
HELM's 'Lewis' land, Mrs. REDMON.

Bk:Pg: 3A:285   Date: 13 Sep 1819   RtCt: 31 May 1820
Joshua OSBURN & John WHITE (trustees of Solomon DAVIS of
MontMd) to David SMITH & Eli PEIRPOINT (Exors. of Thomas
LOVE dec'd). Release of trust on 100+a. Wit: Geo. SWEARINGEN,
Josiah L. DREAN, A. O. POWELL, David LOVETT, H. ELLIOTT,
Craven OSBURN, Jos. H. WRIGHT.

Bk:Pg: 3A:288   Date: 5 Jan 1820   RtCt: 8 May 1820
William NOLAND & wife Catharine of Ldn to Adam ZIMMERMAN of
Ffx. B/S of ½a Lot #71 in Aldie. Wit: Abraham FULTON, Richard F.
PEYTON, Thomas H. BUCKNER, Leven LUCKETT, Burr POWELL.
Delv. to ZIMMERMAN 1 Apr 1824.

Bk:Pg: 3A:290   Date: 8 May 1820   RtCt: 15 Jun 1820
Peter BOSS dec'd. Dower for widow Mary BOSS – lot on SE corner
of King & Loudoun Sts. in Lsbg now occupied by Samuel M. BOSS
(in case of Peter BOSS &c agst John ROSE Admr of Peter BOSS
dec'd).

Bk:Pg: 3A:292   Date: 12 Jun 1820   RtCt: 12 Jun 1820
Hanson ELLIOTT, William TAYLOR, George H. SINCLAIR &
George CARTER. Bond on ELLIOTT as constable.

Bk:Pg: 3A:293   Date: 29 Dec 1819   RtCt: 14 Jun 1820
Dennis McCARTY & wife Margaret of Ldn to George W. McCARTY
of Ldn. B/S of __ on Goose Creek. Wit: George TURNER, John
SMARR, Susan F. SMARR.

Bk:Pg: 3A:294   Date: 18 May 1812   RtCt: 8 Jun 1812/12 Jun 1820

Charles CRIM & wife Catharine of Ldn to Jacob CRIM of Ldn. B/S of 20a (prch/o Ferdinando FAIRFAX) now in possession of Jacob CRIM adj John STATTLER. Wit: R. BRADEN, Abiel JENNERS, Charles CRIM Jr. Delv. to grantee Feb 1822.

Bk:Pg: 3A:297   Date: 25 Jul 1818   RtCt: 9 Nov 1818/10 May 1820

Fanny LEE (Exor of Thomas LEE dec'd) of Ldn to William BRENT Jr. of StafVa and Tench RINGOLD of Washington D.C. BoS for slaves Judy, Will, Hector, Vincent, Menokin, Carpenter, George, Harey, old Billy, old Jem, old Toney, young Toney, Gilbert, Molly, Betty, Armstead, Peggy, Judy and Eve belonging to estate of Thomas LEE dec'd. Wit: Robt. M. NEWMAN, Elizabeth L. CARTER.

Bk:Pg: 3A:299   Date: 29 Jan 1820   RtCt: 20 May 1820

Richard FLING of Ldn to William MEADE of Ldn. Trust for debt using farm animals and household items. Wit: L. P. W. BALCH, W. D. DRISH. Delv to Robert MOFFETT 6 Nov 1820.

Bk:Pg: 3A:301   Date: 25 May 1820   RtCt: 25 May 1820

Samuel DONOHOE & wife Margaret of Ldn to John WILDMAN of Ldn. B/S of 7a on drains of Secolen branch adj DONOHOE & WILDMAN. Delv. to WILDMAN 5 Mar 1821.

Bk:Pg: 3A:303   Date: 25 May 1820   RtCt: 25 May 1820

John WILDMAN & wife Eleanor of Ldn to Samuel DONOHOE of Ldn. B/S of 14a adj WILDMAN, DONOHOE. Delv. to DONOHOE 1 Nov 1821.

Bk:Pg: 3A:305   Date: 11 Mar 1820   RtCt: 11 May 1820

John B. STEVENS & wife Sarah of Ldn to John BRADEN of Ldn. B/S of ¼a in Wtfd on Second St. adj Robert BRADEN, P. McGAVOCK. Wit: Robert BRADEN, Saml. HOUGH Jr. Delv. to J. BRADEN 25 Jun 1837.

Bk:Pg: 3A:307   Date: 15 May 1820   RtCt: 12 Jun 1820

Stephen DANIEL of Fqr to Thomson ASHBY of Fqr. Trust for debt to Thomas BALL (as appearance bail in Sup. Ct of Fqr in Robert HUNTON's Admr. agt. DANIEL and Thadeus MORRIS agst DANIEL) using brick house in Alexandria cnvy/b Aaron BURSON and 15a 'Trap property' with saw mill, grist mill, distillery & house (purchased of Thomson FURR) and slaves James, Miles, John, George, Maria & Winney and farm animals. Wit: Daniel WITHERS, F. W. BROOKE, Thomas C. KELLY.

Bk:Pg: 3A:311   Date: 13 Oct 1819   RtCt: 20 Oct 1819

B. W. SOWER of Ldn to S. B. T. CALDWELL of Ldn. BoS of household items (list given) in house in Lsbg.

Bk:Pg: 3A:313   Date: 9 Jan 1819   RtCt: 2 Jun 1820
William WRIGHT & Daniel STONE (Exors of Anthony WRIGHT
dec'd) to William PAXSON of Ldn. B/S of 5a where Anthony lives on
road from Wtfd to Hllb adj Patterson WRIGHT and 2¾a adj Thomas
PHILIPS. Wit: David CONRAD, Joseph CALDWELL, Amasa
HOUGH. Delv. to Wm. PAXON 30 Aug 1821.

Bk:Pg: 3A:316   Date: 15 Jun 1816   RtCt: 13 Jan 1820
James WHITE & wife Mary, Mahlon JANNEY & wife Rachel, Josiah
WHITE, Robert WHITE & Beniah WHITE of Ldn to Thomas WHITE
of Ldn. B/S of 1/7th of 159a including dower right of Rachel WHITE
(conveyed to John McILHANEY as Admr of James WHITE dec'd for
benefit of heirs by Ferdinando FAIRFAX dated Apr 1798) adj John
MORRIS, Thomas DAVIS, Francis McKEMIE, Samuel
UNDERWOOD, Archibald MORRISON. Wit: Isaac LAROWE,
Rachel WHITE, Joseph McCARTY, Aaron SANDERS, Wm. DARNE,
Geo. SWEARINGEN, A. O. POWELL, Lee W. DURHAM.

Bk:Pg: 3A:320   Date: 30 Nov 1819   RtCt: 27 May 1820
Absalom DENNIS & wife Mary of Ldn to Harman BITZER & John
SINCLAIR of Ldn. Trust for debt to John BURSON using 44¾a
where BURSON now lives cnvy/b BURSON to DENNIS. Wit: Burr
POWELL, Abner GIBSON. Delv. to John BURSON 28 Dec 1832.

Bk:Pg: 3A:323   Date: 7 Oct 1819   RtCt: 22 May 1820
John E. PARMER & wife Merab of Ldn to George W. HENRY of
Ldn. B/S of 4a adj Wtfd, Joseph TALBOTT dec'd. Wit: John H.
McCABE, Samuel HOUGH Jr.

Bk:Pg: 3A:326   Date: 16 May 1820   RtCt: 20 May 1820
William CHILTON & Sarah H. CHILTON of Ldn to Jesse RICE of
Ldn. B/S of 49a adj RICE. Wit: Saml. M. EDWARDS, John
McCORMICK. Delv. to RICE 28 Dec 1825.

Bk:Pg: 3A:328   Date: 7 Feb 1820   RtCt: 15 May 1820
William WENNER & wife Magdalena of Ldn to Jacob KERN of Ldn.
B/S of 1a reserved for Valentine BANTZ out of 111¼a. Wit:
Johnathan WENNER, Adam SANBOWER, Geo. RICKARD, Latimer
ALLDER, Robert BRADEN, Abiel JENNERS. Delv. to KARN
[KERN] 14 Sep 1825.

Bk:Pg: 3A:332   Date: 24 May 1820   RtCt: 16 [?] May 1820
Samuel M. EDWARDS & wife Ann of Ldn to James GARNER of
Ldn. B/S of 2a in Lsbg on N side of Loudoun St adj John MATHIAS.
Wit: Presly CORDELL, Thomas SANDERS.

Bk:Pg: 3A:335   Date: 13 Nov 1819   RtCt: 27 May 1820
John H. BUTCHER & wife Nancy of Ldn to Jehu BURSON of Ldn.
B/S of 108a where Nancy OVERFIELD resided at time of her death.
Wit: Notly C. WILLIAMS, John W. GRAYSON. Delv. to BURSON 30
May 1821.

Bk:Pg: 3A:338   Date: 16 Apr 1819   RtCt: 27 May 1820
William NOLAND & wife Catharine of Ldn to Walter LANGLEY of
Ldn. B/S of 2½a in Aldie adj LANGLEY. Wit: Lewis M. SMITH,
James TURLEY Jr., Amos GULICK, Burr POWELL, Ariss
BUCKNER. Delv. to LANGLEY 13 Nov 1821.

Bk:Pg: 3A:340   Date: 13 Nov 1819   RtCt: 27 May 1820
Edward WILSON & wife Mary Ann of Ldn to John SINCLAIR and
Harmon BITZER of Ldn. Trust for debt to Jehu BURSON using
20¾a on Wancopen branch of Goose Creek by road leading from
Mdbg to Wilson's fulling mill. Wit: Burr POWELL, A. GIBSON.

Bk:Pg: 3A:344   Date: 18 Apr 1820   RtCt: 23 May 1820
William NOLAND & wife Catharine of Ldn to Benjamin HAGERMAN
of Ldn. B/S of Lots #6 & #7 on N side of Mercer St in Aldie. Wit: Burr
POWELL, Ariss BUCKNER.

Bk:Pg: 3A:346   Date: 18 Apr 1820   RtCt: 27 May 1820
William NOLAND & wife Catharine of Ldn to Walter LANGLEY of
Ldn. B/S of Lots #82 & #83 on Mercer St in Aldie. Wit: Burr
POWELL, Ariss BUCKNER. Delv. to LANGLEY 13 Nov 1821.

Bk:Pg: 3A:349   Date: 12 Oct 1819   RtCt: 15 May 1820
Joseph WILDMAN & wife Hannah, David NIXON & wife Rachel of
Ldn to James H. HAMILTON of Ldn. B/S of 46a (from estate of
George NIXON dec'd f/o Hannah). John McCORMICK, Jno. ROSE,
Thos. McCOWATT, Presly CORDELL.

Bk:Pg: 3A:352   Date: 25 Jan 1820   RtCt: 8 May 1820
Mahlon SCHOOLEY of Ldn to John WILLIAMS of Ldn. Trust for debt
to Isaac E. STEER using 41¾a cnvy/b STEER.

Bk:Pg: 3A:356   Date: 11 Mar 1820   RtCt: 8 May 1820
John C. HANDY of Ldn to Charles G. EDWARDS of Ldn. Trust for
debt to Robert BRADEN using lot in Wtfd prch/o Joseph P.
THOMAS.

Bk:Pg: 3A:359   Date: 18 Jun 1819   RtCt: 2 Jun 1820
Jane McCABE, John H. McCABE & wife Mary, Catharine
DOWLING, John NEWTON & wife Harriet (heirs of Henry McCABE
dec'd) of Ldn to Thomas BERKBEY of Ldn. B/S of ½a Lot #4 on S
side of Cornwall St. in Lsbg. Wit: Thomas SANDERS, Saml. M.
EDWARDS. Delv. to Wm. CHILTON pr order 27 Mar 1824.

Bk:Pg: 3A:363   Date: 10 Dec 1813   RtCt: 18 May 1820
Robert PAGE & Charles MAGILL of FredVa and Fleet SMITH of Ldn
(Commrs in case of William Fleming GAINS Exor of Robert PAGE
dec'd of Hanover Co agst Ferdinando FAIRFAX & William Byrd
PAGE) to Carter B. PAGE of RichVa. B/S of 2500a. Wit: H. G.
TUCKER, Alfred H. POWELL, Danl. LEE. Delv to Fleet SMITH pr
order of Jno. B. PAGE filed 26 May 1821.

Bk:Pg: 3A:366   Date: 8 May 1820   RtCt: 10 May 1820
Isaac WRIGHT & wife Susan D. of Ldn to Aaron DAILEY of Ldn. B/S
of 20a below Lsbg on turnpike road (inherited from father William
WRIGHT dec'd) adj Dr. SELDON, Jesse DAILEY. Wit: Presly
CORDELL, Saml. M. EDWARDS.

Bk:Pg: 3A:369   Date: 9 May 1820   RtCt: 10 May 1820
Isaac WRIGHT & wife Susan D. of Ldn to Stacy HAINS of Ldn. B/S
of 14a below Lsbg (inherited from father Wm. WRIGHT dec'd) adj
George FEICHTER. Wit: Presly CORDELL, Saml. M. EDWARDS.

Bk:Pg: 3A:372   Date: 13 May 1820   RtCt: 16 May 1820
Peter BENEDUM & wife Catharine of Ldn to Charles B. BALL of
Ldn. B/S of 4a adj Lsbg, Reuben SCHOOLEY, __ TOWNER, __
BOSS, __ FADLEY, __ HARRIS, __ McNELLEDGE, James RUST.
Wit: Saml. M. EDWARDS, Thomas SANDERS. Bernard HOUGH &
wife Louisa conveyed their rights to the land.

Bk:Pg: 3A:377   Date: 6 May 1820   RtCt: 11 May 1820
William GILHAM of AlexDC to James MILLS of Lsbg. B/S of ¼a on
S side of King St in new addition to Lsbg adj Thos. JACOBS, William
WRIGHT, James DAWSON, John DRISH (cnvy/b John EVANS).

Bk:Pg: 3A:380   Date: 10 Sep 1819   RtCt: 10 Jun 1820
George MARKS & wife Mahala of Ldn to John MARKS of Ldn. B/S
of 29a (from will of Elisha MARKS dec'd) adj road leading to Paris
adj Isaiah MARKS. Wit: Notly C. WILLIAMS, John W. GRAYSON.

Bk:Pg: 3A:383   Date: 21 Jan 1820   RtCt: 8 May 1820
Burr POWELL & wife Catharine to Jesse McVEIGH. B/S of ½ of ¼a
Lot #29 in Mdbg adj John HARRIS. (Leven POWELL in 1793
conveyed to Jesse McVEIGH ½a Lot #29 in Mdbg reserving the
ground rent which McVEIGH conveyed to John HARRIS reserving
ground rent of entire lot). Wit: Francis W. LUCKETT, A. GIBSON.
Delv. to McVEIGH 11 Sep 1820.

Bk:Pg: 3A:387   Date: 13 Jan 1820   RtCt: 8 May 1820
Charles J. KILGOUR & wife Louisa of MontMd to David LOVETT of
Ldn. B/S of 92a (Louisa's part of estate of Elizabeth McILHANEY
dec'd) land called 'Gidney Clerks land'. Wit: John WHITE, Craven
OSBURN. Delv. to David LOVETT 10 Jun 1824.

Bk:Pg: 3A:390   Date: 4 Aug 1819   RtCt: 8 May 1820
William NOLAND & wife Catharine of Ldn to James SIMPSON of
Ldn. B/S of ½a Lot #46 & #47 on Mercer St in Aldie at intersection
with old Snickers Gap road. Wit: Henry McKENZIE, Thos. H.
KERBY, James L. NORRIS. Wit: Burr POWELL, Ariss BUCKNER.

Bk:Pg: 3A:393   Date: 27 Nov 1819   RtCt: 9 Jun 1820
Nathaniel MANNING & wife Euphamia of Ldn to John WRIGHT of
Ldn. B/S of 44a adj William VERTS, Robert BRADEN, Kittoctan
Creek, Samuel EVANS and 75a adj WRIGHT's prch/o George

JANNEY. Wit: Abiel JENNERS, John H. McCABE. Delv. to WRIGHT 17 Mar 1821.

Bk:Pg: 3A:396   Date: 10 Jul 1820   RtCt: 10 Jul 1820
Sheriff Jno. HAMILTON, Benjamin SHREVE, Robert MOFFETT & Edward DULIN. Bond on HAMILTON to collect levies.

Bk:Pg: 3A:397   Date: 10 Jul 1820   RtCt: 10 Jul 1820
Edward DULIN and Benjamin SHRIEVE to Thomas FOUCH, S. C. ROZEL, Rt. BRADEN & Saml. M. EDWARDS. Bond on DULIN as committee in charge of estate of Harriet CRAVEN a lunatick.

Bk:Pg: 3A:397   Date: ___   RtCt: 11 Jul 1820
Robert HAMILTON the elder dec'd. Division – Jane McCABE &c agst James HAMILTON in case of 8 May 1820. Lot #34 in Lsbg to defendant as his full ¼ part of estate. Jane McCABE (Lot #46 in Lsbg), John MATHIAS & children representing their mother Ann MATHIAS formerly HAMILTON (part of Lot #3 in Lsbg), Alexander COOPER & children representing mother Elizabeth (residue of Lot #1 in Lsbg). Divisors: Presly CORDELL, Jacob FADELY, Thomas SANDERS, Saml. M. EDWARDS.

Bk:Pg: 3A:400   Date: 8 Feb 1820   RtCt: 10 Jul 1820
Samuel G. GRIFFITH merchant & wife Mary of BaltMd to City Bank of Baltimore. Trust to City Bank of Baltimore using 1484a in Ldn cnvy/b John W. BRONAUGH and adj 705a in Ffx. Wit: John AISQUITH, Jos. BENSON.

Bk:Pg: 3A:410   Date: 12 Oct 1819   RtCt: 11 Jul 1820
James COLEMAN dec'd. Division of 542a and 151a and slaves in case of Robert NEWMAN & wife Frances late COLEMAN & Charles LEWIS and James LEWIS her trustees, Nancy COLEMAN & Sally COLEMAN an infant by Nancy COLEMAN her next friend, James COLEMAN an infant by C. LEWIS his next friend and Johnson COLEMAN by Johnson CLEVELAND his Guardian & next friend agst John J. COLEMAN of 12 Oct 1819. To complainant Francis (103a Lot #1, slave Bill), complainant Nancy (142a Lot #3, slave James & Rachel), defendant John J. (212a Lot #4, slave Charles), complainant James (60a Lot #6, slaves Charlotte, George & Sampson), complainant Sally (40a Lot #2, slaves Milly & her child Len & Sybol/Silvey), complainant Johnson (40a Lot #5, slave Caroline & her child and Toby). Gives plat and details. Divisors: R'd. H. COCKERILL, Thos. DARNE, Charles COLEMAN.

Bk:Pg: 3A:416   Date: 6 Jun 1820   RtCt: 13 Jun 1820
Isaac HARRIS of Ldn to Richard H. HENDERSON of Ldn. Release on debt to Samuel MURREY of house & lot in Lsbg.

Bk:Pg: 3A:417   Date: 15 Jul 1820   RtCt: 5 Jul 1820
Richard H. HENDERSON & wife Orra Moore of Ldn to Thomas SWANN of AlexDC. B/S of 64a (cnvy/b Joseph VANDEVANTER)

adj Archibald MAINS, __ CALDWELL, Jane MAINS. Wit: Presly CORDELL, Samuel M. EDWARDS.

Bk:Pg: 3A:419   Date: 5 Dec 1818   RtCt: 10 Jul 1820
Mahlon GARNER & wife Nancy, David NIXON & wife Rachel, Joseph HAWKINS & wife Sarah, Joseph WILDMAN & wife Hannah, John NIXON Guardian of George NIXON, Giles CRAVEN Guardian of James NIXON and Thomas BROWN Guardian of John NIXON all of Ldn and William NIXON, William KNOX & wife Mary, Daniel MINOR & wife Plesant and Johnathan NIXON of [Jefferson Co] OH to Presley SANDERS Sr of Ldn. B/S of 16a on Beaverdam (prch/o __ COOMBS by George NIXON the elder dec'd being part of estate of George NIXON undevised and allotted to heirs and children of George NIXON 2nd also dec'd). Wit: Patrick McINTYRE, Samuel M. EDWARDS. Delv. to Presley SAUNDERS Sr. 16 Jan 1822.

Bk:Pg: 3A:425   Date: 16 Feb 1820   RtCt: 13 Jun 1820
Jesse TRAYHORN & wife Harriet of Ldn to William H. DORSEY of Ldn. Trust for debt to Thornton WALKER using ½a cnvy/b WALKER. Wit: William BRONAUGH, Thos. GREGG. Delv. to WALKER 25 Aug 1820.

Bk:Pg: 3A:427   Date: 18 Mar 1820   RtCt: 13 Jun 1820
George TAVENER of Ldn to Aaron BURSON of Ldn. Trust for debt to Aaron BURSON using farm and household items. Wit: John THORNBERRY, Geo. BURSON, Stephen BURSON.

Bk:Pg: 3A:429   Date: 17 Feb 1820   RtCt: 13 Jun 1820
Jesse TRAYHORN & wife Harriet of Union to John H. EVANS of Union. B/S of lot a little N of Union adj Samuel DUNKIN, Isaac BROWN, William H. DORSEY. Wit: William BRONAUGH, Thomas GREGG.

Bk:Pg: 3A:431   Date: 22 Apr 1820   RtCt: 15 Jun 1820
Alfred CLEMENS & wife Matilda of Ldn to David CARTER of Ldn. B/S of 1¾a on road from Scholfield's mill to Lsbg adj James DEWAR. Wit: Notly C. WILLIAMS, Benjamin GRAYSON. Delv. to CARTER 30 May 1822.

Bk:Pg: 3A:433   Date: 6 Nov 1819   RtCt: 24 Jun 1820
David BEATTY of Ldn to Zachariah DULANEY of Ldn. Trust for debt to Robert BRADEN using farm animals and household items. Wit: James G. BROADUS, Noble S. BRADEN, Burr BRADEN.

Bk:Pg: 3A:435   Date: 19 May 1820   RtCt: 13 Jun 1820
Hiram SEATON & wife Nancy of Ldn to Elijah VIOLETT of Ldn. B/S of land which VIOLETT held under lease for life. Wit: Joseph CARR, Cuthbert POWELL.

Bk:Pg: 3A:437   Date: 25 Mar 1820   RtCt: 13 Jun 1820
Garrett WALKER of Ldn to William J. BRONAUGH of Ldn. Trust for debt to Samuel & Joseph HATCHER using 3a. Delv. to Thos.

ROGERS Admr of Saml. HATCHER dec'd sur'g partner of Saml. & Jos. HATCHER 1 Aug 1829.

Bk:Pg: 3A:438   Date: 25 May 1820   RtCt: 14 Jun 1820
Jesse CARTER & wife Hannah of Ldn to Samuel PEUGH of Ldn. B/S of 16a (cnvy/b George TAVENER Jr.) adj J. WHITACRE, James BROWN. Wit: Wm. BRONAUGH, Ben. GRAYSON. Delv. to PEUGH 13 Jul 1832.

Bk:Pg: 3A:440   Date: 1 Apr 1820   RtCt: 14 Jun 1820
John FLETCHER & wife Tacy P. of Culpeper Co Va to Thomas W. SMITH of Ldn. B/S of 1/8th part of 2/3 of estate of John GIBSON dec'd with saw mill, merchant mill including claims to dower rights.

Bk:Pg: 3A:442   Date: 15 Oct 1819   RtCt: 13 Jun 1820
Joseph CARR Esqr of Upperville in Ldn to Joshua HARDY tailor of Upperville in Ldn. B/S of 1a adj Upperville partly occupied by HARDY adj John JAMES' shop lot, Ashbys Gap Turnpike road, Jacob IDEN. Wit: Caldwell CARR, James TURNER, Manly IDEN, Aaron GIBSON, Josiah MINEL.

Bk:Pg: 3A:443   Date: 17 Mar 1820   RtCt: 12 Jun 1820
David JANNEY & wife Elizabeth of Ldn to Joseph H. WRIGHT of Ldn. B/S of ¼a Lot #2 on E side of High St in new addition to Wtfd. Wit: Abiel JENNERS, Samuel HOUGH Jr. Delv. to WRIGHT 29 Mar 1821.

Bk:Pg: 3A:445   Date: 18 Jan 1819   RtCt: 13 Jun 1820
Sanford RAMEY & wife Lydia of Ldn to Elijah VIOLETT of Ldn. B/S of remaining interest in 2/9th of land which Elijah VIOLETT holds under lease for life which belonged to brother John VIOLETT dec'd. Wit: Abiel JENNERS, Jno. H. McCABE.

Bk:Pg: 3A:447   Date: 27 Nov 1819   RtCt: 15 Jun 1820
David ALEXANDER & wife Elizabeth of Ldn to Alfred CLEMMENS of Ldn. B/S of 1¾a on branch of Goose Creek (part of tract prch/o Daniel BROWN) on road from Scholfield's mill to Lsbg adj Jas. DEWAR. Wit: William NOLAND, Chs. LEWIS.

Bk:Pg: 3A:449   Date: 13 May 1820   RtCt: 12 Jun 1820
David LOVETT of Ldn to Thomas STEVENS of Ldn. B/S of ¼a Lots #9, #10, #11 & #12 in German settlement. Wit: William WENNER Jr, Jacob SMITH, Geo. McCABE. Delv. to David STEPHEN pr order 22 Feb 1826.

Bk:Pg: 3A:451   Date: 25 Sep 1819   RtCt: 12 Jun 1820
Abiel JENNERS & wife Deborah of Ldn to John WRIGHT of Ldn. B/S of 382a (cnvy/b John BAKER of Pa) adj Catocton Creek (with encumbrance of trust to secure debt due William COCKING of D.C.) Wit: Samuel HOUGH Jr., John H. McCABE. Delv. to ___ 19 Jul 1822 and delv. to John WRIGHT 17 Mar 1821.

Bk:Pg: 3A:453   Date: 18 Apr 1820   RtCt: 12 Jun 1820
William NOLAND & wife Catharine of Ldn to Thomas H. KERBY of Ldn. B/S of ½a Lots #39, #40, #41 & #42 on N side of Mercer St in Aldie adj Samuel TODD. Wit: Burr POWELL, Ariss BUCKNER.

Bk:Pg: 3A:455   Date: 20 Oct 1817   RtCt: 15 Jun 1820
Edward KELLY of Ldn to Sampson BLINCOE & Jesse TIMMS of Ldn. Trust for debt to George CARTER of Oatlands using 222a (cnvy/b Joseph MOXLEY in 1817).

Bk:Pg: 3A:458   Date: 18 Jan 1820   RtCt: 13 Jun 1820
David JAMES of Ldn to David LOVETT & Turner OSBURN of Ldn. Trust for debt to Balaam OSBURN using 50a adj James BRADFIELD, Timothy TAYLOR, Rufus UPDIKE. Delv. to David LOVETT 5 Jul 1822.

Bk:Pg: 3A:459   Date: 9 Feb 1820   RtCt: 3 Jul 1820
Francis STRIBLING & wife Cecelia of Ldn to Stephen WILSON of Ldn. B/S of 140a (cnvy/b WILSON in Apr 1818) on NW fork of Goose Creek adj Benj. DANIEL, Aaron HOLLOWAY, Richard COPELAND, Abdon DILLON. Wit: Thomas GREGG, Craven OSBURN.

Bk:Pg: 3A:461   Date: 16 May 1820   RtCt: 14 Jun 1820
Benjamin JENKINS & wife Mary of Ldn to Abner HUMPHREY of Ldn. Trust for debt to William JENKINS using 140a where JENKINS resides adj John HANN. Wit: Benjamin GRAYSON, Jno. W. GRAYSON. Delv. to HUMPHREY 11 Jun 1821.

Bk:Pg: 3A:465   Date: 20 May 1820   RtCt: 14 Jun 1820
Solomon VICKORY of Ldn to John S. MARLOW & Robert BRADEN of Ldn. Trust for debt to Frederick SLATS using 2a. Wit: George McCABE, Thomas H. STEPHENS, John FISHEL, Trumon GORE. Delv. to Robert BRADEN 9 Mar 1821.

Bk:Pg: 3A:467   Date: 15 Jun 1820   RtCt: 16 Jun 1820
George RUST Jr. of Ldn to Henry CLAGGETT of Ldn. Trust for debt to William T. T. MASON & Thomson MASON (Exors. of Armstead T. MASON) using 503a on Potomac and road from Lsbg to Nolands Ferry. Delv. to RUST pr order of Wm. T. T. MASON 28 Apr 1824.

Bk:Pg: 3A:470   Date: 8 Nov 1819   RtCt: 10 Jul 1820
Abner WILLIAMS (Admr of Alexander WHITELY dec'd) to William NIXON and Isaac & William STEER (Exors of Benjamin STEER dec'd). Trust for Benjamin STEER dec'd & William PAXSON of Ldn as his security as Admr using farm and household items. Wit: Daniel STONE.

Bk:Pg: 3B:001   Date: 9 Aug 1820   RtCt: 9 Sep 1820
Abraham J. BOSS & wife Ann D. of Lsbg to Samuel M. BOSS of Lsbg. B/S of undivided share of lot & 2-story brick house at NE corner of Loudoun & King St. in Lsbg adj R't HOUGH, Charles BALL, Joshua RILEY, Saml. M. EDWARDS leaving Mary BOSS

wd/o Peter BOSS dec'd and heirs Peter BOSS, Saml. M. BOSS, Daniel C. BOSS, David BOSS & Abraham J. BOSS and Mary HAWKE (now MARTIN) and Wm. HAWKE children & heirs of Margaret HAWKE dec'd d/o Peter BOSS dec'd and Saml BOSS son & heir of Jacob BOSS dec'd s/o Peter BOSS dec'd). Wit: Presley CORDELL, Thomas SANDERS. Delv. to Samuel M. BOSS 24 Aug 1820.

Bk:Pg: 3B:002   Date: 1 Mar 1820   RtCt: 20 Jul 1820
Nathaniel MANNING of Wtfd to Jno. WILLIAMS & Richard WOOD. Request to release of trust for debt to John B. STEPHENS.

Bk:Pg: 3B:003   Date: 1 Mar 1820   RtCt: 20 Jul 1820
J. B. STEVENS to Jesse GOVER & William S. NEALE. Request to release trust for debt to Joseph P. THOMAS.

Bk:Pg: 3B:003   Date: 1 Mar 1820   RtCt: 20 Jul 1820
John PANCOAST to Daniel STONE & John WILLIAMS. Request to release trust for debt from Nathaniel MANNING to Joseph TALBOTT.

Bk:Pg: 3B:003   Date: 8 Nov 1819   RtCt: 10 Jul 1820
Abner WILLIAMS to William PAXSON & Joseph WOOD. Mortgage to secure them as endorsers to Waterford Loudoun Co. using his share of wheat. Wit: Daniel STONE. Delv. to Jacob PAXSON 12 May 1829.

Bk:Pg: 3B:004   Date: 17 Jul 1820   RtCt: 17 Jul 1820
William H. LANE now of Ldn to William D. DRISH of Lsbg. Bond concerning Lot #17 in Lsbg since wife is not in Va to relinquish her rights. Wit: S. BLINCOE, Fielding BROWN, Daniel MATHIAS. Delv. to DRISH 26 Dec 1820.

Bk:Pg: 3B:005   Date: 2 Aug 1820   RtCt: 2 Aug 1820
Samuel SINCLAIR of Ldn to Sheriff John HAMILTON of Ldn. Trust of 53a & grist mill (to be released from jail in cases of Tholemiah RHODES agst SINCLAIR, John MARKS & Wm. H. DORSEY and James CARTER agst SINCLAIR & MARKS). Wit: R. H. HENDERSON, Thomas SANDERS, John McCORMICK, Thomas A. MOORE, A. O. POWELL, Lee W. DENHAM.

Bk:Pg: 3B:006   Date: 1 Jul 1820   RtCt: 28 Jul 1820
Jacob SHOEMAKER of Ldn to mother Mary SHOEMAKER of Ldn. Gift of farm animals and household items. Wit: John W. GRAYSON.

Bk:Pg: 3B:007   Date: 17 Jul 1820   RtCt: 19 Jul 1820
William JOHNSON & wife Margaret of Lsbg to Margaret HAWKE, John HAWKE, Mary Jane HAWKE & Elizabeth HAWKE (infant ch/o Margaret HAWKE dec'd late w/o William HAWKE of Lsbg). B/S of ½a in Lsbg on S side of Lsbg adj Mrs. ASQUITH. Wit: John McCORMICK, Thos. SANDERS.

Bk:Pg: 3B:008   Date: 25 Mar 1820   RtCt: 30 Mar 1820
Andrew BEATTY of Ldn to daughters. Gift to older dau. Elizabeth
BEATTY (negro girl Nancy & horse), to dau. Peggy (negro girl
Susanna). Wit: Wm. H. HANDY, Asa C. WILKINSON, Eli H. HANDY,
John SMARR.

Bk:Pg: 3B:009   Date: 17 Jul 1820   RtCt: 17 Jul 1820
William H. LANE & wife Sarah to William D. DRISH of Lsbg. B/S of
Lot #17 on Market St. in Lsbg. Wit: S. BLINCOE, Fielding BROWN,
Danl. MATHIAS. Delv. to DRISH 26 Dec 1820.

Bk:Pg: 3B:010   Date: 20 Jul 1820   RtCt: 20 Jul 1820
Richard H. HENDERSON of Ldn to Thomas SWAYNE of Ffx.
Release of trust for debt of George JANNEY & wife Susannah.

Bk:Pg: 3B:011   Date: 24 Apr 1820   RtCt: 19 Jul 1820
Joseph EIDSON & wife Mahala of Ldn to William BRONAUGH &
William DENNIS. Trust for debt to Miller HOGE of Ldn using 26¼a
prch/o HOGE. Delv. to BRONAUGH 11 Nov 1822.

Bk:Pg: 3B:012   Date: 29 Aug 1819   RtCt: 19 Jul 1820
Simon A. BINNS & wife Sally of Ldn to George FEICHTER of Ldn.
B/S of ¾a on E side of road from Lsbg to Alexandria where James
THOMAS formerly lived now FEICHTER lives (cnvy/b Enoch
FURR).

Bk:Pg: 3B:013   Date: 1 Mar 1820   RtCt: 20 Jul 1820
Joseph P. THOMAS & wife Sarah of Ldn to John C. HANDY of Ldn.
B/S of tavern & storehouse lot in Wtfd and stable lot in Wtfd (cnvy/b
John B. STEPHENS). Wit: Abiel JENNERS, Robert BRADEN. Delv.
pr order 17 Feb 1823.

Bk:Pg: 3B:015   Date: 30 May 1820   RtCt: 10 Jul 1820
Leven POWELL Jr. dec'd. Division – suit of Susannah Elizabeth
POWELL & Wm. Alexander POWELL (wd/o & s/o Leven POWELL
dec'd) agst Cuthbert POWELL, Jas. L. POWELL & Alfred H.
POWELL infant ch/o Leven POWELL Jr. dec'd by Wm. CHILTON
Guardian. Lot 1 (732a) on S fork of Beaverdam adj William
BRONAUGH, Uriel GLASSCOCK, Daniel BROWN divided into 5 lots
{#1 (200a), #2 (133a), #3 (133a), #4 (133a), #5 (133a)}; Lot 2 (546a)
on Broad Run nr Gumspring divided into 2 lots {#1 (273a), #2
(273a)}; Lot 3 (158a) in Fqr adj town of Hopewell divided into 2 lots
{#179a), #2 (79a)}; Lot 4 (360a) in Fqr adj above lot divided into 2
lots {#1 (180a) #2 (180a)}. Nicely detailed series of plats.
Allotments - widow Mrs. Susanna Elizabeth POWELL (200a, 5¾a &
house in Mdbg, 175a where Philip PALMER now lives, negro
woman Anne); Wm. Alexander POWELL (133a, 79a Hopewell tract,
180a, lot in Dumfries, negro Henry); Cuthbert POWELL (133a, 79a
Hopewell tract, 180a, negro boy Tom); John Leven POWELL (133a,
273a, negro boy Elias, girl Martha Ann); Alfred H. POWELL (133a,
273a, negro boy William and Mary Ann). Divisors: George LOVE,

James HIXSON, James PICKETT, Lloyd NOLAND. Delv to Wm. A. POWELL pr order filed ___.

Bk:Pg: 3B:027   Date: 11 Jul 1820   RtCt: 11 Jul 1820
Francis M. BECKWITH deputy for John S. PEYTON marshall of Sup Ct. at Winchester to Sampson BLINCOE of Ldn. B/S of 446a on Goose Creek adj Saml. ADAMS, Stephen C. ROSZEL. (Chancery of 13 Apr 1820 of Bett, Ben, Mary, Eliza & Jack agst John WINNBUSH Admr of Wm. WINNBUSH dec'd Charles LEWIS Admr of Amos THOMPSON dec'd the trustees of Yale college). Wit: Geo. SWEARINGEN. Delv. to BLINCOE 19 Jan 1822.

Bk:Pg: 3B:029   Date: 13 Jul 1820   RtCt: 15 Jul 1820
James REED of Ldn to Abiel JENNERS of Ldn. Trust for debt to Robert BRADEN using cow and household items.

Bk:Pg: 3B:030   Date: 1 Jun 1820   RtCt: 29 Jul 1820
Charles McKNIGHT to Bernard S. DUFFEY. Trust for debt to William TAYLOR using reversionary interest in 112a from will of William BROWN dec'd now in occupancy of widow Hannah BROWN. Wit: J. T. GRIFFITH, Isaac TAVENNER, Joseph HOUGH. Delv. to TAYLOR 24 Nov 1820

Bk:Pg: 3B:031   Date: 24 Jul 1820   RtCt: 24 Jul 1820
David J. COE of Ldn to Edward M. COE of Ldn. B/S of 70a on Goose Creek on N side of Goose Creek (residue of tract devised by will of father Edward COE dec'd) adj brother John M. COE and 28a wood lot on road from Hoge's mill to Mdbg and interest on tract brother Menan COE prch/o Edward M. COE.

Bk:Pg: 3B:032   Date: 11 Jul 1820   RtCt: 12 Jul 1820
Sampson BLINCOE & wife Martha S. of Ldn to Francis M. BECKWITH deputy for John S. PEYTON marshall of Sup Ct in Winchester. Trust for debt to creditors and legatees of Amos THOMPSON dec'd using interest in estate of Rev. Amos THOMPSON dec'd. Wit: William B. HARRISON, Presley CORDELL. Delv to BECKWITH 13 Oct 1820.

Bk:Pg: 3B:034   Date: 17 Feb 1819   RtCt: 9 May 1820
Sheriff John HAMILTON to John L. DAGG. B/S of Samuel D. DAGG's interest (Samuel in debt James L. NORRIS) in house & Lots #26 & #32 in Mdbg of Robert DAGG (d. intestate leaving children John L., Saml, James, Mary, Sarah, Susan & Clarissa). Wit: E. G. HAMILTON, Jesse McVEIGH, Geo. SWEARINGEN, Ben. SHREVE Jr. Delv. to Towns'd McVEIGH pr order of J. L. DAGG 12 Dec 1820.

Bk:Pg: 3B:036   Date: 25 Mar 1820   RtCt: 10 Jul 1820
David ALEXANDER & wife Elizabeth of Ldn to Presley SAUNDERS of Ldn. B/S of 1a (prch/o Daniel BROWN) on branch of Goose Creek on road from Scholfield's mill by Adam BARR, adj David CARTER. Wit: Charles LEWIS, Wm. NOLAND.

Bk:Pg: 3B:037   Date: 24 Jun 1820   RtCt: 11 Jul 1820
Elizabeth GIBSON of Ldn to Caldwell CARR. Trust for debt to Isaac
NICKOLS Sr., Isaac NICKOLS Jr., William NICKOLS, Stephen
WILSON & Abner GIBSON (as security for her as Guardian of her
children) using 14½a (cnvy/b Moses GIBSON) adj heirs of John
GIBSON dec'd. Delv. to C. CARR 22 Aug 1824.

Bk:Pg: 3B:039   Date: 25 Jul 1820   RtCt: 25 Jul 1820
Mark WOOD of Ldn to Benjamin SHREVE of Ldn. Trust for debt to
Richard H. HENDERSON using ½a lot on N edition & W side of
Market St in Lsbg with house now in possession of John DOVIELL?
and lot prch/o Dr. CLAGETT on E side of Back St.

Bk:Pg: 3B:041   Date: 8 Jul 1820   RtCt: 10 Jul 1820
Jacob R. THOMAS to Asa C. WILKINSON. Trust for debt to John C.
HANDY using household items.

Bk:Pg: 3B:043   Date: 24 Jun 1820   RtCt: 26 Jul 1820
Ferdinando FAIRFAX of Ffx to Robert PATTON Jr. of Ffx. Trust for
debt to Robert BEVERLEY with agent Peter R. BEVERLY of
Alexandria using 500a in both Ldn and JeffVa in Shannondale.

Bk:Pg: 3B:045   Date: 12 Aug 1820   RtCt: 12 Aug 1820
John H. McCABE & wife Mary of Ldn to John HAMMERLY of Ldn.
B/S of ¼a on E side of King St. in E addition to Lsbg adj HAMERLY,
John DRISH. Wit: Thomas SANDERS, Presley CORDELL.

Bk:Pg: 3B:047   Date: 9 May 1820   RtCt: 20 Jul 1820
George JANNEY & wife Susanna of Montgomery Co OH to Thomas
SWAYNE of Ffx. B/S of 34a adj Peter SANDERS, Adam
HOUSHOLDER, __ GRUBB. Wit: Newton KEENE, Adam LYNN, R.
J. TAYLOR.

Bk:Pg: 3B:049   Date: 9 May 1820   RtCt: 20 Jul 1820
George JANNEY & wife Susannah of Montgomery Co OH to
Thomas SWAYNE of Ffx. B/S of 190a on NW fork of Goose Creek
adj Amos GIBSON, David SMITH. Wit: Newton KEENE, Adam
LYNN, R. J. TAYLOR.

Bk:Pg: 3B:051   Date: 20 May 1820   RtCt: 5 Aug 1820
William HERBERT (trustee for Jonathan SCHOFIELD for debt to
David & Jonathan ROSS) of Ffx to Thomas JANNEY of AlexDC. B/S
of 80a on Goose Creek below lime kiln. Delv. to JANNEY 21 Apr
1821.

Bk:Pg: 3B:054   Date: 14 Aug 1820   RtCt: 14 Aug 1820
Eleanor HIXSON. Receipt for full payment from Aaron SANDERS as
her Guardian. Wit: R. BRADEN.

Bk:Pg: 3B:054   Date: 25 Aug 1820   RtCt: 25 Aug 1820
James SAUNDERS of Ldn to Benjamin JACKSON of Ldn. BoS for
slave Bill (sold to SAUNDERS by Wm. BENTON agent for James
MONROE) a slave for life. Wit: Saml M. EDWARDS.

Bk:Pg: 3B:055   Date: 26 Dec 1795   RtCt: 11 Sep 1820
James McILHANEY. Col for slaves Clem, Grace, Pegg, Silvy, Jane & Henney (removed within the last 20 days from MD). Delv. to Robt. OGDEN 30 Aug 1822.

Bk:Pg: 3B:055   Date: 27 Mar 1820   RtCt: 14 Aug 1820
Isaac GRIFFITH to George M. CHICHESTER. B/S of rights to farm nr Nolands ferry adj Edward DULIN, John BEATY (formerly John ELLIOTT who left widow Rebecca who Isaac married). Wit: Doddridge LEE, Thos. GASSAWAY.

Bk:Pg: 3B:056   Date: 11 Sep 1820   RtCt: 11 Sep 1820
Jesse McVEIGH & Richard H. HENDERSON. Bond on McVEIGH as commr. of revenue in 2nd district.

Bk:Pg: 3B:056   Date: 11 Sep 1820   RtCt: 11 Sep 1820
Jesse TIMMS & Stephen C. ROSZELL. Bond on TIMMS as commr. of revenue in 1st district.

Bk:Pg: 3B:057   Date: 14 Sep 1820   RtCt: 14 Sep 1820
John HAMILTON, Robert MOFFETT & William MEAD. Bond on HAMILTON as sheriff to collect the poor rate.

Bk:Pg: 3B:057   Date: 14 Sep 1820   RtCt: 14 Sep 1820
John HAMILTON, Ben SHREVE, Robert MOFFETT, Wm. MEAD, Wm. CARR & Thomson MASON. Bond on HAMILTON as sheriff to collect taxes.

Bk:Pg: 3B:058   Date: 14 Jul 1820   RtCt: 14 Aug 1820
Mary HAWLING & Elizabeth HAWLING of Ldn to Nancy FOUCH (wd/o Isaac FOUCH dec'd) of Ldn. B/S of ½a Lot #41 in Mdbg on Washington & Hamilton Sts (belonging to late Samuel HENDERSON Sr.) with ground rents to Burr POWELL. Wit: Temple FOUCH, William HAWLING, John HAWLING.

Bk:Pg: 3B:060   Date: 5 Sep 1820   RtCt: 5 Sep 1820
John HUTCHISON of PrWm (trustee with Nathan HUTCHISON of Ldn) to Jacob ISH. Release of trust. Wit: John MOUNT, E. G. HAMILTON, Towns'd McVEIGH.

Bk:Pg: 3B:061   Date: 5 Sep 1820   RtCt: 5 Sep 1820
John HUTCHISON of PrWm (trustee with Nathan HUTCHISON) to Jacob ISH of Ldn. Release of trust. Wit: E. G. HAMILTON, John MOUNT, Towns'd McVEIGH.

Bk:Pg: 3B:062   Date: 24 Aug 1820   RtCt: 29 Aug 1820
Thomas SWANN (trustee of Portia w/o William HODGSON) to James H. HOOE. B/S of household items (in 1811 John HOPKINS conveyed to SWANN 5a in Alexandria and unexpired lease of 12a Bellvue land on Potomac and items of furniture in trust for Portia – household items have been removed to Ldn). Wit: Chs. G. ESKRIDGE, Ch. J. LOVE, Towns'd McVEIGH.

Bk:Pg: 3B:063 Date: 5 Aug 1820 RtCt: 11 Sep 1820
Lydia BOSS w/o Peter BOSS in Wayne Co OH. CoE for sale to
Saml. M. BOSS on 6 Apr 1820. Delv. to Saml. M. BOSS 4 Oct 1820.

Bk:Pg: 3B:064 Date: 2 Aug 1820 RtCt: 14 Aug 1820
Ariss BUCKNER of Ldn to Walter JONES. B/S of 158a under L/L to
Owen THOMAS and unexpired lease on 155a to Thomas KEENE
and 145a unexpired lease to Thomas ROOKARD and 183a
unexpired lease to Reuben HUTCHISON and 120a unexpired lease
to Charles STEWART. Wit: Wm. G. ORR, Charles DOUGLASS,
Hugh COCKERILL.

Bk:Pg: 3B:065 Date: 13 Apr 1820 RtCt: 17 Aug 1820
William M. REYNOLDS & wife Mary to Guardian of heirs of Richard
BROOKE dec'd. B/S of 140a cnvy/b __ DOWNEY in trust to said
REYNOLDS (DB RR:480) which REYNOLDS purchased. CoE for
Mary in Augusta Co.

Bk:Pg: 3B:067 Date: 21 Jun 1820 RtCt: 11 Sep 1820
Peter OVERFIELD & wife Deborah to John H. BUTCHER. CoE for
sale of 37a on 16 May 1818. Delv. to BUTCHER 1 Mar 1822.

Bk:Pg: 3B:068 Date: 22 Jul 1820 RtCt: 14 Aug 1820
Swithen NICKOLS (trustee of Samuel & Isaac NICKOLS) to William
LODGE. Release of trust on 150a. Wit: Thomas LODGE, Elizabeth
NICKOLS. Delv to Asa ROGERS pr order filed 19 Nov 1821.

Bk:Pg: 3B:069 Date: 12 Feb 1820 RtCt: 28 Aug 1820
Joseph CAVENS of Ldn to Zachariah DULANY of Ldn. B/S of 30a
lot #2 & 16a lot #7 in div. of estate of Joseph CAVENS dec'd. Delv.
to DULANY 27 Mar 1826.

Bk:Pg: 3B:070 Date: 21 Jun 1820 RtCt: 11 Sep 1820
Samuel OVERFIELD & wife Mary to John H. BUTCHER. CoE for
deed of 20 Nov 1817 for 31a. Wit: John SOMMERVILLE, Jacob
COPLIN. Delv. to BUTCHER 1 Mar 1822.

Bk:Pg: 3B:071 Date: 9 Aug 1820 RtCt: 14 Aug 1820
Craven OSBURNE of Ldn to Robert COCKERAL of Ldn. B/S of
rights to 75a formerly Isaac TALLY dec'd occupied by COCKERAL.

Bk:Pg: 3B:073 Date: 8 Aug 1820 RtCt: 14 Aug 1820
Thornton WALKER & wife Fanny of Ldn to William H. DORSEY of
Ldn. Trust for debt to Caleb N. GALLEHER using ½a lot in Union
where WALKER resides. Wit: Wm. BRONAUGH, John M.
GRAYSON

Bk:Pg: 3B:074 Date: 12 Jul 1820 RtCt: 29 Aug 1820
Benjamin GRAYSON to Nathaniel MANNING & wife Euphamia of
Ldn. Release of trust for debt to Daniel EACHES.

Bk:Pg: 3B:075 Date: 5 Aug 1820 RtCt: 29 Aug 1820
Benjamin GRAYSON to Thomas DRAKE of Ldn. Release on trust
for debt to Isaac LEWIS & James LEWIS of KY.

Bk:Pg: 3B:076   Date: 26 Jun 1820   RtCt: 31 Aug 1820
Jonathan CARTER & John SINCLAIR of Ldn to Moses WILSON of Ldn. Release of trust for debt to Meshack LACEY on 52½a.

Bk:Pg: 3B:078   Date: 23 Mar 1820   RtCt: 14 Aug 1820
John J. COLEMAN of Ldn to Cartwright TIPPETT late of Ldn now of Washington City. B/S of 3a island on Horsepen Run at farm of TIPPETT (cnvy/b Ludwell LEE to father James COLEMAN Jr. and allotted to John J. under decree). Delv. to TIPPETT 11 Mar 1822.

Bk:Pg: 3B:079   Date: 19 Aug 1819   RtCt: 19 Aug 1820
John BOOTH of Jefferson Co Indiana to John BURNHOUSE of Harrison Co OH but now of Ldn. B/S of 1/7th part of tract of David MULL dec'd allotted to Margaret w/o BURNHOUSE. Wit: S. BLINCOE, John MOORE, Daniel MILLER.

Bk:Pg: 3B:080   Date: 7 Sep 1820   RtCt: 7 Sep 1820
William CLINE & wife Margaret of Ldn to George M. CHICHESTER of Ldn. B/S of lot on S side of Cornwall St. in Lsbg adj Wm. H. LANE, John DRISH. Wit: John McCORMICK, Presley CORDELL. Delv. to CHICHESTER 14 May 1827.

Bk:Pg: 3B:082   Date: 1 Feb 1820   RtCt: 14 Aug 1820
John MATHIAS of Ldn to Thomas KIDWELL of Ldn. B/S of 56a Lots #29, #30 & #31 on W side of short hill adj John CONARD. Delv. to KIDWELL 16 Jul 1822.

Bk:Pg: 3B:083   Date: __ Mar 1820   RtCt: 16 Aug 1820
John WALTMAN (of Jacob) & wife Margaret of Ldn to Jacob WALTMAN (of Samuel) of Ldn. B/S of interest in 109a of Samuel WALTMAN dec'd on Catocton Creek adj William PAXSON, John HAMILTON and subject to dower of widow now w/o Levi PRINCE. Wit: Jacob WALTMAN, Manuel WALTMAN, Peter CYST. Delv. to Jacob WALTMAN 2 Jan 1824.

Bk:Pg: 3B:085   Date: 11 Jan 1820   RtCt: 14 Aug 1820
Samuel D. LESLIE of Ldn to Thomas LESLIE of Ldn. B/S of ¾a in Hllb (cnvy/b Jesse EVANS in 1817).

Bk:Pg: 3B:086   Date: 24 Apr 1820   RtCt: 31 Aug 1820
Miller HOGE & wife Tacy of Ldn to Joseph EIDSON of Ldn. B/S of 26¼a (prch/o Moses WILSON) adj Capt. Dennis McCARTY. Wit: Notley C. WILLIAMS, Wm. BRONAUGH.

Bk:Pg: 3B:088   Date: 25 Mar 1820   RtCt: 29 Aug 1820
William WINN to John W. GRAYSON. Trust for debt to Thomas DRAKE using 112a adj William HODGSON, Charles RUSSEL (formerly owned by Isaac & James LEWIS & Geo. RUST Jr). Delv. to DRAKE 26 Nov 1821.

Bk:Pg: 3B:090   Date: 13 Aug 1820   RtCt: 2 Sep 1820
Charles DRISH & wife Susanna of Ldn to Robert MOFFETT of Ldn. B/S of lot in Lsbg on E side of King St. adj __ SHREVE, lease of

heirs of Henry GLASGOW dec'd. Wit: John McCORMICK, Presley CORDELL. Delv. to MOFFETT 21 May 1821.

Bk:Pg: 3B:092   Date: 1 Feb 1820   RtCt: 30 Aug 1820
Adam HOUSHOLDER & wife Sarah of Ldn to Amos JANNEY of Ldn. B/S of 1/7th part of one of the heirs of Amos JANNEY dec'd (f/o Sarah) on E side of short hill and 1/7th part of 2/3 of undivided 161a on road from Lsbg to Nolands ferry except dower rights of Grace JANNEY (wd/o Amos JANNEY the elder dec'd). Wit: Samuel HOUGH Jr., John H. McCABE. Delv. to JANNEY 6 Jun 1821.

Bk:Pg: 3B:094   Date: 9 Aug 1820   RtCt: 14 Aug 1820
Isaac TALLEY & wife Rachel of Ldn to Robert COCKRILLE of Ldn. B/S of 40¼a (part of land of late Mrs. TALLEY which falls to Prudence w/o Robert COCKERILLE and by Robert's prch/o Craven OSBURNE). Wit: Craven OSBURNE, John WHITE. Delv. to COCKERILL 7 Apr 1834.

Bk:Pg: 3B:096   Date: 18 Apr 1820   RtCt: 24 Aug 1820
William NOLAND & wife Catharine of Ldn to Rezin WILCOXEN of Ffx. B/S of 40a adj lease of Saml. LOVE, Andrew RUSSELL, W side of Gum Spring & Centreville road. Wit: James RUST, Henry McKENZIE, James SMARR, Burr POWELL, Ariss BUCKNER.

Bk:Pg: 3B:098   Date: 13 Jan 1820   RtCt: 31 Aug 1820
David LOVETT of Ldn to Francis STRIBLING. Trust for debt to Charles J. KILGORE using 92a (Louisa KILGORE's share in estate of Elizabeth McILHANEY dec'd called 'Gidney's Clerks land'.

Bk:Pg: 3B:101   Date: 9 Aug 1820   RtCt: 14 Aug 1820
Robert Cockerille & wife Prudence of Ldn to Isaac TALLY of Ldn. B/S of 40¼a (fell to Isaac TALLEY in own right and with purchase from brother Josiah TALLEY of their late mother's land). Wit: Ebenezer GRUBB, John WHITE. Delv. to TALLEY 16 Jun 1834.

Bk:Pg: 3B:103   Date: 13 Aug 1820   RtCt: 30 Aug 1820
Amos JANNEY of Ldn to Adam HOUSHOLDER & wife Sarah. B/S of 52a on E side of road from Steer's mill to Ball's mill. Delv. to HOUSHOLDER 5 Jan 1821.

Bk:Pg: 3B:104   Date: 27 May 1818   RtCt: 16 Feb 1820
George RUST Jr. & wife Maria of Ldn to Archibald MAIN of Ldn. B/S of 17a adj __ BENEDUM, __ McINTYRE. Wit: Benj'n SHREVE, Joseph BEARD, Henry T. HARRISON, John McCORMICK, Thos. GREGG. Delv. to MAINS 21 Sep 1822.

Bk:Pg: 3B:106   Date: 19 Aug 1820   RtCt: 31 Aug 1820
John SINCLAIR of Ldn to Humphrey B. POWELL of Ldn. Trust for debt to Abner GIBSON using 5a (from father Jas. SINCLAIR dec'd). Delv. to Hugh SMITH pr order of H. B. POWELL 17 Apr 1822.

Bk:Pg: 3B:108   Date: 25 May 1820   RtCt: 15 Aug 1820
Carter B. PAGE of RichVa to William B. PAGE of Frederick. Trust for debt to John W. PAGE (Admr dbn of Robert PAGE dec'd formerly of

Broadneck, Hanover Co Va) using undivided moiety of 2000a in Ldn and Ffx. Delv. to Fleet SMITH pr order of J. B. PAGE 26 May 1821.

Bk:Pg: 3B:110   Date: 21 Dec 1819   RtCt: 1 Sep 1820
William RICHARDS of Ldn to Moses GIBSON of Ldn. LS of 211½a nr Clifton Mills (prch/o GIBSON). Wit: Thos. P. KNOX, Sydnor BAILEY, Jacob DAYMUD.

Bk:Pg: 3B:113   Date: 18 Apr 1820   RtCt: 14 Aug 1820
Thomas H. KERBY of Ldn to Thomas J. NOLAND of Ldn. Trust for debt to William NOLAND of Ldn using Lots #39, #40, #41 & #42 in Aldie. Delv. to NOLAND 31 Mar 1824.

Bk:Pg: 3B:114   Date: 18 Apr 1820   RtCt: 14 Aug 1820
Henry McKENZIE of Ldn to Thomas J. NOLAND of Ldn. Trust for debt to William NOLAND using Lots #59 & #60 in Aldie.

Bk:Pg: 3B:116   Date: 20 Dec 1819   RtCt: 29 Aug 1820
Moses GIBSON & wife Lydia of Ldn to William RICHARDS of Ldn. B/S of 226a nr Turnpike road on the S and Clifton Mill on the N. Wit: Thos. P. KNOX, Sydnor BAILEY, Jacob DAYMUDE, Benjamin GRAYSON, John W. GRAYSON. Delv. pr order 10 May 1824.

Bk:Pg: 3B:118   Date: 20 Jun 1820   RtCt: 11 Jul 1820
Albert BAYLY of Ldn to Ariss BUCKNER & Charles LEWIS of Ldn. Trust for debt to John BAYLY using 188a adj Reuben HUTCHISON, George B. WHITING, Sampson HUTCHISON. Wit; William THRIFT, Levi G. EWERS, Abraham WARFORD, Eli CARRINGTON. Delv. to John BAILEY 18 Jan 1821.

Bk:Pg: 3B:121   Date: 17 Feb 1820   RtCt: 25 Aug 1820
John H. EVANS of Union to John WEADON of Ldn. Trust for debt to Jesse TRAYHERN using lot a little N of Union adj Samuel DUNKIN, Isaac BROWN. Delv. to Wm. H. DORSEY pr order 20 Nov 1820.

Bk:Pg: 3B:123   Date: 4 Mar 1818   RtCt: 11 Sep 1820
James L. McKENNA & wife Ann Cecelia of AlexDC to Benjamin C. ASHTON & Richard C. PATON of AlexDC. Trust for Ann's benefit using 1400a on Broad Run from Flora LEE (her mother, former w/o Ludwell LEE). Wit: West ASHTON, F. H. KENEDY, Anth'y CREASE. Delv. to E. J. LEE Jr 11 Dec 1820.

Bk:Pg: 3B:129   Date: 26 Apr 1819   RtCt: 11 Sep 1820
Benjamin C. ASHTON & Richard C. NORTON to Robert J. TAYLOR (trustee of James L. McKENNA & wife Ann Cecelia of AlexDC). Trust for debt to Charles T. CHAPMAN using land on broad run. Wit: Anth'y CREASE, West ASHTON, W. C. PAGE, F. H. KENADY. Delv. to E. J. LEE Jr. 11 Dec 1820.

Bk:Pg: 3B:136   Date: 19 Jan 1820   RtCt: 14 Aug 1820
Lewis FRENCH of Ldn to negro George. BoS for his freedom. Wit: Aaron BURSON, Tarlton TAYLOR, Abraham BROWN.

Bk:Pg: 3B:137   Date: 17 Jul 1820   RtCt: 11 Sep 1820
Christopher ROSE & wife Catharine to Henry EVANS. BoS for negro boy Sirus (at death of Martha EVANS entitled to equal share as heir of William EVANS dec'd). Wit: George BEATTY, William HARDEN, Robert COMBS, Robert ROSE.

Bk:Pg: 3B:137   Date: 3 Mar 1820   RtCt: 11 Sep 1820
James MARSH to daughter Phebe VERNON. Gift of horse and household items. Wit: Abraham SKILMAN, William TOMLINSON.

Bk:Pg: 3B:138   Date: 8 Mar 1819   RtCt: 20 Sep 1820
William BENTON attorney in fact for Jas. MONROE to James SAUNDERS. BoS for negro man Bill late the property of Augustine G. MONROE (sold to Jas.) a slave for life. Wit: R. G. SAUNDERS.

Bk:Pg: 3B:138   Date: 28 Jan 1820   RtCt: 27 Sep 1820
Charles B. BALL & wife Lucy T. of Ldn to Jacob FADELY of Ldn. B/S of house & lot in Lsbg at lower corner of lot #6. Wit: Presley CORDELL, Thomas SANDERS. Delv. to FADLEY 2 Nov 1820.

Bk:Pg: 3B:139   Date: 27 Feb 1820   RtCt: 11 Sep 1820
Robert MOORE & wife of Ldn to William VICKERS of Ldn. Trust for debt to Aaron BURSON using land on SE side of Goose Creek opposite George BURSON's mill and household items. Wit: Francis W. LUCKETT.

Bk:Pg: 3B:140   Date: 13 Sep 1820   RtCt: 28 Sep 1820
John MUSTIN & wife Blanche of Frederick Co to James MONROE of Albemarle Co. B/S of interest in lands of Joseph JONES the elder dec'd. 28 Sep 1820

Bk:Pg: 3B:142   Date: 9 Oct 1820   RtCt: 9 Oct 1820
John HAMILTON, Benjamin SHREVE, Robert MOFFETT, Wm. CARR & William MEADE. Bond on HAMILTON as sheriff to collect taxes.

Bk:Pg: 3B:142   Date: 14 Sep 1820   RtCt: ___
Benjamin SHREVE to Robert MOFFETT. PoA for bond of John HAMILTON as sheriff.

Bk:Pg: 3B:143   Date: 29 Feb 1820   RtCt: 7 Oct 1820
John C. HANDY of Ldn to James MOUNT of Ldn. B/S of 147¼a on Goose Creek (allotted as heir of John HANDY dec'd). Wit: Wm. H. HANDY, Asa C. WILKINSON.

Bk:Pg: 3B:145   Date: 4 Oct 1820   RtCt: 9 Oct 1820
John HAMILTON. Commissioned as sheriff.

Bk:Pg: 3B:145   Date: 13 Sep 1820   RtCt: 13 Sep 1820
Jacob KEMERLY/KIMMERLE of Ldn to Thomas GASSAWAY of Lsbg. B/S of 61a (prch/o Samuel CLAPHAM, DB UU:49) less 3-4a sold to John DIXON & David McGAHY.

Bk:Pg: 3B:147   Date: 25 Dec 1819   RtCt: 20 Sep 1820
John CRIDLER & wife Elizabeth of Ldn to Simon SMALE. Trust for debt to Thomas MORALLEE using ½a adj James GAR(D)NER on Market St in Lsbg. Wit: John McCORMICK, Presley CORDELL.

Bk:Pg: 3B:149   Date: 1 Sep 1820   RtCt: 4 Sep 1820
Stephen DANIEL of Fqr to Peter BENEDUM of Ldn. Release of trust of Mar 1815.

Bk:Pg: 3B:151   Date: 18 Feb 1820   RtCt: 11 Sep 1820
Stephen GARRETT & wife Ufamey of Ldn to Christopher ROSE & Robert ROSE of Ldn. B/S of 3½a on Goose Creek (part of Robert CARTER's tract). Wit: John DANIEL, George BEATTY, Robert COMBS, Henry EVINS. Delv. to ROSE 12 Sep 1832.

Bk:Pg: 3B:152   Date: 16 Jan 1820   RtCt: 20 Sep 1820
John CRIDLER & wife Elizabeth of Ldn to Thomas RUSSELL of Ldn. B/S of ½a lot in Lsbg on S side of Market St. adj Simon SMAIL, Thomas R. MOTT (prch/o Thomas B. BEATTY). Wit: John McCORMICK, Presley CORDELL.

Bk:Pg: 3B:154   Date: 20 Sep 1820   RtCt: 20 Sep 1820
John CRIDLER & wife Elizabeth of Ldn to William CARR of Ldn. B/S of land adj John FEICHTER on N side of Loudoun St in Lsbg. Wit: John McCORMICK, Presley CORDELL. Delv. to CARR 28 Nov 1821.

Bk:Pg: 3B:156   Date: 21 Dec 1819   RtCt: 20 Sep 1820
John CRIDLER & wife Elizabeth of Ldn to John FEICHTER of Ldn. B/S of land on N side of Loudoun St in Lsbg adj Peter COALTER's prch/o CRIDLER. Wit: John McCORMICK, Presley CORDELL. Delv. to F[E]ITCHER 27 Dec 1823.

Bk:Pg: 3B:159   Date: 23 Sep 1820   RtCt: 23 Sep 1820
John MONROE & wife Mary of Ldn to William KING of Ldn. B/S of lot on W side of King St in Lsbg (prch/o Jacob FADELY in Dec 1818) adj Robert BENTLEY. Wit: Samuel M. EDWARDS, Presley CORDELL.

Bk:Pg: 3B:161   Date: 8 Sep 1820   RtCt: 8 Sep 1820
John James MATHIAS of Ldn to Thomas SWANN of AlexDC. Trust for debt to Edmund J. LEE using 50a on short hill adj John CONRAD and 68a adj __ DEMORY, __ DERRY. Delv. to E. J. LEE 30 Mar 1821.

Bk:Pg: 3B:164   Date: 5 May 1820   RtCt: 9 Oct 1820
Isaac HOUGH & wife Frances of Cincinnati OH to John HUNT of Cincinnati OH. B/S of ¼a in Hllb (cnvy/b Joseph GREGG attorney for Ruth GREGG) adj William CLENDENING, Thomas LASLY. Wit: John MUNROE, Isaac G. BURNET. Delv. to HUNT 5 Jan 1832.

Bk:Pg: 3B:167   Date: 3 Nov 1820   RtCt: 3 Nov 1820
John A. BINNS to Thomas FLOWERS. Release of mortgage.

Bk:Pg: 3B:167   Date: 21 Jul 1820   RtCt: 9 Oct 1820
Benjamin WHITE of Ldn to Edward OWEN of Ldn of farm animals, household items. Wit: Adin WHITE, Richard WHITE.

Bk:Pg: 3B:168   Date: 21 Jul 1820   RtCt: 19 Oct 1820
Edward OWEN of Ldn to Benjamin WHITE of Ldn. BoS for farm animals, household items. Wit: Adin WHITE, Richard WHITE. Delv. to Benj. WHITE 3 May 1822.

Bk:Pg: 3B:169   Date: 1 Jun 1819   RtCt: 20 Oct 1820
Elizabeth GIBSON of Ldn to David E. BROWN & Mahlon GIBSON of Ldn. LS of Elizabeth's right of dower from late husband John GIBSON dec'd for land nr Upperville. Wit: John M. MONROE, Wm. DUNKIN, Jonah BRADFIELD.

Bk:Pg: 3B:170   Date: 31 Jul 1819   RtCt: 30 Oct 1820
Henry SANDERS & wife Patience of Ldn to William MEAD of Ldn. B/S of 19a adj Peter BENEDUM, Henry SANDERS, William MEAD. Wit: Thos. SANDERS, Saml. M. EDWARDS. Delv. to Jos. MEAD 24 Apr 1843.

Bk:Pg: 3B:173   Date: 6 May 1820   RtCt: 6 Oct 1820
Andrew FENITON & wife Jemima of Ldn to Amos JOHNSON of Ldn. B/S of 8a (lot drawn for Jemima FENITON & her children from John VIOLETT dec'd). Wit: Amos DENHAM, Amy DENHAM, Burr POWELL, A. GIBSON.

Bk:Pg: 3B:175   Date: 10 May 1820   RtCt: 11 Oct 1820
William JENKINS & wife Hannah of Frederick Co to Benjamin JENKINS of Ldn. B/S of 140a (sold to Wm. & Benjamin JENKINS by Peter ROMINE in 1802) adj Spencer PEW, James DILLON. Delv. to Jesse RICHARDS 24 Sep 1852 [or 32?]

Bk:Pg: 3B:177   Date: 14 Oct 1820   RtCt: 16 Oct 1820
Thomas GASSAWAY & wife Henrietta of Ldn to Jacob KEMERLE of Ldn. B/S of 61a (prch/o KEMERLE, except 3-4a sold to John DIXON & David McGAHY).

Bk:Pg: 3B:179   Date: 10 Oct 1820   RtCt: 4 Nov 1820
William KIRK & wife Nancy of Ldn to Benjamin MAULSBY of Ldn. B/S of lot on N side of Market St in Lsbg adj KIRK. Wit: Patrick McINTYRE, Presley CORDELL. Delv. to MAULSBY 28 Nov 1822.

Bk:Pg: 3B:182   Date: 1 Aug 1820   RtCt: 13 Nov 1820
Burr POWELL. Commissioned as sheriff.

Bk:Pg: 3B:183   Date: 9 Oct 1820   RtCt: 15 Nov 1820
Benjamin LESLIE & Joshua OSBURN of Ldn to Richard H. HENDERSON of Ldn. PoA for LESLIE & OSBURN as securities for Saml. LESLIE & Craven OSBURNE as Exors of Thomas LESLIE dec'd. Wit: E. G. HAMILTON, William THRIFT.

Bk:Pg: 3B:183   Date: 12 Nov 1820   RtCt: 12 Nov 1820
Burr POWELL, Leven LUCKET, Noble BEVERIDGE, Abner
GIBSON, Benjamin SHREVE & Jesse McVEIGH. Bond on POWELL
as sheriff to collect taxes.

Bk:Pg: 3B:184   Date: 12 Nov 1820   RtCt: 12 Nov 1820
Burr POWELL, Leven LUCKETT, Noble BEVERIDGE, Abner
GIBSON, Benjamin SHRIEVE & Jesse McVEIGH. Bond on
POWELL as sheriff to collect and make payments.

Bk:Pg: 3B:186   Date: 12 Nov 1820   RtCt: 12 Nov 1820
Burr POWELL, Leven LUCKETT, Noble BEVERIDGE, Abner
GIBSON, Benjamin SHRIEVE & Jesse McVEIGH. Bond on
POWELL as sheriff to pay treasurer.

Bk:Pg: 3B:186   Date: 14 Nov 1820   RtCt: 14 Nov 1820
James SIMPSON, French SIMPSON & John R. ADAMS to Thomas
ROGERS, Arthur ROGERS & Hugh ROGERS (admr of Hamilton
ROGERS dec'd). Bond as security.

Bk:Pg: 3B:188   Date: 14 Nov 1820   RtCt: 16 Nov 1820
L. P. W. BALCH, Patrick McINTYRE & Saml. CLAPHAM. Bond on
BALCH as treasurer of the board of commrs. for educating the poor
children of Ldn.

Bk:Pg: 3B:189   Date: 14 Nov 1820   RtCt: 14 Nov 1820
Charles DUNKIN & Jesse TIMMS. Bond on DUNKIN as constable.

Bk:Pg: 3B:189   Date: 13 Nov 1820   RtCt: 13 Nov 1820
Peter C. RUST, William GILMORE & William WILKINSON. Bond on
RUST as constable.

Bk:Pg: 3B:190   Date: 13 Nov 1820   RtCt: 13 Nov 1820
Ann JAMES and Smith JAMES (insolvents) to Sheriff John
HAMILTON of Ldn. Owes Burr POWELL ass'ee of John CRIDER
and Burr POWELL & Thomas MOUNT ass'ee of Alexander
TURLEY. Turning over all interest in land of husband Jacob JAMES
the father of Smith. Wit: S. BLINCOE, Benj. SHREEVE Jr, Robert
MOFFETT.

Bk:Pg: 3B:192   Date: 7 Nov 1820   RtCt: 7 Nov 1820
Francis TRIPLETT Jr. of Ldn to Jacob WILLIAMS of Ldn. B/S of lot
prch/o Jas. DONAGH adj Charles BINNS.

Bk:Pg: 3B:194   Date: 28 Oct 1820   RtCt: 4 Nov 1820
Amasa HOUGH of Ldn to John RUSE(of Christian) of Ldn. B/S of
Lot #7 on N side of road leading from Wtfd to Quaker meeting
house. Delv. to John RUSE 16 Jan 1821.

Bk:Pg: 3B:196   Date: 2 Nov 1820   RtCt: 7 Nov 1820
Thomas FLOWERS & wife Catharine of Ldn to William CARR of
Ldn. B/S of ¼a in new addition to Lsbg on S side of Loudoun St. Wit:
E. G. HAMILTON, Geo. SWEARINGEN, Saml. M. EDWARDS,
Presley CORDELL. Delv. to CARR 28 Nov 1821.

Bk:Pg: 3B:198   Date: 14 Oct 1820   RtCt: 16 Oct 1820
Jacob KIMMERLE of Ldn to Samuel DAWSON of Ldn. Trust for debt
to Thomas GASSAWAY using 61a (except 3-4a sold to John DIXON
& David McGAHY).

Bk:Pg: 3B:200   Date: 13 Sep 1820   RtCt: 9 Oct 1820
Abiel JENNERS & wife Deborah of Ldn to Michael COOPER of Ldn.
B/S of 114½a formerly owned by Abram BAKER, adj John
WILLIAMS, Robert BRADEN, Patrick McGARVIC. Wit: Robert
BRADEN, Samuel HOUGH Jr.

Bk:Pg: 3B:203   Date: 7 Aug 1820   RtCt: 9 Nov 1820
Elijah WARFORD & mother Mary WARFORD late of Ldn now of
Belmont Co OH to Lewis LYDER of Ldn. B/S of 122a (less 2a
reserve) plantation adj Capt. OSBURN. Wit: William PHILPOT,
Thomas SHAMRON.

Bk:Pg: 3B:205   Date: 1 Jun 1820   RtCt: 28 Oct 1820
Richard MOORE & wife Mary of Henry Co KY to Samuel M.
EDWARDS of Lsbg. B/S of 1a in E addition to Lsbg adj Wm. DODD
(cnvy/b comm. John MATHIAS to Mary MOORE in 1816).

Bk:Pg: 3B:207   Date: 11 Sep 1820   RtCt: 11 Oct 1820
Sheriff John HAMILTON of Ldn to John MARKS of Ldn. B/S of 53a
with mill (land of insolvent Samuel SINCLAIR). Wit: A. O. POWELL,
Lee W. DENHAM, E. G. HAMILTON.

Bk:Pg: 3B:209   Date: 8 Sep 1820   RtCt: 9 Oct 1820
William WILLIAMSON & wife Sarah of Fqr to Townsend D. PEYTON
of Ldn. B/S of 123a adj heirs of John BATTSON, Burr POWELL,
Levin LUCKETT, heirs of Richard CRUPPER. Wit: Burr POWELL, A.
GIBSON. Delv. to Saml. NOLAND pr order 4 Nov 1822.

Bk:Pg: 3B:212   Date: 19 Sep 1820   RtCt: 10 Oct 1820
Burr POWELL of Ldn to Nelson GREEN of Ldn. B/S of ¼a nr Mdbg
on S side of Federal St at Pendleton St. Delv. to Wm. L. POWELL pr
order.

Bk:Pg: 3B:215   Date: 10 Jul 1820   RtCt: 28 Oct 1820
Henry SAUNDERS Sr. & wife Patience of Ldn to James H.
HAMILTON of Ldn. B/S of 14a adj Wm. HALL, __ BENEDUM. Wit:
Thomas YANDERS, Thos. SANDERS, Saml. M. EDWARDS. Delv.
to Jno. DRISH who purchased land of Jas. H. HAMILTON (DB
JJJ:323) 30 May 1826.

Bk:Pg: 3B:218   Date: 13 Sep 1820   RtCt: 9 Oct 1820
Michael COOPER (signed in Dutch) & wife Hannah of Ldn to Joshua
PEWSEY of Ldn. Trust for debt to Abiel JENNERS using 114½a adj
William VIRTZ, Robert BRADEN, Patrick McGARVIC. Wit: Robert
BRADEN, Samuel HOUGH Jr. Delv. to JENNERS 14 Mar 1822.

Bk:Pg: 3B:223   Date: 31 Oct 1820   RtCt: 31 Oct 1820
John J. HARDING (Pres. of Overseers of Poor of Ldn) to Ann
WRIGHT wd/o Wm. WRIGHT dec'd (d. 10 Feb 1818 intestate) of

Ldn. B/S of 1a nr Lsbg (from 20a given by John LITTLEJOHN to Overseers).

Bk:Pg: 3B:227 Date: 31 Oct 1820 RtCt: 31 Oct 1820
John J. HARDING (Pres. of Overseers of Poor of Ldn) to Francis TRIPLETT Jr. of Ldn. B/S of 1a (interest of James DONAGH & wife Heziah conveyed to TRIPLETT) (from 20a given by John LITTLEJOHN to Overseers).

Bk:Pg: 3B:231 Date: 31 Oct 1820 RtCt: 31 Oct 1820
John J. HARDING (Pres. of Overseers of Poor of Ldn) to Charles BINNS of Ldn. B/S of 15a (from 20a given by John LITTLEJOHN to Overseers). Delv. to BINNS 17 May 1836.

Bk:Pg: 3B:235 Date: 31 Oct 1820 RtCt: 31 Oct 1820
John J. HARDING (Pres. of Overseers of Poor of Ldn) to Giles HAMMAT of Ldn. B/S of 1a (from 20a given by John LITTLEJOHN to Overseers). Delv. to HAMMATT 14 Jul 1821.

Bk:Pg: 3B:239 Date: 31 Oct 1820 RtCt: 31 Oct 1820
John J. HARDING (Pres. of Overseers of Poor of Ldn) to John Gill WATT of Ldn. B/S of 1a (from 20a given by John LITTLEJOHN to Overseers).

Bk:Pg: 3B:244 Date: 31 Oct 1820 RtCt: 31 Oct 1820
John J. HARDING (Pres. of Overseers of Poor of Ldn) to Isaac CROSSLEY. B/S of 1a (from 20a given by John LITTLEJOHN to Overseers).

Bk:Pg: 3B:248 Date: 5 Jun 1820 RtCt: 15 Jun 1820
Charlotte E. MASON, John T. MASON Jr., William T. T. MASON & Thomson MASON of Liberia (Exors of Armstead T. MASON dec'd of Ldn) to George RUST Jr of Ldn. B/S of 503a on Potomac adj late Gen. Stephen T. MASON. Wit: Chars. GULLATT, Tasker C. QUINLAN, R. J. FLEMING, George WASHINGTON, William S. SANDERS, Fran's KEARNY, Henry CLAGETT, Geo. M. CHICHESTER, Charles DOUGLAS. Delv. to RUST 3 May 1824.

Bk:Pg: 3B:253 Date: 10 Nov 1820 in New York City RtCt: 11 Dec 1820
Charles Fenton MERCER of Aldie to Lynde CATLIN of New York City. Trust for debt to Isaac BRONSON of New York City using 85a on both sides of little river and main st. of Aldie where MERCER now lives with dwelling house, merchant mill, grist mill, granary, store house, saw mill (includes unexpired 10y LS on 6a to Samuel MILLER) and 480a about 2m down the road (1a with house and garden given to free negro woman he emancipated) and 550a abt 1m from the previous on both sides of bull run as dividing line for Ldn and PrWm (under L/L to James WATTS and Francis D. POMEROY) and 136½a 3m W of Aldie leased to James McVEIGH. Forwarded to clerk PrWm 6 Jan 1821.

Bk:Pg: 3B:259   Date: 6 Dec 1820   RtCt: 6 Dec 1820
Richard H. HENDERSON of Lsbg to William NOLAND of Aldie.
Release of trust for debt to George SMITH of Dumfries using land
where NOLAND resides.

Bk:Pg: 3B:261   Date: 27 Sep 1820   RtCt: 25 Nov 1820
William BEARD of Ldn to Alexander BEARD. BoS for farm animals,
household items. Wit: Thos. BROWN, E. JANNEY. Delv. to Alex'r.
BEARD 30 Aug 1821.

Bk:Pg: 3B:261   Date: 8 Nov 1820   RtCt: 8 Nov 1820
James TRAYHERN (insolvent, in suit of John M. MONROE) of Ldn
to Sheriff John HAMILTON of Ldn. B/S of land in FredVa on sleepy
creek former prop. of father James TRAHERN dec'd. Wit: Saml. M.
EDWARDS, Thomas SANDERS, Giles HAMMAT.

Bk:Pg: 3B:263   Date: 1 Apr 1817   RtCt: 11 Dec 1820
Ferdinando FAIRFAX of Washington to William HERBERT Jr of Ffx.
B/S of ferry lot and land at Harper's ferry now leased by Job
HARDING and 2000a in Shannondale tract in Ldn and ferry called
the rocks with land adj in JeffVa.

Bk:Pg: 3B:265   Date: 9 Nov 1820   RtCt: 14 Nov 1820
Lloyd NOLAND to Richard COCHRAN. Release of trust for debt to
Burr POWELL on 16a nr Mdbg.

Bk:Pg: 3B:267   Date: 14 Oct 1820   RtCt: 13 Nov 1820
William GALLIHER & wife Margery of Ldn to George E. LLOYD of
Union. B/S of ½a (cnvy/b Wm. GALLIHER dec'd & wife Mary in
1812) adj Isaac BROWN, Samuel DUNKIN, John GALLEHER,
Caleb GALLEHER. Wit: Wm. BRONAUGH, John W. GRAYSON.

Bk:Pg: 3B:270   Date: 20 Sep 1820   RtCt: 11 Dec 1820
John BURNHOUSE of Harrison Co OH to John BOOTH Jr. of Ldn.
PoA to receive money from Jacob WERTZ of Ldn from sale of part
of estate of David MULL dec'd allotted to wife Margaret
BURNHOUSE (formerly MULL). Wit: John WAGNER, John
SHOBER, William SMITH. Delv. to Jno. BOOTH 15 Sep 1821.

Bk:Pg: 3B:272   Date: 31 Mar 1820   RtCt: 24 Nov 1820
Smith JAMES & wife Ann of Ldn to Dean JAMES of Ldn. B/S of
rights to undivided land of Jacob JAMES dec'd where Smith now
lives and 3 undivided heirs' parts that Smith prch/o William JAMES.
Wit: Hanson DUTTON, Elizabeth JAMES, William FOX. Delv. to
Dean JAMES 29 Mar 1822.

Bk:Pg: 3B:274   Date: 30 Nov 1820   RtCt: 13 Nov 1820
Joseph PURSEL & wife Susan of Ldn to Nicholas KOONCE of Ldn.
B/S of 1a (cnvy/b Thomas LESLIE) between short hill and blue ridge
where PURSEL now lives adj Ebenezer GRUBB. Wit: Ebenezer
GRUBB, Craven OSBURN. Delv. to KOONCE 23 Sep 1823.

Bk:Pg: 3B:276   Date: 6 Apr 1820   RtCt: 5 Dec 1820
William H. DORSEY & wife Judith of Ldn to Thornton WALKER of Ldn. Trust for debt to Jacob SILCOTT, Joseph GORE & Edward CARTER using lot in Union recently prch/o Caleb N. GALLIHER. Wit: Wm. BRONAUGH, Francis W. LUCKETT.

Bk:Pg: 3B:278   Date: 6 Dec 1820   RtCt: 6 Dec 1820
Richard Key WATTS Jr. of MontMd and Helen G. ROSE of Lsbg. Marriage contract – her property remains only hers, put in trust to John ROSE. Wit: Jno. A. BINNS, Chs. G. ESKRIDGE, Geo. RICHARDS, C. BINNS.

Bk:Pg: 3B:280   Date: 4 Dec 1820   RtCt: 4 Dec 1820
Aaron SANDERS & Charles ELGIN of Ldn (a trustees of Mahlon JANNEY for debt to Thomas R. MOTT) to Richard H. HENDERSON of Ldn. B/S of lot nr Wtfd (prch/o David CONRAD by JANNEY).

Bk:Pg: 3B:282   Date: 22 Oct __   RtCt: ___
Matthew HARRISON dec'd. Division – court order of __ 1818 – widow Catharine HARRISON (376a farm Lot #1 & slaves May, Jacob, Alfred, Mat, Lizzy, Betty & Hary), and to children John T. HARRRISON (208a Lot #2 & slaves Henry & Cate), Thomas J. HARRISON (200a Lot #3 & slaves Nannetta & Charlotte), Burr Wm. HARRISON (267a Lot #4 & slaves Abram, Israel & Joan), Margaret L. HARRISON (279a Lot #5 & slaves George, Sam, Gilbert & Eliza), Maria HARRISON (258a Lot #6 & slaves John, Ann & Martha), Sarah E. HARRISON (207a Lot #7 & slaves Sarah & Violet), Henry T. HARRISON (215a Lot #8 & slaves Nathan & Sarah). Divisors. Chas. LEWIS, Thomas FOUCH, John BAYLY. Gives plat.

Bk:Pg: 3B:290   Date: 3 Jun 1820   RtCt: 8 Dec 1820
Sanford EDMONDS & wife Margaret of Ldn to Peter BOGGESS of Ldn. B/S of lot in Wtfd adj Saml. GOVER, John H. CASSADY. Wit: Robert BRADEN, Abiel JENNERS.

Bk:Pg: 3B:293   Date: 17 Nov 1820   RtCt: 7 Nov 1820
Joseph MEAD & wife Elizabeth of Ldn to Richard H. HENDERSON of Ldn. Trust for debt to George RUST Jr. using tract previously prch/o RUST. Wit: John McCORMICK, Presley CORDELL. Delv. to HENDERSON 4 Feb 1824.

Bk:Pg: 3B:297   Date: 16 Apr 1820   RtCt: 14 Nov 1820
Jesse BURSON & wife Martha of Ldn to William MONROE of Ldn. B/S of 1a where MONROE now resides (part of prch/o Jacob STONEBURNER). Wit: James SINCLAIR, William ELLZEY, Saml. M. EDWARDS. Delv. to MONROE 21 Mar 1822.

Bk:Pg: 3B:299   Date: 26 Oct 1820   RtCt: 20 Nov 1820
William NOLAND & wife Catharine of Aldie to Charles Fenton MERCER of Aldie. B/S of 2a adj Aldie, Langley MERCER, James SWART and 3a in Aldie adj Mercer's mill lot. Wit: Burr POWELL, Abner GIBSON. Delv. to C. F. MERCER 13 Oct 1834.

Bk:Pg: 3B:303 Date: 20 Nov 1820 RtCt: 20 Nov 1820
Charles DRISH & wife Susanna of Ldn to David CARR of Ldn. B/S
of lot & one-story brick house on N side of Cornwall St. in Lsbg adj
DRISH. Wit: Thomas SANDERS, Presley CORDELL. Delv. to CARR
19 Feb 1838.

Bk:Pg: 3B:305 Date: 20 Sep 1820 RtCt: 13 Nov 1820
John BURNHOUSE & wife Margaret of Harrison Co OH to Jacob
VIRTZ of Ldn. B/S of rights to 1/7th part of land of David MULL dec'd
being 1/7th of land allotted to Margaret. Wit: John SHOBER, John
WAGNER, William SMITH.

Bk:Pg: 3B:309 Date: 5 Jun 1820 RtCt: 13 Nov 1820
Lewis HUNT & wife Mary of Ldn to William BRONAUGH of Ldn.
Trust for debts to DUNKIN & LLOYD, Price JACOBS & Thomas H.
GALLIHER using lot in Union cnvy/b Anne GALLEHER. Wit: Thos.
H. WAY, Wm. DUNKIN, Francis W. LUCKETT, John W. GRAYSON.
Delv to Geo. E. LLOYD 22 Mar 1823.

Bk:Pg: 3B:312 Date: 20 Nov 1820 RtCt: 20 Nov 1820
John HARRIS of Ldn to Sheriff Burr POWELL. B/S of house & lot on
Washington St in Mdbg (prch/o Jesse McVEIGH & Burr POWELL) –
surrendered by HARRIS for debts to Abner GIBSON, Wm. GREGG,
Joshua GREGG, John MOORE, Amos JOHNSTON. Delv. to Hugh
SMITH late Dpty Shff 24 Dec 1834.

Bk:Pg: 3B:315 Date: 30 Nov 1819 RtCt: 4 Dec 1820
Joseph LEWIS of Ldn to John HEISKELL of Winchester. Trust for
debt to John MILLER of Winchester using 140a in Piedmont Manor
now occupied with tenant Jeremiah PURDOM. Delv. to MILLER 28
Dec 1821.

Bk:Pg: 3B:318 Date: 6 Oct 1820 RtCt: 9 Dec 1820
John M. MONROE & wife Jane of Union to James CRAIG of Ldn.
Trust for debt to Henry BROWN of Ldn using ½a lot adj Union
(cnvy/b Jesse TRAHERN & wife Hannah). Delv. to BROWN 8 Mar
1823.

Bk:Pg: 3B:320 Date: 2 Sep 1819 RtCt: 14 Aug 1820
Ferdinando FAIRFAX of Washington D.C. to Thomas KIDWELL of
Ldn. B/S of 50a on blue ridge adj __ CLENDEN[ING?], __
PURSELL. Wit: Joseph PURSELL, Robert RUSSELL, Valentine
JACOBS, William HICKMAN. Delv. to KIDWELL 21 Sep 1822.

Bk:Pg: 3B:322 Date: 22 Mar 1820 RtCt: 13 Nov 1820
Nathan NEER & wife Jane of Ldn to Ebenezer GRUBB of Ldn. B/S
of rights to land in occupancy of Edward PAINTER in right of his wife
Guilma PAINTER former w/o Jonathan CONRAD dec'd who devised
lad to Guilma for life with remainder to 3 daus. Jane (now NEER),
Elizabeth (formerly HESS now widow) and Sarah (now NEER). Wit:
Craven OSBURNE, John WHITE. Delv. to GRUBB 4 Jun 1822.

Bk:Pg: 3B:325   Date: 7 Nov 1820   RtCt: 11 Dec 1820
Thomas HILLIARY & wife Jane of PrG to heirs of Walter BROOKES dec'd (widow Susanna BROOKS, Henry BROOKS, Caleb BROOKS, Eliza D. BROOKS, Samuel D. BROOKS, Walter BROOKS, Rufus BROOKS, Thomas D. BROOKS, Arther BROOKS, Susannah BROOKS, Emily BROOKES & Virginia BROOKS) of Ldn. B/S of land formerly of estate of Clement WHEELER dec'd of PrG (devised by WHEELER to son Samuel H. WHEELER and dau. Ann w/o Tilghman HILLIARY the elder, Samuel conveyed to Hilliary, prch/o Tilghman HILLARY the elder and his children Clement T., Thomas, Tilghman the younger, Mary, Sarah, William, Washington & Ann). Wit: Abraham CLARK, Thomas FERRAL by BROOKES.

Bk:Pg: 3B:328   Date: 10 Nov 1820   RtCt: 11 Dec 1820
Clement T. HILLIARY & wife Henrietta B. of PrG to heirs of Walter BROOKS dec'd late of Ldn. B/S (ratifying the sale) of land former prop. of Clement WHEELER dec'd of PrG (formerly lived in Ldn). Wit: John B. WATKINS, William Turner WOOTTON.

Bk:Pg: 3B:330   Date: 11 Sep 1820   RtCt: 13 Nov 1820
John MARTIN & wife Sarah of Ldn to Reuben MURRAY of Fqr. Trust for debt to Alcy SEATON using land prch/o heirs of Elisha POWELL dec'd, adj William LUCKETT. Wit: Burr POWELL, A. GIBSON.

Bk:Pg: 3B:333   Date: 28 Jun 1820   RtCt: 15 Nov 1820
John BOOTH Jr. of Ldn attorney in fact of John BOOTH of Jefferson Co Indiana to John GEORGE of Ldn. B/S of 83a (dev. James BOOTH f/o John by will of Robert BOOTH dec'd). Delv. to John GEORGE Jr. 31 Jul 1851.

Bk:Pg: 3B:334   Date: 21 Sep 1820   RtCt: 14 Nov 1820
Richard COCHRAN of Mdbg to William SWART of Ldn. B/S of 3a above Mdbg on turnpike road (cnvy/b Burr POWELL).

Bk:Pg: 3B:336   Date: 25 Jul 1820   RtCt: 9 Dec 1820
John GREGG & wife Phebe of Ldn to John GIBSON of Ldn. B/S of 39a (1/7th undivided part of 272a of Joseph GIBSON dec'd f/o Phebe) on pantherskin. Wit: Samuel MURRY, Pat'k McINTYRE.

Bk:Pg: 3B:338   Date: 19 Oct 1820   RtCt: 15 Nov 1820
Elizabeth JACOBS of Ldn to Valentine JACOBS of Ldn. B/S of 3a in valley of Between the Hills.

Bk:Pg: 3B:340   Date: 28 Nov 1820   RtCt: 28 Nov 1820
Jesse MILLER of Ldn to Aaron MILLER of Ldn. B/S of rights in 88a in Piedmont Manor (Jesse MILLER with Peter MILLER & wife Margaret, Dal MILLER & wife Mary, John MILLER & wife Catharine & Adam MILLER to underage Aaron in Aug 1818, DB YY:139).

Bk:Pg: 3B:341   Date: 24 May 1820   RtCt: 5 Sep 1820
Elias THRASHER of Ldn to Edward MARLOW of Ldn. Trust for debt to John MARLOW as security for THRASHER's note to John

3a (prch/o George SAGERS Sr) nr Peter
⌐op, Adam SHOVER. Wit: Jno. MATHIAS, Wm.
...artin CORDELL.

Bk:Pg: 3B:343   Date: 9 May 1820   RtCt: 11 Dec 1820
George JANNEY & wife Susanna of MontMd to Joseph MEAD of
Ldn. B/S of 104½a on NW fork of Goose Creek adj Amos GIBSON,
Joseph GORE, Benjamin BRADFIELD. Wit: Newton KEEN, Adam
LYNN, R. J. TAYLOR.

Bk:Pg: 3B:346   Date: 18 Aug 1820   RtCt: 2 Nov 1820
Charles Fenton MERCER of Aldie to Benjamin MOFFETT & wife
Malinda of Mdbg. Exchange of land on Kittocton Mt. adj Leven
LUCKETT, Moses GULICK, Tasker C. QUINLAND for 578a on Ohio
River in Mason Co VA. Wit: Burr POWELL, A. GIBSON.

Bk:Pg: 3B:348   Date: 28 May 1819   RtCt: 13 Nov 1820
James TORBERT & wife Elizabeth, Tunis TYTUS & wife Jane late
TORBERT, John KEITH & wife Sarah late TORBERT and William
TORBERT & wife Hannah to John TORBERT, Thomas TORBERT,
and Thomas FRED & wife Elizabeth. B/S of 14a adj Thomas A.
HEREFORD & Benjamin JENKINS (cnvy/b deed of Samuel
BUTCHER in Jan 1819 to surviving brothers & sisters of Samuel
TORBERT dec'd). Wit: John W. GRAYSON, Thomas GREGG.

Bk:Pg: 3B:351   Date: 22 Nov 1820   RtCt: 7 Dec 1820
William NOLAND & wife Catherine of Ldn to Samuel BAID of New
York City. Trust for debt to J. C. VANDEN HESWEL? of New York
City using 113½a nr Aldie.

Bk:Pg: 3B:356   Date: 28 Nov 1820   RtCt: 9 Dec 1820
John MARKS & wife Lydia of Ldn to Isaac NICHOLS Jr. of Ldn.
Trust for debt to Isaac & Samuel NICHOLS using land adj John
MARKS, George MARKS, road from mill to Paris and 10a. Wit:
Notley C. WILLIAMS, John W. GRAYSON. Delv. to Saml. NICHOLS
Exors 10 Nov 1825.

Bk:Pg: 3B:359   Date: 28 Aug 1817   RtCt: 9 Dec 1820
John Talaiferro BROOKE & James Mercer GARNETT (Admrs of
James MERCER late of Fredericksburg VA) to Francis HEREFORD
of Fqr. B/S of land in both Ldn & Fqr on Little River adj late John
MERCER & his sons James, George and John Francis. Wit: Chs. G.
ESKRIDGE, Jno. MATTHIAS, Thos. R. MOTT, James RUSK.

Bk:Pg: 3B:361   Date: 28 May 1819   RtCt: 3 Jan 1821
Samuel M. EDWARDS (trustee of William HANDY & wife Elenor) of
Lsbg to Richard H. HENDERSON of Lsbg. B/S of 147¼a (trust for
debt to John ROSE & Richard H. HENDERSON). Delv. to
HENDERSON 7 Feb 1826.

Bk:Pg: 3B:363   Date: 30 May 1820   RtCt: 2 Jan 1821
Thornton WALKER & wife Fanny of Ldn to John WEADON of Ldn.
B/S of ½ lot in Union adj Isaac BROWN. Wit: Wm. BRONAUGH, N.
C. WILLIAMS. Delv. to WEADON 11 Jun 1821.

Bk:Pg: 3B:364   Date: 2 Jan 1821   RtCt: 2 Jan 1821
Silas REESE & wife ___ of Ldn to Presley CORDELL of Ldn. Trust
for debt to William CLINE using 30a adj Joseph T. NEWTON,
Patrick McINTYRE. Delv. to CORDELL 26 May 1821.

Bk:Pg: 3B:365   Date: 2 Jan 1821   RtCt: 2 Jan 1821
Jacob FADELY & wife Mary of Ldn to Presley CORDELL. Trust for
debt to William JACOBS using lot on W side of King St in Lsbg
(cnvy/b Wm. JACOBS & wife Catharine and John SHAW Sr & wife
Rebecca). Delv. to John SHAW Jr. 3 Aug 1822.

Bk:Pg: 3B:367   Date: 2 Jan 1821   RtCt: 2 Jan 1821
William JACOBS & wife Catharine and John SHAW Sr (f/o
Catharine) & wife Rebecca of Ldn to Jacob FADELEY of Ldn. B/S of
lot on W side of King St in Lsbg adj William TAYLOR, Joseph
BEARD. Wit: Samuel M. EDWARDS, Thomas SANDERS. Delv. to
FADLEY 23 Jul 1823.

Bk:Pg: 3B:368   Date: 4 Oct 1820   RtCt: 2 Jan 1821
Samuel TUSTIN & wife Mary of Ldn to Joshua RILEY of Ldn. B/S of
lot in Lsbg cnvy/b Joseph SMITH & wife Mary (DB ZZ:28). Wit: Thos.
SANDERS, Samuel M. EDWARDS.

Bk:Pg: 3B:370   Date: 1 Jan 1821   RtCt: 2 Jan 1821
Joshua RILEY & wife Rachel of Lsbg to William GILLMORE of Ldn.
Trust for debt to Samuel BUCK using lot in occupancy of John
MURREY on Loudoun St in Lsbg sold to RILEY by Samuel BUCK.
Wit: Saml. M. EDWARDS, Thomas SANDERS.

Bk:Pg: 3B:372   Date: 11 Dec 1820   RtCt: 1 Jan 1821
Samuel BUCK & wife Mary of Shanandoah Co Va to Joshua RILEY
of Ldn. B/S of Lot #59 in Lsbg excepting life estate of Mrs. ELLIOT
in small log house on lot. Wit: Isaac MILLER, Will M. BAYLEY. Delv.
to RILEY 23 Apr 1823.

Bk:Pg: 3B:374   Date: 1 Jan 1821   RtCt: 2 Jan 1821
Joshua RILEY & wife Rachel of Ldn to Samuel BUCK of
Shanandoah Co Va. B/S of lot cnvy/b Henry GLASGOW (DB
VV:116). Wit: Thomas SANDERS, Samuel M. EDWARDS. Delv. to
grantee 19 Sep 1821.

Bk:Pg: 3B:376   Date: 19 Oct 1820   RtCt: 13 Nov 1820
Israel GIBSON & wife Alcy of Ldn to Thomas P. KNOX of Fqr. Trust
for debts to Euphama HAMILTON, Laban LEMORT, Elizabeth
LEMORT and Laban & Thadius LEMORT (Exors of Lewis LEMORT
dec'd), Aaron BURSON using rights to land as heir of John GIBSON
dec'd where mother Elizabeth GIBSON now resides nr Upperville.

Bk:Pg: 3B:379 Date: 13 Dec 1820 RtCt: 27 Dec 1820
Thomas ROGERS, John HOLMES & wife Mary, Arthur ROGERS and Hugh ROGERS of Ldn to Sampson BLINCOE of Ldn. Trust for debt to Enos GARRETT using rights to land of Hamilton ROGERS (GARRETT sold to Hamilton ROGERS 130a in Diggs Valley who would pay more if survey indicated more land, but ROGERS died without paying anything). Wit: S. BLINCOE, Thos. MORALEE, James GREENLEASE.

Bk:Pg: 3B:382 Date: 21 Dec 1820 RtCt: 22 Dec 1820
Samuel DUNKIN of Ldn to Richard H. HENDERSON of Ldn. Trust for debt to Joseph JANNEY of Alexandria using 88½a (prch/o Nathaniel CRAWFORD in 1804). Wit: Geo. E. LLOYD, W. D. DRISH, Benjn. MAULSBY.

Bk:Pg: 3B:383 Date: 24 Dec 1820 RtCt: 25 Dec 1820
John SHAFFER of Ldn to Robert MOFFETT. Trust for debt to Benjamin SHREVE using negroes Tom, Nace & woman Sidney, farm animals. Wit: Geo. SWEARINGEN, Adam HOUSHOLDER, Wm. SMARR.

Bk:Pg: 3B:385 Date: 8 May 1820 RtCt: 10 May 1820
Aaron DAELEY & wife Mary of Ldn to John A. BINNS of Ldn. Trust for debt to Isaac WRIGHT of Ldn using 21a. Wit: Henry H. HAMILTON, John MARTIN, Asa PECK. Wit: Presley CORDELL, Saml. M. EDWARDS. Delv. to BINNS 25 Nov 1822.

Bk:Pg: 3B:387 Date: 15 Sep 1820 RtCt: 9 Dec 1820
Isaac NICHOLS Jr. of Ldn and John GIBSON of Ldn. Agreement Joseph GIBSON (f/o John) died seized of 272a adj John GIBSON and Joseph CARR now FITZHUGH now owned by NICHOLS (4/7ths) and GIBSON (3/7ths) and John wants to build a mill on 4a. Wit: Joseph BAILES, Thomas REES.

Bk:Pg: 3B:389 Date: 25 Dec 1820 RtCt: 25 Dec 1820
John SHAFFER & wife Mary of Ldn to Francis H. CORCE? of Ldn. Trust for debt to Joseph THOMAS of FredVa using lots & mills prch/o Isaac HOUGH (11a & grist mill) and Presley WILLIAMS (70a & grist mill formerly occupied by John BALL cnvy/b Isaac STEER trustee of Susannah BALL) adj William HOUGH dec'd, Isaac BALL, schoolhouse lot, Reuben HIXSON dec'd and 138a (prch/o Jacob VIRTZ & wife Lucy, Peter VIRTZ & wife Susannah, Michael EVERHEART & wife Christina, John THOMAS & wife Margaret in 1815) and 121a (cnvy/b Lewis P. W. BALCH) and 152a (prch/o Henry WOOLF) and 61½a (prch/o TANKERVILLE) and 55½a (prch/o Ferdinando FAIRFAX). Wit: George HAMMAT, Wm. Jas. HARVEY, Deskin MONROE.

Bk:Pg: 3B:393 Date: 18 Dec 1820 RtCt: 22 Dec 1820
John SHAFFER & wife Mary of Ldn to William VIRTZ Jr. of Ldn. Trust for debt to Conrad BITZER assignee of Presley WILLIAMS of Ldn using 121a (prch/o George SWANK) and 152½a (prch/o Henry

WOOLF) and 61½a (prch/o Earl of Tankerville) and 55½a from Ferdinando FAIRFAX. Wit: Robert BRADEN, Abiel JENNERS. Delv. to VIRTZ 21 Sep 1822.

Bk:Pg: 3B:399 Date: 22 Dec 1820 RtCt: 23 Dec 1820
John SHAFFER of Ldn to Giles HAMMETT of Ldn. Trust for debt to John THOMAS using negro men Tom and Voll, mulatto woman Sidney, farm animals and items. Wit: Chs. G. ESKRIDGE, Wm. James HANLEY, Deskin MONROE. Delv. to THOMAS 2 Jun 1821.

Bk:Pg: 3B:400 Date: 18 Dec 1820 RtCt: 21 Dec 1820
John SHAFFER & wife Mary to Lewis P. W. BALCH of Lsbg. Trust for debt to John THOMAS of Lsbg, Peter COMPHER, Frederick SLATZ, John GEORGE, Emanuel WALTMAN, Philip HEATER using lots mentioned in 3B:393. Wit: Robert BRADEN, Thos. J. MARLOW. Delv. to L. P. W. BALCH pr Geo. RICHARDS 2 Jul 1821.

Bk:Pg: 3B:404 Date: 11 Dec 1820 RtCt: 11 Dec 1820
Aaron BURSON of Ldn to John DUNKIN & wife Ruth. Release of trust for debt to Philip FRY dated May 1815.

Bk:Pg: 3B:406 Date: 11 Dec 1820 RtCt: 11 Dec 1820
Cornelius BENNETT of Ldn to John McCORMACK & William CHILTON of Ldn. Trust for debt to James H. HAMILTON using negro man Hector, farm animals. Delv. to Jno. McCORMICK 25 Sep 1821.

Bk:Pg: 3B:407 Date: 9 Sep 1820 RtCt: 11 Dec 1820
Samuel GOVER of Wtfd to Samuel JACKSON of Wtfd. B/S of lot on W side of Market St in Lsbg prch/o Jesse GOVER. Delv. to JACKSON 30 Jan 1829.

Bk:Pg: 3B:408 Date: 7 Nov 1820 RtCt: 11 Dec 1820
Maurice MOORE to sons Thomas and Pierce MOORE. B/S of rights to carry on and regulate business such as farming, coopering and all other business, making all over to Thomas. Wit: Margaret MOORE, Elizabeth MOORE. Delv. pr order 13 Jan 1826.

Bk:Pg: 3B:409 Date: 5 Sep 1820 RtCt: 11 Dec 1820
Samuel GOVER of Ldn to William KNETTLE of Ldn. B/S of ¼a Lot #9 in new addition of Wtfd. Delv. to NETTLE 5 Mar 1830.

Bk:Pg: 3B:410 Date: 6 Dec 1820 RtCt: 11 Dec 1820
John SINCLAIR of Ldn to Burr POWELL & Abner GIBSON of Ldn. Trust for debts to Noble BEVERIDGE now in hands of sheriff, Robert BRADEN, Robert MONROE ass'ee of John POTTER, Abel JANNEY using 84a – 54a (cnvy/b James SINCLAIR) and 30a (cnvy/b Admrs of James Mercer GARRETT) and 150a in Belmont Co OH from estate of father James SINCLAIR dec'd and negro man Frank abt 37-38y prch/o James SANGSTER and farm and household items. Wit: Thomas ROGERS, Hiram McVEIGH, Benj. SMITH. Delv. to Hugh SMITH per order of Burr POWELL 27 Sep 1821.

Bk:Pg: 3B:413   Date: 28 Jun 1820   RtCt: 12 Dec 1820
John BOOTH Jr. of Ldn attorney for John BOOTH of Jefferson Co
Indiana to James BOOTH of Ldn. B/S of 60a part of tract dev. John
BOOTH by will of Robert BOOTH dec'd.

Bk:Pg: 3B:415   Date: 28 Mar 1820   RtCt: 14 Dec 1820
Jesse CARTER (Admr of Jacob DRAKE dec'd) of Ldn and Sarah
DRAKE (wd/o Jacob DRAKE). Agreement – DRAKE had trust to
Abner HUMPHREY and John W. B. GRAYSON for debt due to
Benjamin GRAYSON Esq. DRAKE's children: Urier, Margaret and
Mary Ann all <21y. Debts paid. Sarah to get 1/3 use of 101½a which
CARTER purchased for Sarah. Wit: Edw'd B. GRADY, Wm.
BRONAUGH, Jno. W. T. BRONAUGH, Benjamin GRAYSON.

Bk:Pg: 3B:416   Date: 13 Dec 1820   RtCt: 14 Dec 1820
William TAYLOR of Ldn to James RUST of Ldn. B/S of 17a adj
RUST nr Lsbg. Delv. to RUST 28 May 1836.

Bk:Pg: 3B:418   Date: 13 Dec 1820   RtCt: 14 Dec 1820
James RUST & wife Sarah of Ldn to William TAYLOR of Ldn. B/S of
6a adj __ ROBERTS, TAYLOR and RUST. Wit: Presley CORDELL,
Thomas SANDERS. Delv. to Joseph MEAD pr order of R. G.
TAYLOR 23 May 1836.

Bk:Pg: 3B:419   Date: 15 Dec 1820   RtCt: 16 Dec 1820
Joseph CAVENS and Zachariah DULANY & wife Mary Eleanor of
Ldn to Benjamin GRUBB of Ldn. B/S of 2a adj William WRIGHT,
road from Wtfd to Nolands Ferry. Wit: Robert BRADEN, Abiel
JENNERS. Delv. to B. GRUBB 14 Aug 1821.

Bk:Pg: 3B:421   Date: 19 Oct 1820   RtCt: 16 Dec 1820
John CRIDELLER & wife Elizabeth of Ldn to William EMMERSON
and Judson EMERSON of Ldn. B/S of lot on N side of Loudoun St in
Lsbg. Wit: John McCORMICK, Presley CORDELL.

Bk:Pg: 3B:423   Date: 26 Sep 1820   RtCt: 16 Dec 1820
Peter BENEDUM & wife Catherine of Ldn to Charles BINNS of Ldn.
B/S of 20a adj Geo. RUST. Wit: Presley CORDELL, Thomas
SANDERS. Delv. to BINNS 19 May 1836.

Bk:Pg: 3B:425   Date: 13 Dec 1820   RtCt: 16 Dec 1820
James GREENLEES & wife Catherine of Ldn to Enos GARRETT of
Ldn. B/S of 11a where GREENLEES now resides. Wit: Samuel M.
EDWARDS, Presley CORDELL. Delv. to GARRETT 24 May 1824.

Bk:Pg: 3B:426   Date: 6 Dec 1820   RtCt: 16 Dec 1820
Aaron MILLER of Ldn to Charles CRIM Sr. of Ldn. B/S of 88a in
Piedmont Manor (cnvy/b Moses MILLER to Peter MILLER Sr.) adj
George SHOEMAKER, Peter VIRTS. Delv. pr order 26 Jul 1824.

Bk:Pg: 3B:428   Date: 26 Sep 1820   RtCt: 16 Dec 1820
Samuel M. EDWARDS (trustee of Peter BENEDUM & wife
Catharine of Ldn for debt to John WALKER of FredMd) to Charles

BINNS of Ldn. B/S of 46a on road to Cobbins Gap. Wit: Presley CORDELL, Thomas SANDERS. Delv. to BINNS 10 May 1836.

Bk:Pg: 3B:430 Date: 16 May 1820 RtCt: 20 Dec 1820
William CHILTON & wife Sarah H. of Ldn to Jesse RICE. Trust of 250a adj Geo. CARTER, Tasker QUINLAN, William CHILTON. Wit: John McCORMICK, Saml. M. EDWARDS.

Bk:Pg: 3B:432 Date: 30 Jul 1820 RtCt: 21 Dec 1820
John MARKS & wife Lydia of Ldn to Benjamin STRINGFELLOW of Ldn. B/S of 50a cnvy/b Stephen McPHERSON, adj George MARKS, Isaiah B. BEANS. Wit: Notley C. WILLIAMS, John W. GRAYSON. Delv. pr order 23 Feb 1823.

Bk:Pg: 3B:434 Date: 21 Dec 1820 RtCt: 22 Dec 1820
John SHAVER & wife Mary of Ldn to William WIRTZ Jr. of Ldn. B/S of 83¾a on Potomac adj Leonard POSTON, Wm. WINNER, Christian BEAGLE. Wit: Robert BRADEN, Abiel JENNERS. Delv. to Wm. WIRTZ Jr. 3 Jul 1820.

Bk:Pg: 3B:436 Date: 21 Dec 1820 RtCt: 22 Dec 1820
George E. LLOYD of Ldn to Richard H. HENDERSON of Ldn. Trust for debt to Joseph JANNEY using house & lot in Union. Delv. to HENDERSON 16 Dec 1830.

Bk:Pg: 3B:437 Date: 18 Dec 1819 RtCt: 8 Jan 1821
William CAMPBELL & wife Margaret of Belmont Co OH to Samuel BEAVERS of Ldn. B/S of interest of Margaret (child and heir) dower land of mother Rebecca REED wd/o James REED dec'd. Delv. to BEAVERS 28 Feb 1825.

Bk:Pg: 3B:439 Date: 17 Apr 1801 RtCt: 9 Jan 1821
Thomas NOLAND (of Philip), Enos NOLAND & wife Ann of FredMd to Solomon DAVIS of FredMd. B/S of 164a on road to Nolands Ferry (bought by Philip NOLAND of Richard ABERRY). Wit: Thos. NOLAND, Thos. AWBERY, James NEALE.

Bk:Pg: 3B:440 Date: 26 Jun 1818 RtCt: 8 Jan 1821
Thomas KIDWELL of Ldn to Thomas SWANN of AlexDC. Trust for debt to John MATHIAS using 2 tracts totaling 99a.

Bk:Pg: 3B:442 Date: 11 Nov 1814 RtCt: 8 Jan 1821
Archibald McVICKERS of Ldn to Stephen GARRET of Ldn. Trust for debt to George BROWN, Robert ROSE & William HARDING of Ldn using 356a where McVICKERS, George BROWN, Enos DRAKE & Thomas HARDESTY now live. Wit: S. BLINCOE, Ed'd HAMMAT, Chs. THRIFT.

Bk:Pg: 3B:443 Date: 14 Mar 1820 RtCt: 8 Jan 1821
William LANE of Ldn to Richard H. LEE of Ldn. Trust for debt to T. C. QUINLAN and M. CHICHESTER using lot & house in Lsbg bought of Mr. OGDEN.

Bk:Pg: 3B:444   Date: 8 Jan 1821   RtCt: 8 Jan 1821
Alexander CORDELL, Adam HOUSEHOLDER, Robert MOFFETT &
Sandford RAMEY. Bond on CORDELL as constable.

Bk:Pg: 3B:444   Date: 9 Jan 1821   RtCt: 9 Jan 1821
George H. ALLDER, Lewis LYDER & Ben. BRADFIELD. Bond on
ALLDER as constable.

Bk:Pg: 3B:445   Date: 23 Aug 1820   RtCt: 8 Jan 1821
Central Bank of Georgetown and Washington to Farmers and
Mechanics Bank of Georgetown. B/S of residue of debt - Joseph
LEWIS Jr. of Ldn in debt to Central Bank with 1 note dated Oct 1817
payable to Thomas T. GANTT now dec'd using 'Clifton' estate.
LEWIS gave trust on land in Jun 1819 to Aaron R. LEVERING,
Elisha RIGGS and William THOMPSON Jr. of Georgetown. Wit: W.
NICHOLLS, Hor'o C. SCOTT, Wm. THOMPSON, James A.
MAGRUDER, Thomas PEABODY.

Bk:Pg: 3B:449   Date: 2 Jan 1821   RtCt: 8 Jan 1821
Robert Alexander WHITACRE. Col from MontMd during last 2
weeks of slaves Phill a yellow man abt 33y, black boy Dory abt 13-
14y, Sopha a black woman abt 20y, yellow girl Milley abt 9y, Charles
a black child 1-2y.

Bk:Pg: 3B:449   Date: 9 Aug 1820   RtCt: 8 Jan 1821
William JENKINS of Ldn. CoE for negro man Adam 44y old. Wit:
Henry HUFF, Edward MARLOW. Delv. to negro Adam 14 Jan 1828.

Bk:Pg: 3B:450   Date: 31 Mar 1818   RtCt: 8 Jan 1821
Nicholas OSBURN of Ldn to Joshua GREGG & Lewis LYDER of
Ldn. Trust for debt to James WARFORD using 125a cnvy/b
WARFORD. Delv. to Joshua GREGG 17 Jan 1823.

Bk:Pg: 3C:001   Date: 7 Dec 1820   RtCt: 8 Dec 1820
Edward DORSEY & wife Mary of Ldn to Robert BRADEN & Daniel
STONE of Ldn. Trust for debt to James NIXON using 19a on E side
of Catocton Creek (prch/o Charles ELGIN in Apr 1818) adj Wm.
JANNEY. Delv. to BRADEN 20 Feb 1824.

Bk:Pg: 3C:003   Date: 11 Jan 1821   RtCt: 9 Feb 1821
Andrew MARTIN of Ldn to M. B. WEEKS & E. G. HAMILTON of
Ldn. Trust for debt to Abner GIBSON using negro woman Noaroh,
boy Daniel, girls Mary & Lete and farm and household items. Delv.
to WEEKS & HAMILTON 20 May 1822.

Bk:Pg: 3C:004   Date: 2 Jan 1820   RtCt: 9 Jan 1821
Richard H. HENDERSON (as commr) of Ldn to George HANCOCK
of FredVa. B/S of 650a Heath's, Hawley's & Foley's Lots in decree
of Alfred G. CARTER to George HANCOCK. Delv. to HANCOCK 12
Mar 1821.

Bk:Pg: 3C:006   Date: 19 Jan 1821   RtCt: 29 Jan 1821
Sydnor BAILEY & John GIBSON Jr. (trustees of John BUCHANAN)
to David NIXON of Ldn. B/S of land on Little Miami on Ohio granted

by Pres. John ADAMS to Peregrine FITZHUGH in 1797 and devised by Michael BUCHANAN to John. Wit: Caldwell CARR, Randolph RHODES, Cuthbert POWELL. Delv. to Wm. CARR 13 Apr 1821.

Bk:Pg: 3C:008   Date: 8 Sep 1820   RtCt: 1 Jan 1821
Henly BOGGESS of Fqr to Sampson BLINCOE of Ldn. Trust for debt to John CARR & Archibald MAINS using 220a devised by will of Samuel BOGGESS dec'd. Wit: Towns'd McVEIGH, R. J. FLEMING, John PEIRCE. Delv. to John CARR 5 May 1823.

Bk:Pg: 3C:010   Date: 16 Oct 1820   RtCt: 8 Jan 1821
Francis PIERPOINT of Ldn to Sanford EDMONDS of Ldn. B/S of lot on E side of Market St in Lsbg (prch/o Richard RICHARDSON).

Bk:Pg: 3C:011   Date: 1 May 1819   RtCt: 16 Jun 1819/8 Jan 1821
John H. CRIDLER & wife Mary to Wm. H. HANDY trustee for Thos. A. DENNIS. Trust for debts to Thomas A. DENNIS, James BOALS, Abraham SKILMAN assignee of Wm. COE, Presley SAUNDERS using property of late father and household items. Delv. to HANDEY 27 Jun 1821.

Bk:Pg: 3C:012   Date: 8 Jan 1821   RtCt: 8 Jan 1821
Tasker Carter QUINLAN of Ldn to George CARTER of Oatlands. B/S of 12a adj lease of Robert CARTER of Naming to SHORES, FIELDS, GORHAM and PARTRIC. Delv. to Wm. L. COCKERILL pr order 27 Feb 1822.

Bk:Pg: 3C:014   Date: 8 Jan 1821   RtCt: 8 Jan 1821
William ALT & wife Susannah of Ldn to Bazil NEWMAN of Ldn. B/S of 47a on Edward's ferry road. Wit: John McCORMICK, Thomas SANDERS.

Bk:Pg: 3C:015   Date: 11 Nov 1820   RtCt: 9 Jan 1821
Amos FERGUSON of Ldn to John SINCLAIR of Ldn. Trust for debt to Margaret ONEAL of MontMd using 150a on Little River where he lives. Wit: John SINCLAIR, James M. BOYD, Henry DYER.

Bk:Pg: 3C:017   Date: 9 Jan 1821   RtCt: 9 Jan 1821
William COOPER (a rep. of Robert HAMILTON dec'd) & wife Eleanor of Lsbg to Alexander COOPER Jr. of Ldn. B/S of lot at corner of Loudoun & Back Sts. in Lsbg. Delv. to Alexr COOPER Jr. 24 Aug 1821.

Bk:Pg: 3C:018   Date: 10 May 1819   RtCt: 10 Jan 1821
George COOPER & wife Mary of Ldn to John AXLINE Jr. of Ldn. B/S of 10a on E side of short hill (prch/o Joseph LEWIS Jr.) adj David MULL. Wit: John H. McCABE, Saml. HOUGH Jr. Delv. to AXLINE 19 Aug 1827.

Bk:Pg: 3C:020   Date: 11 Jan 1821   RtCt: 11 Jan 1821
John BOOTH of Jefferson Co Indiana to Margaret MULL (wd/o David MULL), Geo. MULL & Elizabeth MULL of Ldn. B/S of interest in tract that David MULL prch/o John BOOTH the elder.

Bk:Pg: 3C:021   Date: 27 Dec 1820   RtCt: 12 Jan 1821
Benjamin Dulaney CLAGETT & wife Mary of Ffx to Thomas K.
BEALLE of Ffx. Trust for debt to William C. NEWTON using land on
Potomac allotted to mother Julia CLAGETT referred to in deed by
Benjamin DULANEY & wife Elizabeth dated Dec 1813 in Ffx. Wit:
John CROMWELL, William DAVID, Jos. B. DANIELS.

Bk:Pg: 3C:025   Date: 17 Jan 1821   RtCt: 18 Jan 1821
James RUST to Richard H. HENDERSON. B/S of 12' in front of his
lot.

**Bk:Pg: 3C:025   Date: 22 Jul 1820   RtCt: 27 Nov 1820/16 Jan
1821**
Levi WILLIAMS & wife Sarah of Ldn to David SMITH of Ldn. B/S of
7a on NW fork of Goose Creek adj Benjamin BRADFIELD, Joseph
GORE. Wit: Jesse S. WILSON, Henry T. BAYNE, Stephen WILSON,
Thomas SANDERS, William CARR. Delv. to SMITH 2 Jul 1825.

Bk:Pg: 3C:027   Date: 13 Dec 1820   RtCt: 16 Jan 1821
David SMITH of Ldn to David F. BEALL of Ldn. B/S of 5a on NW
fork of Goose Creek adj BEALL, Elizabeth BOLEN (prch/o Enos
POTTS). Wit: Henry T. BAYNE, Chas. JAMES, William B.
LIVINGSTON.

Bk:Pg: 3C:029   Date: 16 Jan 1821   RtCt: 16 Jan 1821
Levi WILLIAMS & wife Sarah of Ldn to Ann WATKINS of Ldn. B/S of
13a on NW fork of Goose Creek adj Isaac & Samuel NICHOLS,
William ALLEN, Elizabeth BOLEN, David SMITH, Elizabeth DAY
(prch/o Enos POTTS). Delv. pr order 22 Jul 1834.

Bk:Pg: 3C:031   Date: 13 Dec 1820   RtCt: 16 Jan 1821
David F. BEALL & wife Elizabeth of Ldn to David SMITH of Ldn. B/S
of 5a on NW fork of Goose Creek adj SMITH (prch/o William
PIGGOTT). Wit: Presley CORDELL, Thomas SANDERS. Delv. to
SMITH 2 Jul 1825.

Bk:Pg: 3C:033   Date: 22 Jul 1820   RtCt: 16 Jan 1821
David SMITH of Ldn to Levi WILLIAMS of Ldn. B/S of 4a on NW fork
of Goose Creek adj Giles CRAVEN (part of prch/o Stephen
WILSON). Wit: Jesse S. WILSON, Henry T. BAYNE, Stephen
WILSON.

Bk:Pg: 3C:034   Date: 15 Jan 1821   RtCt: 15 Jan 1821
Benjamin SHREVES (trustee of Presley WILLIAMS) of Ldn to Aaron
MILLER of Ldn. B/S of all rights of WILLIAMS to land allotted to
Mary HIXON wd/o Reuben HIXON dec'd (with consent from
WILLIAMS and John SHAFFER whom he owed).

Bk:Pg: 3C:035   Date: 15 Jan 1821   RtCt: 15 Jan 1821
Alexander RICHARDSON & Nelson S. HUTCHISON & wife Lydia of
Ldn to Joseph HILLIARD of Ldn. B/S of 1a nr Lsbg adj John GRAY.
Wit: Saml. M. EDWARDS, Thomas SANDERS.

Bk:Pg: 3C:037 Date: 15 Jan 1821 RtCt: 15 Jan 1821
Presley WILLIAMS & wife Jane of Ldn to Aaron MILLER of Ldn. B/S of all rights of WILLIAMS to land allotted to Mary HIXON wd/o Reuben HIXON dec'd (Mary getting 1/6th part of share). Wit: Thos. SANDERS, Saml. M. EDWARDS. Delv. to MILLER 26 May 1823.

Bk:Pg: 3C:039 Date: 27 Dec 1820 RtCt: 12 Jan 1821
Benjamin Dulaney CLAGET of Ffx to William C. NEWTON. PoA. Wit: Thos. K. BEALL, John CROMWELL, Joseph B. DANIELS, William DAVIS.

Bk:Pg: 3C:040 Date: 24 Aug 1820 RtCt: 15 Jan 1821
Charles F. MERCER (devisee of James MERCER dec'd and of John F. MERCER dec'd) to Mary MASON and John T. MASON (devisees of Stephens T. MASON). B/S of 907a.

Bk:Pg: 3C:044 Date: 11 Jan 1821 RtCt: 5 Feb 1821
Arthur ORRISON & wife Elizabeth of Ldn to Thomas J. NOLAND of Ldn. Trust for debt to William NOLAND of Ldn using 228a on Little River Turnpike road prch/o William NOLAND. Wit: Aris BUCKNER, Robert ARMISTEAD. Delv. to NOLAND 2 May 1834.

Bk:Pg: 3C:046 Date: 5 Feb 1821 RtCt: 5 Feb 1821
Patrick B. MILHOLLAN to Francis H. CANE. Trust for benefit of children Sarah, Ewell, Patrick and Diadama MILHOLLAN using monies due from Robert MOFFETT paid annually from sale of land. Wit: Truman RIDDLE, John MARTIN, John HAWLING.

Bk:Pg: 3C:047 Date: 14 Jul 1820 RtCt: 7 Feb 1821
John V. BUSKIRK of FredVa to Joseph TIDBALL and Isaac BAKER of FredVa. Mortgage of land on Goose Creek with water grist mill and saw mill called 'Ball's mill' cnvy/b TIDBALL to BUSKIRK. Wit: Geo. BRENT, Wm. M. HOLLIDAY. Forwarded to Isaac BAKER 28 Mar 1823.

Bk:Pg: 3C:050 Date: 15 Jan 1821 RtCt: 9 Feb 1821
James H. DULANEY of Ldn to Hugh SMITH of Ldn. Trust for debts to Sarah LANE, Hiram HARROVER, Harry HEATH & Beverly RANDOLPH, William PHILLIPS, Wm. STROTHER, Dawson McCORMACK, James SANDERSON, Robert F. DEGGE, Richard COLEMAN using 250a obtained from late father Benj'n DULANEY adj Jno. P. DULANEY, Wm. VICKERS, Hiram SEATON, Mrs. Jemima LEWIS. Delv. to SMITH 9 Jul 1821.

Bk:Pg: 3C:052 Date: 9 Feb 1821 RtCt: 9 Feb 1821
Thomas CHINN Sr. of Ldn to Richard H. HENDERSON of Ldn. Trust for debt to Walter JENKINS of BaltMd using land in Ldn & Fqr devised from father Thomas CHINN dec'd late of Ldn. Wit: Edw'd HAMMAT, Giles HAMMAT, Thomas A. MOORE.

Bk:Pg: 3C:053 Date: 13 Feb 1821 RtCt: 13 Feb 1821
Thomas FOUCH & wife Sarah of Ldn to son Amos FOUCH of Ldn for benefit of children. B/S of 100a on upper side of Goose Creek. Delv. to Amos FOUCH 30 Apr 1823.

Bk:Pg: 3C:055 Date: 11 Nov 1819 RtCt: 12 Feb 1821
Ferdinando FAIRFAX of Washington to Christopher NEALE of AlexDC. B/S of 586a in Shannondale. Gives plats and details. Wit: E. J. LEE Jr., W. A. HARRIS, M. BAYLY Jr. Delv. to Jno. J. MATHIAS pr order 30 Apr 1821.

Bk:Pg: 3C:059 Date: 27 Mar 1820 RtCt: 20 May 1820
Pat. B. MILHOLLEN to Robert MOFFETT. PoA to agreed cancellation of bargain with Matthew MITCHELL. Delv. to MOFFETT 4 Apr 1822.

Bk:Pg: 3C:060 Date: 17 Mar 1820 RtCt: 20 May 1820
Pat. B. MILHOLLEN & wife Malinda and Robert MOFFETT. Agreement – concerning all lands (300-400a) in possession of Matthew MITCHELL except 10a not in his possession which were inherited from father Pat MILHOLLAND and all lands prch/o Thomas MILHOLLAND, Jonathan MILHOLLAND & from Mary GRANT, lands he bought of John MILHOLLAND yet has no deed. Wit: Tho. R. MOTT, A. O. POWELL, Giles HAMMAT. Delv. to MOFFETT 24 Aug 1821.

Bk:Pg: 3C:062 Date: 13 Oct 1820 RtCt: 12 Feb 1821
Anthony CONNARD & wife Mary of Ldn to David CONNARD of Ldn. B/S of 1a on road from Lsbg to Noland ferry. Wit: Chas. ELGIN, Westwood T. MASON, Wm. WRIGHT. Delv. pr order in DB HHH:78 of 25 Nov 1820.

Bk:Pg: 3C:063 Date: 15 May 1818 RtCt: 12 Feb 1821
David GIBSON to Burr POWELL. Trust of 25 Dec 1813 for use of Nancy GIBSON w/o D. GIBSON during her life. Delv to Hugh SMITH pr order of Burr POWELL 12 Nov 1821.

Bk:Pg: 3C:066 Date: 2 Jan 1821 RtCt: 12 Feb 1821
Florence McCARTY of Ldn to Peter SKINNER of Ldn. B/S of house & lot, farm animals, household items. Wit: Samuel RUSK, Dennis McCARTY, Abraham FULTON. Delv. to SKINNER 7 Apr 1826.

Bk:Pg: 3C:067 Date: 22 Aug 1818 RtCt: 12 Feb 1821
John SCHOOLEY, Wm. H. HOUGH & Daniel STONE (Exors of William HOUGH dec'd) of Ldn to Nero LAWSON Jr of Ldn. B/S of lot in Wtfd adj Nathan MINOR.

Bk:Pg: 3C:069 Date: 3 Oct 1820 RtCt: 12 Feb 1821
John MARKS & wife Lydia of Ldn to Isaiah B. BEANS of Ldn. B/S of 2a (cnvy/b Stephen McPHERSON) adj BEANS. Wit: Notley C. WILLIAMS, John W. GRAYSON.

Bk:Pg: 3C:071   Date: 39 Jan 1821   RtCt: 12 Feb 1821
Joseph RICHARDSON & wife Susan of Ldn to John MARKS of Ldn.
B/S of 8a (part of land formerly owned by Mary OVERFIELD) adj
Charles RUSSELL, Jehu BURSON, Martin OVERFIELD (now in
possession of Edward MUDD and to remain so and extend to his
heirs). Wit: Notley C. WILLIAMS, John W. GRAYSON.

Bk:Pg: 3C:073   Date: 30 Jan 1821   RtCt: 12 Feb 1821
John MARTIN (now in jail for debts) & wife Sarah, Edward MARTIN,
Andrew MARTIN & wife Jemimah and John LEWIS & wife Mary of
Ldn to Francis W. LUCKETT & Minor FURR of Ldn. Trust for debts
to James MACHLAN, John WILKINSON & Gourley REEDER,
Joseph FREDD Admr of Zepheniah ROBERTS, James LEATH Exor
of James LEATH dec'd, JENKINS and LLOYD, Josiah MURREY &
Co, James RUST and Joseph EACHES, Hiram SEATON, William
BARSON & Henry BARSON, HOLY and SUCKLEY, Jos. HILLIARD
ass'ee of Rich'd H. HENDERSON. Samuel CHINN and Hiram
SEATON as security for John MARTIN in Prison Bounds using all
land which their father William MARTIN prch/o William SAVAGE. 36-
37a (prch/o heirs of Elisha POWELL) and 52a he leases where he
now lives and all personal property. Wit: S. BLINCOE, John
CAVINS, Joseph CAVINS, E. G. HAMILTON, Asa ROGERS, John
McCORMICK, Presley CORDELL, Wm. BRONAUGH, A. GIBSON.

Bk:Pg: 3C:079   Date: 6 Jan 1821   RtCt: 12 Feb 1821
Stephanson HIXSON & wife Alice of Ldn to George W. SHAWEN
and David SHAWEN of Ldn. B/S of 5a allotted from lands of Reuben
HIXSON dec'd and 9a on N side of Cotocton Creek. Wit: Robert
BRADEN, Saml. HOUGH Jr. Delv. to David SHAWEN 25 Mar 1826.

Bk:Pg: 3C:081   Date: 19 Aug 1820   RtCt: 12 Feb 1821
Daniel BROWN & wife Rachel of Ldn to Usher SKINNER of Ldn.
B/S of 52½a (cnvy/b Aaron BURSON). Wit: Wm. BRONAUGH,
Francis W. LUCKETT.

Bk:Pg: 3C:083   Date: 13 Feb 1821   RtCt: 13 Feb 1821
Frederick BROOKES of Ldn to Charles BIRD, Alexander
SYMINGTON & George HANDY (firm of Charles BIRD & Co) of
PhilPa. Mortgage on 2a of 14y lease on land of Matthew RUST with
building with 3 carding machines and fulling mill.

Bk:Pg: 3C:084   Date: 13 Feb 1821   RtCt: 13 Feb 1821
John SHAFFER & wife Mary of Ldn to John THOMAS of Ldn. Trust
to David AXLINE, Michael EVERHEART & Manuel AXLINE of Ldn
(as security for SHAFFER in prison bond of NIXON) using 1a (DB
YY:132) and personal items. Delv. to THOMAS 23 Jul 1821.

Bk:Pg: 3C:087   Date: 20 Jan 1821   RtCt: 22 Jan 1821
Thomas CHINN of Ldn to Humphrey B. POWELL of Ldn. Trust for
debt to Abner GIBSON using 95¼a on N side of Ashby's Gap
Turnpike adj Burr POWELL. Wit: Asa ROGERS, Burr WEEKS, H.
SMITH.

Bk:Pg: 3C:089   Date: 30 Jan 1821   RtCt: 14 Feb 1821
Alfred H. POWELL & wife Nancy of FredVa to Joseph LEWIS of
Ldn. B/S of 321a adj former distillery, George GIBSON's shop,
Cuthbert POWELL, road leading to Clifton Mill, Mandly TAYLOR,
road to GIBSON's Mill, Mrs. Sarah R. POWELL, James RUST,
Leven M. POWELL. Gives plat. Delv. to LEWIS 5 Dec 1832.

Bk:Pg: 3C:093   Date: 15 Feb 1821   RtCt: 15 Feb 1821
Lot T. JANNEY of Ldn to Mahlon CRAVEN of Ldn. BoS for farm and
household items. Wit: John PURCEL, John HOLMES.

Bk:Pg: 3C:095   Date: 10 Feb 1821   RtCt: 19 Feb 1821
William B. SHIPLEY of Lsbg to William KING of Lsbg. Trust for use
of wife Nancy L. SHIPLEY & infant son using household items. Wit:
John CARNEY, James McDANIEL.

Bk:Pg: 3C:096   Date: 19 Feb 1821   RtCt: 19 Feb 1821
Marcus HUMPHREY (insolvent) of Ldn to Sheriff Burr POWELL. B/S
of 1/10th interest in 40a in occupancy of widow of Abel MARKS dec'd
and 1/10th interest in 600a in KY in right of wife Peggy late MARKS.
Wit: Fleet SMITH, Wm. JAMES, Wm. James HENLEY.

Bk:Pg: 3C:098   Date: 24 Feb 1821   RtCt: 26 Feb 1821
George SANDERS & wife Elizabeth of Ldn to James WEST of Ldn.
B/S of 4a adj Jacob RUSE. Wit: Robert BRADEN, Abiel JENNERS.
Delv. to WEST 3 Feb 1844.

Bk:Pg: 3C:099   Date: 26 Feb 1821   RtCt: 26 Feb 1821
David BOSS & wife Eliza of MontMd to brother Samuel M. BOSS of
Lsbg. B/S of interest in lot with 2-story brick house on NE corner of
Loudoun & King Sts in Lsbg and lot adj Robert HOUGH, Charles
BALL, Joshua RILEY, Saml. E. EDWARDS (prop. of father Peter
BOSS dec'd leaving his widow Mary BOSS, Peter BOSS, Saml. M.
BOSS, Daniel C. BOSS, Abraham J. BOSS, David BOSS, Mary
HAWKE (now Mary MARTIN) and Wm. HAWKE children of
Margaret HAWKE dec'd d/o Peter dec'd and Saml. BOSS s/o Jacob
BOSS dec'd a s/o Peter dec'd). Wit: Thomas SANDERS, Saml. M.
EDWARDS. Delv. to Saml. M. BOSS 18 May 1821.

Bk:Pg: 3C:102   Date: 24 Feb 1821   RtCt: 26 Feb 1821
George SANDERS & wife Elizabeth of Ldn to Frederick BELTZ of
Ldn. B/S of 36a (in div. of Nicholas SANDERS dec'd). Wit: Robert
BRADEN, Abiel JENNERS. Delv. to BELTZ 13 Aug 1827.

Bk:Pg: 3C:104   Date: 27 Feb 1821   RtCt: 27 Feb 1821
Isaac WRIGHT & wife Susannah of Ldn to Samuel CARR of Ldn.
B/S of two quarters on SW side of Turnpike Road from Lsbg to
Goose Creek Bridge adj William GILMORE, Benjamin SHREVE,
Saml CARR. Wit: S. B. T. CALDWELL, Josiah L. DREAN, Jno.
MOOR[E], Presley CORDELL, Thomas SANDERS.

Bk:Pg: 3C:106   Date: 7 Dec 1820   RtCt: 27 Feb 1821
Yeoman Michael PLAISTER & wife Jane of Ldn to housecarpenter
Craven WALKER of Ldn. B/S of ¼a lot in SE corner of Union
including lot assigned to Margaret CAMPBELL & fractional lot
assigned to Jonathan REID in div. of James REID Sr. dec'd. Wit:
Wm. BRONAUGH, Francis W. LUCKETT. Delv. to Willis TRIPLETT
pr order of WALKER 11 Jun 1821.

Bk:Pg: 3C:108   Date: 27 Feb 1821   RtCt: 27 Feb 1821
Daniel HOWELL of Ldn to George LICKEY of Ldn. Trust for debt to
LICKEY using household items.

Bk:Pg: 3C:110   Date: 12 Feb 1817   RtCt: 2 Mar 1821
Benjamin HOUGH & wife Mary of Ldn to Amasa HOUGH of Ldn.
B/S of 5a (part of tract devised by father William HOUGH dec'd).
Wit: Abiel JENNERS, John H. McCABE. Delv. to HOUGH 27 Mar
1822.

Bk:Pg: 3C:112   Date: 14 Feb 1821   RtCt: 3 Mar 1821
Joseph LEWIS Jr. of Ldn to Richard H. HENDERSON of Ldn. Trust
for debt to Alfred H. POWELL of FredVa using 105a in occupancy of
Mrs. Elizabeth SMITH adj John GEORGE, William EVERHEART
and 70a in occupancy of Jacob VIRTZ adj David AXLINE, Mathias
SMIDLEY, both in Piedmont Manor.

Bk:Pg: 3C:114   Date: 3 Mar 1821   RtCt: 3 Mar 1821
John M. MONROE of Ldn to Sheriff Burr POWELL. B/S of 110a in
Island of New Foundland nr Bergen ins'd? Island (1/20th of tract of
2200a left by will of Capt. John NEWMAN) and house & lot in
Union.

Bk:Pg: 3C:116   Date: 25 Jan 1821   RtCt: 3 Mar 1821
William H. DORSEY of Ldn to Henry BROWN of Ldn. B/S of lot N of
Union with use of well pump and water adj Samuel DUNKIN, Isaac
BROWN (cnvy/b Jesse TRAHERN). Delv. to BROWN 25 Mar 1822.

Bk:Pg: 3C:118   Date: 13 Feb 1821   RtCt: 1 Mar 1821
Peter BENEDUM Jr. of Ldn to John BENEDUM of Ldn. B/S of lot on
N side of Market St in Lsbg to east of late Peter BOSS dec'd. Wit: S.
BLINCOE, John CAVINS, John MURRY.

Bk:Pg: 3C:119   Date: 26 Sep 1820   RtCt: 7 Mar 1821
Peter BENEDUM Jr. of Lsbg to Sampson BLINCOE of Lsbg. Trust
for debt to Henry BENEDUM & John BENEDUM using lot on N side
of Loudoun St in Lsbg adj Peter BOSS dec'd. Wit: Henry
BROOKES, Henry KENT.

Bk:Pg: 3C:121   Date: 20 Feb 1821   RtCt: 8 Mar 1821
John MOUNT & wife Mary Ann of Ldn to William BRONAUGH of
Ldn. Trust for debt to Stephen McGEATH using 102a. Wit: Francis
W. LUCKETT, John W. GRAYSON. Delv. to Wm. H. DORSEY pr
order of BRONAUGH 22 Jun 1822.

3C:123 Date: 1 Feb 1821 RtCt: 8 Mar 1821
_JNT & wife Mary Ann of Ldn to William BRONAUGH of
Ldn. Trust for debt to Ezekiel MOUNT using 102a. Wit: Francis W.
LUCKETT, John W. GRAYSON. Delv. to Wm. H. DORSEY pr order
of BRONAUGH 22 Jun 1822.

Bk:Pg: 3C:126 Date: 8 Mar 1821 RtCt: 8 Mar 1821
John BOOTH Sr. of Ldn to John BOOTH Jr of Ldn. B/S of 26a
(prch/o brother James many years ago but he died without making
deed, willed to James by Robert BOOTH). Delv. to John BOOTH Jr.
22 Jul 1822.

Bk:Pg: 3C:127 Date: 8 Mar 1821 RtCt: 8 Mar 1821
John BOOTH (by John BOOTH Jr. his attorney in fact) of Ldn to
David MULL of Ldn. B/S of rights to land allotted to MULL in division
of David MULL dec'd.

Bk:Pg: 3C:129 Date: 8 Mar 1821 RtCt: 9 Mar 1821
Samuel G. HAMILTON & wife Ann H. of Ldn to George SHEID of
Ldn. B/S of ¾a on S side of Cornwall St in W addition of Lsbg and
Thomas R. SANDERS. Wit: Samuel MURREY, Saml. M.
EDWARDS. Delv. to SHEID 29 May 1822.

Bk:Pg: 3C:131 Date: 1 Jan 1821 RtCt: 9 Mar 1821
Samuel G. HAMILTON & wife Ann H. of Ldn to Thomas R.
SANDERS of Ldn. B/S of ¼a on S side of Cornwall in W addition of
Lsbg adj John BURTON. Wit: Samuel MURREY, Saml. M.
EDWARDS. Delv. to SANDERS 15 Mar 1822.

Bk:Pg: 3C:134 Date: 2 Nov 1820 RtCt: 12 Mar 1821
William JENKINS Sr. Relinquishment of claim to negroes of William
JENKINS Jr.

Bk:Pg: 3C:134 Date: 3 Jan 1821 RtCt: 10 Mar 1821
John JANNEY & wife Susan of Ldn to Adam GRUBB of Ldn. B/S for
rights to 22a of Amos JANNEY dec'd with Adam HOUSHOLDER &
wife Sarah late JANNEY, Mahlon JANNEY & wife Rachel, Elizabeth
JANNEY, Ruth JANNEY, Amos JANNEY & Nathan JANNEY (heirs
of Amos JANNEY dec'd late of Ldn). Wit: Ebenezer GRUBB, Thos.
J. MARLOW, John McCORMICK, Thomas SANDERS. Delv. to
GRUBB 14 Aug 1821.

Bk:Pg: 3C:138 Date: 12 Mar 1821 RtCt: 12 Mar 1821
Simon A. BINNS & wife Sarah to Geo. FICHTER. CoE for deed of
Aug 1819. Wit: Stephen C. ROSZEL & Abner GIBSON.

Bk:Pg: 3C:139 Date: 6 Mar 1820 RtCt: 12 Mar 1821
Thomas A. DENNIS of Ldn to Humphrey B. POWELL of Ldn. Trust
for debt to Burr POWELL, Jesse McVEIGH, Harman BITZER using
66a (cnvy/b George BAYLY) where DENNIS now resides and negro
girl Tacey abt 15y old bought of Joseph ADAMS. Wit: Asa
ROGERS, Jacob MANN, Edwin C. BROWN. Delv. pr order 8 Mar
1830.

Bk:Pg: 3C:141   Date: 21 Aug 1820   RtCt: 12 Mar 1821
Richard KEEN of Ldn to James LEWIS Sr. & John BAYLY of Ldn.
Trust for debt to Charles LEWIS of Ldn using land where he now
lives. Wit: Amos SKINNER, Anthony THORNTON, Asel LEE. Delv.
to LEWIS 9 Jul 1821.

Bk:Pg: 3C:143   Date: 16 Feb 1821   RtCt: 12 Mar 1821
Amos GIBSON & wife Hannah of Ldn to Isaac NICHOLS Jr. &
James HOGE of Ldn. Trust for debt to Isaac & Samuel NICHOLS
using 307½a nr Daniel JANNEY's mill adj Israel JANNEY. Wit:
Notley C. WILLIAMS, John W. GRAYSON. Delv. to Saml. NICHOLS
11 Nov 1824.

Bk:Pg: 3C:147   Date: 10 Feb 1821   RtCt: 12 Mar 1821
Moses GULICK of Ldn to Wm. GILMORE of Ldn. Trust using
negroes Dorchas, Mary, Daniel & Sandy for benefit of wife Martha
GULICK formerly MUDD (devised by John MUDD dec'd former
husband). Wit: Joseph GARRETT, Saml. BUCK.

Bk:Pg: 3C:148   Date: 6 Jun 1820   RtCt: 12 Mar 1821
Elijah VIOLETT & wife Phebe of Ldn to Amos DENHAM of Ldn. B/S
of 73a in Ldn & Fqr on Plumb Run (part of tract by A/L from Robert
FLETCHER) adj Ashby's Gap Turnpike. Wit: O. DENHAM, Israel
GIBSON, John L. STUBBLEFIELD, John W. GRAYSON, Joseph
CARR.

Bk:Pg: 3C:150   Date: 13 May 1820   RtCt: 12 Mar 1821
Elizabeth FINETON of Ldn to Amos DENHAM of Ldn. B/S of interest
in 133a left to Elizabeth by grandfather John VIOLETT subject to L/L
of Elijah VIOLETT. Wit: Jos. CARR, Travis GLASCOCK.

Bk:Pg: 3C:152   Date: 28 Feb 1821   RtCt: 12 Mar 1821
Thomas BISCOE of Ldn to Hugh SMITH. Trust for debt to Jesse
HARRIS using 37a, negro woman Joannah with children Sarah,
Marshall & Caroline, farm and household items.

Bk:Pg: 3C:154   Date: 11 Jan 1821   RtCt: 12 Mar 1821
Daniel JOHNSON of Ldn to Jesse McVEIGH of Ldn. Trust for debt
to David GIBSON using undivided interest in Richard CRUPPER
dec'd and farm and household items. Wit: Jno. N. T. G. E. KEENE,
Thomas H. WEY, A. GIBSON, Hamilton ROGERS, Hugh ROGERS,
Wm. BATTSON. Delv. to McVEIGH 6 Nov 1821.

Bk:Pg: 3C:156   Date: 17 Jun 1818   RtCt: 12 Mar 1821
William NOLAND & wife Catharine of Ldn to Arthur ORRISON of
Ldn. B/S of 228a (prch/o Colin AULT). Wit: Henry McKENZIE, Levi
BARTON, Thomas NOLAND, Burr POWELL, A. GIBSON. Delv. to
ORRISON 30 Jun 1824.

Bk:Pg: 3C:158   Date: 9 Dec 1820   RtCt: 12 Mar 1821
Michael PLAISTER of Ldn to Henry PLAISTER Jr. of Ldn. B/S of
22a in lots in Union (cnvy/b William CAMPBELL & wife Margaret,
James REID & wife Leah, Jonathan REID & wife Elizabeth heirs of

James REID Sr. dec'd) and 3a wood lot, 4a lot and 6a lot. Wit: Wm. BRONAUGH, John W. GRAYSON. Delv. to PLAISTER Jr. 4 Oct 1824.

Bk:Pg: 3C:162   Date: 12 Jan 1821   RtCt: 12 Mar 1821
Nancy CRUPPER of Ldn to Townsend D. PEYTON of Ldn. Trust for debt to David GIBSON as security for debt to Noble BEVERIDGE using life estate from husband Richard CRUPPER dec'd including household items. Wit: Daniel C.JOHNSON, John CRUPPER, Ann JOHNSON.

Bk:Pg: 3C:164   Date: 19 Feb 1821   RtCt: 12 Mar 1821
Nero LOSSON/LAWSON of Ldn to Isaac WALKER & Noble S. BRADEN of Ldn. Trust for debt to Edward DORSEY using lot in Wtfd (prch/o Exors of Wm. HOUGH dec'd). Delv. pr order 12 Apr 1824.

Bk:Pg: 3C:166   Date: __ Mar 1821   RtCt: 12 Mar 1821
Richard TAVENER of Ldn to James GREENLEASE, Enos GARRETT, James TAVENER, Zepheniah DAVIS, Jonah SANDS, Isaiah NICHOLS, Eli TAVENER & Thomas ROGERS of Ldn. B/S of 6 sq poles between George TAVENER Sr. & Richard for purpose of building a schoolhouse and use of spring. Wit: Edw'd DORSEY, Wm. J. BRONAUGH.

Bk:Pg: 3C:167   Date: 8 Mar 1821   RtCt: 12 Mar 1821
Michael RITCHIE of Ldn to Jacob CARNES of Ldn. Trust for debt to Jacob VIRTZ of Ldn using farm animals, household items. Delv. to VIRTZ 12 May 1821.

Bk:Pg: 3C:169   Date: 18 Sep 1820   RtCt: 12 Mar 1821
Albert BAYLEY of Ldn to John BAYLY of Ldn. BoS for negroes Moses, Beck, Lucy, Bob, Willis & Milcey and household furniture. Delv. to John BAYLY 19 May 1821.

Bk:Pg: 3C:170   Date: 7 Mar 1821   RtCt: 12 Mar 1821
Elizabeth GIBSON of Ldn to Caldwell CARR. Trust to secure Isaac NICKOLS Sr., Stephen WILSON, Abner GIBSON, Isaac NICHOLS Jr. & Wm. NICHOLS securities for her as Guardian of Israel GIBSON, Tacy GIBSON now FLETCHER, Emily GIBSON late BROWN dec'd, Mahlon GIBSON, Alice GIBSON & Rebeccah GIBSON orphans of John GIBSON dec'd using farm animals and household items. Delv. pr order 14 Dec 1829.

Bk:Pg: 3C:172   Date: 16 Feb 1821   RtCt: 12 Mar 1821
Enos POTTS & wife Lydia of Ldn to Isaac NICKOLS Jr. & James HOGE of Ldn. Trust for debt to Isaac & Samuel NICKOLS using 73a on N fork of Goose Creek and 80a. Delv. to Saml. NICHOLS 14 Nov 1825.

Bk:Pg: 3C:176   Date: 1 Jan 1821   RtCt: 12 Mar 1821
Abraham FULTON of Ldn to Peter SKINNER of Ldn. B/S of farm animals and household items. Wit: Alexander VEALE, Dennis McCARTY. Delv. pr order DB CCC:66 7 Apr 1826.

Bk:Pg: 3C:177   Date: 17 Jun 1820   RtCt: 12 Mar 1821
David LOVETT of Ldn to Herman HEINZERLING of Ldn. B/S of one rood on E side of LOVETT's plantation. Wit: [foreign name], Wm. WIRE, Juflers? KINGERLING. Delv. to HEINZERLING 22 Jul 1822.

Bk:Pg: 3C:178   Date: 21 Feb 1821   RtCt: 12 Mar 1821
James BATTSON of Fqr to H. B. POWELL of Ldn. Trust for debts to Noble BEVERIDGE, Jacob ISH using 1/8th part of estate of father John BATTSON dec'd. Wit: Hiram McVEIGH. Delv. to POWELL 15 Nov 1822.

Bk:Pg: 3C:180   Date: 28 Feb 1821   RtCt: 12 Mar 1821
Thomas RISBY (old and infirmed) to Abraham SKILLMAN. Trust of household items to secure it to wife Sarah and daughters Rachel & Devicy.

Bk:Pg: 3C:181   Date: 12 Mar 1821   RtCt: 12 Mar 1821
William L. COCKERILL to John J. HARDING of Lsbg. BoS for negro woman Phoebe abt 35y old & her child Milly abt 7y old.

Bk:Pg: 3C:182   Date: 14 Oct 1820   RtCt: 12 Mar 1821
John WEADON of Ldn to Samuel DUNKIN of Ldn. Trust for debt to Joseph LOVETT using ½a lot in Union (cnvy/b Thornton WALKER). Delv. to DUNKIN 25 Jan 1825.

Bk:Pg: 3C:183   Date: 26 Jan 1821   RtCt: 12 Mar 1821
Albert BAYLY & wife Sarah of Ldn to John BAYLY of Ldn. B/S of 188a on old Gumspring road adj George B. WHITING, Reuben HUTCHISON, Sampson HUTCHISON (prch/o John BAYLY DB AAA:116). Wit: Moses DOWDELL, Joseph VANPELT, Richard VANPELT, Wm. VANPELT, Marshall Wm. HORTON. Delv. to John BAYLY 19 May 1821.

Bk:Pg: 3C:185   Date: 28 Feb 1821   RtCt: 12 Mar 1821
David LOVETT of Ldn to William WIRE of Ldn. B/S of one rood on E side of LOVETT's plantation. Wit: Thomas H. STEPHENS, John FISHEL. Delv. to WIRE 19 Dec 1821.

Bk:Pg: 3C:186   Date: 7 Mar 1821   RtCt: 12 Mar 1821
Elizabeth GIBSON of Ldn to Caldwell CARR. Trust for [see DB 3C:170] using 79a dower from husband John GIBSON dec'd. Delv. to CARR 9 Mar 1824.

Bk:Pg: 3C:189   Date: 18 May 1818   RtCt: 12 Feb 1821
David GIBSON of Ldn to Burr POWELL of Ldn. Trust to secure wife Nancy GIBSON using land where his father resides (from inheritance and conveyance by brothers & sisters). Wit: Lloyd NOLAND, H. B. POWELL, Ann W. NOLAND. Delv. to Hugh SMITH pr order of Burr POWELL (DB CCC:63) 12 Nov 1821.

)1 **Date: 12 Mar 1821 RtCt: 13 Mar 1821**
Ldn to Presley CORDELL & Sampson BLINCOE
njamin SHREVE Sr. & Robert MOFFETT as
) as Exor of father William MEADE dec'd and as
Admr of Elizabeth MEADE dec'd and as Guardian of Mary, Joseph
& Martha MEADE using 460a. Delv. to B. SHREVE Jr. 28 Jul 1827.

Bk:Pg: 3C:193 Date: 12 Mar 1821 RtCt: 13 Mar 1821
William MEADE of Ldn to Joseph MEADE of Ldn. B/S of 460a and
undivided interest in 'Ross' place' on Secolon Run and negro man
Jerry, woman Janny & her child Mary, farm and household items.
Wit: Henry SANDERS, E. SUMMERS, R. G. SANDERS. Delv. to
Jos. MEAD 1 Feb 1822.

Bk:Pg: 3C:195 Date: ___ RtCt: 13 Mar 1821
William MEADE of Ldn to Joseph MEADE of Ldn. B/S of interest in
lands in Bedford Co Va willed to Elizabeth MEADE now dec'd in will
of William MEADE dec'd. Wit: Henry SANDERS, E. SUMMERS, R.
G. SANDERS. Delv. to Jos. MEAD 26 Jan 1822.

Bk:Pg: 3C:196 Date: 24 Feb 1821 RtCt: 13 Mar 1821
Noah HIXSON of Ldn to David SHAWEN of Ldn. B/S of 90a allotted
to HIXSON in div. of Reuben HIXON dec'd. Delv. to SHAWEN 25
Mar 1824.

Bk:Pg: 3C:198 Date: 10 Mar 1821 RtCt: 13 Mar 1821
Aaron BURSON of Ldn to Francis W. LUCKETT of Ldn. Trust for
Thomas CLOWE & William VICKERS as security using farm and
household items. Delv. to BURSON 13 Mar 1823.

Bk:Pg: 3C:199 Date: 21 Mar 1821 RtCt: 29 Mar 1821
Patrick JONES of Morgan Co Va to Robert MOFFETT of Ldn. B/S of
lots adj George RUST Jr. (prch/o P. B. MILHOLLAND being part
John MILHOLLAND died seized of and allotted to Patrick JONES
and Sarah JONES now SEARS children of Sarah JONES dec'd).
Delv. to MOFFETT 21 Mar 1821.

Bk:Pg: 3C:201 Date: 10 Mar 1821 RtCt: 9 Apr 1821
Thomas LAWRENCE & wife Louisa of BaltMd to Aaron SANDERS
of Ldn. B/S of 36a Lot #6 on Ketocton Mt. allotted Louisa in div. of
John A BINNS. Wit: A. G. BRYSON, Lyman ADAMS. Delv. to
SAUNDERS 16 May 1827.

Bk:Pg: 3C:203 Date: 14 Mar 1821 RtCt: 14 Mar 1821
Joseph T. NEWTON & wife Nelly S. of Ldn to Elis JENKINS of Ldn.
B/S of 7a. Wit: Presley CORDELL, Thomas SANDERS. Delv. to
JENKINS 16 Jul 1824.

Bk:Pg: 3C:205 Date: 14 Mar 1821 RtCt: 14 Mar 1821
John CAVANS & wife Rachael of Ldn to Joseph CAVANS of Ldn.
B/S of 71a (assigned to Nancy CAVENS now CLEMONS wd/o
Joseph CAVENS dec'd). Wit: Presley CORDELL, John H. McCABE.
Delv. to Jos. CAVINS 10 Aug 1821.

Bk:Pg: 3C:207   Date: 30 Oct 1820   RtCt: 15 Mar 1821
Ludwell LEE of Ldn to Thomas DARNE of Ldn. B/S of 209a on S
side of Horsepen Run adj Francis L. LEE, Richard COCKERILL,
heirs of James COLEMAN. Delv. to DARNE 27 Nov 1823.

Bk:Pg: 3C:209   Date: 16 Mar 1821   RtCt: 16 Mar 1821
Thomas J. HARPER to William J. HANDLEY. Trust for debt to
George W. SHAWEN using farm and household items. Wit: George
HAMMAT, R. H. GOVER, Aaron DIVINE.

Bk:Pg: 3C:211   Date: 19 Mar 1821   RtCt: 19 Mar 1821
Samuel A. TILLETT and Charles BINNS. Agreement concerning
sale to BINNS of all lands (203½a) inherited from will of father Giles
TILLETT dec'd in 3 separate lots inherited from mother of GILES
dec'd and laid off in div. of TILLETT, MANLEY and HEREFORD
heirs of one BERRY dec'd the grandfather of Giles dec'd and other
purchased lots. Wit: E. HAMMAT, Jno. A. BINNS, Thos. RUSSELL.

Bk:Pg: 3C:212   Date: 19 Mar 1821   RtCt: 19 Mar 1821
Anne CLEMMENS of Ldn to Joseph CAVENS of Ldn. B/S of interest
in 12a & 88a allotted Anne in decree to divide land of Joseph
CAVENS dec'd. Delv. to CAVINS 10 Aug 1821.

Bk:Pg: 3C:214   Date: 19 Mar 1821   RtCt: 20 Mar 1821
Thomas J. HARPER (insolvent) of Ldn to Sheriff Burr POWELL.
Turns over 88¾a (HARPER has a life estate in right of wife Margaret
late wd/o Aaron GREGG dec'd) adj Wm. & George GREGG. Wit:
John HAWLING, George HAMMAT, George CRIDLER. Delv. to
POWELL 9 Jul 1821.

Bk:Pg: 3C:215   Date: 19 Mar 1821   RtCt: 20 Mar 1821
Aaron DIVINE of Lsbg to Giles HAMMAT of Lsbg. Trust for debt to
John SURGHNOR of Lsbg using household items.

Bk:Pg: 3C:217   Date: 25 Jan 1821   RtCt: 21 Mar 1821
Joz. WHITE of Ldn to Wm. WHITE of Ldn. BoS for negro man Ellick.
Wit: William TEMPLER.

Bk:Pg: 3C:217   Date: 25 Jan 1821   RtCt: 14 Feb 1821
Joz. WHITE of Ldn to Wm. WHITE of Ldn. BoS for negro girl Maria.

Bk:Pg: 3C:217   Date: 14 Feb 1821   RtCt: 22 Mar 1821
William H. HOUGH & Asa MOORE of Ldn to Samuel E. TAYLOR of
Ldn. Release of trust for debt to Upton REED.

Bk:Pg: 3C:219   Date: 20 Mar 1821   RtCt: 11 May 1821
Langhorn DADE of Ldn to Edwin C. BROWN. Trust for debt to Isaac
KELL using farm and household items. Wit: Jno. KEENE, James
BISCOE. Delv. to COCKRAN pr order of BROWN 13 Jul 1821.

Bk:Pg: 3C:221   Date: 30 Jun 1821   RtCt: 3 Jul 1821
Samuel CLAPHAM & wife Elizabeth of Ldn to Richard H.
HENDERSON & Thomas R. MOTT of Ldn. Trust for debt to
Chandler PRICE of PhilPa using 1600a on Potomac. Wit: H. H.

HAMILTON, Thomas A. MOORE, James H. HAMILTON, Samuel DAWSON. Delv. to Jas. H. HAMILTON 17 Jul 1821.

Bk:Pg: 3C:223   Date: 22 Mar 1821   RtCt: 21 [?] Mar 1821
Westley SEARS & wife Sarah (dau of Sarah JONES dec'd) of Ldn to Robert MOFFETT of Ldn. B/S of ½ of lots on Cotocton Mt. allotted by commrs. of land of John MILHOLLEN dec'd adj. George RUST Jr, MOFFETT. Wit: Robert BRADEN, Abiel JENNERS. Delv. to MOFFETT 18 Feb 1823.

Bk:Pg: 3C:225   Date: 21 Aug 1818   RtCt: 22 Mar 1821
Jozabed WHITE of Ldn to Isaac WALKER of Ldn. Trust for debt to Bank of Valley in Lsbg and endorsers Abiel JENNERS, John BRADEN & Chas. G. EDWARDS using undivided share of 58a.

Bk:Pg: 3C:228   Date: 19 Mar 1821   RtCt: 22 Mar 1821
John F. STRIDER of Jefferson Co to Catharine NISONGER. BoS for tools and household items. Wit: Andrew BELTZ, William McBEE, Nenian R. MOKLELL. Delv. to Christ'n NYSWANGER 12 Apr 1824.

Bk:Pg: 3C:229   Date: 23 Mar 1821   RtCt: 24 Mar 1821
Bernard HOUGH & wife Louisa of Ldn to Joseph HOUGH of Ldn. B/S of 47a. Wit: J. H. McCABE, Presley CORDELL. Delv. to Joseph HOUGH 17 Feb 1827.

Bk:Pg: 3C:231   Date: 12 Mar 1821   RtCt: 12 Mar 1821
Bennett MARKS of Ldn to Joshua OSBURN of Ldn. Trust for debt to Thomas JAMES using 30a adj Alexander HARRISON, William BROWN.

Bk:Pg: 3C:234   Date: 20 Nov 1819   RtCt: 27 Mar 1821
John POTTER & wife Elizabeth of JeffVa to Elizabeth POTTER of Ldn. B/S of ½ of lot in Lsbg between lots of Bernard HOUGH & James GARNER. Wit: Saml. MILLER, Jacob FADLEY, John MULLEN, Samuel J. CRAMER, John H. LEWIS.

Bk:Pg: 3C:236   Date: 23 Feb 1821   RtCt: 27 Mar 1821
Peter R. BEVERLEY of Alexandria D. C. to Joseph LEWIS of Ldn. Release of trust on 203a 'Clifton'.

Bk:Pg: 3C:237   Date: 26 Mar 1821   RtCt: 28 Mar 1821
Joseph WOOD & wife Lydia of Ldn to Mahlon JANNEY of Ldn. B/S of ½a (prch/o Mahlon JANNEY dec'd). Wit: Robert BRADEN, Abiel JENNERS. Delv. to N. S. BRADEN Admr of M. JANNEY 14 Sep 1835.

Bk:Pg: 3C:239   Date: 8 Feb 1821   RtCt: 7 Feb 1821
John SHAFFER of Ldn to L. P. W. BALCH of Lsbg. Trust for debt to George RICKARD & Manuel AXLINE as securities on note to John MANN using rents from Simon SHOEMAKER Jr. on farm in German Settlement and crops. Wit: Geo. RICHARDS, David OGDEN, Thomas LITTLETON. Delv. to BALCH 20 Jul 1821.

Bk:Pg: 3C:241   Date: 26 Mar 1821   RtCt: 28 Mar 1821
James MOORE & wife Rebecca of Ldn to Joseph WOOD of Ldn.
B/S of 4a (prch/o Thos. PHILLIPS). Wit: Robert BRADEN, Abiel
JENNERS.

Bk:Pg: 3C:242   Date: 28 Mar 1821   RtCt: 29 Mar 1821
James GREENLEASE & wife Catharine of Ldn to Richard H.
HENDERSON. Trust for debt to Charles BENNETT using 333a
'William Dudley DIGGES' Valley tract'. Wit: John ROSE, Thomas
SANDERS. Delv. to BENNETT 17 Jun 1822.

Bk:Pg: 3C:246   Date: 29 Mar 1821   RtCt: 29 Mar 1821
John SHAFFER to Benjamin SHREVE. Release of trust on dower
right of Presley WILLIAMS and land of Reuben HIXSON dec'd. Wit:
Rich'd. H. HENDERSON.

Bk:Pg: 3C:246   Date: 24 Mar 1821   RtCt: 2 Apr 1821
James MOORE & wife Rebecca of Ldn to Lewis COALE of Ldn.
B/S of 1a on Ball's Run nr mill race. Wit: Robert BRADEN, Abiel
JENNERS. Delv. to COALE 13 Sep 1822.

Bk:Pg: 3C:248   Date: 26 Mar 1821   RtCt: 2 Apr 1821
Mahlon JANNEY & wife Sarah of Wtfd to Lewis COALE of Wtfd. B/S
of lot nr new addition of Wtfd adj Asa MOORE, Mahlon JANNEY.
Wit: R. BRADEN, Abiel JENNERS. Delv. to COALE 13 Sep 1822.

Bk:Pg: 3C:250   Date: 1 Nov 1820   RtCt: 4 Apr 1821
Ludwell LEE of Ldn to Morien/Moreen FOWLER of Ldn. L/L (lives of
FOWLER, wife Elizabeth) of 78a on paved road from Lsbg to
Georgetown.

Bk:Pg: 3C:252   Date: 5 Apr 1820   RtCt: 4 Apr 1821
Ludwell LEE & wife Eliza to Thomas Herbert MUSE. B/S of 30a adj
James L. McKENNA, old road from Lsbg to Alexandria and 1 adj
15a lot. Delv. to J. J. MATHIAS pr direction of MUSE 13 Aug 1834.

Bk:Pg: 3C:253   Date: 1 Sep 1820   RtCt: 5 Apr 1821
Thomas SWAYNE of Ldn to William HERBERT (agent for estate of
Richard DeBUTTS of Ffx). Mortgage on 190a. Delv. to HERBERT 6
Aug 1821

Bk:Pg: 3C:255   Date: 1 Mar 1821   RtCt: 5 Apr 1821
Patrick McFADEN of Ldn to Capt. Aaron SANDERS. BoS for farm
animals and household items. Wit: D. WHERRY.

Bk:Pg: 3C:257   Date: 15 Mar 1821   RtCt: 5 Apr 1821
John CAVINS of Ldn to Mary PAXSON of Ldn. BoS for farm animals
and household items. Wit: John DAYMUD, Joseph CAVINS. Delv. to
Jos. CAVINS pr order of PAXSON 15 Aug 1821.

Bk:Pg: 3C:257   Date: 20 Mar 1821   RtCt: 5 Apr 1821
Nancy CLEMENS of Ldn to Joseph CAVANS of Ldn. BoS for farm
animals and household items. Wit: John DAYMUDE, John CAVINS.
Delv. to CAVINS 10 Aug 1821.

Bk:Pg: 3C:258   Date: 6 Apr 1821   RtCt: 6 Apr 1821
Samuel G. HAMILTON & wife Ann H. of Ldn to George K. FOX of
Ldn. B/S of ¼a on S side of Cornwall in new addition to Lsbg adj
John BURTON, Catharine DOWLING. Wit: J. H. McCABE, Thomas
SANDERS. Delv. to FOX 6 Mar 1833.

Bk:Pg: 3C:260   Date: 10 Apr 1821   RtCt: 10 Apr 1821
John WEADON, Jacob SILCOTT, Benjn. MITCHELL & Thornton
WALKER. Bond on WEADON as constable.

Bk:Pg: 3C:261   Date: 28 Dec 1820   RtCt: 23 Mar 1821
John SHAVER to Benjamin SHREVE. Release of trust. Wit: Robert
MOFFETT, Manuel AXLINE.

Bk:Pg: 3C:261   Date: 25 Jan 1821   RtCt: 12 Feb 1821
Daniel HARTMAN Trustee to Joseph LEWIS Jr. Release of trust for
Edward McGUIRE.

Bk:Pg: 3C:262   Date: 23 Apr 1821   RtCt: 2 May 1821
Minor FURR & wife Phebe to Sydnor BAILEY & John GIBSON.
Trust for debt to Henley BOGGESS using 2a lot with grist mill &
distillery, 75a of T. BARTLETT, 58a of S. BARTLETT, 3a with
house, 165a, all lots adj each other. Wit: Caldwell CARR, H. SMITH,
Nimrod FURR, John W. GRAYSON, Ben GRAYSON.

Bk:Pg: 3C:266   Date: 2 May 1821   RtCt: 2 May 1821
Elizabeth MULL of Ldn to Jacob WERTZ of Ldn. B/S of 1/7th interest
allotted in land of David MULL dec'd.

Bk:Pg: 3C:267   Date: 2 Apr 1821   RtCt: 2 May 1821
David MULL of Ldn to Jacob WERTZ of Ldn. B/S of 1/7th interest
allotted in land of David MULL dec'd.

Bk:Pg: 3C:268   Date: 3 May 1821   RtCt: 4 May 1821
John BAKER of Washington Co Md to Peter COST & Robt.
BRADEN of Ldn. Trust for debt to Jacob COST of Ldn using 128a
'Osburne lot' adj Wm. GRUBB, __ SHAMBLIN, Richard GRUBB and
114a 'Morrises Lot' and 40a 'Wood Lot' and 70a on W side of Short
Hill adj reps. of David POTTS and 11a lot on N side of Short Hill nr
Dawson's Spring and ¼a lot adj Thos. DAVID, Wm. GRUBB. Delv.
pr order 6 Jun 1825.

Bk:Pg: 3C:272   Date: 28 Apr 1821   RtCt: 4 May 1821
Jacob COST & wife Margaret Magdalene of Ldn to John BAKER of
Ldn. B/S of 6 lots on W side of Short Hill prch/o Abiel JENNERS –
128a 'Osburns Lot', 114a 'Morrises Lot', 40a 'Wood Lot', 70a on W
side of Short Hill, 11a lot on N side of Short Hill nr Dawson's Spring
and ¼a lot adj Thos. DAVIS, Wm. GRUBB. Wit: Robert BRADEN,
Samuel HOUGH Jr. Delv. to Jacob COST 13 Aug 1825.

Bk:Pg: 3C:276   Date: 5 May 1821   RtCt: 5 May 1821
Simon JENKINS of Ldn to John JENKINS of FredMd. Trust for debt
to Eliza SMITH of MontMd using household items.

Bk:Pg: 3C:278 Date: 26 Feb 1821 RtCt: 7 May 1821
John BRADY & wife Sarah of Mdbg to Hugh ROGERS & Hamilton ROGERS of Mdbg. Trust for debt to Elizabeth BOYDE of Mdbg using Lot #23 in Mdbg. Wit: Francis W. LUCKETT, A. GIBSON. Delv. to Jesse McVEIGH 10 Apr 1832.

Bk:Pg: 3C:280 Date: 23 Mar 1821 RtCt: 9 May 1821
Benjamin JENKINS of Ldn and John JENKINS of Ldn. Agreement on farm and household items used to pay debt. Wit: Thos. L. HUMPHREY, Eleanor JENKINS, William JENKINS.

Bk:Pg: 3C:281 Date: 3 May 1821 RtCt: 9 May 1821
Warner WASHINGTON of Frederick Co to Lawrence LEWIS of Ffx. Trust to secure payment using 400a prch/o Mordecai THROCKMORTON.

Bk:Pg: 3C:283 Date: 30 Dec 1820 RtCt: 10 May 1821
William D. DRISH & wife Harriot of Lsbg to Henry CLAGETT of Lsbg. B/S of Lot #17 on Market St. in Lsbg adj John THOMAS. Delv. to CLAGETT 2 May 1823.

Bk:Pg: 3C:285 Date: 23 Mar 1821 RtCt: 9 May 1821
Benjamin SHREVE to John JENKINS. B/S of crops. Wit: Thos. L. HUMPHREY, William JENKINS.

Bk:Pg: 3C:285 Date: 10 May 1821 RtCt: 10 May 1821
Adam BARR & wife Precious of Ldn to Richard H. HENDERSON of Ldn. Trust for debt to Amos JOHNSON of Fqr and John ROBERTS of AlexDC using 10a. Delv. to HENDERSON 13 Oct 1821.

Bk:Pg: 3C:287 Date: 14 Jun 1821 RtCt: 14 Jun 1821
John KEENE, Nelson GREEN & John BOYD. Bond on KEENE as constable.

Bk:Pg: 3C:288 Date: 5 Oct 1820 RtCt: 14 May 1821
Charles J. LOVE of Ffx to Lewis HUTCHISON of Ldn. B/S of 21a. Wit: Thomas WARD Jr., Barton HOOPER.

Bk:Pg: 3C:289 Date: 14 May 1821 RtCt: 15 May 1821
Jas. SIMPSON, Benj'n HAGERMAN, William NOLAND & David J. COE. Bond to William R. McCARTY as security for Jas. SIMPSON as Exor of Henson SIMPSON dec'd. Wit: R. H. HENDERSON.

Bk:Pg: 3C:289 Date: 15 May 1821 RtCt: 15 May 1821
Edward HAMMETT & Reuben SCHOOLEY. Bond on HAMMETT as constable.

Bk:Pg: 3C:290 Date: ___ RtCt: 15 May 1821
John GIBSON dec'd. Division – Lot #1 (91a), Lot #2 37a, Lot #3 (29a). Lot #1 (25½a) with merchant mill, saw mill & miller's house in undivided parts to Elisha JANNEY & wife, Amos GIBSON, Israel GIBSON & Mahlon GIBSON. Lot #2 (19¼a) and Lot #6 (12a) to Thomas W. SMITH. Lot #3 (16a) and Lot #7 (15a) to Alice GIBSON. Lot #4 (16¼a) and Lot #8 (13a) to Rebecca GIBSON. Lot #5 (38a)

to David E. BROWN. Divisors: Cuthbert POWELL, Sydnor BAILEY, Vincent MOSS, Daniel EACHES. Gives plat.

Bk:Pg: 3C:294   Date: 11 Jan 1821   RtCt: 30 Apr 1821
John FEICHTER & wife Martha and John McCABE of Ldn to John CRIDLER of Ldn. B/S of lot on Loudoun St adj CRIDLER on the East, FEICHTER on the W, James GARNER on the N. Wit: Samuel MURREY, Presley CORDELL.

Bk:Pg: 3C:296   Date: 27 Apr 1821   RtCt: 30 Apr 1821
Thomas McCOWAT & wife Elizabeth Lsbg to Samuel MURREY of Lsbg. B/S of part of Lot #20 on King St in Lsbg adj William DRISH. Wit: John McCORMICK, Presley CORDELL. Delv. to Jos. L. MARTIN 5 Apr 1825.

Bk:Pg: 3C:298   Date: 20 Mar 1801   RtCt: 9 Apr 1821
Joseph WOOD & wife Lydia of Ldn to James MOORE of Ldn. B/S of 2a on Ball's Run adj Thomas LACEY dec'd, William HOUGH dec'd (prch/o Mahlon JANNEY dec'd) and 1a across the road and opposite the factory lot. Wit: R. BRADEN, Abiel JENNERS.

Bk:Pg: 3C:300   Date: 19 Apr 1821   RtCt: 30 Apr 1821
Jehu HOLLINGSWORTH (trustee of Levi WILLIAMS) of Ldn to David Fendall BEALE of Ldn. Release of trust for debt to Enos POTTS on 63a.

Bk:Pg: 3C:302   Date: 30 Apr 1821   RtCt: 30 Apr 1821
James RUST (trustee of Levi WILLIAMS) of Ldn to David Fendall BEALE of Ldn. Release of trust for debt to John PANCOAST Trustee on 63a. Delv. to D. F. BEALLE 3 Jun 1825.

Bk:Pg: 3C:303   Date: 22 Mar 1821   RtCt: 28 Apr 1821
Jacob HIBBS & wife Jane of Green Co Pa to Michael EVERHART of Ldn. B/S of undivided interest in 60a from will of Robert BOOTH dec'd. Delv. to Samuel POTTERFIELD trustee in deed 8 Mar 1853.

Bk:Pg: 3C:305   Date: 28 Apr 1821   RtCt: 28 Apr 1821
William FOWKE (insolvent) of Ldn to Sheriff Burr POWELL. Trust on 163a where FOWKE now resides (prch/o Samuel BERKLEY on L/L).

Bk:Pg: 3C:306   Date: 28 Apr 1821   RtCt: 28 Apr 1821
Minor FURR (insolvent) of Ldn to Sheriff Burr POWELL. Trust on 3a & house where FURR lives and adj 75a, adj 58a and 1½a mill and lot (all prch/o Samuel & Thomas BERKLEY on L/L) and 145a adj Enoch FURR, William CARPENTER (prch/o Thomas A. HEREFORD).

Bk:Pg: 3C:308   Date: 28 Apr 1821   RtCt: 28 Apr 1821
Samuel CLAPHAM of Ldn to John FRYE of Ldn. B/S of 1a on E side of Catoctin Mt. adj where FRYE now lives. Delv. to John FRYE 8 May 1823.

Bk:Pg: 3C:309   Date: 24 Mar 1821   RtCt: 27 Apr 1821
William PAXSON & wife Jane of Ldn to Samuel PAXSON of Ldn. B/S of 85a (prch/o Isaac STEER) on Cotocton Creek. Wit: Robert BRADEN, Abiel JENNERS.

Bk:Pg: 3C:311   Date: 3 Mar 1821   RtCt: 27 Apr 1821
William PAXSON & wife Jane of Ldn to Conrad WIRTZ of Ldn. B/S of 27a on Catocton Creek adj Conrad WIRTZ. Wit: Robert BRADEN, Abiel JENNERS.

Bk:Pg: 3C:312   Date: 27 Apr 1821   RtCt: 27 Apr 1821
William SHEID & wife Martina of Ldn to George SHEID of Ldn. B/S of 65a on Cabbin branch. Wit: Presley CORDELL, Thomas SANDERS. Delv. to Geo. SHEID 13 Jul 1824.

Bk:Pg: 3C:314   Date: 24 Mar 1821   RtCt: 27 Apr 1821
William PAXSON & wife Jane of Ldn to Enos WILLIAMS of Ldn. B/S of 183a (prch/o Melchor STRUPE) on Cotocton Creek adj Adam HOUSHOLDER, __ BAKER, __ RAMEY, __ FAWLEY, __ WALTMAN. Wit: Robert BRADEN, Abiel JENNERS. Delv. to Charles WILLIAMS Admr of grantee 11 Mar 1822.

Bk:Pg: 3C:316   Date: 6 Jun 1821   RtCt: 10 Dec 1821
Carter B. PAGE & wife Rebecca of RichVa and John W. PAGE & wife Jane Byrd of FredVa to James GOVAN of Hanover Co Va. B/S of 2500a in Ldn & Ffx on Horsepen Run. Delv. pr order 20 Feb 1822.

Bk:Pg: 3C:319   Date: 8 Jun 1821   RtCt: 10 Dec 1821
William Byrd PAGE to James GOVAN. B/S of one undivided moiety (Carter B. PAGE indebted to John W. PAGE as Admr dbn of Robert PAGE dec'd of Broadneck and trust given William Byrd PAGE for one undivided moiety of 2000a in Ldn & Ffx). Delv. pr order 26 Feb 1822.

Bk:Pg: 3C:321   Date: 6 Jan 1818   RtCt: 25 Apr 1821
Joab & Balaam OSBURN of Ldn to Jesse McVEIGH of Ldn. Trust for debt to William R. McCARTY using 127a (formerly belonging to McCARTY) adj Leven LUCKETT. Delv. to H. B. POWELL pr Jesse McVEIGH 13 Apr 1840.

Bk:Pg: 3C:323   Date: 17 Apr 1821   RtCt: 20 Apr 1821
Abel JANNEY & wife Lydia of Ldn to Isaac NICKOLS Jr. & James HOGUE of Ldn. Trust for debt to Isaac & Samuel NICKOLS using 110a adj John EVANS. Delv. to Samuel NICHOLS Exor 10 Nov 1825.

Bk:Pg: 3C:326   Date: 19 Apr 1821   RtCt: 20 Apr 1821
James COCHRAN & wife Rachel of Ldn to Yardley TAYLOR of Ldn. Trust for debt to Stephen WILSON using 23a (part of tract Benj. BRADFIELD wife's father prch/o Stephen WILSON) on NW fork of Goose Creek. Wit: N. C. WILLIAMS, John WHITE. Delv. to TAYLOR 21 Apr 1822.

Bk:Pg: 3C:328   Date: 26 Mar 1821   RtCt: 9 Apr 1821
Joseph WOOD & wife Lydia of Ldn to James MOORE of Ldn. B/S of
2a in Wtfd at Mahlon St. Wit: Robert BRADEN, Abiel JENNERS.
Delv. to Thos. PHILIPS the Exor 6 Jun 1826.

Bk:Pg: 3C:330   Date: 7 Apr 1820   RtCt: 9 Apr 1821
Abner HUMPHREY & wife Mary of Ldn to Abner Gile HUMPHREY
of Ldn. B/S of 119a adj Asa CARTER, William COX, John
CHAMBLIN, John RALPH, Benjamin GRAYSON. Wit: Benjamin
GRAYSON, John W. GRAYSON.

Bk:Pg: 3C:332   Date: 2 Apr 1821   RtCt: 9 Apr 1821
Ann FITZHUGH to Laurence BATTAILE Jr & wife Ann Maria. B/S of
one undivided interest in lot in Ldn by Ct of PrWm div. Delv. pr order
10 May 1824.

Bk:Pg: 3C:333   Date: 7 Apr 1820   RtCt: 9 Apr 1821
Ann FITZHUGH of Ldn to William C. FITZHUGH of Ldn. B/S of 360a
in Ldn & Fqr (been in possession of Wm for 12y, property of Ann's
late husband) and 40a wood lot. Wit: E. T. HARRISON, Jane C.
HARRISON, Lawrence BATTAILE Jr., Ann Maria BATTAILE.

Bk:Pg: 3C:335   Date: 7 Apr 1821   RtCt: 9 Apr 1821
John RICHARDS & Samuel RICHARDS (Exors of Richard
RICHARDS dec'd) of Ldn to Mahlon FULTON and Robert FULTON
of David. B/S of 105a on Beaverdam (part cnvy/b Benjamin
CUMMINGS in 1794 and part cnvy/b Nathaniel CRAWFORD in
1802) adj Jacob SILCOTT, James Carter DULANEY, William
CARTER. Wit: Seth SMITH. Delv. to Robert FULTON 11 Aug 1823.

Bk:Pg: 3C:336   Date: 21 Oct 1820   RtCt: 9 Apr 1821
William H. DORSEY of Ldn to William BRONAUGH of Ldn. Trust for
debt to James CARTER using slave boy John abt 15y old, boy
William abt 9y old, woman Nelly abt 36y, girl Caroline abt 13y, girl
Sophia abt 11y old. Wit: George W. BRONAUGH, Joseph W.
BRONAUGH.

Bk:Pg: 3C:337   Date: 4 Apr 1821   RtCt: 9 Apr 1821
Thomas A. HEREFORD & wife Margaret of Ldn to Theoderick M.
HEREFORD of Ldn. B/S of 100a at lower end of tract where
Thomas lives adj John HANN, Joshua FRED, John TORBERT.

Bk:Pg: 3C:339   Date: 7 Apr 1821   RtCt: 9 Apr 1821
Samuel HIXSON & wife Ruth of Ldn to Presley CORDELL & Saml.
M. EDWARDS of Ldn. Trust for debt to Robert MOFFETT using 90a
where Samuel now resides (from will of father Timothy HIXON
dec'd) adj Philip C. JONES, Jacob SANDS dec'd. Delv. to
CORDELL 18 Feb 1823.

Bk:Pg: 3C:341   Date: 9 Apr 1821   RtCt: 9 Apr 1821
John H. McCABE & wife Mary of Ldn to James STIDMAN and
Elizabeth SMITH of Ldn. B/S of lot on E side of King St in new

addition of Lsbg adj John HAMMERLY. Wit: Thomas SANDERS, Saml. M. EDWARDS. Delv. to STIDMAN 24 Jun 1831.

Bk:Pg: 3C:343   Date: 4 Apr 1821   RtCt: 9 Apr 1821
Richard CLARK & wife Catharine of Ldn to Charles RIVERS of Ldn. B/S of ¼a adj Abner HUMPHREY. Wit: Benjamin GRAYSON, John W. GRAYSON.

Bk:Pg: 3C:344   Date: 4 Apr 1821   RtCt: 9 Apr 1821
Richard CLARK & wife Catharine of Ldn to John L. GILL of Ldn. B/S of lot & house in Bloomfield adj David THARP, J. McVEIGH and an adj. 1a lot prch/o Isaac RICHARDS. Wit: Benjamin GRAYSON, John W. GRAYSON.

Bk:Pg: 3C:346   Date: 17 Feb 1821   RtCt: 9 Apr 1821
John TORBERT & wife Nancy of Ldn to Thomas DRAKE of Ldn. B/S of 11a adj Thomas A. HEREFORD, Benjamin JENKINS (part of inheritance from brother Saml. TORBERT dec'd). Wit: Benjamin GRAYSON, John W. GRAYSON.

Bk:Pg: 3C:348   Date: 9 Apr 1821   RtCt: 9 Apr 1821
John DRAIN of Ldn to Samuel TUSTIN of Ldn. B/S of lot on E side of Liberty St. in Lsbg adj Thomas BIRKBY.

Bk:Pg: 3C:350   Date: 7 Apr 1821   RtCt: 9 Apr 1821
Abigal ROMINE of Ldn to brother Isaiah ROMINE of Ldn (both ch/o John ROMINE). B/S of 150a (from father's 250a dev. to 11 children) adj James GRADY dec'd. Delv. to Minor ROMINE 25 Sep 1837.

Bk:Pg: 3C:352   Date: 7 Apr 1821   RtCt: 9 Apr 1821
Benjamin KENT & wife Sarah of Ldn to William BLAKELY of Ldn. B/S of 14a (prch/o John ROMINE) adj ROMINE, Jesse JANNEY, Rebecca ROMINE dower lot, Nancy ROMINE. Wit: Benjamin GRAYSON, John W. GRAYSON. Delv. pr order 1 Dec 1823.

Bk:Pg: 3C:354   Date: 2 Apr 1821   RtCt: 9 Apr 1821
Dempsey CARTER & wife Mary Ann of Ldn to Matthew CARPENTER of Ldn. B/S of 103a on Beaverdam adj John W. GRAYSON, Benjamin GRAYSON. Wit: Benjamin GRAYSON, John W. GRAYSON. Delv. to CARPENTER 27 Dec 1824.

Bk:Pg: 3C:356   Date: 4 Apr 1821   RtCt: 9 Apr 1821
Enoch FURR & wife Sarah of Ldn to John K. LITTLETON of Ldn. B/S of 99a on Jeffery's branch adj George RUST. Wit: Benjamin GRAYSON, John W. GRAYSON. Delv. to LITTLETON 12 May 1824.

Bk:Pg: 3C:358   Date: 26 Feb 1821   RtCt: 9 Apr 1821
Elizabeth BOYD of Ldn to John BRADY of Ldn. B/S of Lot #23 in Mdbg on Washington St.

Bk:Pg: 3C:360   Date: 17 Mar 1821   RtCt: 9 Apr 1821
Amos JANNEY of Ldn to Benjamin GRUBB of Ldn. B/S of 30a (prch/o George JANNEY) adj John BOGER, Aaron MILLER. Delv. to GRUBB 3 Jan 1822.

Bk:Pg: 3C:361   Date: 20 Mar 1821   RtCt: 10 Apr 1821
Burr POWELL & wife Catharine of Ldn to Townsend McVEIGH of Ldn. B/S of ½a Lots #57 & #58 in Mdbg adj Hugh SMITH. Wit: Francis W. LUCKETT, A. GIBSON. Delv. to McVEIGH 21 May 1822.

Bk:Pg: 3C:363   Date: 20 Mar 1821   RtCt: 10 Apr 1821
William WOLFORD & wife Susannah of Ldn to Peter COMPHER of Ldn. B/S of 62a (part of prch/o George MULL Mar 1814). Wit: Robert BRADEN, Saml. HOUGH Jr. Delv. to COMPHER 26 Mar 1822.

Bk:Pg: 3C:364   Date: 16 Mar 1820   RtCt: 10 Apr 1821
William CARTER of Ldn to Jesse CARTER and William J. CARTER of Ldn. BoS for farm and household items, crops, tenement now in occupation of Jesse WILLIAMS

Bk:Pg: 3C:366   Date: 15 Jan 1821   RtCt: 10 Apr 1821
William FOWKE of Ldn to William BRONAUGH & Benjamin GRAYSON of Ldn. Trust for debts to William PHILLIPS Admr of Elizabeth FOWKE dec'd, Joseph CARR, Noble BEVERIDGE using negro man Harry abt 30y old, woman Nan abt 40y & her children Hanson & Rachael, lad Levi abt 18y, girl Mary abt 13y, girl Eliza abt 11y, girl Dorcas abt 7y, girl Lucinda abt 5y & boy Landon abt 2y, farm animals and household items.

Bk:Pg: 3C:367   Date: 24 Mar 1821   RtCt: 11 Apr 1821
John H. McCABE and Samuel HOUGH Jr. of Ldn to Samuel M. EDWARDS of Ldn. Trust for debt to Conrad BITZER using 80a adj David JANNEY, Thos. LACEY dec'd, Richard GRIFFITH. Delv. to EDWARDS 10 Apr 1823.

Bk:Pg: 3C:370   Date: 15 Feb 1821   RtCt: 11 Apr 1821
Elizabeth POTTER of Ldn to James GARNER of Ldn. B/S of lot in Lsbg on N side of Loudoun St. adj Samuel CLAPHAM. Delv. to GARNER 5 Jun 1822.

Bk:Pg: 3C:372   Date: 11 Apr 1821   RtCt: 11 Apr 1821
George RUST Jr. & wife Maria C. of Ldn to James RUST of Ldn. B/S of 10a (prch/o David LACEY). Wit: Samuel MURREY, Presley CORDELL.

Bk:Pg: 3C:373   Date: 12 Apr 1821   RtCt: 13 Apr 1821
Nero LAWSON of Ldn to Asa MOORE of Wtfd. Trust for debt to Isaac NICKOLS using lot & brick house in Wtfd adj Nathan MINOR, Amasa HOUGH.

Bk:Pg: 3C:376   Date: 14 Apr 1821   RtCt: 14 Apr 1821
Thomas Randolph MOTT of Ldn to James RUST. Release of trust for debt to Mildred T. BALL, Fayette BALL & Chas. B. BALL (Exors of George W. BALL dec'd) on 169a.

Bk:Pg: 3C:376   Date: 9 Apr 1821   RtCt: 14 Apr 1821
Francis STRIBLING Jr. & wife Cecilia of Ldn to Alexander S. TIDBALL of FredVa. Trust for debt to Farmers Bank using 672a on

NW fork of Goose Creek. Wit: Notley C. WILLIAMS, Craven OSBURN. Delv. to H. B. POWELL pr order on ___.

Bk:Pg: 3C:380   Date: 16 Apr 1821   RtCt: 16 Apr 1821
Jacob FADELY & wife Mary of Ldn to Reuben HUTCHISON of Ldn. B/S of 1a (prch/o Israel LACEY dec'd) adj John TURLEY, Matthew HARRISON dec'd, Turnpike road. Wit: Thomas SANDERS, Thos. GASSAWAY. Delv. to HUTCHISON 19 Oct 1827.

Bk:Pg: 3C:382   Date: 16 Apr 1821   RtCt: 19 Apr 1821
Joab & Balaam OSBURN of Ldn to Joel OSBURN of Ldn. B/S of 127a.

Bk:Pg: 3C:383   Date: 16 Apr 1821   RtCt: 19 Apr 1821
Jesse DODD of Ldn to Robert FULTON Jr. of Ldn. Trust for debt to Mahlon FULTON using blacksmith shop tools, household items.

Bk:Pg: 3C:384   Date: 19 Apr 1821   RtCt: 20 Apr 1821
Charles TAYLOR & wife Nancy of Ldn to William WILSON and Timothy TAYLOR of Ldn. Trust for debt to Stephen WILSON using 42a on NW fork of Goose Creek adj Thomas NICKOLS. Wit: Notley C. WILLIAMS, John WHITE. Delv. to T. TAYLOR pr order of S. WILSON 16 Dec 1830.

Bk:Pg: 3C:387   Date: 16 Apr 1821   RtCt: 20 Apr 1821
James RUST & wife Sally of Ldn to Isaac NICKOLS Jr. & James HOGUE of Ldn. Trust for debt to Samuel NICKOLS using 152a or 153a adj Lsbg and 10a lot adj Lsbg and house & lot in Lsbg and 361a adj John RICHARDS. Wit: Presley CORDELL, Saml. M. EDWARDS. Delv. to Samuel NICHOLS' Exors 10 Nov 1825.

Bk:Pg: 3C:391   Date: 14 May 1821   RtCt: 14 May 1821
George SHEID & wife Rebecca to Anthony SAUNDERS. Trust for debt to Anthony CUNARD (security for SHEID as Guardian of his children Sarah G., James W., John H. & Erasmus W. SHEID) using 65a on N Cabbin branch. Wit: John McCORMICK, Presley CORDELL.

Bk:Pg: 3C:393   Date: 13 Oct 1820   RtCt: 14 May 1821
Casper JOHNS(T)ON to Adam BARR. Loan of farm animals, household items which Casper purchased at constable sale sold by Joseph HOCKINGS. Wit: Jos. HOCKINGS, William DEWAR, Hugh BARR. Delv. to JOHNSTON 3 Feb 1824.

Bk:Pg: 3C:394   Date: 12 May 1821   RtCt: 14 May 1821
Sampson RICHARDS of Ldn to John RICHARDS of Ldn. B/S of interest of wife Elizabeth in land late prop. of her father Henry TAYLOR dec'd.

Bk:Pg: 3C:396   Date: 29 Dec 1820   RtCt: 14 May 1821
Henry T. HARRISON of Ldn to Joshua LEE of Ldn. B/S of interest in 215a (devised of Matthew HARRISON dec'd) adj LEE, Henry SETTLE, Joseph LEWIS dec'd. Wit: Pat'k McINTYRE, Joseph

BEARD, S. WHERRY, Burr W. HARRISON. Delv. to LEE 11 Jul 1822.

Bk:Pg: 3C:397   Date: 28 Apr 1821   RtCt: 14 May 1821
George H. SINCLAIR of Ldn to James M. LEWIS & Edward DULIN(G) of Ldn. Trust for debt to Charles THORNTON as security using dower land allotted to Edith SINCLAIR wd/o Samuel SINCLAIR dec'd, interest in negro man Joseph held in like manner. Wit: Barton LUCAS, Elijah TURNER, Thomas DRAKE. Delv. to THORNTON 30 Oct 1822.

Bk:Pg: 3C:400   Date: 12 May 1821   RtCt: 14 May 1821
John BRIDGES of Ldn to John EVANS of Ffx. Trust for debt to William CHICK using mulatto slaves George abt 15y, Eliza abt 12y, Thornton abt 10y, Thomas abt 7y & Julia abt 4y old, and horses. Wit: Elias WATHEN, W. H. ESKRIDGE, William EVANS.

Bk:Pg: 3C:401   Date: 22 Feb 1821   RtCt: 14 May 1821
Alfred WEEKS of Ldn to Hugh ROGERS. Trust for Jesse McVEIGH (jointly bound to Peyton POWELL) as security using farm animals and furniture. Wit: Towns'd McVEIGH. Delv. to Towns'd McVEIGH 22 May 1822.

Bk:Pg: 3C:403   Date: 2 Apr 1821   RtCt: 14 May 1821
John TOWPERMAN of Ldn to Wm. H. HANDEY of Ldn. Trust for debt to Peter TOWPERMAN using 15a. Wit: Micage JONES, Andrew TOWPERMAN, Jas. HILLARD. Delv to Peter TOWPERMAN 26 Nov 1824.

Bk:Pg: 3C:406   Date: 5 Apr 1821   RtCt: 14 May 1821
Levi PRINCE & wife Elizabeth of Ldn to Levi WATERS of Ldn. B/S of 5a between short hill and Blue Ridge adj John CONARD. Wit: Ebenezer GRUBB, Craven OSBURN. Delv. to WATERS 17 May 1823.

Bk:Pg: 3C:408   Date: 21 Apr 1821   RtCt: 14 May 1821
John DEMORY of Ldn to Nicholas ROPP of Ldn. Trust for debt to Elizabeth EVANS w/o Isaac EVANS (for money paid in B/S by William Dudley DIGGS to DEMORY) using 1½a on W side of short hill. Delv. pr order 17 Apr 1832.

Bk:Pg: 3C:410   Date: 30 Jan 1821   RtCt: 14 May 1821
Joshua B. OVERFIELD & wife Anna of Ldn to Edward B. GRADY. Trust for debt to Joseph RICHARDSON using interest in 1/5th of 22a of portion RICHARDSON & wife were entitled to and where OVERFIELD lived as heirs of Martin & Elizabeth OVERFIELD. Wit: Notley C. WILLIAMS, John W. GRAYSON.

Bk:Pg: 3C:412   Date: 30 Jan 1821   RtCt: 14 May 1821
John MARKS of Ldn to Edward B. GRADY of Ldn. Trust for debt to Joseph RICHARDSON using 8a formerly owned by Mary OVERFIELD and cnvy/b RICHARDSON to MARKS. Wit: Delv. to GRADY 5 Feb 1823.

Bk:Pg: 3C:414   Date: 18 Apr 1821   RtCt: 14 May 1821
Stephen WILSON & wife Hannah of Ldn to David JAMES of Ldn.
B/S of 50a being N end of land prch/o William WEST dec'd, adj
James BRADFIELD, Timothy TAYLOR. Wit: Stacey TAYLOR, David
SMITH, Charles TAYLOR, James COCHRAN Jr., Notley C.
WILLIAMS, John WHITE. Delv. to JAMES 14 Mar 1823.

Bk:Pg: 3C:416   Date: 20 Apr 1821   RtCt: 14 May 1821
Thomas SWAYNE of Ldn to David SHAWEN of Ldn. B/S of 13½a
(prch/o George JANNEY) adj Jacob WINE, E. GRUBB. Delv. to
SHAWEN 25 Mar 1824.

Bk:Pg: 3C:417   Date: 19 May 1821   RtCt: 19 May 1821
Sampson RICHARDS (insolvent) of Ldn to Sheriff Burr POWELL.
B/S of all interest in right of wife Elizabeth to land of father Henry
TAYLOR dec'd. Wit: John HAMILTON, John McCORMICK.

Bk:Pg: 3C:419   Date: 22 May 1821   RtCt: 22 May 1821
Jacob EARHART of Ldn to Sheriff Burr POWELL. B/S of all interest
in undivided 1/9th of 460a in FredVa where father Philip EARHEART
lived called 'Chappel Mill tract' and undivided 1/9th of land in
Harrison Co Va on Steer Creek which father bought of Christian
WIREMAN and 1/9th of land on Valley Creek in Hardin Co KY
convy/b Jacob FUNK to father and 1/7th of in Hardin Co Ky cnvy/b
Frederick KIGER & Jno. FUNK to 7 of the children of Philip
EARHART dec'd .

Bk:Pg: 3C:424   Date: 21 May 1821   RtCt: 22 May 1821
Jacob EARHART of Ldn to Wm. VICKERS of Ldn. B/S of cow and
household items. Wit: Benjn. BURSON, Aaron BURSON.

Bk:Pg: 3C:421   Date: 3 Mar 1821   RtCt: 25 May 1821
William CARTER Sr. to Benjamin GRAYSON Jr. & Notley C.
WILLIAMS of Ldn. Trust for debt to Stephen McPHERSON of Ldn
using adj John HATCHER, John WILKINSON, Isaac COWKILL,
Amos HIBS, Richard RICHARDS dec'd, James CARTER dec'd. Wit:
Jacob SILCOTT, Thomas DRAKE, William J. CARTER Jr. Delv. to
N. C. WILLIAMS 14 Oct 1834.

Bk:Pg: 3C:424   Date: 3 Mar 1821   RtCt: 25 May 1821
William CARTER Sr of Ldn to William CARTER Jr of Ldn. B/S of ½
of lot in Union adj James CARTER dec'd, John HATCHER, John P.
DULANEY, John WILKINSON, Isaac COWGILL, Amos HIBBS,
Richard RICHARDS dec'd (formerly land of Thomas BLACKBURN
dec'd and formerly occupied by Benjamin CUMMINGS & Jeremiah
SANFORD). Wit: Jacob SILCOTT, John W. GRAYSON, Stephen R.
MOUNT, Thomas DRAKE.

Bk:Pg: 3C:426   Date: 3 Mar 1821   RtCt: 25 May 1821
William CARTER Sr. of Ldn to Stephen McPHERSON Jr of Ldn. B/S
of 44a on road from Clifton Mill to Mark's Mill adj Abner

HUMPHREY. Wit: Jacob SILCOTT, John W. GRAYSON, Stephen R. MOUNT, Thomas DRAKE.

Bk:Pg: 3C:428   Date: 25 Aug 1820   RtCt: 26 May 1821
James CAMPBELL & wife Elizabeth of Ldn to Robert CAMPBELL of Ldn. B/S of 67a (part of Diggs' Valley cnvy/b Saml. M. EDWARDS). Wit: Presley CORDELL, Thomas SANDERS.

Bk:Pg: 3C:430   Date: 19 Apr 1821   RtCt: 28 May 1821
John CRIDELER & wife Elizabeth of Ldn to Peter FICHTER of Ldn. B/S of lot in Lsbg on N side of Loudoun St. adj John FICHTER, James GARNER. Wit: Presley CORDELL, Thomas SANDERS.

Bk:Pg: 3C:431   Date: 19 Apr 1821   RtCt: 18 May 1821
Peter FICHTER & wife Susannah of Ldn to John CRIDELER of Ldn. B/S of 14a Lot #7 in div. of Jacob STONEBURNER dec'd (DB YY:304) adj Dr. SELDEN.

Bk:Pg: 3C:433   Date: 25 Aug 1820   RtCt: 28 May 1821
Robert CAMPBELL & wife Jane of Ldn to Richard H. HENDERSON of Ldn. Trust for debt to Saml. M. EDWARDS using 67a (part of Digge's Valley cnvy/b brother James CAMPBELL). Wit: Presley CORDELL, Thomas SANDERS. Forwarded to EDWARDS 18 Nov 1853.

Bk:Pg: 3C:436   Date: 3 May 1821   RtCt: 28 May 1821
John WEST & wife Hannah of Ldn to Benjamin KENT of Ldn. B/S of 15a on NW fork of Goose Creek adj Jonas JANNEY. Wit: Notley C. WILLIAMS, John WHITE.

Bk:Pg: 3C:438   Date: 26 May 1821   RtCt: 29 May 1821
Presley CORDELL (as trustee of Silas REESE) of Ldn to Joseph HILLIARD of Ldn. B/S of 30a adj Joseph T. NEWTON, Patrick McINTYRE (prch/o Enoch FRANCIS from estate of Col. Thos. LEE dec'd and conveyed to REESE). Delv. to HILLIARD 13 Mar 1823.

Bk:Pg: 3C:439   Date: 24 May 1821   RtCt: 29 May 1821
Lewis COALE & wife Phebe of Wtfd to Skipwith COALE of Cecil Co Md. Mortgage of 1a lot & 4 pole lot in new addition of Wtfd (prch/o James MOORE & Mahlon JANNEY). Wit: Robert BRADEN, Abiel JENNERS. Delv. to Lewis COALE pr order of Skipwith COALE 13 Sep 1822.

Bk:Pg: 3C:442   Date: 30 May 1821   RtCt: 30 May 1821
Reuben BAGLEY of Ldn to Philip EVERHEART of Ldn. Trust for debt to John FISHELL of Ldn using farm animals and household items.

Bk:Pg: 3C:443   Date: 26 May 1821   RtCt: 1 Jun 1821
John L. GILL & wife Hannah of Ldn to George W. GRAYSON of Ldn. Trust for debt to Jacob SILCOTT of Ldn using 1¼a lot in Bloomfield (cnvy/b Richard CLARK). Wit: Benjn. GRAYSON, John W. GRAYSON.

Bk:Pg: 3C:446   Date: 29 Aug 1820   RtCt: 9 Apr 1821
Amos JOHNSON & wife Sarah of Mdbg to Benjamin MOFFETT of Mdbg. B/S of ¼a on Madison St. in Mdbg. Wit: Burr POWELL, A. GIBSON.

Bk:Pg: 3C:448   Date: 4 Apr 1821   RtCt: 1 Jun 1821
John L. GILL & wife Hannah of Ldn to George W. GRAYSON of Ldn. Trust for debt to John MARKS of Ldn using 1a (cnvy/b Richard CLARK). Wit: Benjamin GRAYSON, John W. GRAYSON.

Bk:Pg: 3C:450   Date: 12 Mar 1821   RtCt: 2 Jun 1821
John WALTMAN & wife Susana of Ldn to Jacob WALTMAN 3rd of Ldn. B/S of 1/8th share of 109a Samuel WALTMAN died possessed (subject to widow's dower now wife of Levi PRINCE) on Catocton Creek adj William PAXSON, John HAMILTON. Wit: Ebenezer GRUBB, Thomas J. MARLOW. Delv. to Jacob WALTMAN 2 Jan 1824.

Bk:Pg: 3C:452   Date: 19 Mar 1821   RtCt: 7 Jun 1821
Martin KITZMILLER of Ldn to Reuben SCHOOLEY of Ldn. BoS for rights to water under ground from tannery to his brewery. Wit: Math'w MITCHELL.

Bk:Pg: 3C:452   Date: 6 Jun 1821   RtCt: 6 Jun 1821
Mahlon JANNEY & wife Rachel and Amos JANNEY & wife Rachel and John JANNEY & wife Saran [Sarah?] of Ldn to Richard H. HENDERSON of Ldn Trust for debt to Joseph JANNEY of AlexDC using 161a from Amos JANNEY dec'd (father of all three) and adj 8a lot and shares of 130a from brother Nathan and Adam HOUSHOLDER. Wit: E. G. HAMILTON. Wit: Samuel MURREY, Presley CORDELL.

Bk:Pg: 3C:455   Date: 6 Jun 1821   RtCt: 6 Jun 1821
Peter BENEDUM of Ldn and Martin KITZMILLER of Ldn. Agreement to let KITZMILLER put in water pipe to Benedum's spring called The Rock Spring to his tannery. Wit: C. BINNS, Benjn. SHREVE. Delv. to KITZMILLER 2 Oct 1822.

Bk:Pg: 3C:456   Date: 24 Feb 1821   RtCt: 4 Jun 1821
Thomas SWAYNE of Ldn to Ebenezer GRUBB of Ldn. B/S of 20a adj GRUBB. Delv. to GRUBB 4 Jun 1822.

Bk:Pg: 3C:458   Date: 16 Mar 1821   RtCt: 4 Jun 1821
Peter SANDERS & wife Ann of Ldn to Ebenezer GRUBB of Ldn. B/S of 113a on branch of Katocton Creek adj GRUBB, William HOUGH, Adam HOUSEHOLDER. Wit: Abiel JENNERS, Samuel HOUGH Jr. Delv. to GRUBB 4 Jun 1822.

Bk:Pg: 3C:460   Date: 21 Feb 1821   RtCt: 4 Jun 1821
Thomas KIDWELL & wife Elizabeth of Ldn to Ebenezer GRUBB of Ldn. Trust for debt to David POTTS using 11a (cnvy/b John MATHIAS in 1818) and 47a adj other lot on W side of short hill and 56a on W side of short hill. Wit: Craven OSBURN, John WHITE.

Bk:Pg: 3C:464   Date: 5 Jun 1821   RtCt: 5 Jun 1821
Edward M. COE & wife Mary of Ldn to John W. COE of Ldn. B/S of
20a lot adj a 28a wood lot left to John W. by his father Edward COE
dec'd (DB WW:271).

Bk:Pg: 3C:466   Date: 6 Jun 1821   RtCt: 6 Jun 1821
Aaron SANDERS and Charles ELGIN to Mahlon JANNEY. Release
of trust on debt to Thomas R. MOTT on house & lot in Wtfd.

Bk:Pg: 3C:467   Date: 1 May 1820   RtCt: 5 Jun 1821
John James MATHIAS of Ldn to Levi WATERS of Ldn. B/S of 21a
on W side of short hill adj another lot of MATHIAS. Delv. to
WATERS 14 May 1823.

Bk:Pg: 3C:468   Date: 5 Jun 1821   RtCt: 5 Jun 1821
Edward M. COE & wife Mary of Ldn to William COE of Ldn. B/S of
35a (Menan COE late of Ldn died possessed of land on N side of
Goose Creek that was div. to Edward M. COE by will of father
Edward COE dec'd and exchanged but without a deed) adj d/o
Charles SMITH. Wit: Presley CORDELL, Thomas SANDERS.

Bk:Pg: 3C:470   Date: 19 Mar 1821   RtCt: 7 Jun 1821
Samuel M. EDWARDS of Ldn and Martin KITZMILLER of Ldn.
Agreement about pipeline for water to tannery. Wit: Thomas
SANDERS, John H. MONROE.

Bk:Pg: 3C:471   Date: 1 Jun 1821   RtCt: 9 Jun 1821
Jehu BURSON & wife Anna of Ldn to John H. BUTCHER of Ldn.
B/S of 108a (part of lot where Mary OVERFIELD resided and at her
death was purchased by John H. BUTCHER of her heirs and then
sold to BURSON). Wit: Notley C. WILLIAMS, John W. GRAYSON.

Bk:Pg: 3C:474   Date: 11 Jun 1821   RtCt: 11 Jun 1821
William CLENDENNING, Amos HARVEY & Robert RUSSELL. Bond
on CLENDENNING as constable.

Bk:Pg: 3C:474   Date: 26 Mar 1821   RtCt: 11 Jun 1821
Nicholas OSBURN. Oath as Lt. Col. with 2nd Reg. of Cavalry &
Second Div of Va Militia, commission dated 21 Feb 1821.

Bk:Pg: 3C:475   Date: 11 Jun 1821   RtCt: 11 Jun 1821
William ROSE, Johnson CLEVELAND & Richard H. HENDERSON.
Bond on ROSE as constable. Wit: Jno. A. BINNS.

Bk:Pg: 3C:476   Date: 1 Jan 1821   RtCt: 14 May 1821
James VIOLETT & wife Sarah of Ldn to James BOLES of Ldn. B/S
of 45a (Lot 9 in div. of John VIOLET dec'd in 1815) on Pantherskin
Run adj Elijah VIOLETT. Wit: Cuthbert POWELL, Joseph CARR.
Delv. to BOLES 24 Jan 1823.

Bk:Pg: 3C:478   Date: 18 Apr 1821   RtCt: 11 Jun 1821
Stephen WILSON & wife Hannah of Ldn to Thomas HUGHES of
Ldn. B/S of 50a (part of prch/o William WEST dec'd) adj Timothy
TAYLOR, Rufus UPDIKE. Wit: Stacy TAYLOR, David SMITH,
Charles TAYLOR, James COCHRAN Jr., Notley C. WILLIAMS, John

WHITE. Delv. to Samuel HUGHES Exor of Thomas HUGHES 28 Feb 1823.

Bk:Pg: 3C:480   Date: 9 Jun 1821   RtCt: 11 Jun 1821
Minor FURR to Joseph CARR. Trust for debt using farm animals and household items. Delv. to Caldwell CARR 10 Nov 1823.

Bk:Pg: 3C:481   Date: 9 Jun 1821   RtCt: 11 Jun 1821
William FOWKE to Joseph CARR. Trust for debt using farm animals and household items. Delv. to Caldwell CARR 10 Nov 1823.

Bk:Pg: 3C:482   Date: 9 Jun 1821   RtCt: 11 Jun 1821
William FOWKE to Benjamin GRAYSON. Trust for debt giving use for 12 months of negro woman Sucky & her 6 children Mary, Darky, Mariah, Lucy, Landon & Tom and young man Levi and 2 horses (purchased by FOWKE at D. Shff's sale of his prop.).

Bk:Pg: 3C:482   Date: 16 Sep 1820   RtCt: 11 Jun 1821
George SCOTT of Culpeper Co Va to Wm. BRONAUGH of Ldn. Trust for debt to Jacob SILCOTT using farm animals. Wit: Joseph W. BRONAUGH, George W. BRONAUGH.

Bk:Pg: 3C:484   Date: 17 Mar 1821   RtCt: 11 Jun 1821
Daniel O'NEALE & wife Anne of Ldn to John PANCOAST of Ldn. B/S of 33a (prch/o Daniel REESE). Wit: Wm. BRONAUGH, A. GIBSON. Delv. to Exor of John PANCOAST 6 Oct 1834.

Bk:Pg: 3C:486   Date: 31 May 1821   RtCt: 11 Jun 1821
George MARKS & wife Mahala of Ldn to David YOUNG of Ldn. Trust for debt to John PANCOAST Sr. using 200a adj John MARKS (devised by father Elisha MARKS dec'd) on road from Mill to Bloomfield. Wit: Notley C. WILLIAMS, John W. GRAYSON.

Bk:Pg: 3C:489   Date: 30 May 1821   RtCt: 11 Jun 1821
John MARKS & wife Lydia of Ldn to David YOUNG of Ldn. Trust for debt to Joshua PANCOAST of Ldn using 148 (devised by father Elisha MARKS) adj George MARKS, Notley C. WILLIAMS. Wit: Notley C. WILLIAMS, John W. GRAYSON. Delv. to PANCOAST 17 Mar 1824.

Bk:Pg: 3C:492   Date: 12 Jun 1821   RtCt: 12 Jun 1821
Westwood T. MASON & wife Ann of Ldn to Alfred BELT of Ldn. B/S of 241a (devised by father and cnvy/b brothers) adj Thomson MASON. Wit: Thomas SANDERS, John BAYLY. Delv. to BELT 16 May 1835.

Bk:Pg: 3C:494   Date: 9 Jun 1821   RtCt: 13 Jun 1821
Craven WALKER of Ldn to Benjamin MITCHELL Jr. of Ldn. Trust for debt to Willis TRIPLETT and Thornton WALKER (firm of TRIPLETT & WALKER) using negroes Delilah & Mary Ann and farm animals. Wit: Jesse TRAHERN, Felix TRIPLETT.

Bk:Pg: 3C:495   Date: 30 Jun 1821   RtCt: 14 Jun 1821
Joseph RICHARDSON & wife Susan of Ldn to Joshua B. OVERFIELD of Ldn. B/S of 22a undivided tract where Martin &

Elizabeth OVERFIELD formerly lived. Wit: Notley C. WILLIAMS, John W. GRAYSON.

Bk:Pg: 3C:497   Date: 13 Jun 1821   RtCt: 14 Jun 1821
William THATCHER & wife Mary, Jonah THATCHER & wife Mary and Henson ELLIOTT & wife Albinah of Ldn to Calvin THATCHER of Ldn. B/S of rights to 150a of Richard THATCHER dec'd adj James BEST, John LOVE, Isachar BROWN, Jonathan HEATON. Wit: John WHITE, Craven OSBURN.

Bk:Pg: 3C:499   Date: 13 Jun 1821   RtCt: 14 Jun 1821
Calvin THATCHER of Ldn to Charles CHAMBLING & Joshua OSBURN of Ldn. Trust for debt to Henson ELLIOTT of Ldn using above land. Delv. pr order 29 Mar 1826.

Bk:Pg: 3C:502   Date: 29 Jan 1821   RtCt: 11 Jun 1821
Joseph CARR of Ldn to Sarah CANNON of Ldn. LS of 1½a [also given as 1a] on turnpike road passing Ashby's Gap between the two churches in Upperville. Wit: Caldwell CARR, Abner HUMPHREY, Thomas KENNAN, Peter C. RUST. Delv. pr order 27 Feb 1828.

Bk:Pg: 3C:504   Date: 14 Jun 1821   RtCt: 16 Jun 1821
William THATCHER of Ldn to Hanson ELLIOTT of Ldn. BoS for crops. Wit: L. ELLZEY, Jonah THATCHER.

Bk:Pg: 3C:505   Date: 23 Apr 1821   RtCt: 18 Jun 1821
Jacob SKINNER. DoE for wife & woman of colour Suckey who he prch/o Charles CRIMM. Wit: Thomas PHILLIPS, David JANNEY.

Bk:Pg: 3C:506   Date: 26 Jul 1819   RtCt: 18 Jun 1821
Charles CRIM to Jacob SKINNER. BoS for negro woman Suckey. Wit: Thomas WHITE, Thomas PHILLIPS, David JANNEY.

Bk:Pg: 3C:506   Date: 23 Jun 1821   RtCt: 23 Jun 1821
Lindsey THOMAS & wife Nancy to Edward HAMMATT. CoE for Nancy on deed of Mar 1819. Wit: Samuel MURREY, Presley CORDELL. Delv. to Jno. SHAW the present holder of the lot pr order of Edw'd HAMMAT 3 Mar 1823.

Bk:Pg: 3C:507   Date: 4 May 1821   RtCt: 26 Jun 1821
Benjamin D. CLAGETT by attorney in fact William C. NEWTON to John P. MINNIX of Fqr. B/S of 125a (1 moiety of 250a allotted to Julia CLAGETT by Benjamin DULANEY Sr. dec'd in deed of settlement made to Daniel F. DULANEY & William HERBERT & said Benjamin as heir of mother Julia dec'd) now occupied by James H. DULANEY. Wit: Jas. L. PRINCE, William H. DORSETT, Jno. H. DUFFEY.

Bk:Pg: 3C:508   Date: 30 Jun 1821   RtCt: 30 Jun 1821
John SHAFFER of Ldn to Daniel MILLER of Ldn. Agreement – LS of 2 water grist and merchant mills and adj fields for 12 months for MILLER as security for SHAFFER to Henry RUCE & John GRAY. Wit: S. BLINCOE, Robt. BENTLEY, A. G. WATERMAN.

Bk:Pg: 3C:509   Date: 3 Jul 1821   RtCt: 3 Jul 1821
Richard H. HENDERSON to James CAMPBELL. Release of trust for debt to Saml. M. EDWARDS on 67a in Diggs' Valley.

Bk:Pg: 3C:510   Date: 19 Mar 1821   RtCt: 6 Jul 1821
Reuben SCHOOLEY of Ldn to Martin KITZMILLER of Ldn. B/S for privilege of putting a water pipe under ground in direction from Rock Spring to his tannery. Wit: Math'w MITCHELL. Delv. to KITZMILLER 20 Aug 1822.

Bk:Pg: 3C:511   Date: 10 Feb 1821   RtCt: 7 Jul 1821
James COCHRAN Jr. & wife Rachel of Ldn to Benjamin BRADFIELD of Ldn. B/S of 21a adj Bernard TAYLOR, Benjamin BRADFIELD. Wit: Notley C. WILLIAMS, John WHITE. Delv. to BRADFIELD 21 Aug 1824.

Bk:Pg: 3C:513   Date: 22 Jun 1810   RtCt: 12 Nov 1810/9 Jul 1821
Edward KELLY and Mary Ann KELLY of Ldn to Thomas CHAPMAN of Dumfries surviving trustee of William CARR dec'd. Trust for debt to CARR using 186a devised by father Thomas KELLEY who held L/L (all expired but Mary Ann) of Robert CARTER. Wit: Amasa RITICOR, Jacob MARSHALL Jr., Jeremiah SLACK.

Bk:Pg: 3C:515   Date: 9 Jul 1821   RtCt: 9 Jul 1821
Burr POWELL, Richard H. HENDERSON & Wm. CHILTON. Bond on POWELL as Sheriff to collect county poor rate.

Bk:Pg: 3C:516   Date: 9 Jul 1821   RtCt: 9 Jul 1821
Burr POWELL, R. H. HENDERSON & Wm. CHILTON. Bond on POWELL as Sheriff to collect levies.

Bk:Pg: 3C:517   Date: 11 Jun 1821   RtCt: 9 Jul 1821
Subscribers who agree to formation of Leesburg Friendship Fire Company: Charles GULLATT, Everitt SAUNDERS, Jno. T. WILSON, Saml. M. BOSS, Thomas SANDERS, Edward HAMMAT, William H. JACOBS, Abel ORISON, Thomas BIRKBY, Saml. TUSTIN, Aaron BIRD, John MURREY, Joshua REILEY, Geo. HEAD, B. W. SOWER, Wm. WOODDY, Arch McALLISTER, J. H. McCABE, Chas. B. BALL, Rich'd H. LEE, John H. MONROE, James L. MARTIN, Jacob MARTIN, Lewis BEARD, Jno. MOOR, Saml. CARR, Reuben SCHOOLEY, Thos. RUSSELL, Isaac HARRIS, John J. HARDING, Presley FOLEY, John CARNEY, Charles A. GULLATT, S. B. T. CALDWELL, Simon SMALE, Enos WILDMAN, Wm. COOKE, James THOMAS, Jacob FADELY, Geo. RICHARDS, S'n. BLINCOE, Thos. F. TEBBS, Robt. F. LACEY.

Bk:Pg: 3C:518   Date: 22 May 1821   RtCt: 23 May 1821
John H. BREWER & wife Delilah of Ffx to Robert MOFFETT of Ldn. B/S of all interest in former prop. of John MILHOLLAND dec'd which descended through mother Nancy BREWER dec'd sister of John

MILHOLLAND dec'd being 1/3 interest. Wit: Henry GUNNELL, Thomas MOSS. Delv. to MOFFETT 24 Feb 1823.

Bk:Pg: 3C:520   Date: 17 Mar 1821   RtCt: 17 May 1821
Vincent KELLY (insolvent) of Ldn to Sheriff Burr POWELL. B/S for executions from Amos JOHNSON, Cuthbert OWENS using land (1/16th part dev. Mahala KELLY w/o Vincent by will of Wm. MADDUX dec'd subject to deed of trust to Jacob ISH) in Fqr where Hannah MADDUX now lives.

3D:001   Date: 13 Jun 1821   RtCt: 9 Jul 1821
William BEAVERS of Ldn to James BEAVERS of Ldn. B/S of 150a (prch/o Joseph & Samuel BEAVERS Nov 1783, DB N:519). Wit: W. McCARTY, J. BEARD, Amasa RITCER. Delv. to James BEAVERS 17 Sep 1824.

3D:002   Date: 22 May 1821   RtCt: 9 Jul 1821
James TORBERT & wife Elizabeth of Ldn to Richard H. HENDERSON of Lsbg. Trust for Charles F. MERCER of Aldie (security with Joshua PANCOAST on bonds) using 111a on Bartons Branch and Bull Run Mt. where TORBERT now lives (prch/o Jonathan CARTER) adj Mathew RUST, Owen SULLIVAN. Wit: Wm. NOLAND.

3D:007   Date: 10 Jul 1821   RtCt: 10 Jul 1821
Sheriff Burr POWELL of Ldn to John Lewis FANT and Jacob TROUT of FredVa. B/S of 1/9th of Chappel tract in FredVa, 1/9th of 1000a in Harrison Co Va, 1/9th of tract in Harden Co Ky conveyed to father Philip EARHEART and 1/7th of 960a in Harden Co Ky cnvy/b Frederick KIGER & Jno FUNK to Jacob and six of his father's children (interest of insolvent debtor Jacob EARHEART). Delv. to TROUT 30 Jan 1822.

3D:008   Date: 9 Jul 1821   RtCt: 9 Jul 1821
James TORBERT of Ldn to Richard H. HENDERSON of Ldn. Trust for debt to Charles Fenton MERCER as security on debt to James' uncle Joseph CRAWFORD of Montgomery Co Pa.

3D:010   Date: 7 Jul 1821   RtCt: 9 Jul 1821
Thomas CHINN & wife Ann Hendly of Ldn to John MOREN of Ldn. B/S of ¾a above Mdbg on Ashbys Gap Turnpike. Wit: Leven LUCKETT, A. GIBSON. Delv. to MOREN 30 Sep 1822.

3D:012   Date: 7 Jul 1821   RtCt: 11 Jul 1821
William CARTER Sr., William CARTER Jr. and Jesse CARTER & wife Hannah of Ldn to George KEEN of Ldn. B/S of 128a at Xroads of road leading to Union and Clifton Mill adj Mahlon FULTON, Amos HIBBS, Isaac COWGILL. Wit: Benj'n GRAYSON, John W. GRAYSON. Delv. to KEENE 19 Mar 1823.

3D:015   Date: 2 Feb 1821   RtCt: 20 Jul 1821
Lewis HUNT tailor & wife Mary of Union to John JOHNSON of Union. B/S of lot in Union conveyed to HUNT by Annah GALLEHER.

Wit: William BRONAUGH, John W. GRASON. Delv. to JOHNSON 17 May 1822.

3D:016   Date: 26 Sep 1820   RtCt: 21 Feb 1821
Charles BINNS of Lsbg to Samuel M. EDWARDS of Lsbg. Trust for debt to John WALKER of FredMd using 146a and 20a. Delv. to EDWARDS 30 Sep 1822.

3D:018   Date: 28 Apr 1821   RtCt: 21 Jul 1821
Henry BALL of Ldn to William MARLOW of Ldn. Trust for debt to Edward MARLOW (as security on bond on distress to Saml CLAPHAM trustee of R. GRIFFITH) using farm animals and household items. Wit: Benj. THRUCE, John SCHOOLEY.

3D:019   Date: 27 Jul 1821   RtCt: 26 Jul 1821
James HIXSON & wife Sarah of Ldn to Alexander KERR cashier of Bank of the Metropolis of Washington D.C. Trust to bank using 330a (cnvy/b James SINCLAIR in Nov 1801) on little river adj John SINCLAIR, James SINCLAIR. Wit: Leven LUCKETT, William NOLAND.

3D:022   Date: 19 Jul 1821   RtCt: 5 Aug 1821
Yeoman William CARTER Sr., son Jesse CARTER & wife Hannah and son William CARTER of Ldn to yeoman Stephen McPHERSON (of William) of Ldn. B/S of 130a between Union and Bloomfield adj George KEENE, Isaac COWGILL, John WILKINSON, Isaac BROWN; and 4a. Wit: Benj'n GRAYSON, John W. GRAYSON.

3D:024   Date: 6 Feb 1821   RtCt: 6 Aug 1821
Andrew DIVERS of Ldn to Samuel DUNKIN of Ldn. B/S of 158a (under will of grandfather Peter OVERFIELD).

3D:025   Date: 28 Jul 1821   RtCt: 28 Jul 1821
William HAWKE of Ldn and Jane PERFECT of Ldn. Marriage contract – trust to Samuel M. EDWARDS for her use of household items and lot in Lsbg from father Robert PERFECT. Wit: John THOMAS, Giles HAMMAT, John J. MATHIAS.

3D:027   Date: 2 Feb 1821   RtCt: 6 Aug 1821
John JOHNSON & wife Sarah of Ldn to Thos. H. WEY of Ldn. Trust for bonds to Samuel DUNKIN using small portion of lot in Union cnvy/b Annah GALLEHER to JOHNSON. Wit: William BRONAUGH, John W. GRAYSON.

3D:029   Date: 14 Apr 1821   RtCt: 11 Aug 1821
John W. CLARK & wife Emily of Ldn to John DUNKIN of Ldn. B/S of 90¼a adj Geo. MARKS, Thomas TRAYHORN. Wit: Benj. GRAYSON, John W. GRAYSON.

3D:031   Date: 10 Aug 1821   RtCt: 10 Aug 1821
James H. DULANY of Ldn to Richard H. HENDERSON of Ldn. Trust for debt to Jacob SILCOTT and William VICKERS of Ldn as security at Bank of the Valley using share of land from father conveyed in trust to Hugh SMITH for benefit of creditors, adj John P. DULANY,

William VICKERS, Hiram SEATON, Mrs. Jemima LEWIS. Wit: E. G. HAMILTON, A. R. St. CLAIR, Thos. A. MOORE.

3D:032   Date: 18 Dec 1820   RtCt: 6 Aug 1821
Edward DULIN & wife Nancy of Ldn to Truman GORE of Ldn. B/S of 147a adj Jacob TODHUNTER. Wit: Chas. ELGIN, John DRISH, Richards ADAMS, Saml. CLAPHAM, Saml. DAWSON. Delv. to GORE 14 May 1824.

3D:034   Date: 21 Feb 1821   RtCt: ___
William Hardage LANE & wife Sarah of Burlington, Larence Co OH to Joshua HUTCHISON of Ffx. Trust for Harrison FITZHUGH of Ffx (as bond for LANE in Sup. Ct.) using stone brickhouse and lot in Lsbg (prch/o David OGDEN). Wit: Sanford HUTCHISON, Geo. HUTCHISON, William DONALDSON, Solomon BIRKLEY, Joseph WHEELER, L. S. WESTGATE.

3D:037   Date: 14 Aug 1821   RtCt: 14 Aug 1821
John JACKSON (as Exor of John JACKSON Sr. dec'd) to Abiel JENNERS. PoA. Delv. to JENNERS 18 Apr 1824.

3D:038   Date: 16 Aug 1821   RtCt: 16 Aug 1821
James D. FRENCH, Daniel STONE and William CHILTON. Bond on FRENCH as constable.

3D:039   Date: 6 Aug 1821   RtCt: 15 Aug 1821
John MILHOLLAND and Joseph CALDWELL. Division by decree of 13 Jun 1821 – Lot #1 to Joseph CALDWELL (2a), Lot #2 to John MILHOLLEN (5a). Gives plat. John E. PALMER apptd Guardian adletem to infant John MILHOLLAND under 21y old. Divisors: Robert BRADEN, Asa MOORE.

3D:040   Date: 1 Nov 1806   RtCt: 12 Jan 1807/13 Aug 1821
James McPHERSON & wife Elizabeth of Ldn to John DOWLIN of Ldn. B/S of 26a (dev. James from 285a cnvy/b Josiaph SETTLE & wife Elizabeth in Oct 1773 to Stephen McPHERSON dec'd f/o James) adj John GIBSON, Joseph CARR. Wit: Wm. BRONAUGH, Saml. DUNKIN, Benj. GRAYSON, Richard CLARK, Joseph CARR, Saml. BOGGES, John FLEMING, Joshua FLETCHER.

3D:043   Date: 20 Jul 1821   RtCt: 20 Jul 1821
Giles HAMMETT & wife Alice B. of Lsbg to Richard H. HENDERSON of Lsbg. B/S of 1a Lot #3 (part of 21a on N side of Market St sold by Jno. LITTLEJOHN to Overseers of the Poor). Wit: Robert BRADEN, Saml. M. EDWARDS.

3D:045   Date: 20 Jul 1821   RtCt: 20 Jul 1821
Thomas R. MOTT & wife Ann C. of Ldn to Giles HAMMETT of Ldn. B/S of 1a lot on N side of Market St (prch/o Wm. MOXLEY). Wit: Robert BRADEN, Saml. M. EDWARDS.

3D:046   Date: 28 Mar 1821   RtCt: 21 Jul 1821
James SWARTS Sr. & wife Elizabeth of Ldn to David DANIEL & wife Elizabeth of Ldn. B/S of 52a adj William CARR, heirs of Mrs. JONES

and 18a (part of 160a prch/o Burr POWELL). Wit: Robert ARMSTEAD, William NOLAND. Delv. to DANIEL 22 Feb 1826.

3D:049 Date: 3 Mar 1821 RtCt: 21 Jul 1821
Thomas KIDWELL & wife Elizabeth of Ldn to George KOUTZ of Ldn. B/S of 10a on Blue Ridge adj Samuel NEAR, reps of Conrod NEAR. Wit: Ebenzer GRUBB, John WHITE.

3D:051 Date: 24 Mar 1821 RtCt: 2 Aug 1821
Joseph STEER & wife Sarah of Ldn to William PAXSON of Ldn. B/S of 4a nr Wtfd (Lot #1 of those sold by Amos GIBSON) adj David JANNY, Mahlon JANNY, Joseph TALBOTT. Wit: Robert BRADEN, Abiel JENNERS. Delv. to PAXSON 12 May 1829.

3D:053 Date: 24 Mar 1821 RtCt: 2 Aug 1821
Enos WILLIAMS & wife Hannah of Ldn to William PAXSON of Ldn. B/S of Lot #11 in Wtfd (sold by Mahlon JANNY dec'd) adj Thomas LACY, Edward DORSEY. Wit: R. BRADEN, Abiel JENNERS. Delv. to PAXSON 15 May 1829.

3D:054 Date: 10 May 1821 RtCt: 2 Aug 1821
Asa MOORE & wife Ann of Ldn to William PAXSON of Ldn. B/S of 9a (prch/o Anthony CONROD Mar 1803) adj Patterson WRIGHT. Delv. to PAXSON 12 May 1829.

3D:056 Date: 2 May 1821 RtCt: 3 Aug 1821
Yeoman George MARKS & wife Mahala of Ldn to yeoman Stephen McPHERSON (of William) of Ldn. B/S of 24a (granted by late father Elisha MARKS) on Beaverdam adj John DUNKIN on road from Drake's mill to Bloomfield. Wit: N. C. WILLIAMS, John W. GRAYSON.

3D:058 Date: 8 Mar 1821 RtCt: 7 Aug 1821
John WINNER & wife Elizabeth of Ldn to John GEORGE of Ldn. B/S of 1a (interest in 60a dev. John BOOTH by Robert BOOTH and after death to heirs of Thomas STUMP and William CHAMBERS). Wit: Robert BRADEN, Thomas J. MARLOW. Delv. to John GEORGE Jr. 21 May 1851.

3D:060 Date: 10 Aug 1821 RtCt: 10 Aug 1821
Sam'l. M. EDWARDS & wife Ann of Ldn to William GILMORE of Ldn. B/S of 10a (prch/o Patrick McINTIRE) adj GILMORE. Wit: John ROSE, Robert BRADEN.

3D:061 Date: 19 Jul 1821 RtCt: 10 Aug 1821
William NOLAND & wife Catharine of Ldn to James SIMPSON of Ldn. B/S of 1a adj Aldie adj Lot #51. Wit: Ariss BUCKNER, John BAYLY.

3D:063 Date: 17 Aug 1821 RtCt: 18 ___ 1821
John A. WASHINGTON & wife Amelia of Ldn to Richard H. HENDERSON of Ldn. Trust for Samuel M. EDWARDS as security on notes to Edward MARLOW Admr of Arthur BOTLER dec'd, Saml. M. BOSS, John MORTEN, Henry RICKTER, Daniel P. CONROD,

RIGGS & PEABODY and Joseph BEARD using land in Ffx beq. by father Edward WASHINGTON (where he resided), farm animals, farm and household items, negro man Adam, woman Sucky& her 3 children Letty, Charles & Susan, woman Elisa, woman Letty, woman Winny & her child Mary. Delv. to Ffx Co to be recorded.

3D:066   Date: 26 Dec 1820   RtCt: 15 Mar 1821
John A. WASHINGTON of Ldn to Thomas SAUNDERS of Ldn. Trust for debt to Samuel M. EDWARDS and Charles ELGIN of Ldn as security on notes to Elizabeth NOLAND, Wm. T. T. MASON & Thomas MASON (Exors of Genl. A.T. MASON dec'd) using negro man Adam, woman Eliza, woman Sucky & her children Letty, Charles & Susan, woman Winney & her child Mary, woman Granny Lett. Delv. to EDWARDS 27 Jun 1822.

3D:068   Date: 21 Jul 1821   RtCt: 14 Aug 1821
John A. WASHINGTON of Ldn to Thomas SAUNDERS. Trust for Samuel M. EDWARDS as security on bond to Dep. Shff Benjamin SHREVE in suit agst WASHINGTON of Geo. M. CHICHESTER endorsed for use of R'd E. POTTER and suit of Jos. CALDWELL endorsed for benefit of R. S. BLACKLOCK and S. D. HARPER's trustee using farm animals. Delv. to EDWARDS 27 Jun 1822.

3D:070   Date: 31 May 1821   RtCt: 7 Sep 1821
Robert M. POWELL carpenter of Ldn to William VICKERS of Ldn. B/S of 15a (inherited from father Elisha POWELL) adj heirs of William LEITH, James LEITH Sr. dec'd, John MARTIN. Wit: Seth SMITH, Gourley REEDER, Saml. HAMMONTREE. Delv. to VICKERS 16 May 1822.

3D:071   Date: 7 Sep 1821   RtCt: 7 Sep 1821
John SINCLAIR of Ldn (insolvent debtor) to Sheriff Burr POWELL of Ldn. B/S of 85a in trust on little river where SINCLAIR lives, 150a in Belmont Co OH in trust (for executions of by William STUART for use of Isaac HITE, Lewis M. SMITH & Co for use of Fleet SMITH, William SINCLAIR for appearance bail, Elisha JANNEY, Amos JOHNSTON, Braden Morgan & Co assignees of John MOUNT).

3D:073   Date: 16 Aug 1821   RtCt: 10 Sep 1821
David J. COE. Commission as Lt. in 57th Reg. 6th Brigade, 2nd Div of Militia.

3D:073   Date: 10 Sep 1821   RtCt: 10 Sep 1821
Jesse TIMMS and George CARTER. Bond on Timms as commr. of revenue in 1st district.

3D:074   Date: 10 Sep 1821   RtCt: 10 Sep 1821
Jesse McVEIGH and Richard H. HENDERSON. Bond on McVEIGH as commr. of revenue in 2nd district.

3D:074   Date: 10 Sep 1821   RtCt: 10 Sep 1821
Clerk of Ct. Charles BINNS, John A. BINNS and R. H. HENDERSON bond to Wm. B. HARRISON, S. ROZELL, S. C.

ROZELL, Wm. NOLAND, Abiel JENNERS and John M. McCABE.
Bond on BINNS to collect taxes.

3D:075   Date: 7 Jul 1821   RtCt: 7 Sep 1821
Thomas CHINN & wife Ann Henly of Ldn to Barney NICKINGS (free
man of colour) of Ldn. B/S of 2a on N side of Ashby Gap Turnpike
road above Mdbg adj CHINN, heirs of his son Robert CHINN. Wit:
Francis W. LUCKETT, A. GIBSON. Delv. to NICKINS 16 Jan 1827.

3D:077   Date: 19 Jun 1821   RtCt: 7 Sep 1821
Yeoman William VICKERS & wife Anna of Ldn to carpenter Robert
M. POWELL of Ldn. B/S of ½a in Millville (part of lot cnvy/b Daniel
EACHES) adj Benjamin BROOK, Aaron BURSON. Wit: William
BRONAUGH, Francis W. LUCKETT.

3D:078   Date: 15 Dec 1819   RtCt: 5 Sep 1821
Edmund J. LEE & wife Sally of Alexandria to Thompson F. MASON
and Daniel MINOR of Alexandria. Trust for Daniel MINOR as
endorser on note to Farmer's Bank using 600a 'Faws Farm' but
called by LEE as "Ellenlie" abt 2 miles from Lsbg on Leesburg
turnpike. Delv. pr order 4 Feb 1823.

3D:081   Date: 27 Aug 1821   RtCt: 31 Aug 1821
Nathan JANNEY of Ldn to Amos JANNEY of Ldn. B/S of 1/7th part of
land of father Amos JANNEY dec'd under and to E of short hill.

3D:082   Date: ___ 1821   RtCt: 31 Aug 1821
William A. BINNS & wife Nancy of Ldn to Charles BINNS of Ldn. B/S
of 6a adj Simon A. BINNS, Charles BINNS, William A. BINNS, Peter
BENEDUM. Delv. to C. BINNS 7 Aug 1833.

3D:083   Date: 23 Jun 1821   RtCt: 29 Aug 1821
George MULL & wife Elizabeth of Ldn to Jacob WIRTZ of Ldn. B/S
of 1/7th part of land of David MULL dec'd. Wit: Robert BRADEN,
Samuel HOUGH.

3D:085   Date: 27 Aug 1821   RtCt: 28 Aug 1821
Dempsey CARTER & wife Mary Ann of Ldn to Stephen
McPHERSON of Ldn. B/S of 64a adj John H. BUTCHER. Wit:
Benjamin GRAYSON, John W. GRAYSON. Delv. to McPHERSON
14 Feb 1829.

3D:087   Date: 27 Aug 1821   RtCt: 28 Aug 1821
Robert BENTLEY (Admr wwa of Patrick McINTYRE) of Ldn to
Samuel CLAPHAM of Ldn. B/S of 118a on Goose Creek adj ___
EDWARDS. Delv. pr order 14 Jan 1823.

3D:089   Date: 27 Feb 1821   RtCt: 11 Jun 1821
Isaac NICKOLS Jr. and Amos GIBSON of Ldn to Hugh SMITH of
Ldn. B/S of interest of Israel GIBSON as heir of John GIBSON dec'd
(cnvy/b Israel in trust for debt to Benjamin BROOKE). Wit: Jesse
McVEIGH, Edw'd B. GRADY, Abel JANNEY, David CARTER.

3D:089   Date: 9 Aug 1821   RtCt: 28 Aug 1821
David LOVETT of Ldn to Fielder BIRCH of Ldn. B/S of interest in ¾a Lots #6, #7 & #8 in German Settlement adj Thomas STEPHENS. Wit: Saml. COOK, Daniel MILLER, William WENNERS. Delv. to grantor 13 May 1822.

3D:090   Date: 27 Aug 1821   RtCt: 28 Aug 1821
Charles BINNS & wife Hannah of Ldn to Saml. M. EDWARDS of Ldn. Trust for debt to Samuel A. TILLETT using 202a. Delv. to TILLETT 2 May 1826.

3D:092   Date: 25 Aug 1821   RtCt: 27 Aug 1821
Daniel THOMPSON of Ldn and Kimble HICKS. Agreement – to pay within the next year for use of farm and household items purchased by HICKS at sale under execution by the sheriff.

3D:093   Date: 129 Jan 1821   RtCt: 27 Aug 1821
James HIXSON & wife Sarah of Ldn to Benjamin HIXSON of Ldn. B/S of 3a on S side of turnpike road. Wit: William NOLAND, A. GIBSON. Delv. to B. HIXON 28 Aug 1824.

3D:095   Date: 25 Aug 1821   RtCt: 27 Aug 1821
Samuel A. TILLETT & wife Jane of Ldn to Charles BINNS of Ldn. B/S of 202¾a (subject to life estate of Samuel's mother). Wit: Thomas SAUNDERS, Saml. M. EDWARDS. Delv. to BINNS 30 Sep 1822.

3D:097   Date: 25 Aug 1821   RtCt: 25 Aug 1821
John G. MYERS of Ldn to Sheriff Burr POWELL of Ldn. B/S of house & lot in Upperville where he now lives and interest in adj lot which also adj Joseph CARR (for release of MYERS now committed to jail under execution issued in Fqr of Joseph LLOYED agst Wm. FULKINSON and MYERS as security).

3D:098   Date: 24 Feb 1821   RtCt: 25 Aug 1821
John GALLOWAY & wife Mary of Ldn to James ALLDER of Ldn. B/S of interest in estate of William CLAYTON dec'd as a distributee of Nancy CLARK dec'd (5a Lot #8 in div. on N side of turnpike road and 6a Lot #15). Wit: Benjamin GRAYSON, John W. GRAYSON. Delv. to ALLDER 9 Sep 1822.

3D:100   Date: 23 Aug 1821   RtCt: 24 Aug 1821
Wilson C. SELDON & wife Mary of Ldn to Sam'l. A. TILLETT of Ldn. B/S of 25a nr Lsbg. Wit: Thomas SANDERS, Saml. M. EDWARDS. Delv. to Chs. BINNS 26 Apr 1832.

3D:102   Date: 3 Sep 1819   RtCt: 15 Aug 1821
James SCOTT & wife Phebe and Rev. John MINES of Ldn to Charles B. BALL of Ldn. Trust to BALL for promissary note using lot & brick house on N side of Market St in west addition of Lsbg adj reps. of Henry McCABE dec'd. Wit: William SEEDERS, Joseph KNOX, Addison MINES. Delv. to Thomas R. MOTT Exor of Chas. B. BALL dec'd 13 Apr 1824.

3D:105   Date: 22 Aug 1821   RtCt: 22 Aug 1821

John L. GILL to Sheriff Burr POWELL. B/S of house and lot in Bloomfield (GILL in custody under execution agst him and Benjamin JENKINS in suit of Jesse McVEIGH assignee of Burr POWELL). Wit: Henry PEERS, S. BLINCOE, Giles HAMMET.

3D:106   Date: 7 Aug 1821   RtCt: 17 Aug 1821

Francis M. BECKWITH Deputy for John S. PEYTON Marshall of Winchester Chancery District to Harrison FITZHUGH of Ffx. B/S of lot of William H. LANE (held in trust) at intersection of Cornwall & King St. in Lsbg (Suit pending between David OGDEN and William H. LANE – LANE failed to make ordered payments, part was already sold to OGDEN).

3D:107   Date: 18 Mar 1820   RtCt: 22 Mar 1820/17 Aug 1821

William H. LANE now of Lsbg to David OGDEN of Lsbg. B/S of lot in Lsbg previously sold to LANE by OGDEN, adj Casper EKHART. Wit: S. BLINCOE, Thos. MORALLEE, Peter FEICHTER. Delv. to OGDEN 16 Dec 1828.

3D:109   Date: 10 Apr 1821   RtCt: 17 Aug 1821

William CHILTON of Lsbg to Lloyd NOLAND. Trust for loans from Burr POWELL, Cuthbert POWELL Jr. & Alfred H. POWELL (trustees of Sarah CHILTON) using house and ½a lot in Lsbg where he now lives and slaves Jenny, Matilda, Maria, Eliza, Alfred, Jane, Harriet, Henry, Wilson, Hannah and Jess. Wit: Edward B. POWELL, Cuthbert POWELL Jr., John MINES, Leven P. CHILTON. Delv. to Burr POWELL 12 Jun 1822.

3D:111   Date: 15 Jul 1818   RtCt: 17 Aug 1821

Charles Fenton MERCER of Aldie to Humphrey B. POWELL. Trust for Burr POWELL as endorser on notes from Lsbg branch of Bank of the Valley using nr 400a on Kitoctan Mt. adj Capt. ROSE. Wit: A. GIBSON, H. SMITH, Asa ROGERS. Delv. to B. POWELL 14 Apr 1824.

3D:113   Date: 25 Nov 1820   RtCt: 16 Aug 1821

Thomas DRAKE of Ldn to Dempsey CARTER of Ldn. B/S of 61a adj Mordecia THROCKMORTON, William WINN.

3D:115   Date: 23 Nov 1820   RtCt: 16 Aug 1821

John NIXON & wife Jane of Harrison Co Ohio to George RHODES of Ldn. B/S of 22a adj __ CURRY, __ THOMAS, __ BENEDUM. Wit: James FERRELL, John McCONKEY. Delv. to RHODES 9 Apr 1836.

3D:116   Date: 5 Jun 1821   RtCt: 15 Aug 1821

David LOVETT of Ldn to Mary BONTZ of Ldn. B/S of ¼a Lots #45 & #46 in German Settlement. Wit: Feilder BURCH, John GOUER [GOWER], Henry COYSIL [COWSILL]. Delv. to Mary AKEY alias Mary BONTZ 30 May 1826.

3D:117   Date: 15 Aug 1821   RtCt: 15 Aug 1821
George NIXON of Ldn to Thomas BROWN of Ldn. B/S of 4¼a nr
Beaverdam (allotted to George from estate of George NIXON the
elder dec'd). Delv. to BROWN 30 Nov 1826.

3D:119   Date: 23 Dec 1820   RtCt: 14 Aug 1821
Richard H. HENDERSON & wife Orra M. of Ldn to William H.
HANDY of Ldn. B/S of 147¼a. Wit: Samuel MURREY, Thomas
SANDERS.

3D:120   Date: 23 Dec 1820   RtCt: 14 Aug 1821
William H. HANDY & wife Elenor of Ldn to Samuel M. EDWARDS of
Lsbg. Trust for debt to Rich'd H. HENDERSON using above 147¼a.
Wit: William BRONAUGH, A. GIBSON. Delv. to EDWARDS 9 Dec
1825.

3D:123   Date: 12 Apr 1821   RtCt: ___
William NOLAND & wife Catharine of Ldn to James LLOYD of Ldn.
B/S of ½a Lot #74 on Mercer St. in [Mdbg]. Wit: Ariss BUCKNER, J.
BALY.

3D:125   Date: 7 Aug 1821   RtCt: 13 Aug 1821
John HITAFFER of Ldn to John P. DUVAL of Ldn Trust for note to
Hiram McVEIGH and Noble BEVERIDGE using farm and household
items.

3D:126   Date: 21 Mar 1821   RtCt: 13 Aug 1821
Plaisterer Jehu BURSON & wife Anna of Ldn to yeoman John
BURSON of Ldn. B/S of 53a (cnvy/b Josiah GREGG & wife
Margaret) adj Joseph BURSON, George BURSON. Wit: N. C.
WILLIAMS, Jno. W. GRAYSON.

3D:128   Date: 19 Mar 1821   RtCt: 13 Aug 1821
Thomas SINCLAIR and Geo. H. SINCLAIR of Ldn to Charles
THORNTON of Ldn. B/S of 62¼a (interest in land of father Samuel
SINCLAIR dec'd except dower of mother Edith SINCLAIR). Wit: Jos.
KNOTT, Thos. G. JORDON, Thos. DRAKE. Delv. to THORNTON 30
Oct 1822.

3D:129   Date: 11 Aug 1821   RtCt: 13 Aug 1821
Morris MOORE, Thomas MOORE and Pierce MO[O]RE to Sydnor
BAILY and Cuthbert POWELL. Trust for debt to Joseph CARR using
126a leased lots where Morriss now lives adj Elizabeth T.
HARRISON, heirs of Archibald FLEMING dec'd (less a few acres
sold to Cuthbert POWELL) and farm items. Wit: Robert
SINGLETON, Lewis FRENCH, Caldwell CARR. Delv. to C. CARR
by direction of S. BAILY 10 Feb 1823.

3D:131   Date: 8 Aug 1821   RtCt: 13 Aug 1821
John MILLER & wife Catharine of Fqr to Michael RICHARDS of Fqr.
B/S of 4a of timber land and 2½a cleared land (due as heirs of
Susannah HOUSEHOLDER dec'd).

3D:132   Date: 3 Mar 1821   RtCt: 13 Aug 1821
Thomas KIDWELL & wife Elizabeth of Ldn to Samuel NEAR of Ldn.
B/S of 8a on Blue Ridge (part of land prch/o Ferd'o FAIRFAX) adj __
KOONTZ. Wit: Ebenezer GRUBB, John WHITE. Delv. to NEAR 15
Apr 1833.

3D:134   Date: 29 Mar 1821   RtCt: 13 Aug 1821
James SWART(S) Sr. & wife Elizabeth of Ldn to William SWART(S)
of Ldn. Gift of 90a adj Casper JOHNSTON, David DANIELS, William
CARR. Wit: William NOLAND, Robert ARMSTEAD.

3D:136   Date: 21 Apr 1821   RtCt: 13 Aug 1821
Vallentine JACOBS of Ldn to Samuel NEAR of Ldn. B/S of 3a
between short hill and Blue ridge adj Ebenezer GRUBB (transferred
by Elizabeth JACOBS to Vallentine). Delv. to NEAR 15 Apr 1833.

3D:137   Date: 13 Aug 1821   RtCt: 13 Aug 1821
Cornelius VANDEVANTER of Ldn to Thornton WALKER of Ldn.
Trust for Isaac VANDEVANTER and Thomas CLEWS as securities
for debt to John PANCOST using farm animals and items.

3D:138   Date: 3 Oct 1821   RtCt: 3 Oct 1821
William NOLAND & wife Catharine of Ldn to Charles F. MERCER
and Richard HENDERSON & Thomas R. MOTT. Trust for payment
on land where NOLAND lives to J. VANDENHENVILLE of NY,
MERCER is security for executions to Thomas SWANN for the use
of Geo. CARTER thru bonds to Edward S. MARLOW assignee for
William JENKINS, Colin AULD, Charles J. CATLESS, C. & J. P.
THOMPSON, S. COFFER, J. VAUGHN assignee of James
ROBERTSON of PhilPa using land and slaves Ben, Payne, Jacob,
Sucky, Kelly the cook, Kelly, Albert, Ida, Robert, Clarissa and
servants for a term of years Bidwell, Sandy & Sampson.

3D:140   Date: 2 May 1821   RtCt: 28 Aug 1821
Henley BOGGESS of Fqr to Richard H. HENDERSON of Ldn. Trust
for debt to John D. BROWN (agent for the Columbian Factory Co of
Alex) using interest in land from father Samuel BOGGESS dec'd.

3D:142   Date: 4 Jul 1821   RtCt: 11 Sep 1821
Jonathan CARTER and John SINCLAIR (trustees of Moses
WILSON) to Hugh ROGERS. B/S of 20½a on S side of Goose
Creek adj Dennis McCARTY, Joseph EDISON (trust on 52½a dated
Jan 1817 WILSON to CARTER and SINCLAIR is partially unpaid).

3D:143   Date: 11 Sep 1821   RtCt: 13 Sep 1821
Joel OSBURN of Ldn to Balaam OSBURN of Ldn. B/S of 127a on
Goose Creek adj __ BEVERIDGE, Leven LUCKETT, __ TAPSEY.

3D:145   Date: 4 Jun 1821   RtCt: 14 Sep 1821
Joseph LEWIS of Ldn to Peter VIRTS of Ldn. B/S of 101a (prch/o
Ferdinando FAIRFAX) adj Joseph SMITH, John WITTERMAN,
Henry FRY. Wit: John GEORGE, George SHOVER, John GEORGE
Jr. Delv. to VIRTS 10 Jun 1822.

3D:146 Date: 24 Apr 1821 RtCt: 3 Oct 1821
Nicholas ROPP & wife Elizabeth of Ldn to Michael DERRY of Ldn.
B/S of 54 sq perch lot between short hill and Blue ridge adj __
SMITH, __ DEMARY, school house lot. Wit: Ebenezer GRUBB,
John WHITE.

3D:148 Date: 8 Aug 1821 RtCt: 19 Sep 1821
Calvin THATCHER and William THATCHER of Ldn to Stephen
GREGG Jr. of Ldn Trust for debt to Thomas GREGG as security on
bonds using farm and household items. Wit: L. ELLSEY, Joshua
OSBURN, Robert CUMMINGS.

3D:150 Date: 19 Sep 1821 RtCt: 19 Sep 1821
Samuel BUCK & wife Mary of Ldn to Samuel RICHARDSON Sr. of
Ldn. B/S of lot in Lsbg with frame dwelling house, adj H.
GLASSGOW, Samuel M. EDWARDS on S side of Royal St., Peter
BOSS (prch/o J. RILEY). Wit: Thomas SANDERS, John W.
McCABE. Delv. to Wm. ELLZEY atty for RICHARDSON 13 Sep
1822.

3D:151 Date: 28 Aug 1821 RtCt: 28 Sep 1821
George MARKS & wife Mahala of Ldn to Thomas DRAKE of Ldn.
B/S of 25a adj DRAKE nr house where Phenias THOMAS resides,
John MARKS. Wit: James JOHNSTON, Peyton MOORE, Geo. S.
MARKS, Notley C. WILLIAMS, John W. GRAYSON. Delv. pr order 8
Jul 1826.

3D:153 Date: 29 Sep 1821 RtCt: 29 Sep 1821
William WHITE of Ldn to Levi WHITE of Ldn. B/S of 3 roods (part of
tract sold Daniel WHITE by John THRELKELD in 1796) adj
GARDNER's lease. Delv. to Levi WHITE 17 Jan 1823.

3D:154 Date: 29 Sep 1821 RtCt: 29 Sep 1821
Levi WHITE & wife Mary of Ldn to William WHITE of Ldn. B/S of 2a
(part of tract sold Daniel WHITE by John THRELKELD in 1796). Wit:
John McCORMACK, Presley CORDELL. Delv. to William WHITE 19
Oct 1822.

3D:156 Date: 29 Sep 1821 RtCt: 1 Oct 1821
John SHAFFER & wife Mary of Ldn to Emanuel AXLINE. Trust for
debt to Jacob DAVIS using land where SHAFFER now lives, land
where Phillip SWANK lives and land where Daniel AXLINE now
lives. Wit: Richard H. HENDERSON, Geo. HAMMET, Giles
HAMMET.

3D:157 Date: 1 Oct 1821 RtCt: 1 Oct 1821
William GILMORE of Ldn to Barnet HOUGH of Ldn. Release of trust
dated Jul 1813 (DB QQ:369). Delv. to B. HOUGH 7 Apr 1824.

3D:158 Date: 22 Sep 1821 RtCt: 1 Oct 1821
Benjamin SHREVE & wife Nancy of Ldn to William GILMORE of
Ldn. B/S of land where ponds of mill sold by Barnet HOUGH to
GILMORE and Samuel BUCK overflow in land owned by SHREVE

who sued for damages. Wit: Richard H. HENDERSON, W. C. SELDON, Thomas A. MOORE, John McCORMICK, Presley CORDELL. Delv. to SMITH & EDWARDS 4 May 1849.

3D:160 Date: 22 Sep 1821 RtCt: 1 Oct 1821
Barnet HOUGH & wife Looice/Louisa of Ldn to William GILMORE of Ldn. B/S of 123a with grist mill on Tuskarora. Wit: John McCORMICK, John H. McCABE. Delv. to D. G. SMITH & T. W. EDWARDS 4 May 1849.

3D:162 Date: 29 Sep 1821 RtCt: 2 Oct 1821
Joseph CALDWELL & with Eliza of Ky to George RUST Jr of Ldn. B/S of 2a where RUST now lives. Wit: John McCORMICK, Presley CORDELL.

3D:163 Date: 1 Aug 1821 RtCt: 8 Oct 1821
William KIRK & wife Nancy of Belmont Co Oh to Samuel HAMMET of Ldn. B/S of ¼a lot on N side of Market St. in Lsbg adj Benjamin MAULSBY (cnvy/b John PAYNE & wife). Wit: Aug's M. GROVE, Chas. ROBERTSON. Delv. to HAMMATT 15 Sep 1823.

3D:166 Date: 17 Aug 1821 RtCt: 8 Oct 1821
Amos JOHNSTON (who holds interest of John CRIDER and John M. FRYE & wife Emily late Emily CRIDER in the estate of Frederick CRIDER dec'd) orders that Margaret the defendant be appointed Guardian adlitum to defendant William CRIDER and Frederick CRIDER Jr. Jesse McVEIGH and Hugh ROGERS court ordered on 17 Aug 1821 to sell negroes Milly and her children, but could not get negro.

3D:167 Date: 1 Sep 1821 RtCt: ___
Jasper POULSON dec'd. Division – court ordered 14 Aug 1821; widow's dower (40a), Thomas TREBBY & wife Deborah (12a Lot #1), John TREBBY & wife Lydia (12a Lot #2), Agness POULSON (12a Lot #3), Isabella POULSON (10a Lot #4), Elizabeth BOVARD (13a Lot #5), John POULSON (10a Lot #6), Samuel SPENCER & wife Margaret (15a Lot #7), Susannah PIERCE (13a Lot #8), Robert WHITE & wife Mary (12a Lot #9), William POULSON (12a Lot #10). Gives plat. Divisors: Stacy TAYLOR, James LOVE, Joshua OSBURN.

3D:169 Date: ___ Nov 1821 RtCt: ___
Burr POWELL, Cuthbert POWELL, Benjamin SHREVE, Leven LUCKETT and Richard H. HENDERSON. Bond on Burr POWELL as sheriff to collect taxes.

3D:170 Date: 12 Nov 1821 RtCt: 12 Nov 1821
Burr POWELL, Cuthbert POWELL, Benjamin SHREVE, Leven LUCKETT and Richard H. HENDERSON. Bond on Burr POWELL as sheriff to collect levies.

3D:170   Date: 12 Nov 1821   RtCt: 12 Nov 1821
Burr POWELL, Cuthbert POWELL, Benjamin SHREVE, Leven
LUCKETT and Richard H. HENDERSON. Burr POWELL as sheriff
to collect and pay officers fees.

3D:171   Date: 12 Nov 1821   RtCt: 12 Nov 1821
Garrison B. FRENCH, James D. FRENCH and John HOLMES.
Bond on Garrison B. FRENCH as constable.

3D:172   Date: 16 Aug 1821   RtCt: 12 Nov 1821
John SKILLMON. Commission as Ensign in 57th Reg 6th Brigade 2nd
Div. of Militia.

3D:172   Date: 6 Oct 1821   RtCt: 6 Oct 1821
Richard H. HENDERSON (as trustee of Adam BARR) of Ldn to
Casper JOHNSTON of Ldn. B/S of 10a & house (in trust to BARR
for him as security agst debt to Amos JOHNSTON & John
ROBERTS). Delv. to JOHNSON 16 Sep 1824.

3D:173   Date: 10 Feb 1821   RtCt: 8 Oct 1821
Robert CUMMINGS (who m. Sarah d/o John EVANS dec'd) to Abel
JANNEY. B/S of Sarah's 1/8th interest in land of her father (after
death or marriage of her mother). Wit: James M. JANNEY, Phillip
GRIFFITH, Thomas GRIFFITH, Notley C. WILLIAMS, John W.
GRAYSON. Delv. to JANNEY 4 Apr 1823.

3D:175   Date: 26 Oct 1821   RtCt: 3 Nov 1821
George SINCLAIR & wife Margaret of Ldn to John J. MATHIAS of
Ldn. Trust for debt to Samuel CLAPHAM using 100a of Potomac
River. Wit: Saml. DAWSON, James M. LEWIS.

3D:177   Date: 26 Oct 1821   RtCt: 3 Nov 1821
William HAWLING of Ldn to John J. MATHIAS of Ldn. Trust for
bonds to Samuel CLAPHAM using 201a on Potowmac River.

3D:179   Date: 26 Oct 1821   RtCt: 3 Nov 1821
Samuel CLAPHAM & wife Elizabeth of Ldn to William HAWLING of
Ldn. B/S of 201a on Potomac River. Wit: Samuel DAWSON, James
M. LEWIS.

3D:181   Date: 26 Oct 1821   RtCt: 3 Nov 1821
Samuel CLAPHAM & wife Elizabeth of Ldn to George SINCLAIR of
Ldn. B/S of 100a on Potomac River adj __ HAWLING. Wit: James
M. LEWIS, Saml. DAWSON. Delv. to Chas. GULLATT the owner 1
Jul 1843.

3D:183   Date: 1 Nov 1821   RtCt: 2 Nov 1821
Stephen McPHERSON & wife Cecelia of Ldn to Benjamin
GRAYSON of Ldn. B/S of 1a lot on SE side of Washington St in
Bloomfield nr William R. COMB's House. Wit: Benj'n GRAYSON,
John W. GRAYSON.

3D:185   Date: 23 Nov 1821   RtCt: 29 Oct 1821
Moses WILSON to William H. HANDY and Thomas DRAKE. Trust
for debt to William WYNNE using 50a adj Denes McCARTY, John

RUSSELL. Wit: Thomas DRAKE, Absolam DENNIS, James B. WILSON. Delv. to DRAKE 15 Nov 1823.

3D:187   Date: 26 Oct 1821   RtCt: 27 Oct 1821
Dpty Shff Francis M. BECKWITH for marshall John S. PEYTON of Winchester Chancery District (for recovery of money in Ct. suit of 10 Apr 1821 Tilghman HILLEARY agst Susan BROOKS wd/o Walter BROOKE dec'd and children Henry, Caleb, Arthur, Susan, Rufus, Emily and Virginia BROOKE) to Samuel CLAPHAM of Ldn. B/S of 242a (prch/o Phillip NOLAND Jr. & wife Mary by Clement WHEELER in May 1777), 300a (prch/o Josias CLAPHAM & wife Sarah by Clement WHEELER in Aug 1777), 50a (prch/o John SINCLAIR & wife Sarah in Aug 1778) all devised by WHEELER to Samuel H. WHEELER and Ann now w/o Tilghman HILLEARY and WHEELER sold his share to HILLEARY who sold to BROOKE.

3D:190   Date: 24 Oct 1821   RtCt: 26 Oct 1821
Francis M. BECKWITH (acting as commr. under decree of Winchester Chancery district of 2 Dec 1820 in suit of William LANE Jr. Admr. of James LANE dec'd agst Samuel DICKERSON Exor of William SAVAGE dec'd and the devisees of William MARTIN dec'd - John, Edward, Robert, Andrew, Elizabeth and Mary MARTIN) to devisees of William MARTIN dec'd. B/S to convey title of 300a nr Union.

3D:191   Date: 4 Oct 1821   RtCt: 23 Oct 1821
Stephen McPHERSON & wife Sarah of Ldn to Joseph GARRETT of Ldn. B/S of 19a adj Stephen McGEATH, said GARRETT, Samuel & Isaac NICKOLS. Wit: William BRONAUGH, Francis LUCKETT.

3D:193   Date: 14 Jul 1821   RtCt: 19 Oct 1821
Samuel E. TAYLOR & wife Ann of Ldn to Jacob MOCK of Ldn. B/S of 104a (part of tract allotted TAYLOR from Jesse TAYLOR dec'd) adj John TAYLOR, Conrod VIRTS, E. DORSEY. Wit: Robert BRADEN, Abiel JENNERS. Delv. to MOCK 25 Nov 1822.

3D:195   Date: 29 Sep 1821   RtCt: 18 Oct 1821
James TORBERT & wife Elizabeth of Ldn to Charles Fenton MERCER of Aldie. B/S of 112a. Wit: Burr POWELL. A. GIBSON, Samuel TORBERT, Leven LUCKETT. Delv. to MERCER 13 Oct 1834.

3D:197   Date: 3 May 1821   RtCt: 18 Oct 1821
William CLAYTON of Ldn to Martha CLAYTON of Ldn. B/S of 100a derived from will of William CLAYTON dec'd. Wit: Robert ORR, Amos CLAYTON, Townsend CLAYTON.

3D:198   Date: 8 Oct 1821   RtCt: 8 Oct 1821
John SHAFFER & wife Mary of Ldn to Geo. M. SHAWEN and Alexander COUPER Jr. of Ldn. Trust for debt to Jacob DAVIS using 61½a now occupied by Samuel AXLINE and 55½a adj Michael BOGER and 121a now occupied by Phillip SWANK and 152½a now

occupied by Daniel AXLINE. Wit: Giles HAMMETT, Geo. HAMMETT, John HAWLING.

3D:202 Date: 13 Jun 1821 RtCt: 12 Oct 1821
John W. GRAYSON of Ldn to James HOGE of Ldn. Trust for debt to Samuel & Isaac NICHOLS using 84a adj Benjamin GRAYSON, Thomas DRAKE, James CARTER dec'd, Dempsey CARTER, Abner HUMPHREY (prch/o Mahlon CARTER & wife Catharine). Wit: Asa WELLS, Daniel FOLLIN, Phebe COHAGAN, Phebe NICKOLS. Delv. to Wm. HOGUE 14 Mar 1829.

3D:205 Date: 12 Apr 1819 RtCt: 14 Feb 1820/15 Oct 1821
James RUST & wife Sarah and Charles CHAMBLIN & wife Ruth of Ldn to Issacher BROWN of Ldn. B/S of 53a adj Eli McKNIGHT, David LOVETT, Charles CHAMBLIN. Wit: James H. HAMILTON, Patrick McINTYRE, Cravin OSBURN, John WHITE. Delv. to BROWN 30 May 1823.

3D:208 Date: 11 Oct 1821 RtCt: 15 Oct 1821
Ammon HEREFORD & wife Amilia of Culpeper Co Va to James RUST of Ldn. B/S of 36a nr Lsbg on E side of Carolina road adj Samuel HOUGH, Dr. SELDON.

3D:210 Date: 1 Oct 1821 RtCt: 15 Oct 1821
John James MATHIAS of Ldn to David POTTS of Ldn. B/S of 324a on Blue Ridge adj POTTS.

3D:212 Date: 8 Mar 1821 RtCt: 15 Oct 1821
Nathaniel MANNING & wife Euphemia of Ldn to William SUMMERS of Ldn. B/S of 20a (prch/o George SAUNEY) adj John WRIGHT, Jeremiah MILLER. Wit: Abiel JENNERS, Samuel HOUGH Jr. Delv. to SUMMERS 1 Sep 1825.

3D:214 Date: 11 Oct 1821 RtCt: 11 Oct 1821
James MOUNT of Ldn to Rich'd H. HENDERSON and Hugh SMITH. Trust for debt to C. & J. P. Thomson, Thomas Janney & Co, Braden Morgan & Co, Hugh Smith &Co all of Alexandria and John B. FRENCH of __ and John PANCOST of FredMd using 147¼a (cnvy/b William H. HANDY & wife Eleanor in 1819). Delv. to HENDERSON 7 Aug 1823.

3D:216 Date: 11 Sep 1821 RtCt: 9 Oct 1821
Balaam OSBURN of Ldn to Joshua OSBURN of Ldn. Trust for debt to Joel OSBURN using 127a on Goose Creek. Delv. pr order filed by Jas. HAMILTON 8 Mar 1830.

3D:218 Date: 24 Feb 1821 RtCt: 26 Oct 1821
Noah HIXSON of Ldn to John JANNEY (of Amos) of Ldn. B/S of 2a (awarded from land of Reuben HIXSON dec'd) adj David SHAWEN.

3D:220 Date: 4 Aug 1821 RtCt: 12 Oct 1821
Samuel GREGG of Ldn to John HOLMES of Ldn. Trust for debt to Josiah GREGG 113a adj Richard BROWN, and farm animals and household items. Delv. to HOLMES 18 May 1822.

3D:223 Date: 23 Oct 1821 RtCt: 12 Nov 1821
Jesse HARRIS & wife Margaret of Loudoun Co Oh [?] to Thomas
BISCOE of Ldn. B/S of 80a on Goose Creek (part of estate of
George NIXON the elder dec'd not devised by him). Wit: John
CUNNINGHAM, Silas JAGGER. Affidavit from Licking Co. Oh.

3D:225 Date: 7 Nov 1821 RtCt: 12 Nov 1821
Thompson MASON & wife Ann of Ldn to John J. STULL of D.C. and
John ROSE of Ldn. Trust for debt to Farmers and Mechanics Bank
of Georgetown using 162½a 'Liberia' where MASON lives adj
Abraham B. T. MASON and W. T. MASON. Wit: Bernard
SPALDING, Walter NEWTON, Abiel JENNERS, James M. LEWIS.
Delv. to t. MASON pr order 1 May 1824.

3D:229 Date: 9 Nov 1821 RtCt: 9 Nov 1821
Richard H. HENDERSON (as trustee of James H. DULANY) of Lsbg
to Edward HALL of WashDC. B/S of 145a adj William VICKERS,
Jemima LEWIS.

3D:230 Date: 5 Nov 1821 RtCt: 7 Oct 1821
Elizabeth FENTON of Ldn to Hiram SEATON of Ldn. B/S of 56a
including attached 8a wood land on Panther Skin Creek (dev. by
John VIOLETT dec'd to Jemima FENTON and her children). Delv. to
SEATON 28 Oct 1839.

3D:232 Date: 24 Sep 1821 RtCt: 15 Nov 1821
Thomas JANNEY & wife Sarah Elizabeth of AlexDC to Robert J.
TAYLOR of AlexDC. Trust for debt to Alexandria Bank as endorser
for notes of D. & J. ROSS using 8a on Goose Creek with water grist
mill and saw mill. Wit: Henry COOPER, John G. JANNEY, Jno. A.
REED, Newton KEENE, Thomas VOWELL. Delv. to Jonah? ? pr
order of R. T. TAYLOR 11 Nov 1822.

3D:236 Date: 18 Jan 1820 RtCt: 29 Nov 1821
Thomas REED & wife Catharine of Hamilton Co Oh to Samuel
BEAVERS of Ldn. B/S of 1/th interest in 2 lots which Rebecca
REED wd/o James REED dec'd holds a life estate. Delv. to Thomas
BEAVERS Exor of Saml. BEAVERS 16 Mar 1839.

3D:237 Date: 12 Nov 1821 RtCt: 12 Nov 1821
Robert BRADEN and John S. MARLOW (trustees of Solomon
VICKROY) of Ldn to John GEORGE and Frederick SLATES of Ldn.
B/S of 2a adj ___ ROWBOUGH.

3D:238 Date: 3 Aug 1821 RtCt: 16 Nov 1821
George HUFF & wife Elizabeth of Muskingum Co Oh to Conrad
WIRTZ of Ldn. B/S of 2a (HUFF to retain right to use of water of
broad run for mill) adj Sanford RAMEY, Frederick COOPER. Wit:
John PETERS, Moses L. MOORE.

3D:241 Date: 15 Feb 1821 RtCt: 10 Dec 1821
Moses ELY & wife Hannah of East Nottingham, Chester Co Pa to
William REEDER of Ldn. B/S of undivided 1/12th of 103a on

Beaverdam (cnvy/b David LOVETT in Apr 1806 to Joseph GOURLEY dec'd, and devised by GOURLEY to Hannah ELY dec'd {half sister by mother's side of GOURLEY} m/o Moses her only survivor).

3D:244   Date: 4 Aug 1820   RtCt: 10 Dec 1821
Jonathan WILKINSON & wife Patty of Lucerne Co Pa to William REEDER of Ldn. B/S of 1/12th interest in 103a of Joseph GOURLEY (who died intestate leaving 2 bros. & three sis. of whole blood and half brother Jonathan). Wit: Thomas DYER, Rosewell WELLES. Delv. pr order 18 Feb 1823.

3D:246   Date: 10 Aug 1821   RtCt: 12 Nov 1821
Moses GIBSON Sr. of Ldn to Travis GLASSCOCK of Upperville. Trust for debt to Thomas W. SMITH of Upperville using farm animals, farm and household items. Delv. pr order 5 Apr 1824.

3D:248   Date: 1 Feb 1821   RtCt: 12 Nov 1821
John MATHIAS of Ldn to George MILLER of Ldn. B/S of 41a Lots #26 & #27 on W side of Short Hill (reserving right to go thru lots to other lots). Delv. to MILLER 20 May 1824.

3D:249   Date: 12 Nov 1821   RtCt: 12 Nov 1821
Newman SETTLE & wife Elizabeth of Ldn to Daniel SETTLE of Ldn. B/S of 12a (dev. by father) adj Newman SETTLE, Abigail JAMES. Wit: Richard B. SETTLE, Robert CUNNINGHAM, Walter AKERS. Delv. to Newman SETTLE 8 Apr 1823.

3D:250   Date: 11 Jul 1821   RtCt: 12 Nov 1821
John THOMAS Sr. of Ldn to John THOMAS Jr of Ldn. B/S of 150a adj Joseph JANNEY, William LODGE. Wit: N. C. WILLIAMS, Abner JURY, Benj. JACKSON, Ammon EWERS. Delv. to THOMAS Jr. 8 Nov 1822.

3D:252   Date: 12 Nov 1821   RtCt: 12 Nov 1821
John THOMAS (trustee of John SHAFFER) of Ldn to Herman HEINZERLING of Ldn. B/S of 1a (cnvy/b Daniel DAVIS & wife Malinda in May 1817 to SHAFFER).

3D:254   Date: 12 Nov 1821   RtCt: 12 Nov 1821
John THOMAS (trustee of John SHAFFER) of Ldn to Michael EVERHART of Ldn. B/S of 13a (cnvy/b Presley WILLIAMS & wife Jane in Apr 1819 to SHAFFER).

3D:255   Date: 26 Oct 1821   RtCt: 13 Nov 1821
Samuel CLAPHAM & wife Elizabeth to Tilghman HILLEARY & others. Trust to Dpty Marshall Francis M. BECKWITH for Marshall John S. PEYTON of Winchester Chancery District using of land bought from BECKWITH. Wit: Saml. DAWSON, James M. LEWIS. Delv. to F. M. BECKWITH 25 Aug 1825.

3D:257   Date: 12 Nov 1821   RtCt: 12 Nov 1821
George MARKS & wife Mahala of Ldn to Edmund LOVETT of Ldn. B/S of ¼a in Union adj Isaac BROWN, James REED. Wit: Notley C. WILLIAMS, John W. GRAYSON.

3D:259   Date: 11 Apr 1821   RtCt: 12 Nov 1821
Thomas STEVENS & wife Ann of Ldn to James McDANIEL of Ldn. B/S of 2a adj James McDANIEL, Edward McDANIEL. Wit: Robert BRADEN, Abiel JENNERS.

3D:261   Date: 8 Nov 1821   RtCt: 12 Nov 1821
Thomas M. SINCLAIR of Ldn to Sarah WHITE of Ldn. B/S of ½ of house & lot in Hillsboro and interest in additional improvements made by John HOUGH after he owned property.

3D:263   Date: 16 Oct 1821   RtCt: 12 Nov 1821
George H. SINCLAIR of Guernsey Co Ohio to Sarah WHITE of Ldn. B/S of ½ of house & lot in Hillsboro and interest in additional improvements made by John HOUGH after he owned property. Wit: William TAYLOR, Jas. M. BELL.

3D:264   Date: 31 Aug 1821   RtCt: 12 Nov 1821
John WHITACRE & wife Phebe of Ldn to David Young of Ldn. Trust for debt to John PANCOAST Jr. and Joshua PANCOST using 100a and 59a (cnvy/b William BRONAUGH Exor of Sebastian WOOSTER). Wit: William BRONAUGH, N. C. WILLIAMS. Delv. to Joshua PANCOAST 17 Oct 1822.

3D:266   Date: 16 Nov 1821   RtCt: 16 Nov 1821
William AULT & wife Susannah of Ldn to Rich'd H. HENDERSON of Ldn. Trust for debt to Colen AULD & others assignees of Robert CAMPBELL using his ¼ interest in 97a of father William AULT late of Ldn. Delv. to Saml. M. EDWARDS 4 Jan 1823.

3D:269   Date: 7 Nov 1821   RtCt: 17 Nov 1821
George Mason CHICHESTER farmer of Ldn to James B. MURRY merchant of NY. Trust for debt to James THOMPSON merchant of NY using 357a (prch/o John T. MASON by Isaac WHITE) on Limestone. Wit: Charles F. GRIM, Anth'y DEY.

3D:272   Date: 7 Nov 1821   RtCt: 17 Nov 1821
Charles Pendleton TUTT farmer & wife Ann Mason of Ldn to James B. MURRAY merchant of NY. Trust for debt to James THOMSON merchant of NY using undivided ½ of 385a (prch/o Isaac Larowe by TUTT and Charles F. MERCER) on E side of Kittockton Mt. at little Limestone headwaters adj Capt. ROSE, __ ELGIN, George GREGG, Brumfield LONG, James COX, John A. BINNS, __ RAMEY, __ NICKOLS, Nicholas MONEY, Isaac LAROWE. Wit: Anth'y DEY, Charles F. GRIM, Thomas GASSAWAY, Thomas SAUNDERS. Gives plat.

3D:278   Date: 26 Nov 1821   RtCt: 26 Nov 1821

Thomas R. MOTT of Lsbg to William NOLAND of Aldie. Release of trust dated 3 Oct for debt to Charles Fenton MERCER and Richard H. HENDERSON.

3D:279   Date: 12 Nov 1821   RtCt: 10 Dec 1821

James H. HAMILTON & wife Margaret of Ldn to David ENGLISH of WashDC. Trust for debt to James EAKIN of WashDC using 178a (prch/o reps of George NIXON dec'd). Wit: Jno. PETER, Thos. COCORAN, And. ROSS, John McCORMACK, Presley CORDELL. Delv. to EAKIN 1 Jun 1822.

3D:283   Date: 2 Nov 1821   RtCt: 27 Nov 1821

Benjamin BURSON of Ldn to James GREEN of Fqr. Trust for debt to Samuel MURRAY of Fqr using farm animals, household items. Wit: Stephen F. BURSON, Joseph BURSON.

3D:284   Date: 15 Nov 1821   RtCt: 27 Nov 1821

Daniel COCKERIL & wife Esther of Ldn to Richard H. HENDERSON of Ldn. Trust for debt to George RUST using 15a (cnvy/b George JANNY & wife Susannah in Mar 1820, DB AAA:[240]). Wit: Robert BRADEN, Abiel JENNERS.

3D:286   Date: 8 Nov 1821   RtCt: 28 Nov 1821

Benjamin NEALE of Butler Co Ky to William CARR of Ldn. B/S of 414a in Ham[p]shire Co Va adj John BRADY. Delv. to CARR 15 Nov 1822.

3D:287   Date: 29 Mar 1821   RtCt: 28 Nov 1821

James SWART Sr. & wife Elizabeth of Ldn to James SWART Jr of Ldn. Gift of 75¾a on Little River adj __ FURGESON, __ TOLBERT. Wit: Robert ARMSTEAD, Wm. NOLAND. Delv. to James Jr. 13 Sep 1823.

3D:290   Date: 27 Nov 1821   RtCt: 28 Nov 1821

Charles Fenton MERCER of Ldn to Richard SMITH cashier of Office of discount and deposit of the Bank of the U.S. in WashDC. Trust using slaves Mathew prch/o John LINTON, Jack prch/o Charles P. TUTT, Charles prch/o William COOKE, Ralph and Vanessa prch/o James MONROE, Peter a miller devised by father James MERCER, Cato devised by brother John Fenton MERCER (all slave in Ldn) and slaves Maria & her 2 children (3y old and 3m old), Joshua and Daniel (recently purchased by Major Joel CRAWFORD of Metledgeville Ga and to remain in possession of Mrs. Lucinda BETTON in Ga). Delv. to SMITH on ___.

3D:292   Date: 27 Nov 1821   RtCt: 28 Nov 1821

James SWART & wife Elizabeth of Ldn to Charles Fenton MERCER of Aldie. B/S of 30a adj Aldie, Jonah HOOD, Walter LANGLEY, William NOLAND. Wit: Robert ARMISTEAD, William NOLAND. Delv. to MERCER 13 Oct 1834.

3D:294   Date: 1 Nov 1821   RtCt: 29 Nov 1821
Isaac STEER and Asa MOORE to Samuel HOUGH. Release of trust for debt to Lydia, Mary and Sarah HOUGH using 180a. Delv. to Saml. HOUGH 5 July 1826.

3D:296   Date: 29 Nov 1821   RtCt: 30 Nov 1821
James MOUNT & wife Hannah of Ldn to Zachariah DULANY of Ldn. Trust for debt to Nathaniel MANNING and Robert BRADEN assignees of John C. HANDY using 147¼a (cnvy/b HANDY in Feb 1820). Wit: William BRONAUGH, Francis W. LUCKETT.

3D:299   Date: 27 Nov 1821   RtCt: 5 Dec 1821
John MARTIN & wife Sarah of Ldn to Joseph CAVINS of Ldn. B/S of interest in land of Joseph CAVINS dec'd f/o Sarah. Wit: James H. HAMILTON, A. GIBSON. Delv. to Jos. CAVINS 13 Dec 1824.

3D:300   Date: 9 Apr 1821   RtCt: 6 Dec 1821
Thomas MARKS Jr. of Ldn to Thomas NICKOLS of Ldn. Trust for debt to Abel JANNEY using 49a nr Blue Ridge on NW fork of Goose Creek. Delv. to JANNEY 4 May 1824.

3D:303   Date: 7 Dec 1821   RtCt: 7 Dec 1821
Aaron BURSON (insolvent debtor) to Sheriff Burr POWELL. B/S of (due to executions of Thomas SHREVE and William WOOD joint merchants, George S. HOUGH, Thomas S. MARTIN, John D. BROWN agt of Columbian Factory, Charles SLADE, James CARTER, Thomas JANNY, John W. MASSIE and William PATTON and Johnathan BUTCHER joint merchants, Thomas MURPHEY for use of Elisha HALL, George JANNY, Roberson HOUGH, Enoch GLASSCOCK) using 122½a adj Edward CARTER, Francis W. LUCKETT, George BURSON and interest in land in possession of George BURSON and Edward CARTER and interest in deed of trust from Stephen DANIEL to John W. GRAYSON for house and lot in AlexDC.

3D:306   Date: 19 Nov 1821   RtCt: ___
Heirs of William SMALLEY dec'd late of Ldn (Andrew SMALLEY of Adams Co, Oh and David SMALLEY of Highland Co Oh and Joshua SMALLY of Ldn and David SWINGLE & wife Catharine late SMALLEY of Monogalia Co and Isaac HEATH of PrWm, Andrew and Lydia HEATH, Ruhemah McKIM late HEATH, Abel JAMES & wife Sally late HEATH of Ldn, Melinda ___ late HAWLEY & husband ___ of Oh and Nelson, Lamoch, Lucy, Sally, Andrew and Louisa HAWLEY the ch/o Catharine HAWLEY formerly HEATH) to Lewis GRIGSBY. B/S of 115a excluding 4-5a once claimed by Sampson TURLEY (prch/o Thomas COCKERIL) adj road from Baptist meeting house to gum spring, Benjamin JAMES. Delv. to Robert P. SWART 15 May 1832.

3D:308   Date: 12 Nov 1821   RtCt: 8 Dec 1821
Samuel M. EDWARDS (as Commr. of Ct) of Ldn to Richard H. HENDERSON of Ldn. B/S of land sold by Dr. Casper WISTAR of

PhilPa to William CLAYTON dec'd. Delv. to EDWARDS 7 May 1824.

3D:309   Date: 17 Nov 1821   RtCt: 23 Nov 1821
William NETTLE of Ldn to Mary FOX of Ldn. B/S of 80a (cnvy/b Robert BRADEN & Mary FOX as Exor of William FOX dec'd in Nov 1821) adj John WORSTLEY, __ STEER, Joseph WOOD, Joseph WOOD.

3D:310   Date: 17 Nov 1821   RtCt: 23 Nov 1821
Robert BRADEN and widow Mary FOX (Exors of William FOX dec'd) of Ldn to William NETTLE of Ldn. B/S of 80a (prch/o Asa HARRAS & wife Elizabeth Feb 1804) directed by will to be sold.

3D:312   Date: 11 Dec 1821   RtCt: 11 Dec 1821
Report of Commissioners (Joseph DENIAL, Jesse McVEIGH, Stephen C. ROZZLE, A. GIBSON, Saml. M. EDWARDS) of the poor house. 154a farm (54a in good timber, rest cultivated in clover and plaister) with large brick house with 7 rooms offered by Dr. William H. DORSEY connected with adj 75a farm with log building offered by William HANN is most suitable. Contract for payments.

3D:314   Date: 6 Dec 1821   RtCt: 8 Dec 1821
John LIVINGSTON of Ldn to Asa MOORE and Thomas PHILLIPS of Ldn. Trust for debt to John WILLIAMS of Ldn using lot in new addition to Wtfd on Second St adj John MORROW, George HENRY (cnvy/b Exors of Mahlon SCHOOLEY).

3D:317   Date: 26 Nov 1821   RtCt: 26 Nov 1821
Leven W. SHEPHERD of Ldn to James M. LEWIS of Ldn. B/S of undivided interest in 37½a of father Charles SHEPHERD dec'd. Delv. to LEWIS 25 Jan 1825.

3D:318   Date: 11 Dec 1821   RtCt: 11 Dec 1821
John L. DAGG, Charles GULATT and Abner GIBSON. Bond on DAGG of Christian Society of Baptists to perform marriages.

3D:319   Date: 10 Dec 1821   RtCt: 10 Dec 1821
Stephen R. MOUNT and Ezekial MOUNT. Bond on Stephen R. MOUNT as constable.

3D:320   Date: 26 Nov 1821   RtCt: 10 Dec 1821
Aquila VICKERS of Ldn to James PLAISTER of Ldn. Trust for debt to William HART of Ldn using farm animals, farm and household items.

3D:321   Date: 10 Dec 1821   RtCt: 10 Dec 1821
Jacob DIVINE of Ldn to Charles G. EDWARDS and John E. PARMER of Ldn. Trust for debt to Samuel HOUGH Jr. using house & lot occupied by DIVINE in Wtfd (cnvy/b Asa MOORE) adj Elizabeth BOND.

3D:323 Date: 1 Nov 1821 RtCt: 10 Dec 1821
Jacob WINE of Ldn to David SHAWAN of Ldn. B/S of 4a (cnvy/b John A. BINNS in Oct 1807) adj Reuben HIXON dec'd. Delv. to SHAWEN 25 Mar 1824.

3D:325 Date: 12 Jun 1821 RtCt: 10 Dec 1821
Charles G. EDWARDS of Ldn and Isaac WILSON of MontMd. Agreement for payment use of house and lot in Wtfd (prch/o Dr. John H. McCABE) adj Anna BALL, Robert BRADEN and another ¾a lot (prch/o John H. McCABE) adj heirs of Dr. John VANDEVANTER, opposite first lot and unimproved ¼a lot (prch/o Edward DORSEY) nr Presbyterian Meeting house adj Lewis KLEIN and 4a lot in Wtfd adj farms of Samuel HOUGH and Wm. PAXSON. Wit: Daniel STONE, Wm. JENNERS, James W. ROPER.

3D:328 Date: 11 Apr 1820 RtCt: 10 Dec 1821
William NOLAND & wife Catharine of Ldn to Thomas NOLAND of Ldn. B/S of ½a Lot #84 on Mercer St in Aldie. Wit: Burr POWELL, Ariss BUCKNER.

3D:330 Date: 10 Dec 1821 RtCt: 10 Dec 1821
John A. WASHINGTON of Ldn to Richard H. HENDERSON and Samuel M. EDWARDS. Trust to secure payment on crops to Samuel CLAPHAM using interest in unexpired 4y term on farm in German Settlement with crops.

3D:330 Date: 12 Dec 1821 RtCt: 12 Dec 1821
Richard H. HENDERSON (as Admr wwa of William CLAYTON dec'd) of Ldn to James ALLDER of Ldn. B/S of land prch/o James GALLAWAY & wife Mary (1/7th share of land allotted to Nancy CLARKE dec'd ch/o Wm. CLAYTON dec'd). Delv. to ALDER 9 Sep 1822.

3D:332 Date: 20 Aug 1821 RtCt: 20 Aug 1821
John BENEDUM (of John) & wife Nancy of Ldn to Reuben SCHOOLEY Jr. and Giles HAMMET of Ldn. B/S of brick house & lot in Lsbg occupied by Jacob CRIDLER adj reps. of Peter BOSS, George EMERY (cnvy/b Peter BENEDUM Jr.) Wit: Presley CORDELL, Saml. M. EDWARDS.

3D:334 Date: 15 Dec 1821 RtCt: 15 Dec 1821
Joseph BARTON (insolvent debtor) to Sheriff Burr POWELL. B/S of 1¼a adj Benjamin JENKINS, Thomas A. HEREFORD, heirs of Samuel TORBERT, John PERKINS (prch/o Thomas DRAKE) (due to executions of Abraham BUSKIRK, John MARKS, Joseph A. LONG). Wit: S. BLINCOE, Thos. SANDERS, Giles HAMMET.

3D:335 Date: 7 Jun 1821 RtCt: 17 Dec 1821
William HERBERT of Ffx to George KOONTZ and Nicholas KOONTZ of Ldn. B/S of 100a (except mines of metal and minerals) on Blue Ridge adj __ PURCELL, __ GRUBB. Delv. to Nich's KOONTZ 10 Mar 1828.

3D:337   Date: 20 Dec 1821   RtCt: 20 Dec 1821
Robert CURRY & wife Elizabeth of Ldn to George RHODES of Ldn.
B/S of undivided 1/8th interest in 64a currently occupied by
RHODES. Wit: Presley CORDELL, Saml. M. EDWARDS. Delv. to
RHODES 9 Sep 1836.

3D:339   Date: 21 Dec 1821   RtCt: 27 Dec 1821
John L. GILL of Ldn to John WORNELL of Ldn. Trust for James
WORNELL as security on bond to Noble BEVERIDGE using
household items. Delv. to John WORNAL 14 Jan 1832.

3D:341   Date: 26 Nov 1821   RtCt: 27 Dec 1821
Michael EVERHART & wife Christianna of Ldn to Jacob
GOODHART of Ldn. B/S of 13a (cnvy/b John THOMAS trustee of
Jno. SHAFFER in Nov 1821). Wit: Robert BRADEN, Abiel
JENNERS. Delv. to GOODHEART 17 Jul 1829.

3D:343   Date: 27 Dec 1821   RtCt: 27 Dec 1821
David CONNER of Ldn and Ann NEWTON of Ldn. Marriage contract
–Ann's personal household items to be held in trust by Charles
BINNS for her children John C., Elizabeth Lee, Robert C., Charles
C., Henry and Alexander NEWTON.

3D:344   Date: 20 Dec 1821   RtCt: 2 Jan 1822
William ALT & wife Susannah of Ldn to Wadsworth SHEPHERD of
Ldn. B/S of 14¾a above Goose Creek adj David EVELAND, __
EDWARDS. Wit: Presley CORDELL, Thomas SANDERS.

3D:346   Date: 20 Jul 1821   RtCt: 5 Jan 1822
John W. GRAYSON to George M. GRAYSON and Alexander
GRAYSON. Trust for debt to Benjamin GRAYSON Sr. and as
security on notes to John H. BUTCHER and heirs of Mahlon
CARTER dec'd using slaves Phillis abt 40y old & her children
Harriet, Dinah and Pompey, Edmond 27y old, Dinah & her 3 children
Mariah a mulatto girl 10y old, Cyrus abt 4y old and Henry nearly 2y
old, and Charles 6y old and Davy 5y old. Delv. to G. M. GRAYSON
7 Sep 1829.

3D:349   Date: 20 May 1821   RtCt: 8 Jan 1822
Peter DEMORY & wife Mary of Ldn to Michael DERRY of Ldn. B/S
of 1a adj DEMORY, George SMITH. Wit: Ebenezer GRUBB, Craven
OSBURN.

3D:351   Date: 1 Jan 1822   RtCt: 11 Jan 1822
Abiel JENNERS & wife Deborah of Ldn to James MARTIN of Lsbg.
Trust for debt to John MILLER of Winchester using 268a (cnvy/b
George TAVENER Jr. Sep 1819) adj William McGEATH, Joseph
JANNEY dec'd. Wit: John H. McCABE, Presley CORDELL.

3D:354   Date: 21 Feb 1821   RtCt: 4 Dec 1821/12 Jan 1822
Thomas KIDWELL of Ldn to John James MATTHIAS of Ld. Trust for
notes to Jacob SHRIVER assigned to John MATTHIAS using 40a.
Delv. to MATHIAS 10 Sep 1823.

3D:357 Date: 22 Dec 1821 RtCt: 2 Jan 1822
Wadsworth SHEPHERD of Ldn to John J. MATHIAS of Ldn. Trust for debt to William ALT using 14¾a on Goose Creek (cnvy/b William ALT). Delv to MATHIAS 3 Sep 1823.

3D:359 Date: 15 Sep 1821 RtCt: 12 Jan 1822
John DEMORY of Ldn to Philip GROVE of Ldn. B/S of 15a (cnvy/b Samuel GROVE in trust for debt due William DERRY). Delv. to Philip GROVE 28 Aug 1824.

3D:361 Date: 28 Dec 1821 RtCt: 12 Jan 1822
James COCHRAN Jr. & wife Rachel of Ldn to Thomas NICKOLS of Ldn. Trust for debt to Abel JANNEY and John GRAY of Ldn using 61a adj Benjamin BRADFIELD, Bernard TAYLOR (allotted to wife from estate of Jonathan BRADFIELD dec'd). Wit: Asa ROGERS, Malinda TORBERT, Thomas KENT, N. C. WILLIAMS, John W. GRAYSON. Delv. to Abel JANNEY 5 May 1824.

3D:364 Date: 28 Aug 1821 RtCt: 7 Jan 1822
John VanBUSKIRK of FredVa to Thomas CRAMER of FredVa. Mortgage on 'Ball's Mill' (cnvy/b Joseph TIDBALL) on Goose Creek. Wit: Lewis LINDSEY, Thomas KENNON, Nicholas FITZSIMMONS.

3D:366 Date: 8 Feb 1822 RtCt: 8 Feb 1822
Benjamin MAULSBY of Lsbg to Burr W. HARRISON of Lsbg. Trust for debt to John H. CANBY using lot on Market St in Lsbg (prch/o William KIRK & wife Nancy). Wit: Henry PEERS, E. G. HAMILTON, A. R. St. CLAIR. Delv. to CANBY 17 Jun 1822.

3D:367 Date: 5 Feb 1822 RtCt: 8 Feb 1822
John DANIEL & wife Ann of Ldn to David DANIEL of Ldn. B/S of interest in personal estate of Thomas RUSSELL dec'd f/o Ann. Wit: Presley CORDELL, Thomas SANDERS. Delv. to DANIEL 22 Feb 1826.

3D:369 Date: 7 Feb 1822 RtCt: 7 Feb 1822
Thomas GREGG (insolvent debtor) of Ldn to Sheriff Burr POWELL. B/S of interest in estate of David LACY dec'd by virtue of m. with Castelina d/o LACY. (suits of Joshua PUSEY & Thomas B. BEATTY of Ldn, Samuel ALABOUGH of Md). Wit: E. G. HAMILTON, Giles HAMMETT, Amos JANNEY.

3D:370 Date: 9 Jun 1821 RtCt: 5 Feb 1822
John VIOLETT to Joshua HOGUE of Fqr. Trust for Samuel SINGLETON as security in bond by VIOLETT to HOGUE using horses and wagon. Delv. to Townsend McVEIGH 13 Aug 1822.

3D:371 Date: 4 Feb 1822 RtCt: 4 Feb 1822
John MARTIN & wife Mary of Lsbg to Samuel M. BOSS of Lsbg. B/S of Mary's interest in 2-story brick house & lot on SE corner of Loudoun & King St in Lsbg (as heir of Peter BOSS dec'd grandfather of Mary) adj Robert R. HOUGH, Charles B. BALL, Saml. M.

EDWARDS, Joshua RILEY. Wit: Thomas SANDERS, Saml. M. EDWARDS. Delv. to BOSS 7 Jun 1822.

3D:374 Date: 1 Feb 1822 RtCt: 1 Feb 1822
Stephanson HIXSON of Ldn to Richard H. HENDERSON of Ldn. Trust for debt to John BOYER assignee of John BALL against Presley WILLIAMS & HIXSON using 76a from father Reubin HIXSON dec'd. Delv. to HENDERSON 2 Oct 1823.

3D:376 Date: 28 May 1821 RtCt: 15 Sep 1821/30 Jan 1822
Isaac S. GARDNER of Hampshire Co Va to Charles Calvert STUART of Ffx. Trust for benefit Martha GARDNER w/o Isaac using Martha's interest in estate of father William LANE Sr. Wit: Wm. MOSS, Benj. T. HIGGS, Rich'd M. LANE.

3D:378 Date: 31 Aug 1813 RtCt: 10 Jan 1814/30 Jan 1822
Thomas HETHERLY of Adams Co Oh to Cupid ROBINSON of Ldn. B/S of part of lot in Lsbg which HETHERLY prch/o Exors of George CARTER dec'd, adj James WINTERS. Wit: Henry PEERS, Presley CORDELL, B. HOUGH. Delv. to Wm. B. TYLER attorney for ROBINSON 25 Feb 1832.

3D:380 Date: 5 Jul 1821 RtCt: 24 Jan 1822
John W. GRAYSON of Ldn to Elijah HALL of Ldn. Trust for debt to Richard HALL using 85a adj Benjamin GRAYSON, Demsey CARTER, Abner HUMPHREY. Wit: John URTON, John URTON, Gerrard URTON, Normon URTON, Barsheba URTON. Delv. to Elijah HALL 23 Aug 1822.

3D:383 Date: 29 Jan 1822 RtCt: 30 Jan 1822
John SHAFFER of Ldn rented to Emanuel AXLINE his plantation until sold under trust and AXLINE to pay for 1/3 of crop. SHAFER now assigns rent of plantation to Trueman GORE who agrees to pay to Abiel JENNERS, although not enough to pay off debt. Wit: Giles HAMMETT, Daniel MILLER, M. JANNEY.

3D:383 Date: 4 Jun 1821 RtCt: 26 Jan 1822
Aaron BURSON & wife Hester of Ldn to Samuel BECK of Ldn. B/S of 4a adj Thomas TRAYHORNE, Thomas KENT. Wit: Richard K. LITTLETON, Israel B. THOMPSON, Joseph BURSON, John W. GRAYSON, Francis W. LUCKETT. Delv. to BECK 12 Mar 1831 (DB LLL).

3D:385 Date: 25 [Jan] 1822 RtCt: 25 Jan 1822
William SEEDERS of Ldn to Reuben SCHOOLEY of Ldn. BoS for household items. Wit: Samuel HAMMETT, John CARNEY, John SURGHNOR.

3D:385 Date: 21 Jan 1822 RtCt: 24 Jan 1822
Richard SMITH cashier of the Office of Discount and Deposit of the Bank of the U.S. in Wash DC to Thompson MASON of Ldn. Release of trust of May 1821.

3D:387 Date: 17 Jan 1822 RtCt: 21 Jan 1822
John JANNEY (s/o Elisha) of Ldn to John MATHIAS and Joshua OSBURN of Ldn. Trust for debt to Thomas SWANN using 66a adj Hllb, Samuel CLENDENING, Benjamin LASLIE, heirs of William RUSSEL, Mahlon MORRIS. Delv. to MATHIAS 1 Jan 1825.

3D:388 Date: 27 Dec 1821 RtCt: 21 Jan 1822
Peter MILLER & wife Peggy and Daniel MILLER & wife Polly of Culpeper Co to Adam MILLER and Jesse MILLER of Ldn. B/S of interest in 150a of Peter MILLER Sr. late of Ldn dev. wife Catharine during her life. Delv. to Adam MILLER 26 Sep 1822.

3D:390 Date: 30 Nov 1821 RtCt: 19 Jan 1822
Amos JANNEY of Ldn to Benjamin SHREVE and John GRUBB of Ldn. Trust for Adam HOUSHOLDER and John JANNEY of Ldn as securities on ct. bonds of Robinson HOUGH assignee of Geo. S. HOUGH and John D. BROWN and notes to Phillip FRY and Bank of Valley and as Admr of Grace JANNEY dec'd using 130a and 167a and farm animals and items. Wit: Elizabeth JANNEY, John KERT, Joseph KERT, William HAWLING, Samuel DAVIS, John SHAFFER.

3D:392 Date: 18 Dec 1821 RtCt: 14 Jan 1822
Stephen McPHERSON & wife Cecelia of Ldn to George KEEN of Ldn. B/S of 2 lots totaling 134a adj Thomas BLACKBURN, James CARTER dec'd road from Bloomfield to Union, John WILKINSON, Mahlon and Robert FULTON. Wit: Benjamin GRAYSON, John W. GRAYSON. Delv. to KEENE 8 Apr 1823.

3D:394 Date: 4 Jan 1822 RtCt: 18 Jan 1822
John W. GRAYSON of Ldn to Benjamin GRAYSON Sr. of Ldn. B/S of 84½a (cnvy/b Mahlon CARTER & wife Catharine, subject to trusts of Saml. & Isaac NICKOLS and Rich'd HALL) on E side of Beaverdam adj Benj. GRAYSON, Mathies CARPENTER, Abner HUMPHREY. Delv. pr order 10 Aug 1831.

3D:395 Date: 19 Feb 1821 RtCt: 15 Jan 1822
Sheriff Burr POWELL (under relief of insolvent debtors) to Thomas MARKS Jr of Ldn. B/S of tract where Mary MARKS now lives nr Blue Ridge and interest in 600a tract in Ky property of Abel MARKS dec'd and right of Marcus HUMPHREY estate by wife Margaret HUMPHREYS late MARKS d/o Abel.

3D:396 Date: 30 Dec 1821 RtCt: 14 Jan 1822
Amos JOHNSON & wife Sarah of Mdbg to Hiram SEATON of Ldn. B/S of 56a (prch/o Andrew and Jemima FENTON and children, whole interest of JOHNSON (1/3 of all land) of Jemima FENITON and life estate of Jemima in 8a attached lot). Wit: Leven LUCKETT, A. GIBSON. Delv. to SEATON 21 Oct 1840.

3D:397   Date: 22 Nov 1821   RtCt: 14 Jan 1822
Townsend D. PEYTON of Ldn to Leven LUCKETT of Ldn. B/S of
61a adj Moses GULICK, old road to Snickers gap. Wit: Alfred
LUCKET, Leven LUCKETT Jr. Delv. pr order filed WW folio 163.

3D:398   Date: 1 Jan 1821   RtCt: 14 Jan 1822
Bernard MANN & wife Joanna of Mdbg to Leven LUCKETT of Ldn.
B/S of Lot #1 & #2 and part of Lot #3 in Mdbg reserving ground rent
of one lot, using 150a in Fqr occupied by James BAGGERLY. Wit:
Francis W. LUCKETT, Abner GIBSON.

3D:400   Date: 13 Jan 1822   RtCt: 14 Jan 1822
Walter LANHAM to Sydnor BAILY. Trust for debt to Vincent MOSS
and Joseph CARR using 250a adj late Nathaniel MOSS, Pierce
BAILY, William BROUGHTON, Daniel THOMAS. Wit: Caldwell
CARR, Benjamin RUST Jr., Peter CARR.

3D:403   Date: 18 Apr 1820   RtCt: 14 Jan 1822
Thomas LEONARD of Ldn to Thomas NOLAND of Ldn. Trust for
debt to William NOLAND using 12 rood lot on Ashby's Turnpike
Road. Wit: Ludwell LUCKET, Thomas H. KIRBY, Thomas RENAL.

3D:405   Date: 18 Apr 1820   RtCt: 14 Jan 1822
William NOLAND & wife Catharine of Ldn to Thomas LEONARD of
Ldn. B/S of 2 rood lot on N side of Ashby's Gap Turnpike road adj
John B. CAWOOD, David JACKSON. Wit: Burr POWELL, Ariss
BUCKNER.

3D:406   Date: 2 Apr 1821   RtCt: 14 Jan 1822
Thornton WALKER & wife Fanny of Ldn to Craven WALKER of Ldn.
B/S of ½a in Union (cnvy/b Samuel DUNKIN & wife Ann) adj Isaac
BROWN. Wit: Wm. BRONAUGH, Francis W. LUCKETT. Delv. to
WALKER 12 Apr 1824.

3D:407   Date: 3 Apr 1821   RtCt: 14 Jan 1822
Craven WALKER & wife Alsey of Ldn to Benjamin MITCHEL Jr. of
Ldn. Trust for debt to Thornton WALKER using ½a in Union (prch/o
Michael PLASTE[R] & wife in Dec 1820). Wit: John W. GRAYSON,
Francis W. LUCKETT.

3D:409   Date: 10 Jan 1822   RtCt: 14 Jan 1822
Richard H. HENDERSON (Admr of William CLAYTON dec'd) of Ldn
to Amos CLAYTON, Isreal CLAYTON, Jacob LUKE & wife Sarah,
Martha CLAYTON and William CLAYTON of Ldn. B/S of land
(HENDERSON paid balance due to Casper WISTAR dec'd for land
not previously conveyed to William CLAYTON dec'd).

3D:410   Date: 7 May 1821   RtCt: 24 Dec 1821
John P. DUVAL & wife Ann of Ldn to John BEVERIDGE Sr of Ldn.
B/S of 50a (part of 314a divided to devisees of William CARR
dec'd). Wit: Abner GIBSON, Francis W. LUCKETT.

3D:412 Date: 20 Dec 1821 RtCt: 24 Jan 1822
Joseph LEWIS of Ldn to John S. STULL of Georgetown. Trust for debt to John DAVIDSON and Walter SMITH using 203a 'Clifton'. Wit: John J. STULL, W. J. RINGGOLD, Fra. DOGE.

3D:414 Date: 20 Dec 1821 RtCt: 19 Jan 1822
Joseph LEWIS Esqr of Ldn to Richard SMITH of WashDC. Trust for debt to Central Bank of Georgetown using 203a 'Clifton'. Wit: J. J. STULL, William THOMPSON, Jr., W. RINGGOLD. Delv. to SMITH pr order.

3D:417 Date: 3 May 1821 RtCt: 19 Jan 1822
James L. McKENNA & wife Ann Cecelia of Ffx to Benjamin C. ASHTON and Richard C. MORTON. Trust for debt to Clement SMITH using 1400a. Wit: Jonah THOMPSON, Thomas COWELL. Delv. to SMITH 16 Feb 1826.

3D:421 Date: 20 Dec 1821 RtCt: 24 Jan 1822
Joseph LEWIS of Ldn to Richard H. HENDERSON and William THOMPSON Jr. of Georgetown. Trust for debt to Central Bank of Georgetown using 310a (except release rights for 150 where Jonathan McCARTY resides) adj Nathaniel MANNING, Edward McDANIEL dec'd, Thomas TRIBBY, Jonathan McCARTY. Wit: C. SMITH, J. J. STULL, W. RINGGOLD.

3D:424 Date: 29 Nov 1821 RtCt: 20 Jan 1822
William NOLAND & wife Catharine of Aldie to Samuel WARD Jr. and J. C. VandenHEUVELL of NY. Trust for debt to Linde CATLIN and Isaac BRONSON of NY using 45a and 32a (exchange of land between NOLAND and Charles Fenton MERCER of Aldie in 1820). Wit: Leven LUCKETT, Robt. ARMSTEAD.

3D:428 Date: 24 Jun 1819 RtCt: 11 Feb 1822
Joseph LEWIS Jr. of Ldn to Aaron R. LEVERING, Elisha RIGGS and William THOMPSON Jr. of Georgetown. Trust for debt to Central Bank of Georgetown using 203a 'Clifton' (conveyed of Benjamin MYERS.) Wit: James MELVIL, James A. MAGRUDER, Brook MACKALL, Jos. B. FOX.

3D:434 Date: 24 Sep 1821 RtCt: 11 Feb 1822
Turner OSBURN. Oath as Capt. in Cavalry in 56th Reg. and 2nd Div. of Va Militia.

3D:434 Date: 17 Nov 1821 RtCt: 11 Feb 1822
Thomas P. WILLIAMS. Oath as Capt. in 56th Reg. and 2nd Div. of Va Militia.

3D:434 Date: 11Feb 1822 RtCt: 11 Feb 1822
L. P. W. BALCH, Robert MOFFETT and Rich'd H. LEE. Bond to President and directors of the Library fund, with BALCH apptd treasurer of board of school commrs.

3D:435   Date: 14 Aug 1820   RtCt: 12 Mar 1822

Josiah WHITE dec'd. Division –First tract of 88a - Lot #1 (15a) to Thomas WHITE, Lot #2 (11a) to Mahlon JANNEY & wife Rachel, Lot #3 (13½a) to James WHITE, Lot #4 (16a) to Robert WHITE, Lot #5 (16a) to Beniah WHITE, Lot #6 (16a) to Rachel JONES an infant by James WHITE her next friend. Mountain lot of 56a – 6 equal portions of 7a. Gives plat. Divisors: Joshua OSBURN, John WHITE.

3D:438   Date: 27 Mar 1805   RtCt: 13 Mar 1822

Peter HANN dec'd. Division in chancery Josiah GREGG and others vs. Hugh HANN and others. Gives plat – 226a surrounded by land of Elisha MARKS, Jesse HUMPHREY, Joseph BURSON and James DILLON. Widow's dower (75a), Lot #1 (11a) to William HANN, Lot #2 (12a) to Josiah GREGG, Lot #3 (12a) to Hannah HANN, Lot #4 (12a) to John HANN, Lot #5 (12a), Lot #6 (12a), Lot #7 (15a) to Peter HANN, Lot #8 (15a) to Hugh HANN, Lot #9 (15a) to John BURSON, Lot #10 (15a) to Rachel HANN, Lot #11 (16a) to Mathias HANN. Divisors: William BRONAUGH, John PANCOAST, Daniel EACHES, Abner HUMPHREY.

3D:439   Date: 23 Jan 1821   RtCt: 11 Feb 1822

John BOOTH of Jeff Co Indiana to John MULL of Ldn. B/S of 10a Lot #2 in div. of David MULL dec'd and interest of BOOTH in widow Mary MULL's dower.

3D:440   Date: 11 Feb 1822   RtCt: 11 Feb 1822

John WINNER and Jacob WALTMAN (Exors of Emanuel WALTMAN dec'd) of Ldn to Joseph WRIGHT of Ldn. B/S of 11a on E side of short hill nr N end (Lot #4 in survey for Ferdinando FAIRFAX).

3D:441   Date: 11 Feb 1822   RtCt: 11 Feb 1822

John WINNER and Jacob WALTMAN (Exors of Emanuel WALTMAN dec'd) of Ldn to Jacob, John and Joseph EVERHART of Ldn. B/S of 58a on Potomac and N end of short hill. Delv. to Jacob EVERHEART 8 May 1826.

3D:443   Date: 11 Feb 1822   RtCt: 11 Feb 1822

John WINNER and Jacob WALTMAN (Exors of Emanuel WALTMAN dec'd) of Ldn to Jacob KARN and John SMITH of Ldn. B/S of 17a (Lot #5 in survey for Ferdinando FAIRFAX). Delv. to Jacob CARNES 21 Oct 1822.

3D:444   Date: 11 Feb 1822   RtCt: 11 Feb 1822

John WINNER and Jacob WALTMAN (Exors of Emanuel WALTMAN dec'd) of Ldn to Adam SANBOWER of Ldn. B/S of 16a (Lot #3 in survey for Ferdinando FAIRFAX). Delv. to SANDBOWER 25 Aug 1823.

3D:445   Date: 17 Jan 1822   RtCt: 14 Feb 1822

Charles STOVEN & wife Mary of Ldn to William LYNE of Ldn. B/S of 508a (prch/o Anthony THORNTON by STOVEN and Joseph LEWIS with LEWIS conveying his rights) adj William ELLSEY dec'd, __ ASHTON, __ BERRYMAN. Wit: J. BAYLY, Chas. LEWIS, Horrace LUCKET, John L. STOVIN. Delv. to LYNE 7 Oct 1822.

3D:446 Date: 17 Jan 1822 RtCt: 11 Feb 1822
William LYNE of Ldn to Charles STOVEN of Ldn. B/S of 274a on Broad run (cnvy/b Samuel LUCKET, Benjamin JACKSON and Josiah CLAPHAM in Mar 1819). Wit: J. BAYLEY, Chas. LEWIS, Horrace LUCKET, John L. STOVIN. Delv. pr order DB DDD:446, 16 Nov 1848.

3D:447 Date: 17 Jun 1822 RtCt: 11 Feb 1822
William LYNE of Ldn to Charles STOVEN of Ldn. B/S of 12a on S branch of Broad run (cnvy/b Moses and George GULICK in Mar 1819) part of 'Gulick's gum spring'. Wit: J. BAYLY, Chas. Lewis, Harace Lucket, John L. Stovin. Delv. pr order filed DB DDD:447, 16 Nov 1848.

3D:448 Date: 15 Apr 1819 RtCt: 11 Feb 1822
Charles Fenton MERCER of Aldie to Cecelia WALDRON of Aldie. B/S of 1a last lot on E end of town on N side of Main St adj Thomas GHEEN. Wit: Thomas BROWN, Thomas C. BROOKS, Wm. NOLAND. Delv. to Joseph VANPELT pr order 29 Aug 1823.

3D:449 Date: 7 Aug 1821 RtCt: 9 Oct 1821/ 11 Feb 1822
William LYNE of Ldn to Charles LEWIS of Ldn. Trust for Charles LEWIS as security on prch/o land nr gum springs using 274a. Wit: James LEWIS, Saml. HALLING, James McFARLAND, Amos SKINNER.

3D:450 Date: 5 Nov 1821 RtCt: 11 Feb 1822
John LICKEY & wife Elizabeth of Belmont Co Ohio to Isaac EATON of Ldn. B/S of 18a on Katocton Mt. on W side of road from Lsbg to Coe's Mill adj Sampson BLINCOE. Wit: John BARNES, Dan'l. MILLER. Delv. pr order 29 Oct 1833.

3D:451 Date: 17 Jan 1822 RtCt: 11 Feb 1822
William LYNE of Ldn to Charles LEWIS and John BAYLEY. Trust for debt to Charles STOVEN using 215a adj Henry SETTLE. Wit: Horace LUCKETT, James McFARLAND, John L. STOVIN. Delv. to John BAILY and Chas. LEWIS 9 July 1827.

3D:453 Date: 11 Feb 1822 RtCt: 11 Feb 1822
Nathaniel MANNING and David REESE of Ldn to Nathan(iel) GREGG of Ldn. Release of trust for debt to John BROWN using 139½a.

3D:455 Date: 1 Nov 1821 RtCt: 11 Feb 1822
Charles MODISET & wife Sarah of Ldn to Stephen R. MOUNT of Ldn. B/S of ¼a lot and house in Bloomfield adj Joseph BARTON, Richard CLARKE. Wit: Benjamin GRAYSON, John W. GRAYSON.

3D:456   Date: 23 Nov 1821   RtCt: 11 Feb 1822
Joseph BARTON & wife Rachel of Ldn to Stephen R. MOUNT of
Ldn. B/S of ¼a with 2 houses (1 occupied by BARTON and the
other by Robert MAHONY) in Bloomfield adj Jesse McVEIGH
(cnvy/b Abner HUMPHREY). Wit: Benjamin GRAYSON, John W.
GRAYSON.

3D:458   Date: 1 Nov 1821   RtCt: __ Feb 1822
Abner HUMPHREY & wife Mary of Ldn to Joseph BARTON of Ldn.
B/S of ¼a & house in Bloomfield adj Jesse McVEIGH.

3D:459   Date: 17 Jan 1822   RtCt: 11 Feb 1822
John BAYLY of Ldn to William LYNE of Ldn. Release of trust for
debt to Charles LEWIS using 274a.

3D:460   Date: 9 Feb 1822   RtCt: 12 Feb 1822
Stephen R. MOUNT of Ldn to Benjamin GRAYSON Jr. of Ldn. Trust
for debt to John W. GRAYSON of Ldn using ¼a lot & house in
Bloomfield adj Jesse McVEIGH. Delv. to Benj. GRAYSON Jr. 10
Mar 1823.

3D:461   Date: 11 Feb 1822   RtCt: 12 Feb 1822
Mordecai THROCKMORTON & wife Sarah McCarty of Ldn to Enoch
FURR of Ldn. B/S of 58a (prch/o Thomas A. BROOK of Md) adj
Capt. John BEAVERS. Wit: Benj. GRAYSON, John W. GRAYSON.

3D:463   Date: 12 Feb 1822   RtCt: 12 Feb 1822
Thomas A. BROOKE to Enoch FURR. B/S of above 58a which was
mortgaged by Mordecai THROCKMORTON. Wit: Presley FOLY,
John K. LITTLETON. Delv. to John K. LITTLETON 9 May 1836 by
direction of FURR.

3D:464   Date: 13 Feb 1821   RtCt: 13 Feb 1822
Dennis McCARTY & wife Margaret of Ldn to Hugh SMITH of Ldn.
B/S of 11a on S side of Goose Creek (devised by will of father
Thaddeus McCARTY dec'd) adj Hugh ROGERS. Wit: Rich'd H.
HENDERSON, G. W. McCARTY, John MARTIN. Delv. to SMITH 10
Jan 1827.

3D:465   Date: 16 Feb 1822   RtCt: 16 Feb 1822
John MARTIN of Ldn to Sydnor BAILY of Ldn. Trust for debt to
Joseph CARR, Joseph McPHERSON Sr., Amos POLTEN using 12a
and 12a, farm animals and household items. Delv. to C. CARR 8
Oct 1823.

3D:466   Date: 16 Feb 1821   RtCt: 16 Feb 1822
George BURSON of Ldn to Sheriff Burr POWELL. B/S of 63a & mills
(prch/o George JANNEY & wife and Elisha JANNEY) to release
BURSON from jail (executions by ___ RICHARDS Admr. of John
RICHARDS dec'd, Charles SLADE, John D. BROWN, Thomas
JANNEY & Co., Geo. JANNEY, Thomas MURPHEY for use of
Elisha HALL).

3D:467   Date: 24 Oct 1821   RtCt: 19 Feb 1822
Edward MARTIN and Andrew MARTIN & wife Jemima to William
BENTON of Ldn. B/S of interest in 300a under will of William
MARTIN dec'd (f/o John, Edward, Robert, Andrew, Elizabeth and
Mary MARTIN now w/o John LEWIS) (prch/o William SAVAGE but
never rec'd a deed) as heirs of Elizabeth MARTIN dec'd who died
intestate and without issue. Wit: John W. GRAYSON, Townsend
McVEIGH, Hugh SMITH, William BRONAUGH, Francis W.
LUCKETT. Delv. to BENTON 3 Mar 1823.

3D:469   Date: 20 Feb 1822   RtCt: 20 Feb 1822
Reuben SCHOOLEY Jr. of Ldn to Edward HAMMETT of Ldn. B/S of
½ of brick house & lot in Lsbg (cnvy/b John BENEDUM in Aug 1821
to SCHOOLEY and Giles HAMMETT) adj lot of reps. of Peter BOSS,
George Emery

3D:470   Date: 23 Feb 1822   RtCt: 23 Feb 1822
John T. DOWNEY of Ldn to Eli EVANS of Ldn. BoS for farm and
household items. Wit: Thomas SANDERS, Charles GULLATT.

3D:471   Date: 25 Feb 1822   RtCt: 25 Feb 1822
Jacob SHOEMAKER of Ldn to Barbara HARDACRE of Ldn. B/S of
3a on E end of short hill adj Phillip FRY, Charles CRIMM, John
GRUBB, Peter MILLER dec'd. Wit: Asa ROGERS, E. G.
HAMILTON, Alfred A. ESKRIDGE. Delv. to Mordica HARDACRE 23
Nov 1822.

3D:472   Date: 25 Feb 1822   RtCt: 25 Feb 1822
Richard DAWSON of Ldn to George W. HENRY of Ldn. BoS for
household items. Wit: G. RICHARDS, E. G. HAMILTON.

3D:473   Date: 14 Feb 1822   RtCt: 28 Feb 1822
Betsey MURRAY (wd/o Sam'l MURRAY dec'd) and James L.
MARTIN & wife Sally (d/o Sam'l dec'd) of Lsbg to Samuel
DONOHOE, Aaron SANDERS, James HAMILTON, Thomas
BIRKBY, Geo. RHODES, David OGDEN, Thomas SANDERS, Isaac
HAINES, John ROSE and Samuel M. EDWARDS (trustee of
Methodist Episcopal Church in Lsbg). B/S of annuities and rents on
2 tenements now occupied by Robert HOUGH and Samuel CARR
and brick school house and adj lot which adj Joseph
HILLIARD(devised by Samuel MURRAY dec'd for use & benefit of
poor widows and orphans in trust to trustees of Meth. Church). Wit:
Presley CORDELL, John H. McCABE. Delv. to Saml. M. EDWARDS
18 Aug 1831.

3D:476   Date: 16 Feb 1822   RtCt: 1 Mar 1822
John W. GRAYSON of Ldn to William WINN of Ldn. Release of trust
of Mar 1820 for debt to Thomas DRAKE.

3D:477   Date: 16 Feb 1822   RtCt: 1 Mar 1822
William WINN of Ldn to John H. BUTCHER of Ldn. B/S of 116a
(prch/o Turner & Herod OSBURN) at fork of Williams Gap run adj

John HANBY, __ McPHERSON, __ RUSSELL, __ OVERFIELD, William L. LEE.

3D:478 Date: 4 Mar 1822 RtCt: 5 Mar 1822
John R. ADAMS & wife Lucinda of Ldn to Thomas R. MOTT of Ldn. Trust for debt to Bank of the Valley using 200a (cnvy/b Samuel ADAMS in Apr 1817) adj Samuel TILLETT, Sampson BLINCOE, Peter BEEMERSTEFFER. Wit: Presley CORDELL, Thomas SANDERS.

3D:480 Date: 28 Feb 1822 RtCt: 4 Mar 1822
Thomas DRAKE of Ldn to Stephen McPHERSON of Ldn. B/S of 4a on N side of stony hill (cnvy/b John H. BUTCHER).

3D:481 Date: 7 Mar 1822 RtCt: 7 Mar 1822
Samuel WRIGHT of Ldn to Jacob EVERHART, Jacob WALTMAN 2nd, John WENNER and Jacob WALTMAN (of Samuel) of Ldn. Trust for debt to four mentioned above using 131a. Delv. to R. H. HENDERSON pr order 22 Apr 1829.

3D:482 Date: 7 Mar 1822 RtCt: 7 Mar 1822
John GEORGE of Ldn to Samuel WRIGHT of Ldn. Release of trust of Mar 1816 for debt to Emanuel WALTMAN.

3D:483 Date: 2 Mar 1822 RtCt: 8 Mar 1822
Stephen DANIEL & wife Catharine of Ldn to Abiel JENNERS of Ldn. B/S of 2a on N side of Kittocton Mt. (part of land beq. from father Joshua DANIEL). Wit: Benjamin GRAYSON, John W. GRAYSON.

3D:484 Date: 1 Nov 1821 RtCt: ___
George WHITMORE & wife Rachel and Samuel PAXSON & wife Martha of Ldn to Abiel JENNERS of Ldn. B/S of plantation where William WRIGHT died and mountain lot. Wit: Robt. BRADEN, Saml. HOUGH Jr. Delv. to JENNERS 24 Jan 1823.

3D:485 Date: 2 Mar 1822 RtCt: 11 Mar 1822
Jacob MILLER of Ldn to Aaron MILLER of Ldn. Trust for Adam MILLER as security on debt to Samuel NEAR using farm and household items. Wit: Sampson BLINCOE, A. R. St. CLAIR, Alfred A. ESKRIDGE.

3D:487 Date: 16 Mar 1822 RtCt: 16 Mar 1822
Samuel HAMMETT, Rich'd H. HENDERSON and Robert BENTLY. Bond on HAMMETT as constable.

3D:487 Date: 11 Mar 1822 RtCt: 11 Mar 1822
Joseph HOCKING, Daniel LOVETT and Edward WILSON. Bond on HOCKING as constable.

INDEX

Reuben, 216
BAID
Samuel, 184
BAILES
Joseph, 186
BAILEY
Albert, 134, 149
George, 42, 134
John, 149
Peggy, 149
Sydnor, 30, 60, 95, 96, 100, 173, 190, 206, 208
BAILY
John, 251
Pierce, 248
Sydnor, 230, 248, 252
BAKER
___, 209
Abraham, 6, 136
Abram, 178
Catharine, 136
Isaac, 193
John, 4, 5, 21, 163, 206
Joshua, 54
BALCH
L. P. W., 23, 54, 87, 112, 114, 128, 133, 147, 149, 157, 177, 187, 204, 249
Lewis P. W., 29, 37, 44, 60, 75, 83, 84, 91, 92, 101, 186, 187
BALDWIN
John, 61
BALL
Anna, 111, 243
Burgess, 4, 6, 8
Charles, 82, 164, 196
Charles B., 4, 7, 8, 10, 76, 82, 86, 87, 94, 96, 98, 99, 101, 117, 140, 142, 151, 160, 174, 212, 221, 228, 245
Fayette, 4, 8, 140, 212
Frances W., 4
George, 8

George W., 4, 8, 77, 212
Henry, 77, 223
Isaac, 27, 98, 186
James, 33
John, 98, 106, 186, 246
Lucy, 140
Lucy T., 174
Martha D., 4
Mildred T., 4, 8, 212
Ruth, 33, 77
Stephen, 14, 62, 64, 67
Susannah, 156, 186
Thomas, 157
BALY
J., 230
BANTZ
Valentine, 158
BARNES
John, 251
BARNETT
Joseph, 109
Mary, 109
BARNS
Abraham, 18
BARR
Adam, 113, 129, 167, 207, 213, 234
George, 67
Hannah, 77, 79
Hugh, 213
Ketura, 77
Letty, 77
Mahala, 77
Nimrod, 77
Precious, 207
Wicus, 77
BARR
Hugh, 77
BARRY
Catharine, 83
William T., 83
BARSON
Henry, 195
William, 195
BARTLET.
Henry, 118
BARTLETT
Henry, 90
S., 206
T., 206
BARTON

Joseph, 12, 243, 251, 252
Levi, 46, 94, 199
Rachel, 12, 252
BASSETT
Nathan, 36
BATES
Mary, 86
BATTAILE
Ann M., 210
Laurence, 210
Lawrence, 210
BATTSON
Elizabeth, 67, 135
Hannah, 135
James, 14, 55, 67, 135, 201
John, 135, 178, 201
Mahaly, 67
Nancy, 67
Rachel, 67
Sarah, 55
Thomas, 67, 135, 140, 148
William, 199
BAYHAN
W. R., 33
BAYLEY
Albert, 200
J., 251
John, 47, 56, 128, 149, 251
Pierce, 48, 149
William M., 185
BAYLY
Albert, 42, 136, 140, 149, 173, 201
George, 42, 67, 72, 119, 136, 198
J., 251
Jane, 30
John, 16, 18, 28, 37, 69, 72, 80, 119, 133, 134, 136, 137, 140, 173, 181, 199, 200, 201, 219, 225, 252
M., 194
Mary, 72
Mary Ann, 119
Mary L., 42
Mountjoy, 72
Peggy, 119
Peggy C., 72

Pierce, 42, 72, 119,
134, 136, 140
Samuel, 72, 136
Sarah, 136, 140, 149,
201
Sydnor, 138, 139
William, 30
William P., 42
BAYNE
Henry T., 192
BAYNES
Matthew, 50
BEAGLE
Christian, 189
BEALE
David F., 64, 74, 85,
208
Thomas B., 87
Thomas K., 106
BEALES
David F., 104
BEALL
David, 3
David F., 84, 192
Elizabeth, 192
Thomas K., 193
William, 153
BEALLE
Thomas K., 192
William, 153
BEANS
Amos, 1
Isaiah B., 52, 78, 94,
107, 189, 194
James, 14, 64, 76,
84, 85, 107
Martin, 48
Matthew, 48, 50, 51
Nathen, 68
Samuel, 78
Susan, 78
BEARD
Alexander, 180
J., 222
Joseph, 20, 43, 71,
82, 101, 115, 119,
136, 137, 172,
185, 214, 226
Lewis, 115, 221
Orpah, 79
Stephen, 79, 119
William, 180
BEATTY
Andrew, 166

David, 55, 162
Elizabeth, 55, 166
George, 174, 175
John, 55
Mary, 78
Peggy, 166
Rachel, 122
Robert, 55
Thomas, 122
Thomas B., 25, 43,
75, 86, 88, 98,
121, 175, 245
William, 55
BEATY
Andrew, 15
John, 156, 169
BEAVER
John, 130
BEAVERS
James, 3, 124, 222
John, 252
Joseph, 222
Samuel, 13, 102,
189, 222, 237
Thomas, 237
William, 222
BECK
Samuel, 246
BECKWITH
Francis M., 167, 229,
235, 238
BEEMER
George, 115
BEEMERSTEFFER
Peter, 254
BEESEX
Prissy, 4
BELL
Catherine, 9
James M., 239
Joseph D., 9
BELT
Alfred, 32, 219
John, 101
BELTZ
___, 100
Andrew, 204
Frederick, 121, 196
P., 9
BEMENDAFFER
Peter, 18
BENEDUM
___, 172, 178, 229

Catharine, 53, 105,
129, 160, 188
Catherine, 10, 188
Henry, 36, 87, 197
John, 129, 147, 197,
243, 253
Nancy, 243
Peter, 9, 10, 36, 53,
57, 87, 105, 106,
113, 128, 129,
130, 147, 160,
175, 176, 188,
197, 217, 227, 243
BENNEDUM
Peter, 56
BENNET
Joseph, 72
BENNETT
Charles, 23, 36, 84,
91, 122, 205
Cornelius, 44, 119,
187
Henry A., 66
Joseph, 134
Matthew, 27
BENSON
Joseph, 161
BENTLEY
Catharine, 81
Catharine L., 120
Joseph, 81
Robert, 44, 65, 98,
115, 120, 175,
220, 227
BENTLY
Robert, 254
BENTON
William, 124, 168,
174, 253
BERKBEY
Thomas, 159
BERKELEY
Marmaduke, 150
BERKLEY
Ann, 150
George, 18
John L., 37
Lewis, 45
Malinda, 150
Matilda, 150
Samuel, 208
Thomas, 208
BERRY
___, 82, 203

BRIDGES
  Alexander, 61
  Benjamin, 12, 61
  John, 214
  Ketturah, 61
  Kitturah, 12
BRINK
  Samuel, 18
BRISCOE
  Alexander M., 72, 82
  Aquilla, 64, 102
  Matilda P., 72, 82
  Thomas, 156
  William H., 55
BROADUS
  James G., 162
BRONAUGH
  George W., 210, 219
  Jeremiah W., 49, 52,
    82, 110
  John, 57
  John W., 161
  John W. T., 110, 188
  Joseph W., 210, 219
  William, 5, 6, 8, 12,
    13, 18, 23, 24, 25,
    26, 29, 30, 31, 32,
    34, 38, 39, 41, 42,
    43, 44, 46, 47, 49,
    52, 53, 61, 62, 65,
    68, 69, 71, 72, 74,
    76, 77, 78, 80, 82,
    85, 91, 94, 95,
    102, 103, 104,
    106, 110, 113,
    118, 125, 141,
    150, 151, 152,
    155, 162, 163,
    166, 170, 171,
    180, 181, 182,
    185, 188, 195,
    197, 198, 200,
    210, 212, 219,
    223, 224, 227,
    230, 235, 239,
    241, 248, 250, 253
  William J., 34, 162,
    200
BRONSON
  Isaac, 179, 249
BROOK
  Benjamin, 227
  Richard, 90
  Thomas A., 143, 252

BROOKE
  Arthur, 235
  Benjamin, 44, 89, 92,
    95, 100, 155, 227
  Caleb, 235
  Emily, 235
  F. W., 157
  Hannah, 89, 92
  Henry, 235
  James B., 30
  John T., 27, 184
  Richard, 78, 170
  Rufus, 235
  Susan, 235
  Thomas A., 3, 82,
    252
  Virginia, 235
  Walter, 30, 235
BROOKES
  Caleb D., 109
  Eliza D., 3
  Emily, 183
  Frederick, 195
  Henry, 109, 197
  James, 3
  Susannah, 109
  Walter, 3, 109, 183
BROOKS
  Arther, 183
  Caleb, 183
  Eliza D., 183
  Henry, 183
  James B., 3, 30
  Rufus, 183
  Samuel D., 183
  Susan, 235
  Susanna, 183
  Susannah, 183
  Thomas C., 251
  Thomas D., 183
  Virginia, 183
  Walter, 30, 183
BROUGHTON
  William, 248
BROWN
  Abraham, 67, 173
  Abram, 60
  Ann, 89
  Asa, 38
  D. Ellicott, 125
  Daniel, 51, 61, 62,
    76, 78, 163, 166,
    167, 195

David E., 110, 176,
    208
  Douglas, 132
  Edwin C., 67, 198,
    203
  Emily, 200
  Fielding, 53, 87, 99,
    100, 104, 150,
    165, 166
  George, 25, 79, 189
  Hannah, 7, 99, 100,
    167
  Henly, 139
  Henry, 94, 151, 182,
    197
  Isaac, 26, 77, 79, 80,
    96, 118, 128, 141,
    147, 151, 162,
    173, 180, 185,
    197, 223, 239, 248
  Isachar, 220
  Issacher, 236
  James, 5, 87, 96,
    139, 163
  John, 23, 26, 44, 88,
    89, 139, 154, 251
  John D., 231, 241,
    247, 252
  Margaret, 67
  Mary, 61, 80, 102
  Moses, 61, 80, 102,
    108
  Nancy, 77, 120
  Nathan, 11, 120, 123
  Rachel, 51, 76, 78,
    195
  Richard, 53, 82, 236
  Sarah, 44, 76, 79
  Spencer, 43, 52
  Thomas, 11, 12, 23,
    76, 77, 162, 180,
    230, 251
  William, 43, 58, 76,
    94, 102, 130, 167,
    204
BRYSON
  A. G., 202
BUCHANAN
  John, 190
  Michael, 191
BUCK
  Mary, 185, 232
  Mary P., 72

Samuel, 72, 105,
185, 199, 232
BUCKNER
Aris, 1, 6, 8, 18, 193
Ariss, 19, 28, 69, 81,
114, 119, 134,
136, 137, 149,
159, 160, 164,
170, 172, 173,
225, 230, 243, 248
Arris, 21
Arriss, 72
R. B., 8
Thomas H., 156
BULLETT
Benjamin, 6
BUMCROATS
Christiana, 51
John, 50, 51
BUMCROTS
John, 39, 43, 50
BURCH
Feilder, 229
BURKINS
Elizabeth, 75, 122
John, 75, 122, 145
BURNET
Isaac G., 175
BURNHOUSE
Christopher, 50
John, 61, 171, 180,
182
Margaret, 61, 180,
182
BURNHOUSE
Margaret, 171
BURNS
___, 47
Charles, 59
BURR
Hannah, 77
BURSON
Aaron, 31, 44, 61, 62,
110, 118, 125,
134, 137, 151,
157, 162, 173,
174, 185, 187,
195, 202, 215,
227, 241, 246
Ann, 132, 133, 135,
140
Anna, 218, 230
Aron, 27
Benjamin, 215, 240

Esther, 61, 62, 110,
118, 125
George, 26, 32, 44,
103, 118, 155,
162, 174, 230,
241, 252
Hester, 246
James, 31, 118, 125
Jehu, 14, 132, 133,
135, 140, 158,
159, 195, 218, 230
Jesse, 97, 106, 181
John, 158, 230, 250
Johnathan, 103
Jonathan, 26
Joseph, 103, 118,
125, 230, 240,
246, 250
Martha, 181
Mary, 31
Rebecca, 26
Stephen, 162
Stephen F., 240
Susanna, 32, 155
Susannah, 32, 103
BURTON
John, 87, 107, 198,
206
BUSKIRK
Abraham, 243
John V., 193
BUSSARD
Daniel, 150, 152,
154, 155
BUTCHER
Eli, 126
Elizabeth, 75, 122
Hannah, 109, 122
John, 105, 126
John H., 49, 50, 51,
75, 103, 122, 131,
133, 141, 145,
158, 170, 218,
227, 244, 253, 254
Johnathan, 241
Jonathan, 132
Mary, 145
Nancy, 141, 158
Samuel, 75, 81, 109,
122, 126, 148, 184
BUTLER
Moses, 113
BUZZARD
Frederick, 67

BYRD
Jane, 13
BYRNE
Ann, 80
Mary, 80
William, 80
BYRNES
Bethsheba, 11
James, 116
Rachel, 116

CADWALADER
Moses, 88
CADWALLADER
Moses, 89
CALDWELL
___, 162
Eliza, 75, 85, 132,
233
Elizabeth, 26
John, 51, 58, 62, 85
Joseph, 26, 34, 39,
51, 58, 62, 75, 85,
121, 131, 132,
133, 141, 158,
224, 226, 233
Mary, 51, 62, 85
Moses, 26, 51, 62,
121, 141
S. B. T., 157, 196,
221
Samuel B. T., 91
Sarah, 26, 62, 85,
121, 132
Sarah E., 112
William, 26, 28, 51,
62, 85
CAMERLY
Christena, 109
Jacob, 109
CAMP
Isaac, 92
CAMPBELL
Andrew, 102
Asaph, 70, 127
Aseph, 70
Elizabeth, 106, 112,
216
James, 105, 106,
112, 216, 221
Jane, 81, 216
John, 63, 70, 126,
149

Margaret, 24, 61,
189, 197, 199
Robert, 81, 154, 216,
239
William, 24, 61, 189,
199
CANBY
John H., 25, 75, 245
CANE
Francis H., 193
CANNON
Sarah, 220
CARNAHAM
George, 74
CARNES
Jacob, 200, 250
CARNEY
Hiram, 47
John, 196, 221, 246
CARPENTER
Mathies, 247
Matthew, 211
William, 208
CARR
Betsy, 68
C., 252
Caldwell, 56, 57, 59,
80, 95, 163, 168,
191, 200, 201,
206, 219, 220,
230, 248
David, 182
John, 2, 24, 56, 57,
59, 82, 103, 123,
131, 144, 191
Joseph, 56, 57, 80,
88, 89, 92, 95, 96,
97, 115, 116, 162,
163, 186, 199,
212, 218, 219,
220, 224, 228,
230, 248, 252
Mary, 114
Peter, 248
Samuel, 11, 12, 36,
65, 66, 84, 115,
133, 136, 196,
221, 253
Thomas, 21
William, 1, 2, 4, 12,
15, 23, 24, 29, 31,
57, 68, 73, 78, 80,
81, 82, 84, 86,
114, 115, 117,

118, 120, 126,
133, 147, 169,
174, 175, 177,
191, 192, 221,
224, 231, 240, 248
CARRAL
Mary, 20
Patrick, 20
CARRELL
Joseph, 142
CARRINGTON
Eli, 173
CARRUTHERS
Patty, 153, 154
Thomas, 153, 154
CARTER
___, 150
Alfred G., 144, 145,
190
Anna M., 77
Asa, 117, 210
Beach, 80
Catharine, 236, 247
Catherine, 22
Cynthia, 117
David, 57, 76, 97,
104, 113, 143,
162, 167, 227
Demphrey, 3
Dempsey, 86, 112,
117, 211, 227,
229, 236
Demsey, 117, 130,
246
Edin, 26
Edward, 37, 61, 94,
181, 241
Eliza T., 77
Elizabeth, 77, 97
Elizabeth L., 157
Frances L., 77
George, 10, 16, 21,
43, 66, 69, 71, 78,
83, 84, 114, 119,
150, 156, 164,189,
191, 226, 231, 246
Hannah, 163, 222,
223
Henry, 18, 112
James, 22, 165, 210,
215, 236, 241, 247
Jesse, 163, 188, 212,
222, 223
John, 144, 145

Johnathan, 97
Jonathan, 3, 8, 65,
72, 74, 82, 97,
113, 171, 222, 231
Landon, 43, 77, 104
Mahaley, 82
Mahlon, 3, 22, 236,
244, 247
Maria, 77
Mary Ann, 211, 227
Mary Anne, 112, 117
Richard, 82, 112
Robert, 42, 43, 144,
145, 175, 191, 221
St. Ledgar L., 77
Thomas, 37
William, 117, 210,
212, 215, 222, 223
William J., 212, 215
CARTRIGHT
Joseph, 127
CASSADAY
John H., 22, 63
CASSADY
John H., 51, 134, 181
CASSIN
Joseph, 24
CATING
Edward, 18
Martha, 18
CATLESS
Charles J., 231
CATLETT
Charles J., 69
CATLIN
Linde, 249
Lynde, 179
CAVAN
Patrick, 97, 112, 114,
116
Sarah, 111
CAVANS
John, 202
Joseph, 202, 205
Patrick, 86, 119, 131
Rachael, 202
Sarah, 54
CAVEN
John, 117
Joseph, 117
Patrick, 154
CAVENS
Joseph, 152, 170,
188, 202, 203

DAVIDSON
  John, 249
  William, 33
DAVIS
  ___, 56
  Daniel, 27, 238
  Edward, 101
  Elizabeth, 13, 146
  Jacob, 232, 235
  John, 122, 140, 146
  Joseph, 1, 92, 120
  Malinda, 27, 238
  Samuel, 247
  Solomon, 156, 189
  Thomas, 13, 19, 39,
    146, 158, 206
  William, 193
  Zepheniah, 200
DAVISON
  N., 113
DAWES
  Ann D., 15
  Benjamin, 15, 149
  Henry, 123
DAWSON
  James, 53, 65, 73,
    160
  Polly, 53
  Richard, 253
  Samuel, 178, 204,
    224, 234, 238
DAY
  Elizabeth, 154, 192
  Henry, 1
DAYMUD
  Jacob, 173
  John, 205
DAYMUDE
  Jacob, 173
  John, 205
DEBELL
  Dorcas, 81
  Jeremiah, 80
  John, 55, 81
  Sarah, 80
DEButts
  John H., 55
  Richard, 205
DEGGE
  Robert F., 193
DEMARY
  ___, 232
DEMERY
  John, 13, 57

Peter, 13
DEMORA
  John, 21
DEMORY
  ___, 47, 70, 175
  John, 129, 131, 132,
    214, 245
  Mary, 244
  Peter, 129, 244
DENHAM
  Amos, 91, 94, 115,
    116, 128, 138,
    139, 176, 199
  Amy, 176
  Lee H., 120
  Lee W., 111, 118,
    120, 165, 178
  O., 199
  Oliver, 89, 118, 120,
    151
DENIAL
  Joseph, 242
DENNIS
  Absalom, 132, 158
  Absalam, 235
  Mary, 158
  Thomas A., 191, 198
  William, 166
DENNY
  Edmond, 89
DERRY
  ___, 70, 175
  Barbara, 131, 132,
    139
  Catharine, 56
  Jacob, 56
  Michael, 232, 244
  Peter, 47
  Philip, 13, 47, 129,
    139
  William, 6, 20, 56,
    104, 106, 131,
    132, 245
DEWAR
  James, 162, 163
  William, 213
DEY
  Anthony, 239
DICKERSON
  Samuel, 235
DIGGES
  William D., 205
DIGGS
  Eleanorah, 20, 21, 26

Thomas D., 139
  William D., 20, 21,
    26, 51, 91, 105,
    214
DILLON
  ___, 56
  Abdon, 164
  James, 176, 250
DISHMAN
  William, 41
DIVERS
  Andrew, 223
DIVINE
  Aaron, 44, 203
  Jacob, 242
DIXON
  J., 152
  Jacob, 62, 152
  John, 48, 152, 174,
    176, 178
  Samuel, 153
DIXSON
  John, 48, 62
DODD
  Jesse, 213
  John, 122
  William, 178
DOGE
  Francis, 249
DONAGH
  Heziah, 179
  James, 177, 179
DONALDSON
  George, 9
  James W., 9
  John B., 9
  Juliana, 9
  Spencer, 9
  Wesley, 9
  William, 224
  Winifred, 9
DONOHOE
  Margaret, 157
  Mrs., 69
  Samuel, 114, 157,
    253
DORSETT
  William H., 220
DORSEY
  E., 95, 235
  Edward, 39, 44, 58,
    85, 190, 200, 225,
    243
  Judith, 30, 181

Mary, 58, 190
William H., 30, 103,
141, 162, 165,
170, 173, 181,
197, 198, 210, 242
DOUGLAS
Charles, 83, 179
Hugh, 4
William, 68
DOUGLASS
Charles, 113, 170
Hugh, 16, 45
DOVIELL
John, 168
DOWDELL
John, 25
Moses, 201
Teressa, 25
DOWLIN
John, 224
DOWLING
Catharine, 44, 107,
159, 206
Edward, 37, 123, 147
Mrs., 114
DOWNEY
___, 170
Barbara, 78
John T., 253
Robert, 78
DOWNS
Jane, 112, 127
DRAIN
J. L., 8
John, 211
DRAKE
Enos, 189
Jacob, 3, 188
Jonathan, 3
Margaret, 188
Mary A., 188
Sarah, 188
Thomas, 3, 15, 133,
145, 170, 171,
211, 214, 215,
216, 229, 230,
232, 234, 235,
236, 243, 253, 254
Thomas T., 127
Urier, 188
DREAN
J. L., 18, 27, 29, 32,
42, 43, 46, 47, 48,
58, 78, 84

John, 15, 31, 63, 78,
90, 104, 114, 149
John W., 31, 88
Josiah, 104
Josiah L., 61, 68, 74,
79, 87, 92, 93,
106, 109, 111,
119, 120, 140,
156, 196
Nancy, 104, 149
DRISH
Barbary, 109
Charles, 8, 9, 26, 28,
94, 121, 137, 171,
182
Eleanor, 2, 9, 94
Elizabeth, 26
Ellen, 30
Harriet, 96
Harriot, 207
Helen, 30
John, 2, 9, 11, 12, 28,
30, 62, 65, 74, 85,
94, 160, 168, 171,
178, 224
Susanna, 171, 182
Susannah, 8, 28, 137
W. D., 30, 57, 157,
186
William, 10, 30, 208
William D., 7, 11, 12,
30, 31, 75, 79, 85,
93, 94, 96, 99,
120, 127, 129,
135, 165, 166,
184, 207
DUFFEY
Bernard S., 84, 167
John H., 220
DULANEY
B., 55
Benjamin, 192, 193,
220
Daniel F., 220
Elizabeth, 192
James C., 210
James H., 193, 220
John P., 139, 193,
215
L., 92
William, 108
Zachariah, 162
DULANY
Elizabeth, 90

James H., 55, 90,
223, 237
John P., 22, 54, 223
Mary, 154
Mary E., 152, 188
Zachariah, 123, 152,
154, 170, 188, 241
DULIN
Edward, 16, 75, 161,
169, 214, 224
John, 22, 35, 53, 74,
96
Nancy, 224
DUNCAN
Anna, 128
C., 149
Charles, 65, 124
Samuel, 27, 128
DUNHAM
O., 155
DUNICKS
Joshua, 87
DUNKIN
Ann, 248
Charles, 177
John, 149, 152, 187,
223, 225
Ruth, 149, 187
Samuel, 92, 128,
141, 147, 151,
162, 173, 180,
186, 197, 201,
223, 224, 248
William, 110, 125,
176, 182
DUNKIN & LLOYD, 182
DUNN
John, 61
DUNSMORE
Mary, 61
DURHAM
L. W., 93
Lee, 92, 127
Lee W., 37, 140, 142,
158
Nancy, 62
DUTTON
Hanson, 180
DUVAL
Ann, 248
Ann F., 23, 57
Anne F., 68
John P., 24, 45, 57,
68, 230, 248

Jesse, 12, 21, 56, 63, 70, 126, 149, 171
John, 160, 209, 214, 234
John H., 9, 96, 162, 173
John W., 65
Martha, 174
Mary, 21
Mary F., 65
Samuel, 70, 160
Sarah, 234
William, 174, 214

EVELAND
David, 19, 244

EVERHART
Casper, 47
Christiana, 100
Christianna, 244
Jacob, 125, 250, 254
Jasper, 139
John, 125, 250
Joseph, 125, 139, 250
Michael, 13, 33, 100, 139, 140, 208, 238, 244
Philip, 28, 29
Phillip, 39
Sarah, 125

EVERHEART
Christina, 186
Joseph, 140
Michael, 186, 195
Philip, 216
William, 101, 197

EVINS
Henry, 175

EWELL
Jesse, 68

EWERS
Ammon, 238
Barton, 96
David, 108
George, 108
John, 108
Johnathan, 96
Jonathan, 99, 108
Levi G., 173
Nancy, 108
Rachel, 96
Richard, 108
Robert, 108
Sarah, 108

William, 108

EXLINE
David, 34

FADELEY
Jacob, 65, 185

FADELY
Jacob, 17, 18, 24, 69, 81, 82, 123, 161, 174, 175, 185, 213, 221
Mary, 18, 24, 81, 123, 185, 213
Polly, 18, 81, 82

FADLEY
___, 160
Jacob, 17, 123, 204

FAIRFAX
Col., 36
Ferdinando, 29, 37, 43, 48, 50, 54, 56, 63, 98, 100, 114, 126, 149, 157, 158, 159, 168, 180, 182, 186, 187, 194, 231, 250
George W., 93, 103

FAIRHURST
George, 48, 126

FAIRLAMB
J. P., 36

FANT
John L., 222

FARQUHAR
James, 93, 99, 119

FARST
Conrad, 90

FAULEY
John, 98

FAW
Abraham, 54

FAWLEY
___, 209
Jacob, 111

FEARST
Betsey, 90
Conrad, 90

FEICHTER
George, 160, 166
John, 101, 175, 208
Martha, 208
Peter, 109, 229
Susanna, 109

FEITCHER

George, 137

FEITCHTER
George, 36

FELL
Cynthia, 108
Edward, 107, 108
Jane, 108
Jesse, 108
Joseph, 108
Margaret, 107, 108
Samuel, 108

FENDALL
P. R., 90

FENITON
Andrew, 146, 176
Jemima, 146, 176, 247

FENITY
Jemima, 144
Maria, 144

FENTON
Andrew, 94, 247
Elizabeth, 237
Jemima, 237, 247

FERGUSON
Amos, 23, 74, 76, 124, 191
Josias, 56

FERRAL
Thomas, 183

FERRELL
James, 229

FICHTER
George, 198
John, 97, 216
Peter, 216
Susannah, 216

FIELDS
___, 191
Elizabeth, 49
John, 63
Thomas, 49

FINETON
Elizabeth, 199

FINITY
Andrew, 94, 115
Jemima, 115
Maria, 115

FISHEL
John, 164, 201

FISHELL
John, 216

FITZHUGH
___, 186

Ann, 210
Harrison, 122, 224, 229
Peregrine, 191
William C., 210
FITZSIMMONS
Nicholas, 245
FLEMING
Archibald, 230
John, 57, 224
R. J., 30, 125, 179, 191
FLEMMING
Joseph, 60
FLETCHER
John, 163
Joshua, 224
Robert, 199
Tacy, 200
Tacy P., 163
FLING
Richard, 157
FLOWERS
Catharine, 177
Thomas, 36, 144, 147, 175, 177
FOLEY
Presley, 87, 221
FOLLIN
Daniel, 236
FOLY
Presley, 252
FOSTER
Jeremiah, 74
Mary, 114
FOUCH
Amos, 194
Isaac, 169
Nancy, 169
Sarah, 194
Temple, 169
Thomas, 18, 26, 28, 29, 49, 53, 63, 67, 89, 96, 98, 104, 133, 138, 147, 161, 181, 194
FOWKE
Elizabeth, 20, 212
Robert D., 20
William, 208, 212, 219
FOWLER
Elizabeth, 205
Moreen, 205

FOWLES
Zanada, 94
FOX
Amos, 10
Elizabeth F., 116
George, 25
George K., 15, 63, 116, 206
Henry, 88
Joseph, 10
Joseph B., 138, 249
Martina B., 116
Mary, 55, 57, 242
William, 180, 242
FOXALL
Henry, 154, 155
FOXHALL
H. T., 152
Henry, 154
FRANCIS
Enoch, 24, 49, 53, 62, 66, 96, 216
John, 79
Nancy, 53, 96
Thomas, 59
William, 17, 64
FRANK
William, 66
FRASIER
Townsend, 33
FRAZIER
Henry, 92
FRED
Elizabeth, 3, 23, 125, 145, 184
Joseph, 3, 91, 153
Joshua, 3, 153, 210
Mahaly, 146
Thomas, 3, 125, 145, 148, 153, 184
FREDD
Joseph, 195
Thomas, 23
FRENCH
___, 42
Clarinda, 124
Garrison, 54
Garrison B., 19, 119, 121, 234
Garrison D., 27
George W., 54
James, 63

James D., 19, 26, 27, 54, 63, 86, 119, 121, 124, 224, 234
John B., 236
Lewis, 19, 119, 173, 230
Mason, 8, 40
FREY
Emily, 155
John, 94
John M., 155
FRISHER
Isaac, 57
FRY
Catharine, 58
Dolley, 58
Henry, 58, 231
Henry J., 110
Peter, 74
Philip, 32, 34, 58, 116, 187
Phillip, 247, 253
Simon, 58
FRYE
Emily, 233
John, 208
John M., 233
John W., 120
Joseph, 99
Peter, 105
FULKERSON
Amelia, 59, 96
Benjamin, 59
William, 59, 96
FULKINSON
William, 228
FULTON
Abraham, 156, 194, 201
David, 210
George, 33
Mahlon, 210, 213, 222, 247
Robert, 41, 44, 155, 210, 213, 247
FUNK
Jacob, 215
John, 215, 222
FURGESON
___, 240
FURLONG
Henry, 108
FURR
___, 137

Enoch, 3, 48, 130,
140, 153, 166,
208, 211, 252
Minor, 100, 195, 206,
208, 219
Nimrod, 206
Phebe, 206
Sarah, 3, 48, 153,
211
Thompson, 137
Thomson, 157
FURST
Conrad, 90

GAINS
William F., 159
GAITHER
James O., 130
GALES
Thomas, 21
William, 21
GALLAHER
Mary, 128
William, 128
GALLAWAY
James, 243
Mary, 243
GALLEHER
Annah, 96, 128, 222,
223
Anne, 182
Caleb, 180
Caleb N., 96, 170
David, 96
John, 180
Mary, 96
William, 96
GALLIHER
Caleb N., 147, 181
Lucinda, 147
Margery, 180
Mary, 180
Thomas H., 182
William, 180
GALLOWAY
John, 228
Mary, 228
GALT
Peter, 27
GANTT
Daniel, 24, 49, 133
Lucy, 24, 49
Thomas T., 47, 190
GARDNER

___, 232
Isaac S., 17, 246
James, 175
Martha, 17, 246
GARNER
Arther, 136
Arthur, 89
James, 63, 86, 87,
158, 204, 208,
212, 216
Mahlon, 77, 162
Nancy, 77, 162
GARNET
James M., 27
GARNETT
James M., 184
GARRET
Joseph, 5, 46
Stephen, 189
GARRETT
Abel, 5
Elizabeth, 55
Enos, 186, 188, 200
James M., 187
John, 5
Joseph, 5, 34, 96,
199, 235
Nicholas, 12
Samuel, 12
Stephen, 175
Ufamey, 175
GARTH
Dabney C., 86
GASSAWAY
Henrietta, 176
Thomas, 45, 169,
174, 176, 178,
213, 239
GEORGE
Elizabeth, 125
James, 20
John, 13, 28, 38, 60,
111, 125, 183,
184, 187, 197,
225, 231, 237, 254
GHEEN
Narrissa, 94
Thomas, 20, 140,
251
William, 94
GIBBS
James L., 56
William, 20
GIBSON

___, 12
A., 14, 15, 16, 25, 26,
29, 32, 40, 46, 56,
58, 60, 67, 71, 84,
94, 95, 97, 110,
111, 115, 116,
118, 122, 124,
125, 127, 128,
129, 132, 135,
137, 140, 141,
142, 144, 145,
148, 153, 154,
159, 160, 176,
178, 183, 184,
195, 199, 207,
212, 217, 219,
222, 227, 228,
229, 230, 235,
241, 242, 247
Aaron, 163
Abigail, 40
Abner, 3, 9, 23, 28,
32, 40, 41, 42, 47,
55, 59, 64, 67, 70,
71, 94, 111, 121,
123, 153, 158,
168, 172, 177,
181, 182, 187,
190, 195, 198,
200, 242, 248
Alcy, 185
Alice, 95, 200, 207
Amos, 13, 32, 41, 51,
52, 56, 58, 59, 69,
88, 89, 100, 168,
184, 199, 207,
225, 227
Ann, 88, 89, 95
David, 128, 129, 194,
199, 200, 201
Elizabeth, 32, 168,
176, 185, 200, 201
Emily, 200
Evi, 40
George, 40, 56, 196
Hannah, 13, 41, 51,
58, 199
Israel, 100, 185, 199,
200, 207, 227
James, 32, 95, 100
John, 32, 80, 95, 100,
163, 168, 176,
183, 185, 186,

117, 120, 126,
130, 133, 141,
153, 162, 163,
164, 170, 173,
188, 206, 210,
211, 212, 215,
216, 217, 219,
222, 223, 224,
227, 228, 234,
236, 244, 246,
247, 251, 252, 254
Burr, 100
George, 49
George M., 3, 244
George W., 216, 217
John M., 170
John W., 51, 80, 86,
91, 96, 97, 100,
107, 111, 112,
117, 126, 130,
132, 133, 137,
145, 147, 149,
150, 152, 153,
158, 160, 164,
165, 171, 173,
180, 182, 184,
189, 194, 195,
197, 198, 199,
200, 206, 210,
211, 214, 215,
216, 217, 218,
219, 220, 222,
223, 225, 227,
228, 230, 232,
234, 236, 239,
241, 244, 245,
246, 247, 248,
251, 252, 253, 254
John W. B., 17, 18,
22, 48, 188
Mary D., 130
Richard O., 130
William, 3, 17, 111,
130
GREAVE
John, 79
GREE
Charlotte, 94
GREEN
James, 125, 240
Nelson, 155, 178,
207
Thomas, 64, 86
GREENLEASE

Catharine, 112, 205
James, 29, 106, 112,
186, 200, 205
GREENLEES
Catherine, 188
James, 188
GREENUP
Christopher, 29, 31,
41, 42, 43
GREENWALL
___, 68
GREGG
___, 156
Aaron, 203
Castelina, 245
Elisha, 19
George, 19, 203, 239
Hannah, 42, 123
Harriet, 17, 100
John, 42, 48, 96, 183
Joseph, 175
Joshua, 49, 96, 182,
190
Josiah, 230, 236, 250
Mahlon, 82
Margaret, 203, 230
Nathan, 88
Nathaniel, 251
Phebe, 48, 183
Ruth, 175
Samuel, 12, 53, 88,
94, 100, 236
Stephen, 1, 2, 17, 91,
97, 100, 124, 232
Thomas, 1, 2, 5, 10,
11, 18, 19, 34, 38,
39, 40, 41, 42, 45,
47, 48, 52, 53, 54,
56, 62, 63, 64, 65,
74, 80, 81, 84, 87,
88, 94, 97, 104,
106, 107, 108,
110, 113, 119,
120, 123, 126,
141, 142, 147,
151, 154, 162,
164, 172, 184,
232, 245
William, 182, 203
GRIFFITH
Isaac, 135, 169
Israel T., 143, 144,
146
J. T., 167

Mary, 161
Phillip, 234
R., 223
Rebecca, 169
Richard, 34, 144, 212
Samuel G., 161
Sarah P., 144
Thomas, 234
GRIGSBY
Hannah, 38
Lewis, 31, 38, 84,
241
Nathaniel, 84
GRIM
Charles F., 239
GRIMES
Andrew, 29
GROVE
Augustus M., 233
Philip, 245
Samuel, 132, 245
GRUBB
___, 168, 243
Adam, 6, 34, 198
Benjamin, 91, 116,
188, 211
E., 215
Eb., 1
Ebenezer, 33, 37,
104, 106, 127,
129, 139, 146,
172, 180, 182,
198, 214, 217,
225, 231, 232, 244
John, 91, 116, 247,
253
Richard, 19, 206
William, 19, 206
GULATT
Charles, 242
GULICK
Amos, 159
George, 1, 97, 110,
251
Martha, 97, 110, 199
Moses, 31, 97, 110,
184, 199, 248, 251
Sarah, 97, 110
GULLATT
Charles, 9, 86, 102,
179, 221, 234, 253
Charles A., 221
GUNN
James, 29, 47

Milley, 47
GUNNELL
Henry, 222
GUY
Sampson, 15

HADDOX
Barbary, 80
John, 80
HAGERMAN
Benjamin, 16, 159, 207
HAGUE
Jonah, 91
HAINE
Daniel, 20
HAINES
Isaac, 253
HAINS
Joseph, 1, 39, 119
Maria, 1, 30, 39
Stacy, 160
HALE
Henry D., 8
William, 8
HALL
Edward, 237
Elijah, 57, 246
Elisha, 241, 252
James, 49, 57
Josiah, 17, 78
Mary, 78
Richard, 246, 247
William, 178
HALLING
John, 125, 154
Samuel, 251
HAMILTON
ANN, 138, 161
Ann H., 198, 206
Charles, 138
E. G., 107, 111, 113, 119, 120, 127, 140, 167, 169, 176, 177, 178, 190, 195, 217, 224, 245, 253
Erasmus G., 28, 107
Euphama, 185
H. H., 80, 88, 204
Henry H., 73, 87, 126, 186

James, 31, 62, 88, 130, 138, 161, 236, 253
James H., 9, 36, 112, 141, 142, 159, 178, 187, 204, 236, 240, 241
James L., 130, 148
James W., 76
Jane, 138
John, 8, 22, 35, 39, 44, 45, 55, 57, 67, 73, 83, 108, 109, 125, 130, 138, 161, 165, 167, 169, 171, 174, 177, 178, 180, 215, 217
Margaret, 9, 76, 240
Nancy, 147
Robert, 147, 161, 191
S. G., 107
Samuel G., 107, 198, 206
Winifred, 130
HAMMAT
E., 203
Edward, 32, 87, 189, 193, 220, 221
George, 186, 203
Giles, 179, 180, 193, 194, 203, 223
HAMMATT
Edward, 89, 101, 122, 123, 154
Giles, 87, 108
Samuel, 141
HAMMERLY
John, 87, 168, 211
HAMMET
George, 232
Giles, 229, 232, 243
Samuel, 233
HAMMETT
Alice B., 224
Edward, 64, 207, 253
George, 236
Giles, 187, 224, 236, 245, 246, 253
Samuel, 246, 254
HAMMONTREE
Samuel, 226
HAMPTON
Joseph, 97

HANBY
John, 17, 25, 28, 254
HANCHER
James W., 97, 101, 123, 154
HANCOCK
George, 144, 145, 190
HANDEY
Eleanor, 39
John C., 151
William H., 39, 145, 214
HANDLEY
William J., 203
HANDSBY
Frederick, 6
HANDSCHY
Frederick, 48, 71
HANDSHY
Catharine, 51
Catherine, 35
Frederick, 35, 51, 92, 139
HANDY
Eleanor, 95, 236
Elenor, 184, 230
Eli H., 30, 166
George, 195
Given, 30
Hannah, 30
John, 30, 174
John C., 30, 159, 166, 168, 174, 241
William, 184
William H., 1, 7, 30, 48, 94, 95, 104, 119, 132, 166, 174, 191, 230, 234, 236
HANKS
Catherine, 32
Isaiah, 32
Jeremiah, 32
John, 32
Nancy, 32
Styles, 32
HANLEY
William J., 187
HANN
Hannah, 250
Hugh, 250
John, 61, 164, 210, 250

Mathias, 250
Peter, 250
Rachel, 250
William, 242, 250
HANSHY
Frederick, 26
HANSON
James M. C., 151
HARBOUR
Peter, 96
HARDACRE
Barbara, 253
Mordica, 253
HARDEN
William, 174
HARDESTY
Thomas, 189
HARDING
Ann A. B., 118
Job, 180
John, 31, 112
John J., 90, 93, 94,
99, 178, 179, 201,
221
William, 151, 189
William H., 151
HARDY
Joshua, 163
HARL
James, 116
HARNED
William, 21, 92
HARPER
Charles, 90
James, 122
Margaret, 203
S. D., 226
Thomas J., 203
William, 90
HARRAS
Asa, 242
Elizabeth, 242
HARRIS
___, 160
Elizabeth, 40, 142
Isaac, 27, 31, 55, 61,
87, 100, 103, 104,
114, 150, 161, 221
Isabella, 108
Jesse, 4, 8, 77, 79,
82, 105, 199, 237
John, 16, 24, 26, 40,
71, 142, 160, 182
Joseph, 123, 152

Margaret, 4, 79, 237
Peggy, 77
Sarah, 103
W. A., 194
William P., 55
HARRISON
Alexander, 7, 204
Alfred, 84
Burr W., 29, 43, 54,
66, 86, 90, 121,
125, 128, 147,
149, 181, 214, 245
Catharine, 181
E. T., 210
Elizabeth T., 230
Henry, 131
Henry T., 88, 90, 172,
181, 213
Jane C., 210
John P., 15
Margaret L., 181
Maria, 181
Mathew, 49, 112,
113, 133
Matthew, 24, 53, 67,
80, 181, 213
Sarah E., 181
Susannah, 7
Thomas J., 181
William B., 13, 38,
69, 72, 97, 148,
149, 167, 226
HARROP
James, 20
HARROVER
Hiram, 193
HARRRISON
John T., 181
HARRUP
James, 19
HART
John M., 32
Joseph, 12
Thomas, 76
William, 69, 242
HARTMAN
Daniel, 150, 206
HARVEY
Amos, 63, 90, 93,
115, 155, 218
William J., 186
HASKINS
John B., 55
HATCHER

Calvin, 134
Hannah, 2
James, 2, 94
John, 215
Joseph, 2, 20, 60, 67,
68, 162
Rebecca, 47, 68
Rebekah, 20
Samuel, 48, 60, 67,
162, 163
Thomas, 20, 47, 48,
68
William, 47, 48, 68,
134
HAUSER
Abigail, 32
HAWKE
Elizabeth, 165
John, 165
Margaret, 142, 165,
196
Mary, 142, 165, 196
Mary J., 165
William, 142, 165,
196, 223
HAWKINGS
Joseph, 36
HAWKINS
Joseph, 14, 77, 141,
162
Sarah, 77, 162
HAWLEY
Andrew, 241
Barton D., 73, 114
Catharine, 241
Hannah, 114
Lamoch, 241
Louisa, 241
Lucy, 241
Melinda, 241
Nelson, 241
Sally, 241
William J., 88
HAWLING
___, 234
Barton D., 1
Elizabeth, 154, 155,
169
Hannah, 1
Isaac, 80, 154
Jemima, 80
John, 27, 80, 154,
169, 193, 203, 236
Mary, 154, 169

Sarah, 183
Thomas, 183
Washington, 183
William, 183
HILLEARD
Joseph, 68
HILLEARY
Tilghman, 235, 238
HILLERY
Clement T., 6
HILLIARD
Joseph, 33, 87, 91,
192, 195, 216, 253
HILLIARY
Ann, 183
Clement T., 183
Henrietta, 183
Jane, 183
Thomas, 183
Tilghman, 183
HIND
R. H., 115
HIRST
David, 45
Jesse, 76
Richard, 34
HITAFFER
John, 230
HITE
Isaac, 226
HIXON
Alice, 147
F. W. P., 74
Fleming W., 10
James, 58
Margaret, 145
Mary, 147, 156, 192,
193
Reuben, 1, 36, 98,
156, 192, 193,
202, 243
Stephenson, 147
Timothy, 210
widow, 102
William, 1
HIXSON
Alice, 195
Benjamin, 46, 128,
153, 228
Eleanor, 74, 168
James, 128, 167,
223, 228
Margaret, 74, 141
Noah, 202, 236

Reuben, 14, 85, 98,
147, 186, 195,
205, 236
Reubin, 246
Ruth, 210
Samuel, 210
Sarah, 223, 228
Stephanson, 195,
246
Tacey, 153
HOCKING
Joseph, 254
HOCKINGS
Joseph, 213
HODGSON
Portia, 69, 169
William, 69, 169, 171
HOFFMAN
E., 69
Jacob, 69
John, 140
Phebe, 140
HOGE
James, 45, 120, 123,
199, 200, 236
Jesse, 101
Joshua, 20
Miller, 124, 166, 171
Samuel, 80, 84, 142
Tacey, 171
William, 1, 43, 101
HOGUE
Dr., 5
James, 209, 213
Joshua, 245
Mary, 68
Samuel, 77
William, 39, 236
HOLDREN
Cornelius, 21
HOLLIDAY
William M., 193
HOLLIN
John M., 35
HOLLINGSWORTH
Jehu, 25, 43, 45, 52,
208
John, 65
Joseph, 36
HOLLOWAY
___, 56
Aaron, 164
HOLMES

John, 14, 76, 186,
196, 234, 236
Martha, 155
Mary, 186
Rowena, 30
HOLY
___, 195
HOOD
Jonah, 124, 240
HOOE
Bernard, 8
James H., 169
R., 66
HOOFF
John, 66
HOOK
James T., 108
Jane, 148
John B., 108, 148
HOOPER
Barton, 207
HOPKINS
John, 16, 48, 71, 92,
169
William, 88
HORTON
Marshall W., 201
HOSKINS
Matilda, 150
Robert, 150
HOUGH
Amasa, 121, 158,
177, 197, 212
Anne E., 124
B., 246
Barnet, 232, 233
Benjamin, 197
Bernard, 86, 112,
119, 160, 204
Charles, 113
Clarinda, 124
Eleanor, 85, 95
Frances, 175
George S., 241, 247
Isaac, 36, 89, 175,
186
John, 38, 73, 84, 88,
94, 113, 239
John W. T., 124
Joseph, 124, 167,
204
Louisa, 160, 204, 233
Lydia, 7, 94, 96, 241
Mahlon, 13, 123

Reuben, 42, 46, 48, 72, 149, 170, 173, 201, 213
Sampson, 48, 140, 173, 201
Sanford, 224

IDEN
Jacob, 163
Manly, 163
Samuel, 148

IREY
John, 2

ISH
Harriet, 98
Jacob, 16, 48, 49, 169, 201, 222
Peter, 98, 120

JACKSON
Benjamin, 37, 45, 96, 117, 168, 238, 251
David, 248
Elizabeth, 73, 111
Henry, 73, 111
John, 50, 51, 224
Lovel, 34
Lovell, 5
S. H., 38
Samuel, 187

JACOBS
Catharine, 185
Elizabeth, 183, 231
Presley, 52
Price, 182
Thomas, 9, 130, 160
Valentine, 182, 183
Vallentine, 231
William, 185
William H., 221

JAGGER
Silas, 237

JAMES
___, 93
Abel, 6, 74, 241
Abigail, 238
Ann, 177, 180
Benjamin, 6, 21, 55, 134, 241
Charles, 192
Daniel, 136, 150
David, 72, 93, 113, 120, 164, 215
Dean, 1, 10, 114, 180

Elias, 40, 108, 136, 150
Elizabeth, 180
Jacob, 177, 180
John, 95, 114, 163
Johnathan, 150
Jonathan, 136
Levi, 7, 36, 95
Mary, 6
Moses, 6
Nancy, 114
Ruth, 150
Sally, 241
Sarah, 74
Smith, 177, 180
Thomas, 7, 45, 56, 147, 204
William, 1, 10, 114, 180, 196

JAMIESON
Andrew, 116, 118
Mary, 118

JANNEY
___, 29, 147
Abel, 11, 28, 114, 187, 209, 227, 234, 241, 245
Amos, 34, 92, 120, 136, 144, 145, 147, 150, 172, 198, 211, 217, 227, 245, 247
Ann, 76
Daniel, 12, 59, 99, 101, 199
David, 2, 13, 14, 41, 59, 66, 69, 91, 99, 143, 145, 154, 163, 212, 220
E., 180
Elisha, 30, 32, 38, 44, 207, 226, 247, 252
Elizabeth, 2, 13, 14, 59, 66, 69, 91, 101, 143, 145, 163, 198, 247
George, 4, 6, 24, 30, 31, 32, 41, 42, 43, 44, 48, 60, 68, 69, 75, 77, 78, 85, 94, 126, 136, 145, 150, 152, 154, 155, 161, 166,

168, 184, 211, 215, 252
Grace, 172, 247
Hannah, 47, 91, 92, 93, 101
Israel, 13, 35, 99, 101, 199
James M., 234
Jesse, 2, 25, 47, 99, 152, 153, 211
Jessee, 46
John, 38, 76, 85, 103, 152, 198, 217, 236, 247
John G., 237
Jonas, 216
Joseph, 10, 63, 103, 186, 189, 217, 238, 244
Letitia, 133
Lot, 80, 84, 142
Lot T., 196
Lydia, 209
M., 28, 246
Mahlon, 14, 51, 52, 53, 54, 57, 58, 62, 64, 69, 81, 83, 110, 116, 139, 150, 151, 152, 158, 181, 198, 204, 205, 208, 216, 217, 218, 250
Moses, 36
Nathan, 34, 198, 227
Rachel, 83, 158, 198, 217, 250
Ruth, 198
Sarah, 111, 172, 198, 205, 217
Sarah E., 237
Sophia, 84, 142
Stacey, 92, 93, 101
Stephen, 25, 49, 99, 126, 133, 141
Susan, 198
Susana, 154
Susanna, 6, 41, 43, 126, 150, 152, 154, 155, 168, 184
Susannah, 24, 31, 44, 68, 85, 94, 166, 168
Thomas, 71, 132, 168, 236, 237, 252

William, 99, 119, 190
JANNY
David, 225
George, 155, 240, 241
Mahlon, 225
Susannah, 240
Thomas, 241
JEFFERS
Anderson, 126
Harriet, 126
JENKINS
___, 195
Benjamin, 149, 164, 176, 184, 207, 211, 229, 243
Eleanor, 207
Elis, 202
Ellis, 63
Hannah, 176
Henry, 63, 65, 69, 87, 115
Jacob, 67
John, 206, 207
Margaret, 63, 87, 115
Mary, 164
Simon, 206
Walter, 193
William, 164, 176, 190, 198, 207, 231
JENNER
Abiel, 100, 121
JENNERS
Abiel, 1, 3, 4, 5, 6, 8, 9, 10, 12, 13, 14, 15, 16, 19, 21, 22, 24, 26, 27, 28, 33, 35, 39, 40, 42, 44, 46, 50, 51, 52, 53, 55, 57, 59, 60, 61, 62, 63, 64, 66, 69, 71, 77, 78, 79, 81, 82, 83, 85, 86, 90, 91, 92, 93, 95, 96, 100, 101, 105, 111, 113, 117, 120, 123, 124, 129, 130, 136, 137, 138, 140, 141, 143, 144, 145, 151, 152, 153, 154, 157, 158, 161, 163, 166, 167, 178,

181, 187, 188, 189, 196, 197, 204, 205, 206, 208, 209, 210, 216, 217, 224, 225, 227, 235, 236, 237, 239, 240, 244, 246, 254
Deborah, 5, 6, 19, 93, 163, 178, 244
William, 243
JOHNS
Thomas, 18
JOHNSON
___, 111, 119
Amos, 12, 115, 116, 128, 144, 146, 155, 176, 207, 217, 222, 247
Ann, 200
Bazzell, 150
Casper, 20
Daniel, 199
Daniel C., 200
Elizabeth, 46
George, 36, 43
Hugh, 112, 152
James, 20, 46, 112, 152
Jane, 46
John, 46, 96, 128, 222, 223
Margaret, 58, 165
Phebe, 20
Sarah, 217, 223, 247
William, 58, 165
JOHNSTON
Amos, 182, 226, 233, 234
Casper, 213, 231, 234
Elizabeth, 138
George, 52
Hugh, 49, 52, 82
James, 46, 49, 52, 82, 138, 232
Jane, 138
John, 138
William, 137
JOHNSTONE
John, 14
JONES
Elizabeth, 7
Henry, 12, 18

Jehu, 19
John, 7, 22, 29, 49, 124, 155
Joseph, 174
Micage, 214
Mrs., 224
Patrick, 202
Philip, 30
Philip C., 210
Rachel, 250
Richard S., 30
Sarah, 202, 204
Thomas, 96, 125
Walter, 37, 69, 170
JORDON
Thomas G., 230
JURY
Abner, 238
Malinda, 96

KALB
Absalom, 89, 101, 117
John, 89, 101
Susannah, 117
KARN
Jacob, 250
KEARNY
Francis, 179
KEEN
George, 222, 247
Newton, 184
Richard, 199
KEENE
Ann, 150
George, 223
John, 203, 207
John N. T. G. E., 199
Kitturah, 12
Newton, 12, 64, 168, 237
Richard, 150
Thomas, 170
KEITH
John, 184
Sarah, 184
KELL
Isaac, 203
KELLEY
John, 119
Thomas, 221
KELLY
Edward, 164, 221
Mahala, 222

Mary Ann, 221
Thomas C., 157
Vincent, 222
KELLY
 Edward, 21
KEMERLE
 Christina, 152
 Jacob, 152, 176
KEMERLY
 Jacob, 62
KENADY
 F. H., 173
KENEDY
 F. H., 109, 173
KENNAN
 Thomas, 220
KENNEDY
 F. H., 120
KENNER
 Adam, 75
KENNON
 Thomas, 245
KENT
 Ailcy, 87
 Ashford, 87
 Benjamin, 28, 46, 47,
  74, 141, 147, 155,
  211, 216
 Elias, 31, 139
 Elizabeth, 87, 155
 Harrison, 139
 Henry, 197
 John, 155
 Samuel, 155
 Sarah, 47, 74, 155,
  211
 Thomas, 87, 155,
  245, 246
 William, 139
KENWORTHY
 William, 13, 61, 126
KERBY
 Thomas H., 160, 164,
  173
KERN
 Jacob, 158
KERR
 Alexander, 223
KERRICK
 Walter, 45, 46
KERT
 John, 247
 Joseph, 247
KEYSER

William, 113
KIDWELL
 Benjamin, 31
 Elizabeth, 217, 225,
  231
 Nancy, 31
 Tamar, 31
 Thomas, 88, 149,
  171, 182, 189,
  217, 225, 231, 244
KIGER
 Frederick, 215, 222
KILE
 George, 15, 113
 John, 15, 49
 Winney M., 49
KILGORE
 Charles J., 172
 George, 99, 101,
  106, 116
 Louisa, 172
KILGOUR
 Charles J., 160
 Louisa, 160
KILLY
 Edward, 21
KIMMERLE
 Christeana, 152
 Jacob, 102, 127, 152,
  174, 178
KIMMINS
 Thomas, 65
KINCHELOE
 Elizabeth, 9
 James, 9
KING
 Miles, 41
 Patrick, 61, 62
 William, 28, 122, 128,
  175, 196
KINGERLING
 Jurlers, 201
KINN
 Benjamin, 47
 Letetia, 47
 Letty, 47
KIPHART
 John, 142
KIPHEART
 John, 129
KIRBY
 Thomas H., 102, 248
KIRK
 James, 113

Nancy, 176, 233, 245
Robert W., 113
Sarah, 113
William, 176, 233,
 245
KIRKPATRICK
 ___, 152
KITTSMILLER
 Martin, 67
KITZMILLER
 Martin, 87, 114, 217,
  218, 221
KLEIN
 Lewis, 9, 15, 57, 144,
  243
KLINE
 William, 122
KNETTLE
 William, 187
KNOTT
 Joseph, 230
KNOX
 Joseph, 78, 228
 Mary, 38, 77, 162
 Thomas P., 128, 173,
  185
 William, 38, 77, 162
KOONCE
 Nicholas, 180
KOONTZ
 ___, 231
 George, 243
 Nicholas, 243
KOUTZ
 George, 225

LACEY
 Armistead J., 82
 Catharine, 145
 Catharine E., 82
 David, 122, 212
 Huldah, 79
 Israel, 9, 213
 Joseph, 79
 Meshack, 171
 Naomi, 79
 Robert A., 82
 Robert F., 221
 Ruth, 79
 Sarah, 136
 Tacey, 79
 Thomas, 208, 212
 Westwood A., 82
LACY

Castelina, 245
David, 245
Thomas, 225
LAFFERTY
  Ann, 62
  Jacob, 62
  Nancy, 62
LAKE
  Isaac, 16, 25, 46, 141
  Sally, 25, 141
LAKENAN
  Margarett, 35
  Thomas, 35
LAKNON
  Robert, 70
LAMBAG
  Joseph, 87
LANE
  Hardage, 13, 17, 34,
    61
  James, 61, 235
  James B., 12, 17
  Joseph, 113
  Martha, 246
  Matilda, 53
  Richard M., 246
  Sarah, 166, 193, 224
  William, 189, 235,
    246
  William A., 125
  William H., 34, 93,
    98, 112, 122, 165,
    166, 171, 224, 229
LANG
  Thomas, 151
LANGLEY
  Walter, 122, 124,
    137, 159, 240
LANHAM
  Walter, 248
LARMOUR
  Mandaville, 57
LAROWE
  Isaac, 2, 19, 22, 65,
    74, 110, 158, 239
LASLIE
  Benjamin, 247
LASLY
  Thomas, 175
LASSWELL
  Jacob, 21, 42
LAWRENCE
  Anne L., 27
  Louisa, 202

Richard, 27
Thomas, 202
Thomas L., 27
LAWSON
  Nero, 194, 200, 212
LEACHMAN
  William, 57
LEATH
  James, 138, 195
  Patty, 138
LEE
  Ann, 109
  Ann C., 53, 120
  Asel, 199
  Daniel, 159
  Doddridge, 169
  E. J., 173, 175, 194
  Edmond J., 137
  Edmund J., 37, 59,
    66, 84, 98, 110,
    114, 149, 175, 227
  Eliza, 8, 205
  Eliza M., 53
  Fanny, 62, 68, 110,
    113, 117, 118,
    140, 157
  Flora, 32, 53, 109,
    110, 120, 173
  Francis L., 59, 203
  George, 18, 53
  Henry, 151
  Joshua, 19, 213
  Ludwell, 8, 32, 59,
    68, 98, 109, 110,
    146, 171, 173,
    203, 205
  Matilda, 110
  Philip L., 110
  Richard H., 32, 53,
    90, 109, 110, 127,
    128, 133, 189,
    221, 249
  Sally, 227
  Thomas, 157, 216
  Thomas B., 16
  Thomas L., 68, 110,
    118
  William L., 17, 254
LEEDOM
  Hannah, 103
  Thomas, 103
LEFEVER
  Henry, 82
LEIDER

Lewis, 49, 51
LEITH
  James, 40, 64, 67,
    118, 138, 139, 226
  Mary, 64, 65, 67
  Patty, 139
  Sarah, 40
  William, 64, 226
LEMORT
  Elizabeth, 185
  Laban, 185
  Lewis, 185
  Thadius, 185
LEONARD
  Thomas, 248
LESLIE
  Ann, 81, 123
  B., 84
  Benjamin, 38, 147,
    176
  Joseph, 84
  Nancy, 12
  Samuel, 84, 176
  Samuel D., 21, 38,
    103, 147, 171
  Thomas, 12, 81, 92,
    123, 149, 171,
    176, 180
LEVERING
  Aaron R., 190, 249
LEVING
  Aaron R., 138
LEWIS
  C., 161
  Catharine, 41
  Charles, 1, 13, 15,
    18, 19, 21, 37, 39,
    40, 41, 47, 48, 49,
    56, 72, 74, 75,
    101, 114, 119,
    143, 146, 148,
    149, 161, 163,
    167, 173, 181,
    199, 251, 252
  Coleman, 102
  George, 72, 80
  Isaac, 170, 171
  James, 41, 146, 161,
    170, 171, 199,
    214, 251
  James M., 45, 117,
    131, 145, 234,
    237, 238, 242
  James W., 42

Jemima, 193, 224, 237
Joanna, 142
John, 77, 102, 195, 253
John H., 204
Joseph, 22, 26, 47, 56, 67, 97, 100, 102, 138, 148, 150, 182, 190, 191, 196, 197, 204, 206, 213, 231, 249, 250
Lawrence, 207
Mary, 195, 253
Mildred, 77
Mildred A. B., 77
Nancy, 41
Rachel, 72
Rebecca, 102
Sarah, 1
Stephen, 41
Thomas, 91
William, 1
LICKEY
Abigail, 32, 129
Conrad, 81
Elizabeth, 7, 22, 148, 251
George, 30, 81, 129, 197
John, 7, 22, 79, 124, 129, 148, 251
John C., 7, 10, 124
Margaret, 10, 81
William, 29, 32, 80, 81, 129
LICKY
William, 22
LINCH
George, 3
LINDSEY
Lewis, 245
LINTON
John, 240
LITTLE
Charles, 66
R. H., 45, 69, 149
LITTLEJOHN
John, 25, 29, 42, 61, 63, 66, 67, 68, 83, 86, 89, 98, 109, 110, 113, 117,

119, 127, 144, 147, 179, 224
John W., 94
Monica, 61, 63, 67, 98, 109, 117, 147
William M., 99, 109
LITTLETON
John, 16
John K., 211, 252
Richard K., 246
Thomas, 204
LIVINGSTON
John, 61, 78, 242
William B., 192
LLOYD
___, 195
Emery, 140
George E., 128, 180, 182, 186, 189
James, 230
LLOYDS
George E., 55
LLOYED
Joseph, 228
LOCKHART
Josiah, 148
LODGE
Samuel, 78
Thomas, 78, 170
William, 25, 78, 170, 238
LONG
Brumfield, 19, 239
Joseph A., 243
LOSCH
Daniel, 36
LOSH
Daniel, 93
LOSSON
Nero, 133, 200
LOVE
Augusta, 97
Augustine, 23, 65, 76, 97, 105, 113
Charles J., 78, 169, 207
Elizabeth M., 16
Frances P., 78
George, 76, 97, 113, 166
James, 58, 88, 233
Jane, 64
Jane H., 97

John, 11, 93, 150, 220
Martha, 97
Mary, 23, 76, 97, 113
Rebecca, 88
Richard H., 16
Samuel, 172
Sarah, 97
Susanna, 36, 88
Thomas, 1, 156
LOVETT
___, 10
Christian, 22
Christiana, 71
Daniel, 2, 8, 16, 36, 37, 54, 66, 82, 108, 115, 119, 138, 141, 254
David, 1, 37, 38, 39, 73, 84, 105, 106, 126, 135, 148, 156, 160, 163, 164, 172, 201, 228, 229, 236, 238
Edmund, 22, 29, 54, 71, 129, 239
Joseph, 74, 143, 201
LOWE
Edward, 7
Elizabeth, 7
Kitty, 7
Sarah, 7
LUCAS
Barton, 214
LUCKET
Alfred, 248
Francis W., 47
Horrace, 251
Leven, 177
Ludwell, 248
Samuel, 251
LUCKETT
F. M., 61
F. W., 78, 155
Francis, 72, 235
Francis M., 6, 12, 13, 23, 24, 26
Francis W, 212
Francis W., 8, 15, 24, 30, 31, 39, 40, 41, 42, 43, 44, 46, 49, 59, 61, 62, 64, 65, 68, 69, 71, 72, 76, 78, 80, 81, 85, 88,

Henry, 46, 102, 160,
172, 173, 199
McKIM
Ruhemah, 241
William H., 6
McKIMIE
Francis, 32
McKINNEY
John, 151
McKNIGHT
Charles, 167
Deborah, 76
Eli, 51, 76, 236
John, 76
William, 76
McMULLIN
Barbary, 109
Daniel, 109
McNEILL
Hirdin, 108
McNELAGE
___, 114
McNELLEDGE
___, 160
McNIGHT
Eli, 49
William, 7
McPHERSON
___, 254
Cecelia, 81, 234, 247
Cecilia, 94, 95, 98
Celia, 1
Cloe, 28
Elizabeth, 224
James, 28, 224
John, 6, 20, 28, 56,
57
Joseph, 252
Kesiah, 28
Mary, 62
Samuel, 62, 64
Sarah, 235
Stephen, 1, 17, 52,
57, 81, 86, 94, 95,
96, 97, 98, 107,
111, 119, 128,
146, 149, 189,
194, 215, 223,
224, 225, 227,
234, 235, 247, 254
William, 225
McVEIGH
Elizabeth, 16, 128

Hiram, 16, 29, 40,
128, 144, 187,
201, 230
J., 211
James, 179
Jesse, 15, 16, 26, 40,
65, 67, 119, 124,
128, 135, 138,
151, 153, 154,
160, 167, 169,
177, 182, 198,
199, 207, 209,
214, 226, 227,
229, 233, 242, 252
Townsend, 55, 70,
100, 111, 118,
135, 167, 169,
191, 212, 214,
245, 253
Townshend, 132
McVICKER
Archibald, 121, 142
McVICKERS
Archibald, 31, 122,
125, 141, 189
Elizabeth, 31, 122,
141
MEAD
Aquilla, 126
Benjamin, 126
Elizabeth, 181
Joseph, 176, 181,
184, 188, 202
William, 73, 107, 154,
169, 176
MEADE
Elizabeth, 202
Joseph, 202
Martha, 202
Mary, 202
William, 157, 174,
202
MEANS
Archibald, 65
MEEK
John, 127
MEGEATH
Mary, 40
Stephen, 39
MEGETH
Gabriel, 5
Martha, 5
MELLLIN
Amy, 96

MELVIL
James, 249
MELVIN
James, 138
MENDENHALL
Jacob, 1, 13, 78, 100,
119
MERCER
Charles F., 15, 16,
19, 25, 67, 74, 78,
110, 179, 181,
184, 193, 222,
229, 231, 235,
239, 240, 249, 251
Fenton, 153
George, 184
James, 16, 27, 184,
193, 240
John, 153, 184
John F., 184, 193,
240
Joseph, 128
Langley, 181
MERSHON
Joseph B., 156
Thomas, 156
William, 120
METCALF
George, 73
MILBURNE
Jonathan, 8
MILDERN
John, 152
MILHOLLAN
Diadama, 193
Ewell, 193
Patrick, 193
Patrick B., 193
Sarah, 193
MILHOLLAND
John, 194, 202, 221,
222, 224
Jonathan, 194
Malinda, 15
P. B., 202
Pat, 194
Patrick, 15, 35, 63
Patrick B., 130
Thomas, 194
MILHOLLEN
Esther, 66
John, 204
Joseph, 66
Malinda, 194

Patrick, 34, 35, 127
Patrick B., 1, 66, 194
MILHOLLIN
　Esther, 39
　John, 39
　Joseph, 39
MILLER
　___, 97
　Aaron, 85, 89, 93, 99,
　　101, 116, 117,
　　147, 183, 188,
　　192, 193, 211, 254
　Adam, 93, 98, 146,
　　183, 247, 254
　Catharine, 93, 98,
　　146, 183, 230, 247
　Christian, 33, 37
　Dal, 183
　Daniel, 2, 95, 98,
　　171, 220, 228,
　　246, 247, 251
　Elizabeth, 146
　George, 238
　Hannah, 69, 104
　Isaac, 185
　Jacob, 146, 254
　Jeremiah, 51, 68, 236
　Jesse, 93, 99, 146,
　　183, 247
　John, 93, 98, 182,
　　183, 230, 244
　Margaret, 183
　Mary, 37, 95, 98, 183
　Moses, 188
　Peggy, 247
　Peter, 28, 93, 98,
　　116, 146, 183,
　　188, 247, 253
　Polly, 247
　Rachel, 85, 93
　Samuel, 87, 93, 103,
　　104, 155, 179, 204
　Sarah, 37
　Valentine, 37
　William, 49
MILLHOLLAND
　Patrick, 51
　Patrick B., 26
MILLHOLLEN
　Patrick B., 123
MILLHOLLINS
　Patrick, 33
MILLIKIN
　Francis, 21

MILLS
　James, 160
MINEL
　Josiah, 163
MINER
　Nathan, 63
MINES
　A., 151
　Addison, 87, 228
　John, 87, 93, 120,
　　228, 229
　John K., 128
MINK
　___, 147, 150
　Laurence, 24, 33
　Lawrence, 35
MINNIX
　John P., 220
MINOR
　Daniel, 77, 162, 227
　John, 36, 77
　Lucy, 77
　Lucy L., 77
　Nathan, 133, 194,
　　212
　Pleasant, 77
　Plesant, 162
　Spencer, 33
MITCHEL
　Benjamin, 248
MITCHELL
　Benjamin, 206, 219
　Elizabeth, 63, 130
　John, 76
　Mathew, 15, 123, 221
　Matthew, 34, 35, 63,
　　130, 194, 217
MOCK
　Jacob, 143, 235
MODISET
　Charles, 251
　Sarah, 251
MOFFET
　Benjamin, 142
　Malinda, 142
MOFFETT
　Benjamin, 141, 143,
　　184, 217
　Ellen, 104
　Malinda, 184
　Robert, 11, 12, 49,
　　55, 73, 83, 104,
　　107, 109, 113,
　　137, 156, 157,

　　161, 169, 171,
　　174, 177, 186,
　　190, 193, 194,
　　202, 204, 206,
　　210, 221, 249
MOKLELL
　Nenian R., 204
MONEY
　Nicholas, 22, 239
MONROE
　___, 97
　A. G., 18
　Andrew, 122
　Augustine G., 174
　Deskin, 186, 187
　Duskin, 87
　James, 141, 168,
　　174, 240
　Jane, 182
　John, 66, 81, 87, 115,
　　116, 120, 137, 175
　John H., 218, 221
　John M., 82, 139,
　　151, 176, 180,
　　182, 197
　Kitty, 7, 89
　Mary, 115, 120, 175
　Robert, 187
　Thomas W., 102
　William, 7, 181
　William D., 89
MONTEITH
　James, 40
MOOR
　John, 221
MOORE
　Ann, 144, 225
　Asa, 7, 14, 21, 35,
　　36, 41, 47, 62, 81,
　　89, 92, 110, 136,
　　137, 139, 144,
　　203, 205, 212,
　　224, 225, 241, 242
　Benjamin, 33, 35
　Elizabeth, 187
　James, 14, 24, 62,
　　77, 92, 93, 99,
　　110, 120, 137,
　　139, 143, 145,
　　205, 208, 210, 216
　John, 87, 136, 140,
　　171, 182, 196
　Margaret, 187
　Mary, 178

Maurice, 187
Morris, 230
Moses L., 237
Peter, 3
Peyton, 232
Pierce, 187, 230
Rebecca, 205
Rebekah, 99
Richard, 178
Robert, 174
Samuel, 72
Thomas, 100, 187, 230
Thomas A., 80, 109, 121, 132, 140, 145, 165, 193, 204, 224, 233
MORALEE
Thomas, 31, 93, 186
MORALLEE
Thomas, 7, 15, 63, 90, 99, 101, 102, 105, 120, 123, 175, 229
MORAN
Samuel, 40
MOREN
John, 222
MORGAN
John, 34, 54, 89, 123
William, 95
MORRALLEE
Thomas, 87, 154
MORRIS
John, 158
Mahlon, 247
Thadeus, 157
Thomas, 90
MORRISON
Archibald, 28, 77, 158
MORROW
John, 242
MORTEN
John, 225
MORTON
Richard C., 249
MOSS
Ann, 111
Nathaniel, 111, 248
Thomas, 21, 120, 138, 222
Thomas R., 25

Vincent, 111, 208, 248
William, 246
MOTT
Ann C., 224
Mary, 148
Mary C., 81
Thomas, 8, 11
Thomas R., 6, 8, 9, 10, 16, 19, 22, 23, 27, 36, 56, 58, 59, 73, 75, 81, 83, 86, 88, 115, 120, 126, 148, 150, 152, 175, 181, 184, 194, 203, 212, 218, 224, 228, 231, 240, 254
MOUNT
Ezekial, 242
Ezekiel, 65, 198
Hannah, 30, 95, 241
James, 30, 95, 112, 174, 236, 241
John, 79, 169, 197, 198, 226
L. R., 97
Mary A., 197, 198
Mary Ann, 79
Sarah, 79
Stephen R., 127, 215, 216, 242, 251, 252
Thomas, 79, 177
MOXLEY
Jane, 83
Joseph, 21, 164
Joshua, 22
William, 44, 83, 93, 224
MUDD
Edward, 106, 195
John, 199
Martha, 199
MULL
Catharine, 60, 61
David, 60, 61, 86, 124, 139, 140, 171, 180, 182, 191, 198, 206, 227, 250
Elizabeth, 140, 191, 206, 227

George, 140, 191, 212, 227
John, 60, 61, 250
Margaret, 180, 191
Mary, 60, 61, 140, 250
Polly, 60
MULLEN
John, 49, 204
Samuel, 76
MULLENS
Joseph W., 16
MUNROE
John, 175
MUNSELL
Levi, 16
MURPHEY
Thomas, 241, 252
MURRAY
Betsey, 31, 33, 253
James B., 239
Reuben, 183
Sally, 253
Samuel, 13, 17, 31, 33, 103, 240, 253
MURREY
Elizabeth, 127
James, 72
John, 185, 221
Josiah, 195
Samuel, 2, 7, 8, 17, 18, 19, 23, 31, 41, 43, 45, 46, 48, 65, 69, 75, 78, 81, 82, 84, 85, 87, 96, 100, 101, 103, 104, 105, 106, 112, 116, 118, 127, 147, 150, 161, 198, 208, 212, 217, 220, 230
William, 72, 134
MURRY
James, 134
James B., 239
John, 197
Samuel, 183
MUSE
Thomas H., 205
MUSGROVE
Nathan, 87
MUSTIN
Blanche, 174
John, 174

MYERS
  Benjamin, 249
  Charlotte, 82
  John, 82
  John G., 228

NEALE
  Benjamin, 240
  Christopher, 64, 194
  James, 189
  Richard H., 124
  W. S., 50, 64, 75
  William S., 3, 13, 71, 123, 165
NEAR
  Amos, 104
  Conrod, 225
  Henry, 104
  James, 104, 131
  Samuel, 225, 231, 254
  Sarah, 104
NEER
  David, 20, 104
  James, 104
  Jane, 182
  Nathan, 182
  Sarah, 182
Negro
  Abram, 181
  Adam, 60, 190, 226
  Albert, 231
  Alce, 11
  Alfred, 9, 181, 229
  Amy, 20
  Ann, 58, 130, 181
  Anna, 130
  Anne, 166
  Anny, 134
  Arena, 130
  Armstead, 59, 157
  Beck, 200
  Becky, 114
  Belcher, 127
  Ben, 127, 231
  Bessie, 60
  Bet, 3
  Betsy, 115, 130
  Betty, 24, 61, 157, 181
  Bidwell, 231
  Bill, 146, 161, 168, 174
  Billy, 157

  Bob, 138, 200
  Bridget, 59
  Caleb, 2
  Caroline, 49, 54, 146, 161, 199, 210
  Carpenter, 157
  Casar, 130
  Cate, 181
  Catharine, 54
  Cato, 240
  Cealia, 85
  Cebes, 60
  Charity, 9, 11
  Charles, 118, 146, 161, 190, 226, 240, 244
  Charlott, 11
  Charlotte, 114, 146, 161, 181
  Clarissa, 231
  Clarrissa, 3
  Clem, 169
  Cyrus, 54, 244
  Daniel, 190, 199, 240
  Darkus, 11
  Darky, 219
  Davy, 12, 72, 244
  Delilah, 219
  Delilale, 11
  Dick, 11
  Dinah, 11, 244
  Doctor, 102
  Dolly, 29
  Dorcas, 212
  Dorchas, 199
  Dory, 190
  Edmond, 244
  Elias, 108, 166
  Elisa, 226
  Eliza, 11, 108, 181, 212, 214, 226, 229
  Elizabeth, 142
  Ellick, 203
  Emily, 7, 11
  Esther, 60
  Eve, 157
  Fanney, 11
  Fanny, 130
  Flora, 30
  Frank, 20, 142, 187
  Franky, 59
  Gary, 112

  George, 114, 146, 157, 161, 173, 181, 214
  Gilbert, 157, 181
  Grace, 169
  Granny Lett, 226
  Hannah, 7, 11, 115, 146, 229
  Hanson, 212
  Harey, 157
  Harriet, 11, 112, 138, 229, 244
  Harriot, 20, 90
  Harry, 9, 60, 130, 212
  Hary, 181
  Hector, 157, 187
  Heister, 72
  Helen, 138
  Henney, 169
  Henny, 138
  Henrieta, 134
  Henry, 49, 166, 181, 229, 244
  Henson, 138
  Ida, 231
  Iday, 3
  Indy, 59
  Isaiah, 11
  Israel, 181
  Jack, 130, 240
  Jacob, 9, 27, 181, 231
  James, 11, 130, 142, 146, 157, 161
  James West, 121
  Jane, 35, 130, 169, 229
  Janny, 202
  Jefferson, 3
  Jem, 59, 157
  Jenny, 59, 229
  Jeraid, 7
  Jerry, 114, 202
  Jess, 229
  Jesse, 11
  Jim, 9, 12
  Jinny, 49
  Joan, 181
  Joannah, 199
  Joe, 127
  John, 3, 11, 12, 30, 60, 157, 181, 210
  Joseph, 130, 214
  Joshua, 240

Judy, 157
Julia, 214
Julian, 36
Juliet, 134
Kelly, 231
Kingston, 59
Kitty, 12, 72
Landon, 212, 219
Lemmon, 59
Len, 146, 161
Lete, 190
Lethe, 70, 87
Letty, 134, 226
Levi, 212, 219
Lewis, 9
Lizzy, 9, 181
Lorindy, 114
Luce, 12
Lucey, 85
Lucinda, 20, 130, 212
Lucy, 54, 59, 79, 121,
    130, 138, 142,
    200, 219
Malvina, 134
Marcus, 60
Maria, 138, 157, 203,
    229, 240
Mariah, 219, 244
Marlborough, 102
Marshall, 199
Martha, 181
Martha Ann, 166
Mary, 4, 7, 9, 130,
    190, 199, 202,
    212, 219, 226
Mary Ann, 57, 166,
    219
Mason, 85
Mat, 181
Mathew, 240
Matilda, 9, 49, 229
May, 181
Menokin, 157
Milcey, 200
Miles, 157
Mille, 146
Milley, 73, 190
Milly, 60, 161, 201,
    233
Molly, 90, 157
Moses, 88, 90, 200
Moss, 59
Nace, 186
Nan, 212

Nancy, 54, 114, 166
Nannetta, 181
Nathan, 108, 181
Ned, 59
Nelly, 11, 210
Noaroh, 190
Osmond, 60
Patty, 130
Payne, 231
Pegg, 169
Peggy, 59, 157
Pen, 12
Peter, 7, 240
Phebe, 3, 11, 30
Philip, 90
Phill, 134, 190
Phillis, 114, 244
Phoebe, 201
Pompey, 244
Rachael, 146, 212
Rachel, 11, 161
Ralph, 11, 240
Richard, 24, 72, 146
Rippon, 59
Robert, 72, 231
Romelus, 72
Sally, 11
Sam, 4, 12, 20, 70,
    181
Sampson, 60, 146,
    161, 231
Samuel, 60
Samuel Biass, 87
Sandy, 199, 231
Sarah, 9, 59, 130,
    134, 181, 199
Sawney, 130
Sidney, 186, 187
Silve, 146
Silvey, 161
Silvy, 169
Sinah Williams, 87
Sinia, 70
Sirus, 174
Soloman, 80
Solomon, 80
Sopha, 190
Sophia, 210
Stephen, 11, 54, 59
Suckey, 220
Sucky, 58, 138, 219,
    226, 231
Susan, 226
Susanna, 166

Sybol, 161
Sylvy, 134
Tacey, 198
Thomas, 3, 214
Thornton, 214
Tilda, 12
Toby, 146, 161
Tom, 20, 59, 73, 166,
    186, 187, 219
Toney, 157
Trent, 3
Trueman, 7
Uriah, 11
Ury, 134
Vanessa, 240
Vincent, 157
Violet, 181
Violett, 35
Voll, 187
Washington, 11
Westley, 7
Wilfred, 134
Will, 157
William, 130, 166,
    210
Willis, 200
Wilson, 229
Winney, 157, 226
Winny, 226
Yorrick, 79
NEILE
    Alexander, 90
NEISWANGER
    Mrs., 131
NELSON
    John G., 16
    Phil, 134
    Thomas, 45
NETTAL
    William, 85
NETTLE
    William, 85, 242
NEWCOMER
    Catharine, 85
    Catherine, 21
    Emamuel, 85
    Emanuel, 3, 21, 52,
        95, 107, 137
NEWMAN
    Bazil, 129, 191
    Frances, 161
    John, 197
    Robert, 161

Dade P., 6, 111, 125
Elizabeth, 111, 226
Enos, 189
Lloyd, 6, 32, 46, 111,
  125, 137, 167,
  180, 201, 229
Mary, 235
Philip, 189
Phillip, 235
Samuel, 6, 46, 111,
  178
Samuel N., 125
Thomas, 46, 111,
  125, 189, 199,
  243, 248
Thomas J., 173, 193
William, 2, 4, 6, 25,
  31, 34, 35, 39, 46,
  48, 49, 62, 64, 74,
  84, 90, 93, 102,
  104, 111, 115,
  116, 121, 124,
  129, 133, 135,
  142, 143, 156,
  159, 160, 163,
  164, 167, 172,
  173, 180, 181,
  184, 193, 199,
  207, 222, 223,
  225, 227, 228,
  230, 231, 240,
  243, 248, 249, 251
NORRIS
  Eliza, 102
  Ignatius, 9, 31, 127,
    129
  James L., 102, 160,
    167
  Mary, 129
  Nelson, 64, 84, 102
NORRISS
  Ignatius, 83
NORTON
  Edward, 36
  John, 74
  Nathaniel, 74
  Richard C., 108, 120,
    173
NORWOOD
  Richard, 109
NUTT
  William, 128, 144
NYSWANGER
  Christian, 204

O'BANNION
  Samuel, 156
ODEN
  Nathaniel S., 146
OFFUTT
  Charles, 12, 136
  E., 69, 75
  Eli, 57
OGDEN
  David, 87, 122, 204,
    224, 229, 253
  Elizabeth, 122
  Mr., 189
  Robert, 169
OGDON
  David, 112
ONEAL
  Margaret, 191
O'NEALE
  Anne, 219
  Daniel, 219
OREM
  Henry, 93
ORENDUFF
  Martha, 147
ORISON
  Abel, 221
ORR
  Benjamin G., 49
  John D., 151
  Lucinda, 151
  Robert, 235
  William G., 170
ORRISON
  Abel, 55
  Arthur, 193, 199
  Elizabeth, 193
OSBURN
  Abner, 155
  Balaam, 1, 20, 47,
    142, 164, 209,
    213, 231, 236
  Capt., 178
  Craven, 38, 39, 74,
    84, 125, 131, 132,
    134, 135, 146,
    147, 150, 155,
    156, 160, 164,
    180, 213, 214,
    217, 220, 244
  Cravin, 236
  David, 2
  Eleanor, 1, 2, 17

Elizabeth, 134
Herod, 1, 2, 17, 81,
  253
Joab, 20, 47, 209,
  213
Joel, 20, 72, 147,
  152, 213, 231, 236
John, 20
Joshua, 2, 3, 5, 6, 11,
  12, 13, 17, 20, 21,
  23, 33, 34, 37, 38,
  40, 41, 64, 65,
  117, 156, 176,
  204, 220, 232,
  233, 236, 247, 250
Landon, 134
Mary, 20
Morise, 152
Moriss, 147
Morris, 1, 20, 153
Nicholas, 49, 70, 190,
  218
Richard, 11, 20
Sarah, 20
Thomas, 20
Turner, 1, 2, 17, 73,
  81, 164, 249, 253
William, 134
OSBURNE
  Craven, 52, 57, 92,
    122, 125, 131,
    135, 170, 172,
    176, 182
  Hector, 52
  Herod, 52
  Joshua, 1, 37, 44, 45,
    52, 57, 72, 98, 121
  Morris, 93
  Turner, 52, 54
OVERFELT
  Benjamin, 75
OVERFIELD
  ___, 254
  Ann, 131
  Anna, 214
  Benjamin, 50, 51,
    122, 126
  Deborah, 50, 170
  Elizabeth, 133, 141,
    214, 220
  Hudson, 141
  John, 126
  Joshua, 131, 141

Joshua, 26, 117, 178
PEYTON
  D., 8
  Elizabeth D., 66
  Francis, 8, 127
  John S., 167, 229,
    235, 238
  Lettice, 127
  Richard F., 156
  T. D., 46
  Townsend D., 58,
    178, 200, 248
PHILIP
  Thomas, 6
PHILIPS
  Hannah, 109
  Jenkin, 109, 126
  Nancy, 103
  Peter, 115
  Thomas, 35, 41, 47,
    52, 102, 111, 120,
    158, 210
PHILLIPS
  James, 75
  Jenkin, 75, 122
  Nicholas, 90
  Peter, 90
  Thomas, 24, 64, 81,
    89, 136, 205, 220,
    242
  William, 193, 212
PHILPOT
  William, 24, 178
PICKETT
  James, 167
PIERCE
  Alse, 75
  Alsea, 79
  Susannah, 233
  Thomas, 75, 79
PIERPOINT
  Eli, 1
  Francis, 191
  John, 99
  Obed, 122
PIGEON
  Mildred, 85
  William, 85
PIGGOT
  Mason, 90
PIGGOTT
  Isaac, 76
  John, 76
  William, 76, 192

PLAISTER
  Henry, 40, 67, 72, 80,
    199
  James, 40, 64, 67,
    242
  Jane, 118, 197
  Michael, 118, 125,
    197, 199
  Susanna, 72
PLASTER
  Henry, 9
  Michael, 24, 248
PLEASANTS
  Samuel, 63
PLETCHER
  Dolly, 13
  Henry, 13
POISAL
  John, 144
POLEN
  Nathaniel, 156
POLIN
  Ann, 56
  Nathaniel, 56
POLTEN
  Amos, 252
POMEROY
  Francis D., 179
PORTER
  Andrew, 121
POSTON
  Joseph, 95, 96
  Leonard, 189
POTT
  David, 19
POTTER
  Elizabeth, 39, 204,
    212
  John, 39, 187, 204
  Richard E., 226
POTTERFIELD
  Elizabeth, 50, 51
  John S., 82
  Samuel, 139, 208
POTTS
  David, 25, 31, 33, 37,
    149, 206, 217, 236
  Enos, 3, 23, 34, 41,
    43, 44, 45, 52, 53,
    64, 107, 141, 154,
    192, 200, 208
  Hannah, 52
  Isaiah, 28
  John, 37, 139

Jonas, 14, 18, 52, 65,
    116, 121, 122,
    142, 147
Jonus, 76
Joshua, 98
Lydia, 23, 34, 41, 53,
    64, 141, 200
Nancy, 52, 121
Nathan, 31, 52, 81
PHOEBE, 76
Susannah, 52
William, 52
POULSON
  Agness, 233
  Isabella, 233
  Jasper, 233
  John, 233
  William, 233
POULTON
  Ansey, 38
  Anzey, 37
  Charles, 37, 38
  Eleanor, 37, 38
  John, 37, 38
  Martha, 38
  Reed, 37, 134
  Reid, 38
  Ruth, 37, 38, 134
  Thomas, 37, 38, 134
POWELL
  A. O., 109, 118, 119,
    120, 124, 127,
    133, 140, 142,
    156, 158, 165,
    178, 194
  Albert O., 46, 47, 54
  Alfred H., 144, 150,
    159, 166, 196,
    197, 229
  Betty, 64, 65, 67
  Burr, 3, 9, 14, 15, 16,
    18, 21, 23, 25, 26,
    27, 29, 32, 40, 41,
    46, 47, 49, 55, 56,
    58, 59, 60, 64, 67,
    70, 71, 84, 94, 97,
    110, 111, 118,
    122, 123, 124,
    125, 127, 128,
    129, 130, 132,
    135, 137, 140,
    142, 144, 145,
    148, 151, 153,
    156, 158, 159,

Beverly, 193
RAPINE
  Daniel, 20, 21
RASOR
  John, 55
RATCLIFF
  O., 146
  R., 146
  Samuel, 146
RATTIE
  John B., 87
RATTKIN
  John B., 9
RATTS
  George N., 18
RAWLS
  W., 36
RAZOR
  Elizabeth, 103, 105
  George, 105
  Philip, 103, 105
REDMAN
  John, 28
REDMON
  Mrs., 156
REDMOND
  Andrew, 28, 33
  Israel, 28, 33, 55
  John, 33
REED
  Catharine, 102, 237
  Elizabeth, 13
  James, 61, 80, 96,
    102, 128, 167,
    189, 237, 239
  John, 80, 102
  John A., 237
  Johnathan, 102
  Jonathan, 13
  Joseph, 113
  Margaret, 189
  Martha, 80, 102
  Mary, 80, 107
  P. B., 45
  Rebecca, 102, 189,
    237
  Thomas, 102, 237
  Upton, 92, 203
REEDER
  Gourley, 105, 106,
    107, 195, 226
  Joseph, 56
  William, 126, 237,
    238

REES
  Thomas, 186
REESE
  Daniel, 97, 145, 219
  David, 25, 50, 89,
    251
  John, 61
  Linny, 97
  Silas, 7, 72, 96, 185,
    216
  Thomas, 136
REID
  Alfred, 69
  Catherine, 9, 27
  Elizabeth, 199
  James, 24, 61, 118,
    197, 199, 200
  John, 61
  Johnathan, 97
  Jonathan, 61, 197,
    199
  Leah, 199
  Rebecca, 61
  Thomas, 9, 27, 61
REILEY
  Joshua, 221
RENAL
  Thomas, 248
RENOE
  Sarah, 154
  Thomas, 154
RENOLD
  Thomas, 26
REYNOLDS
  Mary, 170
  William M., 170
RHINE
  John, 131
  Mary, 131
  Sarah, 131
RHODES
  G. T., 55
  George, 17, 115,
    122, 229, 244, 253
  Randolph, 37, 121,
    191
  Samuel, 62, 64
  Tholemiah, 165
  William, 68
RHORBACK
  ___, 100
RHORBAUGH
  Adam, 125
  Hannah, 125

RICARD
  Molley, 27
  Simon, 27
RICE
  Bethany, 64
  James, 64, 122, 148
  Jesse, 94, 145, 147,
    158, 189
  Rebecca, 122
RICHARDS
  Anne B., 87
  Elizabeth, 135, 213,
    215
  G., 253
  George, 70, 87, 130,
    181, 187, 204, 221
  Isaac, 124, 211
  Jesse, 176
  John, 18, 210, 213,
    252
  Michael, 230
  Richard, 210, 215
  Sampson, 213, 215
  Samuel, 210
  William, 173
RICHARDSON
  ___, 114
  Alexander, 105, 192
  Joseph, 126, 131,
    195, 214, 219
  Richard, 191
  Samuel, 232
  Susan, 195, 219
  Susannah, 131
RICKARD
  ___, 147
  George, 158, 204
  Mary, 28
  Simon, 28
RICKER
  ___, 150
RICKETTS
  David, 135
  Elizabeth, 138
RICKTER
  Henry, 225
RICORD
  George, 96
RIDDLE
  Truman, 193
RIDDLEMIRE
  ___, 66
RIDENBAUGH
  George, 86

S. C., 161
Sarah, 145
ROZELL
S., 226
S. C., 227
Stephen C., 18
ROZZEL
___, 155
ROZZELL
___, 46
Stephen C., 81
ROZZLE
Stephen C., 242
RUCE
Henry, 220
RUSE
Christian, 14, 71, 177
Jacob, 196
John, 71, 177
Sarah, 71
RUSK
James, 11, 184
Samuel, 194
RUSSEL
Anthony, 102
Charles, 171
James, 106, 129
John, 132
Robert, 23, 106, 130, 143
Samuel, 23
William, 38, 247
RUSSELL
___, 254
Andrew, 172
Ann, 245
Charles, 81, 195
Henry, 6
James, 53, 55, 57, 104, 129
John, 235
Robert, 22, 37, 82, 104, 182, 218
Samuel, 22
Susan, 57
Susannah, 53
Thomas, 175, 203, 221, 245
William, 23
RUST
Benjamin, 16, 248
George, 8, 17, 24, 39, 44, 57, 58, 59, 68, 71, 75, 91,

112, 114, 115, 126, 131, 132, 164, 171, 172, 179, 181, 188, 202, 204, 211, 212, 233, 240
James, 8, 11, 12, 18, 23, 24, 27, 43, 45, 48, 57, 59, 68, 87, 91, 98, 103, 114, 115, 120, 148, 152, 160, 172, 188, 192, 195, 196, 208, 212, 213, 236
John S., 18
Mandley T., 7
Maria, 71, 115, 172
Maria C., 8, 44, 59, 68, 114, 212
Mathew, 222
Matthew, 74, 195
Patty, 74
Peter, 41
Peter C., 95, 177, 220
Sally, 7, 152, 213
Sarah, 8, 68, 115, 188, 236
William, 40, 110
RYAN
Sally, 28

SAGERS
George, 184
SANBOWER
Adam, 158, 250
SANDBOWER
Adam, 27
Christian, 27
John, 27
Molley, 27
SANDERS
Aaron, 62, 84, 145, 150, 152, 156, 158, 168, 181, 202, 205, 218, 253
Abijah, 151
Ann, 96, 110, 111, 217
Britton, 84, 118
Elizabeth, 76, 151, 196
George, 60, 76, 196

Henry, 73, 176, 202
J., 144
John, 60, 76, 89, 155
Leanah, 60
Margaret, 77, 95
Nancy, 32
Nicholas, 196
Patience, 176
Peter, 32, 94, 96, 110, 111, 168, 217
Presley, 162
R. G., 202
Robert H., 84
Susanna, 84
Thomas, 73, 83, 84, 103, 104, 109, 114, 123, 126, 130, 132, 133, 136, 137, 144, 149, 150, 151, 152, 155, 158, 159, 160, 161, 165, 168, 174, 176, 178, 180, 182, 185, 188, 189, 191, 192, 193, 196, 198, 202, 205, 206, 209, 211, 213, 216, 218, 219, 221, 228, 230, 232, 243, 244, 245, 246, 253, 254
Thomas R., 198
William S., 179
SANDERSON
James, 90, 193
SANDS
Esther, 25, 94
Hester, 93
Isaac, 61, 71
Jacob, 210
Jonah, 2, 25, 93, 94, 101, 200
Leven L., 71
SANFORD
A. M., 131
Jeremiah, 215
Margaret, 7
Robert, 117
SANGSTER
James, 187
SAPPINGTON

Sarah G., 106, 116,
213
William, 99, 101, 116,
209
SHEKELL
Abram, 79
SHEKELLS
Theodore, 26
SHEPHERD
Charles, 42, 45, 131,
242
Eleanor, 42
James, 42, 57
Leven W., 142, 242
Wadsworth, 244, 245
SHEWELL
Cynthia, 107, 108
Nathaniel, 107, 108
SHIELDS
Joseph, 68
SHIP
James, 67
SHIPLEY
Isaac, 102, 127
Nancy L., 196
William B., 196
SHOBER
John, 180, 182
SHOEMAKER
Catharine, 50
George, 101, 117,
130, 188
Jacob, 116, 165, 253
Mary, 165
Simon, 50, 51, 204
SHORES
___, 191
SHOVER
George, 231
SHOVER
Adam, 184
Thomas, 54
SHREEVE
Benjamin, 177
SHREIVE
Benjamin, 73
SHREVE
___, 171
B., 43
Benjamin, 11, 12, 43,
71, 73, 75, 89,
109, 121, 126,
135, 137, 161,
167, 168, 169,

172, 174, 177,
186, 196, 202,
205, 206, 207,
217, 226, 232,
233, 234, 247
Nancy, 232
Thomas, 241
William, 49, 57
SHREVES
Benjamin, 192
SHRIEVE
Benjamin, 156, 161,
177
SHRIVER
Jacob, 244
SHULTS
George, 124
SILCOT
Jacob, 28
SILCOTT
Jacob, 92, 119, 181,
206, 210, 215,
216, 219, 223
Jesse, 92
SILLMAN
John, 81
SILVER
William, 97
SIMMONS
Isaac, 33
SIMPSON
Eliza, 46
Elizabeth, 25, 29, 84,
141
French, 29, 177
Hanson, 25
Henley, 74
Henson, 124, 207
James, 15, 16, 22,
25, 29, 46, 71, 74,
84, 124, 141, 153,
160, 177, 207, 225
John, 54, 71, 84
Mary, 29, 84
Samuel, 29
Susanna, 146
SINCLAIR
Amos, 16
Benjamin, 83
Craven, 145
Edith, 16, 214, 230
Esther, 94
George, 9, 16, 38,
73, 84, 234

George H., 150, 156,
214, 230, 239
James, 94, 172, 181,
187, 223
John, 8, 9, 32, 46, 54,
64, 76, 81, 83, 94,
97, 104, 113, 129,
140, 158, 159,
171, 172, 187,
191, 223, 226,
231, 235
Margaret, 234
Ruth, 149
Samuel, 16, 78, 98,
110, 128, 145,
149, 150, 165,
178, 214, 230
Sarah, 235
Seth, 9
Susannah, 94
Thomas, 38, 73, 84,
230
Thomas M., 239
William, 226
SINGLETON
Robert, 100, 230
Samuel, 41, 95, 245
SKILLMAN
Abraham, 11, 12, 201
Violinda, 12
SKILLMON
John, 234
SKILMAN
Abraham, 174, 191
SKINNER
Amos, 20, 149, 199,
251
Jacob, 220
Peter, 194, 201
Phebe, 32
Usher, 195
SLACK
Jeremiah, 221
SLADE
Charles, 241, 252
SLATES
Frederick, 237
SLATS
Frederick, 164
SLATZ
Frederick, 187
SMAIL
Simon, 175
SMALE

Elizabeth, 114, 123
Simon, 104, 114,
123, 175, 221
SMALLEY
Andrew, 241
Catharine, 241
David, 241
William, 241
SMALLWOOD
___, 36
Samuel N., 24
Samuel W., 21
SMALLWOOOD
Samuel W., 20
SMALLY
Joshua, 241
William, 67
SMARR
Andrew, 9
James, 172
John, 120, 156, 166
Susan F., 156
William, 7, 96, 124,
186
SMIDLEY
Mathias, 197
SMITH
___, 232
Ann, 43, 54
Benjamin, 16, 40, 52,
122, 155, 187
C., 249
Charles, 54, 124, 218
Clement, 249
D. G., 233
David, 1, 12, 25, 34,
43, 48, 53, 76, 84,
106, 141, 155,
156, 168, 192,
215, 218
Edmund, 108
Eliza, 206
Elizabeth, 197, 210
Emily, 43, 54
Eve, 131
Fleet, 18, 22, 42, 43,
54, 60, 67, 71, 84,
88, 128, 136, 159,
173, 196, 226
George, 24, 33, 60,
104, 106, 129,
131, 142, 180, 244
H., 195, 206, 229
Henry, 33

Hugh, 26, 54, 55, 60,
129, 130, 141,
172, 182, 187,
193, 194, 199,
201, 212, 223,
227, 236, 252, 253
Jacob, 46, 163
John, 59, 250
Joseph, 14, 63, 118,
127, 129, 143,
185, 231
Lewis M., 159, 226
Major, 150
Martha, 33
Mary, 118, 127, 185
Richard, 240, 246,
249
Ruth, 59
Sarah, 99
Seth, 46, 96, 110,
118, 125, 128,
142, 210, 226
Susannah, 13
Thomas, 33
Thomas W., 57, 163,
207, 238
Walter, 249
William, 49, 52, 82,
83, 88, 99, 180,
182
Smith & Edwards, 233
SMITLY
Mathias, 60
SMYTH
Thomas, 36
SNOOT
Benjamin, 59
SNOWDEN
S., 55
SOCKMAN
Charles, 147
John M., 147
SOLLADY
Frederick, 108
SOMMERVILLE
John, 170
SORBOURNE
Moranda, 25
SOUDER
Philip, 67
SOWER
B. W., 157, 221
SPALDING
Bernard, 237

SPENCE
John, 23, 57, 68
Mary, 57
Mary F., 23, 57, 68
SPENCER
Margaret, 233
Nathan, 68
Samuel, 10, 233
SPRING
Andrew, 67
Jones, 37
ST. CLAIR
A. R., 224, 254
ST.Clair
A. R., 245
STANLEY
Jesse, 126
Lydia, 126
Mary, 126
Michael, 126
STANLY
Samuel, 126
STARBUCK
Hezekiah, 126
STARK
Widow, 156
STATTLER
John, 157
STEAR
Isaac, 6
STEELE
Lewis, 85
STEER
___, 242
Benjamin, 14, 113,
164
Isaac, 7, 13, 15, 16,
50, 62, 64, 98,
102, 164, 186,
209, 241
Isaac E., 35, 64, 65,
148, 159
Joseph, 15, 51, 52,
92, 95, 153, 225
Leah, 148
Phebe, 50, 64
Sarah, 15, 92, 153,
225
William, 113, 164
William B., 14
STEERS
Isaac, 142
STEPHEN
David, 163

Thomas, 125, 146, 184
William, 184
TOWERMAN
John, 148
TOWNER
___, 160
Benjamin T., 104
Eve, 104
TOWPERMAN
Andrew, 214
John, 214
Peter, 132, 140, 214
TRACEY
Nancy, 11
Tamar, 11
TRAHERN
Asa, 96
Hannah, 182
James, 180
Jesse, 141, 182, 197, 219
Samuel, 97
TRAYHERN
James, 180
Jesse, 173
TRAYHORN
Harriet, 151, 162
Jesse, 151, 162
Thomas, 223
TRAYHORNE
Thomas, 246
TREBBY
Deborah, 233
John, 233
Lydia, 233
Thomas, 233
TREHORN
Thomas, 61, 149
TRIBBY
Asahel, 39, 100
Catharine, 100
Catherine, 39
George, 38, 39, 100
James, 37, 38
Johnathan, 100
Jonathan, 38, 39
Joseph, 39, 100
Ruth, 39, 100
Tamar, 37, 38
Thomas, 249
TRIPLET
Thomas, 20
TRIPLETT

___, 19
Benjamin, 96
Cynthia, 41
Cyrus, 59
Elizabeth, 15
Felix, 219
Francis, 25, 28, 35, 96, 103, 120, 122, 177, 179
James L., 89, 120
John, 15, 35
Lucy, 59
M. L., 89
Margaret, 57, 68, 133
Margaret B., 23
Margaret C., 57, 110, 117
Nancy, 35
Nathaniel, 44, 105
Reuben, 9, 58, 95, 97
Reubin, 96
Thomas, 23, 57, 68, 110, 117, 133
Willis, 197, 219
Triplett & Walker, 44
TROUT
Jacob, 222
TUCKER
H. G., 159
James, 25
TULLEY
Joseph, 134
TULLYFRANK
Abraham, 16
TURLEY
Alexander, 177
James, 67, 159
John, 67, 140, 213
Sampson, 28, 80, 241
TURNER
Charles, 85, 107
Elijah, 214
George, 29, 156
James, 32, 163
Malinda, 107
Mary, 32
Nancy, 103
TUSTIN
Mary, 185
Samuel, 87, 104, 114, 118, 185, 211, 221
TUTT

Ann M., 239
Charles P., 19, 110, 239, 240
TUTTLE
Addison, 14
TYLER
Bradley, 31
William B., 246
TYTUS
Jane, 184
Tunis, 184

UNDERWOOD
John, 38
Samuel, 158
UPDIKE
Rufus, 164, 218
UPP
John, 120, 151
URTON
Barsheba, 246
Gerrard, 246
John, 246
Norman, 246

VANANDER
Thomas, 102
VANBUSKIRK
John, 245
VANDEN HESWEL
J. C., 184
VANDENHENVILLE
J., 231
VANDENHEUVELL
J. C., 249
VANDEVANTER
Cornelius, 5, 147, 231
Elizabeth, 4
Isaac, 231
John, 243
Joseph, 4, 5, 6, 161
VANDEVENTER
C., 96
John, 110
Joseph, 122
VANHORN
Ann, 83
VANHORNE
Betsy, 83
Garret, 83
John, 5, 65, 83
Mary, 83
Sarah, 5

VANPELT
  Elizabeth, 69
  Joseph, 201, 251
  Richard, 30, 40, 69,
    201
  William, 40, 201
VAUGHN
  J., 231
VEALE
  Alexander, 201
  Amos, 85
  Catharine P., 85
  Catherine, 88
  Charles, 85, 88
VENIE
  Thomas, 73
VERNON
  Daniel, 30, 128, 129,
    151
  John, 11
  Phebe, 174
  Rebecca, 128
VERTS
  Jacob, 60, 140
  Peter, 99
  William, 160
VERTZ
  Conrad, 36
  Jacob, 125
  William, 6
VICKER
  William, 42
VICKERS
  Ann, 40, 118
  Anna, 227
  Anne, 42, 65
  Aquila, 242
  William, 40, 42, 64,
    65, 118, 142, 174,
    193, 202, 215,
    223, 226, 227, 237
  Williams, 69
VICKORY
  Solomon, 164
VICKROY
  Solomon, 125, 237
VINSEL
  George, 50
VIOLET
  John, 33, 88, 218
  John W., 88
  Juliet A., 88
VIOLETT
  Ashford, 40

Benjamin, 128
Elijah, 28, 40, 56, 91,
  94, 115, 116, 128,
  162, 163, 199, 218
Elizabeth, 116
James, 69, 91, 218
Jemima, 69, 115
John, 19, 28, 46, 94,
  115, 116, 128,
  131, 138, 139,
  144, 146, 163,
  176, 199, 237, 245
John W., 128
Julian, 128
Mary, 19
Phebe, 28, 56, 199
Sarah, 91, 218
Thomas, 69
VIRTS
  Conrod, 235
  Jacob, 39
  Peter, 188, 231
VIRTZ
  Jacob, 182, 186, 197,
    200
  Lucy, 186
  Peter, 14, 186
  Susannah, 186
  William, 178, 186
VOWELL
  Thomas, 237

WAGER
  Catharine, 29
WAGNER
  John, 180, 182
WALDRON
  Cecelia, 251
WALKER
  Alsey, 248
  Benjamin, 96
  Craven, 197, 219,
    248
  Fanny, 141, 170,
    185, 248
  Garret, 5
  Garrett, 5, 34, 83, 97,
    162
  Isaac, 13, 100, 136,
    139, 145, 200, 204
  John, 18, 53, 188,
    223
  Letitia, 18
  Susannah, 139

Thornton, 141, 147,
  152, 162, 170,
  181, 185, 201,
  206, 219, 231, 248
WALTERS
  Mahlon, 58
WALTERS
  Levi, 104
WALTMAN
  ___, 209
  Emanuel, 56, 66,
    187, 250, 254
  Jacob, 35, 48, 54, 66,
    130, 171, 217,
    250, 254
  John, 171, 217
  Manuel, 171
  Margaret, 171
  Rachel, 66
  Samuel, 130, 171,
    217, 254
  Susana, 217
WARD
  Samuel, 249
  Thomas, 207
  Zachariah, 57
WARE
  James, 35
WARFORD
  Abraham, 18, 173
  Elijah, 49, 51, 52, 178
  Elizabeth, 11, 70, 72
  James, 11, 51, 70,
    72, 190
  John, 23, 44, 45, 51,
    70
  Mary, 51, 70, 178
  William, 18
WARNER
  George, 14
  William, 14
WASHINGTON
  Amelia, 225
  Edward, 226
  Fairfax, 130
  George, 179
  John A., 102, 225,
    226, 243
  L., 47
  Perrin, 130
  Warner, 130, 207
WATERMAN
  A. G., 220
WATERS

Ann, 151
Benjamin, 106
Catharine, 60, 104
Diah, 60, 106
Johnathan, 151
Levi, 104, 214, 218
WATHEN
Elias, 214
WATKINS
Ann, 192
John B., 183
WATT
Dewanner, 100, 150
John G., 99, 100,
150, 179
WATTS
James, 67, 179
Mountzion, 28
Richard K., 181
WATTSON
___, 119
WAUGH
Alexander, 89
WAY
Thomas H., 182
WEADEN
John, 27
WEADON
John, 173, 185, 201,
206
William J., 133
WEARING
John, 130
WEATHERBY
Jane, 118, 135, 137
M., 89
WEAVER
Adam, 127
WEEDON
Richard, 79
WEEKS
Alfred, 214
B., 153
Burr, 154, 195
James, 122
M. B., 190
WEEST
John, 98
WELDON
William I., 53
WELLES
Rosewell, 238
WELLS
Asa, 236

WENNER
John, 131, 254
Johnathan, 158
Magdalena, 158
William, 54, 158, 163
WENNERS
William, 228
WERTENBAKER
William, 86
WERTZ
Jacob, 100, 180, 206
Lucy, 100
Peter, 100
Susan, 100
William, 139
WEST
Ann B., 112, 113
Corbin, 93
Elizabeth, 112, 113
Erasmus, 92
Hannah, 216
Isaac, 88
James, 121, 196
John, 216
Joseph, 68
Margaret, 40
Thomas, 40
William, 215, 218
WESTGATE
L. S., 224
WESTWOOD
Wolrich, 41
WETTERMAN
___, 24
WEY
Thomas H., 61, 62,
199, 223
WHALEY
George, 156
WHEELER
Ann, 235
Clement, 183, 235
Joseph, 224
Samuel H., 183, 235
WHELUND
James, 28
WHERRY
D., 205
S., 214
Silas, 118
WHITACRE
J., 163
John, 110, 125, 239
Phebe, 110, 239

Robert A., 190
WHITE
___, 56
Adin, 176
Beniah, 158, 250
Benjamin, 85, 176
Benniah, 28
Betsey, 77
Betsy, 77
Daniel, 232
Elizabeth, 4, 11, 79
George, 79
Isaac, 239
Isaac S., 10, 87
James, 81, 89, 148,
158, 250
John, 20, 25, 37, 38,
39, 40, 45, 47, 49,
51, 52, 56, 57, 70,
74, 76, 81, 98,
100, 122, 125,
129, 131, 132,
135, 139, 148,
150, 156, 160,
172, 182, 209,
213, 215, 216,
217, 219, 220,
221, 225, 231,
232, 236, 250
John R., 143
Josabed, 21
Joseph, 4, 11, 77, 79,
85
Josiah, 6, 25, 56, 92,
158, 250
Jozabed, 3, 14, 34,
52, 95, 136, 137,
203, 204
Levi, 85, 153, 232
Margaret, 3, 14, 34,
137
Mary, 81, 158, 232,
233
Mary M., 87
Nancy, 19, 77, 154
Rachel, 158
Richard, 176
Robert, 37, 158, 233,
250
Robert B., 21
Robert D., 35
Samuel, 77
Sarah, 14, 77, 79,
153, 239

Thomas, 10, 28, 36,
134, 158, 220, 250
William, 11, 14, 19,
77, 85, 136, 153,
154, 203, 232
WHITEHURST
Arthur, 86
Lucretia, 86
WHITELY
Alexander, 164
WHITING
Francis, 41
George B., 45, 137,
149, 173, 201
John, 41
WHITMORE
George, 156, 254
Rachel, 254
WHITTEMORE
William, 79
WILCOXEN
Resin, 135
Rezin, 66, 172
WILDMAN
Aaron, 87
Eleanor, 157
Ellener, 7
Enos, 10, 22, 52, 82,
138, 155, 221
Hannah, 77, 126,
159, 162
Jacob, 70
Jane, 82, 138
Jane D., 22
John, 7, 10, 27, 70,
71, 114, 157
Joseph, 70, 77, 89,
126, 159, 162
Mahaley, 82
Martin, 126
Rebecca, 73
Sarah, 71
William, 82
WILEY
Hugh, 14, 145
William, 14
WILIAMS
Notley C., 17
WILKINSON
Anna, 106, 107
Asa C., 166, 168, 174
Elizabeth, 61, 102,
106, 107, 108
Hannah, 106, 107

John, 107, 108, 195,
215, 223, 247
Jonathan, 238
Joseph, 61, 102, 106,
107
Mary, 106, 107
Patty, 238
William, 30, 102, 177
WILLIAMS
Abner, 35, 64, 164,
165
Charles, 209
Daniel, 143
Elijah, 26
Ellis, 76, 143
Enos, 209, 225
Frances, 25
Francis, 5
Hannah, 225
Jacob, 177
James, 114
Jane, 14, 98, 156,
193, 238
Jesse, 212
John, 14, 26, 34, 35,
36, 51, 52, 56, 62,
77, 78, 85, 99,
100, 110, 111,
119, 120, 123,
143, 153, 159,
165, 178, 242
Joseph, 96
Lener, 76
Levi, 41, 45, 53, 64,
65, 84, 141, 152,
154, 155, 192, 208
Martha, 143
Mary, 143
N. C., 3, 48, 53, 59,
72, 81, 118, 133,
149, 185, 209,
225, 230, 238,
239, 245
Notely C., 40, 62
Notley C., 1, 2, 5, 15,
17, 19, 22, 23, 25,
33, 34, 42, 44, 47,
52, 62, 64, 78, 81,
84, 94, 95, 98,
108, 111, 117,
119, 132, 133,
141, 149, 150,
171, 184, 189,
194, 195, 199,

213, 214, 215,
216, 218, 219,
220, 221, 232,
234, 239
Notly C., 145, 152,
154, 158, 160, 162
Owen, 143
Presley, 14, 89, 91,
98, 156, 186, 192,
193, 205, 238, 246
Rhoda, 143
Richard, 78
Samuel, 60, 96
Sarah, 45, 65, 84,
154, 192
Sinah, 87
Thomas, 88
Thomas P., 249
William, 6, 70
WILLIAMSON
Sarah, 178
William, 178
WILLSON
Edward, 14
John, 14
Moses, 132
WILSON
___, 159
Anna, 7
Betsey, 90
Ebenezer, 90, 93,
115
Edward, 132, 135,
137, 140, 148,
159, 254
Eleanor, 115
Elizabeth, 115
Hannah, 90, 93, 115,
215, 218
Isaac, 243
Jabez, 105, 108
James B., 235
Jesse S., 192
John, 7, 20, 115, 144
John T., 31, 53, 87,
91, 221
Maria, 115
Mary, 115
Mary A., 159
Mary Ann, 132
Moses, 14, 122, 124,
171, 231, 234
Polly, 90
Porter, 115

Thomas N., 130
William, 74

ZIMMERMAN

Adam, 153, 156
Ann, 146
George, 146
Henry, 146

Jacob, 146
Jane, 146
Sarah, 153

Other Books by Patricia B. Duncan:

1850 Fairfax County and Loudoun County, Virginia Slave Schedule

1850 Fauquier County, Virginia Slave Schedule

1860 Loudoun County, Virginia Slave Schedule

*Clarke County, Virginia Will Book Abstracts:
Books A-I (1836-1904) and 1A-3C (1841-1913)*

Fauquier County, Virginia Death Register, 1853-1896

Hunterdon County, New Jersey 1895 State Census, Part I: Alexandria-Junction

Hunterdon County, New Jersey 1895 State Census, Part II: Kingwood-West Amwell

Genealogical Abstracts from The Lambertville Press, *Lambertville, New Jersey:
4 November 1858 (Vol. 1, Number 1) to 30 October 1861 (Vol. 3, Number 155)*

Jefferson County, Virginia/West Virginia Death Records, 1853-1880

Jefferson County, West Virginia Death Records, 1881-1903

Jefferson County, Virginia 1802-1813 Personal Property Tax Lists

Jefferson County, Virginia 1814-1824 Personal Property Tax Lists

Jefferson County, Virginia 1825-1841 Personal Property Tax Lists

1810-1840 Loudoun County, Virginia Federal Population Census Index

1860 Loudoun County, Virginia Federal Population Census Index

1870 Loudoun County, Virginia Federal Population Census Index

Abstracts from Loudoun County, Virginia Guardian Accounts: Books A-H, 1759-1904

Abstracts of Loudoun County, Virginia Register of Free Negroes, 1844-1861

Index to Loudoun County, Virginia Land Deed Books A-Z, 1757-1800

Index to Loudoun County, Virginia Land Deed Books 2A-2M, 1800-1810

Index to Loudoun County, Virginia Land Deed Books 2N-2U, 1811-1817

Index to Loudoun County, Virginia Land Deed Books 2V-3D, 1817-1822

Index to Loudoun County, Virginia Land Deed Books 3E-3M, 1822-1826

Index to Loudoun County, Virginia Land Deed Books 3N-3V, 1826-1831

Index to Loudoun County, Virginia Land Deed Books 3W-4D, 1831-1835

Index to Loudoun County, Virginia Land Deed Books 4E-4N, 1835-1840

Index to Loudoun County, Virginia Land Deed Books 4O-4V, 1840-1846

Loudoun County, Virginia Birth Register, 1853-1879

Loudoun County, Virginia Birth Register, 1880-1896

*Loudoun County, Virginia Clerks Probate Records
Book 1 (1904-1921) and Book 2 (1922-1938)*

(With Elizabeth R. Frain) *Loudoun County, Virginia Marriages after 1850,
Volume 1, 1851-1880*

Loudoun County, Virginia 1800-1810 Personal Property Taxes

Loudoun County, Virginia 1826-1834 Personal Property Taxes

Loudoun County, Virginia Will Book Abstracts, Books A-Z, Dec. 1757-Jun. 1841

*Loudoun County, Virginia Will Book Abstracts, Books 2A-3C, Jun. 1841-Dec. 1879
and Superior Court Books A and B, 1810-1888*

Loudoun County, Virginia Will Book Index, 1757-1946

Genealogical Abstracts from The Brunswick Herald, *Brunswick, Maryland:
Mar. 6 1891-Dec. 28 1894*

Genealogical Abstracts from The Brunswick Herald, *Brunswick, Maryland:
Jan. 4 1895-Dec. 30 1898*

Genealogical Abstracts from The Brunswick Herald, *Brunswick, Maryland:
Jan. 6 1899-Dec. 26 1902*

Genealogical Abstracts from The Brunswick Herald, *Brunswick, Maryland:
Jan. 2 1903-June 29 1906*

Genealogical Abstracts from The Brunswick Herald, *Brunswick, Maryland:
July 6 1906-Feb. 25 1910*

CD: *Loudoun County, Virginia Personal Property Tax List, 1782-1850*